CONTENTS

TO

VOLUME I.

～～～～～～～

～～～～～～～

SINCERE CONVERT.

CHAPTER I.

CHAPTER II.

CHAPTER III.

CHAPTER IV.

CHAPTER V.

CHAPTER VI.

SOUND BELIEVER.

CHAPTER I.

AS THE GREAT CAUSE OF THE ETERNAL PERDITION OF MEN IS OF THEMSELVES, SO THE ONLY CAUSE OF THE ACTUAL DELIVERANCE AND SALVATION OF MAN IS JESUS CHRIST.

a *

CHAPTER II.

EVERY SINNER, BELIEVING IN CHRIST, IS TRANSLATED INTO A
MOST BLESSED AND HAPPY ESTATE. WHAT IS THAT HAPPY
STATE THEY ARE MADE PARTAKERS OF, ANSWERED IN SIX
PARTICULARS, AS FOLLOWS:—

CHAPTER III.

ALL THOSE THAT ARE TRANSLATED INTO THIS BLESSED ESTATE
ARE BOUND TO LIVE THE LIFE OF LOVE, IN FRUITFUL AND
THANKFUL OBEDIENCE UNTO HIM THAT HATH CALLED THEM,

LIFE

OF

THOMAS SHEPARD.

BY

JOHN A. ALBRO, D. D.,

PASTOR OF THE

FIRST CHURCH AND SHEPARD SOCIETY,

CAMBRIDGE, MASS.

THE materials for the ensuing Life of THOMAS SHEPARD have been gathered from his own writings, and from all accessible contemporaneous sources. Besides his printed works, which exhibit his views of religion and the church, and aid us in forming a judgment respecting his mind and character, Mr. Shepard left in MS. an Autobiography, containing brief notices of the principal events in his personal and domestic history, which was first published to the world by Rev. Nehemiah Adams, in 1832, and more recently by Rev. Mr. Young, in " The Chronicles of Massachusetts." The Life of Shepard, as it is called, in Mather's Magnalia, the only one that has ever been written, is but little more than an abridgment of this Autobiography, (the third person being used instead of the first,) with a few quaint, general observations interspersed, which, together, constitute but a meager and unsatisfactory view of the character and influence of this eminent man. In the present work, Mr. Shepard's account of himself has, of course, been relied on, as far as it goes, for facts and dates; but a vast amount of matter, essential to the illustration of his labors, and to a just view of his position in New England, has been drawn from other sources. Several interesting MS. Letters, never before published, which throw much light upon Mr. Shepard's domestic and public life, have, by the permission of Mr. Felt, the accomplished librarian of the Massachusetts Historical Society, been kindly transcribed for the author by Mr. David Pulsifer, the only man, it is believed, who could have deciphered the chirography in which they have been locked up for more than two hundred years. The work is, doubtless, very imperfect, notwithstanding all the pains which have been taken to render it complete; but, as a sincere tribute to the memory of one of New England's best as well as chief fathers, and an attempt to vindicate the principles of those men to whom we owe our civil and religious liberty, it is commended to the children of the Puritans, in the hope that it may be regarded as not entirely destitute of interest, and contribute somewhat to the success of the cause in which we are engaged.

This memoir was originally written for the Massachusetts Sabbath School Society, and may be had, separately, at their Depository.

LIFE

OF

THOMAS SHEPARD.

CHAPTER I.

The shield of faith. — General character and different classes of early N. E. ministers. — Mr. Shepard one of the first class. — His birth. — William Shepard. — A mother's influence. — Sent to reside with his grandparents. Removed to Adthrop. — Whitsun-Ales. — Returns home. — Changes in the family. — Unkind step-mother. —Welsh schoolmaster. — Death of his father. — Education neglected by his mother-in-law. — His brother John offers to edŭcate him. — Goes to a new school. — Diligence in study. — Fitted for college.

VIRGIL, in the eighth book of the Æneid, tells us that the shield which Vulcan, at the request of Venus, made for Æneas, contained in sixteen compartments, or pictures, a prophetic representation of the Roman history from the birth of Ascanius to the battle of Actium.

> " The brethren first a glorious shield prepare,
> Capacious of the whole Rutulian war.
> Some, orb in orb, the blazing buckler frame ;
> Some with huge bellows rouse the roaring flame.
>
> .   .   .   .
>
> With joy the weighty spear the prince beheld,
> But most admired the huge, mysterious shield ;
> For there had Vulcan, skilled in times to come,
> Displayed the triumphs of immortal Rome ;

ix

> There all the Julian line the god had wrought,
> And charged the gold with battles yet unfought." *

A device which must have been as terrible to the enemies of the Trojan hero as it was encouraging to the bearer.

What Virgil here presents as a beautiful poetic idea, the Redeemer of the church has actually realized for us. We have the shield of faith, wherewith to quench all the fiery darts of the wicked, emblazoned with the mighty history,- past and prospective, of his stupendous victories. On one part of its flaming disk we see the story of the ancient dispensation, written for the admonition and encouragement of those who have inherited " the covenants, and the promises, and the service of God;" on another portion, there appears the memorable history of our own New England Patriarchs, from the birth of Puritanism to the permanent and quiet settlement of a pure church in this land, exhibiting the trials, sufferings, conflicts, and triumphs of those Christian heroes who turned this wilderness into a fruitful field; a history which should be kept in perpetual remembrance, and constantly held forth to the world, for the purpose of animating their and our posterity in the labors and conflicts that are before us.†

The ministers and Christians by whom New England was planted, as one of our early historians has remarked, were a chosen company of men, drawn from nearly all the counties of England, not by any human contrivance, but by a peculiar work of God upon their spirits, inspiring them as one man to retire into the wilderness they knew not where, and to suffer in that wilderness they knew not what, for the glory of God,

---

* Ingentem clypeum informunt, unum omnia contra
    Tela Latinorum, septenosque orbibus orbes
    Impediunt.
    Illic res Italas, Romanorumque triumphos
    Haud vatum ignarus, venturique inscias ævi,
    Fecerat ignipotens: illic genus omne futuræ
    Stirpis ab Ascanio, pugnataque in ordine bella.

† See Letters on the Puritans, by J. B. Williams.

and for the good of their children.* "God sifted three nations," says Stoughton, "that he might bring choice wheat into
this wilderness."

These early ministers of New England are divided, by
Mather, into three classes: 1. Those who were ordained and
in the actual exercise of the ministry when they left England,
and were the first to preach the gospel and to establish churches, according to the scriptural model, in this country. 2. Young
scholars, who came over from England with their parents and
friends, and completed their education — already begun at home
— in this country, before the college was in a condition to bestow its honors. 3. Those who came over to New England
after the reestablishment of Episcopacy in the mother country,
and the revival of that persecution which was designed, as
James I. declared, to force the Puritans to conform, or to "harry
them out of the kingdom."

To these Mather adds a fourth class, which he calls, fitly
enough, the "Anomalies of New England," that is, a few ministers from other parts of the world, who proved either so erroneous in their principles, or so scandalous in their lives, or so hostile
to the order of the churches, that they cannot be classed among
our "worthies," and deserve no honorable notice from us.†

Mr. Shepard, whose life we here attempt to delineate, belonged to the first class of ministers, who were instrumental
in laying the foundations and in settling the order of the first
churches in Massachusetts; and although his humility ever
constrained him to take the lowest place, yet in learning, talents, piety, and influence he was not a whit behind the "very
chiefest of the apostles" of Congregationalism in the new world.
He was one of those "wise master builders"— few in number,
but great in all that constitutes true excellence — to whom we
owe whatever of simplicity, strength, or solidity belongs to our
ecclesiastical system, and, we may add, to our civil state. His
name may not be so often pronounced in discourse respecting

* Magnalia, b. iii.   † Ibid. b. iii.

the original constitution of our churches as that of John Cotton, who has been called, and not improperly, the "Father of Congregationalism" in New England; but the part he acted, and the influence he exerted in fashioning these churches according to the "pattern showed in the mount," entitled him to equal honor.   Not inferior to Norton, Hooker, or Davenport, in intellectual strength and logical acuteness, he perhaps excelled them all in that fine, beautiful, practical spirit, which was at that time more needed than even genius, and in contemplating which, we become insensible to the greatness of his talents and the extent of his learning.   Although he was a prominent and an efficient actor in scenes of controversy and public disorder, which stirred up all the fountains of bitterness, such were his candor and tenderness that the odium of persecution was never attached to his memory;   and while subject to like passions, and exposed to the same temptations, as other men, his reputation has descended to us without a blot from the hand of friend or foe.   It is not too much, therefore, to say, that Mr. Shepard was a man whom Massachusetts and New England ought to hold in profound respect; and his life, if it receives any thing like justice from his biographer, will be read with interest and profit by all classes of the community.

THOMAS SHEPARD was born at Towcester, near Northampton, in Northamptonshire, England, on the fifth day of November, 1605.   His own statement, in his Autobiography, is, that he was born "in the year of Christ 1604, upon the fifth day of November, called the Powder Treason day, and at that very hour of the day wherein the Parliament should have been blown up by the Popish priests;" which induced his father to give him this name, Thomas, "because, he said, I would hardly *believe* (an allusion to the scepticism of the apostle Thomas) that ever any such wickedness should be attempted by men against so religious and good a Parliament."   As it is certain that the famous Powder Plot was contrived, if contrived at all, in 1605, and was to have been executed on the fifth day of No-

vember, we are obliged to place Mr. Shepard's birth in this year
and on this day, notwithstanding the contradictory date with
which he begins his account of himself; for it is more likely
that he should have forgotten, at the moment of writing, the exact date of the Powder Plot, than the fact, — so indissolubly associated with his name, — that according to the family record
and tradition, he was born at the very hour when the Parliament was to have been blown up by gunpowder.

The father of the subject of this memoir, William Shepard, was born in Fossecut, a small town near Towcester.
He was bred to the business of a grocer by a Mr. Bland,
whose daughter he married, and by whom he had nine
children : three sons, John, William, and Thomas; and six
daughters, Ann, Margaret, Mary, Elizabeth, Hester, and Sarah.
He seems to have been a wise, prudent, and peace-loving man;
and, toward the close of his life, very prosperous in his business. That he was also a godly man, in the sense in which the
Puritans used that phrase, appears from the fact that he removed to Banbury, in Oxfordshire, for the sole purpose of enjoying the light of an evangelical and effective ministry — a
blessing which, it seems, could not be had at Towcester. A
worldly man, or a mere formalist in religion, was not likely to
sacrifice his temporal interests in order to promote the welfare
of his soul, nor leave a quiet and respectable establishment,
like the English church, for such preaching as was at that time
heard from Puritan pulpits.

In the early training and ultimate development and formation
of a man's mind, the character and influence of his mother are
of preëminent importance. The seed that is to germinate and
bear fruit in mature life, is ordinarily planted by the maternal
hand during the first years of childhood. The influence which
is to surround the growing intellect like an atmosphere, and act
upon it at every stage of its progress, flows most frequently
from the heart near which the young immortal has been nourished; and happy is the child who can remember nothing earlier
than those looks, tones, prayers, and tears which are the natural

expressions of maternal piety. They can never be forgotten;
and amidst the most powerful temptations, and the wildest conflicts of passion, they throng around the soul with warning and
beseeching voice, to withdraw it from danger, or to awaken it to
repentance. Augustine acknowledged that he owed his conversion, under God, to the tears and prayers of his mother ; and
Cecil says that he should have been an infidel, if it had not been
for the quiet but perpetual influence of her whom he loved above
all other beings. Mr. Shepard was blessed with a pious mother.
She was a woman of a tender and affectionate disposition, and
" much afflicted in conscience, sometimes even unto distraction,"
but she was "sweetly recovered," and passed her latter days in
the enjoyment of mental serenity and religious peace. She
prayed much for her children, and especially for Thomas, " her
youngest and best beloved," upon whose mind she seems to have
left the impress of her gentle and pious spirit, as well as of her
tender and scrupulous conscience, which were its most distinguishing characteristics in after life. She died when Thomas
was about four years old ; but young as he was, he was sensible
of the " exceeding love " which she felt for him, and during the
darker season which followed, he remembered her with a corresponding affection.

When Thomas was about three years of age, he was sent to
reside with his grandparents at Fossecut, in order to avoid an
epidemic disease which had begun to prevail at Towcester, and
soon swept away several members, sisters as well as servants,
from his father's family. Fossecut was a small, obscure, and
wicked place — " a most blind town and corner. " The aged
grandfather and grandmother, though in comfortable circumstances as to temporal matters, were very ignorant, and, as
we should naturally infer from the manner in which they dealt
with the little boy committed to their care, very irreligious
people ; for here he was " put to keep geese, and other such
country work," all the while much neglected by those who
should have watched over him. It was not long, however, before
he was removed from the influence of his grandparents, probably

in consequence of this neglect, to the family of his uncle, at Adthrop, an adjoining town. The change seems to have been not much for the better; for Adthrop was "a little blind town;" and while he there received more attention, and was somewhat happier and more contented, he learned to " sing and sport as children did in those parts, and to dance at their Whitsun-Ales," — amusements which were far more pernicious to childhood than " keeping geese, and other such country work." For these sports were not the innocent plays and recreations of children among themselves, which all persons, even the Puritans, morose and gloomy as they are (falsely) represented to have been, must have approved; but those demoralizing wakes, morris dances, May games, revels, etc., recommended and sanctioned by that abomination, " The Book of Sports," which James I., and after him Charles, " out of a pious care for the service of God," and desiring, with filial reverence, to " ratify his blessed father's declaration," ordered to be read in all the churches, for the " encouragement of recreations on the Lord's day." The common people were fond of these sports; but the Puritans, and the more serious portion of the community generally, regarded them with strong disapprobation, not only as grossly profaning the Sabbath, but as being the fruitful source of drunkenness, debauchery, contempt of authority, quarrels, and even murders; and efforts were made, from time to time, by the justices of peace, to have them suppressed, as highly prejudicial to the peace and good government of the country.* It is not strange, therefore, that Shepard, in mature life, should have looked back upon his early childhood, in which he was exposed to the corrupting influence of these sports, as a season of peculiar danger, from which he was mercifully delivered by a kind Providence.

When Thomas returned again to his father's house, which he did after the cause of his removal from home had passed by, he found all things changed, or fast changing, for the worse. His " dear mother" was dead, or died very soon after his return.

* Neal, Hist. Purit. ii. 249.

His sister Margaret, who was very fond of him, married her father's clerk. His sister Ann was married to a Mr. Farmer. And to fill up the measure of his griefs, his father married a second wife, who soon made him aware of the difference between his " own mother and a step-mother." She evidently did not love the little motherless boy, and endeavored to incense his father against him ; " it may be," says Shepard, meekly, " that it was justly so, for my childishness." The neglect at grandfather's, and the " Whitsun-Ales," at the " blind little town " of Adthrop, may have rendered the forlorn child somewhat wayward and troublesome ; but the probability is that the step-mother magnified and misrepresented every fault of the orphan, that her own little Samuel might enjoy a larger share of his father's affection.

After suffering under this domestic tyranny for some time, he was sent to the free school in Towcester. But this was to him the school of " one Tyrannus," or of "Ajax Flagellifer." The master, whose name was Rice, a Welshman, was very severe and irritable ; and he treated the poor boy with such harshness and cruelty, as to extinguish, for the time, all love of learning, and to make him often wish that he might be a " keeper of hogs" rather than a scholar. " Bears," says Pliny, " are the fatter for beating." But this is not always or altogether true of boys, especially of such boys as Thomas Shepard, who, it is presumed, rarely needed chastisement, and was more likely to be injured than benefited by severity. "The fierce, Orbilian way of treating children, too commonly used in schools, is a dreadful curse of God upon our miserable offspring, who are born ' children of wrath.' " It is boasted now and then of a schoolmaster, that such and such a brave man had his education under him. There is nothing said, how many that might have been brave men have been destroyed by him ; how many brave wits have been dispirited, confounded, murdered by his barbarous way of managing them. If a fault must be punished, let instruction, both unto the delinquent and unto the spectator, accompany the correction. Let the odious nature of the sin that has enforced the correction be declared, and let nothing be done in a passion; let all be done with all the evidence of compassion that may be.*

William Shepard — the father — died when Thomas was about ten years of age. During his last sickness, which was short and very distressing, the oppressed and dispirited child, to whom life had begun to present its sternest realities, prayed passionately for his recovery; and he made a solemn resolution to serve God better than he had done, if his prayers might be answered; " as knowing that I should be left alone if he were gone. Yet the Lord took him away by death, and I was left fatherless and motherless, when I was about ten years old." It is not to be inferred from these prayers, that at this early age he entertained any hope that he was a Christian; for children who have been religiously educated will often, under the pressure of affliction, pray very earnestly for relief; but from the fact that he made a solemn covenant " to serve God *better*," if his father might recover, we may presume that he had been under very serious impressions, and had tried to maintain a kind of religion in his life.

Upon the death of his father, he was committed to the care of his mother-in-law, who, in consideration of his portion of one hundred pounds, agreed to maintain and educate him. But he was still doomed to be "much neglected," and to feel more keenly than ever the difference between his "own mother and a step-mother." She, as was to have been expected from her previous conduct, proved faithless to her trust; and at last his brother John — William being now dead — offered to take him, and, for the use of his portion, to bring him up as his own child. " And so I lived with this my eldest brother, who showed much love unto me, and unto whom I owe much; for him God made to be both father and mother unto me."

About this time the cruel Welsh schoolmaster died, and was succeeded in the school by a man of talents and of reputed piety,

---

* Essays to do Good, pp. 172, 173.

b *

who was also employed to officiate as the minister of the town. Although he disappointed the expectations of the people with respect to his piety, and afterwards became an "apostate and an enemy of all righteousness," he seems to have been an able teacher ; for he succeeded in reviving or awakening in the mind of young Shepard — who had conceived such a disgust of study that he had rather " keep hogs or beasts than go to school and learn " — a love of application, and a strong desire to be a scholar. Under this new stimulus, he applied himself with great diligence to the Latin and Greek languages, in which he made rapid progress. He was studious, because he was " ambitious of being a scholar," and of enjoying " the honor of learning." At the same time he seems to have been, to a certain extent, influenced by some higher, if not a truly religious motive ; for once, when he was unsuccessful in taking notes of the sermon, he was troubled about it, and " prayed the-Lord earnestly " for assistance in this exercise ; a fact which, at least, indicates a deep sense of his dependence upon God for success in his studies, and a feeling that he was bound to seek the honor which cometh from above, as well as the " honor of learning." But whatever his ruling passion might have been, and whatever may be inferred as to his religious state at this time, from his general seriousness, we know that he devoted himself to the necessary studies with such diligence, and was enabled to make such progress in them, that before he had reached the age of fifteen, he was pronounced by competent judges to be fit for the university.

CHAPTER II.

Mr. Shepard enters Emmanuel College, Cambridge. — Devotes himself to hard study — Neglects religion. — Becomes proud of a little learning. — Has the small-pox. — Effect of Dr. Chadderton's preaching. — Associates with dissipated young men. — Remonstrated with by religious friends. — Falls into a gross sin. — Effect of this sin upon his conscience. — Dr. Preston. — Deep convictions. — Distressing temptations. — Despair. — Dawning of light. — Letter to a friend. — Increasing light. — Change of life. — Peace of mind. — Application to study. — Graduates with honor.

THE brother of Mr. Shepard, having undertaken the care of his education, was anxious to send him to college. But probably the expense of a collegiate course exceeded, at that time, his pecuniary means ; and the portion of one hundred pounds, of which he had the use, would hardly defray the charges of a residence at either of the universities. At this moment, so critical and decisive in the life of the almost friendless scholar, Mr. Cockerill, a fellow of Emmanuel College, Cambridge, and a native of Northamptonshire, came to Northampton upon a visit to his friends ; and having satisfied himself, by a personal examination, that Shepard was worthy of patronage, encouraged his brother to send him to Cambridge, promising to use his influence there in his behalf. Other persons, connected with the university, interested themselves in this application, and although he was, in his own opinion, "very raw and young," he was admitted to Emmanuel College as a pensioner in the year 1619. During the early part of his college course, Mr. Cockerill, who had so kindly encouraged and befriended him, was his tutor. Thus this chosen vessel, forsaken of father and mother, and cast helpless upon the world was, by "a secret hand of Providence," taken out of "that profane and ignorant town of Towcester," the "worst town, I think, in the world," and graciously provided for in Cambridge, "the best place for knowledge and learning," where he was prepared, by a severe discipline, for an arduous and important service in the church of God.

Up to this period, although he seems to have been at times deeply serious, and to have been in the habit of praying frequently under the pressure of affliction, he was evidently destitute of a saving knowledge of the truth. During the first two years of his college life he devoted himself to hard study, greatly neglecting religion and the practice of secret prayer, (which he had hitherto observed,) except at times, when his early religious impressions revived with considerable force, and he was induced to pay some attention to the concerns of his soul. The effect of a little learning was what is often witnessed upon minds of his order. When in his third year he became sophister, he began to be "foolish and proud," and to exhibit himself in public as a disputer about things which he afterwards saw he "did not then know at all, but only prated about them." Time and more learning corrected this folly, and made him one of the humblest, as he was one of the devoutest of men. It would be well if he had more imitators in the feelings with which he looked back upon this stage of his intellectual development. "There is nothing more lamentable," says Luther, in his Table Talk, "than the pride and ambition of many young preachers, who wish to shine as logicians, rhetoricians, etc., and become so finical and obscure in their preaching, that neither the people nor themselves know what they are about. A young lawyer, in his first year, is a Justinian; in his second year he is a doctor; in the third a licentiate; in the fourth a bachelor; in the fifth a student."

But Mr. Shepard was not left to neglect the interests of his soul in his ambition to shine as a scholar and a "disputer of this world." In his second year he was brought near to the grave by the small-pox, which had awakened him, in some measure, to a sense of his guilt and danger. The preaching of Dr. Chadderton, the master of Emmanuel College, especially upon a sacrament day, also produced a deep impression upon his mind. And a few months afterwards he heard Mr. Dickinson, in the chapel, discourse upon the words, "I will not destroy it for ten's sake," with a powerful effect upon his conscience. But these serious impressions gradually disappeared, and he unfortunately fell into the society of some dissipated young men, who endeavored to counteract and destroy all the influence of those pious preachers. He even, for a time, went with them in their time-wasting and soul-destroying amusements and pleasures, and seemed fast making shipwreck of faith and a good conscience. But he was not suffered to continue long in this thoughtless state. Upon one occasion, a pious student, with whom he chanced to be walking, described to him "the misery of every man out of Christ," and faithfully admonished him of his guilt and danger. This awakened, and for a time checked him in his course of folly and sin. At another time he happened to be present when several pious persons were conversing upon the wrath of God, revealed from heaven against all unrighteousness and ungodliness of men, which they spoke of under the figure of a consuming fire, intolerable and eternal. This conversation revived and strengthened the solemn impressions which had been previously made upon his mind, and led him to resume the practice of secret prayer, as a means of escaping from that wrath to come which he so much feared.

But he had not yet seen the evil of his heart, nor felt that conviction of sin which prostrates the soul before the throne of grace in godly sorrow that worketh repentance unto life. The effect of the conversations referred to soon wore off, as other serious impressions had done, until an event occurred which revived them all with overwhelming force, and made him feel, as he had never felt before, the need of atoning blood to cleanse him from all sin. The sin of Peter, and its immediate effect, are left upon the sacred record to show us the depth to which men may fall if left to themselves, — to encourage the penitent sinner to return with tears to the Saviour against whom he has sinned, — and to exhibit the riches of divine grace, which can rescue the soul from the deepest degradation; and for the same reasons we

record the fact which follows, earnestly admonishing the reader
to beware of using it as an encouragement to sin, lest his "bands
be made strong," and repentance be hid from his eyes. As the
fears which had been awakened by the solemn addresses of his
pious friends gradually subsided, Shepard again associated with
the loose and dissipated students of his own and of other colleges,
and frequently joined them in their intemperate carousals; until, at length, upon a Saturday night, he drank so freely that
he became grossly intoxicated, and was carried, in a state of
insensibility, to the chambers of a student of Christ's College, where he awoke to consciousness late on Sabbath morning, sick, and completely prostrated from the effects of this
debauch.

The moral impression of a fall like this is very different
upon different persons. Some of those dissolute young men,
probably, thought of that night's excess only as a matter to be
laughed about at their next convivial meeting. Not so with
Shepard. Filled with confusion and shame by the recollec-
tion of his "beastly carriage," he hurried away into the fields,
and there hid himself, during the whole of that dreadful Sabbath,
from every eye but that of God. The particular sin, however,
which made him afraid, and drove him, like Adam, into concealment, not only awakened him to pungent sorrow for this act,
but opened his eyes to see the exceeding sinfulness of his whole
life, and the necessity of repentance for all his sins. It was a
day long to be remembered, for it was the commencement of a
new life. In that solitude, where he lay trembling like a culprit,
"the Lord, who might justly have cut me off in the midst of my
sin, did meet me with much sadness of heart, and troubled my
soul for this and other sins, which then I had leisure to think
of, and made me resolve to set upon a course of daily meditation about the evil of sin and my own ways." Let those who
are disposed to speak lightly or scornfully of the early transgressions of eminent Christians, remember the bitter tears with
which they were lamented and abandoned.

But with all this trouble of mind, and compunction on account of actual sins, he had not yet obtained a true self-knowledge, nor seen the hidden evils of his heart. To this deeper and clearer view of himself as a sinner, he was led by the preaching of Dr. Preston, one of the most able theologians and preachers of his time, who became master of Emmanuel College in 1622. Shepard, hearing the preaching of Dr. Preston spoken of as "most spiritual and excellent," by Samuel Stone and others, listened attentively to the instructions of this celebrated divine, hoping to find here that guidance in the way of righteousness which he so much needed. The first sermon which he heard from Dr. Preston was upon the words, "Be ye transformed by the renewing of your mind," (Rom. xii. 2;) in which the nature of a change of heart was clearly unfolded. Under this discourse, "the Lord so bored my ears as that I understood what he spake; the secrets of my soul were laid open before me, and the hypocrisy of all the good things I thought I had in me, as if one had told him of all that ever I did — of all the turnings and deceits of my heart." So clearly was he made to see himself, — his secret sins — the whole frame and temper of his mind, — that he thought Dr. Preston the "most searching preacher in the world;" and with profound gratitude to God, and love for the preacher, he began in earnest to seek for that radical conversion and renewal, the nature of which had been so clearly exhibited to him.

This new birth, however, was not to be for Shepard, as it appears to be in some cases, a speedy or an easy work. Many pass from a state of sin and condemnation to the light, liberty, and hope of the children of God, in such a way that their whole experience in relation to this change may be expressed in the words of the blind man whom the Saviour suddenly and by a miraculous touch restored to sight — "Whereas I was blind, now I see." But Shepard's conviction of sin had been exceedingly pungent and distressing, and his progress to a state of reconciliation and peace with God was rough, protracted, and painful. He was beset with fears of death and "the terrors of God's wrath." In his daily meditation, "constantly every

evening before supper," he found the Lord ever teaching
him something concerning himself, or the divine law, or the
vanity of the world, which he never saw before, and which
filled him with perplexity and overwhelming solicitude. He
was also assaulted by sharp temptations. At one time he felt
" a depth of atheism and unbelief in the main matters of salvation," — whether the Scriptures were the word of God, —
whether Christ was the Messiah, — whether there was a God.
At another time he " felt all manner of temptations to all
kinds of religions, not knowing which to choose." At last he
heard of Grindleton, and was in danger of falling into Per-
fectionism, Familism, Antinomianism, or whatever that system
was called which afterwards made such havoc in the infant
churches of New England. He did not really adopt or believe
any of the absurd doctrines of the Familists, but only went so
far in these " miserable fluctuations and straits of his soul "
as to question " whether that glorious state of perfection might
not be the truth," and whether old Mr. Rogers's " Seven Treatises," and the " Practice of Christianity," — books which were
then esteemed as containing very sound theology, — " might not
be legal," and these writers " legal men ; " a singular hallucina-
tion, from which he was soon delivered by reading in one of the
Familist books the astounding doctrine, that a Christian is so
swallowed up in the spirit, " that what action soever the spirit
moves him to commit, suppose adultery, he may do it, and it is
no sin to him." This passage, like an overdose of poison,
operated exactly contrary to its nature and design. Tempted as
he was to " all kinds of religion," he could not digest this doctrine of devils ; and the horrible absurdity of the proposition
awakened in him an intense abhorrence of the whole system to
which it belonged, which in after years, and in more critical times,
rendered him a most determined and successful opposer of Antinomianism, as we shall see in the progress of this biography.

In the mean time, the other temptations by which he was led
to doubt the genuineness of Christ's miracles, and, in short, the
truth of divine revelation, continued with unabated, if not with

increasing, severity; so that, at last, having questioned whether Christ did not cast out devils by Beelzebub, he conceived the dreadful idea that he had committed the unpardonable sin, and was abandoned to hopeless apostasy and destruction. And now, "the terrors of God began to break in, like floods of fire," into his soul. He saw, as he then thought, in these rebellious doubts, and in this chaotic darkness of mind, the fruits of "God's eternal reprobation." He thought of God as "a consuming fire and an everlasting burning," and himself as a "poor prisoner, led to that fire." And these thoughts of eternal reprobation and torment so distressed him, especially "at one time, upon a Sabbath day, at evening," that he became well nigh distracted, and was strongly tempted, like Judas, to anticipate his doom, and, by suicide, hurry to his own place.

During eight dark and dismal months, these "fiery darts of Satan" were incessantly hurled at his peace, and there seemed to be no help for his poor soul in God or man; for he was afraid of God, and was ashamed to speak of these things to any experienced Christian. Three things, according to Luther, are necessary to form a theologian — namely, study, prayer, and temptation. And doubtless Shepard's gloomy passage through this "slough of despond" was necessary to give him a clear and an affecting view of his misery and helplessness as a sinner; to fix more firmly in his mind those doctrines which he was subsequently to preach; to make him humble under the honor that awaited him, and to fit him to apply the promises of the gospel judiciously to distressed consciences. Like Luther, he learned the true divinity by being "hunted into the Bible" and to the throne of grace; and he was eminently fitted to sympathize with the afflicted, by those horrible temptations which almost broke his spirit and drove him to despair. At the same time, his peculiar experience, both in his descent into these "depths of Satan," and in the manner of his deliverance from them, tended to give to his preaching and writings, that "legal" aspect, which there will be occasion to speak of more particularly hereafter.

His conflicts were now drawing to a close, and light was about to dispel the horror of that darkness in which his mind had been so long shrouded. When he was at the worst, not knowing what to do, and not daring to disclose his feelings to any person, it occurred to him that he should do as Christ did in his agony. The Saviour prayed earnestly, and an angel came down to comfort him ; and this seemed to be the only way of relief. Shut up to this, he fell down in agonizing supplication, and " being in prayer, I saw myself so unholy, and God so holy, that my spirit began to sink ; yet the Lord recovered me, and poured out a spirit of prayer upon me for free mercy and pity ; and in the conclusion of the prayer, I found the Lord helping me to see my unworthiness of any mercy, and to leave myself with him, to do with me what he would. And then, and never till then, I found rest ; and so my heart was humbled, and I went with a staid heart to supper late that night, and so rested here, and the terrors of the Lord began to assuage sweetly."

To a friend who afterwards inquired of him how the atheistical thoughts which had tormented him were removed, he thus writes : " The Lord awakened me, and bid me beware lest an old sore break out again. And this I found, that strength of reason would commonly convince my understanding that there was a God ; but I felt it utterly insufficient to persuade my will of it, unless it was by fits, when, as I thought, God's Spirit moved upon the chaos of these horrible thoughts ; and this, I think, will be found a truth. I did groan under the bondage of those unbelieving thoughts, looking up and sighing to the Lord, that if he were as his works and word declared him to be, he would please to reveal himself by his own beams, and persuade my heart, by his own Spirit, of his essence and being, which, if he would do, I should account it the greatest mercy that ever he showed me. And, after grievous and heavy perplexities, when I was by them almost forced to make an end of myself and sinful life, and to be my own executioner, the Lord came between the bridge and the water, and set me, out of anguish of spirit, to pray unto him for light in the midst of so great darkness. In which time, he revealed himself, manifested his love, stilled all those raging thoughts, so that, though I could not read the Scripture without blasphemous thoughts before, now I saw a glory, a majesty, a mystery, a depth in it, which fully persuaded; and which light — I desire to speak it to the glory of his free grace, seeing you call me to it — is not wholly put out, but remains, while I desire to walk closely with him, unto this day. And thus the Lord opened my eyes, and cured me of my misery; and if any such base thoughts come (like beggars to my door) to my mind, and put these scruples to me, I used to send them away with this answer: Why should I question that truth which I have both known and seen?" *

To the period referred to in this extract the conversion of Mr. Shepard must be assigned; but he did not at once obtain full assurance and a settled peace. The firm earth upon which he had at length landed seemed to heave under him like the stormy sea where he had been so long tossed, and, for a while, he walked unsteadily and with fear. When his distracting doubts and dreadful apprehensions of God's wrath were gone, he still felt his unworthiness, his bondage to self and the world, his unfitness for any good work, and was oppressed with the dread of losing what God had already wrought in him. But walking, on one occasion, in the fields, "the Lord dropped this meditation" into his mind, with a distinctness and force which made it appear almost like an address: "Be not discouraged because thou art so vile, but make this double use of it: first, loathe thyself the more; secondly, feel a greater need, and put a greater price, upon Jesus Christ, who only can redeem thee from all sin." This thought greatly encouraged him, and he was thus enabled to "beat Satan with his own weapons."

His outward life was now wholly changed. He abstained from all appearance of evil. He no longer associated with the gay and the thoughtless; and he felt it to be his duty, not only to exhibit an example of holy living, but to labor in all appropriate

* Select Cases Resolved, pp. 44, 45.

ways for the conversion of his fellow-students. So much progress he had made without any direct assistance from human instructors, and without obtaining any assurance of his pardon and acceptance with God. He had been working out his salvation with fear and trembling, alone ; and although his face was toward Zion, and his feet in the way of the divine precepts, he needed, like Apollos, that some one should expound unto him the way of God more perfectly, and to lead him to take those views of Christ, and of his redemptive work, which were necessary to a cheerful hope, and an appropriation of the promises of grace.

At this stage of his experience, and in this state of mind, Dr. Preston providentially preached a sermon upon 1 Cor. i. 30 : " But of him are ye in Christ Jesus, who of God is made unto us wisdom, and righteousness, and sanctification, and redemption ; " in which he showed that there is in Christ an ample supply for all our spiritual wants, and that this treasure is designed for the benefit of all Christians. " And when he had opened how all the good, all the redemption I had, was from Jesus Christ, I did then begin to prize him, and he became very sweet to me." Although he had often heard Christ freely offered by ministers before, if men would receive him as their Lord and Saviour, yet he had found his heart " ever unwilling to accept of Christ upon those terms." But now Christ became precious to his soul, and he found it easy to comply with the conditions upon which all the blessings of redemption were promised.

He was not, however, entirely free from all fears and doubts. But he found the Lord constantly " revealing free mercy," and showing him that all his ability to believe in Christ, and to accept of him, was in this grace of God. He saw that Christ obeyed the law, not on his own account, but to work out and bring in " everlasting righteousness" for poor sinners who had none of their own — a righteousness which is sufficient to " justify the ungodly who believeth in Jesus." He saw, also, that " to as many as received him, to them gave he power to become the sons of God," and he felt that the Lord had given him " a heart to receive Christ with a naked hand." And so, after many conflicts and questionings, he obtained that peace of God which passeth knowledge, and commenced that life of faith, which, as the shining light, shone brighter and brighter unto the perfect day.

Although these religious exercises must have occupied a considerable portion of his time, and have rendered all human learning and worldly honor comparatively worthless, yet he seems to have maintained a highly respectable standing in college; and after the decided change which has been described took place, and religion began to shed its light and peace upon his soul, a rapid development of his intellectual powers became evident. There is nothing that gives such elevation, strength, and enlargement to the mind as the practical reception of the word of God under the influence of the Holy Spirit. "The fear of the Lord is the beginning of wisdom, and the knowledge of the holy is understanding." Shepard, in common with many others, felt the invigorating effect of that heavenly knowledge; and in after years, when young men consulted him with respect to their studies, he was accustomed to refer to this influence of religion upon his own mind, and to advise them to spend a considerable portion of their time in communing with their own hearts and with God, a practice which he had found so beneficial in all his intellectual efforts. Thus, at peace with God, — with a definite object of pursuit before him, — and in the diligent application of himself to all his studies, — he continued through the remainder of his college life. He took his bachelor's degree in 1623 — not far from the time, as we should judge, when he experienced the radical change in his religious feelings above described; and in 1625, when he had finished his course of study, he left college, with a high reputation for scholarship, and with the usual honors of the university.

c *

CHAPTER III.

MR. SHEPARD became master of arts in the year 1627. About six months before taking his degree, he went to reside in the family of Thomas Weld, (then of Tarling, in the county of Essex, and afterwards ordained the first minister of the church in Roxbury,) where he received much aid in his theological studies, and encouragement in his Christian course. Here he became acquainted with Thomas Hooker, who about that time was appointed a lecturer at Chelmsford, in Essex, from whose able and discriminating ministry he derived great advantage. While engaged in his studies and preparation at Tarling, he became " very solicitous what would become of him," when he had taken his master's degree; for then his "time and portion would be spent," and he would be left without resources, and with small hope of finding any employment for which he was fitted.

The religious condition of England, at that time, was very dark and perplexed; and the prospects of pious young men, who, like Thomas Shepard, desired to serve God and their generation in the gospel ministry, were exceedingly discouraging. Although the picture of those times has been often drawn, and the circumstances which compelled our fathers to abandon, not only the church in which they had been educated, but the country that gave them birth, have been often and eloquently described, yet it may not be amiss to give, in this place, a brief

sketch of the history of that gloomy period, that our youthful
readers may clearly understand what it was that made Mr.
Shepard so " solicitous what should become of him," and why he
could not devote his talents and piety to the work of the ministry in Protestant England.

At the beginning of the reign of Henry VIII., who ascended
the throne of England in the year 1509, the English church
was a branch of that Papal hierarchy which had extended its
power over the civilized world, and like the great red dragon
of the Apocalypse, had swept away a large part of the stars of
heaven, and cast them to the earth, rendering the skies black,
and the night hideous. During the long and tyrannical reign
of that apostate church, however, there were a few faithful
witnesses for the truth who testified and were persecuted, like
Antipas, even in the region where " Satan's seat" was. In the
valleys of the Alps, the Waldenses, uncorrupted by the errors
and unawed by the power of Rome, retained the doctrines and
observed the discipline of the primitive church. The history of
these people is, indeed, somewhat obscure; but from their own
declarations, corroborated by the confessions of some of their
worst enemies, it appears highly probable that they could trace
the origin of their churches back to the age of the apostles, and
that their religious doctrines and practices were substantially
those which long afterwards were adopted and maintained by
the English Puritans. They rejected the books of the Apoc-
rypha from the sacred canon. They kept the Sabbath very
strictly. They were extremely careful of the religious education of their children. They denied the supremacy of the pope,
the lawfulness of indulgences, auricular confession, prayers for
the dead, transubstantiation, invocation of saints, and the worship
of the Virgin Mary. They abhorred the mass, the doctrine of
purgatory, and, in short, all the unscriptural ceremonies, superstitions, and abominations of the Papacy. They committed the
pastoral care of their churches to ministers freely chosen by
themselves, who were expected, in conformity to the apostolic
injunction, to be examples to the flock, in word, in conversation,

in faith, in purity, in charity. Their whole aim seems to have been to realize in their form of ecclesiastical government, and in the lives both of the clergy and of the people, that sanctity and godly simplicity which characterized the commencement of the church, and which were so beautifully exhibited in the precepts and example of Jesus Christ.*

Thus, three hundred years before the reformation, we find a company of sturdy reformers, who had never bowed the knee to Baal, — a remnant according to the election of grace, — who prepared the way and furnished the means for the final overthrow of " that man of sin," that " son of perdition," who " exalteth himself above all that is called God, or that is worshipped." They were the Protestants of the twelfth century, and were called *Cathari*, pure, on account of the professed purity of their doctrines and life, just as our fathers were afterwards in scorn styled *Puritans*, for their opposition to the errors and corruptions of their times.

The reformation, which many erroneously suppose to have commenced in the sixteenth century, was nothing more than the rejection of doctrines and practices which men, in the course of ages, had ignorantly or wickedly added to the religion of Christ. And this work was commenced by the faithful servants of God as soon as the evil began. The great Head of the church had never left himself without a few witnesses, at least, to testify against the errors that were constantly mingling with his truth. The Romanists ask, with an air of triumph, " Where was your religion before Luther's reformation ? " We answer, that in the darkest times of the antichristian apostasy, the true church, and the doctrines which Luther, and Calvin, and our fathers preached, were found among the Waldenses, three hundred years before the time of Luther ; and they were but the successors and representatives of still earlier reformers, who protested, with what strength th ey had, against the encroachments of the " man of sin." It was from these people that the

---

* Mosheim, Eccl. Hist. cent. 12, ch. 12.

doctrines of the reformation were disseminated in England and on the continent; and had it not been for them, perhaps neither Wickliff, in the fourteenth century, nor Luther, in the sixteenth, would have appeared as reformers. During the fierce persecutions to which they were constantly exposed, in the thirteenth century, from the Papal church, some of them fled into Germany; while others, turning to the west, found refuge in England. Raymond Lollard, one of the leading men among the Waldenses, promulgated their doctrines in the land of our fathers, where they were called " Lollards ; " and where, from the fact that, so late as the year 1619, there was a tower standing in London, which, in consequence of its use as a place of confinement for those who professed their religion, was called " The Lollard's Tower," it would seem that they did not wholly escape the malice of that antichristian power which consumed their fathers and brethren, as heretics, in Italy.

The doctrines held by the Waldenses were received and taught by John Wickliff, the earliest of the English reformers. Wickliff was born about the year 1324. He was educated at Queen's College, Oxford, in which he was afterwards professor of divinity, and was, for a time, minister of Lutterworth, in the diocese of Lincoln. He was a profound scholar, and an eloquent preacher. Though born and educated amidst all the darkness of Popery, he preached, substantially, the same doctrines which were afterwards maintained by the Puritans ; and one hundred and thirty years before the reformation, vindicated those great principles, which, under the preaching of Luther, Calvin, and others, enlightened the world, and produced that movement toward religious and civil liberty which must eventually be enjoyed by all nations. He wrote nearly two hundred volumes ; but his greatest work was the translation of the New Testament into English.

Wickliff died in 1384. After his death, the university published the following testimony concerning him : " That from his youth to the time of his death, his conversation was so praiseworthy, that there never was any spot or suspicion reported of it; that in his reading and preaching he behaved like a stout and valiant champion of the faith, and that he had written in logic, philosophy, divinity, morality, and the arts, without an equal." Without, however, supposing that Wickliff was either immaculate in life, or absolutely free from theological errors, we may regard him as a bold defender of fundamental truths, and the "morning star" of the reformation in England.

In the year 1425, after he had been dead more than forty years, the Council of Constance ordered all his works to be collected and burnt, together with his bones. This diabolical order was executed by Richard Fleming, Bishop of Lincoln, who caused the remains of the excommunicated reformer to be dug up, burnt, and the ashes to be thrown into a brook. "Thus," says Fuller, "this brook hath conveyed his ashes into Avon, Avon into Severn, Severn into the Narrow Seas; they into the main ocean. And thus the ashes of Wickliff are the emblem of his doctrine, which is now disseminated all the world over." * The number of his disciples increased so greatly after his death, that new and more severe laws were made against heretics, in the hope — vain as all such hopes must be — that force would prevent the spread of truth, and the dungeon and the stake put an end to the efforts of Christians to rescue the people from the thralldom of error. Fox, the martyrologist, referring to the posthumous persecution of Wickliff, remarks, "that as there is no counsel against the Lord, so there is no keeping down truth, but it will spring and come out of dust and ashes, as appeared in this man. For they digged up his body, burnt his bones, and drowned his ashes; yet the word of God and truth of his doctrine, with the fruit and success of his labors, they could not burn, and they remain, for the most part, to this day." †

About eight years after Wickliff's death, his followers presented a remonstrance to the English Parliament, in which they

---

* Church History, b. iv. p. 171.   † Acts and Monuments, i. 606.

speak of Romanism just as Shepard did, two hundred and fifty years later. They say that when the church of England began to mismanage her temporalities, in conformity to the precedent of Rome, faith, hope, and charity began to take leave of her communion; that the English priesthood, derived from Rome, and pretending to a power superior to angels, is not the priesthood which Christ settled upon his apostles; that the enjoining celibacy upon the clergy was the occasion of scandalous irregularities in the church; that the pretended miracle of transubstantiation runs the great part of Christendom upon idolatry; that exorcisms and benedictions, pronounced over bread and oil, wax and incense, over the stones of the altar, the holy vestments, the miter, the cross, and the pilgrim's staff, have more of necromancy than of religion in them; that the union of the offices of prince and bishop, prelate and secular judge, in the same person, and making the rector of a parish a civil officer, is a plain mismanagement, and puts a kingdom out of the right way; that prayer made for the dead is a wrong ground for charity and religious endowments, and therefore all the charities of England stand upon a wrong foundation; that pilgrimages, prayers, and offerings, made to images and crosses, have nothing of charity in them, and are near of kin to idolatry; that auricular confession makes the priests proud, and lets them into the secrets of the penitent, gives opportunity for intrigues, and that this, as well as the doctrine of indulgences, is attended with scandalous consequences; that the vow of single life, undertaken by women in the church of England, is the occasion of horrible disorders.* These were sound doctrines, and well put to the reason and conscience of the Parliament; but they wrought no change, and rendered it no safer to preach or practice them. Persecution raged against the Lollards, — as all who desired a reformation of the church were now called, — under Henry V.; but the more they were persecuted, the more they increased, and they sowed the whole of England with good seed, which, nourished

* Collier, Eccl. Hist. i. cent. 14.

by the blood of the martyrs, has continued to bring forth good fruit to this day.

The first rupture between the English church and the Papal hierarchy, and the commencement of what has been called the reformation in England, were occasioned, not by a change of religious opinions either in the ruling powers, or the great mass of the people, but by causes purely selfish and worldly. Henry VIII., a man not only destitute of all personal religion, but possessed of all the vile and abominable passions which can degrade humanity, wished to obtain from the pope a divorce from his queen, Katharine, that he might, with the sanction of the church, marry Anne Boleyn, who had been an attendant upon the queen. The ground which he assigned for this divorce was so absurd that even the pope, unscrupulous as he was in respect to other matters, and strongly as he was inclined to grant the request of his powerful subject, could not be prevailed upon to sanction it. Whereupon Henry, not to be defeated in his cruel purpose, resolved to make himself the supreme head of the English church.

His first act of retaliation upon the pope was a proclamation, in which all persons were forbidden to purchase any thing from Rome, under the severest penalties. In 1534, being the twenty-sixth year of his reign, the act of supremacy, which took from the pope all authority and power over the church in England, and gave to the king all authority whatever in ecclesiastical affairs, was passed by the Parliament. This act declares that " the king, his heirs, and successors, kings of England, shall be taken, accepted, and reputed the only SUPREME HEAD of the church of England; and shall have and enjoy, annexed and united to the imperial crown of this realm, as well the title and style thereof, as all the honors, immunities, profits, and commodities, to the SUPREME HEAD of the church belonging; and shall have full power and authority to visit, repress, redress, and amend all such errors, heresies, abuses, contempts, and enormities, whatsoever they be, which, by any manner of spiritual authority or jurisdiction, ought or may be lawfully reformed, repressed, ordered, redressed, counseled, restrained, or amended, most to the pleasure of Almighty God, and increase of virtue in Christ's religion, and for the conservation of peace, unity, and tranquillity of this realm, any usage, custom, foreign law, foreign authority, prescription, or any thing or things, to the contrary notwithstanding."

This act was the commencement of what has been called the "Reformation" in England. But it was not such an act as the state of the church demanded. It was conceived in sin, and brought forth in iniquity. It gave no relief to burdened consciences, nor freedom to the souls that were crying from under the altar. It made no change in doctrine, nor breathed any new life into the dead formalities of the old religion. It simply transferred the church, like a flock of sheep, from a rapacious pope to a brutal and licentious king; and gave to a civil, instead of an ecclesiastical tyrant, the sole power of reforming abuses, heresies, and errors, without the slightest regard to the rights of conscience, or the laws of Jesus Christ. It was an act which, in banishing the pope, banished the King of Zion from his appropriate domain, and enthroned one who might be called literally, a "*man of sin*," in the church, — for he was one of the most wicked of men, — authorizing him, as God, to sit in the temple, and to usurp the authority of God. It was continually fortified, and its provisions extended, by subsequent acts of Parliament. In the thirty-seventh year of this reign, a law was passed which declares "that archbishops, bishops, archdeacons, and others, have no manner of jurisdiction ecclesiastical, but by, under, and from the king's authority, the only undoubted supreme head of the church of England, to whom, by Holy Scripture, all authority and power is wholly given to hear and determine all manner of causes whatsoever, and to correct all manner of heresies, errors, vices, and sins whatever; and to all such persons as his majesty shall appoint thereunto." * Under this law chancelors,

* Neal, Hist. Purit. ii. ch. 1.   Peirce, Vindication of Dissenters, pp. 7–9. Hume, Hist. Eng., A. D. 1534.

commissioners, and other officers, never heard of in the primitive church, were appointed; and, to secularize the church as effectually as possible, the king, in the exercise of his unlimited power, committed all the most important ecclesiastical matters to laymen. This exorbitant power in the political head of the church was confirmed in the reign of Edward VI., of Queen Elizabeth, of James I., and of Charles II.; and until the reign of William and Mary, all clergymen were compelled to acknowledge it in the oath of supremacy — an oath which transferred their allegiance, as Christians, from Christ to the King of England, and made them traitors to the cause which all true ministers are bound by a more solemn and stringent oath to defend at all hazards.

Although the church of England was thus effectually separated from the church of Rome, and emancipated from the authority of the pope, the great body of the inferior clergy, and of the people, countenanced and encouraged by many leading men both in the church and state, adhered firmly to the old opinions and practices; and although, during the reign of this capricious and cruel tyrant, there was much confiscation of church property, and persecution of Roman Catholics, there was but very little reformation from the worst corruptions of Popery. How could the church be purified by such a beast as Henry VIII., and by time-serving men like Cranmer, who were always ready to become the tools of a power that neither feared God nor regarded man?

Edward VI., a youth of very different disposition and temper from his father, — of visible piety even, — ascended the throne in 1547. Under his reign some change for the better was effected in the condition of the oppressed and suffering church. Two of the statutes against the Lollards, and several oppressive Popish laws, were repealed, and others, more favorable to truth and liberty, enacted by the Parliament which assembled soon after the accession of the young king. A committee of divines was appointed to examine and reform the worship of the church, who, finding the clergy generally incapa-

ble of composing either sermons or prayers, set forth a book
of Homilies, and a Liturgy for their use. This change in the
worship of the church was the foundation of that uniformity
which was subsequently established by the government, and
exacted with such unsparing rigor by those in power, that
many of the most pious and useful ministers in England, like
Shepard and his associates, who had conscientious scruples
respecting the propriety of some of these offices, were obliged to
abandon the ministry, or, like the woman of the Revelation, flee
into the wilderness, where God had prepared a place for them.

Nothing can be more certain than that, in the first and purest
age of the church, there was no such thing as a uniform liturgy,
which all worshipers were *obliged* to use and conform to. Very
few forms appear to have been used for three hundred years,
and those were not *imposed* upon the people by ecclesiastical or
civil power. In those times Christian worship consisted of
hymns, — prayers, — (which, as Tertullian says, were offered
sine monitore, quia de pectore, without a prompter, because they
came from the heart,) — the reading of the Scriptures, — and
the celebration of the Lord's supper. It was not until the fourth
century that set forms were introduced, and ministers were forbidden to use any prayers in the churches except such as were
composed by able men, or approved by the synods; and even
this innovation, as Shepard remarks, grew out of the gross and
palpable ignorance of the ministry in those contentious and
heretical times, and was enforced in order to prevent the scandalous scenes which were common in churches where the pastors
were incapable of preaching or praying to the edification of the
people.

By degrees, however, the worship of the church, which, from
the beginning, had been very simple, notwithstanding the forms
that had from time to time been introduced, began, as Burnet
remarks, to be thought too naked, unless " put under more artificial rules, and dressed up with much ceremony; " and therefore
various rights and ceremonies, better fitted to please the eye

and strike the imagination than to promote the godly edifying
of the worshiper, were continually added. Still there was no
universal uniformity of worship. Every bishop adopted that
form which he thought best adapted to the times and to the temper of his own people. And this diversity continued until the
Bishop of Rome, among other acts of usurpation, pretended
that it belonged to the mother church to furnish a model of
doctrine and of worship, to which all the churches in Christendom
ought to conform. But even under the dominion of the pope,
there was great diversity in the forms of worship, and *absolute
uniformity* was never effected until it was forced upon the
English church after its separation from Rome.

The committee of divines who prepared the English Liturgy under Edward VI. found a great variety of forms, and
much diversity in respect to worship, existing in the church.
In the south of England there was the Liturgy of Sarum; in the
north, that of the Duke of York; in South Wales, that of
Hereford; in North Wales, that of Bangor; in the diocese of
Lincoln, one which was peculiar to that see. The committee
collected all these offices, — this "copper counterfeit coin," —
as Shepard calls it, — "of a well-grown Antichrist, whereby he
cheated the churches when he stole away the golden legacy
of Christ," — with the design of forming out of them a new
Liturgy, which should be used in all parts of the country, and
by every congregation. They thought that entire uniformity,
both in doctrine and worship, was necessary to the purity and
peace of the church; and were determined that the diversity
which had been tolerated in the darkest times of Popery should
no longer be allowed in Protestant England. They attempted
what was at once unreasonable, unnecessary, and impracticable;
and forged fetters for the people, which, if they did not crush
the life of devotion out of the church, would one day be burst
asunder with violence and universal tumult. Had they drawn
up various forms for those whose feeble piety needed assistance,
and left something to the judgment, discretion, and conscience

of those who had begun to "breathe the pure air of the Holy Scriptures," the church might have been united, and New England remained for some centuries longer in the possession of its original inhabitants.

The first service book, or Liturgy of Edward VI., was gathered from the Popish Breviary, Ritual, and Missal, with but slight alterations or improvements. They did not, says Burnet, mend every thing that required it, but left the office of the mass as it was, only adding to it that which made it a communion. While many of the Romish superstitions were omitted, some were retained; the committee going "as far as they could in reforming the church," and hoping "that they who should come after would, as they might, do more." * They felt, honestly, no doubt, that it was a great advantage to the people to hear prayers in their native language, rather than in an unknown tongue. They wished to have the people united; and aimed to convert Papists to the English church by a form of worship which should differ as little as possible from that to which they had been accustomed. Those who desired a real reformation did all that they could; and those who were Papists at heart were satisfied to have a Liturgy which made no fundamental change. Among other things, the vestments in which the Romish priests officiated were retained, against the judgment of many pious persons, who thought that these surplices, copes, and other rags and symbols of Popery, should be confined to the pope's wardrobe. It was urged that these garments belonged to the idolatry of the mass, and had been used to set it off with more pomp and show, and ought not, therefore, to be used in a church professing to be apostolical. But to this the reformers replied, that the priest's garments, under the Mosaic dispensation, were white, and this seemed to be a fit emblem of the purity and decency becoming priests under the gospel. Moreover, it was said that the clergy were extremely poor, and could not afford to dress themselves decently; and as the people, vibrating

* Preface to the Liturgy of Edward VI.

d *

from the extreme of blind submission to the clergy, were inclined
to despise them, and to make light of their sacred functions, if
they were to officiate in their own garments they would bring
the divine offices into contempt. These considerations were
deemed conclusive, and so it was resolved that the use of the
Popish vestments should be continued, and made obligatory upon
all officiating clergymen.*

A more thorough reformation of the church — a reformation
which should leave none of the vain pomp and foolish pageant-
ry of Romanism behind — a reformation which should make
all the rites, ceremonies, and doctrines of the church conform-
able to the rules laid down by Christ and his apostles, and
suffer nothing to be required of men but what was clearly
sanctioned by the authority of God's word — was needed ; and
by many, even by Edward himself, greatly desired. And had
those in power followed the light of the Scriptures, which was
then beginning to shine upon the church, purging out the
old leaven of Popery, and every thing in doctrine or worship
which they themselves acknowledged was unscriptural, there
would have been no dissent except among the advocates of
an antichristian hierarchy. But, as Edward, in his vain efforts
to realize his idea of a reformation, sadly complained, those
bishops who ought to carry forward this work, "some for Papis-
try, some for ignorance, some for age, some for their ill name,
some for all these," were men "unable to execute discipline,"
and it was therefore "a thing unmeet for them to do." †

It was lamentably true, as Mrs. Hutchinson, in her interesting Memoirs of her husband, finely remarks, "that when the
dawn of the gospel began to break upon England, after the
dark night of the Papacy, the morning was more cloudy there
than in other places, by reason of the state interest which
was mixing and working itself into the interests of religion,
and which, in the end, quite wrought it out. For Henry

---

* Burnet, Hist. Reform. ii. 75, 76.

† Neale, Hist. Purit. i. 53.   Burnet, Hist. Reform. ii. 69, 427.

VIII., who by his royal authority cast out the pope, did not intend that the people of the land should have any ease of oppression, but only change their foreign yoke for homebred fetters, dividing the pope's spoils between himself and his bishops, who cared not for their father at Rome, so long as they enjoyed their patrimony and their honors at home, under another head." *

Under the reign of Mary, the sister of Edward, the English church reverted to Popery; and Protestants, indiscriminately, suffered the most severe and unrelenting persecution.

On the accession of Elizabeth, in 1558, all real Protestants in the nation entertained strong hopes that the work of reform, which was begun (with whatever motives) by her father, which was promoted to the extent of his power by her brother Edward, and which had been not only retarded, but reversed, by her sister Mary, of bloody memory, would be resumed and speedily completed. But all hopes founded upon the accession of a professedly Protestant queen were destined to be sadly disappointed.

The nation was, at this time, divided into three parties of very unequal size: the *Papists*, the *State Protestants*, and a small, but continually increasing, number of *truly religious people*, who were afterwards branded with the name of Puritans. The great body of the people of England, says Macaulay, had no fixed opinion as to the matters of dispute between the churches. "Each side had a few enterprising champions, and a few stout-hearted martyrs; but the nation, undetermined in its opinions and feelings, resigned itself implicitly to the guidance of the government, and lent to the sovereign, for the time being, an equally ready aid against either of the extreme parties. They were sometimes Protestant, sometimes Catholic, sometimes half Protestants, half Catholics. They were in a situation resembling that of those borderers whom Sir Walter Scott has described with so much spirit, —

"Who sought the beeves that made their broth,
In Scotland and in England both."

* Memoirs of Colonel Hutchinson, i. 105.

The religion of England was thus a mixed religion, like that of the Samaritan settlers described in the Second Book of Kings, " who feared the Lord, and served their own gods ; " like that of the Judaizing Christians, who blended the doctrines of the synagogue with those of the church ; like that of the Mexican Indians, who, for many generations after the subjugation of their race, continued to unite with the rites learned from their conquerors the worship of the grotesque idols which had been adored by Montezuma and Gautimozin." *

All the English clergy, who were really Protestant at heart, made vigorous exertions, in the beginning of the reign of Elizabeth, to separate the church more entirely from the influence of Popery ; but the queen, who controlled all the affairs of the church as well as of the state, was very differently inclined. Though educated as a Protestant, and professing, from her early years, to feel strong dislike of the Papacy, and love to the cause of truth, she was, in opinion, " little better than half a Protestant." She loved magnificence in religion as well as in every thing else, and, to the last, cherished a great fondness for those rites and ceremonies of the Romish church which her father had retained. " She had no scruple about conforming to that church, when conformity was necessary to her own safety ; and she had professed, when it suited her, to be wholly a Catholic." She always kept a crucifix, with wax lights burning around it, in her private chapel. The service of the church had been too much stripped of ornament and display to suit her taste, and its doctrines were made too narrow for her opinions ; in both, therefore, she made alterations, to bring them into greater conformity to the Papacy. Instead of carrying the reformation of Edward further, she often repented that it had been carried so far. Accordingly she directed the committee of divines, who were appointed, in 1559, to review the Liturgy of Edward, to strike out all passages that could be offensive to the pope, and to make the people easy about the corporeal presence of Christ in the

* Macaulay's Essays, i. 178, 179.

sacrament, but to say not a word in favor of the stricter Protestants, a respectable body both of the clergy and the laity, who were anxious to bring the reformation to that state which Protestants abroad regarded as the scriptural model.

In the year 1559, the Parliament passed an " act for the uniformity of common prayer, and service of the church, and administration of the sacraments ; " by one clause of which all ecclesiastical jurisdiction was again given up to the crown ; and the queen was empowered, with the advice of her commissioners, or metropolitan, to ordain and publish such other rites or ceremonies as might, in her opinion, be most for the advancement of God's glory, the edifying of his church, and the due reverence of Christ's holy mysteries and sacraments ; without which clause, reserving to the queen power to make what alterations she pleased, she told Archbishop Parker she would not have passed the act. The oppressive use that was made of the enormous power thus conferred upon a queen, who declared that she hated the Puritans worse than she did the Papists, we see in the history of those times. Elizabeth was resolved that all should conform to her worship, or suffer the severest penalties of the law; and she persecuted the conscientious Nonconformists with a cruelty which proved that her profession of hatred was sincere. She did not burn them, as her sister Mary did the heretics of her time, but she subjected them to hardships more terrible than death.

In the exercise of her boundless prerogative, she instituted that engine of persecution, the court of " High Commission ; " and no less than five courts of this name were established with increasing severity. The power of these tribunals was brought to bear with terrible effect upon the Puritans. A great many faithful ministers were suspended from their livings, deposed, fined, imprisoned, and their families and interests ruined, for refusing to conform to the established ritual. They were frequently imprisoned without any previous complaint, and sometimes without any knowledge of the charges upon which they

were arrested; they were refused bail, and often suffered a long
and tedious confinement before they were brought to trial.
They were not only denied the privilege of trial by jury, but
condemned without being confronted by the witnesses against
them. On the most insnaring questions, multiplied and arranged
in the most artful manner, they were obliged to answer instantly
upon oath, with the rack or the prison distinctly in view. The
horrible character of these inquisitorial examinations is well
described by Lord Burleigh, in a letter to Archbishop Whitgift: "I have read over your twenty-four articles, formed in
Romish style, of great length and curiosity, to examine all manner of ministers in this time, without distinction of persons,
to be executed, and I find them so curiously penned, so full of
branches and circumstances, that I think the Inquisition of Spain
used not so many questions to comprehend and to trap their
priests."

After the convocation of 1562 had framed the Thirty-nine
Articles, and, by a majority of one, decided to retain all the
ceremonies which had given so much offence to every real Protestant, the bishops began to enforce upon the clergy subscription to the Liturgy and ceremonies, as well as to the articles
of faith. The penalty for refusing to subscribe was expulsion
from their parishes. Three hundred ministers, of pious and exemplary lives, some of them eminent for their talents and learning, refused to subscribe, and were deprived of their livings.
Unwilling to separate from a church in which the word and the
sacraments were in substance administered, though disfigured
and defiled by some Popish superstitions, some of these deprived
ministers continued to preach, as they had opportunity, in places
where the ceremonies could be safely dispensed with, though
they were excluded, of course, from all ecclesiastical preferment.

Many of the common people were as strongly opposed to the
use of the clerical vestments, and other relics of Popery, as the
ministers, and, believing it to be unlawful to countenance such

superstitions even by their presence, would not enter the churches where they were used. It now became a question of great interest and importance, for those who were qualified and desirous to preach the gospel, as well as for those who wished to hear it in its purity, what their duty was in this posture of affairs. In the year 1572, a solemn consultation was held by them upon this subject; and after prayer and earnest debate respecting the lawfulness and necessity of separating from the established church, they came to this result: "That, since they could not have the word of God preached, nor the sacraments administered, without idolatrous gear, and since there had been a separate congregation in London, and another at Geneva, in Queen Mary's time, which used a book and order of preaching, administration, and discipline which Calvin had approved of, and which was free from the superstition of the English service, therefore it was their duty, in their present circumstances, to break off from the public church, and to assemble, as they had opportunity, in private houses, or elsewhere, to worship God in a manner that might not offend the light of their consciences." Another question was discussed at this meeting, namely, whether they should use so much of the Common Prayer and service of the church as was not offensive; or, since they were cut off from the church of England, at once to set up the purest and best form of worship most consonant to the sacred Scriptures, and to the practice of the foreign reformers. They concluded to do the latter; and accordingly laid aside the English Liturgy altogether, and adopted the service book used at Geneva. This has been called the epoch of the *Separation*, as the year 1562 was of *Nonconformity*.*

In the year 1581, the Parliament passed an act imposing a fine of 20*l.* a month on every person who refused to attend the Common Prayer; and it was not long before there was occasion to inflict this ruinous penalty. The afflicted Puritans appealed to the queen, to both houses of Parliament, to the Convocation,

---

* Neal, Hist. Purit. i. 154.

and to the bishops, but could obtain no relief. Several ministers were imprisoned for the inexcusable crime of asking for a little relief from the rigor with which they were pursued to ruin. Members of Parliament were sent to the Tower for speaking in favor of the miserable Puritans. Bills, passed in the House of Commons for their relief, were sent for by the queen, and cancelled: and the Parliament was peremptorily forbidden to meddle with ecclesiastical affairs.

Wearied out with this unrelenting persecution, which drove so many of the most useful ministers into obscurity, and discouraged by the stern rejection of all their petitions for relief, the Puritans began to despair of any further reformation of the church by the ruling powers; and in one of their assemblies came to this conclusion: " That, since the magistrate could not be induced to reform the discipline of the church by so many petitions and supplications, therefore, after so many years' waiting, it was lawful to act without him, and to introduce a reformation in the best manner they could." *

That portion of the Puritan party, however, to which our fathers belonged, did not voluntarily and schismatically separate from the church, like Brown and others, who renounced all communion with the establishment, not only in ceremonies and prayers, but in hearing the word and sacraments, and refused to recognize it as a true church, or its ministers as true ministers of the gospel. The Nonconformists generally did not deserve the name of Brownists, which they sometimes bore through the ignorance or malice of their enemies. They doubtless agreed with the separatists in opposing the tyranny and superstitions of the hierarchy, and in maintaining their right to worship God according to the dictates of their consciences enlightened by the Scriptures ; but they did not acknowledge him as their father, nor, in fact, did they agree with him in principle. The final exclusion of both parties from the parent church was brought about by the same cause, namely, the oppression which they suffered

* Neal, i. 303.

from the bishops; but sameness of origin is no proof of identity in doctrine. "No marvel," says Cotton, "if we take it ill to be called Brownists, in whole or in part; for neither in whole nor in part do we partake of his schism. He separated from churches and from saints; we only from the world, and that which is of the world. We were not baptized into his name, and why should we be called by his name? The Brownists did not beget us to God, or to the church, or to their schism — a schism which as we have lamented in them, as a fruit of misguided, ignorant zeal, so we. have ever borne witness against it since our first knowledge of it."*

The truth is, that while the Puritans deprecated and dreaded separation from the church, and labored in all suitable ways to avoid the necessity of going out of it, there was an evident determination on the part of the ruling powers to get rid of those, whom, for fleeing from their tyranny, they condemned as separatists. It was the opinion of the stricter reformers generally, that they might consistently retain their connection with the parent church, which they acknowledged to be a true church; that the restraint of arbitrary human laws upon their privileges, and the imposition by such laws of corrupt members, canons, and ways of worship, destroyed neither their rights nor their Christian character; and that since a separation was not allowed by the reigning powers, and the organization of purer churches within the kingdom was impracticable, they ought to remain in the church, groaning under their burdens, and laboring for her reformation. But the reigning powers were very willing to have these conscientious people excluded from the fellowship of a church which they loved with all her faults.

Archbishop Sheldon once said to a gentleman, who expressed much regret that the door was made so strait that many sober ministers could not enter, "It is no cause of regret at all; if we had thought so many of them would have conformed, we would have made it still straiter."

* Way of the Congregational Churches, p. 10.

The sin of schism, therefore, which has been so often charged upon our Congregational fathers, does not lie at their door. Laud himself, the greatest enemy the Puritans ever had, lays it down as a maxim, that "schism is theirs whose the *cause* of it is; and *he* makes the separation who gives the *first cause* of it, not he that makes an actual separation upon a just cause preceding." "They who talk so much of sects and divisions," says Locke, "would do well to consider whether those are not most authors and promoters of sects and divisions, who impose creeds and ceremonies, and articles of men's making, and make things not necessary to salvation the necessary terms of communion; excluding and driving from them such as, out of conscience and persuasion, can not assent and submit to them, and treating them as if they were utter aliens from the church of God, and such as were deservedly shut out as unfit to be members of it; who narrow Christianity with bounds of their own making, which the gospel knows nothing of; and often, for things in themselves confessedly indifferent, thrust men out of their communion, and then punish them for not being of it." *

CHAPTER IV.

Sketch of English ecclesiastical history continued. — Accession of James I. — Hopes of the Puritans. — Hampton Court conference. — No change in the Liturgy. — Conformity enjoined by proclamation. — James's speech to his first Parliament. — Bishop Bancroft's measures. — Puritans divided into two classes, Conformists, and Nonconformists. — Vindication of Nonconformists. — Story from Roman history. — John Hampden's refusal to pay ship money. — Grand result of persecution.

THE harassed and helpless Puritans had looked forward with hope to the accession of James I. He was a member of the Presbyterian church of Scotland and had often professed much

* Letters on Toleration.

sympathy with them in their afflictions. Not anticipating the change that would be wrought in his theological notions by the prelate's maxim, "No bishop, no king," nor dreaming of the effect which would be produced upon his "northern constitution" by the "southern air of the bishop's breath," they expected that he would at once relieve them of these burdens. He ascended the throne of England in 1603; and whether he had always been a hypocrite, or whether he became intoxicated by the flattery of the hypocritical bishops, certain it is, that all the cheering expectations of those who regarded themselves as his brethren in the faith of Christ, were at once blasted by the contemptuous and oppressive course which he adopted toward them. Upon his arrival in England, a petition, signed by eight or nine hundred ministers of the gospel, "his majesty's most humble subjects," praying, not for a "disorderly innovation, but a godly reformation," in the ceremonies and discipline of the church, was presented to him.

This called forth a bitter attack upon the Puritans from the bishops and the universities, and produced a controversy, which after a few months was silenced by a royal proclamation, in which the king declared his attachment and adherence to the established church; but graciously encouraged the petitioners to hope for a conference, in which the nature and extent of their grievances would be examined. This conference, or, as it should rather be called, the trial and condemnation of the Puritans, was held at Hampton Court, on the 14th of January, 1604, and hence called the "Hampton Court Conference."

A very full and graphic account of this conference is found in Fuller's Church History of England. The king sat as moderator; but in the discussion he became the chief speaker in defence of the oppressive proceeding of the church, and assailed the Nonconformists with much coarse, vulgar, and abusive language. The church was represented by nearly all the bishops and deans; and Dr. Reynolds, Dr. Sparks, Mr. Knewstubs, and Mr. Chadderton, men eminent for piety and learning, and held in high respect by the people, appeared in behalf of the Nonconformists.

On the first day of the conference, the king made a sort of gratu-
latory address to the bishops and deans by themselves, in which
he expressed his joy that he had not, like Henry VIII., Edward
VI., and Queen Elizabeth, to alter all things, but merely to confirm what he found well settled; that he had been brought, by
God's good providence, into the promised land, where religion
was purely professed, and where he could sit among grave,
learned, and reverend men, not as before, *"elsewhere,"* (not
deigning to name poor Scotland,) a king without state, without
honor, without order, where beardless boys would sometimes
brave him to his face; and declared his purpose to be, like a
good physician, to examine and try the complaints of the people,
and fully to remove the occasions of them if scandalous; to cure
them if dangerous; to take knowledge of them if but frivolous;
thereby to cast a sop into the mouth of Cerberus, that he might
bark no more; and if any thing should be found necessary to
be redressed, that it should be done "without any visible alteration."

On Monday, January 16, the advocates of the Nonconformists
were admitted to the conference, and the king made a "pithy
speech," winding up with an address to these four opposers of
conformity, whom he had heard were the "most grave, learned,
and modest of the *aggrieved sort,"* professing himself ready to
hear what they had to object, and commanding them to begin.

Dr. Reynolds. "All things disliked or questioned may be
reduced to these four heads: 1. That the doctrine of the church
might be preserved in purity, according to God's word. 2. That
good pastors might be placed in all the churches to preach the
same. 3. That the church government might be sincerely administered according to God's word. 4. That the Book of Common Prayer might be fitted to more increase of piety. For the
first, may your majesty be pleased, that the articles of religion
concluded on in 1562 be explained where obscure, and enlarged
where defective." And here the doctor referred to Articles 16,
23, and 25, as needing revision.

Bishop of London. (Bancroft.)   "May it please your majesty, that the ancient canon may be remembered, *Schismatici contra episcopos non sunt audiendi*. And there is another decree of a very ancient council, that no man should be permitted to speak against that whereunto he hath formerly subscribed. And as for you, Dr. Reynolds, and your sociates, how much are ye bound to his majesty's clemency, permitting you, contrary to the statute primo Elizabethæ, so freely to speak against the Liturgy and discipline established. Fain would I know the end you aim at, and whether you be not of Mr. Cartwright's mind, who affirmed that we ought in ceremonies rather to conform to the Turks than to the Papists. I doubt you approve his position, because here appearing before his majesty in Turkey gowns, not in your scholastic habits, answering to the order of the universities."

The King. "My lord bishop, something in your passion I may excuse, and something I must mislike. I may excuse you thus far, that I think you have just cause to be moved, in respect that they traduce the well-settled government, and also proceed in so indecent a course, contrary to their own pretense, and the intent of this meeting. I mislike your sudden interruption of Dr. Reynolds, whom you should have suffered to have taken his liberty; for there is no order, nor can be any effectual issue of disputation, if each party be not suffered, without chopping, to speak at large." . . .

Dr. Reynolds. "The catechism in the Common Prayer Book is too brief, and that by Mr. Nowell, late Dean of Paul's, too long for novices to learn by heart. I request, therefore, that one uniform catechism may be made, and none other generally received."

The King. "I think the doctor's request very reasonable, yet so that the catechism may be made in the fewest and plainest affirmative terms that may be. And herein I would have two rules observed. First, that curious and deep questions be avoided in the fundamental instruction of a people. Secondly, that there should not be so general a departure from the Papists, that every thing should be accounted an error in which we agree with them."

e *

Dr. Reynolds. "Great is the profanation of the Sabbath, and contempt of your majesty's proclamation, which I earnestly desire may be reformed."

This motion was unanimously agreed to.

Dr. Reynolds. "May it please your majesty that the Bible be new translated; such translations as are extant not answering the original." And he instanced in three particulars.

Bishop of London. "If every man's humor might be followed, there would be no end of translating."

The King. "I profess I could never yet see a Bible well translated in English. I wish some special pains were taken for a uniform translation, which should be done by the best learned in both universities; then reviewed by the bishops, presented to the privy council, lastly ratified by royal authority, to be read in the whole church, and no other. To conclude this point, let errors in matters of faith be amended, and indifferent things be interpreted, and a gloss added to them. A church with some faults is better than an innovation. And surely, if these were the greatest matters that grieved you, I need not have been troubled with such importunate complaints." . . .

Dr. Reynolds. "And now to proceed to the second general point, concerning the planting of learned ministers; I desire they be in every parish."

The King. "I have consulted my bishops about it, whom I have found willing and ready herein. But as *subita evacuatio* is *periculosa,* so *subita mutatio.* It can not presently be performed, the universities not affording them." . . .

Bishop of London. "Because this, I see, is a time of moving petitions, may I humbly present two or three to your majesty? First, that there may be amongst us a praying ministry, it being now come to pass, that men think it the only duty of ministers to spend their time in the pulpit. I confess, in a church newly to be planted, preaching is most necessary; not so in one long established, that prayer should be neglected."

The King. "I like your motion exceeding well, and dislike the hypocrisy of our time, who place all their religion in the ear, whilst prayer, so requisite and acceptable, if duly performed, is accounted and used as the least part of religion."

Bishop of London. "My second motion is, that until learned men may be planted in every congregation, godly homilies may be read therein."

The King. "I approve your motion, especially where the living is not sufficient for the maintenance of a learned preacher. Also where there be multitudes of sermons, there I would have homilies read divers times." . . .

Lord Chancellor. "Livings rather want learned men, than learned men want livings; many in the universities pining for want of places. I wish, therefore, some may have single coats (one living) before others have doublets, (pluralities,) and this method I have observed in bestowing the king's benefices."

Bishop of London. "I commend your honorable care that way, but a doublet is necessary in cold weather. My last motion is, that pulpits may not be made Pasquils, wherein every discontented fellow may traduce his superiors."

The King. "I accept what you offer, for the pulpit is no place of personal reproof. Let them complain to me, if injured." . . .

Dr. Reynolds. "I come now to SUBSCRIPTIONS, as a great impeachment to a learned ministry, and therefore entreat that it may not be exacted as heretofore; for which many good men are kept out, though otherwise willing to subscribe to the statutes of the realm, articles of religion, and the king's supremacy." . .

Mr. Knewstubs. "I take exceptions to the cross in baptism, whereat the weak brethren are offended, contrary to the counsel of the apostle, (Rom. xiv. and 2 Cor. viii.)"

The King. "*Distingue tempora, et concordabunt Scripturæ.* Great the difference between those times and ours. Then, a church not fully settled; now, ours long established. How long will such brethren be weak? Are not forty-five years sufficient for them to grow strong in? Besides, who pretends this weakness? We require not the subscription of laics and idiots, but of preachers and ministers, who are not still, I trow, to be fed with milk, being enabled to feed others. Some of them are strong enough, if not headstrong; conceiving themselves able enough to teach him who last spake for them, and all the bishops in the land."

Mr. Knewstubs. "It is questionable whether the church hath power to institute an outward significant sign."

Bishop of London. "The cross in baptism is not used otherwise than a ceremony." . . .

The King. "I am exceeding well satisfied on this point, but would be acquainted about the antiquity of the use of the cross."

Dr. Reynolds. "It hath been used ever since the apostles' time. But the question is, how ancient the use thereof hath been in baptism."

Dean of Westminster. "It appears out of Tertullian, Cyprian, and Origen, that it was used *in immortali lavacro.*"

Bishop of Winchester. "In Constantine's time it was used in baptism."

The King. "If so, I see no reason but we may continue it." . . .

Mr. Knewstubs. "If the church hath such a power, the greatest scruple is, how far the ordinance of the church bindeth, without impeaching Christian liberty."

The King. "I will not argue that point with you, but answer as kings in Parliament, *Le roy s'avisera.* This is like Mr. John Black, a beardless boy, who told me, the last conference in Scotland, that he would hold conformity with his majesty in matters of doctrine, but every man for ceremonies was to be left to his own liberty. But I will have none of that. I will have one doctrine, one discipline, one religion, in substance and ceremony. Never speak more to that point, how far you are bound to obey."

Dr. Reynolds. "Would that the cross, being superstitiously abused in Popery, were abandoned, as the *brazen serpent* was stamped to powder by Hezekiah, because abused to idolatry."

The King. "Inasmuch as the cross was abused to superstition in time of Popery, it doth plainly imply that it was well used before. I detest their courses, who peremptorily disallow of all things which have been abused in Popery, and know not how to answer the objections of the Papists when they charge us with novelties, but by telling them we retain the primitive use of things, and only forsake their novel corruptions. Secondly, no resemblance between the brazen serpent — a material, visible sign — and the sign of the cross made in the air. Thirdly, Papists, as I am informed, never did ascribe any spiritual grace to the cross in baptism. Lastly, *material crosses*, to which the people fell down in time of Popery, (as the idolatrous Jews to the brazen serpent,) are already demolished, as you desire."

Mr. Knewstubs. " I take exception at the wearing of the surplice, a kind of garment used by the priests of Isis."

The King. " I did not think, till of late, it had been borrowed from the heathen, because commonly called *a rag of Popery.* Seeing now we border not upon heathens, neither are any of them conversant with, or commorant among us, thereby to be confirmed in paganism, I see no reason but for comeliness' sake it may be retained." . . .

Dr. Reynolds. " I desire, that according to certain provincial constitutions, the clergy may have meetings every three weeks."

The King. " If you aim at a Scottish Presbytery, it agreeth as well with monarchy as God and the devil. Then Jack, and Tom, and Will, and Dick shall meet and censure me and my council. Therefore I reiterate my former speech, *Le roy s'avisera :* stay, I pray, for one seven years, before you demand, and then if you find me grow pursy and fat, I may perchance hearken unto you, for that government will keep me in breath, and give me work enough. . . . I shall here speak of one matter more, somewhat out of order, but it skilleth not. Dr. Reynolds, you have often spoken for my supremacy, and it is well. But know you any here, or elsewhere, who like of the present government ecclesiastical, and dislike my supremacy ? "

Dr. Reynolds. " I know none."

The King. . . . " My lords the bishops, I may thank you

that these men plead thus for my supremacy. They think they can not make good their party against you but by appealing unto it; but if once you were out, and they in, I know what would become of my supremacy; for, No Bishop, no King. I have learnt of what cut they have been, who, preaching before me since my coming into England, passed over with silence my being supreme governor in causes ecclesiastical. Well, doctor, have you any thing else to say?"

Dr. Reynolds. "No more, if it please your majesty."

The King. "If this be all your party hath to say, I will make them conform themselves, or else I will harry them out of the land, or else do worse."

Here ended the second day's conference. The third was held on the Wednesday following. After some discourse between the king, the bishops, and the lords respecting the proceedings of the Court of High Commission, the four Nonconformists were called in, and such alterations in the Liturgy as the bishops, by the advice of the king, had made, were read to them, and to which their silence was taken for consent.

The King. "I see the exceptions against the Communion Book are matters of weakness; therefore, if the persons reluctant be discreet, they will be won betimes, and by good persuasions: if indiscreet, better they were removed, for by their factions many are driven to be Papists. From you, Dr. Reynolds, and your associates, I expect obedience and humility, (the marks of honest and good men,) and that you would persuade others abroad by your example."

Dr. Reynolds. "We here do promise to perform all duties to bishops as revered fathers, and to join with them against the common adversary, for the quiet of the church."

Mr. Chadderton. "I request that the wearing of the surplice and the cross in baptism may not be urged on some godly ministers in Lancashire, fearing, if forced unto them, many, won by their preaching of the gospel, will revolt to Popery."

The King. "It is not my purpose, and I dare say it is not the bishop's intent, presently, and out of hand, to enforce these things, without fatherly admonitions, conferences, and persuasions, premised." . . .

Mr. Knewstubs. "I request the like favor of forbearance to some honest ministers in Suffolk. For it will make much against their credit in the country to be now forced to the surplice and cross in baptism."

Archbishop of Canterbury. "Nay, sir."

The King. "Let me alone to answer him. Sir, you show yourself an uncharitable man. We have here taken pains, and, in the end, have concluded on unity and uniformity, and you, forsooth, must prefer the credits of a few private men before the peace of the church. This is just the Scotch argument, when any thing was concluded which disliked some humors. Let them either conform themselves shortly, or they shall hear." * . . .

After a few words respecting ambuling and sitting communion, this famous — if it should not rather be called infamous — conference ended; and with it all the hopes which the Puritans had cherished of relief from the intolerable bondage in which they were held by the bishops. Fuller remarks, that in this conference some thought that James "went above himself;" that the Bishop of London, the violent Bancroft, "appeared even with himself;" and that Dr. Reynolds "fell much beneath himself." But we must remember that the report of those proceedings was originally made by a professed enemy of the Puritan divines, who was as much inclined to flatter the pedantic vanity of the king, and to glorify the bishops, as he was to misrepresent the character and the arguments of those whom he hated. "When the Israelites go down to the Philistines to whet all their iron tools, no wonder if they set a sharp edge on their own, and a blunt one on their enemies' weapons," as Fuller charitably observes. The Archbishop of Canterbury went so far as to declare his belief that his majesty spoke by the especial assistance of God's Spirit; and Bancroft "appeared only even with him-

* Fuller's Church History, book x. pp. 7–21.

self," when he exclaimed, "I protest that my heart melteth with
joy, that Almighty God, of his singular mercy, hath given us
such a king, as, since Christ's time, the like hath not been."
But Sir J. Harrington, who was present, remarked, in reference
to the archbishop's blasphemous flattery, that the spirit by which
that king spoke was "rather foul mouthed;" that he used
expressions which it would not be decent to repeat; and that
he resorted to abuse rather than argument, bidding the petitioners to "away with their sniveling." James himself, in a letter to
some nameless Scotch correspondent, describes the part he played
in the conference in the following style: "We have kept such
a revell with the Puritans here this two days as was never heard
the like. Quhaire I have pepered them as soundlie as yee have
done the Papists thaire. It were no reason, that those that will
refuse the airy-sign of the cross after baptism should have their
purses stuffed with any more solid and substantial crosses. . . . .
I have such a book of theirs as may well convert infidels, but it
shall never convert me, except by turning me more earnestly
against thayme."

We can see clearly enough through all the clouds of prejudice
and passion in which that scene has been enveloped, that the
demands of the Puritans were perfectly reasonable, and presented in the humblest and most unobjectionable manner; while
on the part of the king and the bishops, there was not even the
appearance of a desire to heal the divisions of the church by
modifying the arbitrary and tyrannical measures which produced
them, but, on the contrary, a manifest determination to make the
Puritans conform to every thing contained in a semi-Popish Liturgy,.or, as James himself once called it, "an ill-said mass in
English," by the terror of fines, imprisonment, and banishment
from their country. This conference seems to have been a providential opportunity for healing the distractions of the church,
and of establishing a true Christian union upon the basis of God's
word. But it was wickedly lost through the worldly policy of
the bishops, and the arbitrary principles and cowardice of the
king, who flattered the hierarchy to secure its support of the

throne, and feared the Puritans for their resistance to his sovereign will. Had the ruling powers at this time followed the advice of some of the wisest and most pious divines in their own church, or the example of the reformers abroad who took the Scriptures, and not a corrupt tradition, for their guide in the work of reformation, they might have prevented a division as disgraceful as it was disastrous in its consequences to them.

But they, in their blindness, deemed it best to retain every thing which troubled the consciences of the most devout portion of the church. The only good thing done by them at this conference was, consenting to a new translation of the Bible, or rather a careful revision and comparison of all the translations then in use. A very few trifling alterations in the prescribed service were agreed upon by the king and the bishops ; and then a royal proclamation was issued, commanding all the people to conform to the doctrines and discipline of the established church, as the only form to be tolerated in the kingdom, and admonishing the malcontents not to expect any further alteration or relief. The Common Prayer Book was accordingly printed, with these inconsiderable amendments, and the proclamation prefixed, like the cherubim with flaming sword guarding the tree of life.

James opened his first Parliament with a characteristic speech, in which he acknowledged the Romish church to be " our Mother Church," and professed his willingness to meet the Papists half way, for the sake of bringing about a union of the two religions, at the same time denouncing the Puritans as a " sect insufferable in any well-governed commonwealth." The convocation, which sat at the same time, were very active in laying snares, and preparing weapons, for the unfortunate sect thus placed under the curse of the realm. They drew up a book of one hundred and forty canons, according to which, suspension and deprivation being regarded as too light a punishment for the enormous sin of Nonconformity, all who refused to conform were, *ipso facto*, excommunicated and cast out, as heathen and publicans, from the fellowship and protection of both church and state. By these canons all Nonconformists were rendered incapable of bringing actions at law for the recovery of their legal debts; were, by process of the civil courts, to be imprisoned for life, or until they should give satisfaction to the church; were to be exposed to every form of temporal evil in this world, and to be denied Christian burial after death; and if the power of the bishops had extended into the other world, would have been eternally excluded from the fellowship of just men made perfect. These canons were ratified by the king, who, at the same time, commanded that they should be diligently observed and executed; that every parish minister should read them over once every year in his church, before divine service; and that all persons having ecclesiastical jurisdiction should see them put in execution, and not fail to inflict the full penalty upon every one who should purposely violate or neglect them.*

On the death of Archbishop Whitgift, who, though an enemy and a persecutor of the Puritans, was, comparatively, a moderate man, Bancroft, Bishop of London, who was the most irascible and abusive speaker, next to the king, in the Hampton Court conference, succeeded to the archiepiscopal chair. Bancroft was a man of a savage temper and most arbitrary principles; and what Whitgift strove to accomplish by comparatively mild measures, he resolved to do at once by an exterminating rigor. He revived the persecution with such severity that, in 1605, the year of Mr. Shepard's birth, about three hundred ministers were silenced, turned out from their parishes, or otherwise punished, for refusing subscription; and yet of the sufferers in eight bishoprics, no account was taken. These ministers had preached in the church from ten to thirty years; and, in many churches, the ceremonies had been laid aside for a long time. Some of these ministers were excommunicated and imprisoned, and others forced into exile — "harried out of the kingdom," as James insolently threatened they should be, if they did not conform.

* Bennet, Mem. ch. iii.   Neal, Hist. Purit. i. 422.

Under the intolerant measures now adopted and inflexibly adhered to, many good men strove to conform, and succeeded in convincing themselves that they were doing God service in conforming to the established order. Hence those who most earnestly desired to see a thorough reformation of the church were divided into two parties, distinguished at the time, and well known since, as *Conformists* and *Nonconformists.* Of the first class was Dr. Reynolds, who, at the Hampton Court conference, solemnly promised "to perform all duties to bishops, as reverend fathers, and to join with them against the common adversary, for the quiet of the church." Dr. Sparks, also, another of the representatives of Puritanism in that unhappy conference, to which the petitioners were called, "not to have their scruples removed," but to hear the king's "pleasure propounded," went home a convert to the doctrine of the bishops, and soon after published a Treatise of Unity and Uniformity. "Henceforward," says Fuller, "many cripples in conformity were cured of their former halting therein, and those who knew not their own, till they knew the king's mind, in this matter, for the future, quietly digested the ceremonies of the church." Of the latter class were our Congregational fathers, who were willing to suffer the loss of all things rather than conform to a ritual of human origin, imposed with irresistible human power.

It has been often urged, in reproach of the Nonconformists, that while they cordially consented to the *doctrines* of the church, which were the only essential things, they obstinately refused to perform a few *ceremonies,* which were in themselves indifferent; and professing to honor the church as their "dear mother," blindly fled from her communion, and put her very existence in jeopardy for the sake of getting rid of an "airy cross," and some genuflections which could do no one any harm.

There would be some appearance of justice in this charge, if the ceremonies in question had been regarded, at that time, by any party, as indifferent things. But nothing is more evident than that both the government and the Puritans considered the question of absolute and universal conformity a question of life and death. The only ground upon which the church can be in any degree justified in its unyielding demands is, that she regarded every part of the prescribed Liturgy essential. If those rites and ceremonies were, in the judgment of the government, really indifferent matters, it was most unjust and cruel on their part to command every adult person in England to practice them against the scruples of even a weak conscience, upon pain of ruinous fines, imprisonment, or perpetual banishment. It is said that Dr. Burgess, once preaching before King James, and touching lightly upon the ceremonies, related the following story, by which he intended to illustrate, in a quiet way, the inhumanity of the bishops in persecuting the Puritans : Augustus Cæsar was once invited to dinner by a Roman senator, who was distinguished for his wealth, power, and magnificent living. As the emperor entered the house, he heard a great outcry, and, upon looking about, he saw several persons dragging a man after them, with the design, apparently, of killing him, while the poor fellow was begging most piteously for mercy. The emperor demanded the cause of that violence, and was told that their master had condemned this man to the fish ponds for breaking a very valuable glass. He commanded a stay of the execution ; and when he came into the house, asked the senator whether he had glasses that were worth a man's life. He answered, being a great connoisseur in such things, that he owned glasses which he valued at the price of a province. The emperor desired to see these marvelous glasses, and was taken to a room where a large number were displayed. He saw that they were indeed beautiful to the eye, but knowing that they had been, and might still be, the cause of much mischief, he dashed them all to atoms, with this expression: " Better that all these perish than one man." The bishops, however, for whose especial benefit this story was told, were greatly enraged, instead of being convinced by the illustration. They thought the ceremonies worth the lives of a thousand men ; and they succeeded in getting the doctor silenced for daring to think otherwise.

On the other hand, the nonconforming Puritans, if they

could have regarded these things as indifferent in themselves, could no longer regard them as indifferent when they were imposed by the state, under severe penalties, as essential to the acceptable worship of God. They did not object to the use of forms of prayer; there were many things in the Common Prayer Book which they could use with a good conscience; and if any latitude had been allowed, they would never have separated from the church. But they saw the mischief of human authority in relation to religious worship, and could not acknowledge that the magistrate had power to impose a body of mere ceremonies upon those whom Christ had freed from the bondage of the ceremonial law. "We reject," says one of those Nonconformists, "those forms of prayer and of public worship which are imposed upon the consciences of men by human power, as *essential parts* of divine service. Although as to the matter of them they might be lawfully observed, yet by the manner in which they are introduced, they become the instruments of cruelty, and occasions of outrageous tyranny over the best and most worthy sons of the church." *

And when we remember that this book contained the only form of worship allowed in England, — that every part of it, without exception, was made a matter of necessity, and not of choice, — that not only the ministers were required to use the whole of it, but that every adult person in the kingdom was obliged to be present at the celebration of this service, and to take an active part in the worship by repeating a certain form of words, and performing certain rites and ceremonies, — the refusal of our fathers to conform seems not only defensible, but imperatively demanded by their higher relation to Christ. For, as Shepard well observes, the very yielding of conformity to such a service would "miserably cast away the liberty purchased by Christ for his people, inthrall the churches to Antichrist, and lift up the power of Antichrist in his tyrannous usurpation upon the churches of Christ." †

* Apol. ch. vii. Q. 2.　　　　　　　† Treatise of Liturgies, Preface.

*f**

When Hampden, a few years later, resisted the illegal re-
quirement of Charles I. with respect to ship money, and for
a few shillings was willing to plunge the nation into a civil war,
he was hailed as a noble champion of civil liberty. Why, then,
should our fathers be branded as narrow-minded bigots, and
wicked disturbers of the peace of the church, for refusing obedience to demands which no human governor has a right to
make, and asserting a liberty guarantied by the great charter
of the kingdom of God?

But the Puritans did not consider the Common Prayer Book,
in all its parts, a matter of *indifference in itself*, and to be
resisted only because it was imposed by the secular power without warrant from the Scriptures. While they freely acknowledged that God might be acceptably worshiped by forms of
prayer, they regarded this particular book as unsuitable for public
worship, and as a grievous burden upon their consciences. The
grounds of their objection to the use of this liturgy were, that it
was taken from the Roman Mass Book, which had been the
means, in their opinion, of filling the church with idolatry and
superstition, and though purged from some of the greater
abominations of the mass, could not be used without sanctioning
the idolatrous worship of Rome ; that it claimed for human
rulers unlimited power to decree rights and ceremonies for the
church — a power which obviously belongs to Christ alone, as
the Lord and Lawgiver of the church ; that it set apart many
holidays, and instituted feasts which were enforced in the spiritual courts by civil penalties ; that it annexed human ceremonies
to certain parts of worship which savored strongly of idolatry,
and therefore not to be tolerated in the church, as the surplice,
the sign of the cross in baptism, kneeling before the bread
and wine in the Lord's supper, etc. Kneeling at the sacrament
was especially offensive to them, because it was a gesture required by the Papists as an act of adoration, the object of which
was the real body of Christ, supposed to be present in the bread
and wine. " The mass," says John Drury, " is the greatest idol
in the world, and the act of kneeling was brought in at the

Popish communion to worship that idol.   We ought not to symbolize with them in that act of worship ; we ought not to follow the corruption of an ordinance when we have Christ's practice made known to us.   It is not lawful to mix the acts of God's true worship with the chief act of an idol worship, such as is kneeling at the mass.   For the meaning and purpose of kneeling is adoration ; the object of adoration is the body and blood of Christ, supposed to be in the elements.   But if we believe no such real presence as they have fancied, then we make void the object of adoration, and consequently the act intended towards it is disannulled also." *

We see, then, that conformity was not a question of mere expediency, but of right and wrong, of obedience and sin.   " We are not," said our fathers, " to dissemble with God nor men. Our separation were needless and sinful, if we did not consider conformity sinful in some degree.   And in that case, to practice it is to tell the world, if sincerity be left among men, that we account it all lawful or tolerable to us, though not simply eligible. We therefore dare not, by practice, violate our consciences, and so destroy our avowed principles.   Nor will persons of any candor and Christian charity think this a humor of opposition ; for they know that among us have been, and are, men of sober minds and tried integrity ;   men of good sense and learning ; men of great ability and usefulness in church and state ; men who relished also the comforts of their life and families as others do ;   men who greatly valued an opportunity of serving their generation, and their dear Redeemer in the gospel ministry ; men who would not for trifles expose themselves to poverty, contempt, obscurity, prisons, merciless fines, exile, and death itself.   This were a humor indeed." †

It is sad to contemplate the intolerant and oppressive measures adopted by one part of the church against another, and to witness the calamitous effects which resulted from the persecuting

* Model of Church Government, pp. 40, 41. 1648.
† Letter of Nonconforming Ministers, p. 7. 1701.

spirit of those times — the fines, imprisonments, banishments, deaths, by which the faith and patience of the saints were so severely tried; but at the same time it is instructive and consoling to direct our thoughts to what time has shown to have been the ultimate design of Providence, in permitting those disastrous scenes to exist. A new world was to be created. A pure church was to be planted far away from the enormous corruptions and abuses of old Christendom; and persecution was to people the wilderness with a chosen generation, — a royal priesthood, — who should worship God in the spirit, and magnify the divine law by holy obedience.

The authors of the Epistle dedicatory to Shepard's Clear Sunshine of the Gospel upon the Indians of New England have given a beautiful expression to this thought: " That God, who often makes men's evil of sin serviceable to the advancement of the riches of his grace, has shown that he had merciful ends in the malicious purpose which drove our fathers from England. As he suffered Paul to be cast into prison, to convert the jailer; to be shipwrecked at Melita, to preach to the barbarians; so he suffered their way to be stopped up here, and their persons to be banished hence, that he might open a passage for them in the wilderness, and make them instruments to draw souls to him, who had been so long estranged from him. . . . It was the end of the adversary to suppress, but God's to propagate, the gospel; theirs to smother and put out the light, God's to communicate and disperse it to the uttermost corners of the earth. . . . And if the dawn of the morning be so delightful, what will the clear day be? If the first fruits be so precious, what will the whole harvest be? If some beginnings be so full of joy, what will it be when God shall perform his whole work, when the whole earth shall be full of the knowledge of the Lord, as the waters cover the sea, and east and west shall sing together the song of the Lamb? " *

* Clear Sunshine, Preface, pp. 3, 4.

CHAPTER V.

Mr. Shepard at Mr. Weld's. — Dr. Wilson's lecture. — Nature of a lec-
tureship. — Mr. Shepard requested by the ministers of Essex to accept
the lecture. — Lecture established for three years at Earles-Colne. —
First sermon. — Method of preaching. — Effect of his ministry. — Opposition arises. — Lecture transferred to Towcester. — Continues to preach
at Earles-Colne. — Summoned to London by Bishop Laud. — Interview
with the bishop. — Silenced. — Character of Laud. — Studies the subject
of conformity at Earles-Colne. — Laud comes into the County of Essex.
— Second interview with the bishop. — Commanded to leave the place.

Such, as has been described in the preceding chapters, was
the religious condition of England, and such the prospects of
pious young men who desired to devote themselves to the work
of the ministry, at the time when Thomas Shepard was waiting
at Mr. Weld's, in Essex, for his master's degree, " solicitous
what would become of him." But while he was thus waiting in
painful suspense, the Lord was in secret preparing a place and a
work for him ; so that when he was ready and prepared to enter upon his chosen employment, he was unexpectedly called to
preach the gospel under circumstances most favorable to his usefulness, though not in a way to gratify a worldly ambition, or to
awaken hope of preferment in the national establishment.
Just at this time, Dr. Wilson, a pious physician, a brother, it is
supposed, of John Wilson, afterwards pastor of the first church
in Boston, had resolved to establish a lecture in some town in
that county, with an income of thirty pounds a year for its maintenance — a lecture which Mr. Weld and several other ministers,
with the concurrence, as it appears, of Dr. Wilson, urged Mr.
Shepard to accept, and to " set it up in a great town in Essex,
called Cogshall."

In order to understand the position and duties of a lecturer,
at that period, as distinguished from the office and work of a
clergyman, it may be necessary to give a brief account of the
nature of the lectures here referred to, and of the circumstances

in which they had their origin. "Many parts of the country," says Carlyle, "being thought by the more zealous among the Puritans insufficiently supplied with able and pious preachers, a plan was devised, in 1624, for raising by subscription, among persons grieved at the state of matters, a fund for buying in such 'lay impropriations' as might offer themselves, for supporting good ministers therewith, in destitute places, and for otherwise encouraging the ministerial work. The originator of this scheme was Dr. Preston, a man of great celebrity and influence in those days. His scheme was found good. The wealthy London merchants, almost all of them Puritans, took it up, and by degrees the wealthier Puritans over England at large. Considerable funds were subscribed for this object, and vested in 'Feoffees,' who afterwards made some noise in the world under that name. They gradually purchased some advowsons, or impropriations, such as came to market, and hired, or assisted in hiring, a great many lecturers. These lecturers were persons not generally in full priest's orders, being scrupulous about the ceremonies, but in deacon's or some other orders, with permission to preach, or 'lecture,' as it was called, whom, accordingly, we find lecturing in various places, under various conditions, in the subsequent years; often in some market town, on market days, on Sunday afternoons as supplemental to the regular priest, when he might be idle, or given to white and black surplices; or as 'running lecturers,' now here, now there, over a certain district. They were greatly followed by the serious part of the community, and gave proportional offense in other quarters. In a few years, they had risen to such a height that Laud took them seriously in hand, and, with patient detail, hunted them mostly out; nay, brought the Feoffees themselves and their whole enterprise into the Star Chamber, and there, with emphasis enough and heavy damages, amid huge clamor from the public, suppressed them." *

The lecture of Dr. Wilson, which Mr. Weld and other Puritan ministers of Essex were anxious that Mr. Shepard should

---

* Letters and Speeches of Oliver Cromwell, i. 50.

accept, was one of the kind here described. Of so much importance did they deem this lecture, and so much confidence did they feel in Mr. Shepard's piety, and ability to render it useful to the people, that they set apart a day of fasting and prayer for the purpose of seeking divine direction as to the place where it should be established. Toward the evening of that day, they began to consider whether Mr. Shepard should go to Cogshall or to some other town in that region. Most of the ministers were in favor of establishing the lecture at Cogshall, because it was a town of considerable importance, had great need of evangelical preaching, and was, so far as they knew, the only place where it was especially desired. Mr. Hooker, however, objected to this place, on the ground that Mr. Shepard was altogether too young and inexperienced for such a work at that time; and moreover that the clergyman of Cogshall was a cunning, malicious old man, an enemy of the Puritans, who, although he was apparently in favor of having a lecture established there, yet would be likely to give a young and inexperienced man, like Mr. Shepard, a great deal of trouble; remarking, in his quiet way, that it was always "dangerous and uncomfortable for little birds to build under the nests of old ravens and kites."

While the ministers were actually engaged in discussing this subject, the people of Earles-Colne, a town in the same county, having heard that a free lecture was to be established somewhere in the county of Essex, and believing that it would be a great blessing to that "poor town," sent a deputation to Tarling, where the ministers were assembled, who arrived just as the question was about to be decided, with an urgent request that the lecture might be established there for three years, that being the time to which its continuance in any place was limited; because it was presumed by the founders that if the lecture was to be the means of doing any good, its beneficial influence would become manifest within three years, and then, if it was taken away, the people in a populous town would be willing to maintain it themselves; but if, on the other hand, no good was accomplished in so long a time, it would be a waste of the funds to continue it in that place any longer. In view of this earnest, and, as it seemed, providential application, the ministers felt somewhat as Peter did, when, after anxiously meditating upon the vision he had seen upon the house top, the messengers of Cornelius presented themselves, with a request which he interpreted as a divine intimation of his duty. They at once decided that the lecture should go to Earles-Colne; advising Mr. Shepard to accept this providential call, and if, after preaching there a while, he found the people favorably disposed toward him and desirous of his services, to remain in that place during the time fixed for the continuance of the lecture there.

Mr. Shepard saw clearly that it was his duty to comply with the advice of his friends. This appointment opened to him a door of usefulness earlier and more effectually than he had anticipated, without, at the same time, subjecting him to many of those annoyances to which the regular ministers were constantly liable; and though the salary connected with this lecture was small, it was sufficient to enable him, for the present, to subsist with comparative comfort. It was a very hopeful undertaking. And it was no small honor for one who, in his own opinion, was "so young, so weak, inexperienced, and unfit for so great a work," to be called into this difficult service "by twelve or sixteen judicious ministers of Christ." He moreover regarded it as a manifestation of divine goodness, never to be forgotten, that when he "might have been cast away upon some blind place, without the help of any ministry" about him, or have been "sent to some gentleman's house, to be corrupted with the sins in it," the Lord should place him in the best county in England, viz., Essex, and locate him "in the midst of the best ministry in the country, by whose monthly fasts and conferences" he found much assistance and encouragement in his arduous work.

Accordingly he resolved to go to Earles-Colne. After taking his degree of master of arts, in 1627, and receiving deacon's orders, "sinfully," as he afterward thought, of the Bishop of Peterborough, he repaired to the scene of his future labors. He was cordially welcomed and entertained by a Mr. Cosins, a schoolmaster in the town, "an aged, but a godly and cheerful Christian," the only person, indeed, in the place who seemed to have "any godliness," by whose counsel, sympathy, and coöperation, the spirit of the young and timid preacher was greatly refreshed and strengthened. His first sermon was upon 2 Cor. v. 19, and was so acceptable to the people, that they united in giving him a formal invitation in writing to remain and lecture to them agreeably to the terms of his appointment. From this unanimity and earnestness, so unusual in those times, he inferred that it was the Lord's will that he should labor in that place. Still he was fearful that he should not be suffered by the superior powers to pursue his work in peace. In order, therefore, to avoid molestation from that quarter, he "sinfully," according to his own subsequent interpretation of the act, procured a license to officiate as a lecturer, from the register of the Bishop of London, before his name and character were much known — a license which, for a time, enabled him to preach without hinderance or suspicion on the part of the bishop and his officers.

Mr. Shepard entered upon his work at Earles-Colne with great zeal. His sole object in preaching was, according to the commission given to the apostle, to turn his hearers "from darkness to light, and from the power of Satan unto God." In order to accomplish this end most effectually and speedily, he endeavored, first of all, to "show the people their misery;" next, to exhibit "the remedy, Jesus Christ;" and finally, to show "how they should walk answerable to his mercy, being redeemed by Christ." This course of preaching, accompanied, as it evidently was, by a sincere, earnest, and prayerful spirit in the preacher, — "the Lord putting forth his strength in my extreme weakness," — soon began to produce the most happy results. The people who had walked in darkness, and among whom there seemed to be but one man who "had any godliness," were enlightened in respect to the distinguished doctrines of the gospel, and many, both in Earles-Colne and in the region around, were converted. Among the most valuable fruits of his ministry were the two sons of Mr. Harlakenden, Richard and Roger; the latter of whom came to New England with his spiritual father, and was of great service to him in his labors here.

Such a ministry as this, lifting up its voice like a trumpet amidst the smooth preaching and dead formalism of the church, showing the people their transgression, and making them feel their misery, could not, at that period, be long tolerated by the ruling powers. " Satan began to rage." The commissaries, registers, and others, began to threaten the faithful preacher, taking it for granted that he was a " nonconformable man," whose mouth must be stopped ; though at that time, not having studied the subject of conformity, he " was not resolved either way, but was dark in these things." But notwithstanding the violent opposition that arose on all sides, " the Lord, having work to do in the place," sustained him, " a poor ignorant thing," against all the threatenings of the commissaries, and the " malice of the ministers round about," and " by strange and wonderful means," kept him in the field until the work was done.

When the three years for which the lecture had been established at Earles-Colne were expired, the people, having learnt to appreciate the blessing of a faithful ministry, were unwilling to part with the instrument of so much good, and at once raised, by subscription, a salary of about forty pounds a year, to induce him to remain with them. This unexpected movement satisfied him that it was his duty to continue his ministrations in that place ; and, as the lecture must be transferred to some other town, he used his influence to have it established at Towcester, — the place of his birth, — " the worst town in the world," in his opinion, believing that he could confer no greater benefit upon his " poor friends " there than by sending to them a faithful preacher of the gospel. Dr. Wilson consented to Mr. Shepard's proposal, and Mr. Stone, afterwards the able colleague of Mr. Hooker, both at Cambridge and Hartford, was sent with the lecture to Towcester, " where the Lord was with him," and many souls were converted by his faithful ministry.

Mr. Shepard continued to preach at Earles-Colne for about six months after the transfer of the lecture to Towcester ; when the storm, which had been long gathering, burst upon him, and drove him from his work in that place. Laud, having succeeded Bancroft as Bishop of London, began to look sharply after these lecturers, and to enforce entire conformity to the established ceremonies with a rigor beyond that of any of his predecessors. It was not likely that such a man as Shepard could long escape persecution, when a very worthy minister was called before the Court of High Commission, and severely censured for merely expressing in a sermon his belief that the night was approaching, because "the shadows were so much longer than the body, and ceremonies more in force than the power of godliness." Accordingly, on the 16th of December, 1630, Mr. Shepard was summoned to London, like a culprit, to answer for his conduct at Earles-Colne. The bishop did not ask him whether he had subscribed, or was willing to subscribe and conform, but taking it for granted that he was an obstinate Nonconformist, after abusing Dr. Wilson for setting up a lecture, and the lecturer for daring to preach in his diocese, forbade the further exercise of his ministerial gifts in that bishopric; and moreover threatened the poor man with a speedy and violent interruption if he attempted to preach any where else.

This interview between the haughty bishop and the humble preacher is best described in the language of the sufferer himself. "As soon as I came in the morning, about eight of the clock, falling into a fit of rage, he asked me what degree I had taken in the university. I answered him that I was master of arts. He asked of what college. I answered, of Emmanuel. He asked how long I had lived in his diocese. I answered, three years and upward. He asked who maintained me all this while, charging me to deal plainly with him, adding, withal, that he had been more cheated and equivocated with, by some of my malignant faction, than ever was man by Jesuit. At the speaking of which words he looked as though blood would have gushed out of his face, and did shake as if he had been haunted with an ague fit, to my apprehension, by reason of his extreme malice and secret venom. I desired him to excuse me. He fell then to threaten me, and withal to bitter railing, calling me all to nought, saying, 'You prating coxcomb, do you think all the learning is in your brain?' He then pronounced his sentence thus : 'I charge you that you neither preach, read, marry, bury, or exercise any ministerial function in any part of my diocese; for if you do, and I hear of it, I'll be upon your back, and follow you wherever you go, in any part of the kingdom, and so ever-lastingly disenable you.' I besought him not to deal so in regard of a poor town. And here he stopped me in what I was going on to say. 'A poor town! You have made a company of sedi-tious, factious bedlams; and what do you prate to me of a poor town?' I prayed him to suffer me to catechize on the Sabbath days in the afternoon. He replied, 'Spare your breath; I'll have no such fellows prate in my diocese. Get you gone; and now make your complaint to whom you will.' So away I went; and blessed be God that I may go to HIM."

Nothing can exceed the shameful violence and brutality of the bishop but the meekness and humility of the defenceless victim. "The Lord saw me unfit and unworthy to be continued there any longer," — this is his own self-condemning language respect-ing the oppressive treatment which he had received from a nar-row-minded and unfeeling man, — "and so God put me to silence there, which did somewhat humble me; for I did think it was for my sins the Lord set him thus against me."

The character of Laud, who holds a prominent place in the history of those times when good men were treated worse than felons for refusing to conform to human ceremonies in the wor-ship of God, has been very differently drawn by the friends and the enemies of the Puritans. In the flattering portrait by Clarendon, he appears as an angel of light, and with the beauty of a holy martyr; in the rough sketch of Prynne, whose colors were mixed up with his own blood, he is represented as one of the most hateful incarnations of the spirit of evil. We must make allowance for the sweeping expressions of men whom the bishop had caused to be set in the pillory, cropped, branded with hot irons, imprisoned, fined, and banished, for the sake of what

they verily believed to be the cause of truth. But after making
all necessary allowance, it seems impossible to regard him with
any feeling but that of detestation. When we read Shepard's
description of the manner in which he silenced one of the most
pious, humble, and promising young men in the church of England at that time, — a description which probably would have
answered for many similar scenes, — we can not wonder that
Winthrop should call him " our great enemy," or that Shepard,
forbidden, like the apostles by the Jewish rulers, to " speak at
all, or to teach in the name of Jesus," should represent him as
" a man fitted of God to be a scourge to his people." Laud
was born in 1573, at Reading, in Berkshire, and educated at
St. John's College, Oxford, of which he subsequently became
the president, and the munificent patron. He was made Bishop
of St. David's, in Wales, in 1621, — afterward Bishop of London, — and finally, upon the death of Abbot, in 1633, Archbishop of Canterbury. There was, indeed, as Fuller says,
" neither order, office, degree, nor dignity, in college, church,
nor university, but he passed through it," and in every station
he exhibited the same overweening partiality for the ceremonies
of the church, and the same bitter hostility toward the Puritans, who would not bow down to his idol. If he was not, as
Shepard calls him, " a fierce enemy of all righteousness," he
was certainly the avowed enemy of the most righteous persons
in the church, and a cruel persecutor of every one who showed
by his life that he preferred the power of godliness to a vain
ceremony. He had a zeal for the externals of religion which
consumed the spirit of piety, and an ambition to increase the
political power of the church which did not hesitate to trample upon the most sacred rights of man. He was evidently a
man of a narrow intellect and a bad heart. He was envious,
passionate, vindictive, cruel, and implacable. In the Star
Chamber he always advocated the severest measures, and " infused more vinegar than oil into all censures " against the
victims of church authority. " For this individual," says an
eminent writer, " we entertain a more unmitigated contempt

g *

than for any other character in our history. His mind had not
expansion enough to comprehend a great scheme, good or bad.
His oppressive acts were not, like those of the Earl of Straf-
ford, parts of an extensive system. They were the luxuries
in which a mean and irritable disposition indulges itself from
day to day — the excesses natural to a little mind in a great
place. While he abjured the innocent badges of Popery, he
retained all its worst vices — a complete subjection of reason to
authority, a weak preference of form to substance, a childish
passion for mummeries, an idolatrous veneration for the priestly
character, and, above all, a stupid and a ferocious intolerance." *
It is only necessary to add that, after inflicting upon the defense-
less Puritans all the evil in his power, he died a violent death,
being beheaded, upon a charge of high treason, on the 10th of
January, 1645, in the seventy-second year of his age. He ascended the scaffold " with a cheerful countenance, imputed by his
friends to the *clearedness*, by his foes to the *searedness*, of his
conscience. The beholders that day were so divided between
bemoaners and insulters, that it was hard to decide which of
them made up the major part of the company." †

Having been thus unexpectedly silenced, and forbidden to
preach or to perform any ministerial act within the realm of England, with no means of subsistence, with no employment, with no
hope of being able to promote the cause which he had most at
heart, with the withering sentence of the bishop upon him. Mr.
Shepard seemed to be really in an evil case. But though persecuted, he was not forsaken ; though cast down, he was not
destroyed. The Harlakendens, some of whom had been the
subjects of renewing grace under his preaching, showed their
affection and gratitude by affording him an asylum in their hos-
pitable mansion, and were " so many fathers and mothers " to
him. The people of Earles-Colne, also, mindful of the good
which had been done among them by his faithful labors, were

---

* Macaulay's Essays, 1, 10, 84
† Fuller, Church History, book xi., p. 215.

desirous that he should remain in the place, and were ready to contribute to his comfort, though he could be of no service to them as a minister of the gospel. Here he remained about six months; and as he was shut out from all active employment, he improved his enforced leisure in looking more carefully into the order of worship to which he was required to conform — a subject respecting which he had until now been undecided. The more he studied, the more clearly he saw "the evil of the English ceremonies, cross, surplice, and kneeling," and the less disposed to adhere to a church that made conformity to such things an indispensable condition of its fellowship, and used its power so tyrannically against all who had conscientious scruples about them.

Mr. Shepard's course in relation to this matter was not at all singular. Many of the most distinguished Puritans of that time, and of a somewhat later period, were, for a while, undecided respecting their duty as to the ceremonies, were willing to conform to many things which they could not altogether approve, were greatly distressed at the idea of separating from their mother church, which, with all her faults, still retained, substantially, the true Christian doctrine. This was Philip Henry's state of mind. He was disposed to remain in the church, and to conform as far as possible; but the treatment he received convinced him that the assumption of human authority in matters of religion was a great evil, and made him practically, though not nominally, an Independent.* In his Diary for February 16, 1673, the following passage occurs: "Mr. Leigh at chapel. Discourse at noon not altogether suitable to the Sabbath, concerning ceremonies; but something said in public led to it, viz., that the magistrate hath power in imposing *gestures* and *vestures*." So Baxter, one of the most candid and conscientious of men, was driven farther and farther from the English church, by the doctrine, so cruelly reduced to practice, that the state has the right to fix the mode

* Letters on the Puritans, by J. B. Williams.

in which men shall worship God, and by the impudent plea of " men's good, and the order of the church," in justification of acts of inhumanity and uncharitableness.* John Corbet, the author of " Self-employment in Secret," who was turned out of his living at Bramshot, in Hampshire, was another whom violent and compulsory treatment compelled to study the subject of conformity with great care and impartiality. Many parts of conformity, says Baxter, he could have yielded to, but not *all*, and nothing less than all would satisfy the bishops.†

While Mr. Shepard was thus engaged in examining this subject, which had become one of vital importance, and forming his views of duty in relation to the ceremonies, his old enemy, Bishop Laud, coming into the country upon a visitation, and learning that he was still at Earles-Colne, cited him to appear before the court at Peldon; " where I appearing, he asked me what I did in the place. I told him I studied. He asked me what. I told him the fathers. He replied, I might thank him for that; yet he charged me to depart the place. I asked him whither should I go. To the university, said he. I told him I had no means to subsist there. Yet he charged me to depart the place." It was at this visitation that Mr. Weld, who had been suspended from his ministry about a month before, was formally excommunicated, and thus, to use the bishop's expression, " everlastingly disenabled." Mr. Rogers, of Dedham, was, at the same time, required to subscribe; and, as he could not conscientiously do this, he was, like a multitude of other pious and faithful ministers, suspended and silenced.

---

* Baxter's Remains, 131, fol. 1696.
† Sermon at the Funeral of J. Corbet.

CHAPTER VI.

It was now evident that Mr. Shepard's work at Earles-Colne, where he had first become acquainted with the burden and the glory of the cross, was finished ; and that he must prepare for a speedy departure, if he would escape the effects of the bishop's indignation. But whither should he go ? There were no means of subsistence for him at the university. He could no longer preach in the diocese of London ; and he had been threatened with persecution if he attempted to preach any where else in England. But he was under the guidance of a Providence in whose wisdom he could implicitly trust ; and during this trying scene his mind seems to have been kept in perfect peace with respect to the question where he should go, and what he should do. The situation of chaplain in a gentleman's family, in Yorkshire, had been offered to him ; but he was unwilling to leave his present post until actually forced away by circumstances which he could not control. These circumstances had now occurred ; and he was watching for the indications of the divine will in relation to his future course.

A few days after he had been peremptorily commanded, by an authority which he could not resist, to leave Earles-Colne, the bishop was to hold a visitation in Dunmore, in Essex ;· and Mr. Weld, Mr. Daniel Rogers, Mr. Ward, Mr. Marshall, and

Mr. Wharton, all standing in jeopardy every hour, "consulted together, whether it was best to let such a swine root up God's plants in Essex, and not give him some check." In what way they expected to give "a check" to such a man as Laud does not appear; but it was agreed upon privately, at Braintree, that they would speak to the bishop, and, if possible, to arrest this work of devastation.

Mr. Shepard and Mr. Weld, traveling together to the place where the bishop was to hold his visitation, discussed the expediency of emigrating to New England. But, upon the whole, they concluded that it would be better to go by the way of Scotland into Ireland, and endeavor to find there a place where they might safely and profitably exercise their ministry. When they came to the church where the bishop was to preach, Mr. Weld, who had been already excommunicated, stopped at the door, not being permitted to stand within consecrated walls; but Mr. Shepard, upon whom the anathema had not yet been pronounced, went boldly in. Sermon being ended, Mr. Weld drew near to hear the bishop's speech, supposing that, as divine service was over, even an excommunicated person might listen to an ordinary address. He was, however, mistaken. The bishop saw him, and, turning upon him with his accustomed violence, demanded why he was "on this side New England," and how he, who, by excommunication, had become a heathen and a publican, dared to stand upon holy ground. Mr. Weld meekly pleaded in excuse, that, if he had sinned, it was through ignorance, and begged to be forgiven. The bishop, however, was not in a forgiving mood, and Mr. Weld was committed to the pursuivant, and bound over in the sum of one hundred marks, to answer, before the Court of High Commission, for the crime of desecrating a church by his presence, as "an example" and a warning to all such persons in future.*

While this shameful scene was being enacted, Mr. Shepard, coming into the crowd, heard the bishop inquiring about him,

* Chronicles of Massachusetts, 522, note.

and found that the pursuivant, having arrested Mr. Weld, was anxious to get hold of his companion, as the worst of the two. Several persons who were friendly to Mr. Shepard, hearing his name pronounced, and seeing that the bishop had resolved to make "an example" of him also, urged him to retire without delay ; but, as he hesitated, and lingered upon this dangerous ground, not knowing what to do, a Mr. Holbeech, a pious school-master of Felsted, in Essex, seeing his danger, seized him, and drew him forcibly out of the church. This was no sooner done than the apparitor called for Mr. Shepard, and, as he was no where to be seen, the pursuivant was sent in haste to find and arrest him. But Mr. Holbeech, who seems to have had more energy and presence of mind upon this occasion than his friend, " hastened our horses, and away we rid as fast as possible ; and so the Lord delivered me out of the hand of that lion a third time."

Mr. Shepard was now a fugitive, not from justice, but from the savage officers of that most iniquitous Star Chamber, in which, if no fault whatever could be proved, it was ruin to a man's person and purse to be tried. He had, as has been said, received an invitation to act as chaplain to a gentleman's family in Yorkshire, which he had declined to accept until the bishop had actually driven him away from Earles-Colne. Soon after his flight from Dunmore, he received a letter from Ezekiel Rogers, then living at Rowley, in Yorkshire, renewing this invitation, and urging him to come into that county, where he would be " far from the hearing of the malicious Bishop Laud," who had threatened him, if he preached any where in his diocese. The family referred to was that of Sir Richard Darley, of But-tercrambe, in the north riding of Yorkshire. As a compensation for his services, the knight offered to board and lodge him, and the two sons of Sir Richard, Henry and Richard Darley, prom-ised, for their part, a salary of twenty pounds a year. The letters, moreover, which he received from Yorkshire, presented an inducement of a higher nature, for they came " crying with that voice of the man of Macedonia, ' Come and help us.' " Un-

der these circumstances, Mr. Shepard could not be doubtful as
to the path of duty, and he resolved to "follow the Lord to so
remote and strange a place." When he was ready to depart,
Sir Richard considerately sent a man to be his guide in a journey which, at that time, was not only tedious, but somewhat
hazardous; and with "much grief of heart," he "forsook Essex
and Earles-Colne, going, as it were, he knew not whither;" and
the affectionate people, who had for a season rejoiced in his
light, "sorrowing most of all for the words which he spake,
that they should see his face no more."

In this journey he had occasion to remember the Saviour's
words, "Pray that your flight be not in winter." They traveled
on horseback, and were five or six days upon the road. The
weather was cold and stormy. The rivers in Yorkshire were
much swollen by the rains, and hardly passable. The ways
were rough, and on several occasions the travelers were in great
danger. At last they came to a town called Ferrybridge, on the
River Aire, "where the waters were up, and ran over the bridge
for half a mile together." Here they hired a guide to conduct
them over the bridge. "But when he had gone a little way, the
violence of the water was such, that he first fell in, and after him
another man, who was near drowning before my eyes. Whereupon my heart was so smitten with fear of the danger, and my
head so dizzied with the running of the water, that had not the
Lord immediately upheld me, and my horse also, and so guided
it, I had certainly perished." They had proceeded but a short
distance upon the bridge, when Mr. Shepard fell into the river,
but was able to keep his seat upon his horse, which, being a
very good one, with great effort soon regained its footing upon
the bridge. Mr. Darley's man, also, in his efforts to save Mr.
Shepard, fell in, and was near drowning, but at last extricated
himself from his perilous situation. After much difficulty, they
reached a house upon the opposite side of the river, where they
changed their clothes, and "went to prayer," blessing God for
"this wonderful preservation." He looked now upon his life
as a new existence granted to him, which he "saw good reason

to give up unto God and his service. And truly the Lord, that had dealt only gently with me before, now began to afflict me, and to let me see how good it was to be under his tutoring."

It was late on Saturday evening when they reached York. Stopping only for some slight refreshment, they went on to Buttercrambe, the seat of Sir Richard, about seven miles farther, where, at a late hour, very wet, cold, and weary, they at last arrived. The reception which Mr. Shepard met at the house of Sir Richard Darley was in one respect all that he could have anticipated; for all his wants were promptly attended to, and he was lodged in the "best room in the house." But the religious condition of the family, and the manner in which he found some of its members employed near Sabbath morning when he arrived, must have been more chilling to his heart than the cold rain had been to his frail body. To his utter astonishment and dismay, he found "divers of them at dice and tables," and learnt, with unspeakable sorrow, that, although he was expected to preach on the morrow, no preparation had been made to receive him "as becometh saints." He was hurried to his lodgings, and on the next day, worn out with the fatigue of a perilous journey, sad at heart, and almost dead with despondency, he preached his first sermon in that place; with what effect is not known, but can easily be conjectured. It is not strange that while he was comfortably provided for in external respects, he should feel that he had fallen upon evil days, and that he was "never so sunk in spirit as about this time." For he was now far from all his friends. He was in a "profane house," where there seemed to be no fear of God. He was in a "vile, wicked town and country." He was "unknown and exposed to all wrongs." He felt "insufficient to do any work;" and, to render his situation as comfortless as possible, "the lady was churlish." Yet even here he was not altogether forsaken and desolate. The lady might treat him contemptuously, but Sir Richard was kind; and he found in the house three friendly servants — Thomas Fugill, who was one of the principal settlers of New Haven, in 1638, — Ruth Bushell, after-

wards married to Edward Mitchenson, both of whom came to
New England, and were members of the church in Cambridge, —
and Margaret Touteville, a relative of Sir Richard, — by whose
kind attentions the unexpected trials to which he was exposed
were in some measure alleviated.

Soon after Mr. Shepard became a resident in this family, the
daughter of Sir Richard Darley was married to " one Mr.
Alured, a most profane young gentleman," upon which occasion,
according to custom, a sermon was required from the chaplain.
This was the commencement of what may be called a revival in
that " profane house." Under the discourse, " the Lord first
touched the heart of Mistress Margaret with very great terrors
for sin and her Christless estate." Immediately other members
of the family, among whom were Mr. and Mrs. Alured, began
to inquire what they must do to be saved. These convictions
resulted in hopeful conversion; and the whole family, if not
savingly renewed, were, at least, thoroughly reformed, and
brought to the regular performance of external duties. This
seems to have been the limit of Mr. Shepard's success in that
place. For although Mather says that God quickly made him
instrumental of a blessed change in the neighborhood, as well as
in the family, — the profanest persons thereabouts being touched
with the efficacy of his ministry, and prayer with fasting succeeding to their former wildness, — yet Mr. Shepard himself,
who best knew the results of his preaching, declares that while
most of the members of Sir Richard's family were converted, or,
at least, greatly changed, he knew of " none in the town, or
about it, who were brought home."

While Mr. Shepard was thus faithfully laboring to enrich this
family with the blessings of the gospel, the Lord was preparing
for him one of the greatest of earthly blessings — a pious and
devoted wife. For three years, while he resided at Earles-
Colne, he had made it a subject of earnest prayer that the Lord
would carry him to a place " where he might find a meet yoke-
fellow." His prayer was now answered. He found in Margaret Touteville — then about twenty-seven years of age — a

woman every way suited to aid him in his arduous work. She was " a most humble woman," — " a very discerning Christian," — " amiable and holy," — " endued with a very sweet spirit of prayer," — and upon the whole, " the best and the fittest person in the world" for such a man as Shepard. Sir Richard, with his whole family, favored the connection, not only giving their cordial consent to his union with their kinswoman, but generously increasing her marriage portion; and in 1632, after a residence of about a year in the family, he was happily married to one, who, in his " exiled condition in a strange place," and in his hardships and dangers, was ever to him an " incomparably loving " and faithful wife.

Mr. Shepard now found it expedient to remove from Buttercrambe. His wife was unwilling to remain in Sir Richard's family after her marriage; and besides, it soon became impossible for him to continue his labors in that place, for Bishop Neile, a rigid ceremonialist, coming to York and hearing of him, peremptorily forbade his preaching there any longer unless he would subscribe, which, with his conscience now becoming fully enlightened, he could not do. At this crisis he received an invitation to preach at Heddon, a town in Northumberland, about five miles from Newcastle upon the Tyne. It was a poor place, and afforded but little prospect of a comfortable subsistence. But it was the only field of labor open to him at that time; and as the people were anxious to obtain his services, — especially as there he would be far from the residence of any bishop, a matter of the greatest importance to a preacher who could not subscribe, — he resolved to go. Accordingly, accompanied by Mr. Alured, he went to Heddon, not without painful apprehensions of danger from the efforts of his enemies, and his " poor wife full of fears." But all his fears were not realized. He experienced, as he expected, some hardship and inconvenience; but he found some kind Christian friends, among the most valuable of whom were Mrs. Fenwick, who gave him the use of a house, and Mrs. Sherbourne, who contributed largely to his maintenance. His labors in Heddon, and in the adjoining towns, were abundant, and accompanied by the divine blessing. Many of his hearers were converted; and those who already loved the truth were greatly strengthened by his vigorous piety and enlightening ministry. He found time also to study more thoroughly the subject of church government and order, and to form his opinions more fully in relation to the ceremonies, and the "unlawful standing of bishops." He thus became more and more sensible of the great errors of the established church, and better fitted for the work of building up the tabernacle of God in the wilderness, to which he was soon to be called.

After preaching at Heddon for about a year, he removed — for what reason is not known — to a neighboring town. But he was soon forced to leave that place by a clergyman who came with authority to forbid his preaching publicly any longer. In this new and unexpected trouble, application was made by his friends to Morton, Bishop of Durham, for liberty to continue his ministry among them; but the bishop, although he seems to have been disposed to grant this request, acknowledged that he dared not give his sanction to the preaching of a man whom Laud had undertaken to silence. Mr. Shepard therefore went from place to place, and preached wherever he could do so without danger, until at last he was obliged to confine himself to private exposition in the house of Mr. Fenwick. During this dismal and trying season, his first child, whom he named Thomas, was born, — the mother having been in great peril for four days, through the unskillfulness of her physician. To have been deprived of such a wife in that "dark country," and when he was struggling with innumerable difficulties and dangers, would have broken his spirit, and the Lord mercifully spared him this affliction. But the shadow of such an evil falling upon him amidst all his other trials humbled him in the dust, reminded him of all his delinquencies and broken resolutions, drew him nearer to God, and excited him to greater diligence and faithfulness in his great work.

Mr. Shepard had now been "tossed from the south to the north of England," and could neither go farther in that direction, nor preach the gospel publicly where he was. He therefore began to consider the case of conscience, frequently put by the martyrs in the bloody days of Queen Mary — whether it was not his duty to abandon his country altogether, and seek in a new world not only a refuge for himself, but a place where he might labor securely, and with hope, for the advancement of the Saviour's kingdom. The thoughts of many pious persons in England had, for some time, been turned toward this country, where, it was believed, the Lord was about to plant the gospel, and to establish a pure church. Cotton, Hooker, Stone, and Weld, the intimate friends of Mr. Shepard, together with many of their people, had already fled to New England; and many others were preparing to follow them into the wilderness, where they could worship God according to his word. Under these circumstances, Mr. Shepard "began to listen to a call to New England."

For taking this decisive step he saw many weighty reasons. He had no call to any place in England where he could preach the gospel, nor any means of subsistence for himself and family. He saw many pious people leaving their country, and going forth, like Abraham, they knew not whither, at the call of God and conscience. He was urged by those who had already gone, and by many who wished to go to New England, to abandon a country where he could no longer be useful as a minister of Christ, and aid them in their holy enterprise by his wisdom and piety. He "saw the Lord departing from England when Mr. Hooker and Mr. Cotton were gone," and anticipated nothing but misery if he were left behind. He was convinced of the evil of the ceremonies, and of the inexpediency, if not the sin, of mixed communion in the sacraments of the church as then administered, while at the same time he deemed it "lawful to join with them in preaching." He felt it to be his duty to enjoy, if possible, the benefit of all God's ordinances, and to seek them in a foreign land, if they could not be found at home. He was exposed to fine, imprisonment, and all manner of persecution, and he saw no divine command to remain and suffer, when the Lord had providentially opened a way of escape. He regarded, however,

h *

not so much his own personal quiet and safety as "the glory of those liberties in New England," which the people of God seemed about to enjoy, and the influence which he might exert in securing and defending them. It was urged by some who did not wish to emigrate, that he might remain in the north of England, and preach privately; but he was convinced that this would expose him to danger, and he was not satisfied that it was his duty to hazard his personal liberty, and the comfort and safety of his family, for what was by all classes deemed a disorderly manner of preaching, when he might exercise his talent publicly and honorably in New England. Finally, he considered how sad a thing it would be, if he should die, to leave his wife and child in "that rude place of the north, where there was nothing but barbarous wickedness," and "how sweet it would be to leave them among God's people," however poor.

These considerations appeared to him of sufficient weight to justify his speedy departure, "before the pursuivants came out" to render his escape impracticable. And afterward, when the removal of the New England Puritans was spoken of, by some of their brethren at home, as a treacherous and cowardly flight from the duty of suffering, the same reasons, substantially, were assigned by him, in his answer to Ball, as a complete vindication of their conduct. "Was it not," he says, "a time when human worship and inventions were grown to such an intolerable height, that the consciences of God's people, enlightened in the truth, could no longer bear them? Was not the power of the tyrannical prelates so great, that, like a strong current, it carried every thing down stream before it? Did not the hearts of men generally fail them? Where was the people to be found that would cleave to their godly ministers in their sufferings, but rather thought it their discretion to provide for their own quiet and safety? What would men have us do in such a case? Must we study some distinctions to salve our consciences in complying with so manifold corruptions in God's worship? or should we live without God's ordinances, because we could not partake in the corrupt administration of them? It is true we might have suffered; we might easily have found the way to have filled the prisons; and some had their share in these sufferings. But whether we were called to this when a wide door of liberty was set open, and our witnesses to the truth, through the malignant policy of those times, could not testify openly before the world, but were smothered up in close prisons, we leave to be considered. We can not see but the rule of Christ to his apostles, and the practice of God's saints in all ages, may allow us this liberty as well as others — to fly into the wilderness from the face of the dragon. The infinite and only-wise God hath many works to do in the world; and, by his singular providence, he gives gifts to his servants, and disposes them to his work as seems unto him best. If the Lord will have some to bear witness by imprisonment, mutilation, etc., he gives them spirits suitable to this work, and we honor them in it. If he will have others instrumental to promote reformation in England, we honor them, and rejoice in their holy endeavor, and pray for a blessing upon them and their labors. And what if God will have his church built up also in these remote parts of the world, that his name may be known to the heathen, or whatsoever other end he has, and for this purpose will send forth a company of weak-hearted Christians, who dare not stay at home to suffer, why should we not let the Lord alone, and rejoice that Christ is preached, howsoever and wheresoever?"*

Having fully resolved to leave England at the first favorable opportunity, Mr. Shepard took leave of his friends in the north, where he had labored for about a year; and in the beginning of June, 1634, accompanied by his wife, child, and maid servant, he left Newcastle secretly, for fear of the pursuivants, on board a coal vessel bound to Ipswich, the principal town in Suffolk. He remained a short time in Ipswich, first in the family of Mr. Russell, and then with his friend Mr. Collins, both of whom were afterward prominent members of the church in Cambridge. From Ipswich he made a journey to Earles-Colne, where he

---

* Treatise of Liturgies, Pref. pp. 4–6.

lived very privately in the family of Mr. Harlakenden, from whom he received every attention which his forlorn situation required. Here he passed the summer of 1634. This period, in which he was "so tossed up and down," having no permanent place of residence, and being obliged to keep himself concealed from the notice of the bishops, he found "the most uncomfortable and fruitless to his own soul especially," that he ever experienced. He therefore longed to be in New England as soon as possible; and, as a number of friends, among whom was John Norton, were preparing to emigrate at the close of that summer, he determined to accompany them. The ship in which they expected to sail was the Hope, of Ipswich, and the time fixed for their departure was the early part of September. Although the season was so far advanced that they must arrive on the bleak coast of New England toward the beginning of winter, yet as dangers thickened around them, — as the master, Mr. Gurling, was an able seaman and very friendly to the emigrants, — as the ship was a large and good one, — and as they were assured by the captain that he would certainly sail at the time appointed, — they were willing to encounter the perils of the voyage at that season.

All necessary arrangements having been made, Mr. Shepard repaired, with his family, to Ipswich, for the purpose of embarking. The ship, however, was not ready to sail, and they were detained six or eight weeks beyond the time agreed upon. The company were now in great perplexity and distress. The winter was rapidly approaching, and the voyage becoming every day more dangerous. They were surrounded by enemies, and constantly liable to be discovered and arrested by the savage pursuivants. Some of them feared that this detention might be a divine chastisement sent upon them for "rushing onward too soon." Mr. Shepard was for a while in great heaviness of soul, and had many fears and doubts in relation to this enterprise. He had gone too far to relinquish the voyage, and the only alternative was to proceed; but from that time he resolved "never to go about a sad business in the dark, unless God's call, within as well as without" was "very strong, and clear, and comfortable."

While the company were thus anxiously and impatiently waiting for the ship to sail, Mr. Shepard and Mr. Norton were kindly concealed and provided for in the house of a worthy man, who exerted himself nobly, and at some hazard to himself, in their behalf. Many of the pious people in the town resorted privately to these men of God for instruction. At the same time their enemies were eagerly watching for them, and using all possible means to entrap and apprehend them. These hunters of souls, failing in all their efforts to draw their prey into the open field, and being restrained by law from breaking into the asylum to which they had fled, at last persuaded a young man, who lived in the house where Mr. Shepard lodged, by a large sum of money, to promise that, at a certain hour of a night agreed upon, he would open the door for their peaceable entrance into this sanctuary. The youth, who was frequently in the presence of Mr. Shepard, and heard the words of grace and the fervent prayers which he uttered, became deeply impressed with the thought that this was a holy man of God; and that to betray him into the hands of his enemies would be a heinous crime. He began to repent of his bargain. As the night in which he was to execute his wicked purpose drew near, he became greatly agitated with sorrow, fear, and regret, insomuch that his master noticed the remarkable change in his appearance and conduct, and questioned him as to the cause of his apparent distress. At first he was unwilling to reveal the truth, and for some time evaded the inquiries of the family; but at length, by the urgent expostulations of his master, he was brought to confess with tears, that on such a night, he had promised to let in men to apprehend the godly minister. Mr. Shepard was immediately conveyed away to a place of safety by his friends; and when the men came at the time appointed, the bird had escaped from the snare of the fowler. Not finding the door unbolted, as they expected when they raised the latch, they thrust their staves under it to lift it from its hinges; but being observed by some persons whom the good man of the house had prudently employed for that purpose, they precipitately fled, lest they should be arrested and dealt with as housebreakers.*

CHAPTER VII.

On the 16th of October, 1634, Mr. Shepard and his friends sailed from Harwich, a seaport in Essex, at the mouth of the River Stour. They had proceeded but a few leagues, when, the wind suddenly changing, they were obliged to cast anchor in a very dangerous place. The wind continued to blow all night, and, on the morning of the 17th, became so violent that the ship dragged her anchors, and was driven upon the sands near the harbor of Harwich, where she was for some time in the most imminent peril. To add to their distress, one of the sailors, in endeavoring to execute some order, fell overboard, and was carried a mile or more out to sea, apparently beyond the reach of any human aid. The ship and crew were at that moment in so much danger, that no one could be spared to go in search of him, if, indeed, the boat could have lived a moment in the sea that was breaking around them; and when the immediate danger to the ship was over, no one on board supposed that the poor man was alive. He was, however, discovered floating upon the waves at a great distance, though it was known that he was not able to swim; and three seamen put off in the boat, at the

* Johnson's Wonder-working Providence, ch. 29.

hazard of their lives, to save him. When they reached him, though he was floating, — supported, as it were, by a divine hand, — he exhibited no signs of life; and having taken him on board, they laid him in the bottom of the boat, supposing him to be dead. One of the men, however, was unwilling to give up his shipmate without using all the means in their power for his resuscitation. Upon turning his head downward, in order to let the water run out, he began to breathe; in a few moments, under such treatment as their good sense suggested, he was able to move and to speak; and by the time they reached the ship, he had recovered the use of his limbs, having been in the water more than an hour. This incident is interesting mainly on account of the prophetic use that was made of it by one of the passengers, probably either Mr. Shepard or Mr. Norton, in his efforts to encourage the desponding company. "This man's danger and deliverance," said he, " is a type of ours. We are in great danger, and yet the Lord's power will be shown in saving us."

The event corresponded to the prediction, and the strong faith of the man of God, like that of Paul, in his stormy voyage to Rome, was rewarded by the deliverance which it confidently expected. The ship, that was driving rapidly toward the shore, and actually touching the sands with her keel, was, by some means, turned about, and beaten back toward Yarmouth Roads, "an open place at sea, fit for anchorage, but otherwise a very dangerous place." Here they came to anchor, and hoped to ride out the gale. But on Saturday morning, October 18, the storm increased in violence, and the wind from the west blew with such destructive fury, that the day was long known among the inhabitants of the coast as the *Windy Saturday.* Many vessels were cast away in this storm; and among them the collier which brought Mr. Shepard from Newcastle, the captain and all his men being lost. When the wind arose, the anchors were thrown out; but the cables parted immediately, and the ship drifted rapidly toward the sands, where her destruction seemed inevitable. The master gave up all for lost, and the passengers resorted to prayer. Guns were fired for assistance from the town; but, although thousands were spectators of their danger, and large rewards were offered to any who would venture their lives to save the passengers and crew, yet so dreadful was the storm that that no one could be prevailed upon to volunteer in this service. It was known among the crowd that gazed from the walls of Yarmouth upon this terrible scene, that the ship was full of Puritan emigrants, and therefore a peculiar interest was felt in the catastrophe which seemed to await her — some fervently praying that the Lord would deliver his people from the danger that threatened them, and others, probably, impiously rejoicing in their anticipated destruction. One man, an officer of some kind, ventured to give expression to the feelings which were cherished by many. With a spirit of prophecy somewhat like that of Balaam when he was constrained to bless with his mouth the people whom he cursed in his heart, he scoffingly exclaimed, that he "pitied the poor collier in the road," — referring to the coal vessel in which Mr. Shepard had sailed from Newcastle, — "but for the Puritans in the other ship he felt no concern, for their faith would save them."

And their faith — or rather the Lord in whom they trusted, and for whose glory they had encountered perils by sea as well as by land — did save them, in a remarkable way and by unexpected means. The captain and the sailors had lost all presence of mind; and believing that the storm was preternatural, and that the ship was bewitched, they made use of the only means of escape they could think of, which was nailing two red-hot horseshoes to the mainmast as a charm.* But there was on board a drunken fellow, "no sailor, though he had often been to sea," who had taken it into his head to accompany these pious people to New England, to whose cool judgment they now, under God, owed their deliverance. Instead of nailing horseshoes to the mast, he advised that it should be cut away, as the only possible method of saving the ship. The captain and the crew, bewildered by terror, were incapable of listening to advice; and

* Johnson, Hist. N. Eng. ch. 29.

at last Cock, — for that was the man's name, — assuming the responsibility, called for hatchets, and encouraging the company and the seamen, who were "forlorn and hopeless of life," they cut the masts by the board, just at the moment when all had given themselves up for lost, expecting "to see neither New nor Old England, nor faces of friends any more."

When the mast was down, a small anchor, which remained, was thrown out; but it being very light, the ship dragged, and continued to drift rapidly toward the shore. The sailors, supposing that the anchor was gone, or that it would not hold, pointed to the devouring sands, where so many vessels had been ingulfed, and bade the passengers behold the place where their graves should shortly be. The captain declared that he had done all that he could, and desired the ministers to pray for help from above. Accordingly, Mr. Norton, with the passengers, two hundred in number, in one place, and Mr. Shepard, with the mariners upon deck, "went to prayer," and committed their "souls and bodies unto the Lord that gave them." Immediately after prayer, the violence of the wind began to abate, and the ship ceased to drift. The last anchor was not lost, as they thought, but was dragged along, plowing the sand by the violence of the wind, which abating after prayer, though still violent, "the ship was stopped just when it was ready to be swallowed up of the sands." They were still, however, in great danger, for the wind was high, and though the anchor had brought the ship up, yet the "cable was let out so far that a little rope held the cable, and the cable the little anchor, and the little anchor the great ship in this great storm." When one of the company, whose faith was stronger than cable or tempest, saw how strangely they were preserved, exclaimed, "That thread we hang by" — for so he called the rope attached to the cable — "will save us." And so, indeed, it did, "the Lord showing his dreadful power, and yet his unspeakable rich mercy toward us, who heard, nay, helped us, when we could not cry, through the disconsolate fears we had, out of these depths of seas and miseries." This deliverance was so great, and so mani-

festly wrought in answer to prayer, that Mr. Shepard thought, if
he ever reached the shore again, he should live like one risen
from the dead ; and he desired that this mercy, to him and his
family, might be remembered to the glory of God, by his " children and their children's children," when he was dead, and could
not " praise the Lord in the land of the living any more."

They remained on board during the night in comparative safety, — the storm continuing to abate, — but in a very comfortless
condition.   Many were sick, " many weak and discouraged," and
there were " many sad hearts."   On Sabbath morning, October
19, they went on shore.   The Puritans were very strict in their
observance of the Sabbath ; and Mr. Shepard thought that they
were in too much haste to leave the ship, and that they ought to
have spent the day on board in praising the Lord for his signal
interposition in their behalf.   But there were many feeble persons among them who were unable to engage in religious exercises, and had need of refreshment on shore ; and besides, they
were " afraid of neglecting a season of providence in going
out while they had a calm ; " for they were held, as it were,
by " a thread," and if the wind should rise again, they might all
find their graves in the sands.   Mr. Shepard and his family left
the ship in the first boat that was sent from the town to take off
the passengers.   And here they were visited by a new and more
bitter affliction.   They were saved from the devouring waters to
be smitten by the sudden and mysterious death of their only
child, now about a year old.   In the passage from the ship to
the shore, he was seized with vomiting, which no means they
could use, although they had all necessary medical aid at
Yarmouth, could check.   After lingering for a fortnight in
great distress, he died, and was buried at Yarmouth.   The
funeral was conducted very privately ; and it was no small
aggravation of the sorrow which they felt for the loss of their
first born, that Mr. Shepard dared not be present, lest the pursuivants should discover and apprehend him.   For as soon as
they were ashore, says Scottou, " two vipers designed not only
to leap upon the hands " of Shepard and Norton, " but to seize

their persons. But how strangely preserved is not unknown to *some of us.*" *

It is interesting to learn what were the feelings and exercises of such a man as Mr. Shepard under afflictions like these; for the inward experiences of such minds furnish great lessons for us. There was no murmuring under the rod. The feeling of his heart was that of a loving child kindly chastised by a tender father; and he saw in every blow a manifestation of divine love, and a corrective of his waywardness. As if the Lord "saw that these waters were not sufficient to wash away my sinfulness, he cast me into the fire. He showed me my weak faith, pride, carnal content, immoderate love of creatures, of my child especially, and begat in me some desires and purposes to fear his name. I considered how unfit I was to go to such a good land as New England with such an unmortified, hard, dark, formal, hypocritical heart; and therefore no wonder if the Lord did thus cross me." He even began to fear — such was his tenderness of conscience, and desire to walk in all the commandments and ordinances of the Lord blameless — that his affliction came, in part, for "running too far in a way of separation from the mixed assemblies in England," though this, of all his sins, must have been the smallest, for he did not forsake the church until he was driven from it by arbitrary force; and he always believed and declared — what none of the Puritans ever denied — that there were "true churches in many parishes in England," and also true ministers of the gospel, whose preaching he never refused to hear when he had opportunity.

One effect of these afflictions — the sudden death of his only child, and the tremendous storm which seemed like a frown of Providence upon their voyage — was to diminish very much his desire of emigrating to New England, and to make him almost willing to remain and suffer at home. This state of mind, how-

---

* Chronicles of Mass. 540, note.

ever, did not continue long.   When he remembered that he had
been tossed from one end of England to the other ; that there was
no place in his native land where he could preach the gospel ;
that, so long as he refused conformity to the errors and corruptions
of the church, nothing but "bonds and afflictions" awaited him ;
that a "door of escape" was providentially opened ; and that, in
this distant land, he should not only be beyond the reach of the
bishops, but find a place where he might labor for the cause of
Christ, — his desire to emigrate revived, and he resolved that,
as soon as practicable, he would make another attempt to place
the ocean between him and his persecutors.

   In the mean time, he was in great distress, not knowing where
to go, nor what to do.   The Philistines were upon him.   There
seemed to be no place of safety.   He could neither labor for a
subsistence, nor could his friends, without great danger, minister
effectually to his necessities.   In this time of need, — the most
trying and apparently hopeless he had ever experienced, —
Roger Harlakenden and his brother Samuel, having heard of
his escape from the dangers of the sea, and of worse dangers to
which he was still exposed upon land, visited him, and refreshed
his spirit by their sympathy and assistance.   While casting
about where to spend the winter that was approaching, Mr.
Bridge, minister of Norwich, kindly offered him an asylum in
his family.   But a Mrs. Corbet, an aged and eminently pious
woman, who lived about five miles from Norwich, fearing that
Mr. Bridge might hazard his liberty by harboring the fugitive,
invited him to occupy a house of hers, then vacant, at Bastwick,
a small hamlet in the county of Norfolk.   And she not only furnished him with a house which "was fit to entertain any prince,
for fairness, greatness, and pleasantness," but, in various ways,
endeavored to render the season of his detention and confinement as comfortable as possible.   Here, with his wife and a few
friends, — Mr. Harlakenden defraying the whole expense of
housekeeping, — he passed the winter of 1634–5, far from the
notice of his enemies, and solaced by "sweet fellowship one with

another, and also with God." Nor was he idle in this comfortable retreat. For, although he could not preach publicly, he could employ his pen for the instruction and consolation of his afflicted friends, and, by diligent study, prepare himself for that service to which he was soon to be called, in the new world. It was during this season that he wrote the little work, first published at London in 1648, entitled " SELECT CASES RESOLVED," in a letter to a pious friend, who had fallen into doubt and difficulty respecting the questions therein discussed. In the title pages of the first two editions, this letter is said to have been sent from New England; but, from several expressions at the commencement and at the close, it is evident that it was written in England, and upon the eve of his departure from that country; for he says, ' It may possibly be my dying letter to you before I depart from hence and return to Him, as not knowing but our last disasters and sea straits, of which I wrote to you, may be but the preparation for the execution of the next approaching voyage." And again, in the conclusion : " I thank you heartily for improving me this way of writing, *who have my mouth stopped from speaking*," — a calamity which certainly never befell him in New England, — " and remember, when you are best able to pray for yourself, to look after me and mine, and all that go with me on the mighty waters; and then to look up and sigh to heaven for me, that the Lord would, out of his free grace, but bring me to that good land, and those glorious ordinances, and that there I may but behold the face of the Lord in his temple " — a request which he never had occasion to make after landing on these shores. Of this letter, written in a time of great trial, and coming from a mind itself needing all the consolations of friendship and religion, it is only necessary to say, in the language of those who first gave it to the public, that it is " so full of grace and truth, that it needs no other epistle commendatory than itself," and no one who desires to walk comfortably with God, in his general and particular calling, can study these answers, in which acuteness, depth, piety, and Christian experience are so eminently and happily blended, without becoming a wiser and a holier man.*

Early in the spring of 1635, Mr. Shepard, accompanied by his friend Harlakenden, went up to London, in order to make all necessary preparation for another attempt to leave England. During the journey, which seems to have been somewhat protracted, he was nearly deprived of his faithful and devoted wife. At the house of Mr. Burroughs, a Puritan minister, where they stopped about a fortnight, Mrs. Shepard, being near her confinement, " fell down from the top of a pair of stairs to the bottom ; yet the Lord kept her, and the child also, from that deadly danger." Upon their arrival at London, in the very neighborhood of their " great enemy," Laud, and not knowing where to hide themselves, a Mrs. Sherbourne provided a " very private place " for them ; where, on Sunday, April 5, 1635, their second son was born, whom they named Thomas, after his brother who died at Yarmouth. The mother soon recovered, but the child was sickly, and at one time they thought he would have died of a sore mouth. Mr. Shepard had more confidence in prayer than in the physician's skill ; and in the night he was " stirred up to pray " for the life of the child, and " that with very much fervor, and many arguments ; " and thus, after a sad, heavy night, the Lord shined upon him in the morning, and he found the sore mouth, which was thought to be incurable, " suddenly and strangely amended." They had not been long in London before their hiding-place was discovered by their enemies, and in order to escape from the " vipers " that were ready to fasten upon them, they removed by night to a house belonging to Mr. Alurcd, which, providentially, stood empty. The pursuivants, who were sent to apprehend Mr. Shepard, were a little too late : for, upon entering the place where he had been secreted, they found that the whole family had gone, no one knew whither ; and thus once more the Lord delivered his faithful servant from the snares which had been laid for him.

---

* Prefaces to Select Cases Resolved.

In the closest retirement, but not without much sympathy and many tokens of love from Christian friends, Mr. Shepard and his family passed the summer of 1635 in London. Toward the close of the summer, — Mrs. Shepard and the child having recovered their strength in some measure, — they began to prepare again for their removal to New England. The reasons which had led them to this decision the year before still existed, with perhaps increasing force ; and it became more and more evident, every day, that there was no longer any place or duty for them in England. Several "precious friends" were resolved, and waiting to sail with Mr. Shepard, among whom were Roger Harlakenden, Mr. Champney, Mr. Wilson, Mr. Jones, afterward colleague with Mr. Bulkley, at Concord, besides many pious people who were ready to follow their persecuted ministers to the ends of the earth, in order to enjoy the gospel in its purity. All necessary arrangements having been made, on the 10th of August, 1635, — a day to be remembered by the people of this commonwealth, — the company embarked on board the ship Defense, of London, commanded by Captain Thomas Bostock, and commenced their voyage, "having tasted much of God's mercy in England, and lamenting the loss of our native country, when we took our last view of it."

Mr. Shepard, it has been said, embarked in disguise, and under the assumed name of his brother, " John Shepard, husbandman." The authority for this statement is found in a list of passengers who came over in the Defense, taken from a manuscript volume, discovered in the Augmentation Office, so called, by Mr. Savage, in the year 1842, which contains the names of persons permitted to embark at the port of London, between Christmas, 1634, and the same period in the following year. In this list we have, among others, the names of John Shepard, husbandman, aged thirty-six, Margaret Shepard, thirty-one, and Thomas Shepard, three months. Samuel Shepard appears as a servant of Roger Harlakenden. Neither Mr. Wilson nor Mr. Jones is mentioned, though they were certainly on board ; but Sarah Jones, aged thirty-four, with her children, is named among the

passengers.* It is probable that Mr. Shepard did embark under the name of his brother John, though, as he was born in
1605, he could have been but thirty years of age when he came
to this country, and Margaret seems to have been somewhat
younger. We know that great efforts were at that time made to
prevent the ministers from leaving England. As early as 1629,
Mr. Higginson, writing from Salem, exhorted his friends to come
quickly, for if they lingered too long, "the passages of Jordan,
through the malice of Satan, might be stopped." Cotton, Hooker, and Stone, who came in 1633, with great difficulty eluded the
vigilance of the pursuivants, and escaped from the country.
Richard Mather was obliged to conceal himself until the vessel
was at sea. In April, 1637, a proclamation was issued "to
restrain the disorderly transportation of his majesty's subjects to
the colonies without leave," commanding that "no license
should be given them without a certificate that they had taken
the oaths of supremacy and allegiance, and had conformed to the
discipline of the church of England." † The danger, therefore,
to which Mr. Shepard, in common with others, was exposed, was
great enough to render concealment desirable and necessary.
How far any one is justifiable in assuming the name of another
for the purpose of avoiding danger, or of doing a good work, is
a question of casuistry which every reader will decide according to his light; but all candid persons who become familiar with
the character of Shepard, and with the circumstances in which
he was placed, must be convinced that he intended to act conscientiously, and that if he did not, as he confessed, belong to that
class of martyrs to whom God gave "a spirit of courage and
willingness to glorify him by sufferings at home," he was at
least a sincere lover of truth, and foremost among those holy
men who were prepared to "go to a wilderness, where they
could forecast nothing but care and temptation," for the sake of
enjoying Christ in his ordinances, and of propagating the

* Mass. Hist. Coll. xxviii. 268, 269, 273.
† See Chronicles of Massachusetts, pp. 260, 428, notes.

gospel in its divine purity. If any think that he erred in not boldly facing the terrors of the Star Chamber, "let him that is without sin among them cast the first stone at him."

The ship in which they embarked was old, rotten, and altogether unfit for such a voyage. In the first storm they encountered, she sprung a leak, which exposed them to imminent peril; and they were on the point of returning to port, when, with much difficulty, they succeeded in repairing the damage. They had a stormy and rough passage. The infant Thomas, who, at their embarkation, was so feeble that the parents and friends feared he could not live until they reached New England, was much benefited by the sea; but the mother, worn out by constant watching, hardship, and exposure, at last took a cold, terminating in consumption, which, in a few months, consigned her to an early grave. Among other incidents of the voyage, Mrs. Shepard's miraculous preservation from "imminent and apparent death" ought not to be passed over in silence. In one of the violent storms which they experienced, she was, by the sudden lurching of the ship, thrown head foremost, with the child in her arms, directly toward a large iron bolt; and "being ready to fall, she felt herself plucked back by she knew not what," whereby both she and the child escaped all injury — a wonderful interposition, which Mr. Shepard and others who witnessed it could ascribe to nothing but "the angels of God, who are ministering spirits for the heirs of life."

On the 2d day of October, 1635, after fifty-four wearisome days upon the sea, they came in sight of the land where they hoped to find rest both for the body and the soul; and on the third they landed safely at Boston, "with rejoicing in God after a longsome voyage," and amidst the hearty congratulations of numerous friends, whose houses were hospitably thrown open for their accommodation. Mr. Shepard and his family were kindly provided for at the house of Mr. Coddington, then treasurer of the colony, where they remained until after the Sabbath; and on Monday, October 5, they removed to Newtown, which was to be their future field of labor and their quiet home.

CHAPTER VIII.

Sketch of the early history of Newtown. — Organization of the second
church in Newtown. — Death of Mrs. Shepard. — Sickness of Thomas.
— Antinomian controversy. — Mr. Shepard's position and influence in this
controversy. — First Synod in Newtown. — Mr. Hooker's objections. —
Result of Synod.

NEWTOWN, afterward called Cambridge, was selected as the
site of a town which the settlers intended to fortify, and make
the metropolis of the Massachusetts colony. In the spring of
the year 1631, Winthrop, who had the year preceding been
chosen governor, came to this place, and set up the frame of a
house upon the spot where he first pitched his tent. The deputy governor, Dudley, completed a house for himself, and removed
his family, with the expectation that this was to be the seat of
government. The town was laid out near Charles River, in
squares, the streets intersecting each other at right angles. It
soon became evident, however, that Boston was to be the chief
place of commerce; and the neighboring Indians, having ceased
their hostility, and made overtures of perpetual friendship with
the colonists, Governor Winthrop removed the frame of his
house to Boston, and the scheme of a fortified town here was
abandoned.

But, though the design of making Newtown the capital of the
colony was given up, it remained still under the especial care
and direction of the government. The annual election of governor and magistrates was, for some time, held here; and, in
1632, the General Court appropriated sixty pounds, to be raised
by the several plantations, toward erecting a palisade about it.
The first settlers of the town, though few in number, were, generally, in good circumstances; and they soon received a valuable
accession by the arrival of a company, recently from England,
who had commenced a settlement at Braintree, but who, by
direction of the General Court, removed to Newtown in August,

1632. Winthrop calls them "Mr. Hooker's company," from which it may be inferred that they were from that part of the county of Essex where Mr. Hooker was settled. Mr. Hooker, however, did not come over with this company, and the people of Newtown had as yet no minister; but they erected a meeting house, preparatory to the settlement of the ministry and the ordinance of the gospel among them, feeling, as one of the early fathers remarks, that a country, however beautiful and prosperous, without a gospel ministry, is "like a blacksmith without his fire."

Mr. Hooker, in company with Mr. Cotton and Mr. Stone, arrived in the month of September, 1633, and on the 11th of October following, he, with Mr. Stone for his assistant, was ordained over the people of Newtown, many of whom had sat under his ministry in England, and after their settlement here had never ceased to importune him to come and take the pastoral charge of them. In May, 1634, the people of Newtown, being, as they alleged, straitened for room, and having obtained leave of the General Court to look out a place, either for extension or removal, sent several of their number to Agawam and Merrimack, to find, if possible, a more suitable location for their growing community. Not succeeding to their satisfaction in this attempt, they petitioned for leave to remove to the banks of the Connecticut River, where they were certain of finding ample territory and a fruitful soil. The subject was earnestly discussed in the General Court for several days. The principal arguments in favor of granting the petition were — that the people, without more land for their cattle, could not maintain their minister, or receive any more of their friends who might be disposed to come and assist them; that, if the fertile country upon the Connecticut were not speedily occupied by a colony from Massachusetts, the Dutch or the English might take possession of it, which would be very undesirable; that the towns in the colony were located too near each other; and finally, that they were strongly inclined, and, in fact, had made up their minds, to go — a reason as conclusive, perhaps, as any other. In addition to the avowed grounds of their desire to remove so far from the parent colony, some have ventured to add one which they never avowed, and probably never thought of, namely, that Mr. Hooker's light would shine more brightly, and be more conspicuous, if it were farther from the golden candlestick of the church in Boston.

On the other hand, a variety of reasons were urged against their removal. It was said that, being united in one body with the Massachusetts colony, and being bound by oath to seek the good of the commonwealth, it would be wrong, in point of conscience, to allow them to separate from their brethren; that the colony was weak, and constantly in danger of being attacked by its enemies, and therefore could not afford to spare so large a number of their most influential citizens; that the departure of Mr. Hooker would not only draw away many from the colony, but divert to a distant part of the country friends who would otherwise settle here; that, by removing, they would be exposed to great danger, from the Dutch, — who claimed the Connecticut country, and had already built a fort there, — from the Indians, and from the English government, which would not permit them to settle without a patent in any place to which the king laid claim; that they might be accommodated at home by enlargement from other towns, or by removal to any other place within the patent; and finally, that it would be the removal of a candlestick out of its place, which was a calamity by all means to be avoided if possible.

When the question was taken, the governor and two assistants voted in the affirmative; the deputy governor, together with the other assistants and all the deputies, in the negative. At this stage of the business, a controversy arose between the Court of Magistrates and the deputies respecting the legal effect of this vote, not necessary to be described here. It is sufficient to say that the proceedings of the court were brought to a stand; and so great, in their opinion, was the importance of the question respecting " the negative voice," which divided them, that a day of fasting and prayer for divine direction was set apart by public authority. Accordingly, the 18th day of September was observed by all the churches in the colony. On the 24th of the same month, the court again met at Newtown. Mr. Hooker was requested to deliver a discourse upon the important occasion; but he declining on the ground that his personal interest in the question rendered him unfit for this service, the delicate and difficult task was, by desire of the whole court, performed by Mr. Cotton. He chose for his text Haggai ii. 4, from which he took occasion to describe the nature, or the strength, as he termed it, of the magistracy, of the ministry, and of the people. The strength of the magistracy he asserted to be their authority; of the ministry, their purity; and of the people, their liberty; showing that each of these had a negative voice in relation to the other, and yet the right of ultimate decision was in the whole body of the people; answering all objections, and exhorting the people to maintain their liberties against all unjust and violent attempts to take them away.

This discourse gave great satisfaction to all parties. The court resumed its discussions in a better and more forbearing spirit; and although the deputies were not satisfied that the negative voice should be left to the magistrates, yet the subject was by common consent dropped for that time. The result was, that the people of Newtown, seeing how unwilling their brethren were that they should remove to Connecticut, came forward and accepted such lands as had been offered for their accommodation, by Boston and Watertown. This arrangement, however, was not long satisfactory. The people of Newtown, having fixed their eyes and their minds upon the fine country upon the Connecticut, soon began to revive the project of removal, and many in the neighboring towns being desirous of joining them in this enterprise, the General Court at length gave them leave to remove whither they would, on condition of their remaining under the jurisdiction of Massachusetts.

The place selected by the agents of Newtown was called by the natives Suckiaug, where, toward the close of the year 1635, a plantation was commenced by a few of their number, the great body of the people, with their ministers, intending to follow them during the ensuing year. Accordingly, early in the summer of 1636, Messrs. Hooker and Stone, with about one hundred persons, composing the whole, or very nearly the whole of the congregation, left Newtown, and traveled through a pathless wilderness to the place which they had chosen as their inheritance. They had no guide but their compass. Like the patriarchs, they drove before them their flocks and herds, and fed upon the milk of their kine by the way. After a long and tedious journey, they reached Suckiaug, on the Connecticut, and laid the foundation of the city of Hartford.

Upon the removal of Mr. Hooker's congregation, Mr. Shepard and those who accompanied him, about sixty in all, purchased the houses thus left vacant, to dwell in until they should find a more suitable place for a permanent settlement. The majority, however, soon became desirous of remaining at Newtown, and were unwilling to remove farther, "partly because of the fellowship of the churches; partly because they thought their lives were short, and removals to new plantations full of troubles; partly because they found sufficient for themselves and company." They therefore resolved to remain, and without further delay to organize themselves into a church for the enjoyment of those gospel privileges which they had suffered so much to secure. The necessary arrangements were accordingly made, and on the 1st day of February, 1636, corresponding to February 11, new style, a public assembly was convened, and a church, the first permanent one in Cambridge, and the eleventh in Massachusetts, was duly organized. The following account of this solemn transaction, given by an eye witness, is exceedingly interesting for the light which it throws upon the manner of constituting churches in the time of our fathers.

"Mr. Shepard, a godly minister come lately out of England, and divers other good Christians, intending to raise a church body, came and acquainted the magistrates therewith, who gave their' approbation. They also sent to all the neighboring churches for their elders to give their assistance, at a certain day, at Newtown, when they should constitute their body. Accordingly, at this day, there met a great assembly, where the proceeding was as followeth: Mr. Shepard and two others — who were after to be chosen to office — sat together in the elders' seat. Then the elder of them began with prayer. After this Mr. Shepard prayed with deep confession of sin, etc., and exercised out of Eph. v. 27, 'That he might present it to himself a glorious church,' etc., and also opened the cause of their meeting. Then the elder desired to know of the churches assembled what number were needful to make a church, and how they ought to proceed in this action. Whereupon some of the ancient ministers, conferring shortly together, gave answer: That the Scripture did not set down any certain rule for the number. Three, they thought, were too few, because by Matt. xviii. an appeal was allowed from three; but that seven might be a fit number. And, for their proceeding, they advised that such as were to join should make confession of their faith, and declare what work of grace the Lord had wrought in them; which accordingly they did, Mr. Shepard first, then four others, then the elder, and one who was to be deacon, — who had also prayed, — and another member. Then the covenant was read, and they all gave a solemn assent to it. Then the elder desired of the churches, that, if they did approve them to be a church, they would give them the right hand of fellowship. Whereupon Mr. Cotton, upon short speech with some others near him, in the name of their churches, gave his hand to the elder, with a short speech of their assent, and desired the peace of the Lord Jesus to be with them. Then Mr. Shepard made an exhortation to the rest of his body, about the nature of their covenant, and to stand firm to it, and commended them to the Lord in a most heavenly prayer. Then the elder told the assembly that they were intended to choose Mr. Shepard for their pastor, (by the name of the brother who had exercised,) and desired the churches, that, if they had any thing to except against him, they would impart it to them before the day of ordination. Then he gave the churches thanks for their assistance, and so left them to the Lord." * - Mr. Shepard's ordination, or rather installation, took place soon after, but the exact date of it is not known. It was probably deferred, as Mather suggests, on account of the lateness of the hour, and for the purpose of having ample time for the performance of those solemnities which they thought suitable to such an occasion.

Mr. Shepard's ministry in Newtown commenced under the pressure of heavy domestic affliction. Within a fortnight after the organization of the church, his wife Margaret, whose health had been for some time rapidly failing, was taken from him by death. It had been her great desire to see her husband in a place of safety among God's people, and to leave her child under the pure ordinances of the gospel. Her desire was granted. Having been received into the fellowship of the church, having given up her dear child in the ordinance of baptism, and having witnessed the hopeful beginning of the work for which she had sacrificed all the comforts of life, and even life itself, she was enabled to say, with Simeon of old, " Lord, now lettest thou thy servant depart in peace, for mine eyes have seen thy salvation." The precious ordinances for which she had pined, amidst the privations and dangers of their wandering life, were the means of greatly cheering her under the wasting power of disease, and of filling her soul with a sense of God's love, which continued until the last breath. Nothing can be more beautiful or touching than Mr. Shepard's reference to the baptism of his son, and to the early death of his " incomparably loving," amiable, and pious wife — a passage which many a baptized child may read with tears. " On the 7th of February, God gave thee the ordinance of baptism, whereby God is become thy God, and is beforehand with thee, that whenever thou shalt return to God, he will undoubtedly receive thee : this is a most high and happy privilege, and therefore bless God for it. And now, after this had been done, thy dear mother died in the Lord, departing out of this world to another, who did lose her life by being careful to preserve thine ; for in the ship thou wert so feeble and froward both in the day and night, that hereby she lost her strength, and at last her life. She hath made also many a prayer and shed many a tear for thee; and this hath been oft her request, that if the Lord did not intend to glorify himself by thee, that he would cut thee off by death rather than to live to dishonor him by sin. And therefore know it, that if thou shalt turn rebel against God, and forsake him, and care not for the knowledge of him, nor believe in his Son, the Lord will make all these mercies woes; and all thy mother's prayers, tears, and death, to be a swift witness against thee at the great day." *

The child to whom this affecting appeal was made was afterward brought very low by a humor which filled his mouth, lips, and cheeks with blisters, so that it was difficult for him to take sufficient nourishment to sustain life. When the humor left his mouth, it seized upon his eyes, and in a short time he became quite blind, "with pearls upon both eyes, and a white film, insomuch that it was a dreadful sight unto all the beholders of him, and very pitiful." None but a father can realize the distress which Mr. Shepard felt at the prospect that his only son was to be blind through the remainder of his life. But he was mercifully spared this severe affliction. When he had become convinced that he must have "a blind child to be a constant sorrow to him till his death," and was made contented to "bear the indignation of the Lord, because he had sinned," resolving now to "fear nor grieve no more, but to be thankful, nay, to love the Lord, suddenly and strangely, by the use of a poor weak means, namely, the oil of white paper," the child was restored to sight again, to the great joy of the father, who regarded the cure as a gracious answer to his earnest prayers. The manner in which Mr. Shepard used this event to awaken the gratitude of his child, when, in after years, he should learn how wonderfully he had been preserved from one of the greatest temporal calamities, is worthy of remembrance. " Now,

* Introduction to Autobiography.

*j**

consider, my son, and remember to lift up thine eyes to heaven, to God, in everlasting praises of him, and dependence upon him; and take heed thou dost not make thine eyes windows of lust, but give thine eyes, nay, thy heart, and whole soul, and body, to him that hath been so careful of thee when thou couldst not care for thyself."

These domestic afflictions were soon followed by trials of another sort, which, to a minister of Christ so deeply interested in the prosperity of the church as Mr. Shepard was, were, perhaps, more difficult to be borne with patience, and called for a larger measure of grace. He found that the people of God are exposed to "perils in the wilderness," as well as in the crowded thoroughfares of the world, and that Christ may be as deeply wounded in the house of his friends as among the armies of the aliens. The church at Newtown had been organized but a short time, and had but just begun to enjoy the liberty and the rest for which so many sacrifices had been made, when the peace of all the churches in the colony was violently disturbed by the opinions and practices of the Antinomians, which were first promulgated in this part of the world by Mrs. Hutchinson. As Mr. Shepard bore a distinguished part in that controversy, and exerted no small influence in bringing it to a triumphant conclusion, a few words respecting its origin and effects may here be expected.

Mr. Hutchinson, who had been an intimate friend and a great admirer of Mr. Cotton in England, came to Boston, with his wife, in the autumn of 1634. Mrs. Hutchinson was a woman of a masculine understanding, and of fiery zeal in religion. Mr. Cotton, whom she held in the highest estimation and respect, said of her, at an early period of her residence here, that " she was well beloved," and that " all the faithful embraced her conference, and blessed God for her fruitful discourses " — a commendation which, if she ever deserved, she soon forfeited, by her gross heresies in doctrine and in practice. At Boston she was treated with great respect, not only by Mr. Cotton, but by other distinguished persons, among whom was Mr. Vane, who, in 1636, was chosen governor of the colony, in the room of Winthrop. It was natural that the high consideration in which she was held by the leading men in the church and state should awaken her vanity, and give her great influence with the people. In imitation of the brethren of the church of Boston, who held weekly meetings for religious conference, she soon established a meeting of women at her house, in obedience, as she pretended, to the apostolical precept that "the aged women should be teachers of good things;" and especially that they should "teach the young women to be sober." The novelty of this proceeding among the Puritans, who, in obedience to another apostolical injunction, had never suffered "a woman to speak in the church," together with the reputation of the innovator, soon collected an audience of sixty or eighty women at her house every week, to hear her prayers, her exhortations, and her explanations — seldom, probably, correct — of Mr. Cotton's sermons.

In these meetings, held professedly for the purpose of promoting the edification of the younger women, but designed to diffuse a new light among the men also, Mrs. Hutchinson was not long satisfied to be the humble expositor of Mr. Cotton's doctrines, but soon ventured to broach some opinions of her own, which, however, she pretended to confirm by an unfair and fraudulent use of Mr. Cotton's authority. The fundamental position which she assumed, and maintained with a fierce enthusiasm, was, that a Christian should not look to any Christian graces, or to any conditional promises made to faith or sanctification, as evidence of God's special grace and love toward him, — this being a way of works, — but, without the appearance of any grace, faith, holiness, or change in himself, must rest upon an absolute promise made in an immediate revelation to his soul. In connection with this doctrine, and as the legitimate results of it, she taught that the Holy Ghost dwells personally in a justified person; that the command to work out our salvation with fear and trembling is addressed to none but such as are under the covenant of works; that personal holiness is not to be regarded as a sign of a justified state; that there is no such thing as inherent righteousness;

that immediate revelations respecting future events are to be expected by believers, and should be received as equally authoritative and infallible with the Scriptures ; together with many other
absurd and foolish notions, which it would seem that none but persons extremely ignorant, or partially insane, could possibly believe.

That Mrs. Hutchinson received these opinions from Mr. Cotton, as she and her followers pretended, is not credible.   It
is true that Mr. Cotton at one time entertained a too favorable opinion of the piety and talents of this enthusiastic innovator, and for a while bore no decided testimony against the
errors that were dividing and distracting the church.   The consequence was, that he was claimed by both parties in this controversy ; the Antinomians declaring that their doctrines were legitimate inferences from his preaching, and had his sanction ; the
Orthodox, on the other hand, affirming that he adhered to the
common faith, and disavowed their heretical sentiments.   This
state of the public mind called for an open and explicit declaration of his sentiments, which, as soon as he fully understood the
use made of his authority by the Antinomians, he made, to the
satisfaction of his brethren, and to the dismay and discomfiture
of the heretics.   He at once, as is usual in such cases, became
the object of the hatred and reproaches of the party which he
had seemed — and only seemed — to favor.   They called him a
coward, who dared not avow his real principles ; a double-minded man, who taught one thing in the pulpit, and another in private conference; a blind guide, who had lost all insight into the
spirit of the gospel; and so bitter, and at the same time so vulgar, was the hatred with which they persecuted the good man,
that one of the party sent him a pound of candles, with the impudent intimation that he was in " great need of light."

It has been sometimes said, in later times, that this Antinomian controversy was a strife, a mere jargon of words, while
the parties were really of one mind respecting justification and
sanctification.   But a careful examination will show that it was
a strife between two different and opposite gospels, and exhibited
totally different grounds of hope to sinners.   The Antinomians

were heretics of the worst and most dangerous sort. By their mode of advancing free grace, says Shepard, they denied and destroyed all evidence of inherent grace in us; by crying up Christ, they destroyed the use of faith to apply to him; by advancing the spirit and revelations by the spirit, they destroyed or weakened the revelation by the Scriptures; by depending on Christ's righteousness and justification without the works of the law, they destroyed the use of the law, and made it no rule of life to a Christian; by imagining an evidence by justification, they destroyed all evidence by effectual vocation and sanctification. Their opinions were "mere fig leaves to cover some distempers and lusts lurking in men's hearts;" and hence it was that after they regarded themselves as once sealed, and consequently in Christ, and had received the witness, they never doubted, though they fell into the foulest and most scandalous sins; and to renew their repentance they spoke of, as a sign of great weakness.*

Absurd, licentious, and destructive as these opinions were, they spread among the people with astonishing rapidity; and wherever they took root they produced the bitter fruits of alienation, hatred, and slander. The converts to the new opinions were, as Shepard justly called them, "the scourges of the land, and the most subtle enemies of the power of godliness." By their clamor "the ancient and received truths came to be darkened, God's name to be blasphemed, the church's glory diminished, many godly persons grieved, many wretches hardened, deceiving and being deceived, growing worse and worse." They labored to destroy the reputation of all those ministers who held the commonly-received doctrines, stigmatizing them as legal preachers who were under a covenant of works, who never knew Christ themselves, and who could not be the instruments of bringing men into the light and liberty of the gospel. They encouraged ignorant men and women to become preachers, and applauded their ministrations as more effectual than that of any of the "black coats" — as they contemptuously styled the reg-

* New England's Lamentations for Old England's Errors, p. 4.

ular ministers — who had been at what they facetiously called the "ninniversity." They opposed the marching of the troops that had been raised to assist the people of Connecticut against the Pequods, upon the ground that the officers and soldiers were too much under a covenant of works.

In an incredibly short time, this fanatical spirit divided not only the church of Boston, but a large number of the churches of Massachusetts and Plymouth. The people became disaffected toward the ministers, and prejudiced against all their public and private instruction. Many who had been converted, apparently by the instrumentality of these ministers, in England, — who had followed them into this wilderness to sit under their ministrations, — who had been, like the Galatians, ready to pluck out their own eyes, and give them to their pastors, — now forsook their parish churches, and greedily listened to the ravings of insanity or ignorance. Some of the leading men in the colony, among whom were Vane, Coddington, and others, took sides with these disturbers of the peace. Families, as well as churches, were divided and alienated. It became common, says Winthrop, to distinguish men by being under a covenant of grace, or a covenant of works, as in other countries, between Protestants and Papists. The mischief spread into all associations, civil as well as religious, "insomuch that the greater part of this new transported people stood still, many of them gazing one upon another, like sheep let loose to feed on fresh pasture, being stopped and startled in their course by a kennel of devouring wolves. The weaker sort wavered much, and such as were grown Christians hardly durst discover the truth they held one unto another. The fogs of error increasing, the bright beams of the glorious gospel of our Lord Christ, in the mouth of his ministers, could not be discerned through the thick mists by many; and that sweet, refreshing warmth, that was formerly felt from the Spirit's influence, was now turned, in these errorists, to a hot inflammation of their own conceited revelations, ulcerating, and bringing little less than frenzy or madness to the patient." *

* Wonder-working Providence, p. 100.

In the midst of all this excitement and confusion, Mr. Shepard continued steadfast in the faith ; and through his vigilance, faithfulness, and discriminating ministry, the church of Newtown was preserved from the least taint of this heresy. He had been somewhat familiar with the doctrines and spirit of the Antinomians in his younger days, in England, and he had sufficient "light to see through these devices of men's heads," which many of his brethren, able as they were, wanted ; and though it was a sad disappointment to him to be called so soon into the heat of controversy, and "a most uncomfortable time to live in contention" with those who professed to be disciples of Christ, yet it was a duty he could not shun ; and he had the satisfaction and the honor of being a principal instrument in bringing this unhappy excitement to an end.

One of the means by which he destroyed the influence of the heretics in his own congregation was the delivery of that admirable course of sermons upon the parable of the ten virgins, which, after his death, were published by his son Thomas, assisted by his successor, Mr. Mitchel. They were commenced in 1636, when the leaven of Familism, or Antinomianism, was most powerfully at work among the people, and finished in 1640, when it was mostly purged away ; and were designed to refute the impudent heresy of that time, and establish the assaulted truth. They constitute the largest, and, in some respects, the most valuable of his works, and are eminently adapted to expose all false religion, while real Christians will find in them abundant instruction and encouragement. In the celebrated "Treatise on the Religious Affections," President Edwards makes a freer use of this book than of any other. His whole work is pervaded by its spirit, and he acknowledges, by nearly a hundred quotations, his obligations to Mr. Shepard for some of his profoundest thoughts. He rendered another important service to the colony during that stormy season by his election sermon.

By the help of the pious Johnson, we obtain a glimpse of Mr. Shepard in the pulpit, as well as of his mode of handling this knotty subject. In the course of this "dismal year of 1636," a pious man, who, like many others, had left his native land to enjoy the liberty of the gospel here, arrived in New England, expecting to find the wilderness blossoming as the rose under the labors of the able ministers who had preceded him; but, to his amazement, he found the whole country in a state of confusion, and was at once addressed in a new theological language which was entirely unintelligible to him. "Take here," says Johnson, in his rude, quaint manner, referring to this man, "the sorrowful complaint of a poor soul in miss of its expectation at landing, who, being encountered with some of these errorists at his first landing, when he saw that good old way of Christ rejected by them, and he could not skill in that new light which was the common theme of every man's discourse, he betook him to a narrow Indian path, in which his serious meditations soon led him where none but senseless trees and echoing rocks make answer to his heart-easing moan. 'O,' quoth he, 'where am I become? Is this the place where those reverend preachers are fled, that Christ was pleased to make use of to rouse up his rich graces in many a drooping soul? Here have I met with some that tell me I must take a naked Christ. O, woe is me; if Christ be naked to me, wherewith shall I be clothed? But methinks I most wonder they tell me of casting off all godly sorrow for sin, as unbeseeming a soul that is united to Christ by faith. And there was a little nimble-tongued woman among them, who said she could bring me acquainted with one of her own sex that would show me a way, if I could attain it, even revelations, full of such ravishing joy, that I should never have cause to be sorry for sin, so long as I live; and as for her part, she had attained it already. "A company of legal professors," quoth she, "lie poring on the law which Christ hath abolished, and when you break it, then you break your joy; and now no way will serve your turn but a deep sorrow." These, and divers other expressions, intimate unto me that here I shall find little increase in the graces of Christ, through the hearing of his word preached, and other of his blessed ordinances. O, cunning devil, the Lord Christ rebuke thee, that, under the

pretense of a free and ample gospel, shuts out the soul from par-
taking with the divine nature of Christ, in that mystical union of
his blessed Spirit, creating and continuing his graces in the soul.
My dear Christ, it was thy work that moved me hither to come,
hoping to find thy powerful presence in the preaching of the
word, although administered by sorry men, subject to like infirmities with others of God's people; and also by the glass of the
law, to have my sinful, corrupt nature discovered daily more and
more, and my utter inability to any thing that is good, magnifying
hereby the free grace of Christ, who, of his good will and pleasure, worketh in us to will and to do, working all our works in us
and for us. But here they tell me of a naked Christ. What is
the whole life of a Christian, but, through the power of Christ,
to die to sin, and to live to holiness and righteousness, and to that
end to be diligent in the use of means?'

"At the uttering of this word, he starts up from the green bed
of his complaint, with resolution to hear some one of these able
ministers preach, whom report had so highly valued, before his
will should make choice of any one principle. Then, turning his
face to the sun, he steered his course toward the next town; and,
after some small travel, he came to a large plain. No sooner
was he entered thereon, but hearing the sound of a drum, he
was directed toward it by a broad, beaten way. Following this
road, he demands of the next man he met what the signal of
the drum meant. The reply was made, they had as yet no bell
to call men to meeting, and therefore made use of a drum.
'Who is it,' quoth he, 'lectures at this town?' The other re-
plies, 'I see you are a stranger, new come over, seeing you
know not the man: it is one Mr. Shepard.' 'Verily,' quoth the
other, 'you have hit the right. I am new come over, indeed, and
have been told, since I came, that most of your ministers are legal
preachers; only, if I mistake not, they told me this man preached
a finer covenant of works than the others. But, however, I
shall make what haste I can to hear him. Fare you well.'
Then, hastening thither, he crowdeth through the thickest, where
having staid while the glass was turned up twice, the man was

metamorphosed, and was fain to hang down the head often, lest his watery eyes should blab abroad the secret conjunction of his affections, his heart crying loud to his Lord's echoing answer, to his blessed Spirit, that caused the speech of a poor, weak, pale-complexioned man to take such impression in his soul at present, by applying the word so aptly, as if he had been his privy councilor; clearing Christ's work of grace in the soul from all those false doctrines which the erroneous party had affright-ed him withal; and he resolves, the Lord willing, to live and die with the ministers of New England, whom he now saw the Lord had not only made zealous to stand for the truth of his discipline, but also for the doctrine, and not to give ground one inch." *

The Antinomian excitement reached its greatest height to-ward the close of the year 1636 and the beginning of 1637. Though defeated at the annual election in their attempt to con-tinue Vane — the head of their party — in the office of governor, the Antinomians were powerful enough to menace the safety of the state as well as of the churches. They were every where bold, impudent, and restless. When they were complained of in the civil courts for misdemeanors, or summoned before the church for question or censure, they had many respectable and influen-tial persons to defend them, and to protest against any sentence, civil or ecclesiastical, which might be passed against them ; and when they were condemned, there were enough to raise a mutiny against the government on their behalf. Great efforts were made, both by magistrates and ministers, to heal this plague in the church. Innumerable sermons were preached against the erroneous doctrines. Conferences were held with the leaders of the fanatics, sometimes privately before the elders, sometimes publicly before the whole congregation, where they had liberty to say all that could be said in defense of their sentiments, and were heard with great patience. Every thing which individual influence could do was done to root out these pestilent opinions, and to restore peace to the distracted colony.

* Wonder-working Providence, pp. 100–104.

At length, when all hope of removing this evil by the usual means was given up, the General Court, in consultation with the ministers, determined to call a synod of all the churches in New England, for the purpose of settling this controversy, agreeably to the example of the primitive church, referred to in the Acts of the Apostles. Three things were judged expedient as a necessary preparation for this great measure ; a general fast, to seek the divine presence with the synod ; a collection of all the erroneous opinions, amounting to above eighty, which it might be necessary to discuss ; and a friendly conference with Mr. Cotton, respecting any expressions of his which might have seemed to give countenance to the errors that were troubling the country.

These preparatory steps having been taken, the proposed synod was convened at Newtown, August 30, 1637. That Mr. Shepard was a prominent agent in procuring this synod, and a very influential member of it, is evident from many circumstances, particularly from the fact that Mr. Hooker, in April preceding, addressed to him a letter dissuading him from using his influence in its behalf. " Your general synod," says Mr. Hooker, " I can not yet see either how reasonable or how salutary it will be for your turn, for the settling and establishing the truth in that honorable way as were to be desired. My ground is this : they will be chief agents in the synod who are chief parties in the cause ; and for them only who are prejudiced in the controversy to pass sentence against cause or person — how improper ! how unprofitable ! My present thoughts run thus : That such conclusions which are most extra, most erroneous, and cross to the common current, send them over to the godly learned to judge in our own country, and return their apprehensions. I suppose the issue will be more uncontrollable. If any should suggest this was the way to make the clamor too great and loud, and to bring a prejudice upon the plantations, I should soon answer, There is nothing done in corners here but it is openly there related ; and in such notorious cases, which can not be kept secret, the most plain and naked relation ever causeth the truth

most to appear, and prevents all groundless and needless jealous-
ies, whereby men are apt to make things more and worse than
they are." * We have no letter of Mr. Shepard in reply to
this ; but it can not be doubted that he did answer these arguments against the propriety of determining the disputed points
by a synod, and it was his answer, probably, that changed Mr.
Hooker's thoughts in relation to this matter. However that
may be, it is certain that the Connecticut pastor afterward
took a different view of the subject, and judged it expedient
to attend the synod, and to take a leading part in all its proceedings.

The synod, consisting of all the ministers and messengers of
the New England churches, together with a few who had recently arrived, but were yet unsettled, was organized by the choice
of Mr. Hooker and Mr. Buckley, joint moderators. The first
session was opened by Mr. Shepard with one of his " heavenly
prayers." After the organization of the synod, the erroneous
opinions which had been spread through the country, some of
them, as Cotton declared, blasphemous, some incongruous, and
all unsafe, together with the texts of Scripture which had been
perverted in support of them, and certain " unsavory speeches,"
that had been used in the heat of dispute, were read and fully
discussed, and finally unanimously condemned. The synod
continued in session about a month, and all the Antinomians,
who desired it, had liberty to be present, and freedom of speech,
restrained only by the laws of order and decency. There was,
says Shepard, " a most wonderful presence of Christ's spirit in
that assembly," and the general result of its deliberations was,
that, through the grace and power of Christ, the pernicious
errors which had well nigh brought the church to desolation
" were discovered, — the defenders of them convinced and
ashamed, — the truth established, — and the consciences of the
saints settled." The public condemnation of these errors, and
the testimony of the synod against them, were subscribed by

* Huchinson's Hist. Mass. vol. i.

nearly all the ministers and messengers present; but some, among whom was Mr. Cotton, while they reprobated the leading doctrines of the Antinomians, and all the monstrous inferences from them, as sincerely and as deeply as any members of the synod, declined subscribing the Result, because *subscription* was a word of ill omen among the Puritans. The doings of the synod, sustained by the zealous coöperation of the ministers and the uninfected portion of the churches, finally resulted in the restoration of sound doctrine and of good order among the people. All the churches accepted the result, and generally with entire unanimity, with the exception of the church in Boston. Mr. Wheelwright and Mrs. Hutchinson, the leaders of the Antinomian party, together with a few of their followers, after civil and ecclesiastical process, were excommunicated, banished, or at least forced from the colony, (Mr. Vane having previously returned to England,) not for their errors of opinion alone, but on account of the disorganizing and destructive influence which the public maintenance of those errors exerted upon the peace and welfare of the community. Many of the ignorant and enthusiastic people, who had been misled by the appearance of eminent piety in their new guides, when those who had seduced them into error were gone, returned penitently to the churches and the ministry which they had abandoned, and were received by their brethren into renewed fellowship, with joy and gratitude to God for his healing mercy; and Mr. Wheelwright himself, after seven years of banishment, publicly confessed and renounced his errors, and was restored to his former standing in church and state, which he enjoyed for nearly forty years, with the reputation of a humble and worthy minister of Christ. Thus terminated the first great temptation of our fathers in the wilderness — an event which, through the ignorance of some, and the perverse spirit of others, has been frequently spoken of to the reproach, not of the guilty tempters, but of those wise and holy men, who, by the word of God, and prayer, effectually resisted the evil, and preserved the churches from one of the worst and most destructive forms of errors. " And so the Lord," says

k *

Shepard, " within one year, wrought a great change among us, having delivered the country from war with the Indians and Familists, who rose and fell together."

CHAPTER IX.

Mr. Shepard's vigilance with respect to the manner of organizing churches. — Gathering of the church at Dorchester. — Letter to Richard Mather. — Interest in education. — Commencement of Harvard College. — Why the college was placed at Newtown. — Difficulty with Mr. Eaton. — Marries Joanna Hooker. — Death of Mr. Harlakenden. — Mr. Shepard's work interrupted by sickness. — Letter of Mr. Bulkley. — How employed at this time.

WHILE Mr. Shepard was thus watchful over the interests of his own flock, and zealous in the public vindication of the true doctrines of grace against the abominable errors of the Antinomians, his advice and assistance were often sought in the organization of new churches in the colony ; and in such cases, as a wise master builder, he was careful to see that the materials with which he built were of the right kind, and that they were securely placed upon the " foundation of the apostles and prophets, Jesus Christ himself being the chief corner stone." One instance will serve as a specimen of his wisdom and fidelity in this respect. In the early part of this " dismal year of 1636," while a multitude of " chaffy hypocrites " and ignorant fanatics were thronging into the country, and many of the churches were suffering under the deadly influence of unsound members, he was called to attend a council for the organization of the second church in Dorchester, a great part, if not the whole, of the first having removed to Connecticut.

The confession of faith, laid before the council by Mr. Mather, was found to be orthodox and satisfactory ; but when the persons who were to constitute the church came to relate their experience, the elders refused to organize them, on the ground that they were " not meet, at present, to be the foundation of a church." Many of them built their hope upon " dreams, and ravishes of the spirit by fits;" or upon mere "external reformation;" or "upon their duties and performances;" wherein they discovered "three special errors: 1. That they had not come to hate sin because it was filthy, but only left it because it was hurtful. 2. That they had never truly closed with Christ, or, rather, Christ with them, but had made use of him only to help the imperfection of their sanctification and duties, and had not made him their wisdom, righteousness, sanctification, and redemption. 3. That they expected to believe by some power of their own, and not only and wholly from Christ." * Mr. Shepard, whose experience of God's work of grace in the heart was widely different from this, deeming their evidences unscriptural and delusive, successfully opposed their organization into a church at that time. After his return home, he wrote the following letter to Mr. Mather, vindicating the course which he pursued at the council, and exhibiting his views respecting the materials of which churches should be formed. It is a letter which is not without deep significance and interest at the present day, when the same errors of experience are common, and many churches have a far greater proportion of wood, hay, and stubble, than of gold and precious stones, in their composition.

" DEAR BROTHER:

" As it was a sad thing to us to defer the uniting of your people together, so it would add affliction to my sorrow, if that yourself, (whom the Lord hath abundantly qualified and fitted for himself,) and church, and people should take to heart too much so solemn a demur and stop to the proceedings of those that were to be united to you. For what would this be but a privy quarreling with the wise providence of our God, who knows what physic is best to be given, and a grieving indeed for that good hand of God in which we ought abundantly to rejoice; for I am confident of it, that there is nothing in this cup so bitter, but, by waiting a while, yourself and people will find such sweetness in

* Winthrop's Journal, i. 184.

the bottom and conclusion of it, as shall make you and them a double amends.

"David had a great desire to build the temple, and he was content with the sad message of the prophet, he must not do it, his son should. It was quite honor enough unto him to provide stuff for it. I persuade myself the Lord intends to do more for you, and by you, in the place where the Lord hath set you, and that he will honor you with a more glorious service than that of Solomon; to build him a temple, not of stones, but of saints, elect and precious. Yet you know how many years Solomon waited before the temple came to be erected.

"All the stones of it were hewn and hammered out in Mount Lebanon, so that no ax or hammer was heard knocking while the temple was a-building. (1 Kings vi. 7.) O, let not a little waiting be sad or grievous to you, while your people are preparing themselves, or the Lord, rather, is preparing them, to be built on the foundation stone; that when you meet again together, there may not be any hammer heard, any doubt made, any pause occasioned, by any neglect of them in not seeking to gather their evidences better, both to quiet their own souls before the Lord, and to satisfy the consciences of other men.

"As for myself, I was very loth to speak, but I thought — and I have found it since — that I should neither be accounted faithful to the church that sent me, neither should I manifest the tenderness of the good of your people, if I had not spoken what I did. I did confess, and do confess still, that although there were divers weaknesses in most, which I did and do willingly, with a spirit of love, cover and pass by, as knowing what I am myself, yet there were three of them, chiefly, that I was not satisfied scarce in any measure with their profession of faith. Not but that I do believe upon your own trial of them — which, I persuade myself, will not be slighty in laying a foundation — but that they might have grace, yet because we came not here to find gracious hearts, but to see them too. It is not faith, but a visible faith, that must make a visible church, and be the foundation of visible communion; which faith, I say, because my weakness could not see in some of them by their profession, I therefore spake what I did with respect to yourself, and tenderness also to them, that so they might either express themselves more fully for satisfaction of the churches, — which I did chiefly desire, — or if there were not time for this, that they might defer till another time, which you see was the general vote of all the churches. Which course I have thought, and do think, hath this threefold good wrapped up in it.

"1. That if your people, then doubtful to us, be indeed sincere, this might make them more humble, and make them search themselves more narrowly, and make them cast away all their blurred evidences, and get fairer and show better, and so find more peace, and keep more close to God than ever before. And on the contrary, if they be unsound, that this might be a means to discover them; for either you will find them proud, passionate, and discontented at this, — which I believe is far from all of them, — or else you will see that this doth little good, and works little upon them; which unto my own self would be a shrewd evidence of little or no grace, if the majesty and presence of God in so many churches so ready to receive you should work no more awe, nor sad laying to heart such a sentence as this hath been. For believe it, brother, we have been generally mistaken in most men and in great professors; these times have lately shown, and this place hath discovered, more false hearts than ever we saw before. And it will be your comfort to be very wary and very sharp in looking to the hearts and spirits of those you sign yourself unto, especially at first, lest you meet with those sad breaches which other churches have had, and all by want of care and skill to pick forth fit stones for so glorious a foundation as posterity to come may build upon and bless the Lord.

"2. By this means others will not be too forward to set upon this work, who, after sad trial, will be found utterly unfit for it. For it is not a work for all professors, nor for all godly men, to lay a foundation for a church, for many godly men may have some odd distempers that may make for the ruin of the building, therefore not fit for a foundation; many godly men are weak and simple, and unable to discern, and so may easily receive in such as may afterward ruin them, hence unfit to lay a foundation. Not that I judge thus of your people. I dare not think so; but if those that be fit have been thus stopped in their way, how will this make others to tremble and fear in attempting this work, less able than yourselves!

" 3. By this means, I believe and hope that the communion of saints will be set at a higher price, when it is seen that it is not an honor that the Lord will always put on, nor bestow and give away unto his own people. I do therefore entreat you in the Lord, that you would not hang down your head, but rejoice at this good providence of the Lord, which will abound so much to his praise and your future peace. Neither let it discourage you, nor any of your brethren, to go on in the work for after times; but having looked over their own evidences a little better, and humbled their souls for this, and thirsting the more after the Lord in his temple and ordinances, while with David they are deprived for a season of them, that hereafter you would come forth again, (it may be some of your virgins have been sleeping, and this may awaken them,) with your lamps trimmed, your lamps burning, your wedding garments on to meet the bridegroom. And if others will fall and sleep again, and not get their oil when they have had this warning, what do they do but discover themselves to be but foolish ones, who, though they knock hereafter, and cry, Lord, Lord, it may be Christ nor his spouse will never let them in.

" Thus with my unfeigned love to all your brethren, whom I honor and tender in the Lord, with my poor prayers for you and them, that in his time he would unite and bring you together, I rest, in great haste,

Your brother in Christ,

THOMAS SHEPARD.*

" From NEWTOWN, (Cambridge,)
       " April 2, 1636."

---

* Transcribed from the original MS. in the Mass. Hist. Soc., by Rev. N. Adams, D. D.

The answer of Mr. Mather to this faithful and truly apostolical letter was worthy of a Puritan and a Christian. Instead of
that self-sufficient and insubordinate spirit with which adverse
decisions of councils are now frequently met by ministers and
churches, Mr. Mather acknowledges the justness of the rebuke,
cordially submits to the authority of the council, and expresses
the deepest gratitude for the faithfulness of his brethren.
" As for what you spake that day," he says to Mr. Shepard,
" I bless the Lord for it. I am so far from any hard thoughts
toward you for the same, that you have, by your free and faithful dealing that day, endeared yourself in my esteem more than
ever, though you were always much honored and very dear to
me. And blessed be the name of the Lord forever, that put it
into your hearts and mouths, all of you, to express yourselves as
you did ; for we now see our unworthiness of such a privilege
as church communion is, and our unfitness for such a work as to
enter into covenant with himself, and to be accepted of his
people. . . . If the counterfeiting Gibeonites were made
hewers of wood and drawers of water, because they beguiled
Israel to enter into league and covenant with them, when they
were not the men that they seemed to be, it is as much as we are
worthy of, that we may be hewers of wood, etc., for the churches
here, because we attempted a league and covenant with our
churches, and were not worthy of such a matter, nor meet to be
covenanted with, though — blessed be the Lord for it — the
heads of the congregation of the Lord's Israel here were not so
hasty, and rash, and credulous as they were in the days of Joshua.
. . . But you will say, Why, then, did you present yourself
with the people before the Lord and the churches ? I will tell you
the truth therein. They pressed me into it with much importunity, and so did others also, till I was ashamed to deny any longer,
and laid it on me as a thing to which I was bound in conscience
to assent to ; because if I yielded not to join, there would be,
said they, no church at all in this place ; and so a tribe, as it
were, should perish out of Israel, and all through my default.
This kind of arguing, meeting that inward vainglory, which I

spake of before, was it that drew me forward, and prevailed against the consciousness of my own insufficiency, and against that timorousness that I sometimes found in myself. . . . It was pride that induced me to yield to their importunity, because I was desirous to have the praise and glory of being tractable and easy when entreated, and not to be noted for a stubborn and of a stiff spirit. . . . But why, then, did we bring stones so unhammered and unhewn — evidences of faith no fairer, etc.? In this, sir, you lay your finger upon our sore directly; neither can we here put in any other plea but guilty. The good Lord pardon, saith Hezekiah, every one that prepareth his heart to seek God, though he be not cleansed according to the purification of the sanctuary. Let us beg the help of your prayers for pardon herein, as Hezekiah did pardon for that people, and for more grace and care that, if we ever come forth again for the same purpose, — which, for my part, I am much afraid to do, — we may not come to the dishonor of God, and grief of his saints, as at the last time we did. The Lord render you a rich and plentiful reward for your love and faithfulness.

" To my dear friend and loving brother,
—— Mr. Thomas Shepard, at Newtown."

Nothing can be more beautiful than the temper exhibited in these letters. We hardly know which to admire most, the Christian faithfulness and love of the pastor of Cambridge, or the meekness, humility, and thankfulness for reproof, expressed by the pious minister of Dorchester. " Let the righteous smite me," says the Psalmist; " it shall be a kindness; and let him reprove me; it shall be an excellent oil, which shall not break my head; for yet my prayer also shall be in their calamities." Mr. Shepard, upon receiving Mr. Mather's reply, must have felt as Paul did when he witnessed the effect of his Epistle upon the Corinthians. " Though I make you sorry with a letter, I do not repent, though I did repent; for I perceive that the same epistle hath made you sorry, though it were but for a season. . . . For ye were made sorry after a godly manner, that ye might receive damage by us in nothing." It is necessary only to add, that the people of Dorchester, humbled and instructed by the opinion and faithful dealing of the council, " came forth again," in the month of August following, for the purpose of being organized into a church, not now " to the dishonor of God," or " to the grief of his saints," but with the approbation and sanction of their scrupulous brethren, and to the glory of the Redeemer. Mr. Mather was immediately ordained pastor of the church, and continued to preside over it with distinguished ability and success, until his death in 1669, in the seventy-third year of his age.

But Mr. Shepard did not confine his care and labors to the churches. Among the institutions which he regarded as of pre-eminent importance, and which it was his earnest desire to see established in the colony, was a college, to be, as he expresses it, " a nursery of knowledge in these deserts, and a supply for posterity." The great object of our fathers, in coming to this country, was not merely to escape fines and imprisonment for Nonconformity. They wished, it is true, for liberty to worship God according to the dictates· of their own consciences, and they shrunk with a natural dread from the severe penalties of laws which they could not obey without sin; but they had a nobler object than personal safety. They had conceived the idea of a Christian commonwealth, widely different, in its form and principles, from any that then existed in the world; and this idea they began to realize as soon as they set foot upon these shores. Besides, therefore, the instruction which their children received at the fireside, and in the primary schools, they wanted an institution for the education and training of young men for the learned professions, and especially for the Christian ministry, without which all their labor and sacrifices would be in vain. The important stations occupied by the able and learned founders of the church and state would soon be vacant; and even if a sufficient number of scholars could be procured from the parent country to fill them, yet those who were educated abroad, under an entirely

different religious and political constitution, could not be so
thoroughly acquainted with the grounds of the civil and religious
institutions, nor so much attached to the interests of the colony,
as children who were born and educated here. As soon, therefore, says one of the early settlers, as " God had carried us safely
to New England, and we had builded our houses, provided necessaries for our own livelihood, reared convenient places for God's
worship, and settled the civil government, one of the next things
we longed for and looked after was, to advance learning and
to perpetuate it to posterity, dreading to leave an illiterate ministry to the churches, when our present ministers shall lie in the
dust." *

The plan of founding a college in Massachusetts was brought
before the General Court at its session at Newtown in September, 1636. It was then resolved that such an institution should
be immediately commenced, and the sum of four hundred pounds
was immediately appropriated as the beginning of a fund for its
endowment — a grant which, inadequate as it confessedly was, yet
considering the poverty of the colony, and the distractions produced by the " war with the Indians and the Familists," which
was then raging, must be regarded as very liberal.

The place selected for the college was Newtown, which, in
honor of the university where most of the early New England fathers were educated, was thenceforth called Cambridge.
For this choice of Newtown as the seat of the new university
there were two weighty reasons. One was, that through the
influence of Mr. Shepard, under God, the congregation in this
place had been preserved from the contagion of Antinomianism, which was then threatening the utter dissolution of the Boston church, and had begun to contaminate many other churches
in the colony. The other is thus stated by Johnson : " To
make the whole world understand that spiritual learning was
the thing they chiefly desired, to sanctify the other, and make
the whole lump holy, and that learning, being set upon its right

---

* New England's First Fruits, p. 12.

object, might not contend for error instead of truth, they chose this place, being then under the orthodox and soul-flourishing ministry of Mr. Thomas Shepard; of whom it may be said, without any wrong to others, the Lord by his ministry hath saved many a hundred souls." *

The fund created by the grant of the General Court was, in 1639, enlarged by the donation of between seven and eight hundred pounds from John Harvard of Charlestown, — being half of his estate, — together with the whole of his library of two hundred and sixty volumes; and in honor of him, as the chief benefactor, the institution was named Harvard College.† Nathaniel Eaton, brother of Theophilus Eaton of New Haven, was the first instructor in this infant seminary. He was intrusted with the management of the funds, as well as with the instruction of the students. The funds he squandered, and toward his pupils he manifested a disposition at once cruel and mean. For his abusive treatment of his usher, Mr. Briscoe, and for some other sins as great, though not so notorious, he was dismissed from office, fined twenty pounds for the satisfaction of Briscoe, excommunicated by the church of Cambridge, and finally compelled to leave the colony.‡

In this unhappy and disgraceful affair, Mr. Shepard, at first, innocently enough, took the wrong side. Eaton professed, " eminently, yet falsely and most deceitfully," to be a Christian ; and the good pastor of Cambridge, who knew no guile, was for a long time ignorant of his great wickedness. On one occasion he beat poor Briscoe with " a walnut-tree plant, big enough to have killed a horse," until the whole neighborhood was alarmed by the cry of murder. Mr. Shepard, rushing into the house at the outcry, and seeing Briscoe with his knife in his hand, took it for granted that the usher, and not the master, was to blame, and immediately complained of him to the governor, "for his insolent speeches, and for crying out murder, and drawing his knife ; " demanding that he should be required to make a public

---

* Wonder-working Providence, 164.
† Winthrop's Journal, ii. 81, 342.   ‡ Ibid. i. 308.

acknowledgment of his violence.   And when Eaton, after much labor with him in private, had reluctantly confessed his guilt, Mr. Shepard, and several of the elders, "came into court, and declared how, the evening before, they had taken pains with him to convince him of his faults;" that he had "freely and fully acknowledged his sin;" that they "hoped he had truly repented," and therefore "desired of the court that he might be pardoned and continued in his employment; alleging such further reasons as they thought fit." *   But Mr. Shepard was not long deceived in respect to Eaton's real character.   He soon saw things in their true light, and cordially assented to the sentence by which the hypocrite was expelled from office, and cut off from the fellowship of the church; mourning deeply over this great scandal to the cause of truth, and especially lamenting his own "ignorance, and want of wisdom and watchfulness," in relation to the guilty man.   Eaton fled from the colony, and afterward sent for his wife and children to come to him in Virginia.   Her friends in Cambridge urged her to delay the voyage for a while; but she resolved to go, and the vessel in which she sailed was never heard of afterward.†   This disaster deeply affected Mr. Shepard; and though he was in no sense chargeable with the sad fate of this unhappy family, he called himself to account as if he were in some measure guilty of their blood.   In his diary, under date of June 3, 1640, he says, "When tidings came to me of the casting away of Mrs. Eaton, I did learn this lesson — whenever any affliction came, not to *rub up my former, old, true humiliation,* but to be more humbled; for I saw I was very apt to do the first.   And I blessed God for the light of this truth."

Mr. Shepard's first wife, who had shared with him the dangers of persecution in England, and the hardships of his flight to the asylum which had been providentially prepared for him in this country, died, as has been already stated, in February, 1636; and his son Thomas, then about ten months old, was

---

placed under the care of a Mrs. Hopkins, who was probably one of the company that came over with them. For a season, therefore, while he was engaged in these public labors, amidst the distracting controversies, and other evils, which, as a leading man in the colony, he could not avoid, his own house was left unto him desolate; and he was obliged to encounter afflictions abroad, without those comforts of home to which he had been accustomed in his former trials, and which his usually feeble health rendered necessary.

It was natural, therefore, that he should think of another connection, and endeavor to rekindle the fire upon his own hearth. "A prudent wife," the sacred writer tells us, "is from the Lord;" and Mr. Shepard soon obtained this great blessing. In the month of October, 1637, he married Joanna, the eldest daughter of his early friend and counselor, Mr. Hooker, with whom he had been long acquainted, and whose extraordinary fitness for the station she was required to fill he fully understood. This connection proved to be eminently suitable; and all the expectations which he and his friends had formed respecting her as a wife, as a mother, and as a helper in the great work which was at that time tasking and exhausting his energies, were much more than realized.

The year after his marriage, he suffered a great loss in the death of his early and devoted friend Roger Harlakenden. The family of Harlakenden, as the reader will remember, had been the protectors and supporters of Mr. Shepard, when, in England, he was hunted from place to place by the pursuivants, and obliged to hide himself from the wrath of the bishops. The two brothers, Richard and Roger, having been converted under his preaching, were ever among his warmest friends; and Roger, unwilling to be separated from the powerful and " soul-flourishing ministry" which had been so highly blessed to his soul, came and settled with his pastor in Cambridge. Mr. Shepard calls him a "most dear friend, and precious servant of Jesus Christ." He was of such reputation in the colony that he was three times chosen assistant; and his influence must have been

*

of the greatest service to the church and its minister. He died of small-pox, November 17, 1638, being only twenty-seven years of age. "He was," says Winthrop, "a very godly man, and of good use both in the commonwealth and in the church. He was buried with military honors, because he was lieutenant colonel. He left behind a virtuous gentlewoman and two daughters. He died in great peace, and left a sweet memorial behind him of his piety and virtue." *

Soon after the death of Mr. Harlakenden, Mr. Shepard himself was brought to the borders of the grave by a disease, which was probably brought on by over-exertion, hardship, and grief. The manner in which he himself speaks of it leads us to this conclusion. "I fell sick," he says, "after Mr. Harlakenden's death, my most dear friend, and most precious servant of Jesus Christ; and when I was very low, and my blood much corrupted, the Lord revived me; and after that took pleasure in me, to bless my labors, so that I was not altogether useless nor fruitless." That his sickness — whatever might have been its nature — was so severe as to bring death very near, apparently, not only to his *own* mind, but also to awaken painful apprehensions in the public mind respecting his danger, is evident from a letter addressed to him by Mr. Bulkley, one of the moderators of the late synod, soon after his recovery.

"DEAR SIR: I hear the Lord hath so far strengthened you, as that you were the last Lord's day at the assembly. The Lord go on with the work of his goodness toward you. Being that now the Lord hath enabled you thus far, I desire a word or two from you, what you judge concerning the teachers in a congregation, whether the administration of discipline and sacraments do equally belong unto them with the pastor, and whether he ought therein equally to interest himself. I would also desire you to add a word more concerning this, viz., what you mean by the *execution* of discipline, when you distinguish it from the *power*. We have had speech sometimes concerning the church's power in matters of discipline, wherein you seemed to put the power itself into the hands of the church, but to reserve the execution to the eldership. I would see what you comprehend under the word *execution*. I would gladly hear how the common affairs of the church stand with you. I am here shut up, and do neither see nor hear. Write me what you know. Let me also know how Mr. Phillips doth incline, whether toward you or otherwise ; and what way Mr. Rogers is like to turn, whether to stay in these parts or to go unto Connecticut. I wrote to you not long ago, advising you to consider *quid valent humeri ;* I know not whether you answered that letter. The Lord in mercy bless all your labors to his church's good. Remember my love to Mrs. Shepard, with Mrs. Harlakenden.

Grace be with you all.

Yours in Christ Jesus,

P. BULKLEY.*

"February 12, 1638."

From this letter, it is evident, not only that Mr. Shepard's illness had been such as to interrupt his public labors, and excite some degree of alarm among his friends, but also, incidentally, that his labors in the pulpit, and with the pen, were so great as, perhaps, to retard his complete recovery, and to render necessary some fraternal advice that he should spare himself a little. "I wrote you not long ago, advising you to consider *quid valent humeri*" — what your shoulders are able to bear ; a caution which he seems not to have laid to heart, for he continued to labor beyond his strength, and to take upon his shoulders a weight which they were not able to sustain. His laborious preparation for preaching, and his public labors for the good of the churches and the prosperity of the commonwealth, were probably the burden which Mr. Bulkley feared he would not be able to bear.

As to those points of ecclesiastical order upon which Mr. Bulkley asks for information, no reply from Mr. Shepard has been

---

* Hutchinson's MS. Papers, vol. i., in Mass. Hist. Soc. Library.

preserved; but his opinions in relation to them are fully expressed in his published works. What they were will be seen when we come to speak of the services which Mr. Shepard rendered in settling the principles upon which the early Congregational churches were organized.

CHAPTER X.

Mr. Shepard on the point of removing to Matabeseck. — Cause of his embarrassments. — Letter from Mr. Hooker. — State of Mr. Shepard's mind during this season. — Extracts from his diary. — Difficulty removed. — Birth of children. — Samuel Shepard. — Letters from Mr. Hooker.

IN the year 1640, Mr. Shepard, in addition to his other afflictions, was plunged into almost inextricable embarrassment with respect to his affairs, which had well nigh compelled him to remove to some other plantation, or to return to England. This embarrassment was occasioned by the depressed state of the colonists with respect to the means of meeting their pecuniary obligations. The influx of settlers had ceased in consequence of the change of affairs in England; and this sudden check to immigration had an immediate effect upon the price of cattle, etc. While the inhabitants continued to multiply, a farmer, who could spare but one cow in a year out of his stock, used to clothe his family with the price of it at the expense of the new comers; when this failed, they were put to great difficulties.* Some of the colonists, in the prospect of a thorough reformation in England, began to think of returning to their native land. "Others, despairing of any more supply from thence, and yet not knowing how to live there if they should return, bent their minds wholly to removal to the south parts, supposing they should find better means of subsistence there, and for this end put off their estates here at very low rates. These things, together with the scarcity of money, caused a sudden and very great abatement of the prices

* Hutchinson, Hist. Mass. i. 92.

of all our commodities. Corn was sold ordinarily at three shillings the bushel, a good cow at seven or eight pounds, and some at five, and other things answerable, whereby it came to pass that men could not pay their debts, for no money nor beaver were to be had ; and he who last year, or but three months before, was worth one thousand pounds, could not now, if he should sell his whole estate, raise two hundred pounds, whereby God "taught us the vanity of all outward things!" "The scarcity of money made a great change in all commerce. Merchants would sell no wares but for ready money. Men could not pay their debts, though they had enough. Prices of cattle fell soon to the one half and less, yea, to a third, and after, to one fourth part."* For the relief of the people, at this season of unexpected trial, the court, in October, 1640, ordered that, for all new debts, corn should be a legal tender ; Indian corn to be received at four shillings, summer wheat at six shillings, rye and barley at five shillings, and pease at six shillings per bushel; and that upon all executions for old debts, the officer should take land, houses, corn, cattle, fish, or other commodities, and deliver the same in full satisfaction to the creditor at such prices as should be fixed by three intelligent and indifferent men, to be chosen, one by the creditor, another by the debtor, and the third by the marshal; the creditor being at liberty to make choice of any goods in the possession of the debtor, and if there were not sufficient goods to discharge the debt, then he might take house or land.†

What the exact amount of Mr. Shepard's nominal salary was, at this time, is not known ; but from the report of a committee, appointed a few years later to make inquiries in relation to the maintenance of ministers in the vicinity of Cambridge, a tolerably accurate idea may be formed as to his means of subsistence. Mr. Hobart, of Hingham, received ninety pounds a year, one third in wheat, one third in corn, and the remainder in pease. Mr. Mather, of Dorchester, received one hundred pounds, pay-

---

* Winthrop's Journal, II. 21, 18.
† Winthrop's Journal, II. 7. Felt's Massachusetts' Currency, p. 23.

able in corn, and in work as he might have occasion for it   Mr. Eliot and Mr. Danforth, of Roxbury, sixty pounds each, in corn; Mr. Allen, of Dedham, sixty pounds, in corn and work; Mr. Flint and Mr. Thompson, of Braintree, fifty-five pounds each, in corn; Mr. Wilson, of Medfield, sixty pounds, in corn. Mr. Shepard's salary was not, probably, greater than that of his friends in the neighboring towns, nor paid in a different manner. And when the scarcity of money became so great that the corn, in which his salary was paid, could neither be sold for cash nor exchanged at the merchant's for the various other necessaries of life, nor — until the order of court above referred to — made a legal tender for any debt, his situation, as well as that of all the ministers in the colony, who had no means of subsistence except their stipulated amount of corn, must have been well nigh desperate.   And if, in addition to the unavoidable pressure which had come upon him, any of the people — before the price of corn, as part of the circulating medium, had been fixed by the court — unfairly charged their minister the price which this commodity bore the year before, when it had suddenly fallen to one third, or to one quarter, of its former value, and, as Winthrop says, " would buy nothing," the evil would, of course, be greatly aggravated.   Reduced to great extremity with respect to his maintenance, Mr. Shepard contemplated a removal to Matabeseck, a settlement upon the Connecticut River, which was afterward called Middletown.   To this step he was urged by Mr. Hooker, his father-in-law, in the following interesting letter, never before published, which strongly insinuates that there had been some injustice and unfair dealing, as well as poverty, among the people, with respect to the payment of their debts.

" DEAR SON: Since the first intimation I had from my cousin Samuel, when you were here with us, touching the number and nature of your debts, I conceived and concluded the consequences to be marvelous desperate, in the view of reason, in truth, unavoidable, and yet insupportable ; such as were likely to ruinate the whole. For why should any send commodities, much less come themselves, to the place, when there is no justice amongst men to pay for what they take, or the place is so forlorn and helpless, that men can not support themselves in a way of justice, and therefore there is neither sending nor coming, unless they will make themselves and substance a prey? And hence to weary a man's self to wrestle out an inconvenience, when it is beyond all possibilities which are laid before a man in a rational course, is altogether bootless and fruitless, and is to increase a man's misery, not to ease it. Such be the mazes of mischievous hazards, that our sinful departures from the right and righteous ways of God bring upon us, that, as birds taken in an evil net, the more they stir, the faster they are tied. If there was any sufficiency to make satisfaction in time, then respite might send and procure relief; but, when that is wanting, delay is to make many deaths of one, and to make them all more deadly.

"The first and safest way for peace and comfort is to quit a man's hand of the sin, and so of the staying of the plague. Happy is he that hath none of the guilt in the commission of evils sticking to him. But he that is faulty, it will be his happiness to recover himself by repentance, both sudden and seasonably serious; and when that is done in such hopeless occasions, it is good to sit down under the wisdom of some word. That which is crooked nobody can make straight, and that which is wanting none can supply, (Eccl. i. 15 ;) and then seek a way in heaven for escape, when there is no way on earth that appears. You say that which I long since supposed; the magistrates are at their wit's end, and I do not marvel at it.

"But is there, then, nothing to be done, but to sink in our sorrows? I confess here to reply, and that upon the sudden, is wholly beyond all my skill. Yet I must needs say something, if it be but to breathe out our thoughts, and so our sorrows. I say ours, because the evil will reach us really more than by bare sympathy. Taking my former ground for granted, that the weakness of the body is such that it is not able to bear the disease longer, but is like to grow worse and more unfit

for cure, — which I suppose is the case in hand, — then I can
not see but of necessity this course must be taken: —

" 1. The debtors must freely and fully tender themselves and
all they have into the hands, and be at the mercy and discretion,
of the creditors. And this must be done nakedly and really. It
is too much that men have rashly and unjustly taken more than
they were able to repay and satisfy ; therefore they must not add
falsehood and dissimulation when they come to pay, and so not
only break their estate, but their consciences finally. I am afraid
there be old arrearages of this nature that lie yet in the dark.

" 2. The churches of the commonwealth, by joint consent and
serious consideration, must make a privy search what have
been the courses and sinful carriages which have brought in
and increased this epidemical evil; pride and idleness, excess in
apparel, building, diet, unsuitable to our beginnings or abilities ; what toleration and connivance at extortion and oppression ; the tradesman willing the workman may take what he
will for his work, that he may ask what he will for his commodities.

" 3. When they have humbled themselves unfeignedly before the Lord, then set up a real reformation, not out of
politic respects, attending our own devices, but out of plainness, looking at the rule, and following that, leave the rest to
the Lord, who will ever go with those who go his own way.

" *His præmissis :* I can not see in reason, but if you can sell,
and the Lord afford you any comfortable chapmen, but you
should remove. For why should a man stay until the house
fall on his head ? or why continue his being there where in
reason he shall destroy his substance ? For were men merchants, how can they hold it, when men either want money
to buy withal, or else want honesty, and will not pay ? The
more honest and able any persons or plantations be, their
rates will increase, stocks grow low, and their increase little or
nothing. And if remove, why not to Matabeseck ? For may
be the gentlemen will not come, and that is most likely ; or,

if they do, they will not come all; or if all, is it not probable but they may be entreated to abate one of the lots? or,
if not abate, — if they take double lots, — they must bear
double rates: and I see not but all plantations find this a main
wound, they want men of abilities and parts to manage their
affairs, and men of estate to bear charges. I will tell thee
mine whole heart: considering, as I conceive, your company
must break, and considering things *ut supra*, if you can sell,
you should remove.

"If I were in your places, I should let those that must and
will transplant themselves as they see fit, in a way of providence and prudence. I would reserve a special company, — but
not many, — and I would remove hither. For I do verily think
that either the gentlemen will not come, or, if they do, they may
be over-entreated not to prejudice the plantation by taking too
much. And yet, if I had but a convenient spare number, I do
believe that would not prove prejudical to any comfortable subsistence; for able men are most fit to carry on occasions by their
persons and estates with most success. These are all my thoughts;
but they are *inter nos;* use them as you see meet. I know to
begin plantations is a hard work; and I think I have seen as
much difficulty, and come to such a business with as much dis-
advantage, as most men could do, and therefore I would not
press men against their spirits. When persons do not choose a
work, they will be ready to quarrel with the hardness of it. This
only is to me beyond exception: if you do remove, considering
the correspondence you have here of hearts, and hands, and
helps, you shall never remove to any place with the like advantage. The pillar of fire and cloud go before you, and the Father
of mercies be the God of all the changes that pass over your
head." . . .   *Totus tuus,*

                                                    T. HOOKER.[*]
"Nov. 2, 1640.

        "*Sint mutuæ preces in perpetuum.*"

        [*] Hutchinson's MS. Papers, vol. i. pp. 37–40.
VOL. I.   *m*

In a subsequent letter, but without date, Mr. Hooker refers again to the subject of Mr. Shepard's removal.

"Touching your business at Matabeseck; this is the compass of it: Mr. Fenwick is willing that you and your company should come thither upon these terms: Provided that you will reserve three double lots for three of the gentlemen, if they come; that is, those three lots must carry a double proportion to that which yours take. If they take twenty acres of meadow, you must reserve forty for them; if thirty, threescore for them. This is all we could obtain, because he stays one year longer in expectation of his company, at the least some of them; and the like hath been done in Quinipiack, and hath been usual in such beginnings. Therefore we were silent in such a grant, for the while. Consider, and write back your thoughts. I am now weary with writing, and I suppose you will be with reading. The blessing of Him that dwelt in the bush dwell with you forever.   *Totus tuus,*

T. HOOKER." *

The general state of Mr. Shepard's mind in view of this contemplated removal, and the painful circumstances which had brought him into these straits, may be inferred from some remarks found in his diary during this gloomy season.

"February 14, 1640. When there was a church meeting to be resolved about our going away, viz., to Matabeseck, I looked on myself as poor, and as unable to resolve myself or to guide others or myself in any action, as a beast; and I saw myself in respect of Christ as a brute is in respect of a man. And hence I left myself on Christ's wisdom."

It is a peculiar feature in all Mr. Shepard's references to his trials, that he never complains of outward difficulties, — never manifests any impatience under his losses and privations, — never blames those by whom he has been made to suffer, — but always condemns himself, and makes every untoward event in

---

* Hutchinson's MS. Papers, vol. i.

his life a means of humbling and bringing him nearer to God. When he was silenced and driven forth as a fugitive by Bishop Laud, he thought it was "for his sins" that the Lord thus set his adversaries against him.

It is, indeed, impossible to discover, by reading his diary, how great, or of what kind, his external trials were ; or even whether, at this time, there were any particularly trying circumstances in his condition ; and it was not until after long examination, and a very fortunate accident, as it might be called, that the extract above, standing as it does without any explanation, was found to relate to embarrassments which threatened the very existence of his congregation in Cambridge. As illustrations of this feature, the following passages, taken almost at random from his diary during this season, may be given : —

"December 1. *A small thing troubled me.* Hence I saw, that though the Lord had made me that night attain to that part of humiliation to see that I deserved nothing but misery, yet I fell short in this other part, viz., to submit to God in any crossing providence or command, but had a spirit soon touched and provoked. I saw also that the Lord let sin and Satan prevail there, that I might see my sin, and be more humbled by it, and so get strength against it."

"January 11. In the morning the Lord presented to me *the sad state of the church ;* which put me upon a spirit of sorrow for my sins as one cause, and to resolve in season to go visit all families. But first to begin with myself, and go to Christ, that he may begin to pour out his ointment on me, and then to my wife, and then to my family, and then to my brethren."

"January 30. When I was in meditation, I saw, *when Christ was present, all blessings were present ;* as where any were without Christ present, there all sorrows were. Hence I saw how little of Christ was present in me. I saw I did not cease to be and live of myself, that Christ might be and live in me. I saw that Christ was to do, counsel, and direct, and that I should be wholly diffident of myself, and careful for this, that he might be all to me. Hence I blessed Christ for showing me this, and mourned for the want of it."

"February 1. When I was on my bed a Monday morning, the Lord let me see that I was nothing else but a mass of sin, and that all I did was very vile. Which when my heart was somewhat touched with, immediately the Lord revealed himself to me in his fullness of goodness, with much sweet affection. The Lord suddenly appeared, and let me see there was strength in him to succor me, wisdom to guide, mercy in him to quicken, Christ to satisfy; and so I saw all my good was there, as all evil was in myself."

"February 9. I considered, when I could not bring Christ's will to mine, I was to bring mine to his. But then it must be thus: 1. That if ever he gives my desire, it will be infinite mercy, and so his will is good. 2. If he doth not, yet I deserved to be crossed, and to feel nothing but extremity."

It is probable that, at the church meeting referred to February 14, the plan of removing to Matabeseck was throroughly discussed, and in view of expected relief finally given up. For on the next day, February 15, we find the following entry in his diary: " I was in prayer, and in the beginning of it, that promise came in, ' *Seek me, and ye shall live.*' Hereupon I saw I had cause to seek him only, always; because there was nothing else good, and because he was always good. And my heart made choice of God alone, and he was a sweet portion to me. And I began to see how well I could be without all other things with him; and so learnt to live by faith." Again, under date of March 2, 1641, he says, " I was cast down with the sight of our unworthiness in this church, deserving to be utterly wasted. But the Lord filled my heart with a spirit of prayer, not only to desire small things, but with a holy boldness to desire great things for God's people here, and for myself, viz., that I might live to see all breaches made up, and the glory of the Lord upon us; and that I might not die, but live to show forth God's glory to this and the children of the next generation. And so I rose from prayer with some confidence of an answer — 1. Because I saw Christ put it into my heart to ask; 2. Because he was true to hear all prayer."

Still later, we find the following passage : —

"October 29. *I was much troubled about the poverty of the churches ;* and I saw it was such a misery as I could not well discern the cause of, nor see any way out. Yet I saw we might find out the cause of any evil by the Lord's stroke. Now, he struck us in outward blessings, and hence it is a sign there was our evil: 1. In not acknowledging all we have from God, (Hos. ii. 8 ;) 2. In not serving God in having them ; 3. In making ourselves secure and hard hearted ; for lawful blessings are the secret idols, and do most hurt ; and it is then a sign our greatest hurt lies in having, and that the greatest good lies in God's taking them away from us. Whereupon I, considering this, did secretly content myself that the Lord should take all from us, if it might be not in wrath, but in love, hereby to glorify himself the more, and to take away the fuel of our sin. I saw that, if the Lord's people could be joyfully content to part with all to the Lord, prizing the gain of a little holiness more than enough to overbalance all their losses, that the Lord then would do us good."

One more extract from his meditations at this time will suffice. " July 23. As I was riding to the sermon, (lecture at Charles-town,) my heart began to be much disquieted by seeing almost all men's souls and estates out of order, and many evils in men's hearts, lives, courses. Hereupon *my heart began to withdraw itself from my brethren and others.* But I had it secretly suggested to me, that Christ, when he saw evils in any, he sought to amend them, did not presently withdraw from them, nor was not perplexed and vexed only with them. And so I considered, if I had Christ's Spirit in me, I should do so. And when I saw that the Lord had thus overcome my reasonings and visited me, I blessed his name. I saw, also, the night before this, that a child of God, in his solitariness, did *wrestle against temptation,* and so overcome his discontent, pride, and passion."

This event in the life of Mr. Shepard is exceedingly interest-ing, not only as throwing light upon the trials and hardships to which our fathers in the ministry were subjected in the early

m *

days of New England, but especially as it brings out, in a strik-
ing manner, a prominent and beautiful feature of Mr. Shepard's
piety. The purity of gold is tested by the crucible; and this
trial of a faith " more precious than of gold that perisheth," developed a state of mind which, amidst the abounding hypocrisy and
selfishness of the world, it is most delightful to contemplate. The
manner in which he stayed himself upon God, and rebuked his
discontent, and quietly continued his labors, under a burden of
debt and of want, which, upon ordinary principles, would have
justified his removal, may serve as a model of ministerial patience
and faithfulness for us at the present day. Ministers are doubtless subjected to many trials growing out of an insufficient maintenance; and the people may be more or less in fault for the embarrassments which distract their pastors. But a hasty removal
to Matabeseck is not the only cure; nor will impatience, and discouragement, and complaint make the burden any lighter. If, in
such circumstances, a minister can, like Shepard, make the troubles of his outward estate the means of rendering him more
humble, more prayerful, more submissive to the will of God,
more desirous of glorifying Christ by a faithful service, he may
live to see " all breaches made up, and the glory of the Lord
upon him." He will not die of starvation, but " live to show
forth God's glory to this and the children of the next generation." More of the spirit of our fathers, under the unavoidable pressure of Providence, or the injustice and selfishness of the
people, would in the end produce a great change in the state of
things; would render the ministry more permanent, and more respected, and the people more just and benevolent; would give the
lie to the charge that ministers labor merely for hire, and produce
in the public mind a deep conviction that those who preach the
gospel are really the servants of Him, " who, though rich, for
our sakes became poor, that we, through his poverty, might be
rich." The injustice of the people in withholding an ample
support, when it is in their power to give it, is not hereby justified, but rebuked in the most effectual manner; and perhaps
nothing would be so likely to make the altar rich enough in

external offerings to supply all the wants of those who minister at it, as that supreme regard to the interests of the church and the honor of Christ, of which Shepard gives us such a beautiful example.

Of Mr. Shepard's domestic affairs, subsequent to the period referred to above, little is known, except what he has incidentally told us in his invaluable but too brief account of himself. That he suffered many privations in consequence of the general poverty of the people, is probable ; and that amidst all his afflictions he labored with a zeal that consumed him, is certain. In October, 1641, he says, " I was very sad to see the *outward wants of the country*, and what would become of me and mine, if we should want clothes and go naked, and give away all to pay our debts. Hereupon the Lord set me upon prizing *his love*, and the Lord made me content with it. And there I left myself, and begged this portion for myself and for my child, and for the church." Again : " Oct. 2. On Saturday night and this morning I saw, and was much affected with, God's goodness unto me, the least of my father's house, *to send the gospel to me*. And I saw what a great blessing it would be to *my child*, if he may have it, that by my means it comes to him. And seeing the glory of this mercy, the Lord stirred up my heart to desire the blessing and presence of his ordinances in this place, and the continuance of his poor churches among us, looking on them as means to preserve and propagate the gospel. And my heart was, for this end, very desirous of mercy, outward and inward, to sustain them, for his own mercy's sake. And so I saw one strong motive to pray for them, even for posterity's sake, rather than in England, where so much sin and evil was abounding, and where children might be polluted. And I desired to honor the Lord better, that I might make him known to this generation." Again : " Oct. 9. On Saturday morning I was *much affected for my life ;* that I might live still to seek, that so I might see God, and make known God before my death." These extracts from his diary, a book of choice thoughts, worthy to be the daily companion of every minister, show that with respect to his appropriate work he was diligent, and, notwithstanding his outward trials, contented.

During the nine years which elapsed between Mr. Shepard's second marriage and the death of his excellent wife, three children were born to him. The first, a boy, died "before he saw the sun, even in the very birth." The second, Samuel, was born October 18, 1641, at the time of Mr. Shepard's greatest domestic privation and difficulty. The third was also a son, named John, who, after a brief and sickly life of four months, "departed on the Sabbath morning, a day of rest, to the bosom of rest."

With respect to Samuel, we find the following reference in the diary, from which several passages have been already quoted : —

"October 18. On Monday morning my child was born. And when my wife was in travail, the Lord made me pray that she might be delivered, and the child given in mercy, having had some sense of mercy the day before at the sacrament. But I began to think, What if it should not be so, and her pains be long, and the Lord remember my sin ? And I began to imagine, and trouble my heart with fear of the worst. And I understood at that time that my child had been born, and my wife delivered in mercy already. Hereupon I saw the Lord's mercy, and my own folly to disquiet my heart with fear of what never shall be, and not rather to submit to the Lord's will; and come what can come, to be quiet there. When it was born, I was much affected, and my heart clave to the Lord, who gave it. And thoughts came in that this was the beginning of more mercy for time to come. But I questioned, Will the Lord provide for it ? And I saw that the Lord had made man (especially the church and their posterity) to great glory, to praise him, and hence would take care of him. . . . And I saw God had blessings for all my children ; and hence I turned them over to God."

This son, whom Mr. Shepard and his friends were wont to call " Little Samuel," was brought up in the family of his grandfather Hooker, at Hartford. We catch a glimpse of him by means of a delightful letter from Mr. Hooker to Mr. Shepard, without date, but written, as we should judge from a passage in it, just before the second meeting of the synod which agreed upon the platform, and probably after the death of Samuel's mother.

"DEAR SON: This being the first messenger which I understand comes into your coasts, I was glad to embrace the opportunity, that I might acquaint you with God's dealings and our own condition here. The winter hath been exceeding mild and favorable above any that ever yet we had since we came into these ends of the earth. Thus the Lord is pleased to cross the conceits of the discontented, and accommodate the comforts of his servants beyond their expectations, and is able to do the like in other things, were we as fit to receive them as he is willing to dispense them to us. Myself, wife, and family enjoy our wonted health. My little Sam is very well, and exceedingly cheerful, and hath been so all this time, — grows a good scholar. The little creature hath such a pleasing, winning disposition, that it makes me think of his mother almost every time I play with him. . . .

> *Totus tuus,*
>
> T. HOOKER.*

" *Saluta salutandos* Mr. Cotton, Mr. Dunster, etc."

In another letter, apparently subsequent to the preceding, Mr. Hooker again speaks with a grandfather's tenderness of his " Little Sam:" —

" My little bed-fellow is well. I bless the Lord, and I find what you related to be true; the colder the weather grows, the more quiet he lies. I shall hardly trust any body with him but mine own eye. Young ones are heavy headed, and if once they fall to sleep they are hard to awake, and therefore unfit to help. My wife wishes you, by advice, to give something to little John, to prevent the jaundice. Preventing physic is best. By

* Hutchinson's MS. Papers, vol. i. p. 90.

this time I am weary with writing, and I suppose you may be so with reading. My eyes grow dim, and my hand much worse, though never good, and therefore my pen is very unpleasant; yet I could not but communicate my thoughts with you, according to my custom.

"My wife and friends salute you. Sam remembers his duty; is very thankful for his things you sent, which are received.

"The blessing of Heaven be with you.

Totus tuus,

T. HOOKER.*

"September 17, 1646."

It is only necessary to add, that Samuel Shepard was graduated at Harvard College in 1658; was ordained the third minister of Rowley in 1662, and died April 7, 1668, at the early age of twenty-seven. "He was," says Mr. Mitchel, "a pious, holy, meditating, able, choice young man — one of the first three. He was an excellent preacher, and most dearly beloved at Rowley. The people would have plucked out their eyes to have saved his life."

CHAPTER XI.

Mr. Shepard's plan for procuring funds for the support of indigent students. — Defense of the Nine Positions. — Letter from Mr. Hooker. — Character of the answer to Ball. — Mr. Cotton's opinion of the work. — Influence of Mr. Shepard in procuring the Cambridge Platform. — Letter from Mr. Hooker. — Character of the platform. — Commendation of Higginson and Oakes. — Birth of a son, and sudden death of Mrs. Shepard.

IN consequence of the general poverty and destitution of the colony referred to in the foregoing chapter, which had almost driven Mr. Shepard from Cambridge, the college, in whose prosperity he felt the deepest interest, was in a languishing condition.

* Hutchinson's MS. Papers, vol. i. p. 100.

Its funds were altogether insufficient to accomplish the purpose for which it was founded; and such was the scarcity of money, that many young men, who were desirous of obtaining a liberal education, were utterly unable to meet the expense of a residence at Cambridge. At this crisis, Mr. Shepard, ever foremost in promoting the cause of religious education in the colony, conceived the plan of procuring voluntary contributions of corn — money being out of the question — from all parts of New England, for the maintenance of indigent students. When the commissioners of the united colonies of Massachusetts, Plymouth, Connecticut, and New Haven met at Hartford, in 1644, Mr. Shepard, being in Connecticut, laid his plan before that body in the following noble memorial: —

"To the honored Commissioners: —

"Those whom God hath called to attend the welfare of religious commonwealths have been prompt to extend their care for the good of public schools, by means of which the commonwealth may be furnished with knowing and understanding men in all callings, and the church with an able minister in all places; without which it is easy to see how both these estates may decline and degenerate into gross ignorance, and consequently into great and universal profaneness. May it please you, therefore, among other things of common concernment and public benefit, to take into your consideration some way of comfortable maintenance for that school of the prophets that now is. For although hitherto God hath carried on the work by a special hand, and that not without some evident fruit and success, yet it is found by too sad experience, that, for want of some external supplies, many are discouraged from sending their children, though pregnant and fit to take the least impression thereunto; others that are sent, their parents enforced to take them away too soon to their own homes too oft, as not able to minister any comfortable and seasonable maintenance therein; and those that are continued, not without much pressure, generally, to the feeble abilities of their parents or other private friends, who bear the burden therein alone. If, therefore, it were recommended by you to the freedom of every family that is able and willing to give, throughout the plantations, to give but the fourth part of a bushel of corn, or something equivalent thereto; and to this end, if every minister were desired to stir up the hearts of the people, once in the fittest season of the year, to be freely enlarged therein; and one or two faithful and fit men appointed in each town to receive and seasonably to send in what shall be thus given by them, — it is conceived, that, as no man would feel any grievance hereby, so it would be a blessed means of comfortable provision for the diet of divers such students as may stand in need of some support, and be thought meet and worthy to be continued a fit season therein. And because it may seem an unmeet thing for this one to suck and draw away all that nourishment which the like schools may need in after times in other colonies, your wisdom may therefore set down what limitation you please, or choose any other way you shall think more meet for this desired present supply. Your religious care hereof, as it can not but be pleasing to Him whose you are, and whom you now serve, so fruit hereof may hereafter abundantly satisfy you that your labor herein hath not been in vain." *

This memorial was received by the commissioners with much favor. They cordially approved of Mr. Shepard's plan, and ordered that it should be recommended to the deputies of the several General Courts, and to the elders within the four colonies, to call for a voluntary contribution of one peck of corn, or twelve pence in money, or its equivalent in other commodities, from every family — a recommendation which was adopted by the courts, and very generally responded to with great alacrity by the people, suitable persons being appointed in all the towns to receive and disburse the donations.†

Thus, through the influence of Mr. Shepard, the first charitable provision for the support of indigent scholars in New

---

* Hazard's State Papers, vol. ii. p. 17.   † Winthrop's Journal, ii. 214.

England was made at Cambridge ; and a noble example of zeal for the advancement of learning was exhibited, amidst poverty hardship, and sufferings, that might easily have been pleaded in excuse for the indefinite postponement of this work. Massachusetts, in later times, has produced many liberal benefactors of Harvard and other colleges, but none deserving of higher honor than Shepard, and those public-spirited men whom he inspired with a zeal in behalf of this institution, which carried them to the extent of their power, " yea, and beyond their power," in supplying its wants.

At this period of his life, Mr. Shepard was equally zealous and successful in the work of establishing and vindicating those principles, and that ecclesiastical polity, which have ever distinguished Massachusetts as a religious commonwealth. In connection with Cotton, Hooker, and Norton, he exerted a controlling influence in organizing and settling the Congregational churches upon that foundation where they have stood until this day.

In the year 1636, a number of Puritan ministers in England, having been informed that the churches of New England had adopted a new mode of discipline, which many deemed erroneous, and which they themselves had formerly disliked, addressed to them a letter containing nine questions or propositions, upon which their mature opinion was requested ; at the same time assuring them, that, if their answer was satisfactory, they should receive the right hand of fellowship ; if otherwise, their error should be pointed out and condemned.

The propositions which the New England ministers were understood to have adopted, and which they were now required to defend or to renounce, were the following, viz. : That a prescribed form of prayer, and set Liturgy, is unlawful ; that it is not lawful to join in prayer, or to receive the sacrament, where a prescribed Liturgy is used ; that the children of godly and approved Christians are not to be baptized until their parents become regular members of some particular congregation ; that the parents themselves, though of approved piety, are not to be received to the Lord's supper until they are ad-

mitted as members ; that the power of excommunication is so in
the body of the church, that what the major part shall decide
must be done, though the parties, and the rest of the assembly,
are of another mind ; that none are to be admitted as members
unless they promise not to depart or to remove without the consent of the congregation ; that a minister is so the minister of a
particular congregation, that, if they dislike him unjustly, or
leave him, he ceases to be their minister ; that one minister can
not perform any ministerial act in another congregation ; that
members of one congregation may not communicate in another.

This letter was immediately answered in a pamphlet containing the views of the New England ministers upon these points,
which were the same, in substance, as those maintained in Cotton's " Way of the Congregational Churches," and afterward
more fully unfolded and vindicated in " The Power of the
Keys." To this answer a reply was, at the request of the English brethren, drawn up by Mr. John Ball, minister of Whitmore,
near Newcastle, in Staffordshire, entitled " A Trial of the New
Church Way in New England and in Old." The first copy of
this reply, sent in 1640, having miscarried, another was prepared, which, after much delay, finally came to hand about the
year 1644. The manifold errors respecting the ecclesiastical
polity of our fathers, and the gross misrepresentations of the
principles and practices of these churches, which this book contained, induced Mr. Shepard, with the coöperation of Mr. Allen,
of Dedham, to attempt a thorough discussion of these points,
which he did in an elaborate treatise, entitled " A Defense of
the Answer made unto the Nine Questions or Positions sent
from New England, against the Reply thereto by that Reverend
Servant of Christ, Mr. John Ball, entitled ' A Trial of the New
Church Way in New England and in Old ;' wherein, besides a
more full Opening of sundry Particulars concerning Liturgies,
Power of the Keys, Matter of the Visible Church, etc., is more
largely handled that Controversy concerning the Catholic
Church ; tending to clear up the Old Way of Christ in New

England Churches." The first edition of this book was printed at London, in 1648. In a subsequent edition, printed in 1653, this long and cumbrous title was abridged, and the name of Mr. Allen omitted, while the preface is subscribed with both names, as in the first edition.*

In this treatise, Mr. Shepard explains and defends the views of our New England fathers, respecting the worship and discipline of the church, with extraordinary learning, ability, and acuteness. Mr. Hooker, in a letter to Mr. Shepard, written about the time that the Questions made their appearance, had expressed the fear " that the first and second questions, touching a stated form of prayer," would " prove very hard to make any handsome work upon ; " and that " a troublesome answer might be returned to all the arguments." The answer to the Nine Positions had admitted that a form of prayer is not in itself unlawful ; and Mr. Hooker feared, that, in defending this admission, Mr. Shepard would expose himself and his brethren to the charge of inconsistency.

Notwithstanding Mr. Hooker's fears and forebodings, Mr. Shepard succeeded in making very " handsome work " upon all the points respecting which the author of the letter required satisfaction ; and gave an answer to Mr. Ball's reply, which, so far from involving the Congregationalists in difficulty, was the means of silencing the objections which had been made against them, and of satisfying the English brethren that their position was impregnable. He shows clearly that what Mr. Ball had stigmatized as " A New Church Way " was in truth no other than the " old church way of godly reformers ; " that " the mending of some crooks in an old way " does not make a new road ; and that, in the constitution of the New England churches, both with respect to worship and discipline, the true scriptural model had been constantly kept in view.

On the subject of a Liturgy, there was a slight shade of difference between Mr. Shepard and his father-in-law. Mr. Hooker

* Hanbury's Historical Memorials, iii. 33.

thought it would be better to maintain that "all set forms are unlawful, either in public or in private," than to defend Mr. Cotton's position. In a letter to Mr. Shepard, he says, " Mr. Ball, I suppose, hath a right and true cause to defend in the former part of his book, and handles it well; and though I think it may receive another return, because there is some room for a reply, yet if he hit it in that, I suppose the next rejoin will silence. Only I confess, I had rather defend the cause upon this supposal — that all set forms are unlawful either in public or in private, than to retire to that defense of Mr. Cotton's; that it is lawful to use a form in private, or occasionally in public, but not ordinarily; for, to my small conceit, he doth in such a distinction *tradere causam*, and that fully. For if I may use a form in private, then a form hath not the essence of an image in it, against the second commandment, for that is not to be used at all; then a stated form is not opposite to the pure worship in spirit and truth, for then it should not be used in private; then to bring in a book for the performance of this duty is not to bring in an altar, for that would be unlawful in private. Again: if lawful to use a printed prayer in private, then hath it the essentials of true prayer; then it is not of the same nature with preaching a printed sermon, or reading a homily, because neither of these have the essentials of preaching: hence a man may exercise the gift of prayer, and the graces of the Spirit in so praying, because it is a lawful prayer." *   .   .   .

Mr. Shepard, without discussing the question whether all forms of prayer, under all circumstances, are unlawful, declares that this was not the question upon which the Congregationalists separated from the church of England. It was the particular Liturgy of that church, — which " was the same that was in Popery for substance," having been " gathered out of the Mass Book," which required many unscriptural ceremonies and idolatrous gestures, — which was never commanded by God, but imposed upon the church by the " insolent tyranny of the usurping

* Hutchinson's MS. Papers, vol. i.

prelates," — which had been "greatly abused unto idolatry and superstition," — which made every part of its complex service a matter of life and death, — which was upheld and enforced by the whole physical power of the state, — it was *this* Liturgy that they renounced and condemned as a corrupt service book, which had been too long tolerated in the English churches. Mr. Ball had made a false issue in discussing the lawfulness of forms of prayer in general, while the whole controversy turned upon the lawfulness of submitting to this particular Liturgy. "All of us could not concur," says Mr. Shepard, "to condemn all set forms as unlawful; yet we could in this, namely, that though some set forms may be lawful, yet it will not follow that this of the English Liturgy is." It became necessary, therefore, to "distinguish of forms, and so touch the true Helena of this controversy; and therefore if any shall observe Mr. Ball's large defense of set forms in general, they shall find those wings spread forth in a very great breadth to give some shelter and warmth to that particular Liturgy then languishing, and hastening, through age and feebleness, toward its last end." *

With respect to the discipline of the New England churches, Mr. Shepard clearly distinguishes Congregationalism from Brownism, (or Independency,) on the one hand, and from Presbyterianism on the other. Brownism, he shows, places the entire government of the church in the hands of the people, and drowns the voice of the pastors in a major vote of the brethren, who were content, as Ward of Ipswich wittily observed, that the elders should "sit in the saddle, if they might hold the bridle." Presbyterianism, on the contrary, commits the whole power of discipline to the presbytery of each church, or to the common presbytery of many churches combined together by mutual consent, thus swallowing up the interests of the people of every congregation in the majority of the presbyteries; while, in the organization of the Congregational churches, both extremes are here shown to be avoided by a wise and judicious distribution of

* Defense of Nine Positions, ch. ii., passim.

n *

power into different hands, which neither subjects the people to the arbitrary decision of the pastors, nor merges the authority of the pastors in the will of the majority.*

Mr. Shepard here distinguishes between the *power* and the *execution* of discipline — the point upon which Mr. Buckley requested information in the letter which has been already referred to. It belongs to the brethren, or body of the church, to censure an offending brother by admonition, suspension, or excommunication, as his offense may require; but in handling offenses before the church, it is the prerogative of the pastor to declare the counsel and will of God respecting the matter, and to pronounce sentence by the authority of Christ with the consent of the brethren.† "We distinguish," says Mr. Shepard, "between power and authority. There is a power, right, or privilege which is not authority, properly so called. The first is in the whole church, by which they have right to choose officers, receive members, etc. Authority, properly so called, we ascribe only to the officers, under Christ, to rule and govern, whom the church must obey." ‡

It was falsely imputed to the Congregationalists, he says, that they "set up a popular government, making the elders of the church no more but moderators, and that ministers received their power from the people, were their servants, and administered in their name, when we oft profess the contrary — that all authority, properly so called, is in the hands of the elders, and the liberty of the people is to be carried in a way of subjection and obedience to them in the Lord." § The office of the pastor, as he describes it in another place, "is the immediate institution of Christ; the gifts and the power belonging thereto are from Christ immediately, and therefore he ministers in his name, and must give account to him; and yet his outward call to this office, whereby he hath authority to administer the holy things of Christ to the

---

* Defense of Nine Positions, ch. xiv.
† Cambridge Platform, ch. x.
‡ Defense of Nine Positions, p. 129.
§ Preface to Defense of Nine Positions, p. 13.

church, is from Christ by his church; and this makes him no more the servant of the church than a captain, by leave of the general, chosen by the band of soldiers, is the servant of his band." " If," he goes on to say, " the power, privilege, and liberty of the people be rightly distinguished from the authority of the offi- cers, as it ought, a dim sight may easily perceive how the exe- cution of the keys, by the officers authoritatively, may stand with the liberties of the people in their place, obediently follow- ing and concurring with their guides, so long as they go along with Christ their King, and his laws ; and cleaving in their obe- dience to Christ, and dissenting from their guides, only when they forsake Christ in their administrations. If there need any ocular demonstration hereof, it is at hand in all civil adminis- trations wherein the execution of laws and of justice is in the hands of the judges, and the privilege, power, or liberty of the people in the hands of jurors. Both sweetly concur in every case, both civil and criminal. Neither is the use of a jury only to find the fact done, or not done, — as some answer this instance, — but also the nature and degree of the fact, in reference to the law that awards answerable punishments ; as, whether the fact be simple theft or burglary, murder or manslaughter, etc. ; and so in cases of damages, costs in civil cases, etc. ; whereby it appears that, although the power and privilege of the people be great, yet the execution, authoritatively, may be wholly in the officers." * From these principles it followed, as the platform afterward declared, that all church acts proceed after the man- ner of a mixed administration, in such a way that no church act can be regarded as valid without the consent of both.†

Every thing, in short, necessary to a clear understanding of the discipline and order of the early New England churches, is explained and vindicated in this treatise, with a degree of learn- ing and ability unsurpassed in any work of our Puritan fathers ; and no one can read it attentively without assigning to its authors

* Defense of Nine Positions, pp. 130, 131
† Cambridge Platform, ch. x.

a high place among the controversial writers of that age.   The
estimation in which this work was held by Mr. Shepard's contemporaries may be inferred from a single sentence in Cotton's
eloquent Latin Preface to Norton's Answer to Apollonius, written in 1645, and printed at London in 1648.   After speaking of
the labors of Hooker, Davenport, and Mather with high commendation, he refers to Shepard and Allen, as men of eminent
piety, distinguished for erudition, and powerful preachers, who
had accomplished a great work for the church, by happily solv-
ing some of the abstrusest points of ecclesiastical discipline in the
answer to Ball; and whose arguments, uttered in the spirit of
piety, truth, and the love of Christ, were adapted to conciliate
opposers, and recommend the order of our churches to all
readers.*

Upon the principles so ably unfolded and defended in
this treatise, and in others already referred to, although
not digested into a system, nor formally adopted, the churches
of Massachusetts were founded, and all ecclesiastical affairs conducted, from the time of Mr. Cotton's arrival, in 1633, until the
adoption of the Cambridge Platform in 1648.   Mr. Shepard's
personal agency in the production of this digest of the principles
and uses of the churches does not appear very clearly in the history

---

* Sepharedus (qui vernaculo idiomate Shepardus) una cum Allenio
fratre, fratrum dulce par, uti eximia pietate florent ambo, et eruditione non
mediocri, atque etiam mysteriorum pietatis prædicatione (per Christi
gratiam) efficaci admodum, ita egregiam navarunt operam in abstrusissimis
disciplinæ nodis feliciter enodandis : et dum rei sponsum parent, atque
nunc etiam edunt Domino Baleo, non illi quidem satisfactum eunt (qui
satis jam aperte videt in beatifica Agni visione, introitus omnes atque
exitus, formas et leges cœlestis Hierusalem) sed iis omnibus, qui per univer-
sam Britanniam in ecclesiis Christi peregrinantur, et rei disciplinariæ studi-
osius appellerunt.   Verba horum fratrum uti suaviter spirant pietatem,
veritatem, charitatem Christi ; ita speramus fore, (per Christi gratiam,) ut
multi qui a disciplina Christi alieniores erant, odore horum unguentorum
Christi effusorum delibati atque delincti, ad amorem ejus et pellecti et per-
tracti, eam avidius accipiant, atque amplexentur.

of those times; but there are several circumstances from which we may reasonably infer that it was very great. It has already been stated that Mr. Shepard was at Hartford in 1644, and laid before the commissioners for the united colonies, who met there at that time, a memorial touching some provision to be made for indigent students in Harvard College. Now, it so happened, that, at that meeting of the commissioners, the idea of a public confession of faith, and a plan of church government, to be approved by the churches in a general synod, and published as a book of doctrine and discipline, was, so far as we know, first suggested and discussed.* Nothing is more probable than that Mr. Shepard suggested this plan to the commissioners, and urged them to adopt some measure by which it could be properly brought before the court and the churches.

Be this, however, as it may, the commissioners at that time took the first step toward the convocation of the synod which produced the Cambridge Platform, by agreeing to lay this subject before the General Court of Massachusetts. Accordingly, in the year 1646, a bill was brought into the General Court for calling a synod, to accomplish the end proposed by the commissioners. The magistrates readily passed the bill; but there was a question among the deputies whether the court could legally require the churches to send their pastors and delegates to such a synod; and a fear was expressed that if the civil authority should thus interpose in ecclesiastical matters, a precedent might be established which would justify the court in attempting to enforce upon the churches a uniformity entirely subversive of Christian liberty. It was also objected that the sole purpose of the proposed synod was to construct a platform of discipline for all the churches, to be reported to the General Court for its approval, which seemed to imply that either the court or the synod had power to compel the churches to practice what should be thus established and recommended. In view of these objections, and from deference to the fears of those deputies who offered them,

* Hazard's State Papers, II. 24.

it was finally ordered that the synod should be called by way of a recommendation, and not of a command, addressed to the churches.*

Mr. Hooker, writing to Mr. Shepard respecting the great object of this synod, expresses his views of the plan, and his fears lest the authority of the magistrate and the binding power of synods should be pressed too far.

"DEAR SON : We are now preparing for your synod. My years and infirmities grow so fast upon me, that they wholly disenable to so long a journey ; and because I can not come myself, I provoke as many elders as I can to lend their help and presence. My brother Stone and my cousin Stebbings come from our church, and I think the rest of the elders of the river will accompany them. The Lord Christ be in the midst among you by his guidance and blessing. . . . I have returned, and do renew thanks for the letter and copy of the passages of the synod. I wish there may not be a misunderstanding of some things by some, or that the binding power of synods be not pressed too much. For — I speak it only to yourself — he that adventures far in that business will find hot and hard work, or else my perspective may fail, which I confess may be : my eyes grow dim. I could easily give way to arguments that urge the help of a synod to counsel ; but as for more, I find no trouble in my thoughts to answer all I ever yet heard propounded. I find Mr. Rutherford and Apollonius to give somewhat sparingly to the place of the magistrate to put forth power in the calling of synods ; wherein I perceive they go cross to some of our most serious and judicious writers ; and, if I mistake not, they cross their own principles sometimes. I confess I am apt to give too much to the supreme magistrate in some men's thoughts, and I give not much to the church's authority. However, I shall not trouble you with my thoughts ; *qui bene latuit bene vixit.* I could have wished that none of the copies sent to us had been sent to

---

* Hubbard's Hist. N. Eng. ch. 58.

England; the reason my brother Stone will relate when he sees you; for it is too large, and not so safe to commit to paper. The blessing of Heaven be with you.

" Entreat Mr. Eliot to send me some grafts of a great yellow apple he hath, which I liked exceedingly when I was with him the last time.   *Totus tuus,*

T. Hooker." *

The synod met at Cambridge in the autumn of the year 1646; but so late in the season, and so few of the pastors invited from the other colonies were able to be present, that, after a session of fourteen days, it was adjourned to the 8th day of June of the following year, 1647.

They met according to adjournment; but at the time of meeting a great sickness was prevailing in the country, and it was again adjourned to the 30th of September, 1648. At this meeting of the synod, the confession of faith, and platform of church government, after thorough discussion, were adopted and laid before the General Court for their approval; and the court, at its next session, formally accepted and approved the platform, declaring that it was what the churches had hitherto practiced; and, in their judgment, as to its essential principles, altogether in accordance with the word of God. Thus the Cambridge Platform became a part of the laws and usages of the commonwealth of Massachusetts, and, for substance, is still followed by the Congregational churches throughout New England.

Of this work it is scarcely possible to speak too highly. It was the production of men distinguished for preëminent talents, learning, and piety, — for their sacrifices and sufferings in the cause of religious liberty, — and for their untiring zeal for the prosperity of the church; and, as a whole, may be pronounced the most scriptural and excellent model of church government which has been framed since the time of the apostles. The fathers of New England, both civil and religious, regarded it,

* Huchinson's MS. Papers, vol. i.

and the authors of it, with extraordinary respect; and if in these days there are any who profess to hold it in slight estimation, it is because they are either unacquainted with its real character, or have forsaken the faith and order of the Puritans. "We who saw the persons, who, from our famous colonies, assembled in the synod that agreed upon the Platform of Church Discipline," — such is the language of Higginson and Hubbard, near the close of that century, — " can not forget their excellent character. They were of great renown in the nation from which the Laudian persecution exiled them. Their learning, their holiness, their gravity struck all men with admiration. They were Timothys in their houses, Chrysostoms in their pulpits, Augustines in their disputations. The prayers, the studies, the humble inquiries, with which they sought after the mind of God, were as likely to prosper as any men's on earth. And the sufferings wherein they were confessors for the name and the truth of our Lord Jesus Christ, add unto the arguments which would persuade us that our gracious Lord would reward and honor them with communicating much of his truth unto them. The famous Brightman had foretold that God would yet reveal more of the true church state to some of his faithful servants, whom he would send into the wilderness, that he might have communion with them ; and it was eminently accomplished in what was done for and by the men of God that first erected churches for him in this American wilderness." *

If the ecclesiastical principles, so clearly developed in the platform, were solemnly reaffirmed by a body, which, like the synod that formed it, should represent the Congregational churches of New England, and this book — with such modifications as time and change have rendered necessary — were universally received as authoritative in respect to church discipline, many growing evils might, perhaps, receive a check, and the unity and strength of our denomination be greatly promoted. Such a movement, devoutly to be wished by all who love the institutions

* Higginson's and Hubbard's Testimony to the Order of the Churches.

of the Puritans, may possibly find favor with the churches ; and Cambridge, the ancient place of synods, may again witness a gathering like that of 1648. In the mean time, the more closely we adhere to the scheme of ecclesiastical polity set forth by that venerable assembly, the more confidently may we expect that Congregationalism will maintain its ascendency in New England, and commend itself to the consciences and the hearts of intelligent Christians throughout our country.

While Mr. Shepard was thus engaged in labors abundant and fruitful for the advancement of the great work which he and his noble associates came into " these ends of the earth " to do, he was visited by an unexpected and grievous calamity. On the 2d day of April, 1646, the Lord gave him another son, but took away his " most dear, precious, meek, and loving wife, in childbed, after three weeks lying in," leaving him again desolate in his trials. Mrs. Shepard, from all that can be learnt of her, seems to have been worthy of the tender epithets which her bereaved husband here bestows upon her. She was evidently a woman of superior mind and attainments, of great prudence, of an exceedingly amiable disposition, and of eminent piety. " This affliction," says Mr. Shepard, " was very great. She was a woman of incomparable meekness of spirit, toward myself especially, and very loving; of great prudence to care for and order my family affairs, being neither too lavish nor sordid in any thing, so that I knew not what was under her hand. . . . The Lord hath made her a great blessing to me to carry on matters in the family with much care and wisdom. . . . She had an excellency to reprove for sin, and discern the evils of men. She loved God's people dearly, and was studious to profit by their fellowship, and therefore loved their company. She loved God's word exceedingly, and hence she was glad she could read my notes, which she had to muse on every week. She had a spirit of prayer beyond ordinary of her time and experience. She was fit to die long before she did die, even after the death of her first born, which was a great affliction to her. But her work not being done then, she lived almost nine years with me,

and was the comfort of my life to me ; and the last sacrament
before her lying in seemed to be full of Christ, and thereby fitted
for heaven. She did oft say she should not outlive this child ;
and when her fever first begun, by taking some cold, she told me
that we should love one another exceedingly, because we
should not live long together. Her fever took away her sleep ;
want of sleep wrought much distemper in her head, and filled it
with fantasies and distractions, but without raging. The night
before she died, she had about six hours' unquiet sleep. But
that so cooled and settled her head, that when she knew none
else, so as to speak to them, yet she knew Jesus Christ, and
could speak to him ; and therefore, as soon as she awakened out
of sleep, she broke out into a most heavenly, heart-breaking
prayer after Christ, her dear Redeemer, for the Spirit of life, and
so continued praying, to the last hour of her death, ' Lord, though
I am unworthy, one word — one word,' etc., and so gave up the
ghost. Thus the Lord hath visited and scourged me for my
sins, and sought to wean me from this world. But I have ever
found it a difficult thing to profit even but a little by the sorest
and sharpest afflictions."

CHAPTER XII.

THE labors and influence of Mr. Shepard, and of those good
men with whom he was associated, were directed chiefly, as has
been seen in the foregoing chapters, to the accomplishment of
their first great undertaking, which was to found a truly Chris-

tian commonwealth in New England, where they and their posterity might enjoy civil and religious freedom. But they did not forget or neglect another important work, which was to preach the gospel to the natives of this country, and to bring these poor outcasts to the knowledge of God. Many persons ignorant of the history of those times, and disposed to find fault with our fathers, not only with but without cause, have severely censured them for what has been called their unjust and cruel treatment of the poor Indians, their utter neglect of the wants, both temporal and spiritual, of the original owners of the soil, whom they violently expelled, and the selfishness which characterized all their treatment of those to whom they owed their comfortable home on these shores. This is not the place for the defense of the colonists from this charge, or for the history of early Indian missions in New England. That work belongs appropriately to the Life of Eliot, the "Apostle to the Indians." The only object in referring to the subject here is, to show how deeply Mr. Shepard was interested in all efforts to civilize and Christianize the natives of Massachusetts. It will suffice to say — and the facts will warrant the assertion — that the government and the churches of this state, in their deep poverty and innumerable hinderances, did very much — as much, probably, in proportion to their ability — for the propagation of the gospel among the Indians on this part of the continent, as is done now, with all our means, for the conversion of the heathen abroad or at home. It is a fact which will ever be remembered to the glory of God, and to the praise of our fathers, that the first Protestant mission to the heathen, since the time of the apostles, was commenced among the Indians in the town of Cambridge in Massachusetts; and that the first translation of the Bible by an Anglo-Saxon into a heathen language was made by John Eliot, pastor of the church in Roxbury, and printed at Cambridge, where the first Protestant sermon in a pagan tongue was delivered. Legal provision was made by the government for the support of preaching among these Indians. Schools were established for the instruction of their children. Courts were established for the especial purpose of protecting their rights, and of punishing trespasses against them. Great and good men, among whom Eliot and Shepard stand preëminent, devoted themselves to the difficult work of establishing the institutions of the gospel among them, and leading them to obedience to the laws of Christ. A college building was erected at Cambridge expressly for the purpose of giving to Indian youth a liberal education, that they might become teachers, ministers, and magistrates among their countrymen; and although this design proved abortive, the failure was owing not to any want of zeal in those who commenced it, but to the inherent and insurmountable difficulty of the work itself. Not a foot of land, for which an owner could be found, was ever taken by the early settlers without ample remuneration; and if we hear of Indian wars, they were wars in which the colonists were compelled to defend their lives and their lawful possessions against the unprovoked attacks of savage and relentless foes. It was one part of their original design, as we have said, to "advance the honor of God, of their king and country, by this settlement, without injury to the native inhabitants." They meant "to take nothing but what the Indians were willing to dispose of; nor to interfere with them, except for the maintenance of peace among them, and the propagation of Christianity."

Mr. Shepard, if not the most prominent agent in this good work, was nevertheless a most zealous and faithful promoter of it. There was probably no one, except Mr. Eliot, to whom the Indians were more indebted for those measures which concerned their civil or their spiritual welfare. The first missionary station, where Mr. Eliot statedly preached to them, was fixed at Nonantum, in Cambridge, in the year 1646. Mr. Shepard watched over the infant church gathered there with parental solicitude and kindness. He frequently attended the weekly lecture held by Mr. Eliot; and although he could not preach in the Indian language, yet several tracts, written by him for this purpose, were translated by his friend, and he was thus enabled to teach them the rudiments of the oracles of God. And thus Cambridge has the honor of furnishing not only the first heathen mission, but the first Protestant tract, and the first Protestant translation of the Bible in a heathen language.

Mr. Shepard has given an interesting account of the progress of the work in and about Cambridge, in a letter to a friend in England, which was afterward published under the title of " The Clear Sunshine of the Gospel breaking forth upon the Indians in New England," designed especially to describe the effect of Mr. Eliot's labors, but incidentally exhibiting his own interest and agency in the mission. During the winter, he was confined at home ; but on the 3d of March, 1647, he attended the Indian lecture, " where Mr. Wilson, Mr. Allen, of Dedham, Mr. Dunster, beside many other Christians, were present ; on which day, perceiving divers of the Indian women well affected, and considering that their souls might stand in need of answers to their scruples as well as the men's, we did therefore desire them to propound any questions they would be resolved about, by first acquainting their husbands, or the interpreter privately themselves ; whereupon we heard two questions thus orderly propounded. At this time there were sundry others propounded of very good use ; in all which we saw the Lord Jesus leading them to make narrow inquiries into the things of God, that so they might see the reality of them. I have heard few Christians, when they begin to look toward God, make more searching questions that they might see things really, and not only have a notion of them. . . . From this 3d of March until the end of this summer, I could not be present at the Indian lectures ; but when I came the last time, I marveled to see so many Indian men, and women, and children in English apparel ; they being at Noonanetum generally clad, especially upon lecture days, which they have got, partly by gift, from the English, and partly by their own labors, by which some of them have very handsomely appareled themselves, and you would scarce know them from English people. . . . There is one thing more which I would acquaint you with, which happened this summer, viz. : June 9, the first day of the synod's meeting at Cambridge, where the forenoon was spent in hearing a sermon preached by one of the elders, Ezekiel Rogers, of Rowley, as a preparation to the work of the synod. The afternoon was spent in hearing an Indian lecture, where there was a great confluence of Indians from all parts to hear Mr. Eliot; which we conceived not unseasonable at such a time, — partly that the reports of God's work begun among them might be seen and believed of the chief who were then sent, and met from all the churches of Christ in the country, who could hardly believe the reports they had received concerning these new stirs among the Indians, — and partly hereby to raise up a greater spirit of prayer for the carrying on of the work begun upon the Indians, among all the churches and servants of the Lord. . . . When the sermon was done, there was a convenient space of time spent in hearing those questions which the Indians publicly propounded, and in giving answers to them. . . . That which I note is this: that their gracious attention to the word, the affections and mourning of some of them under it, their sober propounding of divers spiritual questions, their aptness to understand and believe what was replied to them, the readiness of divers poor naked children to answer openly the chief questions in the catechism which were formerly taught them, and such like appearances of a great change upon them, did marvelously affect all the wise and godly ministers, magistrates, and people, and did raise their hearts up to a great thankfulness to God; very many deeply and abundantly mourning for joy, to see such a blessed day, and the Lord Jesus so much known and spoken of among such as never heard of him before." . . .

Toward the latter part of this year, 1647, Mr. Shepard, together with Mr. Eliot and Mr. Wilson, were invited by the inhabitants of Yarmouth to meet with some of the elders of Plymouth colony for the purpose of settling, if possible, a difficulty which had been of long standing among them, and which threatened to divide and destroy the church in that place. " Wherein," says Mr. Shepard, " the Lord was very merciful to us and them, in binding them up beyond our thoughts in a very short time, in giving not only that bruised church, but the whole town also, a hopeful beginning of a settled peace and future quietness. But Mr. Eliot, as he takes all other advantages of times, so he took this, of speaking with and preaching to the poor Indians in those remote places about Cape Cod." " Thus you have a true, but somewhat rent and ragged relation of these things ; it may be most suitable to the story of naked and ragged men. . . . If any in England doubt of the truth of what was formerly writ, or if any malignant eye shall question or vilify this work, they will now speak too late ; for what was here done at Cambridge was not set under a bushel, but in the open sun, that what Thomas would not believe by the report of others, he might be forced to believe by seeing with his own eyes, and feeling Jesus Christ thus risen among them with his own hand." *

On the 8th of September, 1647, Mr. Shepard married, for his third wife, Margaret Boradel, by whom he had one son, Jeremiah, born August 11, 1648, and who, after his death, became the wife of Jonathan Mitchell, his successor in the church at Cambridge.

Mr. Shepard's work upon earth was now almost finished, and his useful life was rapidly drawing to a close. His health had at no period of his life been very vigorous, and he was liable to frequent attacks of illness. He was, as Johnson tells us, " a poor, weak, pale-complexioned man, whose physical powers were feeble, but spent to the full ; " and he says of himself, that he was " very weak, and unfit to be tossed up and down, and to bear persecution." It is astonishing that with such a feeble body he was able to endure so many " afflictions and temptations," and to perform such an amount of intellectual and other labor. In August, 1649, upon his return from a meeting of ministers at Rowley, he took a severe cold, which terminated in quinsy, accompanied by fever, and in a few days " stopped a silver trumpet from whence the people of God had often heard the joyful sound of the gospel." He died August 25, 1649, in the forty-fourth year of his age, universally lamented by the whole

* Clear Sunshine, etc., passim.

colony, in whose service he had exhausted àll his powers. "The next loss," says Johnson, "was the death of that famous preacher of the Lord, Mr. Hooker, pastor of the church at Hartford, and Mr. Phillips, pastor of the church at Watertown, and the holy, heavenly, soul-affecting, soul-ravishing minister, Mr. Thomas Shepard, pastor of the church at Cambridge, whose departure was very heavily taken by all the people of Christ round about him; and now New England, that had such heaps upon heaps of the riches of Christ's tender, compassionate mercies, being turned from his dandling knees, began to read their approaching rod, in the bend of his brow and frowns of his former favorable countenance toward them." *

The words of the dying are generally regarded as deeply significant; and the last expressions of a soul on the verge of heaven are treasured up and repeated by the living as revelations from the inner sanctuary of truth. The nature of the disease of which Mr. Shepard died perhaps prevented him from speaking much upon his death bed; and many things which he may have said have not, probably, been reported to us. A few precious sayings, however, have been preserved, and, coming across the gulf of two hundred years, sound like a voice from heaven. "O, love the Lord Jesus Christ very much," said he to those who stood by his bed side watching his ebbing breath; "that little part which I have in him is no small comfort to me now." The pious Baily, of Watertown, has preserved in his diary a sentence from those dying lips which is worthy to form the practical maxim of every minister. To several young ministers who visited him just before his decease he said, "Your work is great, and calls for great seriousness. As to myself, I can say three things .hat the study of every sermon cost me tears; that before I preached a sermon, I got good by it myself; and that I always went up into the pulpit as if I were to give up my account to my Master." "O that my soul," adds Baily, "may remember and practice accordingly." †

* Wonder-working Providence, p. 213.
† Extract from Baily's Diary, in Mather's Magnalia.

Among his dying words, and perhaps not less indicative of his spiritual state than those already quoted, we may place his last will. It was dictated to his friends Daniel Gookin and Samuel Danforth but a few moments before his spirit departed; and in the calmness with which he disposed of all his worldly substance for the benefit of the living, while he gave up his soul to God in the assurance of a glorious immortality, through the merits of Jesus Christ, we see the true character and the all-pervading influence of his personal religion. It had been his aim through life to do all things to the glory of God; and when he came to die, it seemed to him as much an act of piety to take thought for the welfare of those whom he was to leave behind as to meditate upon the crown that awaited him in heaven.

"On the 25th day of the 6th month, (August,) 1649, Mr. Thomas Shepard, pastor of the church at Cambridge, being of perfect memory, and having his understanding clear, made his last will and testament in the presence of Daniel Gookin and Samuel Danforth.

"Upon the day and year above written, about two o'clock in the morning, he, feeling his spirits failing, commanded all persons to avoid the room except those before named, and then desiring their attendance, spake distinctly unto them as followeth, or words to like effect: —

"'I desire to take this opportunity to make my will, and I intreat you to observe what I speak, and take witnesses to it.

"'1. I believe in the everlasting God the Father, and his eternal Son Christ Jesus, and communion of the Holy Spirit; and this God I have chosen for my only portion: and in the everlasting mercies of this same God, Father, Son, and Holy Spirit, I rest and repose my soul.

"'2. All my whole temporal estate (my debts being first paid) I leave with my dear wife, during her estate of widowhood; that she may with the same maintain herself, and educate my children in learning, especially my sons Thomas and Samuel.

"'3. In case my wife marry again, then my will is, that my

wife shall have such a proportion of my estate as my executors shall judge meet. And also I give unto her the gold which is in a certain box in my study.

"'4. The residue of my estate I give and bequeath to my four children, as followeth, viz.: (1.) A double portion to my eldest son, Thomas, together with my best silver tankard, and my best black suit and cloak, and all my books, manuscripts and papers; which last named, viz., books, manuscripts and papers, although the property of my son Thomas, yet they shall be for the use of my wife and my other children. (2.) To my son Samuel a single portion, together with one of my long silver bowls. (3.) To my son John I bequeath a single portion, with the other long silver bowl. (4.) To my son Jeremiah a single portion, and my other silver tankard.

"'5. I give and bequeath, as a legacy to my beloved friend Mr. Samuel Danforth, my velvet cloak and ten pounds.

"'6. I give unto the elders, to be equally divided, five pounds that Mr. Pelham oweth me.

"'7. I give unto my cousin Stedman five pounds.

"'8. I give to Ruth Mitchenson, the elder, ten pounds.

"'Lastly, I do hereby appoint my dear friends and brethren, Daniel Gookin, Edward Collins, Edward Goffe, and Samuel Danforth, to be executors of this my last will and testament.'

DANIEL GOOKIN,
SAMUEL DANFORTH." *

Thus died Thomas Shepard, in the peace of God that passeth all understanding, which kept his mind and his heart through Jesus Christ. There is something in this dying scene which reminds of one of the most beautiful and affecting incidents in the life of that Saviour whom Shepard so much resembled. " When Jesus, therefore, saw his mother, and the disciple stand-

---

* The inventory of Mr. Shepard's estate, consisting of lands, furniture, and library, amounted to eight hundred and ten pounds nine shillings one penny. His books, — about two hundred and sixty in number, — together with several MSS., were valued at one hundred pounds.

ing by whom he loved, he saith to his mother, Woman, behold
thy son! Then saith he to the disciple, Behold thy mother!
And from that hour that disciple took her unto his own house."

Mr. Shepard was buried at Cambridge amidst the regrets and
the tears of a congregation and a college that owed, under God,
their existence and their prosperity to his devoted labors and sacrifices. But "no man [now] knoweth of his sepulcher." Such
have been the changes which time and accident have produced,
that no stone remains to mark the place of his rest, nor is it possible to identify the grave that holds his precious dust. His
friend, Mr. Buckley, as an expression of his love and grief,
wrote a Latin elegy upon the occasion of his death, of which
Mather has preserved two lines, as a comprehensive epitaph,
descriptive at once of his faithfulness and of his success in his
ministry.

> "Nominis, officiiq; fuit concordia dulcis;
> Officio pastor, nomine Pastor erat."

> His name and office sweetly did agree,
> Shepard by name, and in his ministry.

That Mr. Shepard must have been a powerful and an efficient
preacher might be inferred from what we know of his spiritual
preparation for the ministry; of the purity and elevation of
his personal religion; of his close and humble walk with God;
of his devotion to the interests of his flock, — if we had not the
testimony of contemporaries who were eye witnesses and heart witnesses of the effects which his preaching produced. When we
are told that he always finished his preparation for the pulpit by
two o'clock on Saturday afternoon, believing "that God would
curse that man's labors who goes lumbering up and down in the
world all the week, and then upon Saturday afternoon goes to his
study, whenas God knows that time were little enough to pray in,
and weep in, and get his heart into a frame fit for the approaching Sabbath," — when we know that he wept in the composition
of his sermons, — that he went into the pulpit as if he expected
there to give up his account of his stewardship, — that he always derived some spiritual benefit from his discourses before he
delivered them to his people, — and that the conversion of his

hearers was the great end of his preaching, — we are sure that
his sermons must have been effective, and, like the word of God,
of which they were but the echo, quick and powerful, sharper
than any two-edged sword, piercing even to the dividing asunder
of the joints and marrow, and laying bare the thoughts and
intents of the heart. That intense zeal in the service of God, —
that unreserved self-consecration to the work of turning man
from darkness to light, — that holy patience in tribulation, —
that baptism of sermons in tears, — those " heavenly prayers," —
could not but render him

     " A son of thunder and a shower of rain."

And this inference is justified and confirmed by those who saw
and felt the power of his preaching. " This year," 1649, says
Morton, " that faithful and eminent servant of Christ, Mr.
Thomas Shepard, died. He was a soul-searching minister of the
gospel. By his death, not only the church and people of Cambridge, but also all New England, sustained a very great loss.
He not only preached the gospel profitably and very successfully,
but also hath left behind him divers worthy works of special use
in reference to the clearing up of the state of the soul to God
and man ; the benefit whereof those can best experience who
are most conversant in the improvement of them, and have God's
blessing on them therein to their soul's good." * There is a
tradition, received by Mr. Prince from the old men of his day,
and by him handed down to us, that he " scarce ever preached a
sermon but some one or other of his congregation were struck
with great distress, and cried out in agony, ' What shall I do to
be saved ; ' and that though his voice was low, yet so searching
was his preaching, and so great a power attending, as a hypocrite could not easily bear it, and it seemed almost irresistible." †
Johnson can not find epithets enough to express his personal
excellence, nor language to set forth the wonderful effects of
his public ministrations : " that gracious, sweet, heavenly-mind-

* Morton's New England Memorial, p. 169.
† Prince's Sermons, published by Erskine, p. 60.

ed, and soul-ravishing minister," being the common, and apparently inadequate terms in which he speaks of the pastor of Cambridge; "in whose soul," says the enthusiastic eulogist, "the Lord shed abroad his love so abundantly, that thousands of souls have cause to bless God for him, even at this very day, who are the seal of his ministry; and he a man of a thousand, endued with abundance of true, saving knowledge for himself and others."

But perhaps the most discriminating and competent witness to Mr. Shepard's power in the pulpit is Jonathan Mitchel, who, if not converted, was certainly greatly enlightened, and aided in his inquiries after truth, by his ministry. Mr. Mitchel, as Mather tells us, kept a journal of his inward life, a few extracts from which are preserved in the Magnalia. On one occasion he made this entry: "I had hardly any savor on my spirit before God; but a terrible and most excellent sermon of Mr. Shepard awakened me. He taught me that there are some who seem to be found and saved by Christ, and yet afterward they perish. These remarks terrified me. I begged of God that he would have mercy on me, and accomplish the whole work of his grace for me." * On another occasion he thus writes: " Mr. Shepard preached most profitably. That night I was followed with serious thoughts of my inexpressible misery, wherein I go on, from Sabbath to Sabbath, without God and without redemption." † Mr. Mitchel succeeded Mr. Shepard, and his first sermons were full of lamentations over the loss which he and the people had suffered in the extinction of " that light of New England." On one occasion, when referring to the few years which he had lived under Mr. Shepard's ministry, he said, " Unless it had been four years living in heaven, I know not how I could have more cause to bless God with wonder than for those four years." ‡ After all, perhaps the general impression which he produced upon the people to whom he preached, the character of the piety which grew up under his ministrations, and the spiritual state of the church, furnish the best proofs of his power. Mr. Mitchel was,

---

* Magnalia, B. iv. pp. 168, 169.   † Ib.   ‡ Ib. B. iv. p. 172.

at first, very reluctant, even when urged by Mr. Shepard upon his death bed, to occupy the pulpit of his illustrious teacher; and the only consideration which finally induced him to accept the pastoral charge of that congregation was, as he himself declared, " that they were a gracious, savory-spirited people, principled by Mr. Shepard, liking a humbling, mourning, heart-breaking ministry and spirit; living in religion, praying men and women." A preacher who could make such a man as Mitchel feel that he was living for four years in heaven, and leave such an impression upon a whole people, must have been, to use the language of the venerable Higginson, a " Chrysostom in the pulpit," and a " Timothy in his family," and in the church.

As a writer, Mr. Shepard deservedly holds a high rank among the most able divines which Puritanism — fruitful in great men — has ever produced. His works are controversial, doctrinal, and practical. He was " an Augustine in disputation," as well as a Chrysostom in the pulpit; and, like a scribe well instructed, he produced several works which are of permanent value for doctrine and instruction in righteousness. His " THESES SAB-BATICÆ," or " Doctrine of the Sabbath," is a masterly discussion of the *morality*, the *change*, the *beginning*, and the *sanctification* of the Sabbath. It is the substance of several sermons upon the fourth commandment, and was thrown into the scholastic form of theses, or short propositions, at the earnest request, and for the particular use, of the students in the college. Afterward, at the desire of all the elders in New England, the work was somewhat enlarged, and published in its present form in 1649. It is now very rare, not more than two or three copies being known to be extant. With respect to the precise time at which the Christian Sabbath begins, he differed slightly from some of the elders; and Mr. Allen, together with several others, wrote friendly argumentative letters to him upon that point; but the question seems to be of too little interest or importance to call for any remark in this place. Of the " ANSWER TO BALL" we have already spoken. The Preface to that book contains an admirable exposition of the grounds upon which our fathers proceeded in their great enterprise in New England, and if republished by itself, as it was a great many years ago, would be an invaluable tract for the times.

About three months before his death, he wrote a letter to a friend upon the subject of infant baptism, in which he felt a deep interest. It was published in 1663, at the earnest request of many who had heard of its effect upon the person to whom it was addressed, under the title of " The Church Membership of Children, and their Right to Baptism, according to that holy and everlasting covenant of God established between himself and the faithful, and their seed after them, in their generations." Of all the works upon infant baptism — and they are many — which have been written in New England, this letter of Shepard's may be regarded as one of the most able and satisfactory.

Mr. Shepard's style is often rugged, but full of passages of sweet and quiet beauty, which makes the reader think of pure water gushing from some craggy rock, or of flowers springing up on the side of a rough pathway. He utters great thoughts without any apparent preparation or effort, as if they were ever present and most familiar to his mind, and amidst his most elevated or abstruse reasoning, continually surprises and delights the reader with utterances which seem to come from the heart of a little child. In his polemics there is no bitterness. He never takes an unfair advantage of an opponent, nor uses abusive language in the place of argument. He is always serious, candid, frank, and charitable. He held and taught the distinguishing doctrines of grace, which Calvin before him had discussed ; but he never presents them as dry dogmas, nor uses any language respecting them which is calculated to wound, unnecessarily, a serious mind. He always appears lovely in the most terrible passages ; and makes one feel the influence of his gentle spirit, while he sends the truth with overwhelming power to the conscience. He was a Puritan and a Congregationalist ; but in maintaining and defending his position against those whose words were " drawn swords," his spirit is always unruffled, and his remonstrances, though uttered with earnestness, convey no venom into the wound which they produce.

There is a class of persons, who, while they do ample

justice to Mr. Shepard's talents, learning, and piety, yet complain much of what they term the severe, legal, discouraging aspect of some of his *practical writings* — particularly those in which he exhibits the conditions of salvation, and endeavors to lead a sinner to Christ. The remarks of a recent English author upon this alleged characteristic of Shepard's works exhibit all the objections that have ever been made against them. "The Treatises of S. and D. Rogers, Th. Hooker, and the New England Shepard," says he, "can not be read without grave exceptions. For in these valuable writers, — and others might be named, — amidst much that is superexcellent, there are statements as to the constitution of a Christian which look austere ; which, by checking the freeness of salvation, become, though contrary to intention, stumbling blocks, and the occasion of mental trouble. Instead of at once directing sinners, as the apostles did, to the finished atonement, — to the propitiatory work of Christ, — of urging them to take God at his word, — to receive the testimony given of his Son, and so to possess joy and peace in believing, these good men seem to have been infected with the ancient errors, which confined evangelical teaching to the initiated. They evidently thought a routine of tedious preparation needful before coming to the Saviour. Qualifications, therefore, unknown to the word of God, were prescribed, and rules laid down, which not merely concealed great and precious promises, but savored of a legal spirit, and kept out of view that death unto the law which is the life of evangelical obedience." *

In this general charge of austere and legal teaching, which, as this writer says, obscures the promises and grace of the gospel, we do not distinctly perceive the points wherein Mr. Shepard is supposed to be erroneous. But in Giles Firmin's " Real Christian," a book which was written expressly for the purpose of correcting the errors of the " Sincere Convert," — one of Mr. Shepard's most practical works, — the dangerous doctrines are set forth, and controverted at length. In this book Mr. Shepard teaches that the preparatory work which every sinner must ex-

* Letters on the Puritans, by J. B. Williams, p. 170.

perience before he can receive the grace of God in Christ, includes *conviction of sin, compunction,* and *humiliation ;* that the sinner must be satisfied with the will of God, though his suit should be unsuccessful; that the soul must be so humbled as to be willing that Christ should dispose of it according to his pleasure ; that the sinner must seek the glory of God's grace above his own salvation ; and that in this work of conviction, compunction, and humiliation, we must be so thoroughly divested of all self-confidence and disposition to dictate to God, that he shall appear supremely excellent, though we may never partake of his love.

Firmin thought that a person under *such* a preparatory work was as good a Christian as he could be if he were actually united to Christ. In a letter to Mr. Shepard, he expressed his surprise at the doctrine that an act of grace or of obedience should be required of a person under a *preparatory* work, than which, he conceived, none greater could be performed by a real Christian ; and he declared that he knew no act of self-denial in the gospel like this quiet submission to the justice and sovereignty of God, irrespective of any assurance of pardon and acceptance; and this, too, under the *preparatory* work of humiliation !

This doctrine, Mr. Firmin thought, must be a great stumbling block in the way of sinners, and occasion great perplexity in all readers who believed it to be true. And he seems to have known one serious person, besides himself, who was much troubled by this "constitution of a Christian." "Preaching once abroad," he says, "I closed up the point in hand, by applying it to what Mr. Shepard had delivered, to see how these doctrines agreed. A gentleman and a scholar, meeting me some time after, gave me thanks for the close of my sermon. I asked him why. He told me that he had a maid servant who was very godly, and reading of that particular in Mr. Shepard's book which I opposed, she was so cast down, and fell into such trouble, that all the Christians who came to her could not quiet her spirit." * That is, this poor, godly servant maid could not be

* Real Christian, Preface, pp. 4, 5.

p *

freed from trouble of mind, occasioned by the doctrine that she must be truly convinced of sin, be deeply humbled, and submit implicitly to the will of God, until she was convinced, by Mr. Firmin, that Shepard, though an eminently learned and holy man, was mistaken in relation to that matter!

Before attempting to suggest an answer to these objections, it may be well to remark that the book called the " Sincere Convert" was, perhaps, of all Mr. Shepard's works, the least satisfactory to himself; not because its fundamental doctrines were doubtful to his own mind, but because it had not received that revision from his own hand which every work requires, and was, moreover, barbarously printed. " It was," says Mr. Shepard, in a letter to Mr. Firmin, " a collection of notes in a dark town in England, which one procuring of me, published without my will or privity. I scarce know what it contains ; nor do I like to see it, considering the many typographical errors, most absurd, and the confession of him that published it, that it comes out mutilated and altered from what was first written." * And this was said in October, 1647, a year after the English publisher, in his fourth edition, declared that the book had been " corrected and much amended by the author " !

Mr. Shepard, however, while he thus almost disowned the " Sincere Convert," did not disavow, but vindicated the doctrine here called in question. Though it was a " ragged child," as he sometimes called it, it spoke upon this point, at least, the sentiments of its author. In a letter to Mr. Firmin, he says, " I do not think this (that is, unconditional submission to the will of God) is the highest measure of grace, as you hint, any further than as any peculiar work of the Spirit is high ; for upon a narrow inquiry, it is far different from that readiness of Paul and Moses, out of a principle of love to Christ, to wish themselves anathematized for Israel's sake ; which is a high pitch indeed." And he closes his letter thus : " Let my love end in breathing out this desire : Preach humiliation. Labor to possess men with a sense of wrath to come, and misery. The gospel consolations

---

* Real Christian, p. 215.

and grace, which some would have dished out as the dainties of the times, and set upon the ministry's table, may possibly tickle and ravish some, and do some good to them that are humbled and converted already. But if axes and wedges, withal, be not used to hew and break this rough, uneven, bold, yet professing age, I am confident the work and fruit of those men's ministry will be at best mere hypocrisy; and they shall find it, and see it, if they live to see a few years more." *

Mr. Shepard here touches the root of the matter. A ministry, to be truly fruitful, must show to the people their transgressions; and that doctrine that does not humble the sinner and require unconditional submission, while it offers redeeming grace, though it were preached by an angel from heaven, is anathematized by the gospel. " Some souls can relish none but mealy-mouthed preachers, who come with soft, and smooth, and toothless words, (byssina verba, byssinis viris.) But these times need humbling ministries; and blessed be God that there are any. For where there are no law sermons, there will be few gospel lives; and were there more law preaching by the men of gifts, there would be more gospel walking both by themselves and the people. To preach the law, not in a forced, affected manner, but wisely and powerfully, together with the gospel, as Christ himself was wont to do, is the way to carry on all three together, viz., *sense of misery*, — the *application of the remedy*, — and *the returns of thankfulness and duty*. Nor is any doctrine more comforting than this humbling way of God, if rightly managed." †

Mr. Shepard had an able defender of his doctrines, as well as a worthy successor to his ministry, in Jonathan Mitchel, who drank into the spirit of that theology which exalts God while it abases man, and carried out in his preaching the views of his master. " I have," he says, " no greater request for myself and for you, than that God would make us see things as they really are, and pound our hearts all to pieces, and make sin most bitter, and Christ most sweet, that we might be both humbled and com-

* Real Christian, pp. 19, 56.

† Preface to Shepard's Sermons on Ineffectual Hearing of the Word, by G. Greenhill and S. Mather.

forted to purpose. An imperfect work of the law, and then an imperfect work of the gospel, is the bane and ruin of these days. Some fears and affections, and then some hopes of mercy, without finding full rest and satisfaction in Christ alone, men rest in, and perish." *

Whatever may be said of the legal tone of Mr. Shepard's writings, by those who think that " the God of terror, the Thunderer from Sinai, must fold up his lightnings prettily, and muffle his thunder in an easily-flowing, poetical measure," they doubtless exhibit in a masterly manner those distinguishing doctrines of grace which have ever been, as they will ever be, the true and only foundation of the sinner's peace.

It may be interesting to the reader to learn in what light these writings were regarded when they were more known than they are now, by men most competent, by profound acquaintance with the Scriptures, to judge correctly of their merits. And first, hear how William Greenhill speaks of that " ragged child," in the edition of 1692. " The author is one of singular piety, inward acquaintance with God, skilled in the deceits of men's hearts, able to enlighten the dark corners of the little world, and to give satisfaction to staggering spirits. The work is weighty, quick, and spiritual; and if thine eye be single in perusing it, thou shalt find many precious, soul-searching, soul-quickening, soul-enriching truths in it; yea, and be so warned and awakened, as that thou canst not but bless God for the man and the matter, unless thou be possessed with a dumb devil." † White, in his " Power of Godliness," mentions, among the best means and helps for acquiring a holy character, together with other books, Shepard's " Sincere Convert," and " Sound Believer." Steele, in his " Husbandman's Calling," advises the Christian farmer to purchase some *choice* books, and read them well, and recommends Shepard's " Sound Believer," as one of peculiar value. ‡ Hugh Peters exhorts his daughter to read, among other books mentioned in his letter, Shepard's " Sincere Convert," for the

---

* Letter to an Anxious Inquirer, 1649.
† Preface to Sincere Convert, p. 9.
‡ Letters on the Puritans, by J. B. Williams.

purpose of having her " understanding enlightened with the
want of Christ and his worth." * Rev. James Frazier, of Scotland, in 1738, thus speaks of Shepard's writings: " The Lord
hath blessed the reading of practical writings to me, and thereby
my heart hath been put into frame, and much strength and light
gotten ; such as Isaac Ambrose, Goodwin, Mr. Gray, and very
much by Rutherford's, above others ; but most of all, by Mr.
Thomas Shepard, of New England, his works. He hath, by
the same Lord, been made the ' Interpreter, one of a thousand ; '
so that, under Christ, I have been obliged to his writings as
much, and more, than to any man's whatever, for awakening,
strengthening, and enlightening my soul. The Lord made him a
well of water to me in all my wilderness straits." † Our own
Edwards, a man whose religious experience was as genuine and
as deep as that of any divine whom New England or the world has
produced, was more indebted to Shepard's Sermons on the Parable of the Ten Virgins, in the preparation of his " Treatise
concerning the Religious Affections," than to any other human
production whatever, as is shown by the fact that out of one
hundred and thirty-two quotations from all authors, upward of
seventy-five are from Mr. Shepard. To finish this catalogue of
eminent men who have borne testimony to the truth and power of
Mr. Shepard's practical writings, we repeat what old Mr. Ward,
of Ipswich, once said to Giles Firmin, his son-in-law, respecting
one of the prominent characteristics of his preaching and writing. " When Mr. Shepard comes to deal with hypocrites, he
cuts so desperately, that men know not how to bear him; he
makes them all afraid that they are all hypocrites. But when
he comes to deal with a tender, humble soul, he gives comfort so
largely, that we are afraid to take it." And Mr. Firmin himself
says, that the book which he so severely reviews is, for the most
part, " very solid, quick, and searching, cutting very sharply,"
and by no means a book for " an unsound heart to delight in." ‡
Of the character of Mr. Shepard's personal religion, after

* Hanbury's Memorials, 111, 573.
† Preface to Select Cases, etc., by T. Prince, 1774.
‡ Real Christian, p. 216.

what has been said in the foregoing account of his life, it is unnecessary to speak at length. The best moral portrait of him
that we have is drawn, unconsciously, by himself in his diary, to
which more than one reference has been made. It is a journal,
as David Brainerd justly remarks, in which true religion is de-
lineated in a very exact and beautiful manner; and in reading
this expression of his most secret feelings, — never, certainly,
designed to be made public, — we may see what he regarded as
the religion of a minister of Christ, the state he endeavored to
attain, and the difficulties he encountered in his way to heaven.
The humiliation, the submission to the will of God, the deep
sense of unworthiness, the desire to advance the glory of God
above all selfish considerations, which he preaches to others
in his works, he here shows that he himself experienced. The
joys which from time to time sprang up in his soul, in view of
redeeming mercy, were evidently not the self-created comforts
of a deceived heart that had never been truly broken for sin, but
the peace of God which came to fill a heart purified as a temple
for the Most High. It is a journal which every minister might
study with profit; and any one who should find his mind respond-
ing to these profound utterances of a heavenly mind, might, without much danger of disappointment, hope to be made an instrument
of promoting the glory of God in the conversion of sinners.

Upon the whole, when we consider the rich Christian experience which Mr. Shepard attained; the sacrifices which he
cheerfully made for the sake of Christ and the gospel; the great
amount of ministerial and other labor which he performed, with
feeble health and manifold hinderances; the attainments which
he made in sanctity, and the knowledge of divine things; the
able theological works he produced; and the influence, felt even
now, which he exerted in building up the churches of New England, — and all this ere he had passed the meridian of life, — we
must regard him as one of the brightest ornaments of the church,
and hold his memory in profound and grateful remembrance.

> "A sacred man, a venerable priest,
> Who never spake and admiration missed.

Of good and kind he the just standard seemed ;
Dear to the best, and by the worst esteemed.
His wit, his judgment, learning, equal rise ;
Divinely humble, yet divinely wise;
He triumphed o'er our souls, and, at his will,
Bid this touched passion rise, and that be still ;
Released our souls, and made them soar above,
Winged with divine desires and flames of heavenly love."

The following is a very brief account of Mr. Shepard's Family and Writings : —

Mr. Shepard left three sons : —

THOMAS, born April 5, 1635, at London ; graduated at Harvard College, 1653 ; ordained pastor of the church in Charlestown, April 13, 1659 ; died of small-pox, December 22, 1677, aged 43.

SAMUEL, born at Cambridge, October 18, 1641 ; graduated at Harvard College, 1658 ; ordained over the church at Rowley, as its third pastor, 1665 ; died April 7, 1668, in the twenty-seventh year of his age.

JEREMIAH, born August 11, 1648; graduated at Harvard College, 1669 ; ordained at Lynn, October 6, 1679 ; died June 2, 1720, aged 72, after a ministry of forty-one years.

Mr. Shepard's third wife, Margaret Boradel, after his death, married Jonathan Mitchel, his successor in the church of Cambridge.

Anna, the daughter of Thomas Shepard of Charlestown, was married, in 1682, to Daniel Quincy. They had one son, named John Quincy, born July 21, 1689. Elizabeth, the daughter of John Quincy, married William Smith, the minister of Weymouth. Abigail, the daughter of William Smith, married John Adams, afterward president of the United States, and was the mother of John Quincy Adams, who was thus a descendant, in the sixth generation, from Thomas Shepard of Cambridge.*

* Chronicles of Massachusetts, p. 558, note.

Of Mr. Shepard's books, the children of his mind, the following is believed to be a tolerably correct list, with the dates, so far as known, of their respective editions : —

1. SERMONS ON THE PARABLE OF THE TEN VIRGINS. Folio, London, 1695.

2. ANSWER TO BALL. Quarto, London, 1648.

3. THESES SABBATICÆ. Quarto, London, 1649.

4. SINCERE CONVERT. London. Several editions, — the last, London, 1692.

5. SOUND BELIEVER.

6. CHURCH MEMBERSHIP OF CHILDREN. Cambridge, 1663.

7. NEW ENGLAND'S LAMENTATION for Old England's Errors. London, 1645.

8. CLEAR SUNSHINE OF THE GOSPEL BREAKING UPON THE INDIANS. London, 1648.

9. SELECT CASES RESOLVED. London and Edinburgh, 1648.

10. THE LITURGICAL CONSIDERATOR, in reply to Dr. Gauden. London, 1661.

11. CAUTION AGAINST SPIRITUAL DRUNKENNESS ; Sermon.

12. SUBJECTION TO CHRIST IN ALL HIS ORDINANCES, etc.; the best way to preserve liberty.

13. INEFFECTUAL HEARING OF THE WORD.

14. SINGING OF PSALMS a Gospel Ordinance, 1647.

15. MEDITATIONS and SPIRITUAL EXPERIENCES. A Diary from November, 1640, to December, 1641.

16. FIRST PRINCIPLES OF THE ORACLES OF GOD. London and Edinburgh, 1648.

17. THE SAINT'S JEWEL. 16mo., London, 1692.

The Bible used by Mr. Shepard is in the possession of the Rev. William Jenks, D. D. It has the Hebrew of the Old Testament, without points, and the Greek of the New. It exhibits marks of use. On the title page, at the bottom, after the name of a previous possessor, is Shepard's name, an autograph, thus : Thomas Shepard. ἐν τϐτοις ἴσθι. Immanuel. For this account of Shepard's Bible I am indebted to the kindness of Rev. Dr. Jenks.

THE

SINCERE CONVERT:

DISCOVERING THE SMALL NUMBER OF

TRUE BELIEVERS,

AND THE GREAT DIFFICULTY OF

SAVING CONVERSION;

WHEREIN IS EXCELLENTLY AND PLAINLY OPENED THESE
CHOICE AND DIVINE PRINCIPLES:

1. THAT THERE IS A GOD, AND THIS GOD IS MOST GLORIOUS.
2. THAT GOD MADE MAN IN A BLESSED ESTATE.
3. MAN'S MISERY BY HIS FALL.
4. CHRIST THE ONLY REDEEMER BY PRICE.
5. THAT FEW ARE SAVED, AND THAT WITH DIFFICULTY.
6. THAT MAN'S PERDITION IS OF HIMSELF.

BY

THOMAS SHEPARD,

CAMBRIDGE, NEW ENGLAND.

CORRECTED AND AMENDED BY THE AUTHOR.

" Strait is the gate, and narrow is the way, which leadeth unto life;
and few there be that find it."   MATT. vii. 14.

BOSTON:
DOCTRINAL TRACT AND BOOK SOCIETY.

1853.

TO THE

CHRISTIAN READER.

IN these evil and perilous times, God hath not left us without some choice mercies. Our sins abound, and his mercies superabound. The Lord might justly have spoken those words of death against us which of old he did against the Jews — I have taken away my peace from this people, loving kindness and mercies; which had he pulled from us, we had cause enough to mourn with Rachel, and to refuse comfort; for all our happiness lies wrapped up in peace, loving kindness, and mercy. But God is yet good unto Israel, (Ps. lxxiii. 1;) he commands deliverances for Jacob, (Ps. xliv. 4;) he overrules all the powers of darkness, (Ps. lxxvi. 10,) and tells the sons of Belial (men of corrupt minds and cursed practice) that they shall proceed no further, but that their folly shall be manifest unto all. (2 Tim. iii. 8, 9.) He makes all enemies, all devils, all creatures to further his own glory, and the good of his peculiar people. When times are naught and dangerous, he saith, Come, my people, enter into thy chambers, and shut thy doors about thee; hide thyself, as it were, for a little moment, till the indignation be overpast. (Isa. xxvi. 10.) If troubles threaten life, he saith, " When thou passest through the waters, I will be with thee, and through the rivers, they shall not overflow thee ; when thou walkest through the fire, thou shalt not be burnt, neither shall the flames kindle upon thee; for I am the Lord thy God." (Isa. xliii. 3.) When enemies are incensed, fears and sorrows multiplied, he saith, " Fear thou not, for I am with thee; be not dismayed, for I am

3

thy God; I will strengthen thee, I will help thee; yea, I will uphold thee with the right hand of my righteousness. Behold, all they that were incensed against thee shall be ashamed and confounded, they shall be as nothing; and they that strive with thee shall perish." (Isa. xl. 10, 11.) Such words of comfort and life doth God speak unto his. And among other mercies, he stirs up the spirits of his servants to write many precious truths and tracts, to further the everlasting good of his beloved ones. If the bottomless pit be open, and smoke rise thence, to darken the air and obscure the way of the saints, (Rev. v. 2,) heaven also is opened, (Rev. xi. 19,) and there are lightnings and voices, to enlighten their spirits and direct their paths. Had ever any age such lightnings as we have? Did ever any speak, since Christ and his apostles, as men now speak? We may truly and safely say of our divines and writers, The voice of God, and not of man : such abundance of the Spirit hath God poured into some men, that it is nôt they, but the Spirit of the Father that speaks in them.

What infinite cause hath this age to acknowledge the unspeakable mercy of God in affording us such plenty of spiritual tractates, full of divine, necessary, and conscience-searching truths, yea, precious, soul-comforting, and soul-improving truths! such whereby head, heart, and soul-cheating errors are discovered and prevented; such as soundly difference true grace from all seemings and paintings. No time, no nation, exceeds us herein. And shall we, that abound in truths, be penurious in praises? Consider, reader, whether spiritual truths be not worthy of thy choicest praises. Every divine truth is one of God's eternal thoughts; it is heaven born, and bears the image of God. Truth is the glory of the sacred Trinity. Hence the Spirit is called Truth, (John xvi. 13,) Christ is called Truth, (John xiv. 6,) and God himself is said to be the God of truth. (Deut. xxxii. 4.) It is so delightful to him, that his eyes are always upon the truth. (Jer. v. 3.) And when the only-wise God would have men make a purchase, he counsels them to buy the truth. And is it not good counsel? Is it not a good purchase? Can you bestow your pains or lay out your money better? If you be dead in sins and trespasses, truth is the seed of a new life, of a heavenly birth. (James i. 18.) If you be in any bondage, truth can make you free. (John viii. 32.) If compassed about with enemies, truth can shield thee. (Ps. xci. 4.) If you be full of filthy thoughts and lusts, or any impurities, the truth can sanctify you. (John xvii. 17.) If darkness and faintness possess your souls, truth is *lumen et pabulum animæ* — "the light and life of the soul." (Ps. cxix. 105.)

Let us, then, advance our thoughts of truth, and rate it above all sublunary things, and buy it, though it cost us all. It is no simony, it is not too dear; you cannot overvalue truth. It is sister to the peace of God, which passeth all understanding. See how God himself estimates his word and truth. (Ps. cxxxviii. 2,) " Thou hast magnified thy word above all thy name." Whatsoever God is known by, beside his word, is beneath his word. Take the whole creation, which is God's name in the greatest letters, it is nothing to his word and truth. Therefore Christ tells the Pharisees, it is easier for heaven and earth to pass than one tittle of the law to fail. If the least jot or tittle of the law be prized by God above all the world, let us take heed of undervaluing the great and glorious truths of the gospel, and settle it as a law upon our hearts that we can never overprize or yield sufficient praise for any truth. Men can praise God for the blessings of the field, the seas, the womb, and of their shops; but where is the man that praises God for his blessing of blessings — for TRUTH — for good books, for heavenly treatises? Men seldom purposely lift up their hearts and voices to heaven, to praise God for the riches of knowledge bestowed upon them. In good books you have men's labor and God's truth. The tribute of thanks is due for both, that God enables men to so great labors, and that he conveys such precious treasures through earthen vessels. David thought it his duty to praise God for truth, (Ps. cxxxviii. 2,) and hath left it on record for our imitation. He saw such excellency, and found so much sweet gain in truth, that he must break out in praises for it.

1 *

Reader, give over thy old way of slighting and censuring men's labors. Experience hath long since told thee, that no good comes that way. Now learn to turn thy prejudices into praises, and prove what will be the fruit of honoring and praising God for truths dispensed by his faithful servants. Let me tell thee, this is a chief way to keep truth still among us. If truths be not received with the love of them, and God honored for them, presently strong delusions come, and truth must suffer or fly. God hath made good that promise in Jeremy. He hath revealed unto us abundance of peace and truth; and we, through ingratitude, have forfeited both. Our peace is shaken; and who can promise himself, with Hezekiah, There shall be peace and truth in my days? Peace may fail thee, but let not truth. Every good Christian may and should say, with the good king, There shall be *truth* in my days, if not *peace* and *truth*. I will so far honor truth, as to receive the love of it. I will hold it fast by faith, hold it forth by practice, praise God daily for it, and venture all in defence of it. So did the martyrs, whose memory is sweet, and whose regard is great. It is better suffering for truth than with truth: yet if truth must suffer, or can die, better it is to die with truth than outlive it. But that truth may live, and we live by truth, let us magnify God much for truth, for his word and good books that spring thence. Some probably may say, It's enough to praise God for his word. Other books are not *tanti*. Wilt thou praise God for the sea, and be unthankful for the rivers and springs? Wilt thou lift up thy voice for the great waters, and be silent for the silver drops and flowers? If the former rain affect thee, be not ungrateful for the latter. God would have man to value his servants, and praise him for their labors. But they have errors in them. Be it so. Shall we refuse to praise God for the flowers and the corn, because there be some weeds in the garden, and thistles in the field? Prejudice not thyself: buy, read, take thy delight. Here is a garden without weeds, a cornfield without cockle or darnel, thorn or thistle. Art thou a *sincere convert?* Here are truths suitable, solid, and wholesome. Thou mayest feed and feast without fear.

The author is one of singular piety, inward acquaintance with God, skilled in the deceits of men's hearts, able to enlighten the dark corners of the little world, and to give satisfaction to staggering spirits. His work needs not the purple of another's commendation to adorn it. But because custom, not necessity, (for it is truth's prerogative to travel without a passport,) — I say, because custom causeth truth to crave and carry epistles commendatory, know that the work is weighty, quick, and spiritual. And if thine eye be single in perusing it, thou shalt find many precious, soul-searching, soul-quickening, and soul-enriching truths in it; yea, be so warned and awakened, as that thou canst not but bless God for the man and matter, unless thou be possessed with a dumb devil.

To conclude: Christian reader, take heed of unthankfulness. Spiritual mercies should have the quickest and fullest praises. Such is this work; thou foresawest it not, thou contributest nothing to the birth of it. It is preventing mercy. By it, and other of the same nature, God hath made knowledge to abound; the waters of the sanctuary are daily increased, and grown deep. Let not the waters of the sanctuary put out the fire of the sanctuary. If there be no praise, there is no fire. If thy head be like a winter sun, full of light, and heart like a winter's earth, without fruit, fear lest thy light end in utter darkness, and the tree of knowledge deprive thee of the tree of life. The Lord grant thou mayest find such benefit by this work as that thy heart may be ravished with truth, and raised to praise God to purpose, and made to pray, Lord, still send forth thy light and truth, that they may lead us. So prays

Thine in Christ,

W. GREENHILL.

INTRODUCTION.

The knowledge of divinity is necessary for all sorts of men — both to settle and establish the good, and to convert and fetch in the bad. God's principles pull down Satan's false principles set up in man's head, loved and believed with men's hearts, and defended by their tongues. Whilst strongholds remain unshaken, the Lord Jesus is kept off from conquering of the soul.

Now, spiritual truths are either such as tend to enlarge the understanding, or such as may work chiefly upon the affections. I pass by (in this knowing age) the first of these, and, being among a people whose hearts are hard enough, I begin with the latter sort; for the understanding, although it may literally, yet it never savingly, entertains any truth, until the affections be herewith smitten and wrought upon.

I shall, therefore, here prosecute the unfolding of these divine principles : —

First, that there is one most glorious God.

Secondly, that this God made all mankind at first in Adam in a most glorious estate.

Thirdly, that all mankind is now fallen from that estate into a bottomless gulf of sin and misery.

Fourthly, that the Lord Jesus Christ is the only means of redemption of this estate.

Fifthly, that those that are saved out of this woful estate by Christ are very few, and that these few are saved with much difficulty.

Sixthly, that the greatest cause why so many die and perish in this estate is from themselves : either, —

1. By reason of their bloody ignorance, they know not their misery ; or, —

2. By reason of their carnal security, they feel not, they groan not under their sin and misery.

3. By reason of their carnal confidence, they seek to help themselves out of their misery by their own duties, when they see or feel it ; or, —

4. By reason of their false faith, whereby they catch hold upon, and trust unto, the merits of Christ too soon, when they see and feel they cannot help themselves.

8

THE SINCERE CONVERT.

DISCOVERING THE SMALL NUMBER OF TRUE BELIEVERS.

CHAPTER I.

THAT THERE IS A GOD, AND THIS GOD IS MOST GLORIOUS.

Exod. xxxiii. 18, "I beseech thee, show me thy glory."

THIS is the first divine truth, and there are these two parts considerable in it : —

1. That there is a God.
2. That this God is most glorious.

I will begin with the first part, and prove, omitting many philosophical arguments, that there is a God — a true God ; for every nation almost in the world, until Christ's coming, had a several god. Some worshiped the sun, some the moon, — called by Ezekiel the Queen of Heaven, which some made cakes unto, — some the whole heavens, some worshiped the fire, some the brute beasts, some Baal, and some Molech. The Romans, saith Varro, had six thousand gods ; who, imprisoning the light of nature, were given up to sins against nature, either to worship idols of man's invention, as the ignorant, or God and angels in those idols, as the learned did. But these are all false gods.

I am now to prove that there is one true God, the Being of beings, or the first Being. Although the proving of this point seems needless, because every man runs with the cry and faith, There is a God, yet few thoroughly believe this point. Many of the children of God, who are best able to know men's hearts, because they only study their hearts, feel this temptation, Is there a God ? bitterly assaulting them sometimes. The devil will sometimes undermine, and seek to blow up, the strongest walls and bulwarks. The light of nature indeed shows that

9

there is a God; but how many are there that, by foul sins against their conscience, blow out and extinguish almost all the light of nature! and hence, though they dare not conclude, because they have some light, though dim, yet, if they saw their heart, they might see it secretly suspect and question whether there be a God. But grant that none questions this truth, yet we that are builders must not fall to a work without our main props and pillars. It may appear, therefore, that there is a God from these grounds:—

First, from the works of God. (Rom. i. 20.) When we see a stately house, although we see not the man that built it, although also we know not the time when it was built, yet will we conclude thus: Surely some wise artificer hath been working here. Can we, when we behold the stately theater of heaven and earth, conclude other but that the finger, arms, and wisdom of God hath been here, although we see not him that is invisible, and although we know not the time when he began to build? Every creature in heaven and earth is a loud preacher of this truth. Who set those candles, those torches of heaven, on the table? Who hung out those lanterns in heaven to enlighten a dark world? Who can make the statue of a man, but one wiser than the stone out of which it is hewn? Could any frame a man but one wiser and greater than man? Who taught the birds to build their nests, and the bees to set up and order their commonwealth? Who sends the sun post from one end of heaven to the other, carrying so many thousand blessings to so many thousands of people and kingdoms? What power of man or angels can make the least pile of grass, or put life into the least fly, if once dead? There is, therefore, a power above all created power, which is God.

Secondly, from the word of God. There is such a majesty stirring, and such secrets revealed in the word, that, if men will not be wilfully blind, they cannot but cry out, "The voice of God, and not the voice of man." Hence Calvin undertakes to prove the Scripture to be the word of God by reason, against all atheists under heaven. Hast thou not thought sometimes, at a sermon, the minister hath spoken to none but thee, and that some or other hath told the minister what thou hast said, what thou hast done, what thou hast thought? Now, that word which tells thee the thoughts of thy heart can be nothing else but the word of an all-seeing God, that searcheth the heart.

Again: that word which quickeneth the dead is certainly God's word; but the word of God ordinarily preached quickeneth the dead; it maketh the blind to see, the dumb to speak, the deaf to hear, the lame to walk, those that never felt their sins to load them to mourn, those that never could pray to breathe out unutterable groans and sighs for their sins.

Thirdly, from the children begotten of God; for we may read in men's foreheads, as soon as ever they are born, the sentence of death; and we may see by men's lives what hellish hearts they have. Now, there is a time that some of this monstrous brood of men are quite changed, and made all new; they have new minds, new opinions, new desires, new joys, new sorrows, new speeches, new prayers, new lives, and such a difference there is betwixt these and others, that they are hated by others, who loved them well while they loved their sins. And whence came this strange change? Is it from themselves? No; for they hated this new life and these new men once themselves. Is it because they would be credited thereby? No; it is to be hated of father, mother, friends, and maligned every where. Is it out of simplicity, or are their brains grown crazy? They were indeed once fools, and I can prove them all to be Solomon's fools; but even simple men have been known to be more wise for the world, after they have been made new. But, lastly, is it now from a slavish fear of hell, which works this alteration? Nothing less; they abhor to live like slaves in Bridewell, to do all for fear of the whip.

Fourthly, from God's register, or notary, which is in every man; I mean, the conscience of man, which telleth them there is a God; and although they silence it sometimes, yet in time of thunder, or some great plague, as Pharaoh, or at the day of death, then they are near God's tribunal, when they acknowledge him clearly. The fearful terrors of conscience prove this, which, like a bailiff, arrests men for their debts; ergo, there is some creditor to set it on: sometimes, like a hangman, it torments men; ergo, there is some strange judge that gave it that command. Whence arise these dreadful terrors in men? Of themselves? No, surely; all desire to be in peace, and so to live and sleep in a whole skin. Comes it from melancholy? No; for melancholy comes on by degrees; these terrors of conscience surprise the soul suddenly at a sermon, suddenly after the commission of some secret foul sin. Again: melancholy sadness may be cured by physic; but many physicians have given such men over to other physicians. Melancholy sadness may be borne, but a wounded spirit who can bear? Thus you see that there is a God.

Objection. Who ever saw God, that every one is thus bold to affirm that there is a God?

Answer. Indeed, his face never was seen by mortal man, but his back parts have been seen, are seen, and may be seen by all the world, as hath been proved.

Object. All things are brought to pass by second causes.

Ans. 1. What though? Is there no master in the house, because the servants do all the work? This great God maintains state by doing all the creatures subjection; yet sometimes we may cry out in beholding some special pieces of his administration, Here is the finger of God.

2. What though there be such confusion in the world as that shillings stand for pence, and counters stand for pounds, the best men are bought and sold at a low rate, and worst men prized and preferred; yet if we had eyes to see and conceive, we should see a harmony in this discord of things. God is now like a wise carpenter, but hewing out his work. There is a lumber and confusion seemingly among us; let us stay till the day of judgment, and then we shall see infinite wisdom in fitting all this for his own glory, and for the good of his people.

Object. But if there be a God, why hears he not his people's prayers? Why doth he forget them when they have most need of him?

I answer, Noah's dove returns not presently with an olive branch of peace in his mouth. Prayer sometimes that speeds well returns not presently, for want of company enough to fetch away that abundance of mercy which God hath to give. The Lord ever gives them their asking in money or money worth, in the same thing or a better. The Lord ever gives his importunate beggars their desires, either in pence by little and little, or by pounds; long he is many times before he gives, but payeth them well for their waiting.

This is a use of reproof to all atheists either in opinion or practice.

First. In opinion; such as either conclude or suspect there is no God. O, blasphemous thoughts! Are there any such men? Men! nay, beasts; nay, devils; nay, worse than devils, for they believe and tremble. Yet the fool hath said in his heart, There is no God. (Ps. xiv. 1.) Men that have little heads, little knowledge, without hearts, as scholars sometimes of weak brains, being guided only by their books, seeing how things come by second causes, yet cannot raise their dull thoughts to the beholding of a first cause. Great politicians are like children, always standing on their heads, and shaking their heels against heaven : these think religion to be but a piece of policy, to keep people in awe : profane persons desiring to go on in sin, without any rub or check for sin, blow out all the light of nature, wishing there were no God to punish, and therefore willing to suspect and scruple that not to be which indeed is. Those also that have sinned secretly, though not openly against nature, or the light of conscience. God smites men for incest, sodomy, self-pollution, with dismal blindness. Those also that are notorious worldings, that look no higher than their barns, no farther than their shops; the world is a pearl in their eye; they can not see a God.

Lastly. I suspect those men that never found out this thief, this sin, that was bred and born with them, nor saw it in their own hearts, but there it lies still in some dark corner of their souls, to cut their throats — these kind of men sometimes suspect there is no God. O, this is a grievous sin! for if no God, no heaven, no hell, no martyrs, no prophets, no Scriptures. Christ was then a horrible liar, and an impostor. Other sins wrong and grieve God, and wound him, but this sin stabs the very heart of God; it strikes at the life, and is (as much as lies in sinful man) the death of God; for it saith, There is no God.

Secondly. This reproveth atheists in practice, which say there is a God, and question it not, but in works they deny him. He that plucks the king from his throne is as vile as he that saith he is no king. These men are almost as bad as atheists in opinion. And of such dust heaps we may find in every corner, that in their practice deny God; men that set up other gods in God's room; their wealth, their honor, their pleasure, their backs and bellies to be their gods; men that make bold to do that against this true God which idolaters dare not do against their idol gods; and that is, continually to wrong this God; men that seek not for all they want by prayer, nor return all back again to God by praise.

A second use is, for exhortation. O, labor to see and behold this God. Is there a God, and wilt thou not give him a good look? O, pass by all the rivers, till thou come to the spring head; wade through all creatures, until thou art drowned, plunged and swallowed up with God. When thou seest the heavens, say, Where is that great Builder that made this? When thou hearest of mutations of kingdoms, say, Where is the Lord of hosts, the great Captain of these armies? When thou tastest sweetness in the creature, or in God's ordinances, say, Where is sweetness itself, beauty itself? Where is the sea of these drops, the sun of these beams? O that men saw this' God! it's heaven to behold him; thou art then in a corner of hell, that canst not, dost not see him: and yet what is less known than God? Methinks, when men hear there is a God about them, they should lie groveling in the dust, because of his glory. If men did see him, they would speak of him. Who speaks of God? Nay, men can not speak to God; but as beggars have learnt to cant, so many a man to pray. O, men see not God in prayer; therefore they can not speak to God by prayer. Men sin and God frowns, (which makes the devils to quake;) yet men's hearts shake not, because they see him not.

Use 3. O, make choice of this God as thy God. What though there be a God; if it be not thy God, what art thou the better? Down with all thy idol gods, and set up this God. If there be any creature that ever did thee any good, that God set not a work for thy good, love that; think on that as thy God. If there be any thing that can give thee any succor on thy death bed, or when thou art departed from this world, take that to be thy God. Thou mightest have been born in India, and never have heard the true God, but worshiped the devil for thy god. O, therefore, make choice of him alone to be thy God; give away thyself wholly and forever to him, and he will give away his whole self everlasting unto thee. Seek him weeping, and thou shalt find him. Bind thyself by the strongest oaths and bonds in covenant to be his, and he will enter into covenant with thee, and so be thine. (Jer. l. 3, 5.)

The fourth use is, a use of comfort to them that forsake all for this God. Thou hast not lost all for nought, thou hast not cast away substance for shadows, but shadows for somewhat. (Prov. viii. 18.) When all comfort is gone, there is a God to comfort thee. When thou hast no rest here, there is a God to rest in; when thou art dead, he can quicken thee; when thou art weak, he is strong; and when friends are gone, he will be a sure one to thee.

Thus much of the first part of this doctrine, or divine truth, *That there is a God.* Now, it followeth to show you that this God is a *most glorious God,* and that in four things he is glorious.

1. In his essence. 2. In his attributes. 3. In his persons. 4. In his works.

1. He is glorious in his essence. Now, what this glory is no man or angel hath, doth, or ever shall know; their cockle shell can never comprehend this sea; he must have the wisdom of God, and so be a God, that comprehendeth the essence of God; but though it can not be comprehended what it is, yet it may be apprehended that it is incomprehensible and glorious; which makes his glory to be the more admired, as we admire the luster of the sun the more in that it is so great we can not behold it.

2. God is glorious in his attributes, which are those divine perfections whereby he makes himself known unto us. Which attributes are not qualities in God, but natures. God's wisdom is

God himself, and God's power is God himself, etc. Neither are they divers things in God, but they are divers only in regard of our understanding, and in regard of their different effects on different objects. God punishing the wicked is the justice of God; God compassionating the miserable is the mercy of God.

Now, the attributes of God, omitting curious divisions, are these:—

1. He is a Spirit, or a spiritual God, (John iv. 24;) therefore abhors all worship, and all duties performed without the influence of the Spirit; as to confess thy sins without shame or sorrow, and to say the Lord's prayer without understanding — to hear the word that thou mayest only know more, and not that thou mayest be affected more — O, these carcasses of holy duties are most odious sacrifices before God.

2. He is a living God, whereby he liveth of himself, and gives life to all other things. Away, then, with thy dead heart to this principle of life to quicken thee, that his almighty power may pluck thee out of thy sepulcher, unloose thy grave clothes, that so thou mayest live.

3. He is an infinite God, whereby he is without limits of being. (2 Chron. vi. 18.) Horrible, then, is the least sin that strikes an infinite, great God, and lamentable is the estate of all those with whom this God is angry; thou hast infinite goodness to forsake thee, and infinite power and wrath to set against thee.

4. He is an eternal God, without beginning or end of being. (Ps. lxxx. 1.) Great, therefore, is the folly of those men that prefer a little short pleasure before this eternal God; that, like Esau, sell away an everlasting inheritance for a little pottage — for a base lust and the pleasure of it.

5. He is an all-sufficient God. (Gen. xvii. 1.) What lack you, therefore? you that would fain have this God, and the love of this God, but you are loth to take the pains to find him, or to be at cost to purchase him with the loss of all? Here is infinite, eternal, present sweetness, goodness, grace, glory, and mercy to be found in this God. Why post you from mountain to hill, why spend you your money, your thoughts, time, endeavors, on things that satisfy not? Here is thy resting-place. Thy clothes may warm thee, but they can not feed thee; thy meat may feed thee, but can not heal thee; thy physic may heal thee, but can not maintain thee; thy money may maintain thee, but can not comfort thee when distresses of conscience and anguish of heart come upon thee. This God is joy in sadness, light in darkness, life in death, heaven in hell. Here is all thine eye ever saw, thine heart ever desired, thy tongue ever asked, thy mind ever

conceived. Here is all light in this sun, and all water in this sea, out of whom, as out of a crystal fountain, thou shalt drink down all the refined sweetness of all creatures in heaven and earth forever and ever. All the world is now seeking and tiring out themselves for rest; here only it can be found.

6. He is an omnipotent God, whereby he can do whatever he will. Yield, therefore, and stand not out in the sinful or subtle close maintenance of any one sin against this God so powerful, who can crush thee at his pleasure.

7. He is an all-seeing God. He knows what possibly can be or may be known: approve thyself, therefore, to this God only, in all thy ways. It is no matter what men say, censure, or think of thee. It is no matter what thy fellow-actors on this stage of the world imagine. God is the great Spectator that beholds thee in every place. God is thy Spy, and takes complete notice of all the actions of thy life; and they are in print in heaven, which that great Spectator and Judge will open at the great day, and read aloud in the ears of all the world. Fear to sin, therefore, in secret, unless thou canst find out some dark hole where the eye of God can not discern thee. Mourn for thy secret neglect of holy duties; mourn for thy secret hypocrisy, whoredom, profaneness, and, with shame in thy face, come before this God for pardon and mercy. Admire and wonder at his patience, that, having seen thee, hath not damned thee.

8. He is a true God; whereby he means to do as he saith. Let every child of God, therefore, know to his comfort, that whatever he hath under a promise, shall one day be all made good; and let all wicked men know, whatever threatening God hath denounced, whatsoever arrows are in the bowstring, will one day fly and hit, and strike deep, and the longer the Lord is a-drawing, the deeper wound will God's arrow (that is, God's threatening) make.

9. He is a holy God. Be not ashamed, therefore, of holiness, which if it ascend above the common strain of honesty, the blind and mad world accounts it madness. If the righteous (that is, those that be most holy) be scarcely saved, where shall the ungodly and the sinner appear? (1 Pet. iv 18.) Where? Not before saints nor angels, for holiness is their trade; not before the face of the man Christ Jesus, for holiness was his *meat and drink;* not before the face of a blessed God, for holiness is his nature; not in heaven, for no unclean thing crawls there; they shall never see God, Christ, saints, angels, or heaven, to their comfort, that are not holy. Wear, therefore, that as thy crown now, which will be thy glory in heaven; and if this be to be vile, be more vile.

10. He is a just and merciful God; just in himself, and so will punish all sin; merciful in the face of Christ, and so will punish no sin, having already borne our punishments for them. A just God against a hard-hearted sinner, a merciful God towards a humble sinner. God is not all mercy and no justice, nor all justice and no mercy. Submit to him, his mercy embraceth thee. Resist him, his justice pursues thee. When a child of God is humbled indeed, commonly he makes God a hard-hearted, cruel God, loth to help; and saith, Can such a sinner be pardoned? A wicked man, that was never humbled, makes God a God of lies — one that (howsoever he speaks heavy words, yet he is a merciful God and) will not do as he saith, and he finds it no difficult work to believe the greatest sin may be pardoned. Conceive, therefore, of him as you have heard.

Thirdly. God is glorious in his persons, which are three: Father begetting, Son begotten, and the Holy Ghost, the third person, proceeding. Here the Father is called the Father of glory, (Eph. i.;) Christ is called the Lord of glory, (1 Cor. ii;) and the Spirit is called the Spirit of glory. (1 Pet. iv.) The Father is glorious in his great work of *election;* the Son is glorious in his great work of *redemption;* the Holy Ghost is glorious in his work of *application:* the Father is glorious in choosing the house, the Son is glorious in buying the house, the Spirit is glorious in dwelling in the house — that is, the heart of a poor, lost sinner.

4. He is glorious in his works — in his works of creation, and in his works of providence and government. Wonder, therefore, that he should so vouchsafe to look upon such worms, such dung-hills, such lepers as we are; to provide, protect, to slay his Son; to call, to strive, to wait, to give away himself and all that he is worth, unto us. O, fear this God when you come before him. People come before God in prayer as before their fellows, or as before an idol. People tremble not at his voice in the word. A king or monarch will be served in state; yet how rudely, how slovenly do men go about every holy duty! Thus much of the first principal head, *That there is one most glorious God.* Now we are to proceed to the second.

2*

CHAPTER II.

THAT THIS GOD MADE ALL MANKIND AT FIRST IN A MOST GLORIOUS AND HAPPY ESTATE, LIKE UNTO HIMSELF.

For the opening of which assertion I have chosen this text, (Eccl. vii. 29,) *God made man righteous ;* which clearly demonstrates, —

That God made all mankind at first in Adam, in a most glorious, happy, and righteous estate. Man, when he came first out of God's mint, shined most glorious. There is a marvelous glory in all creatures, (the servants and household stuff of man ;) therefore there was a greater glory in man himself, the end of them. God calleth a parliament, and gathers a council, when man was to be made ; and said, " Come, let us make man in our own image," as though all the wisdom of the Trinity should be seen in the creation of man.

Wherein did the glory and blessedness of man appear ?

In the impression of God's image upon him. (Gen. i. 26.) Can there be any greater glory for a Joseph, for a subject, than to be like his prince ?

What was the image of God ?

The schoolmen and fathers have many curious (yet some necessary) though difficult questions about this. I will omit all theirs, and tell you only what is the apostle's judgment, (Col. iii. 20,) out of which this general description of God's image may be thus gathered : It is man's perfection of holiness, resembling God's admirable holiness, whereby only man pleaseth God.

For all other inferior creatures did carry the marks and footsteps of God's power, wisdom, goodness, whereby all these attributes were seen. One of the most perfect attributes, his holiness, he would have men only appear in, and be made manifest by man, his best inferior creature, as a king's wisdom and bounty appears in managing the affairs of all his kingdom ; but his royal, princely, and most eminent perfections appear in the face and disposition of his Son, next under him. But more particularly this image of God appeared in these four particulars : —

1. In man's understanding. This was like unto God's. Now, God's image here chiefly consisted in this particular, viz. : As God saw himself, and beheld his own infinite, endless glory and excellency, so man was privy to God's excellency, and saw God most gloriously ; as Moses, though a sinful man, saw him face to face, much more Adam, a perfect man. God, loving man, could do no less than reveal himself to man.

2. In his affections. The image of God chiefly appeared in two things : —

First. As God, seeing himself, loved himself, so Adam, seeing God, loved this God more than the world, more than himself. As iron put into the fire seems to be nothing but fire, so Adam, being beloved of God, was turned into a lump of love, to love God again.

Secondly. As God delighted in himself, so did Adam delight in God, took sweet repose in the bosom of God. Methinks I see Adam rapt up in continual ecstasies in having this God.

3. In his will. The image of God chiefly appeared in two things : —

First. As God only willed himself as his last end, so did Adam will God as his last end, not as man doth now.

Secondly. As God willed nothing but good, so did Adam will nothing, though not immutably, but good; for God's will was his.

4. In his life, God's image did appear thus : that, even as God, if he had assumed man's nature, would have lived outwardly, so did Adam ; for God would have lived according to his own will, law, and rule : so did Adam. Adam's body was the lantern through which holiness, like a lamp burning in his heart, shined. This was God's image, by means of which, as it is said in the description, he pleased God, similitude being the ground of love ; and hence God did most dearly love him, and highly honor him to be Lord over all creatures. No evil (continuing in that estate) could hurt him ; here was no sorrow, no sickness, no tears, no fears, no death, no hell, nor ever should have been if there he had stood.

Objection. How was this estate ours ?

Answer. As Christ's righteousness is a believer's by imputation, though he never performed it himself, so Adam's righteousness and image were imputed to us, and accounted ours ; for Adam received our stock or patrimony to keep it for us, and to convey it to us. Hence, he proving bankrupt, we lost it. But we had it in his hands, as an orphan may have a great estate left him, though he never receive one penny of it from him that was his guardian, that should have kept it for him, and conveyed it to him.

Here see the horrible nature of sin, that plucks man down by the ears from his throne, from his perfection, though never so great. Adam might have pleaded for himself, and have said, Although I have sinned, yet it is but one and the first fault. Lord, behold, I am thy first born. O, pity my poor posterity, who are forever undone if thou forgivest not. Yet see, one sin weighs him down and all his posterity, as we shall hear, into eternal ruin.

Hence learn how justly God may require perfect obedience to all the law of every man, and curse him if he can not perform it, because man was at first made in such a glorious estate, wherein he had power given him to please God perfectly. God may, therefore, require this debt of perfect obedience. Now man is broke, and in prison ; in hell he must lie forever, if he can not pay justice every farthing, because God trusted him with a stock which if he had well improved, he might have paid all.

See what cause every man hath to lament his miserable estate he is now fallen into. For beggars' children to live vagrants and poor is not so lamentable as for a great prince's children to become such. One never in favor with the prince grieves not as he doth that was once in favor, but now cast out. Man is now rejected of God that was beloved of God. He is now a runagate up and down the earth that was once a prince and lord of all the world. This is one aggravation of the damned's sorrow. O, the hopes, the means, the mercies that once I had ! Can these, do these lament for the loss of their hopes and common mercies ? Lord, what hearts, then, have men that can not, do not, that will not lament the loss of such special high favors, now gone, which once they had ? It is said that those that saw the glory of the first temple wept when they saw the glory of the second, and how inferior it was to the first. You that either have the temple of God begun to be repaired in you, or not begun at all, O, think of the temple burnt, the glory of God now vanished and lost.

This speaks comfort to all God's people. If all Adam's posterity were perfectly righteous in him, then thou that art of the blood royal, and in Christ art perfectly righteous in him much more, inasmuch as the righteousness of the second Adam exceeds the first, so art thou more happy, more holy in the second Adam than ever the first in himself was. He might lose all his righteousness ; but the second Adam can not, hath not ; so that, if Christ may be damned, then thou mayest ; else not.

This likewise reproveth three sorts of people : —

1. Such as are ashamed of holiness. Lord, what times are we fallen into now ? The image of God, which was once men's glory, is now their shame ; and sin, which is men's shame, is now their glory. The world hath raised up many false reports of holy courses, calling it folly and preciseness, pride, hypocrisy, and that, whatsoever shows men may make, they are as bad as the worst, if their sins were writ in their foreheads. Hence it cometh to pass that many a man, who is almost persuaded to be a new man, and to turn over a new leaf, dares not, will not, for

shame of the world, enter upon religious courses. What will they think of me then? saith he. Men are ashamed to refuse to drink healths, and hence maintain them lawful. Our gallants are ashamed to stay a mile behind the fashion; hence they will defend open and naked breasts and strange apparel, as things comely. O, time servers! that have some conscience to desire to be honest, and to be reputed so, yet conform themselves to all companies. If they hear others swear, they are ashamed to reprove them; they are ashamed to enter the lists of holy discourse in bad company; and they will pretend discretion, and we must not cast pearls before swine; but the bottom of the business is, they are ashamed to be holy. O, fearful! Is it a shame to be like God? O, sinful wretches! It is a credit to be any thing but religious, and, with many, religion is a shame. I wonder with what face thou darest pray, or with what look thou wilt behold the Lord of glory at the last day, who art ashamed of him now, that will be admired of all men, angels, and devils then? Dost thou look for wages from Christ that art ashamed to own Christ, or to wear his livery?

2. It reproves them that hate holiness, which is more than to be ashamed of it.

3. It reproves them that content themselves with a certain measure of holiness. Perfect holiness was Adam's image, whereby he pleased God; and shall a little holiness content thee?

Now, there are these three sorts of them: —

1. The formalist, who contents himself with some holiness, as much as will credit him.

The form and name of religion is *honos*, honor sometimes; but the power and practice of it is *onus*, a burden; hence men take up the first, and shake off the second. And indeed the greatest part take up this course: if they have no goodness, they should be the shame, scorn, and table talk of the times; therefore every man will, for his honor's sake, have this form. Now, this form is according to the mold wherein he is cast. If his acquaintance be but civil, he will be like them; if they be more exact, as to pray, read, confer, he will not stay one inch behind them. If to be better than his companions, to bear the bell before them, will credit him, he will be so, whatever it cost him; but yet he never will be so exact in his course as to be hated for it, unless he perceives the hatred he contracts from some men shall be recompensed with the more love and credit by other men. He disguiseth himself according to the places or company he comes into. King Joash was a good man so long as Jehoiada the priest lived. If a little religion will serve to credit men, that shall serve for that time; if more in another place, you shall then have them commending good men, good sermons, good books, and drop forth two or three good sentences. What will they think of him then? They cover themselves over with these fig leaves of common honesty to cover their nakedness; they bait all their courses over with honesty, that they may catch, for they fish only for credit. One may trap these people thus: Follow them in their private houses, there is worldliness, passion, looseness; and to their private chambers, there they ordinarily neglect or snuffle over duties to their private vain thoughts. In this tyring house you shall then see these stage players; their shop windows are shut; here no honesty is to be seen scarce, because their gain, their respect, comes not in at this door, where none beholds them. Let either minister or any faithful friend search, try, discover, accuse, and condemn these men as rotten, though gilded, posts, as unsound, hollow-hearted wretches, their hearts will swell like toads, and hiss like snakes, and bark like dogs, against them that thus censure them, because they rob them of their God they served, their gain is gone.

2. The guilty, self-condemned sinner, that goes further than the formalist, and contents himself with so much holiness as will quiet him; and hence all the heathen have had some religion, because they had some conscience to trouble them. This man, if he hath lived in foul sins, and begins to be racked and troubled for them, he will then confess and forsake those sins. But how? As a dog doth his meat; not because he hates his carrion, but because he fears the cudgel. He performs holy duties, not because he will use them, but because he must use them; there is no quiet else. If conscience be still, he omits duties; if conscience cry and stir, he falls to duties, and so hath his good mood as conscience hath his fits. They boast and crow over hypocrites, because the holiness they have is not a bare show. No; but it is to stop thy conscience, and only to quiet the clamors of that. Thou dost bribe, and so quiet (the bailiff) thy conscience, by thy praying, hearing, and sorrowing; but God, thy Judge, hath heavy things to lay to thy charge, before whom thou shalt shortly with dread appear.

3. The pining and devout hypocrite, that, being pursued with the fear of hell, goes further, and labors for just so much holiness as will save him only, and carry him to heaven at last. Hence the young man in the gospel came with that great question to Christ, which many unsound hearts come with to ministers

now — what he should do to inherit eternal life. These people set up such a man in their thoughts to be a very honest man, and one doubtless that shall be saved; and hence they will take him to be their copy and sampler, and labor to do as he doth, and to live just as he lives, and to hold opinions as he holds, and so hope to be saved. They will ask, very inquisitively, What is the least measure of grace, and the least grain of faith? and the best sermons are not such as humble them most, but such as flatter them best; wherein they may hear how well good desires are accepted of by God; which if they hear to be of that virtue to save them, God shall be served only with good desires, and the devil in their actions all their lives.

Thus they make any thing serve for God; they labor not after so much holiness as will honor Christ, but after just so much as will bear their charges to heaven, and save themselves. For this is one of the greatest differences betwixt a child of God and a hypocrite. In their obedience, the one takes up duties out of love to Christ, to have him ; and hence he mourns daily, because Christ is no greater gainer by him ; the other out of love to himself, merely to save his own soul ; and hence he mourns for his sins, because they may damn him. Remember that place, therefore, 1 Cor. xv. ult.

Lastly. Labor to get this image of God renewed again. Honest men will labor to pay their debts; this is God's debt. How do men labor to be in the fashion ! Better to be out of the world than out of the fashion. To be like God is heaven's fashion, angels' fashion, and it will be in fashion one day, when the Lord Jesus shall appear ; then, if thou hast the superscription and image of the devil, and not the image of God upon thee, God and Christ will never own thee at that day. Labor, therefore, to have God's image restored again, and Satan's wash out ; seek not, as many do, to purchase such and such a grace first. But, —

1. Labor to mortify and subdue that sin which is opposite in thine heart to that grace. First put off the old man, and then put on the new. (Eph. iv.)

2. Labor for a melting, tender heart for the least sin. Gold is then only fit to receive the impression when it is tender and is melted ; when thine heart is heated, therefore, at a sermon, cry out, Lord, now strike, now imprint thine image upon me !

3. Labor to see the Lord Jesus in his glory. For as wicked men, looking upon the evil example of great ones in the world, that will bear them out, grow like them in villainy, so the very beholding the glorious grace in Christ, this great Lord of glory, transformeth men into this image. (2 Cor. iii. 17, 18.) As the glass, set full against the sun, receives not only the beams, as all

other dark bodies do, but the image of the sun, so the understanding, with open face beholding Christ, is turned into the image and likeness of Christ. Men nowadays look only to the best men's lives, and see how they walk, and rest here. O, look higher to this blessed face of God in Christ as thine own. As the application of the seal to the wax imprints the image, so to view the grace of Christ as all thine imprints the same image strongly on the soul. I come now to the third principal head in order, which I shall insist upon, out of Rom. iii. 23 : " All have sinned and deprived of the glory of God."

CHAPTER III.

THAT ALL MANKIND IS FALLEN BY SIN FROM THAT GLORIOUS ESTATE HE WAS MADE IN, INTO A MOST WOFUL AND MISERABLE CONDITION.

THE devil abusing the serpent, and man abusing his own free will, overthrew Adam, and in him all his posterity, by sin. (Gen. iii. 1–3 etc.)

Now, man's misery appears in these two things : —

1. His misery in regard of sin.
2. His misery in regard of the consequences of sin.

1. His misery in regard of sin appears in these particulars : —

1. Every man living is born guilty of Adam's sin. Now, the justice and equity of God, in laying this sin to every man's charge, though none of Adam's posterity personally committed it, appears thus : —

First. If Adam standing, all mankind had stood, then it is equal, that he falling, all his posterity should fall. All our estates were ventured in this ship; therefore, if we should have been partakers of his gains, if he had continued safe, it is fit we should be partakers of his loss too.

But, secondly. We are all in Adam, as a whole country in a parliament man; the whole country doth what he doth. And although we made no particular choice of Adam to stand for us, yet the Lord made it for us ; who, being goodness itself, bears more good will to man than he can or could bear to himself ; and being wisdom itself, made the wisest choice, and took the wisest course for the good of man. For this made most for men's safety and quiet; for if he had stood, all fear of losing our happy estate had vanished ; whereas, if every man had been left to stand or fall for himself, a man would ever have been in fear of falling.

And again: this was the sure way to have all men's states preserved; for having the charge of the estates of all men that ever should be in the world, he was the more pressed to look the more about him, and so to be more watchful, that he be not robbed, and so undo and procure the curses of so many thousands against him. Adam was the head of mankind, and all mankind naturally are members of that head; and if the head invent and plot treason, and the head practice treason against the king or state, the whole body is found guilty, and the whole body must needs suffer. Adam was the poisoned root and cistern of all mankind: now, the branches and streams being in the root and spring originally, they therefore are tainted with the same poisoned principles. If these things satisfy not, God hath a day coming wherein he will reveal his own righteous proceedings before men and angels. (Rom. ii. 4.)

O that men would consider this sin, and that the consideration of it could humble people's hearts! If any mourn for sin, it is for the most part for other foul actual sins; few for this sin that first made the breach, and began the controversy betwixt God and man. Next unto the sin against the Holy Ghost, and contempt of the gospel, this is the greatest sin that crieth loudest in God's ears for vengeance, day and night, against a world of men. For now men's sins are against God in their base and low estates; but this sin was committed against Jehovah, when man was at the top of his preferment. Rebellion of a traitor on a dunghill is not so great as of a favorite in court. Little sins against light are made horrible. No sin, by any man committed, was ever against so much light as Adam had. This sin was the first that ever displeased God. Drunkenness deprives God of the glory of sobriety; whoring, of chastity; but this sin darkens the very sun, defaces all the image of God, the glory of man, and the glory of God in man; this is the first sin ever did thee mischief. This sin, like a captain, hath gathered together all those troops and swarms of sins that now take hold upon thee. Thank this sin for a hard heart thou so much complainest of; thank this sin for that hellish darkness that overspreads thee. This hath raised Satan, death, judgment, hell, and heaven against thee.

O, consider these sins that are packed up in this evil. 1. Fearful apostasy from God like a devil. 2. Horrible rebellion against God in joining sides with the devil, and taking God's greatest enemies' part against God. 3. Woful unbelief, in suspecting God's threats to be true. 4. Fearful blasphemy in conceiving the devil (God's enemy and man's murderer) to be more true in his temptations than God in his threatening. 5. Horrible pride, in thinking to make this sin of eating the forbidden fruit to be a step and a stair to rise higher, and to be like God himself. 6. Fearful contempt of God, making bold to rush upon the sword of the threatening secretly, not fearing the plague denounced. 7. Horrible unthankfulness, when God had given him all but one tree, and yet he must be fingering that too. 8. Horrible theft, in taking that which was none of his own. 9. Horrible idolatry, in doting upon and loving the creature more than God the Creator, who is blessed forever.

You, therefore, that now say, No man can say, Black is your eye, you have lived civilly all your days, look upon this one grievous sin, take a full view of it, which thou hast never shed one tear for as yet, and see thy misery by it, and wonder at God's patience; he hath spared thee who wast born branded with it, and hast lived guilty of it, and must perish forever for it, if the Lord from heaven pity thee not.

But here is not all. Consider, secondly, every man is born stark dead in sin. (Ephes. ii. 1.) He is born empty of every inward principle of life, void of all grace, and hath no more good in him (whatsoever he thinks) than a dead carrion hath. And he is under the power of sin, as a dead man is under the power of death, and can not perform any act of life ; their bodies are living coffins to carry a dead soul up and down in.

It is true, (I confess,) many wicked men do many good actions, as praying, hearing, alms deeds ; but it is not from any inward principle of life. External motives, like plummets on a dead (yet artificial) clock, set them a-running. Jehu was zealous, but it was only for a kingdom ; the Pharisees gave alms only to be seen of men. If one write a will with a dead man's hand deceased, that will can not stand in any law ; it was not his will, because it was not writ by him, by any inward principle of life of his own. Pride makes a man preach, pride makes a man hear, and pray sometimes. Self-love stirs up strange desires in men, so that we may say, This is none of God's act by his grace in the soul, but pride and self-love. Bring a dead man to the fire, and chafe him, and rub him, you may produce some heat by this external working upon him ; but take him from the fire again, and he is soon cold ; so many a man that lives under a sound minister, under the lashes and knock of a chiding, striving conscience, he hath some heat in him, some affections, some fears, some desires, some sorrows stirred ; yet take him from the minister and his chafing conscience, and he grows cold again presently, because he wants an inward principle of life.

Which point might make us to take up a bitter lamentation for every natural man. It is said, (Ex. xii. 30,) "That there was a great cry in Egypt, for there was not a house wherein there was not one found dead." O Lord, in some towns and families, what a world of these are there! Dead husband, dead wife, dead servants, dead children, walking up and down with their sins, (as fame saith some men do after death,) with grave clothes about them; and God only knows whether ever they shall live again or not. How do men lament the loss of their dead friends! O, thou hast a precious soul in thy bosom stark dead; therefore lament thine estate, and consider it seriously.

First. A dead man can not stir, nor offer to stir; a wicked man can not speak one good word, or do any good action, if heaven itself did lie at the stake for doing it, nor offer to shake off his sins, nor think one good thought. Indeed, he may speak and think of good things, but he can not have good speeches, nor good thoughts; as a holy man may think of evil things as of the sins of the times, the thought of those evil things is good, not evil, so *e contra.*

Secondly. A dead man fears no dangers, though never so great, though never so near. Let ministers bring a natural man tidings of the approach of the devouring plagues of God denounced, he fears them not.

Thirdly. A dead man can not be drawn to accept of the best offers. Let Christ come out of heaven, and fall about the neck of a natural man, and with tears in his eyes beseech him to take his blood, himself, his kingdom, and leave his sins, he can not receive this offer.

Fourthly. A dead man is stark blind, and can see nothing, and stark deaf, and hears nothing, he can not taste any thing; so a natural man is stark blind, he sees no God, no Christ, no wrath of the Almighty, no glory of heaven. He hears the voice of a man, but he hears not the voice of God in a sermon; "he savoreth not the things of God's Spirit."

Fifthly. A dead man is senseless, and feels nothing: so cast mountains of sin upon a wicked man, he feels no hurt until the flames of hell break out upon him.

Sixthly. A dead man is a speechless man; he can not speak unless it be like a parrot.

Seventhly. He is a breathless man: a natural man may say a prayer, or devise a prayer out of his memory and wit, or he may have a few short-winded wishes; but to pour out his soul in prayer, in the bosom of God, with groans unutterable, he can not. I wonder not to see so many families without family prayer. Why? They are dead men, and lie rotting in their sins.

Eighthly. A dead man hath lost all beauty : so a mere natural man hath lost all glory ; he is an ugly creature in the sight of God, good men, and angels, and shall one day be an abhorring to all flesh.

Ninthly. A dead man hath his worms gnawing him : so natural men have the worm of conscience breeding now ; which will be gnawing them shortly.

Lastly. Dead men want nothing but casting into the grave : so there wants nothing but casting into hell for a natural man. So that, as Abraham loved Sarah well while living, yet when she was dead, he seeks for a burying-place for her to carry her out of his sight. So God may let some fearful judgment loose, and say to it, Take this dead soul out of my sight, etc. It was a wonder that Lazarus, though lying but four days in the grave, should live again. O, wonder thou that ever God should let thee live, that hast been rotting in thy sin twenty, thirty, perhaps sixty years together.

III. Every natural man and woman is born full of all sin, (Rom. i. 29,) as full as a toad is of poison, as full as ever his skin can hold ; mind, will, eyes, mouth, every limb of his body, and every piece of his soul, is full of sin ; their hearts are bundles of sin ; hence Solomon saith, " Foolishness is bound up in the heart of a child ;" whole treasures of sin. " An evil man, (said Christ,) out of the evil treasure of his heart, bringeth forth evil things ;" nay, raging seas of sin. The tongue is a world of mischief. What is the heart then ? " For out of the abundance of the heart the tongue speaketh :" so that, look about thee and see, whatever sin is broached, and runs out of any man's heart into his life through the whole world, all those sins are in thine heart ; thy mind is a nest of all the foul opinions, heresies, that ever were vented by any man ; thy heart is a foul sink of all atheism, sodomy, blasphemy, murder, whoredom, adultery, witchcraft, buggery ; so that, if thou hast any good thing in thee, it is but as a drop of rosewater in a bowl of poison ; where fallen it is all corrupted.

It is true thou feelest not all these things stirring in thee at one time, no more than Hazael thought he was or should be such a bloodsucker, when he asked the prophet Elisha if he were a dog ; but they are in thee like a nest of snakes in an old hedge. Although they break not out into thy life, they lie lurking in thy heart ; they are there as a filthy puddle in a barrel, which runs not out, because thou happily wantest the temptation or occasion to broach and tap thine heart ; or because of God's restraining grace by fear, shame, education, and good company, thou art restrained and bridled up, and therefore when one came to comfort that famous picture, pattern, and monument of God's justice by seven years' horror, and grievous distress of conscience, when one told him he never had committed such sins as Manasses, and therefore he was not the greatest sinner since the creation, as he conceived, he replied, that he should have been worse than ever Manasses was, if he had lived in his time, and been on his throne.

Mr. Bradford would never have looked upon any one's lewd life with one eye, but he would presently return within his own breast with the other eye, and say, " In this my vile breast remains that sin, which, without God's special grace, I should have committed as well as he." O, methinks this might pull down men's proud conceits of themselves, especially such as bear up and comfort themselves in their smooth, honest, civil life ; such as through education have been washed from all foul sins ; they were never tainted with whoredom, swearing, drunkenness, or profaneness; and here they think themselves so safe, that God can not find in his heart to have a thought of damning them.

O, consider of this point, which may make thee pull thine hair from thine head, and turn thy clothes to sackcloth, and run up and down with amazement and paleness in thy face, and horror in thy conscience, and tears in thine eyes. What though thy life be smooth, what though thy outside, thy sepulcher, be painted? O, thou art full of rottenness, of sin, within. Guilty, not before men, as the sins of thy life make thee, but before God, of all the sins that swarm and roar in the whole world at this day, for God looks to the heart; guilty thou art therefore of heart whoredom, heart sodomy, heart blasphemy, heart drunkenness, heart buggery, heart oppression, heart idolatry ; and these are the sins that terribly provoke the wrath of Almighty God against thee. (Is. lvii. 17.) " For the iniquity of his covetousness," saith our translation, " I smote him ; " but the Hebrew renders it better — " For the iniquity of his concupiscence " (which is the sin of his heart and nature) " I smote him." As a king is angry and musters up his army against rebels, not only which brings his soldiers out to fight, but who keeps soldiers in their trenches ready for to fight. These sins of thine heart are all ready armed to fight against God at the watchword or alarm of any temptation. Nay, I dare affirm and will prove it, that these sins provoke God to anger, and are as bad, if not worse, than the sins of thy life. For, —

1. The sin of thine heart or nature is the cause, the womb that contains, breeds, brings forth, suckles all the litter, all the

troop of sins that are in thy life; and therefore, giving life and being to all other, it is the greatest sin.

2. Sin is more abundantly in the heart than in the life. An actual sin is but a little breach made by the sea of sin in thine heart, where all sin, all poison, is met and mingled together. Every actual sin is but as a shred broken off from the great bottom of sin in the heart; and hence Christ saith, " Out of the abundance of the heart the mouth speaketh; and out of the evil treasure of the heart we bring forth evil things." A man spending money (I mean sin in the life) is nothing to his treasure of sin in the heart.

3. Sin is continually in the heart. Actual sins of the life fly out like sparks, and vanish; but this brand is always glowing within : the toad spits poison sometimes, but it retains and keeps a poisonful nature always. Hence the apostle calls it " sin that dwells in me," that is, which always lies and remains in me. So that, in regard of the sins of thy heart, thou dost rend in pieces and break, 1. All the laws of God. 2. At one clap. 3. Every moment of thy life. O, methinks the thought of this might rend a heart of rock in pieces; to think I am always grieving God at all times, whatsoever I do.

4. Actual sins are only in the life and outward porch; sins of the heart are within the inward house. One enemy within the city is worse than many without; a traitor on the throne is worse than a traitor in the open field. The heart is Christ's throne. A swine in the best room is worse than in the outward house. More I might say; but thus, you see, sins of the life are not so bad, nor provoke God's wrath so fiercely against thee, as the sins of thine heart. Mourn, therefore, not so much that thou hast not been so bad as others are, but look upon thy black feet — look within thine own heart, and lament that, in regard of thy sins there, thou art as bad as any; mourn not so much merely that thou hast sinned, as that thou hast a nature so sinful, that it is thy nature to be proud, and thy nature to be vain and deceitful, and loathe not only thy sins, but thyself for thy sin, being brimful of unrighteousness. But here is not all. Consider fourthly.

IV. That whatever a natural man doth is sin; as the inside is full, so the outside is nothing else but sin, at least in the sight of a holy God, though not in the sight of blind, sinful men. Indeed, he may do many things, which, for the matter of them, are good; as he may give alms, pray, fast, come to church: but as they come from him they are sin; as a man may speak good words, but we can not endure to hear him speak, because of his stinking breath which defiles them. Some actions indeed, from their general nature, are indifferent, for all *indiffer-ences* lie in *generals*; but every deliberate action, considered *in individuo*, with all its circumstances, as time, place, motive, end, is either morally good or morally evil, as may be proved easily; morally good in good men, morally evil in unregenerate and bad men. For let us see particular actions of wicked men.

1. All their thoughts are only evil, and that continually. (Gen. vi. 5.)

2. All their words are sins, (Ps. l. 16;) their mouths are open sepulchers, which smell filthy when they are opened.

3. All their civil actions are sins, as their eating, drinking, buying, selling, sleeping, and ploughing. (Prov. xxi. 4.)

4. All their religious actions are sins, as coming to church, praying, (Prov. xv. 8, 9; xxviii. 9,) fasting and mourning: roar and cry out of thyself till doomsday, they are sins. (Is. lviii.)

5. All their most zealous actions are sins, as Jehu, who killed all Baal's priests: because his action was outwardly and mate-rially good, therefore God rewarded him with temporal favors; but because he had a hawk's eye to get and settle a kingdom to himself by this means, and so was theologically evil, therefore God threatens to be revenged upon him. (Hosea i. 4.)

6. Their wisdom is sin. O, men are often commended for their wisdom, wit, and parts; yet those wits, and that wisdom of theirs, are sin. (Rom. viii.) The wisdom of the flesh is enmity against God.

Thus all they have or do are sins; for how can he do any good action whose person is filthy? "A corrupt tree can not bring forth good fruit:" thou art out of Christ; therefore all thy good things, all thy kindnesses done unto the Lord, and for the Lord, as thou thinkest, are most odious to him. Let a woman seek to give all the content to her husband that may be, not out of any love to him, but only out of love to another man, he abhors all that she doth. Every wicked man wants an inward principle of love to God and Christ, and therefore, though he seeks to honor God never so much, all that he doth being done out of love to himself, God abhors all that he performs. All the good things a wicked man doth are for himself, either for self-credit or self-ease, or self-content, or self-safety; he sleeps, prays, hears, speaks, professeth for himself alone; hence, acting always for himself, he committeth the highest degree of idolatry; he plucks God out of his throne, and makes himself a god, because he makes himself his last end in every action; for a man puts himself in the room of God as well by making him-self his *finis ultimus*, as if he should make himself *primum principium.* Sin is a forsaking or departing from God. Now, every natural man remaining always in a state of separation from God, because he always wants the bond of union, which is faith, is always sinning; God's curse lies upon him; therefore he brings out nothing but briers and thorns.

Objection. But thou wilt say, If our praying and hearing be sin, why should we do these duties? We must not sin.

Answer 1. Good duties are good in themselves, although, coming from thy vile heart, they are sins.

2. It is less sin to do them than to omit them; therefore, if thou wilt go to hell, go in the fairest path thou canst in thither.

3. Venture and try; it may be God may hear, not for thy prayers' sake, but for his name's sake. The unjust judge helped the poor widow, not because he loved her suit, but for her importunity; and so be sure thou shalt have nothing if thou dost not seek. What though thou art a dog, yet thou art alive, and art for the present under the table. Catch not at Christ, snatch not at his bread, but wait till God give thee him; it may be thou mayest have him one day. O, wonder then at God's patience, that thou livest one day longer, who hast all thy lifetime, like a filthy toad, spit thy venom in the face of God, that he hath never been quit of thee. O, look upon that black bill that will one day be put in against thee at the great day of account, where thou must answer with flames of fire about thine ears, not only for thy drunkenness, thy bloody oaths and whoring, but for all the actions of thy short life, and just so many actions so many sins.

Thou hast painted thy face over now with good duties and good desires; and a little honesty, amongst some men, is of that worth and rarity, that they think God is beholding to them, if he can get any good action from. But when thy painted face shall be brought before the fire of God's wrath, then thy vileness shall appear before men and angels. O, know it, that as thou dost nothing else but sin, so God heaps up wrath against the dreadful day of wrath.

Thus much for man's misery in regard of sin.

Now followeth his misery in regard of the consequents or miseries that follow upon sin. And these are, 1. Presence. 2. Future.

First. Man's present miseries, that already lie on him for sin, are these seven; that is, —

First. God is his dreadful enemy. (Ps. v. 5.)

Question. How may one know another to be his enemy?

Answer 1. By their looks. 2. By their threats. 3. By their blows. So God, —

1. Hides his face from every natural man, and will not look upon him. (Is. lix. 2.)

2. God threatens, nay, curseth every natural man. (Gal. iii. 10.)

3. God gives them heavy, bloody lashes on their souls and bodies.

Never tell me, therefore, that God blesseth thee in thine outward estate; no greater sign of God's wrath than for the Lord to give thee thy swing, as a father never looks after a desperate son, but lets him run where he pleases. And if God be thine enemy, then every creature is so too, both in heaven and earth.

Secondly. God hath forsaken them, and they have lost God. (Eph. ii. 12.) It is said, that, in the grievous famine of Samaria, doves' dung was sold at a large price, because they wanted bread. O, men live and pine away without God, without bread, and therefore the dung of worldly contentments are esteemed so much of, thou hast lost the sight of God, and the favor of God, and the special protection of God, and the government of God. Cain's punishment lies upon thee in thy natural estate; thou art a runagate from the face of God, and from his face thou art hid. Many have grown mad to see their houses burnt, and all their goods lost. O, but God, the greatest good, is lost. This loss made Saul cry out in distress of conscience, (1 Sam. xxviii. 15,) The Philistines make war against me, and God is departed from me; the loss of the sweetness of whose presence, for a little while only, made the Lord Jesus Christ cry out, My God, my God, why hast thou forsaken me? whereas thou hast lost God all thy lifetime. O, thou hast a heart of brass, that canst not mourn for his absence so long. The damned in hell have lost God, and know it, and so the plague of desperate horror lieth upon them; thou hast lost God here, but knowest it not, and the plague of a hard heart lieth upon thee, thou that canst not mourn for this loss.

Thirdly. They are condemned men, condemned in the court of God's justice, by the law which cries, Treason, treason against the most high God, and condemned in the court of mercy, by the gospel, which cries, Murder, murder against the Son of God, (John iii. 18;) so that every natural man is damned in heaven, and damned on earth. God is thy all-seeing, terrible Judge; conscience is thine accuser, a heavy witness; this world is thy jail; thy lusts are thy fetters. In this Bible is pronounced and writ thy doom, thy sentence. Death is thy hangman, and that fire that shall never go out thy torment. The Lord hath in his infinite patience reprieved thee for a time; O, take heed and get a pardon before the day of execution come.

Fourthly. Being condemned, take him, jailer; he is a bondslave to Satan, (Eph. ii. 3;) for, His servants ye are whom ye obey, saith Christ. Now, every natural man doth the devil's drudgery, and carries the devil's pack; and howsoever he saith he defieth the devil, yet he sins, and so doth his work. Satan hath overcome and conquered all men in Adam, and therefore they are under his bondage and dominion. And though he can not compel a man to sin against his will, yet he hath power, —

First. To present and allure man's heart by a sinful temptation.

Secondly. To follow him with it, if at first he be something shy of it.

Thirdly. To disquiet and rack him, if he will not yield, as might be made to appear in many instances.

Fourthly. Besides, he knows men's humors, as poor wandering, beggarly gentlemen do their friends in necessity, (yet in seeming courtesy,) he visits and applies himself unto them, and so gains them as his own. O, he is in a fearful slavery who is under Satan's dominion, who is, —

1. A secret enemy to thee.

2. A deceitful enemy to thee, that will make a man believe (as he did Evah, even in her integrity) that he is in a fair way, when his condition is miserable.

3. He is a cruel enemy or lord over them that be his slaves, (2 Cor. iv. 3;) he gags them so that they can not speak, (as that man that had a dumb devil,) neither for God, nor to God, in prayer; he starves them, so as no sermon shall ever do them good; he robs them of all they get in God's ordinances, within three hours after the market, the sermon is ended.

4. He is a strong enemy. (Luke xi. 21.) So that if all the devils in hell are able to keep men from coming out of their sins, he will: so strong an enemy, that he keeps men from so much as sighing or groaning under their burdens and bondage. (Luke xi. 21.) When the strong man keeps the palace, his goods are in peace.

Fifthly. He is cast into utter darkness; as cruel jailers put their prisoners into the worst dungeons, so Satan doth natural men, (2 Cor. iv. 3, 4;) they see no God, no Christ; they see not the happiness of the saints in light; they see not those dreadful torments that should now in this day of grace awaken them and humble them. O, those by-paths which thousands wander from God in, they have no lamp to their feet to show them where they err. Thou that art in thy natural estate, art born blind, and the devil hath blinded thine eyes more by sin, and God in justice had blinded them worse for sin, so that thou art in a corner of hell, because thou art in utter darkness, where thou hast not a glimpse of any saving truth.

Sixthly. They are bound hand and foot in this estate, and can not come out, (Rom. v. 6; 1 Cor. ii. 14;) for all kind of sins, like chains, have bound every part and faculty of man, so that he is sure for stirring; and those are very strong in him, they being as dear as his members, nay, as his life, (Col. iii. 7;) so that when a man begins to forsake his vile courses, and purposeth to become a new man, devils fetch him back, world enticeth him, and locketh him up; and flesh saith, O, it is too strict a course; farewell, then, merry days and good fellowship. O, thou mayest wish and desire to come out some time, but canst not put strength to thy desire, nor endure to do it. Thou mayest hang down thy head like a bulrush for sin, but thou canst not repent of sin; thou mayest presume, but thou canst not believe; thou mayest come half way, and forsake some sins, but not all sins; thou mayest come and knock at heaven's gate, as the foolish virgins did, but not enter in and pass through the gate; thou mayest see the land of Canaan, and take much pain to go into Canaan, and mayest taste of the bunches of grapes of that good land, but never enter into Canaan, into heaven, but thou lie bound, hand and foot, in this woful estate, and here thou must lie and rot like a dead carcass in his grave, until the Lord come and roll away the stone, and bid thee come out and live.

Lastly. They are ready every moment to drop into hell. God is a consuming fire against thee, and there is but one paper wall of thy body between thy soul and eternal flames. How soon may God stop thy breath! There is nothing but that between thee and hell; if that were gone, then 'farewell all. Thou art condemned, and the muffler is before thine eyes. God knows how soon the ladder may be turned; thou hangest but by one rotten twined thread of thy life, over the flames of hell every hour.

Thus much of man's present miseries.

Now followeth his future miseries, which are to come upon him hereafter.

I. They must die either by a sudden, sullen, or desperate death, (Ps. lxxxix. 48,) which though it is to a child of God a sweet sleep, yet to the wicked it is a fearful curse proceeding from God's wrath, whence, like a lion, he tears body and soul asunder; death cometh hissing upon him like a fiery dragon with the sting of vengeance in the mouth of it; it puts a period to all their worldly contentments, which then they must forsake, and carry nothing away with them but a rotten winding sheet. It is the beginning of all their woe; it is the captain that first strikes the stroke, and then armies of endless woes follow after. (Rev. vi. 2.) O, thou hadst better be a toad, or a dog, than a man, for there's an end of their troubles when they are dead and gone; they fall not as men from a steep hill, not knowing where they shall fall: now repentance is too late, especially if thou hadst lived under means before; it is either cold repentance, when the body is weak, and the heart is sick, or a hypocritical repentance, only for fear of hell; and therefore thou sayest, "Lord Jesus, receive my soul." Nay, commonly then, men's hearts are most hard, and therefore men die like lambs, and cry not out; then it is hard plucking thy soul from the devil's hands, to whom thou hast given it all thy life by sin; and if thou dost get it back, dost thou think that God will take the devil's leavings? Now thy day is past, and darkness begins to overspread thy soul; now flocks of devils come into thy chamber, waiting for thy soul, to fly upon it as a mastiff dog when the door is opened. And this is the reason why most men die quietly that lived wickedly, because Satan then hath them as his own prey; like pirates, who let a ship pass that is empty of goods, they shoot commonly at them that are richly loaden. The Christians, in some parts of the primitive church, took the sacrament every day, because they did look to die every day. But these times wherein we live are so poisoned and glutted with their ease, that it is a rare thing to see the man that looks death steadfastly in the face one hour together: but death will lay a bitter stroke on these one day.

II. After death they appear before the Lord to judgment, (Heb. ix. 27;) their bodies indeed rot in their graves, but their souls return before the Lord to judgment. (Eccles. xii. 7.) The general judgment is at the end of the world, when both body and soul appear before God, and all the world to an account. But there is a particular judgment that every man meets with after this life, immediately at the end of his life, where the soul is condemned only before the Lord.

You may perceive what this particular judgment is, thus, by these four conclusions: —

1. That every man should die the first day he was born, is clear; for "the wages of sin is death;" in justice, therefore, it should be paid of a sinful creature as soon as he is born.

2. That it should be thus with wicked men, but that Christ begs their lives for a season. (1 Tim. iv.) He is the Saviour of all men; that is, not a Saviour of eternal preservation out of hell, but a Saviour of temporal reservation from dropping into hell.

3. That this space of time, thus begged by Christ, is that season wherein only a man can make his peace with a displeased God. (2 Cor. vi. 2.)

4. That if men do not thus within this cut of time, when death hath despatched them, judgment only remains for them; that is, then their doom is read, their date of repentance is out, then their sentence of everlasting death is passed upon them, that never can be recalled again. And this is judgment after death. "He that judgeth himself," saith the apostle, (1 Cor. xi. 31,) "shall not be judged of the Lord." Now, wicked men will not judge and condemn themselves in this life; therefore, at the end of it, God will judge them. All natural men are lost in this life, but they may be found and recovered again; but a man's loss by death is irrecoverable, because there is no means after death to restore them, there is no friend to persuade, no minister to preach, by which faith is wrought, and men get into Christ; there is no power of returning or repenting then; for night is come, and the day is past.

Again: the punishment is so heavy that they can only bear wrath, so that all their thoughts and affections are taken up with the burden. And, therefore, Dives cries out, "I am tormented." O that the consideration of this point might awaken every secure sinner! What will become of thine immortal soul when thou art dead? Thou sayest, I know not; I hope well. I tell thee, therefore, that which may send thee mourning to thy house, and quaking to thy grave, if thou diest in this estate, thou shalt not die like a dog, nor yet like a toad; but after death comes judgment; then farewell friends when dying; and farewell God forever, when thou art dead.

Now, the Lord open your eyes to see the terrors of this particular judgment; which if you could see, (unless you were mad,) it would make you spend whole nights and days in seeking to set all even with God.

I will show you briefly the manner and nature of it in these particulars.

1. Thy soul shall be dragged out of thy body, as out of a foul prison, by the devil, the jailer, into some place within the bowels of the third heavens, and there thou shalt stand stripped of all friends, all comfort, all creatures before the presence of God, (Luke ix. 27;) as at the assizes, first the jailer brings the prisoners out.

2. Then thy soul shall have a new light put into it, whereby it shall see the glorious presence of God, as prisoners brought with guilty eyes look with terror upon the judge. Now thou

seest no God abroad in the world, but then thou shalt see the Almighty Jehovah, which sight shall strike thee with that hellish terror and dreadful horror, that thou shalt call to the mountains to cover thee — "O rocks, rocks, hide me from the face of the Lamb." (Rev. vi. ult.)

3. Then all the sins that ever thou hast or shalt commit shall come fresh to thy mind; as when the prisoner is come before the face of the judge, then his accusers bring in their evidence; thy sleepy conscience then will be instead of a thousand witnesses, and every sin then, with all the circumstances of it, shall be set in order, armed with God's wrath round about thee. (Ps. l. 21.) As letters writ with juice of oranges can not be read until it be brought unto the fire, and then they appear, so thou can not read that bloody bill of indictment thy conscience hath against thee now; but when thou shalt stand near unto God, a consuming fire, then what a heavy reckoning will appear! It may be thou hast left many sins now, and goest so far, and profitest so much, that no Christian can discern thee; nay, thou thinkest thyself in a safe estate; but yet there is one leak in thy ship that will sink thee; there is one secret, hidden sin in thine heart, which thou livest in, as all unsound people do, that will damn thee. I tell thee, as soon as ever thou art dead and gone, then thou shalt see where the knot did bind thee, where thy sin was that now hath spoiled thee forever, and then thou shalt grow mad to think — O that I never saw this sin I loved, lived in, plotted, perfected mine own eternal ruin by, until now, when it is too late to amend!

4. Then the Lord shall take his everlasting farewell of thee, and make thee know it too. Now God is departed from thee in this life, but he may return in mercy to thee again; but when the Lord departs with all his patience, to wait for thee no more, nor shall Christ be offered thee any more, no Spirit to strive with thee any more, and so shall pass sentence, though haply not vocally, yet effectually upon thy soul, the Lord saying, "Depart, thou cursed," thou shalt see indeed the glory of God that others find, but to thy greater sorrow shalt never taste the same. (Luke xiii. 28.)

5. Then shall God surrender up thy forsaken soul into the hands of devils, who, being thy jailers, must keep thee till the great day of account; so that as thy friends are scrambling for thy goods, and worms for thy body, so devils shall scramble for thy soul. For as soon as ever a wicked man is dead, he is either in heaven or in hell. Not in heaven, for no unclean thing comes there. If in hell, then amongst devils there shall be thine eternal lodging, (1 Pet. iii. 19;) and hence thy forlorn soul shall

lie mourning for the time past, *now* it is too late to recall again; groaning under the intolerable torments of the wrath of God present, and amazed at the eternity of misery and sorrow that is to come; waiting for that fearful hour when the last trump shall blow, and then body and soul meet to bear that wrath, that fire that shall never go out. O, therefore, suspect and fear the worst of thyself now; thou hast seldom or never, or very little, troubled thy head about this matter, whether Christ will save thee or not, thou hast such strong hopes and confidence already that he will. Know that it is possible thou mayest be deceived; and if so, when thou shalt know thy doom after death, thou canst not get an hour more to make thy peace with God, although thou shouldest weep tears of blood. If either the muffler of ignorance shall be before thine eyes, — like a handkerchief about the face of one condemned, — or if thou art pinioned with any lust, or if thou makest thine own pardon, proclaimest (because thou art sorry a little for thy sins, and resolvest never to do the like again) peace to thy soul, thou art one that after death shalt appear before the Lord to judgment. Thou that art thus condemned now, dying so, shalt come to thy fearful judgment after death.

There shall be a general judgment of soul and body at the end of the world, wherein they shall be arraigned and condemned before the great tribunal seat of Jesus Christ. (Jude 14, 15. 2 Cor. v. 10.) The hearing of judgment to come made Felix to tremble; nothing of more efficacy to awaken a secure sinner than sad thoughts of this fiery day.

But thou wilt ask me how it may be proved that there will be such a day.

I answer, God's justice calls for it. This world is the stage where God's patience and bounty act their parts, and hence every man will profess and conceive, because he feels it, that God is merciful. But God's justice is questioned; men think God to be all mercy, and no justice; all honey, and no sting. Now, the wicked prosper in all their ways, are never punished, but live and die in peace; whereas the godly are daily afflicted and reviled. Therefore, because this attribute suffers a total eclipse almost, now, there must come a day wherein it must shine out before all the world in the glory of it. (Rom. ii. 5.)

The second reason is from the glory of Christ. He was accused, arraigned, condemned by men; therefore he shall be the Judge of them. (John v. 27.) For this is an ordinary piece God's providence towards his people; the same evil he casts them into now, he exalts them into the contrary good in his time. As the Lord hath a purpose to make Joseph ruler over all

Egypt, but first he maketh him a slave, God had a meaning to make Christ Judge of men, therefore first he suffers him to be judged of men.

Quest. But when shall this judgment day be?

Ans. Though we can not tell the day and hour particularly, yet this we are sure of, that when all the elect are called, for whose sake the world stands, (Is. i. 9,) when these pillars are taken away, then woe to the world; as when Lot was taken out of Sodom, then Sodom was burnt. Now, it is not probable that this time will come as yet; for first Antichrist must be consumed, and not only the scattered visible Jews, but the whole body of the Israelites, must first be called, and have a glorious church upon earth. (Ezek. xxxvii.) This glorious church Scripture and reason will enforce, which when it is called shall not be expired as soon as it is born, but shall continue many a year.

Quest. But how shall this judgment be?

Ans. The apostle describes it. (1 Thess. iv. 16, 17.)

1. Christ shall break out of the third heaven, and be seen in the air, before any dead arise; and this shall be with an admirable shout, as when a king cometh to triumph among his subjects, and over his enemies.

2. Then shall the voice of the archangel be heard. Now, this archangel is Jesus Christ himself, as the Scripture expounds, being in the clouds of heaven; he shall, with an audible, heaven-shaking shout, say, "Rise, you dead, and come to judgment!" even as he called to Lazarus, "Lazarus, arise!"

3. Then the trump shall blow; and even as at the giving of the law (Ex. xix.) it is said the trumpet sounded, much more louder shall it now sound, when he comes to judge men that have broken the law.

4. Then shall the dead arise. The bodies of them that have died in the Lord shall rise first; then the others that live shall (like Enoch) be translated and changed. (1 Cor. xv.)

5. When thus the judge and justices are upon their bench at Christ's right hand, on their thrones, then shall the guilty prisoners be brought forth, and come out of their graves, like filthy toads, against this terrible storm. Then shall all the wicked, that ever were or ever shall be, stand quaking before this glorious Judge, with the same bodies, feet, hands, to receive their doom.

O, consider of this day, thou that livest in thy sins now, and yet art safe; there is a day coming wherein thou mayest and shalt be judged.

1. Consider *who* shall be thy Judge. Why, mercy, pity, goodness itself, even Jesus Christ, that many times held out his

bowels of compassion toward thee. A child of God may say, Yonder is my brother, friend, husband; but thou mayest say, Yonder is mine enemy. He may say at that day, Yonder is he that shed his blood to save me; thou mayest say, Yonder he comes whose heart I have pierced with my sins, whose blood I have despised. They may say, " O, come, Lord Jesus, and cover me under thy wings." But thou shalt then cry out, " O rocks, fall upon me, and hide me from the face of the Lamb."

2. Consider the manner of his coming. (2 Thess. i. 7.) He shall come in flaming fire — the heavens shall be on a flame — the elements shall melt like scalding lead upon thee. When a house is on fire at midnight in a town, what a fearful cry is there made! When all the world shall cry, Fire! fire! and run up and down for shelter to hide themselves, but can not find it, but say, O, now the gloomy day of blood and fire is come; here's for my pride, here's for my oaths, and the wages for my drunkenness, security, and neglect of duties.

3. In regard of the heavy accusations that shall come against thee at that day. There is never a wicked man almost in the world, as fair a face as he carries, but he hath, at some time or other, committed some such secret villainy, that he would be ready to hang himself for shame if others did know of it; as secret whoredom, self-pollution, speculative wantonness, men with men, women with women, as the apostle speaks. (Rom. i.) At this day all the world shall see and hear these privy pranks, then the books shall be opened. Men will not take up a foul business, nor end it in private; therefore there shall be a day of public hearing; things shall not be suddenly shuffled up, as carnal thoughts imagine, viz., that at this day, first Christ shall raise the dead, and then the separation shall be made, and then the sentence passed, and then suddenly the judgment day is done. No, no; it must take up some large quantity of time, that all the world may see the secret sins of wicked men in the world; and therefore it may be made evident from all Scripture and reason, that this day of Christ's kingly office in judging the world will last happily longer than his private administration now (wherein he is less glorious) in governing the world. Tremble, thou time server; tremble, thou hypocrite; tremble, thou that livest in any secret sin under the all-seeing eye of this Judge; thine own conscience indeed shall be a sufficient witness against thee, to discover all thy sins at thy particular judgment; but all the world shall openly see thine hidden, close courses of darkness, to thine everlasting shame at this day.

4. In regard of the fearful sentence that then shall be passed

4 *

upon thee : "Depart, thou cursed creature, into everlasting fire, prepared for the devil and his angels." Thou shalt then cry out, "O, mercy, Lord! O, a little mercy!" "No," will the Lord Jesus say, "I did indeed once offer it you, but you refused; therefore depart." Then thou shalt plead again, "Lord, if I must depart, yet bless me before I go." "No, no; depart, thou cursed." "O, but, Lord, if I must depart cursed, let me go into some good place." "No; depart, thou cursed, into hell fire." "O Lord, that's a torment I can not bear; but if it must be so, Lord, let me come out again quickly." "No; depart, thou cursed, into everlasting fire." "O Lord, if this be thy pleasure, that here I must abide, let me have good company with me." "No; depart, thou cursed, into everlasting fire, prepared for the devil and his angels." This shall be thy sentence; the hearing of which may make the rocks to rent; so that, go on in thy sin and prosper, despise and scoff at God's ministers and prosper, abhor the power and practice of religion, as a too precise course, and prosper; yet know it, there will a day come when thou shalt meet with a dreadful Judge, a doleful sentence. Now is thy day of sinning; but God will have shortly his day of condemning.

5. When the judgment day is done, then the fearful wrath of God shall be poured out, and piled upon their bodies and souls, and the breath of the Lord, like a stream of brimstone, shall kindle it, and here thou shalt lie burning, and none shall ever quench it. This is the execution of a sinner after judgment. (Rev. xxi. 8.)

Now, this wrath of God consists in these things : —

1. Thy soul shall be banished from the face and blessed sweet presence of God and Christ, and thou shalt never see the face of God more. It is said (Acts xx.) that "they wept sore, because they should see Paul's face no more." O, thou shalt never see the face of God, Christ, saints, and angels more. O, heavy doom, to famish and pine away forever without one bit of bread to comfort thee, one smile of God to refresh thee! Men that have their sores running upon them must be shut up from the presence of men sound and whole. O, thy sins, like plague sores, run on thee; therefore thou must be shut out like a dog from the presence of God and all his people. (2 Thess. i. 9.)

2. God shall set himself like a consuming infinite fire against thee, and tread thee under his feet, who hast by sin trod him and his glory under foot all thy life. A man may devise exquisite torments for another, and great power may make a little stick to lay on heavy strokes; but great power stirred up to strike from great fury and wrath makes the stroke deadly. I tell thee, all

the wisdom of God shall then be set against thee to devise torments for thee. (Micah ii. 4.) There was never such wrath felt or conceived as the Lord hath devised against thee that livest and diest in thy natural estate; hence it is called "wrath to come." (1 Thess. i. ult.) The torment which wisdom shall devise the almighty power of God shall inflict upon thee, so as there was never such power seen in making the world as in holding a poor creature under this wrath, that holds up the soul in being with one hand, and beats it with the other, ever burning like fire against a creature, and yet that creature never burnt up. (Rom. ix. 22.) Think not this cruelty; it is justice. What cares God for a vile wretch, whom nothing can make good while it lives? If we have been long in hewing a block, and we can make no meet vessel of it, put it to no good use for ourselves, we cast it into the fire. God heweth thee by sermons, sickness, losses, and crosses, sudden death, mercies, and miseries; yet nothing makes thee better. What should God do with thee but cast thee hence? O, consider of this wrath before you feel it. I had rather have all the world burning about my ears than to have one blasting frown from the blessed face of an infinite and dreadful God. Thou canst not endure the torments of a little kitchen fire on the tip of thy finger, not one half hour together. How wilt thou bear the fury of this infinite, endless, consuming fire in body and soul throughout all eternity?

3. The never-dying worm of a guilty conscience shall torment thee, as if thou hadst swallowed down a living poisonful snake, which shall lie gnawing and biting thine heart for sin past, day and night. And this worm shall torment by showing the cause of thy misery; that is, that thou didst never care for Him that would have saved thee; by showing thee also thy sins against the law, by showing thee thy sloth, whereby thy happiness is lost. Then shall thy conscience gnaw to think, So many nights I went to bed without prayer, and so many days and hours I spent in feasting and foolish sporting. O, if I had spent half that time, now misspent, in praying, in mourning, in meditation, yonder in heaven had I been. By showing thee also the means that thou once hadst to avoid this misery. Such a minister I heard once, that told me of my particular sins, as if he had been told of me; such a friend persuaded me once to turn over a new leaf; I remember so many knocks God gave at this iron heart of mine, so many mercies the Lord sent; but, O, no means could prevail with me. Lastly, by showing thee how easily thou mightest have avoided all these miseries. O, once I was almost persuaded to be a Christian; but I suffered my

heart to grow dead, and fell to loose company, and so lost all. The Lord Jesus came unto my door and knocked ; and, if I had done that for Christ which I did for the devil many a time to open at his knocks, I had been saved. A thousand such bites will this worm give at thine heart, which shall make thee cry out, O, time, time ! O, sermons, sermons ! O, my hopes and my helps are now lost that once I had to save my lost soul !

4. Thou shalt take up thy lodging forever with devils, and they shall be thy companions. Him thou hast served here, with him must thou dwell there. It scares men out of their wits almost to see the devil, as they think, when they be alone ; but what horror shall fill thy soul when thou shalt be banished from angels' society, and come into the fellowship of devils forever !

5. Thou shalt be filled with final despair. If a man be grievously sick, it comforts him to think it will not last long. But if the physician tell him he must live all his lifetime in this extremity, he thinks the poorest beggar in a better estate than himself. O, to think, when thou hast been millions of years in thy sorrows, then thou art no nearer thy end of bearing thy misery than at the first coming in ! O, I might once have had mercy and Christ, but no hope now ever to have one glimpse of his face, or one good look from him any more.

6. Thou shalt vomit out blasphemous oaths and curses in the face of God the Father forever, and curse God that never elected thee, and curse the Lord Jesus that never shed one drop of blood to redeem thee, and curse God the Holy Ghost that passed by thee and never called thee. (Rev. xvi. 9.) And here thou shalt lie, and weep, and gnash thy teeth in spite against God and thyself, and roar, and stamp, and grow mad, that there thou must lie under the curse of God forever. Thus, I say, thou shalt lie blaspheming, with God's wrath like a pile of fire on thy soul burning, and floods, nay, seas, nay, more, seas of tears, (for thou shalt forever lie weeping,) shall never quench it. And here, which way soever thou lookest, thou shalt see matter of everlasting grief. Look up to heaven, and there thou shalt see (O !) that God is forever gone. Look about thee, thou shalt see devils quaking, cursing God, and thousands, nay, millions, of sinful, damned creatures crying and roaring out with doleful shriekings, O, the day that ever I was born ! Look within thee ; there is a guilty conscience gnawing. Look to time past ; O, those golden days of grace and sweet seasons of mercy are quite lost and gone ! Look to time to come ; there thou shalt behold evils, troops and swarms of sorrows, and woes, and raging waves, and billows of wrath come roaring upon thee.

Look to time present; O, not one hour or moment of ease or refreshing, but all curses meet together, and feeding upon one poor lost immortal soul that never can be recovered again! No God, no Christ, no Spirit to comfort thee, no minister to preach unto thee, no friend to wipe away thy continual tears, no sun to shine upon thee, not a bit of bread, not one drop of water to cool thy tongue.

This is the misery of every natural man. Now, do not thou shift it from thyself, and say, God is merciful. True, but it is to very few, as shall be proved. It is a thousand to one if ever thou be one of that small number whom God hath picked out to escape this wrath to come. If thou dost not get the Lord Jesus to bear this wrath, farewell God, Christ, and God's mercy forever. If Christ had shed seas of blood, set thine heart at rest; there is not one drop of it for thee, until thou comest to see, and feel, and groan under this miserable estate. I tell thee, Christ is so far from saving thee, that he is thine enemy. If Christ were here, and should say, Here is my blood for thee, if thou wilt but lie down and mourn under the burden of thy misery, and yet for all his speeches, thy dry eyes weep not, thy stout heart yields not, thy hard heart mourns not, as to say, O, I am a sinful, lost, condemned, cursed, dead creature; what shall I do? dost not think but he would turn away his face from thee, and say, O, thou stony, hard-hearted creature, wouldest thou have me save thee from thy misery, and yet thou wilt not groan, sigh, and mourn for deliverance to me, out of thy misery? If thou likest thine estate so well, and prizest me so little, perish in thy misery forever.

O, labor to be humbled day and night under this thy woful estate. Thou art guilty of Adam's grievous sin: will this break thine heart? No. Thou art dead in sin, and top-full of all sin: will this break thine heart? No. Whatsoever thou doest, hast done, shalt do, remaining in this estate, is sin: will this break thine heart? No. God is thine enemy, and thou hast lost him: will this break thine heart? No. Thou art condemned to die eternally; Satan is thy jailer; thou art bound hand and foot in the bolts of thy sins, and cast into utter darkness, and ready every moment to drop into hell: will this break thine heart? No. Thou must die, and after that appear before the Lord to judgment, and then bear God's everlasting, insupportable wrath, which rends the rocks, and burns down to the bottom of hell. Will this break thine hard heart, man? No. Then farewell Christ forever; never look to see a Christ, until thou dost come to feel thy misery out of Christ. Labor therefore for this, and the Lord will reveal the brazen serpent, when thou art in thine own sense and feeling, stung to death with the fiery serpents.

So I come to open the fourth principal point.

CHAPTER IV.

THAT THE LORD JESUS CHRIST IS THE ONLY MEANS OF REDEMPTION AND DELIVERANCE OUT OF THIS ESTATE.

"In whom we have redemption through his blood," (Eph. i. 7,) which plainly demonstrates that

"Jesus Christ is the only means of man's redemption and deliverance out of his bondage and miserable estate."

And this is the doctrine I shall now insist upon.

When the Israelites were in bondage and misery, he sends Moses to deliver them. When they were in Babylon, he stirred up Cyrus to open the prison gates to them; but when all mankind is under spiritual misery, he sends the Lord Jesus, God and man, to redeem him. (Acts iv. 12.)

Question. How doth Christ redeem men out of this misery?

Answer. By paying a price for them. (1 Cor. vi. ult.) God's mercy will be manifested in saving some, and his justice must be satisfied by having satisfaction or price made and paid for man's sin. Hence Christ satisfieth God's justice, —

First. By standing in the room of all them whom mercy decreeth to save. A surety standeth in the room of a debtor. (Heb. vii. 22.) As the first Adam stood in the room of all mankind fallen, so Christ standeth in the room of all men rising, or to be restored again.

Secondly. By taking from them in whose room he stood the eternal guilt of all their sins, and by assuming the guilt of all those sins unto himself. (2 Cor. v. 22.) Hence Luther said Christ was the greatest sinner by imputation.

Thirdly. By bearing the curse and wrath of God kindled against sin. God is holy, and when he seeth sin sticking only by imputation to his own Son, he will not spare him, but his wrath and curse must he bear. (Gal. iii. 13.) Christ drinks up the cup of all the elect at one draught, which they should have been sipping and drinking, and tormented with, millions of years.

Fourthly. By bringing into the presence of God perfect righteousness, (Rom. v. 21;) for this also God's justice required perfection, conformity to the law, as well as (perfect satisfaction) suffering for the wrong offered to the Lawgiver. Justice thus requiring these four things, Christ satisfies justice by performing them, and so pays the price.

1. Christ is a Redeemer by strong hand. The first redemption by price is finished in Christ's person, at his resurrection; the second is begun by the Spirit in man's vocation, and ended at the day of judgment; as money is first paid for a captive in Turkey, and then because he can not come to his own prince himself, he is fetched away by strong hand.

Here is encouragement to the vilest sinner, and comfort to the self-succorless and lost sinner, who have spent all their money, their time, and endeavors upon those duties and strivings that have been but poor physicians to them. O, look up here to the Lord Jesus, who can do that cure for thee in a moment which all creatures can not do in many years. What bolts, what strong fetters, what unruly lusts, temptations, and miseries art thou locked into? Behold, the Deliverer is come out of Sion, having satisfied justice, and paid a price to ransom poor captives, (Luke iv. 18 ;) with the keys of heaven, hell, and thy unruly heart in his hand, to fetch thee out with great mercy and strong hand. Who knows but thou poor prisoner of hell, thou poor captive of the devil, thou poor shackled sinner, mayest be one whom he is come for? O, look up to him, sigh to heaven for deliverance from him, and be glad and rejoice at his coming!

This strikes terror to them, that though there is a means of deliverance, yet they lie in their misery, never groan, never sigh to the Lord Jesus for deliverance; nay, that rejoice in their bondage, and dance to hell in their bolts ; nay, that are weary of deliverance; that sit in the stocks when they are at prayers ; that come out of the church, when the tedious sermon runs somewhat beyond the hour, like prisoners out of a jail, that despise the Lord Jesus, when he offers to open the doors, and so let them out of that miserable estate. O, poor creatures! is there a means of deliverance, and dost thou neglect, nay, despise it? Know it, that this will cut thine heart one day, when thou art hanging in thy gibbets in hell, to see others standing at God's right hand, redeemed by Christ: thou mightest have had share in their honor; for there was a Deliverer come to save thee, but thou wouldest have none of him. O, thou wilt lie yelling in those everlasting burnings, and tear thy hair, and curse thyself: From hence might I have been delivered, but I would not. Hath Christ delivered thee from hell, and hath he not delivered thee from thine alehouse? Hath Christ delivered thee from Satan's society, when he hath not delivered thee from thy loose company yet? Hath Christ delivered thee from burning, when thy fagots, thy sins, grow in thee? Is Christ's blood thine, that makest no more account of it, nor feelest no more virtue from it, than in the blood of a chicken? Art thou redeemed? Dost thou hope by Christ to be saved, that didst never see, nor feel, nor sigh under thy bondage? O, the devils will keep holiday (as it were) in hell, in respect of thee, who shalt mourn under God's wrath, and lament. O, there was a means to deliver us out of it, but thou shalt mourn forever for thy misery. And this will be a bodkin at thine heart one day, to think there was a Deliverer, but I, wretch, would none of him. Here, likewise, is matter of reproof to such as seek to come out of this misery from and by themselves. If they be ignorant, they hope to be saved by their good meaning and prayers. If civil, by paying all they owe, and doing as they would be done by, and by doing nobody any harm. If they be troubled about their estates, then they lick themselves whole by their mourning, repenting, and reforming. O, poor stubble, canst thou stand before this consuming fire without sin? Canst thou make thyself a Christ for thyself? Canst thou bear and come from under an infinite wrath? Canst thou bring in perfect righteousness into the presence of God? This Christ must do, else he could not satisfy and redeem. And if thou canst not do thus, and hast no Christ, desire and pray that heaven and earth shake till thou hast worn thy tongue to the stumps; endeavor as much as thou canst, and others commend thee for a diligent Christian; mourn in some wilderness till doomsday; dig thy grave there with thy nails; weep buckets full of hourly tears, till thou canst weep no more; fast and pray till thy skin and bones cleave together; promise and purpose with full resolution to be better; nay, reform thy head, heart, life, and tongue, and some, nay, all sins; live like an angel; shine like a sun; walk up and down the world like a distressed pilgrim going to another country, so that all Christians commend and admire thee; die ten thousand deaths; lie at the fireback in hell so many millions of years as there be piles of grass on the earth, or sands upon the sea shore, or stars in heaven, or motes in the sun; I tell thee, not one spark of God's wrath against thy sin shall be, can be, quenched by all these duties, nor by any of these sorrows, or tears; for these are not the blood of Christ. Nay, if all the angels and saints in heaven and earth should pray for thee, these can not deliver thee, for they are not the blood of Christ. Nay, God, as a Creator, having made a law, will not forgive one sin without the blood of Christ; nay, Christ's blood will not do it neither, if thou dost join never so little that thou hast or dost unto Jesus Christ, and makest thyself or any of thy duties copartners with Christ in that great work of saving thee. Cry out, therefore, as that blessed martyr did, None but Christ, none but Christ.

Take heed of neglecting or rejecting so great salvation by Jesus Christ. Take heed of spilling this potion, that only can cure thee.

But thou wilt say, This means of redemption is only appointed for some: it is not intended for all, therefore not for me; therefore how can I reject Christ?

It is true, Christ spent not his breath to pray for all; (John xvii. 9,) "I pray for them; I pray not for the world, but for them which thou hast given me, for they are thine;" much less his blood for all; therefore he was never intended as a Redeemer of all; but that he is not intended as a Deliverer of thee, how doth this follow? How dost thou know this?

But secondly, I say, though Christ be not intended for all, yet he is offered unto all, and therefore unto thee; and the ground is this chiefly:—

The universal offer of Christ ariseth not from Christ's priestly office immediately, but from his kingly office, whereby the Father having given him all power and dominion in heaven and earth, he hereupon commands all men to stoop unto him, and likewise bids all his disciples, and all their successors, to go and preach the gospel to every creature under heaven. (Matt. xxviii. 18, 19.) For Christ doth not immediately offer himself to all men as a Saviour, whereby they may be encouraged to serve him as a king; but first as a king commanding them to cast away their weapons, and stoop unto his scepter, and depend upon his free mercy, acknowledging, if ever he save me, I will bless him; if he damn me, his name is righteous in so dealing with me.

But that I may fasten this exhortation, I will show these four things:—

I. The Lord Jesus is offered to every particular person; which I shall show thus: What hast thou to say against it, that thou dost doubt of it? It may be thou wilt plead, —

O, I am so ignorant of myself, God, Christ, or his will, that surely the Lord offers no Christ to me.

Yes, but he doth, though thou liest in utter darkness. Our blessed Saviour glorified his Father for revealing the mystery of the gospel to simple men, neglecting those that carried the chief reputation of wisdom in the world. The parts of none are so low as that they are beneath the gracious regard of Christ. God bestoweth the best fruits of his love upon mean and weak persons here, that he might confound the pride of flesh the more. Where it pleaseth him to make his choice, and to exalt his mercy, he passeth by no degree of wit, though never so uncapable.

But thou wilt say, I am an enemy to God, and have a heart

so stubborn and loth to yield, I have vexed him to the very heart by my transgressions.

Yet he beseecheth thee to be reconciled. Put case, thou hast been a sinner, and rebellious against God ; yet so long as thou art not found amongst malicious opposers, and underminers of his truth, never give way to despairing thoughts; thou hast a merciful Saviour.

But I have despised the means of reconciliation, and rejected mercy.

Yet God calls thee to return: "thou hast played the harlot with many lovers ; yet turn again to me, saith the Lord." (Jer. iii. 1.) Cast thyself into the arms of Christ, and if thou perish, perish there ; if thou dost not, thou art sure to perish. If mercy be to be had any where, it is by seeking to Christ, not by turning from him. Herein appears Christ's love to thee, that he hath given thee a heart in some degree sensible ; he might have given thee up to hardness, security, and profaneness — of all spiritual judg-ments the greatest. But he that died for his enemies will in no wise refuse those the desire of whose soul is toward him. When the prodigal set himself to return to his father, his father stays not for him, but meets him in the way. If our sins dis-please us, they shall never hurt us; but we shall be esteemed of God to be that which we desire and labor to be. (Ps. cxlv. 19.)

But can the Lord offer Christ to me, so poor, that have no strength, no faith, no grace, nor sense of my poverty ?

Yes, even to thee; why should we except ourselves, when Christ doth not except us ? " Come unto me, all ye that are weary and heavy laden." We are therefore poor, because we know not our riches. We can never be in such a condition wherein there will be just cause of utter despair. He that sits in darkness, and seeth no light, no light of comfort, no light of God's countenance, yet let him trust in the name of the Lord. Weaknesses do not debar us from mercy; nay, they incline God the more. The husband is bound to bear with the wife, as being the weaker vessel; and shall we think God will exempt himself from his own rule, and not bear with his weak spouse?

But is this offer made to me, that can not love, prize, nor desire the Lord Jesus ?

Yes; to thee. Christ knows how to pity us in this case. We are weak, but we are his. A father looks not so much at the blemishes of his child as at his own nature in him ; so Christ finds matter of love from any thing of his own in us. A Chris-tian's carriage toward Christ may in many things be very offensive, and cause much strangeness ; yet, so long as he resolves not upon any known evil, Christ will own him, and he Christ.

O, but I have fallen from God oft, since he hath enlightened me ; and doth he tender Christ to me ?

Thou must know that Christ hath married every believing soul to himself, and that, where the work of grace is begun, sin loses strength by every new fall. If there be a spring of sin in thee, there is a spring of mercy in God, and a fountain daily opened to wash thy uncleanness in. Adam (indeed) lost all by once sinning ; but we are under a better covenant, — a covenant of mercy, — and are encouraged by the Son to go to the Father every day for the sins of that day.

If I was willing to receive Christ, I might have Christ offered to me ; but will the Lord offer him to such a one as desires not to have Christ ?

Yes ; saith our Saviour, "I would have gathered you as the hen gathereth her chickens under her wings, and you would not." We must know a creating power can not only bring something out of nothing, but contrary out of contrary ; of un-willing, God can make us a willing people. There is a promise of pouring clean water upon us, and Christ hath taken upon him to purge his spouse, and make her fit for himself.

What hast thou now to plead against this strange kindness of the Lord in offering Christ to thee? Thou wilt say, it may be, —

O, I fear time is past ! O, time is past ! I might once have had Christ, but now mine heart is sealed down with hardness, blindness, unbelief. O, time is now gone !

No ; not so. See Isaiah lxv. 1–3 : "All the day long God holdeth out his hands to a backsliding and rebellious people." Thy day of grace, thy day of means, thy day of life, thy day of God's striving with thee and stirring of thee, still lasts.

But if God be so willing to save, and so prodigal of his Christ, why doth he not give me Christ, or draw me to Christ ?

I answer, What command dost thou look for to draw thee to Christ but this word, Come ? O, come, thou poor, forlorn, lost, blind, cursed nothing ; I will save thee ; I will enrich thee ; I will forgive thee ; I will enlighten thee ; I will bless thee ; I will be all things unto thee, do all things for thee. May not this win and melt the heart of a devil ?

II. Upon what condition may Christ be had ?

Make an exchange of what thou art or hast with Christ for what Christ is or hath ; and so taking him, (like the wise mer-chant the pearl,) thou shalt have salvation with him.

Now, this exchange lieth in these four things chiefly : —

First. Give away thyself to him, head, heart, tongue, body, soul, and he will give away himself unto thee, (Cant. vi. 3 ;) yea, he will stand in thy room in heaven, that thou mayest triumph and say, I am already in heaven, glorified in him ; I see God's blessed face in Christ ; I have conquered death, hell, and the devil in him.

Secondly. Give away all thy sins to Christ, confess them, leave them, cast them upon the Lord Jesus, so as to receive power from him to forsake them, and he will be made sin for thee to take them away from thee. (1 John i. 9.)

Thirdly. Give away thine honor, pleasure, profit, life, for him ; he will give away his crown and honor, life and all, to thee. (Luke xviii.) Let nothing be sweet unto thee but him, and nothing shall be sweet unto him but thee.

Fourthly. Give away thy rags, forsake thine own righteousness, for him ; he will give away all his robes and righteousness to thee. (Phil. iii. 8, 9.) Thou shalt stand as glorious in the sight of God, howsoever thou art a poor snake in thyself, as an angel, nay, as all the angels, because clothed with his Son Christ Jesus his righteousness.

Now, tell me, will you have Christ ? He is offered to you. Yes, you will all say ; yea, with all mine heart. But will you have him upon these terms, upon these four conditions ?

Now, because men will flatter themselves, and say, Yes, —

III. I will show you four sorts of people that reject Christ thus offered.

First. The slighting unbeliever, that, when he hears of an offer of Christ, and should wonder at the love of the Lord in doing this, he makes nothing of it, but goes from the church, and says, We must give ministers the wall in the pulpit, and, poor men, they must have somewhat to say and preach for their living ; there was a good plain sermon to-day ; the man seems to mean well, but I think he be no great scholar ; and so makes no more of the offer of Christ than of the offer of a straw at their feet. If a good bargain be offered them, they will forget all their business to accomplish that ; yet they make light of this offer. (Matt. xxii. 5.)

Secondly. The desperate unbeliever, that, seeing his sins to be so great, and feeling his heart so hard, and finding but little good from God, since he sought for help, like Cain fleeth from the presence of the Lord ; like a mad lion he breaks his chains of restraining grace, and runneth roaring after his prey, after his cups, queans, lusts, etc., and so will not honor Christ with such a great cure of such great sins, that he shall never have the credit of it, nor will be beholding to him for such a kindness.

Thirdly. The presumptuous unbeliever, that, seeing what sins he hath committed, and, it may be, having a little touch and some sorrow for his sins, catcheth at Christ, hoping to be saved by him before ever he come to be loaden with sin as the greatest evil, or God's wrath kindled against him as his greatest curse, and so, catching at Christ, hopes he hath Christ, and, hoping he hath Christ already, shuts out Christ for the future, and so rejects him. (Micah iii. 11.) You shall have these men and women complain never of the want, but only of the weakness, of their faith, and they will not be beaten off from thence ; let them hear never so much of their misery, nor see never so much of their sin, yet they will not be beaten off from trusting to Christ.

Fourthly. The tottering, doubtful unbeliever ; one that is in a question whether he had best have Christ or no. He sees some good in Christ that he would gladly have him for, as, Then I shall have heaven, and pardon, and grace, and peace ; and yet he sees many things he dislikes with Christ, as, namely, Then farewell merry meetings, pastimes, cards and dice, pleasure and sinful games ; and hence they totter this way and that way, not knowing whether they had best have Christ or no. (James i. 6, 7.) These people reject Jesus Christ.

IV. And now come and see the greatness of this sin.

1. It is a most bloody sin ; it is a trampling under foot the blood of the Son of God. (Heb. x. 21.)

2. It is a most dishonoring sin ; for as by the first act of faith a man glorifieth God by obeying all the law at an instant in Christ, so by rejecting him thou dost break all those laws of God in an instant, and so dost dishonor him.

3. It is a most ungrateful sin ; it is despising God's greatest love, which the Lord takes most heavily.

4. It is a most inexcusable sin ; for what have you to cast against Jesus Christ? O, my sins are so great, thou wilt say. But take Christ, his blood will wash thee from all thy sins.

O, but my heart is hard, and my mind blind.

Yea, but take me, and I will break thine heart, open thine eyes. A new heart is God's gift, and he hath promised to create it in us.

O, but then I must forsake all my pleasures.

Thou shalt have them fully, continually, infinitely in Christ.

O, but I can not take Christ.

O, but Christ can give thee a hand to receive him, as well as give away himself.

5 *

5. It is a most heavy sin. What sin will gripe so in hell as this? (John iii. 19.) God the Father shall strike the devils for breaking the law of the creation; but God the Son shall strike thee, and the Comforter himself shall set himself against thee, for despising the means and offers of redemption. The devils might never have had mercy, but thou shalt think with anguish, and vexation, and madness of heart, I might have had a Christ; he was offered unto me. Mercy wooed this stubborn, proud heart to yield. But, O, rock of adamant that I was! it did not affect me. O, fly speedily to this city of refuge, lest the pursuer of blood overtake thee.

Away, then, out of yourselves, to the Lord Jesus. Heaven and earth leave thee, and have forsaken thee: now, there is but one more that can do thee good, and deliver thy soul from endless sorrow: go to him, and take hold on him, not with the hand of presumption and love to thyself, to save thyself, but with the hand of faith, and love to him, to honor him.

I am well enough already: what tell you me of Christ?

This is the damning sin of these times: when men have Christ offered unto them, foretelling them else of wrath to come, they say they are well; hence, feeling no judgment here, they fear no wrath hereafter; hence, being well, they feel no need of Christ; hence, till they die, they never seek out for a Saviour. Men will not come into the ark already made for them before the flood arise. The world makes so much of those it nurseth up, that they are unwilling to come to heaven, when they are called to come home.

But it may be Christ hath not redeemed me, nor shed his blood for me; therefore why should I go to him?

It may be, it is true; may be not; yet do thou venture, as those, (Joel ii.,) "Who knows but the Lord may return?" It is true, God hath elected but few, and so the Son hath shed his blood, and died but for a few; yet this is no excuse for thee to lie down and say, What should I seek out of myself for succor? Thou must in this case venture and try, as many men amongst us do now, who, hearing of one good living fallen, twenty of them will go and seek for it, although they know only one shall have it. Therefore say as those lepers in Samaria, If I stay here in my sins, I die; if I go out to the camp of the Syrians, we may live; we can but die, however: if I go out to Christ, I may get mercy; however, I can but die, and it is better to die at Christ's feet than in thine own puddle. Content not yourselves therefore with your bare reformation, and amending your lives; this is but to cross the debt in thine own book; it remaineth uncancelled in the creditor's book still: but go, take, offer up this eternal sacrifice before the eyes of God the Father, and cry guilty at his bar, and look for mercy from him; sigh under thy bondage, that as Moses was sent unto the Israelites, so may Christ be sent into thy soul. Rest not therefore in the sight or sense of a helpless condition, saying, I can not help myself, unless Christ doth: sigh unto the Lord Jesus in heaven for succor, and admire the Lord forever, that when there was no help, and when he might have raised out of the stones children to praise him, yet he should send his Son out of his bosom to save thee. So much for this particular.

The fifth divine principle follows to be handled.

CHAPTER V.

THAT THOSE THAT ARE SAVED ARE VERY FEW; AND THAT THOSE THAT ARE SAVED ARE SAVED WITH VERY MUCH DIFFICULTY.

"STRAIT is the gate and narrow is the way that leadeth unto life, and few there be that find it." (Matt. vii. 14.)

Here are two parts: —

1. The paucity of them that shall be saved: few find the way thither.

2. The difficulty of being saved: strait and narrow is the way and gate unto life.

Hence arise two doctrines: —

1. That the number of them that shall be saved is very small. (Luke xiii. 24.) The devil hath his drove, and swarms to go to hell, as fast as bees to their hive. Christ hath his flock, and that is but a little flock; hence God's children are called jewels, (Mal. iii. 17,) which commonly are kept secret, in respect of the other lumber in the house; hence they are called strangers and pilgrims, which are very few in respect of the inhabitants of the country through which they pass; hence they are called sons of God, (1 John iii. 2;) of the blood royal, which are few in respect of common subjects.

But see the truth of this point in these two things: —

First, look to all ages and times of the world; secondly, to all places and persons in the world; and we shall see few men were saved.

1. Look to all ages, and we shall find but a handful saved. As soon as ever the Lord began to keep house, and there were but two families in it, there was a bloody Cain living, and a good Abel slain. And as the world increased in number, so in wickedness. Gen. vi. 12, it is said, "All flesh had corrupted their

ways," and amongst so many thousand men, not one righteous but Noah and his family, and yet in the ark there crept in a cursed Cham.

Afterwards, as Abraham's posterity increased, so we see their sin abounded. When his posterity was in Egypt, where, one would think, if ever men were good, now it would appear, being so heavily afflicted by Pharaoh, being by so many miracles miraculously delivered by the hand of Moses, yet most of these God was wroth with, (Heb. iii. 12,) and only two of them, Caleb and Joshua, went into Canaan, a type of heaven. Look into Solomon's time, what glorious times? what great profession was there then? Yet, after his death, ten tribes fell to the odious sin of idolatry, following the command of Jeroboam, their king. Look further into Isaiah's time, when there were multitudes of sacrifices and prayers, (Is. i. 11 ;) yet then there was but a remnant; nay, a very little remnant, that should be saved. And look to the time of Christ's coming in the flesh, (for I pick out the best time of all,) when one would think, by such sermons he preached, such miracles he wrought, such a life as he led, all the Jews would have entertained him ; yet it is said, "He came unto his own, and they received him not." So few, that Christ himself admires at one good Nathaniel, "Behold an Israelite in whom there is no guile." In the apostles' time, many, indeed, were converted, but few comparatively, and amongst the best churches many bad, as that at Philippi. (Phil. iii. 18.) Many had a name to live, but were dead, and few only kept their garments unspotted. And presently, after the apostles' time, "Many grievous wolves came and devoured the sheep ; " and so, in succeeding ages, (Rev. xii. 9,) all the earth wondered at the whore in scarlet.

And in Luther's time, when the light began to arise again, he saw so many carnal gospelers, that he breaks out in one sermon into these speeches : "God grant I may never live to see those bloody days that are coming upon an ungodly world." Latimer heard so much profaneness in his time, that he thought verily doomsday was just at hand. And have not our ears heard censuring those in the Palatinate, where (as it is reported) many have fallen from the glorious gospel to Popery, as fast as leaves fall in autumn? Who would have thought there had lurked such hearts under such a show of detesting Popery as was among them before? And at Christ's coming, shall he find faith on the earth?

2. Let us look into all places and persons, and see how few shall be saved. The world is now split into four parts, Europe,

Asia, Africa, and America; and the three biggest parts are drowned in a deluge of profaneness and superstition; they do not so much as profess Christ; you may see the sentence of death written on these men's foreheads. (Jer. x. ult.) But let us look upon the best part of the world, and that is Europe; how few shall be saved there ! First, the Grecian church, howsoever, now in these days, their good patriarch of Constantinople is about a general reformation among them, and hath done much good, yet are they for the present, and have been for the most part of them, without the saving means of knowledge. They content themselves with their old superstitions, having little or no preaching at all. And for the other parts, as Italy, Spain, France, Germany, for the most part they are Popish; and see the end of these men. (2 Thess. ii. 9–12.) And now amongst them that carry the badge of honesty, I will not speak what mine ears have heard and my heart believes concerning other churches : I will come into our own church of England, which is the most flourishing church in the world ; never had church such preachers, such means; yet have we not some chapels and churches stand as dark lanterns without light, where people are led with blind, or idle, or licentious ministers, and so both fall into the ditch ?

Nay, even amongst them that have the means of grace, but few shall be saved. It may be sometimes amongst ninety-nine in a parish, Christ sends a minister to call some one lost sheep among them. (Matt. xiii.) Three grounds were bad where the seed was sown, and only one good. It is a strange speech of Chrysostom in his fourth sermon to the people of Antioch, where he was much beloved, and did much good — How many do you think, saith he, shall be saved in this city? It will be a hard speech to you, but I will speak it ; though here be so many thousands of you, yet there can not be found a hundred that shall be saved, and I doubt of them too ; for what villainy is there among youth! what sloth in old men ! and so he goes on. So say I, Never tell me we are baptized, and are Christians, and trust to Christ; let us but separate the goats from the sheep, and exclude none but such as the Scriptures doth, and sets a cross upon their doors, with, Lord, have mercy upon them, and we shall see only a few in the city shall be saved.

1. Cast out all the profane people among us, as drunkards, swearers, whores, liars, which the Scripture brands for black sheep, and condemns them in a hundred places.

2. Set by all civil men that are but wolves chained up, tame devils, swine in a fair meadow, that pay all they owe, and do

nobody any harm, yet do none any great good; that plead for themselves, and say, Who can say, Black is mine eye? These are righteous men, whom Christ never came to call. "For he came not to call the righteous, but sinners, to repentance."

3. Cast by all hypocrites, that like stageplayers, in the sight of others, act the part of kings and honest men; when, look upon them in their tyring house, they are but base varlets.

4. Formal professors and carnal gospelers, that have a thing like faith, and like sorrow, and like true repentance, and like good desires, but yet they be but pictures; they deceive others and themselves too. (2 Tim. iii. 5.)

Set by these four sorts, how few then are to be saved, even among them that are hatched in the bosom of the church!

First. Here, then, is a use of encouragement. Be not discouraged by the name of singularity. What! do you think yourself wiser than others? and shall none be saved but such as are so precise as ministers prate? Are you wiser than others, that you think none shall go to heaven but yourself? I tell you, if you would be saved, you must be singular men, not out of faction, but out of conscience. (Acts xxiv. 16.)

Secondly. Here is matter of terror to all those that be of opinion that few shall be saved; and therefore, when they are convinced of the danger of sin by the word, they fly to this shelter: If I be damned, it will be woe to many more beside me then; as though most should not be damned. O, yes, the most of them that live in the church shall perish; and this made a hermit which Theodoret mentions to live fifteen years in a cell in a desolate wilderness, with nothing but bread and water, and yet doubted, after all his sorrow, whether he should be saved or not. O, God's wrath is heavy, which thou shalt one day bear.

Thirdly. This ministereth exhortation to all confident people, that think they believe, and say, they doubt not but to be saved, and hence do not much fear death. O, learn hence to suspect and fear your estates, and fear it so much that thou canst not be quiet until thou hast got some assurance thou shalt be saved. When Christ told his disciples that one of them should betray him, they all said, "Master, is it I?" But if he had said eleven of them should betray him, all except one, would they not all conclude, Surely, it is I? If the Lord had said, Only few shall be damned, every man might fear, It may be it is I; but now he says most shall, every man may cry out and say, Surely it is I. No humble heart but is driven to and fro with many stinging fears this way; yet there is a generation of presumptuous, brazen-faced, bold people, that confidently think of themselves, as the Jews of the Pharisees, (being so holy and strict,) that if God save but two in the world, they shall make one.

The child of God, indeed, is bold as a lion; but he hath God's spirit and promise, assuring him of his eternal welfare. But I speak of divers that have no sound ground to prove this point, (which they pertinaciously defend,) that they shall be saved. This confident humor rageth most of all in our old professors at large, who think, that is a jest indeed, that having been of a good belief so long, that they now should be so far behindhand as to begin the work, and lay the foundation anew. And not only among these, but amongst divers sorts of people whom the devil never troubles, because he is sure of them already, and therefore cries peace in their ears, whose consciences never trouble them, because that hath shut its eyes; and hence they sleep, and sleeeping dream that God is merciful unto them, and will be so; yet never see they are deceived, until they awake with the flames of hell about their ears; and the world troubles them not; they have their hearts' desire here, because they are friends to it, and so enemies to God. And ministers never trouble them, for they have none such as are fit for that work near them; or if they have, they can sit and sleep in the church, and choose whether they will believe him. And their friends never trouble them, because they are afraid to displease them. And God himself never troubles them, because that time is to come hereafter. This one truth, well pondered and thought on, may damp thine heart, and make thy conscience fly in thy face, and say, " Thou art the man;" it may be there are better in hell than thyself, that art so confident; and therefore tell me, what hast thou to say for thyself, that thou shalt be saved? In what thing hast thou gone beyond them that "think they are rich and want nothing, who yet are poor, blind, miserable, and naked?"

Thou wilt say, haply, first, I have left my sins I once lived in, and am now no drunkard, no swearer, no liar, &c.

I answer, Thou mayest be washed from thy mire, (the pollution of the world,) and yet be a swine in God's account, (2 Pet. ii. 20;) thou mayest live a blameless, innocent, honest, smooth life, and yet be a miserable creature still. (Phil. iii. 6.)

But I pray, and that often.

This thou mayest do, and yet never be saved. (Is. i. 11.) To what purpose is your multitude of sacrifices? Nay, thou mayest pray with much affection, with a good heart, as thou thinkest, yet a thousand miles off from being saved. (Prov. i. 28.)

But I fast sometimes, as well as pray.

So did the scribes and Pharisees, even twice a week, which could not be public, but private fasts. And yet this righteousness could never save them.

But I hear the word of God, and like the best preachers.

This thou mayest do too, and yet never be saved. Nay, thou mayest so hear, as to receive much joy and comfort in hearing, nay, to believe and catch hold on Christ, and so say and think he is thine, and yet not be saved; as the stony ground did, (Matt. xiii.,) who heard the word with joy, and for a season believed.

I read the Scriptures often.

This you may do too, and yet never be saved; as the Pharisees, who were so perfect in reading the Bible, that Christ needed but only say, " It hath been said of old time;" for they knew the text and place well enough without intimation.

But I am grieved and am sorrowful, and repent for my sins past.

Judas did thus, (Matt. xxvii. 3;) he repents himself with a legal repentance for fear of hell, and with a natural sorrow for dealing so unkindly with Christ, in betraying not only blood, but innocent blood. True humiliation is ever accompanied with hearty reformation.

O, but I love good men and their company.

So did the five foolish virgins love the company, and (at the time of extremity) the very oil and grace of the wise; yet they were locked out of the gates of mercy.

But God hath given me more knowledge than others, or than I myself had once.

This thou mayest have, and be able to teach others, and think so of thyself too, and yet never be saved.

But I keep the Lord's day strictly.

So did the Jews, whom yet Christ condemned, and were never saved.

I have very many good desires and endeavors to get to heaven.

These thou and thousands may have, and yet miss of heaven. Many shall seek to enter in at that narrow gate, and not be able.

True, thou wilt say, Many men do many duties, but without any life or zeal; I am zealous.

So thou mayest be, and yet never be saved, as Jehu. Paul was zealous when he was a Pharisee, and if he was so for a false religion, and a bad cause, why, much more mayest thou be for a good cause; so zealous as not only to cry out against profaneness in the wicked, but civil honesty of others, and hypocrisy of others, yea, even of the coldness of the best of God's people; thou mayest be the fore horse in the team, and the ringleader of good exercises amongst the best men, (as Joash, a wicked king, was the first that complained of the negligence of his best officers in not repairing the temple,) and so stir them up unto it; nay, thou mayest be so forward as to be persecuted, and not yield an inch, nor shrink in the wetting, but mayest manfully and courageously stand it out in time of persecution, as the thorny ground did: so zealous thou mayest be, as to like best of and to flock most unto the most zealous preachers, that search men's consciences best, as the whole country of Judea came flocking to John's ministry, and delighted to hear him for a season; nay, thou mayest be zealous as to take sweet delight in doing of all these things. (Is. lviii. 2, 3,) "They delight in approaching near unto God," yet come short of heaven.

But thou wilt say, True, many a man rides post that breaks his neck at last; many a man is zealous, but his fire is soon quenched, and his zeal is soon spent; they hold not out; whereas I am constant, and persevere in godly courses.

So did that young man; yet he was a graceless man. (Matt. xix. 20,) "All these things have I done from my youth; what lack I yet?"

It is true, hypocrites may persevere; but they know themselves to be naught all the while, and so deceive others; but I am persuaded that I am in God's favor, and in a safe and happy estate, since I do all with a good heart for God.

This thou mayest verily think of thyself, and yet be deceived and damned, and go to the devil at last. "There is a way," saith Solomon, "that seemeth right to a man, but the end thereof is the way of death." For he is a hypocrite not only that makes a seeming outward show of what he hath not, but also that hath a true show of what indeed there is not. The first sort of hypocrites deceive others only; the latter, having some inward yet common work, deceive themselves too. (James i. 26,) "If any man seem to be religious," (so many are, and so deceive the world;) but it is added, "deceiving his own soul." Nay, thou mayest go so fairly, and live so honestly, that all the best Christians about thee may think well of thee and never suspect thee, and so mayest pass through the world, and die with a deluded comfort that thou shalt go to heaven and be canonized for a saint in thy funeral sermon, and never know thou art counterfeit till the Lord brings thee to thy strict and last examination, and so thou receivest that dreadful sentence, "Go, ye cursed." So it was with the five foolish virgins, that were never discovered by the wise, nor by themselves, until the gate of grace was shut upon them. If thou hast, therefore, no better evidences to show for thyself, that thine estate is good, than these, I will not give a pin's point for all thy flattering false hopes of being saved. But it may be thou hast never yet come so far as to this pitch ; and if not, Lord, what will become of thee ? Suspect thyself much, and when, in this shipwreck of souls, thou seest so many thousands sink, cry out, and conclude, It is a wonder of wonders, and a thousand and a thousand to one, if ever thou comest safe to shore.

O, strive, then, to be one of them that shall be saved, though it cost thee thy blood and the loss of all that thou hast ; labor to go beyond all those that go so far and yet perish at the last. Do not say that, seeing so few shall be saved, therefore this discourageth me from seeking, because all my labor may be in vain. Consider that Christ here makes another and a better use of it. (Luke iii 24.) Seeing that "many shall seek and not enter, therefore," saith he, "strive to enter in at the strait gate." Venture, at least, and try what the Lord will do for thee.

Wherein doth the child of God, and so how may I, go beyond these hypocrites that go so far ?

In three things principally.

First. No unregenerate man, though he go never so far, let him do never so much, but he lives in some one sin or other, secret or open, little or great. Judas went far, but he was covetous. Herod went far, but he loved his Herodias. Every dog hath his kennel ; every swine hath his swill, and every wicked man his lust. For no unregenerate man hath fruition of God to content him, and there is no man's heart but it must have some good to content it ; which good is to be found only in the fountain of all good, and that is God, or in the cistern, and that is in the creatures. Hence, a man having lost full content in God, he seeks for and feeds upon contentment in the creature which he makes a god to him ; and here lies his lust or sin, which he must needs live in. Hence, ask those men that go very far, and take their penny for good silver, and commend themselves for their good desires — I say, ask them if they have no sin. Yes, say they ; who can live without sin ? And so they give way to sin, and therefore live in sin. Nay, commonly, all the duties, prayers, care, and zeal of the best hypocrites are to hide a lust, as the whore in the Proverbs, that wipes her mouth, and goes to the temple, and pays her vows ; or to feed a lust, as Jehu his zeal against Baal was to get a kingdom. There remains a root of bitterness in the best hypocrites, which, howsoever it be lopped off sometimes by sickness or horror of conscience, and a man hath purposes never to commit again, yet there it secretly lurks ; and, though it seemeth to be bound and conquered by the word, or by prayer, or by outward crosses, or while the hand of God is upon a man, yet the inward strength and power of it remains still ; and therefore, when temptations, like strong Philistines, are upon this man again, he breaks all vows, promises, bonds of God, and will save the life of his sin.

Sécondly. No unregenerate man or woman ever came to be poor in spirit, and so to be carried out of all duties unto Christ. If it were possible for them to forsake and break loose forever from all sin, yet here they stick, as the scribes and Pharisees ; and so, like zealous Paul before his conversion, they fasted and prayed, and kept the Sabbath, but they rested in their legal righteousness, and in the performance of these and the like duties. Take the best hypocrite, that hath the most strong persuasions of God's love to him, and ask him why he hopes to be saved. He will answer, I pray, read, hear, love good men, cry out of the sins of the time. And tell him again that a hypocrite may climb these stairs and go as far, he will reply, True, indeed ; but they do not what they do with a sound heart, but to be seen of men. Mark, now, how these men feel a good heart in themselves and in all things they do ; and therefore feel not a want of all good, which is poverty of spirit; and therefore here they fall short. (Is. lxvi. 2.) There were divers hypocrites forward for the worship of God in the temple ; but God loathes these, because not poor in spirit ; to them only, it is said, the Lord will look. I have seen many professors very forward for all good duties, but as ignorant of Christ, when they are sifted, as blocks. And if a man (as few do) know not Christ, he must rest in his duties, because he knows not Christ, to whom he must go and be carried if ever he be saved. I have heard of a man that, being condemned to die, thought to escape the gallows, and to save himself from hanging, by a certain gift he said he had of whistling. So men seek to save themselves by their gifts of knowledge, gifts of memory, gifts of prayer ; and when they see they must die for their sins, this is the ruin of many a soul, that, though he forsake Egypt and his sins and flesh pots there, and will never be so as he hath been, yet he never cometh into Canaan, but loseth himself and his soul in a wilderness of many duties, and there perisheth.

Thirdly. If any unregenerate man come unto Christ, he never gets into Christ, that is, never takes his eternal rest and lodging in Jesus Christ only. (Heb. iv. 4.) Judas followed

Christ for the bag; he would have the bag and Christ too. The young man came unto Christ to be his disciple; but he would have Christ and the world too. They will not content themselves with Christ alone, nor with the world alone, but make their markets out of both, like whorish wives, that will please their husbands and others too. Men in distress of conscience, if they have comfort from Christ, they are contented; if they have salvation from hell by Christ, they are contented; but Christ himself contents them not. Thus far a hypocrite goes not. So much for the first doctrine observed out of the text. I come now to the second.

Doctrine 2. That those that are saved are saved with much difficulty; or it is a wonderful hard thing to be saved.

The gate is strait, and therefore a man must sweat and strive to enter; both the entrance is difficult, and the progress of salvation too. Jesus Christ is not got with a wet finger. It is not wishing and desiring to be saved will bring men to heaven; hell's mouth is full of good wishes. It is not shedding a tear at a sermon, or blubbering now and then in a corner, and saying over thy prayers, and crying God mercy for thy sins, will save thee. It is not, Lord, have mercy upon us, will do thee good. It is not coming constantly to church. These are easy matters. But it is a tough work, a wonderful hard matter, to be saved. (1 Pet. iv. 18.) Hence the way to heaven is compared to a race, where a man must put forth all his strength, and stretch every limb, and all to get forward. Hence a Christian's life is compared to wrestling. (Eph. vi. 12.) All the policy and power of hell buckle together against a Christian; therefore he must look to himself, or else he falls. Hence it is compared to fighting. (2 Tim. iv. 7.) A man must fight against the devil, the world, himself, who shoot poisoned bullets in the soul, where a man must kill or be killed. God hath not lined the way to Christ with velvet, nor strewed it with rushes. He will never feed a slothful humor in man, who will be saved if Christ and heaven would drop into their mouths, and if any would bear their charges thither. If Christ might be bought for a few cold wishes and lazy desires, he would be of small reckoning amongst men, who would say, Lightly come, lightly go. Indeed, Christ's yoke is easy in itself; and when a man is got into Christ, nothing is so sweet; but for a carnal, dull heart, it is hard to draw in it; for

There are four strait gates which every one must pass through before he can enter into heaven.

1. There is the strait gate of humiliation. God saveth none

but first he humbleth them. Now, it is hard to pass through the gates and flames of hell; for a heart as stiff as a stake to bow; as hard as a stone to bleed for the least prick; not to mourn for one sin, but all sins; and not for a fit, but all a man's lifetime. O, it is hard for a man to suffer himself to be loaden with sin, and pressed to death for sin, so as never to love sin more, but to spit in the face of that which he once loved as dearly as his life. It is easy to drop a tear or two, and be sermon sick; but to have a heart rent for sin and from sin, this is true humilitation; and this is hard.

2. The strait gate of faith. (Eph. i. 19.) It is an easy matter to presume, but hard to believe in Christ. It is easy for a man that was never humbled to believe and say, It is but believing; but it is a hard matter for a man humbled, when he sees all his sins in order before him, the devil and conscience roaring upon him, and crying out against him, and God frowning upon him, now to call God Father, is a hard work. Judas had rather be hanged than believe. It is hard to see a Christ as a rock to stand upon, when we are overwhelmed with sorrow of heart for sin. It is hard to prize Christ above ten thousand worlds of pearl; it is hard to desire Christ, and nothing but Christ; hard to follow Christ all the day long, and never to be quiet till he is got in thine arms, and then with Simeon to say, "Lord, now lettest thou thy servant depart in peace."

3. The strait gate of repentance. It is an easy matter for a man to confess himself to be a sinner, and to cry to God forgiveness until next time; but to have a bitter sorrow, and so to turn from all sin, and to return to God, and all the ways of God, which is true repentance indeed, this is hard.

4. The strait gate of opposition of devils, the world, and a man's own self, who knock a man down when he begins to look toward Christ and heaven.

Hence learn, that every easy way to heaven is a false way, although ministers should preach it out of their pulpits, and angels should publish it out of heaven.

Now, there are nine easy ways to heaven, (as men think,) all which lead to hell.

1. The common broad way, wherein a whole parish may all go abreadth in it; tell these people they shall be damned, their answer is, Then woe to many more besides me.

2. The way of civil education, whereby many wild natures are by little and little tamed, and like wolves are chained up easily while they are young.

3. Balaam's way of good wishes, whereby many people will

6 *

confess their ignorance, forgetfulness, and that they can not make such shows as others do, but they thank God their hearts are as good, and God for his part accepts (say they) the will for the deed. And, " My son, give me thy heart ; " the heart is all in all, and so long they hope to do well enough. Poor deluded creatures thus think to break through armies of sins, devils, temptations, and to break open the very gates of heaven with a few good wishes ; they think to come to their journey's end without legs, because their hearts are good to God.

4. The way of formality, whereby men rest in the perform- ance of most or of all external duties without inward life. (Mark i. 14.) Every man must have some religion, some fig leaves to hide their nakedness. Now, this religion must be either true religion or the false one ; if the true, he must either take up the power of it, — but that he will not, because it is burdensome, — or the form of it ; and this being easy, men embrace it as their God, and will rather lose their lives than their religion thus taken up. This form of religion is the easiest religion in the world ; partly because it easeth men of trouble of conscience, quieting that : Thou hast sinned, saith conscience, and God is offended ; take a book, and pray, keep thy conscience better, and bring thy Bible with thee; now, conscience is silent, being charmed down with the form of religion, as the devil is driven away (as they say) with holy water; partly, also, because the form of religion credits a man, partly because it is easy in itself ; it is of a light carriage, being but the shadow and picture of the substance of religion ; as now, what an easy matter it is to come to church ! They hear (at least outwardly) very attentively an hour and more, and then to turn to a proof, and to turn down a leaf : here is the form. But now to spend Saturday night, and all the whole Sabbath day morning, in trimming the lamp, and in getting oil in the heart to meet the bridegroom the next day, and so meet him in the word, and there to tremble at the voice of God, and suck the breast while it is open ; and when the word is done, to go aside privately, and there to chew upon the word, there to lament with tears all the vain thoughts in duties, deadness in hearing, this is hard, because this is the power of godliness, and this men will not take up : so for private prayer ; what an easy matter is it for a man to say over a few prayers out of some devout book, or to repeat some old prayer, got by heart since a child, or to have two or three short-winded wishes for God's mercy in the morning and at night ! this form is easy. But now to prepare the heart by serious meditation of God and man's self, before he prays, then to come to God with a bleeding, hunger-starved heart, not

only with a desire, but with a warrant, I must have such or such a mercy, and there to wrestle with God, although it be an hour or two together for a blessing, this is too hard; men think none do thus, and therefore they will not.

Fifthly. The way of presumption, whereby men, having seen their sins, catch hold easily upon God's mercy, and snatch comforts before they are reached out unto them. There is no word of comfort, in the book of God, intended for such as regard iniquity in their hearts, though they do not act it in their lives. Their only comfort is, that the sentence of damnation is not yet executed upon them.

Sixthly. The way of sloth, whereby men lie still, and say, God must do all. If the Lord would set up a pulpit at the alehouse door, it may be they would hear oftener. If God will always thunder, they will always pray; if strike them now and then with sickness, God shall be paid with good words and promises enough, that they will be better if they live; but, as long as peace lasts, they will run to hell as fast as they can; and, if God will not catch them, they care not, they will not return.

Seventhly. The way of carelessness, when men, feeling many difficulties, pass through some of them, but not all, and what they can not get now, they feed themselves with a false hope they shall hereafter; they are content to be called precisians, and fools, and crazy brains, but they want brokenness of heart, and they will pray (it may be) for it, and pass by that difficulty; but to keep the wound always open, this they will not do; to be always sighing for help, and never to give themselves rest till their hearts are humbled, that they will not: "These have a name to live, yet are dead."

Eighthly. The way of moderation, or honest discretion, (Rev. iii. 16,) which, indeed, is nothing but lukewarmness of the soul; and that is, when a man contrives, and cuts out such a way to heaven as he may be hated of none, but please all, and so do any thing for a quiet life, and so sleep in a whole skin. The Lord saith, "He that will live godly must suffer persecution." No, not so, Lord. Surely, (think they,) if men were discreet and wise, it would prevent a great deal of trouble and opposition in good courses; this man will commend those that are most zealous, if they were but wise; if he meet with a black-mouthed swearer, he will not reprove him, lest he be displeased with him; if he meet with an honest man, he will yield to all he saith, that so he may commend him; and when he meets them both together, they shall be both alike welcome (whatever he thinks) to his house and table, because he would fain be at peace with all men.

Ninthly, and lastly. The way of self-love, whereby a man, fearing terribly he shall be damned, useth diligently all means whereby he shall be saved. Here is the strongest difficulty of all, to row against the stream, and to hate a man's self, and then to follow Christ fully.

I come now to the sixth general head, proposed in order to be considered.

CHAPTER VI.

THAT THE GRAND CAUSE OF MAN'S ETERNAL RUIN, OR WHY SO MANY ARE DAMNED, AND SO FEW SAVED BY CHRIST, IS FROM THEMSELVES.

"WHY will ye die?" (Ezek. xxxiii. 11.) The great cause why so many people die, and perish everlastingly, is because they will; every man that perisheth is his own butcherer or murderer. (Matt. xxii. 27. Hosea ix.) This is the point we propose to prosecute at present.

Question. The question here will be, how men plot and perfect their own ruin.

Answer. By these four principal means, which are the four great rocks that most men are split upon; and great necessity lieth upon every man to know them; for when a powder plot is discovered, the danger is almost past. I say, there are these four causes of man's eternal overthrow, which I shall handle largely, and make use of every particular reason, when it is open and finished.

First. By reason of that bloody black ignorance of men, whereby thousands remain wofully ignorant of their spiritual estate, not knowing how the case stands between God and their souls, but thinking themselves to be well enough already, they never seek to come out of their misery till they perish in it.

Secondly. By reason of man's carnal security, putting the evil day from them, whereby they feel not their fearful thralldom, and so never groan to come out of the slavish bondage of sin and Satan.

Thirdly. By reason of man's carnal confidence, whereby they shift to save themselves by their own duties and performances, when they feel it.

Fourthly. By reason of man's bold presumption, whereby men scramble to save themselves by their own seeming faith, when they see an insufficiency in duties, and an unworthiness in themselves for God to save them.

I will begin with the first reason, and discover the first train whereby men blow up themselves, which is this: they know not this misery, nor that fearful, accursed, forlorn state wherein they lie, but think and say they shall do as well as others; and therefore, when any friend persuadeth them to come out of it, and shows them the danger of remaining in such a condition, what is their answer? I pray you save your breath to cool your broth. Every vat shall stand on his own bottom. Let me alone; I hope I have a soul to save as well as you, and shall be as careful of it as you shall or can be. You shall not answer for my soul. I hope I shall do as well as the precisest of you all.

Hence, likewise, if the minister come home to them, they go home with hearts full of outcries against the man, and their tongue dipped in gall against the sermon. God be merciful unto us if all this be true! Here's harsh doctrine enough to make a man run out of his wits, and to drive me to despair. Thus they know not their misery, and not knowing, (they are lost and condemned creatures under the everlasting wrath of God,) they never seek, pray, strive, or follow the means whereby they may come out of it, and so perish in it, and never know it till they awake with the flames of hell about their ears. They will acknowledge, indeed, many of them, that all men are born in a most miserable estate; but they never apply particularly that general truth to themselves, saying, I am the man; I am now under God's wrath, and may be snatched away by death every hour; and then I am undone and lost forever.

Now, there are two sorts of people that are ignorant of this their misery.

First. The common sort of profane, blockish, ignorant people.

Secondly. The finer sort of unsound, hollow professors, that have a peacock's pride, that think themselves fair and in very good estate, though they have but one feather on their crest to boast of.

I will begin with the first sort, and show you the reasons why they are ignorant of their misery; that is, for these four reasons:—

First. Sometimes because they want the saving means of knowledge. There is no faithful minister, no compassionate Lot, to tell them of fire and brimstone from heaven for their crying sins; there is no Noah to forewarn them of a flood; there is no messenger to bring them tidings of those armies of God's devouring plagues and wrath that are approaching near unto them; they have no pilot — poor forsaken creatures — to show them their rock; they have either no minister at all to teach them, either because the parish is too poor, or the church living too great to maintain a faithful man, (the strongest asses carrying the greatest burdens commonly.) O, woful physicians ! Sometimes they be profane, and can not heal themselves; and sometimes they be ignorant, and know not what to preach, unless they should follow the steps of Mr. Latimer's Frier ; or, at the best, they shoot off a few popguns against gross sins; or if they do show men their misery, they lick them whole again with some comfortable, ill-applied sentences, (but I hope better things of you, my brethren,) the man's patron may haply storm else. Or else they say commonly, Thou hast sinned ; comfort thyself, but despair not; Christ hath suffered ; and thus skin over the wound, and let it fester within, for want of cutting it deeper. I say, therefore, because they want a faithful watchman to cry, Fire, fire, in that sleepy estate of sin and darkness wherein they lie, therefore whole towns, parishes, generations of men are burnt up, and perish miserably. (Lam. ii. 14.)

Secondly. Because they have no leisure to consider of their misery, when they have the means of revealing it unto them, as Felix. (Acts xxiv. 25.) Many a man hath many a bitter pill given him at a sermon, but he hath no leisure to chew upon it. One man is taken up with suits in law, and another almost eaten up with suretyship, and carking cares how to pay his debts, and provide for his own ; another hath a great charge and few friends, and he saith the world is hard, and hence, like a mole, roots in the earth, week days and Sabbath days. The world thus calling them on one side, and lusts on another, and the devil on the other side, they have no leisure to consider of death, devil, God, nor themselves, hell, nor heaven. The minister cries and knocks without, but there is such a noise and lumber of tumultuous lusts and vain thoughts in their hearts and heads, that all good thoughts are sad, unwelcome guests, and are knocked down presently.

Thirdly. Because, if they have leisure, they are afraid to know it. Hence people cry out of ministers, that they damn all, and will hear them no more, and they will not be such fools as to believe all that such say : the reason is, they are afraid to know the worst of themselves ; they are afraid to be cut, and therefore can not endure the chirurgeon; they think to be troubled in mind, as others are, is the very high road to despair ; and therefore, if they do hear a tale, how one, after hearing of a sermon, grew distracted, or drowned or hanged himself, it shall be an item and a warning to them as long as they live, for troubling their hearts about such matters. Men of guilty consciences (hence) fly from the face of God, as prisoners from the judge, as debtors from the creditor. But if the Lord of hosts can catch you, you must and shall feel with horror of heart that which you fear a little now.

Fourthly. Because, if they be free from this foolish fear, they can not see their misery, by reason that they look upon their estates through false glasses, and by virtue of many false principles in their minds, they cheat themselves.

Which false principles are these principally ; I will but name them.

First. They conceive God, that made them, will not be so cruel as to damn them.

Secondly. Because they feel no misery, (but are very well,) therefore they fear none.

Thirdly. Because God blesseth them in their outward estates, in their corn, children, calling, friends, &c., would God bless them so, if he did not love them ?

Fourthly. Because they think sin to be no great evil, — for all are sinners, — so this can not mischief them.

Fifthly. Because they think God's mercy is above all his works, though sin be vile, yet conceiving God to be all mercy, all honey, and no justice, they think they are well.

Sixthly. Because they think Christ died for all sinners, and they confess themselves to be great ones.

Seventhly. Because they hope well, and so think to have well.

Eighthly. Because they do as most do, who, never crying out of their sins while they lived, and dying like lambs at last, they doubt not, for their parts, but, doing as such do, they shall die happily, as others have done.

Ninthly. Because their desires and hearts are good, as they think.

Tenthly. Because they do as well as God will give them grace, and so God is in the fault only if they perish.

These are the reasons and grounds upon which profane people are deceived.

Now, it followeth to show the grounds on which the finer sort miscarry.

Secondly. Hollow professors cheat and cozen their own souls. It is in our church as it is in an old wood, where there are many tall trees ; yet cut them and search them deeply, they prove pithless, sapless, hollow, unsound creatures. These men twist their own ruin with a finer thread, and can juggle better than the common sort, and cast mists before their own eyes, and so cheat their own souls. It is a minister's first work to turn

men from darkness into this light, (Acts xxvi. 18,) and the
Spirit's first work to convince men of sin. (John xvi. 9.) And
therefore it is people's main work to know the worst at first of
themselves.

Now, the cause of these men's mistaking is threefold.

First. The spiritual madness and drunkenness of their understanding.

Secondly. The false, bastard peace begot and nourished in the
conscience.

Thirdly. The sly and secret distempers of the will.

First. There are these seven drunken distempers in the
understanding or mind of man, whereby he cometh to be most
miserably deceived.

First. The understanding's arrogancy. You shall never see
a man mean and vile in his own eyes, deceived, (Ps. xxv. 9;)
but a proud man or woman is often cheated.   Hence proud Ha-
man thought surely he was the man whom the king would honor,
when, in truth, it was intended for poor Mordecai.   For pride
having once overspread the mind, it ever hath this property — it
makes a penny stand for a pound, a spark is blown up to a flame,
it makes a great matter of a little seeming grace; and therefore
the proud Pharisee, when he came to reckon with himself, he
takes his poor counter, — that is, "I am not as other men, nor as
this publican,"— and sets it down for one thousand pounds; that is,
he esteems of himself as a very rich man for it; so many a
man, because he hath some good thing in himself, as he is pitiful to
the poor, he is a true man though a poor man; he was never
given to wine or women; he magnifieth himself for this title,
and so deceives and overreckons himself.   There are your
Bristow stones like diamonds, and many cheaters cozen country
folks with them that desire to be fine, and know not what diamonds are; so many men are desirous to be honest, and to be
reputed so, not knowing what true grace means.   Therefore
Bristow stones are pearls in their eyes.   A little seeming grace
shines so bright in their eyes, that they are half bewitched by it
to think highly of themselves, although they be but glittering,
seeming jewels in a swine's snout.   A cab of doves' dung was
sold in Samaria's time of famine at a great rate; a man living
in such a place, where all about him are either ignorant, or profane, or civil, a little moral honesty (dung in respect of true
grace) goes a great way, and is esteemed highly of, and he is as
honest a man as ever lived.   To a man that looks through a red
glass, all things appear red; a man looking upon himself through
some fair spectacles, through some one good thing which he hath

in himself, appears fair to him. It is said, (Luke xx. ult.,) "The Pharisees devoured widows' houses. Might not this racking of rents make them question their estates? No. Why? They for pretense made long prayers: so many men are drunk now and then, but they are sorry; they can not but sin, but their desires are good; they talk idly, but they live honestly; they do ill sometimes, but they mean well. Thus, when some good things are seen in themselves, pride puffs them up with an overweening conceit of it, and so they cozen their souls.

Secondly. The understanding's obstinacy; whereby the mind, having been long rooted in this opinion, that I am in a good estate, will not suffer this conceit to be plucked out of it. Now, your old rooted, yet rotten professors, having grown long in a good conceit of themselves, will not believe that they have been fools all their lifetime, and therefore now must pull down and lay the foundation again; and hence you shall have many say of a faithful minister, that doth convince and condemn them and their estate to be most woful, What shall such an upstart teach me? Doth he think to make me dance after his pipe, and to think that all my good prayers, my faith, my charity, have been so long abominable and vile before God? No silver can bribe a man to cast away his old traditional opinions and conceits, whereby he cheats himself, till Christ's blood do it. (1 Pet. i. 18.) And hence the woman of Samaria objected this against Jesus Christ, that their old "fathers worshiped in that mountain," and therefore it was as good a place as Jerusalem, the place of God's true worship. (John iv. 20.) Men grow crooked and aged with good opinions of themselves, and can seldom or never be set straight again. Hence such kind of people, though they would fain be taken for honest, religious Christians. yet will never suspect their estates to be bad themselves, neither can they endure that any other should search or suspect them to be yet rotten at the heart: and are not those wares and commodities much to be suspected, nay, concluded to be stark naught, which the seller will needs put upon the chapman without seeing or looking on them first? It is a strong argument we produce against the Papist's religion to be suspected to be bad, because they obtrude their opinions on their followers, to be believed without any hesitation or dispute about them, either before or after they have embraced them: certainly thy old faith, thy old prayers, thy old honesty, or form of piety, are counterfeit wares, that can not endure searching; because thou wilt not be driven from this conceit, I am in a good estate, I have been so long of this good mind, and therefore will not begin to doubt now. It is to be feared that such kind of people, as I have much observed, are either notoriously ignorant, or have some time or other fallen into some horrible secret, grievous sins, as whoredom, oppression, or the like, the guilt of which, lying yet secretly on them, makes them fly from the light of God's truth, which should find them out, quarreling both against it and the ministers that preach it. (Rom. ii. 8.) And therefore, as it is with thieves when they have any stolen goods brought within doors, they will not be searched or suspected, but say, they are as honest men as themselves that come to search; for they fear, if they be found out, that they shall be troubled before the judge, and may hardly escape with their lives: so many old professors, when the minister comes to search them, they clap to the doors upon the man and truth too, and say, they hope to be saved as well as the best of them all: the reason is, they are guilty; they are loth to be troubled and cast down by seeing the worst of themselves, and think it is hard for them to go to heaven and be saved, if they have been in a wrong way all their lifetime. An honest heart will cry after the best means, "Lord, search me," (John iii. 20,) and open all the doors to the entertainment of the straitest, strictest truths.

Thirdly. The understanding's obscurity, or ignorance of the infinite exactness, glorious purity, and absolute perfection of the law of God; whence it cometh to pass that this burning lamp, or bright sun of God's law, being set and obscured in their minds, rotten glowworms of their own righteousness, doing some things according to the law of God, shines and glisters gloriously in their eyes, in the dark nighttime of dismal darkness, by doing of which they think to please God, and their estates are very good. "I was alive," saith Paul, (Rom. vii. 9,) "without the law;" and he gives the reason of it, because sin did but sleep in him, like a cutthroat in a house where all is quiet. Before the law came, he saw not that deadly secret score of corruption, and that litter of rebellion that was lurking in his heart, and therefore thought highly of himself for his own righteousness. The gospel is a glass to show men the face of God in Christ. (2 Cor. ii. ult.) The law is that glass that showeth a man his own face, and what he himself is. Now, if this glass be taken away, and not set before a deformed heart, how can a man but think himself fair? And this is the reason why civil men, formalists, almost every one, think better of themselves than indeed they are, because they reckon without their host; that is, they judge of the number, nature, and greatness of their sins by their own books, by their own reason; they look not God's debt book, God's exact laws over, and compare themselves therewith; if they did, it would amaze the stoutest heart, and pluck down men's plumes, and make them say, Is there any mercy so great as to pass by such sins, and to put up such wrongs, and to forgive such sins and debts, one of which alone may undo me, much more so many?

Fourthly. The understanding's security or sleepiness, whereby men never reflect upon their own actions, nor compare them with the rule; although they have knowledge of the law of God, yet it is with them as it is with men that have a fair glass before them, but never beholding themselves in the glass, they never see their spots. This is the woe of most unregenerate men; they want a reflecting power, and light to judge of themselves by. (Jer. viii. 6.) You shall have them think on a sermon, Here is for such a one, and such a one is touched here; when it may be the same sermon principally speaks of them; but they never say, This concerneth me; I was found out through the goodness of the Lord to-day, and surely the man spake unto none but unto me, as if somebody had told him what I have done. And hence you shall find out many lame Christians, that will yield to all the truths delivered in a sermon, and commend it too, but go away and shake off all truths that serve to convince them. And hence many men, when they examine themselves in general, whether they have grace or no, whether they love Christ or no, they think yes, that they do with all their hearts; yet they neither have this grace nor any other, whatever they think, because they want a reflecting light to judge of generals by their own particular courses. For tell these men that he that loves one another truly, will often think of him, speak of him, rejoice in his company, will not wrong him willingly in the least thing; now, ask them, if they love Christ thus. If they have any reflecting light, they will see where they have one thought of Christ, they have a thousand on other things. Rejoice! nay, they are weary of his company in word, in prayer. And that they do not only wrong him, but make a light matter of it when it is done. All are sinners, and no man can live without sin. Like a sleepy man, (fire burning in his bed straw,) he cries not out, when others happily lament his estate, that see afar off, but can not help him. (Is. xlii. 25.) A man that is to be hanged the next day may dream over night he shall be a king. Why? Because he is asleep, he reflects not on himself. Thou mayest go to the devil, and be damned, and yet ever think and dream that all is well with thee. Thou hast no reflecting light to judge of thyself. Pray therefore that the Lord would turn your eyes inward, and do not let the devil and delusion shut you out of your own house, from seeing what court is kept there every day.

Fifthly. The understanding's impiety, whereby it lessens and vilifies the glorious grace of God in another ; whence it comes to pass, that this deluded soul, seeing none much better than himself, concludes, If any be saved, I shall no doubt be one. (Is. xxvi. 10, 11.) Men will not behold the majesty of God in the lives of his people ; many a man being too light, yet desirous to go and pass for current, weighs himself with the best people, and thinks, What have they that I have not? what do they that I do not? And if he see they go beyond him, then he turns his own balance with his finger, and makes them too light, that so he himself may pass for weight.

And this vilifying of them and their grace, judging them to be of no other metal then other men, appears in three particulars.

First. They raise up false reports of God's people, and nourish a kennel of evil suspicions of them ; if they know any sin committed by them, they will conclude they be all such; if they see no offensive sin in any of them, they are then reputed a pack of hypocrites ; if they are not so uncharitable, (having no grounds,) they prophesy they will hereafter be as bad as others, though they carry a fair flourish now.

Secondly. If they judge well of them, then they compare themselves to them, by taking a scantling only by their outside, and by what they see in them ; and so, like children, seeing stars a great way off, think them no bigger nor brighter than winking candles. They stand afar off from seeing the inside of a child of God; they see not the glory of God filling that temple ; they see not the sweet influence they receive from heaven, and that fellowship they have with their God; and hence they judge but meanly of them, because the outside of a Christian is the worst part of him, and his glory shines chiefly within.

Thirdly. If they see God's people do excel them, that they have better lives, better hearts, and better knowledge, yet they will not conclude that they have no grace, because it hath not that stamp, that honest men's money hath. But this prank they play ; they think such and such good men have a greater measure and a higher degree of grace than themselves, yet they dare be bold to think and say their hearts are as upright, though they be not so perfect as others are; and so vilify the grace that shines in the best men, by making this gold to differ from their own copper, not essentially, but gradually, and hence they deceive themselves miserably ; not but that one (star or) sincere Christian differs from another in glory ; I speak of those men only that never were fixed in so high a sphere as true honesty dwells, yet falsely father this bad conclusion, that they are upright for their measure, that they have not the like measure of grace received as others have.

Sixthly. The understanding's idolatry, whereby the mind sets up, and bows down to a false image of grace; that is, the mind, being ignorant of the height and excellency of true grace, takes a false scantling of it, and so imagines and fancies, within itself, such a measure of common grace to be true grace, which the soul easily having attained unto conceives it is in the estate of grace, and so deceives itself miserably. (Rom. x. 3.)   And the mind comes to set up her image thus : —

First. The mind is haunted and pursued with troublesome fears of hell; conscience tells him he has sinned, and the law tells him he shall die, and Death appears, and tells him he must shortly meet with him ; and if he be taken away in his sins, then comes a black day of reckoning for all his privy pranks, a day of blood, horror, judgment, and fire, where no creature can comfort him. Hence saith he, Lord, keep my soul from these miseries : he hopeth it shall not prove so evil with him, but fears it will.

Secondly. Hereupon he desireth peace and ease, and some assurance of freedom from these evils.   For it is a hell above ground ever to be on the rack of tormenting fears.

Thirdly. That he may have ease, he will not swagger his trouble away, nor drown it in the bottom of the cup, nor throw it away with his dice, nor play it away at cards, but desires some grace, (and commonly it is the least measure of it too.)   Hereupon he desires to hear such sermons and read such books as may best satisfy him concerning the least measure of grace; for, sin only troubling him, grace only can comfort him soundly.   And so, grace, which is meat and drink to a holy heart, is but physic to this kind of men, to ease them of their fears and troubles.

Hereupon, being ignorant of the height of true grace, he fancieth to himself such a measure of common grace to be true grace. As, if he feels himself ignorant of that which troubles him, So much knowledge will I then get, saith he.   If some foul sins in his practice trouble him, these he will cast away, and so reforms. If omission of good duties molest him, he will hear better, and buy some good prayer book, and pray oftener.   And if he be persuaded such a man is a very honest man, then he will strive to do as he doth; and now he is quieted.

When he hath attained unto this pitch of his own, now he thinks himself a young beginner, and a good one too; so that if he dieth, he thinks he shall do well; if he liveth, he thinks and hopes he shall grow better; and when he is come to his own

7 *

pitch, he here sets down his staff, as fully satisfied. And now, if he be pressed to get into the estate of grace, his answer is, That is not to be done now: he thanks God that care is past. The truth is (beloved) it is too high for him; his own legs could never carry him thither, all his grace coming by his own working, not by God Almighty's power. Let a man have false weights, he is cheated grievously with light gold. Why? Because his weights are too light, so these men have too light weights to judge of the weight of true grace; therefore light, clipped, cracked pieces cheat them. Hence you shall have those men commend pithless, sapless men, for very honest men as ever break bread. Why? They are just answerable to their weights. Hence I have not much wondered at them who maintain that a man may fall away from true grace; the reason lieth here: They set up to themselves such a common work of grace to be true grace, from which no wonder that a man may fall. Hence Bellarmine saith, That which is true grace, *veritate essentiæ*, only, may be lost; not that grace which is true, *veritate firmæ soliditatis*, which latter, being rightly understood, may be called special grace, as the other common grace. Hence also you shall have many professors hearing a hundred sermons never moved to grow better. Hence likewise you shall see our common preachers comfort every one, almost, that they see troubled in mind, because they think presently, they have true grace, now they begin to be sorrowful for their sins. It is just according to their own light weights.

For the Lord's sake take heed of this deceit. True grace (I tell you) it is a rare pearl, a glorious sun clouded from the eyes of all but them that have it, (Rev. ii. 17;) a strange, admirable, almighty work of God upon the soul, which no created power can produce; as far different, in the least measure of it, from the highest degree of common grace, as a devil is from an angel; for it is Christ living, breathing, reigning, fighting, conquering in the soul. Down, therefore, with your idol grace, your idol honesty; true grace never aims at a pitch; it aspires only to perfection. (Phil. iii. 12, 13.) And therefore Chrysostom calls St. Paul *insatiabilis Dei cultor* — a greedy, insatiable worshiper of the Lord Almighty.

Seventhly. The understanding's error is another cause of man's ruin. And that is seen principally in these five things, these five errors or false conceits: —

First. In judging some trouble of mind, some light sorrow for sin, to be true repentance; and so, thinking they do repent, hope they shall be saved. For sin is like sweet poison; while a man is drinking it down by committing it, there is much pleasure in it; but after the committing of it, there is a sting in it, (Prov. xxiii. 31, 32;) then the time cometh when this poison works, making the heart swell with grief; sorry they are at the heart, they say, for it; and the eyes drop, and the man that committed sin with great delight now cries out with grief in the bitterness of his soul, O that I, beast that I am, had never committed it! Lord, mercy, mercy! (Prov. v. 3, 4, 11, 12.) Nay, it may be they will fast, and humble and afflict their souls voluntarily for sin; and now they think they have repented, (Is. lviii. 3,) and hereupon when they hear that all that sin shall die, they grant this is true indeed, except a man repent, and so they think they have done already. This is true; at what time soever a sinner repents, the Lord will blot out his iniquity: but this repentance is not when a man is troubled somewhat in mind for sin, but when he cometh to mourn for sin as his greatest evil, and if he should see all his goods and estate on a light fire before him; and that not for some sins, but all sins, little and great; and that not for a time, for a fit and away, (a land flood of sorrow,) but always like a spring never dry, but ever running all a man's lifetime.

Secondly. In judging the striving of conscience against sin to be the striving of the flesh against the spirit; and hence come these speeches from carnal black mouths; the spirit is willing, but the flesh is weak. And hence men think, they, being thus compounded of flesh and spirit, are regenerate, and in no worse estate than the children of God themselves. As sometime I once spake with a man, that did verily think that Pilate was an honest man, because he was so unwilling to crucify Christ; which unwillingness did arise only from the restraint of conscience against the fact. So, many men judge honestly, yet simply, upon such a ground of themselves: they say, they strive against their sins, but, Lord be merciful unto them, they say, the flesh is frail. And hence Arminius gives a diverse interpretation of the seventh chapter to the Romans from ordinary divines; concerning which Paul speaks in the person of an unregenerate man, because he observed divers graceless persons (as he saith himself) having fallen, and falling commonly into sins against conscience, to bring that chapter in their own defense and comfort, because they did that which they allowed not, (ver. 15,) and so it was not they, but sin that dwelled in them.

And so many among us know they should be better, and strive that they may grow better, but, through the power of sin, can not; conscience tells them they must not sin, their hearts and lusts say they must sin; and here, forsooth, is flesh and spirit.

O, no, here is conscience and lust only by the ears together; which striving, Herod, Balaam, Pilate, or the vilest reprobate in the world may have. Such a war argueth not any grace in the heart, but rather more strength of corruption, and more power of sin in the heart; as it is no wonder if a horse run away when he is loose; but when his bit and his bridle are in his mouth, now to be wild, argueth he is altogether untamed and subdued. Take heed, therefore, of judging your estate to be good, because of some backwardness of your hearts to commit some sins, though little sins; for thy sins may be, and it is most certain are, more powerful in thee than in others that have not the like strugglings, because they have not such checks as thou hast to restrain thee. Know, therefore, that the striving of the spirit against the flesh is against sin because it is sin; as a man hates a toad, though he be never poisoned by it; but the striving of thy conscience against sin is only against sin because it is a troubling or a damning sin. The striving of the spirit against the flesh is from a deadly hatred of sin. (Rom. vii. 15.) But thy striving of conscience against sin is only from a fear of the danger of sin. For Balaam had a mind to curse the Israelites, for his money's sake; but if he might have had a house full of silver and gold, (which is a goodly thing in a covetous eye,) it is said, he durst not curse them.

Thirdly. In judging of the sincerity of the heart, by some good affection in the heart. Hence many a deluded soul reasons the case out thus with himself: Either I must be a profane man, or a hypocrite, or an upright man. Not profane, I thank God; for I am not given to whoring, drinking, oppression, swearing; nor hypocrite, for I hate these shows, I can not endure to appear better without than I am within; therefore I am upright. Why? O, because my heart is good; my affections and desires within are better than my life without; and whatever others judge of me, I know mine own heart, and the heart is all that God desires. And thus they fool themselves. (Prov. xxviii. 26.) This is one of the greatest causes and grounds of mistake amongst men that think best of themselves: they are not able to put a difference between the good desires and strong affections that arise from the love of Jesus Christ.

Self-love will make a man seek his own good and safety; hence it will pull a man out of his bed betimes in the morning, and call him up to pray; it will take him and carry him into his chamber toward evening, and there privately make him seek, and pray, and tug hard for pardon, for Christ, for mercy: Lord, evermore give us of this bread! But the love of Christ makes a man desire Christ and his honor for himself, and all other things for Christ. It is true, the desires of sons in Christ by faith are accepted ever; but the desires of servants, men that work only for their wages out of Christ, are not.

Fourthly. In judging of God's love to them, by aiming sometimes at the glory of God. Is this possible, that a man should aim at God's glory, and yet perish? Yes, and ordinarily too: a man may be liberal to the poor, maintain the ministry, be forward and stand for good things, whence he may not doubt but that God loves him: but here is the difference — though a wicked man may make God's glory in some particular things his end, yet he never makes it, in his general course, his utmost and last end. A subtle apprentice may do all his master's work, but he may take the gain to himself, or divide it betwixt his master and himself, and so may be but a knave, as observant as he seems to be: so a subtle heart (yet a villainous heart) may forsake all the world, as Judas did, may bind himself apprentice to all the duties God requires outwardly at his hands, and so do good works; but what is his last end? It is that he might gain respect or place, or that Christ may have some part of the glory, and he another. Simon Magus would give any money sometimes that he could pray so well, know so much, and do as others do; and yet his last end is for himself: but "how can you believe, if you seek not that glory that comes from God?" saith Christ. There is many seek the honor of Christ; but do you seek his honor only? Is it your last end, where you rest and seek no more but that? If thou wouldest know whether thou makest Christ's glory thy last end, observe this rule: —

If thou art more grieved for the eclipse of thine own honor, and for thine own losses, than for the loss of God's honor, it is an evident sign thou lovest it not, desirest it not as thy chiefest good, as the last end, for thy *summum bonum*, and therefore dost not seek God's honor in the prime and chiefest place. Sin troubled Paul more than all the plagues and miseries of the world. Indeed, if thy name be dashed with disgrace, and thy will be crossed, thy heart is grieved and disquieted: but the Lord may lose his honor daily by thine own sins, and those that be round about thee, but not a tear, not a sigh, not a groan to behold such a spectacle: as sure as the Lord lives, thou seekest not the Lord's name or honor as thy greatest good.

Fifthly. In judging the power of sin to be but infirmity; for if any thing trouble an unregenerate man, and makes him call his estate into question, it is sin, either in the being or power of it. Now, sin in the being ought not, must not, make a man question his estate, because the best have that left in them that will humble them, and make them live by faith; therefore the power of sin only can justly thus trouble a man. Now, if a man do judge of this to be only but infirmity, which the best are compassed about withal, he can not but lie down securely and think himself well. And if this error be settled in one that lives in no one known sin, it is very difficult to remove; for let the minister cast the sparks of hell in their faces, and denounce the terror of God against them, they are never stirred. Why? Because they think, Here is for you that live in sin, but as for themselves, although they have sins, yet they strive against them, and so can not leave them; for we must have sin as long as we live here, they say. Now, mark it, there is no surer sign of a man under the bloody reign and dominion of his lusts and sins, than this — that is, to give way to sin, (though never so little and common,) nor to be greatly troubled for sin, (for they may be a little troubled,) because they can not overcome sin. I deny not but the best do sin daily; yet this is the disposition of Paul, and every child of God — he mourneth not the less, but the more for sins; though he can not quite subdue them, cast them out, and overcome them. As a prisoner mourns the more that he is bound with such fetters he can not break, so doth every one truly sensible of his woful captivity by sin. This is the great difference between a raging sin a man will part withal, and a sin of infirmity a man can not part withal: a sin of infirmity is such a sin as a man would, but can not part with it, and hence he mourns the more for it; a raging sin is such a sin as a man, haply by virtue of his lashing conscience, would sometimes part withal, but can not, and hence mourns the less for it, and gives way to it. Now, for the Lord's sake, take heed of this deceit; for I tell you, those sins you can not part withal, if you groan not day and night under them, (saying, O Lord, help me, for I am weary of myself and my life,) will certainly undo you. You say, you can not but speak idly, and think vainly, and do ill, as all do sometimes; I tell you, those sins shall be everlasting chains to hold you fast in the power of the devil, until the judgment of the great day.

And thus much of the understanding's corruption, whereby men are commonly deluded. Now followeth the second.

Secondly. In regard of the false, bastard peace begot in the conscience. Why should the camp tremble when scouts are asleep? or give false report when the enemies are near them? Most men think they are in a safe estate, because they were never in a troubled estate; or if they have been troubled, because they have got some peace and comfort after it. Now, this false peace is begot in the heart by these four means:—

1. By Satan.
2. By false teachers.
3. By a false spirit.
4. By a false application of true promises.

I. By Satan, whose kingdom shall fall if it should be divided, and be always in a combustion ; hence he laboreth for peace. (Luke xi. 24,) "When the strong man keepeth the palace, his goods are in peace ; " that is, when Satan, armed with abundance of shifts and carnal reasonings, possesseth men's souls, they are at peace. Now, look as masters give their servants peace, even so the devil.

1. By removing all things that may trouble them ; and, —

2. By giving unto them all things that may quiet and comfort them, as meat, drink, rest, lodging, &c., so doth Satan deal with his slaves and servants.

First. By removing those sins which trouble the conscience ; for a man may live in a sin, and yet never be troubled for that sin ; for sin against the light of conscience only troubles the conscience. As children that are tumbling and playing in the dust, they are not troubled with all the dust, nay, they take pleasure to wallow in it ; but only with that (whether it be small or great) that lights in their eyes. And hence that young man came boasting to Christ that he had kept all the commandments from his youth ; but went away sorrowful, because that dust, that sin he lived in with delight before, fell into his eyes, and therefore he was troubled. Now, mark the plot of the devil, when he can make a man live, and wallow, and delight in his sins, and so serve him ; and yet will not suffer him to live in any sin against conscience, whereby he should be troubled, and so seek to come out of this woful estate, he is sure this man is his own ; and now a poor deluded man himself goes up and down, not doubting but he shall be saved. Why ? Because their conscience (they thank God) is clear, and they know of no one sin they live in, they know nothing by themselves that may make them so much as suspect their estate is bad. (Matt. ix. 13,) " I came not to call the righteous, but sinners, to repentance ; " that is, such a one as in his own opinion is fish-whole ; every sin being a child of God's sickness, he is never without some kind of sorrow ; but some sins only being a natural man's sickness, they being removed, he recovers out of his former sorrow, and grows well again, and thinks himself sound : the Lord Jesus never came to save such, therefore Satan keeps possession of them. For the Lord's sake, look to this subtlety : many think themselves in a good estate, because they know not the particular sin they live in ; whereas Satan may have stronger possession of such as are bound with his invisible fetters and chains, when those that have their pinching bolts on them may sooner escape.

Secondly. By giving the soul liberty to recreate itself in any sinful course, wherein the eye of conscience may not be pricked and wounded. Servants, when they are put always to work, and never can go abroad, are weary both of work and master; that master pleaseth them that giveth them most liberty. To be pent up all the day long in doing God's work, watching, praying, fighting against every sin, this is a burden, this is too strict; and because that they can not endure it, they think the Lord looks not for it at their hands. Now, Satan gives men liberty in their sinful courses; and this liberty begets peace, and this peace makes them think well of themselves. (2 Pet. ii. 19.) There are many rotten professors in these days, that, indeed, will not open their mouths against the sincere-hearted people of God; yet they walk loosely, and take too much liberty in their speeches, liberty in their thoughts, liberty in their desires and delights, liberty in their company, in their pastimes, and that sometimes under a pretense of Christian liberty; and never trouble themselves with these needless controversies : To what end, or in what manner, do I use these things? Whereas the righteous man feareth alway, considering there is a snare for him in every lawful liberty : May not I sin in my mirth, in my speaking, in my sleeping? O, this liberty that the devil gives, and the world takes, besots most men with a foolish opinion that all is well with them.

Thirdly. By giving the soul good diet, meat and drink enough, what dish he likes best. Let a master give liberty, yet his servant is not pleased, unless he have meat, and drink, and food; so there is no wicked man under heaven, but as he takes too much liberty in the use of lawful things, so he feedeth his heart with some unlawful secret lust, though all the time he live in it, it may be, it is unknown to him. (Luke xvi.) Dives had his dish, his good things, and so sang himself asleep, and bade his soul take his ease and rest; yea, observe this : diet is poisoned in itself, but ever commended to the soul as wholesome, good, and lawful. They christen sin with a new name, as popes are at their election; if he be bad, they call him sometimes Pius; if a coward, Leo, etc. So covetousness is good husbandry; company-keeping, good neighborhood; lying to save their credit from cracking, but a handsome excuse; and hence the soul goes peaceably on, and believes he is in a good estate.

Fourthly. By giving the soul rest and sleep, that is, cessation sometimes from the act of sin; hence they are hardly persuaded that they live in sin, because they cease sometimes from the act of sin; as no man doth always swear, nor is he always drunk, nor always angry. They think only their falls, in these or the like sins, are slips and falls which the best men may have sometimes, and yet be a dear child of God. O, Satan will not always set men at his work; for if men should always have their cups in their hands, and their queans in their arms; if a covetous man should always root in the earth, and never pray, never have good thoughts, never keep any Sabbath; if a man should always speak idly, and never good word drop from him, a man's conscience would never be quiet, but shaking him up for what he doth; but by giving him respite for sinning for a time, Satan getteth stronger possession afterward; as Matt. xii. 43. When the unclean spirit is gone out of a man, it returns worse. Samson's strength always remained, and so doth sin's strength in a natural man, but it never appears until temptation come.

Fifthly. By giving the soul fair promises of heaven and eternal life, and fastening them upon the heart. Most men are confident their estate is good; and though God kills them, yet will they trust in him, and can not be beaten from this. Why? O, Satan bewitcheth them; for as he told Evah by the serpent, she should not die, so doth he insinuate his persuasions to the soul, though it live in sin, he shall not die, but do well enough as the precisest. Satan gives thus good words, but woful wages — the eternal flashes of hell.

II. By false teachers, who, partly by their loose examples, partly by their flattering doctrines in public, and their large charity in private, daubing up every one, (especially he that is a good friend unto them,) for honest and religious people; and if they be but a little troubled, applying comfort presently, and so healing them that should be wounded, and not telling them roundly of their Herodias, as John Baptist did Herod. Hereupon they judge themselves honest, because the minister will give them the beggarly passport; and so they go out of the world, and die like lambs, wofully cheated. (Matt. xxiv. 11.) Look abroad in the world and see what is the reason so many feed their heart with confidence they shall be saved, yet their lives condemn them, and their hearts acquit them. The reason is, such and such a minister will go to the alehouse, and he never prays in his family, and he is none of these precise, hot people, and yet as honest a man as ever lives, and a good divine, too. Ahab was miserably cheated by four hundred false prophets. Whilst the minister is of a loose life himself, he will wink at others and their faults, lest in reproving others he should condemn himself, and others should say unto him, "Physician, heal thyself." Thieves of the same company will not steal from one another, lest they trouble thereby themselves. And hence they give others false cards to sail by, false rules to live by; their unconscionable large charity is like a gulf that swalloweth ships, (souls I mean,) tossed with tempests and not comforted. (Is. liv. 7, 8.) And hence all being fish that cometh to their net, all men think so of themselves.

III. A false spirit. This is a third cause that begets a false peace. As there is a true "Spirit that witnesseth to our spirits that we are the sons of God," (Rom. viii. 15,) so there is a false spirit, just like the true one, witnessing that they are the sons of God. (1 John iv. 1.) We are bid to try the spirits. Now, if these spirits, were not like God's true Spirit, what need trial? As, what need one try whether dirt be gold, which are so unlike each other? And this spirit I take to be set down, Matt. xxiv. 23. Now, look as the true Spirit witnesseth, so the false spirit, being like it, witnesseth also.

First. The Spirit of God humbles the soul; so before men have the witness of the false spirit, they are mightily cast down and dejected in spirit, and hereupon they pray for ease, and purpose to lead new lives, and cast away the weapons, and submit. (Ps. lxvi. 3.)

Secondly. The Spirit of God in the gospel reveals Jesus Christ and his willingness to save; so the false spirit discovereth Christ's excellency, and willingness to receive him, if he will but come in. It fareth with this soul as with surveyors of lands, that take an exact compass of other men's grounds, of which they shall never enjoy a foot. So did Balaam. (Num. xxiv. 5, 6.) This false spirit showeth them the glory of heaven and God's people.

Thirdly. Hereupon the soul cometh to be affected, and to taste the goodness and sweetness of Jesus Christ, as those did, (Heb. vi.;) and the soul breaks out into a passionate admiration: O that ever there should be any hope for such a vile wretch as I am, and have been! and so joys exceedingly, like a man half way rapt up into heaven.

Fourthly. Hereupon the soul, being comforted after it was wounded, now calleth God my God, and Christ my sweet Saviour; and now it doubts not but it shall be saved. Why? Because I have received much comfort after much sorrow and doubting, (Hos. viii. 2, 3;) and yet remains a deluded, miserable creature still. But here mark the difference between the witness of each spirit. The false spirit makes a man believe he is in the state of grace, and shall be saved, because he hath tasted of Christ, and so hath been comforted, and that abundantly. But the true Spirit persuades a man his estate is good and safe, because he hath not only tasted, but bought this Christ, as the wise merchant in the gospel, that rejoiced he had found the pearl, but yet stays not here, but sells away all, and buys the pearl. Like two chapmen that come to buy wine; the one tastes it, and goeth away in a drunken fit, and so concludes it is his; so a man doth, that hath the false spirit; but the true-spirited man doth not only taste, but buys the wine, although he doth not drink it all down when he cometh to taste it; yet he having been incited by tasting to buy it, now he calls it his own. So a child of God tasting a little of God, and a little of Christ, and a little of the promises at his first conversion, although he tastes not all the sweetness that is in God, yet he forsakes all for God, for Christ, and so takes them lawfully as his own.

Again : the false spirit, having given a man comfort and peace, suffers a man to rest in that state; but the true Spirit, having made the soul taste the love of the Lord, stirreth up the soul to do and work mightily for the Lord. Now the soul crieth out, What shall I do for Christ, that hath done wonders for me? If every hair on my head were a tongue to speak of his goodness, it were too little. (Neh. viii. 10,) "The joy of the Lord is our strength." (Ps. li. 12,) "Uphold me with thy free spirit;" or, as the Chaldean paraphrase hath it, thy "kingly spirit;" the spirit of adoption in God's child is no underling, suffering men to lie down, and cry, My desires are good, but flesh is frail. No, it is a kingly spirit, that reigns where it liveth.

IV. False applying of true promises is the last cause of false peace. And when a man hath God's Spirit within, and God's hand and promise (as he thinks) for his estate, now he thinks all safe. This did the Jews ; they said, "We have Abraham to our Father;" and so reputed themselves safe, God having made them promise, "I will be a God of thee and of thy seed." But here is a difference between a child of God's application of them and a wicked man's. The first applieth them so to him, as that he liveth upon them, and nothing but them; and to whom doth the dug belong, but to the child that lives upon it? The other lives upon his lusts, and creatures, and yet catcheth hold on the promise.

By these four means is begot a bastard, false peace.

Thus much of the second cause of man's deceiving himself — false peace in the conscience.

Now followeth the third.

III. The corruptions and distempers of the will, which is the third cause why men deceive themselves; which are many. I will only name three.

First. When the will is resolved to go on in a sinful course, and then sets the understanding a-work to defend it. Whence it fareth with the soul as with a man that cometh to search for stolen goods, who, having received a bribe beforehand, searcheth every where but where it is, and so the man is never found out to be what he is. So a man having tasted the sweetness of a sinful course, (which pleasure bribes him,) he is contented to search into every corner of his heart, and to try himself, as many do, except there where his darling lust lies; he sits upon that, and covers it willingly from his own eyes, as Rachel did upon stolen gods, and so never finds out himself. (John iii. 20,) A man that hath a mind to sleep quietly, will cause the curtains to be drawn, and will let some light come in, but shuts out all that, or so much as may hinder him from sleeping; so a man, having a mind to sleep in some particular sinful course at his ease, will search himself, and let some light come into his mind.

And hence many profane persons, that know much, (their opinions are orthodox, their discourse savory,) yet do they know little of themselves, and of those sins and lusts that haunt them, which they must part with; because this light troubleth them, it hinders them from sleeping in their secure estate, and therefore they draw the curtain here. Hence many men, that live in those sins of the grossest usury, finding the gain, and tasting the sweet of that sin, will read all books, go to all those ministers they suppose that hold it lawful, and so pick up and gather reasons to defend the lawfulness of the sin, and so, because they would not have it to be a sin, find out reasons whereby they think it no sin; but the bottom is this — their will hath got the bribe, and now the understanding plays the lawyer; and hence men live in the most crying sins, and are sure to perish, because they will not know they are in an error.

Secondly. When the will sets the understanding a-work to extenuate and lessen sin; for many, when they see their sins, yet make it small by looking at the false end of their optic glass; they think such small matters never make any breach between the Lord and their souls. Hence they say, The best man sins seven times a day; and who can say, My heart is clean? What is the reason that a child of God hath little peace, many times after commission of small sins? O, it is because they see the horrible nature of the least sin; small wrongs against so dear, so great a friend as the Lord is, it cuts their hearts; yet a carnal heart is never troubled for great sins, because they make a light matter of them.

Thirdly. Willful ignorance of the horrible wrath of God. Hence men rush on in sin as the horse into the battle. Hence men never fear their estates, because they know not God's wrath hanging over them. Coldest snakes, when they are frozen with cold, never sting nor hurt; one may carry a nest of them in his bosom; but bring them to the fire, then they hiss and sting: so sin, when it is brought near God's wrath, (that devouring fire,) it makes men cry out of themselves, Then I am undone! O, I am a lost creature! But being not thus heated, sin never makes a man cry out of himself.

These are the causes why men are ignorant of their woful, miserable estate; which ignorance is the first rock, or the first powder plot, that spoils thousands.

Yet there are three more dangerous, because more secret.

Now followeth the second reason of man's ruin. By reason of man's carnal security, whereby men can not be affected with, nor so much as have hearts to desire to come out of their misery when they know it; for, if a man's mind understand his misery, yet if the heart be hard or sleepy, and not affected, loaded, wounded, humbled, and made to groan under it, he will never greatly care to come out of it. (Is. xxix. 9, 10.) Now, this is the estate of many a soul; he doth know his misery, but by reason of the sleepy, secure, senseless spirit of slumber, he never feels it, nor mourns under it, and so comes not out of it.

Now the reasons of this security are these: —

Because God pours not out the full measure of his wrath upon men, because he kindles not the pile of wrath that lies upon men, it is reserved, and concealed, not revealed from Heaven; and so long, let God frown, ministers threaten, and smaller judgments drop, yet they will never seek shelter in Jesus Christ, but sleep in their sins, until God rain down floods of horror, blood, fire; until God's arrows stick in men's hearts, they will never seek out of themselves unto Jesus Christ. (Eccl. viii. 11.) So long as God's plagues were upon Pharaoh, he giveth fair words, and Moses must be sent to pray for him; but when God's hand is taken away, now Pharaoh's heart is hardened: so long as God's sword is in his scabbard, men have such stout hearts that they will never yield; God must wound, and cut deep, and stab, and thrust to the very heart, else men will never yield, never awaken, till God's fists be about men's ears, and he is dragging them to the stake; men will never awake and cry for a pardon and deliverance of their woful estate.

Secondly. Because if they do in part feel, and so fear God's wrath, they put away the evil day far from them; they hope

8 *

they shall do better hereafter, and repent some other time, and therefore they say, Soul, eat, drink, follow thy sports, cups, queans; thou hast a treasure of time which shall not be spent in many years, (Is. xxii. 12, 13;) that look as it is with the wax, let it be of never so pliable a disposition, and the fire never so hot, yet if it be not brought near the fire, and be held in the fire, it never melts, but still remains hard; so it is here. Let a man or woman have never so gentle or pliable a nature, and let God's wrath be never so hot and dreadful in their judgments, yet if they make not the day of wrath present to them, if they see it not ready every moment to light upon their hearts, they are never melted, but they remain hard hearted, secure, sleepy wretches, and never groan to come out of their woful estate; and this is the reason why many men, that have many guilty consciences, though they have many secret wishes and purposes to be better, yet never cry out of themselves, nor ever seek earnestly for mercy, till they lie upon their death beds; and then, O the promises they ply God with! Try me, Lord, and restore me once more to my health and life again, and thou shalt see how thankful I will be! because that now they apprehend wrath and misery near unto them. (Heb. iii. 13.)

Thirdly. Because they think they can bear God's wrath, though they do conceive it near at hand, even at the very doors; men think not that hell is so hot, nor the devil so black, nor God so terrible as indeed he is. And hence we shall observe the prophets present God's wrath as a thing intolerable before the eyes of the people, that thereby they might quench all those cursed conceits of being able to bear God's wrath. (Nahum i. 9.) And hence we shall have many men desperately conclude they will have their swing in sin, and if they perish, they hope they shall be able to bear it; it is but a damning they think, and hence they go on securely. O, poor wretches! the devil scares and fears all the world, and at God's wrath the devils quake, and yet secure men fear it not, they think hell is not so terrible a place.

Fourthly. Because they know no better an estate. Hence, though they feel their woful and miserable condition, yet they desire not to come out of it. Although men find hard lodging in the world, hard times, hard friends, hard hearts, yet they make a shift with what they find in this miserable inn, until they come to hell; for such a man, pursued by outward miseries, or inward troubles, there stays; O, miserable man, that makes shift till he come to hell! They may hear of the happy estate of God's people, but not knowing of it experimentally, they stay where they are. (Job iv. 14.)

Take a prince's child, and bring it up in a base house and place, it never aspires after a kingdom or crown; so men hatched in this world, knowing no better an estate, never cast about them to get a better inheritance than that they scramble for here. Wives mourn for the long absence of their beloved husbands, because they know them and their worth. God may absent himself from men weeks, months, years, but men shed not one tear for it, because they never tasted the sweetness of his presence. It is strange to see men take more content in their cups and cards, pots and pipes, dogs and hawks, than in the fellowship of God and Christ, in word, in prayer, in meditation; which ordinances are burdens and prison unto them. What is the reason of it? Is there no more sweetness in the presence of God's smiling in Christ than in a filthy whore? Yes; but they know not the worth, sweetness, satisfying goodness of a God. Some sea fish, (say they,) if once they come into fresh water, will never return again, because they now taste a difference between those brackish and sweet waters: so is it here; if men did but once taste the happiness of God's people, they would not for a thousand worlds be one half hour in their wild, loose sea again.

Fifthly. Because, if they do know a better estate, yet their present pleasures, their sloth, doth so bewitch them, and God's denials, when they seek unto him, do so far discourage them, that they sleep still securely in that estate. A slothful heart, bewitched with present ease, and pleasures, and delights, considering many a tear, many a prayer must it make, many a night must it break its sleep, many a weary step must it take towards heaven and Christ, if ever it come there, grows discouraged, and deaded, and hard-hearted in a sleepy estate, and had rather have a bird in the hand than two in the bush; Israelites wished that they were at their onions and garlic again in Egypt. Was there no Canaan? Yes; but they wished so because there were walls built up to heaven, and giants, sons of Anak, in the land, difficulties to overcome. O, slothful hearts! Secondly. Because God sometimes put them to straits, and denied them what they sought for, they were of such a waspish, testy, sullen spirit, that, because the Lord had them not always on his knees, they would run away; so many a man meets with sorrow enough in his sinful, dropsy, drunken estate; he hears of Heaven, and a better estate, yet why goes he to his lusts and flesh pots again? O, because there are so many difficulties, and blocks, and hinderances in his way; and because they pray and find not ease, therefore they eat, drink, laugh, sport, and sleep in their miserable estate still. (Matt. vii. 14.) Therefore men walk in the broad way, because the other way to life is strait and narrow; it is a plague, a burden, a prison, to be so strict; men had rather sit almost an hour in the stocks than be an hour at prayer; men had rather be damned at last than sweat it out and run through the race to receive a crown; and hence men remain secure.

Sixthly. Because of the strange, strong power of sin, which bears that sway over men's souls that they must serve it, as prisoners stoop to their jailers, as soldiers that have taken their pay, their pleasure of sin, must follow it as their captain, though they go marching on to eternal ruin; nay, though doomsday should be to-morrow, yet they must and will serve their lusts. As the Sodomites, when they were smitten with blindness, which tormented their eyes as though they had been pricked with thorns, (for so the Hebrew word signifies,) even when destruction was near, they groped for the door. Men can not but sin, though they perish for sin; hence they remain secure.

Seventhly. Despair of God's mercy: hence, like Cain, men are renegades from the face of God; men think they shall never find mercy when all is done; hence they grow desperately sinful; like those Italian senators, that, despairing of their lives, when upon submission they had been promised their lives, yet, being conscious of their villainy, made a curious banquet, and at the end of it every man drank up his glass of poison, and killed himself; so men feeling such horrible hard hearts, and being privy to such notorious sins, they cast away lives, and heaven, and soul for lost, and so perish wofully, because they lived desperately, and so securely.

Eighthly. Because men nourish a blind, false, flattering hope of God's mercy: hence many knowing and suspecting that all is naught with them, yet having some hope they may be in a good estate, and God may love them, hence they lie down securely, and rest in their flattering hope. Hence observe, those people that seldom come to a conclusion, to a point, that either they are in the state of grace or out of it, that never come to be affected, but remain secure in their condition, they commonly grow to this desperate conclusion: that they hope God will be merciful unto them; if not, they can not help it; like the man that had on his target the picture of God and the devil; under the first he wrote, *Si tu non vis*, if thou wilt not; under the other he wrote, *Ipse rogitat*, here is one will.

Ninthly. Because men bring not their hearts under the hammer of God's word to be broken, they never bring their consciences to be cut. Hence they go on still securely with festered consciences. Men put themselves above the word, and their hearts above the hammer; they come not to have the minister to humble them, but to judge of him, or to pick some pretty fine thing out of the word, and so remain secure sots all their days: for if ever thy heart be broken, and thy conscience be awaked, the word must do it; but people are so sermon-trodden, that their hearts, like footpaths, grow hard by the word.

Tenthly. Because men consider not of God's wrath daily, nor the horrible nature of sin; men chew not these pills: hence they never come to be affected nor awakened.

Awaken, therefore, all you secure creatures; feel your misery, that so you may get out of it. Dost thou know thine estate is naught, and that thy condemnation will be fearful, if ever thou dost perish? and is thine heart secretly secure, so damnably dead, so desperately hard, that thou hast no heart to come out of it? What! no sigh, no tears? Canst thou carry all thy sins upon thy back, like Samson the gates of the city, and make a light matter of them? Dost thou see hell fire before thee, and yet wilt venture? Art thou worse than a beast which we cannot beat nor drive into the fire if there be any way to escape? O, get thy heart to lament and mourn under thy miseries; who knows then but the Lord may pity thee? But O, hard heart! thou canst mourn for losses and crosses, burning of goods and houses, yet though God be lost, and his image burnt down, and all is gone, thou canst not mourn. If thine heart were truly affected, the pillow would be washed with thy tears, and the wife in thy bosom would be witness of thy heart-breakings in midnight for those sins which have grieved the Spirit of God many a time; thou couldst not sleep quietly nor comfortably without assurance. If you were sick to death, physicians should hear how you do; and if you were humbled, we should have you in the bitterness of your spirit cry out, "What shall we do?" But know it, thou must mourn here or in hell. If God broke David's bones for his adultery, and the angels' backs for their pride, the Lord, if ever he saves thee, will break thine heart too.

Question. But thou wilt say, How shall I do to get mine heart affected with my misery?

Answer. 1. Take a full view of thy misery. 2. Take special notice of the Lord's readiness and willingness to receive thee yet unto mercy; for two things harden the heart: 1. False hope, whereby a man hopes he is not so bad as indeed he is. 2. No hope, whereby a man, when he sees himself so notoriously bad, thinks there is no willingness in the Lord to pardon or receive such a monster of men to mercy; and, if neither the hammer can break thy stony heart, nor the sunshine of mercy melt it, thou hast a heart worse than the devil, and art a spectacle of the greatest misery, 1. In regard of sin. 2. In regard of God's wrath.

First. In regard of sin. Thou hast sinned, and that grievously, against a great God. Thou makest no great matter of this : no ; but, though it be no load to thee, it is load on the Lord's heart, (Is. i. 24,) and time will come he will make the whole sinful world, by rivers of fire and blood, to know what an evil it is ; for, —

1. In every sin thou dost strike God, and fling a dagger at the heart of God. 2. In every sin thou dost spite against God ; for, if there were but one only thing wherein a man could do his friend a displeasure, was not here spite seen if he did that thing ? Now tell me, hath not the Lord been a good friend unto thee ? Tell me, wherein hath he grieved thee ? and tell me, in what one thing canst thou please the devil, and do God a displeasure, but by sin ? Yet, O hard heart, thou makest nothing of it. But consider, thirdly, in every sin thou dost disthrone God, and settest thyself above God ; for, in every sin, this question is put, ¡Whose will shall be done, God's will or man's ? Now, man by sin sets his own will above the Lord's, and so kicks God (blessed forever, adored of millions of saints and angels) as filth under his feet. What, will this break your hearts ?

Consider, then, of God's wrath, the certainty of it, the unsupportableness of it, — how that, dying in thy sins and secure estate, it shall fall ; for, when men cry, Peace, peace, then cometh sudden destruction at unawares. Pray, therefore, to God to reveal this to thee, that thine heart may break under it. Secondly, consider the Lord's mercy and readiness to save thee, who hath prepared mercy, and entreats thee to take it, and waiteth every day for thee to that end.

The third reason of man's ruin is that carnal confidence, whereby men seek to save themselves, and to scramble out of their miserable estate by their own duties and performances, when they do feel themselves miserable. The soul doth as those (Hos. v. 13) men when they be wounded and troubled : they never look after Jesus Christ, but go to their own waters to heal themselves, like hunted harts when the arrow is in them. (Rom. ix. 31, 32.)

For the opening of this point, I shall show you these two things : —

1. Wherein this resting in duties appears.
2. Why do men rest in themselves ?

First. This resting in duties appears in these eleven degrees : —

1. The soul of a poor sinner, if ignorantly bred and brought up, rests confidently in superstitious vanities. Ask a devout Papist how he hopes to be saved; he will answer, by his good works. But inquire, further, What are these good works? Why, for the most part, superstitious ones of their own inventions, (for the crow thinks her own bird fairest,) as whipping themselves, pilgrimage, fasting, mumbling over their Paternosters, bowing down to images and crosses.

2. Now, these being banished from the church and kingdom, then men stand upon their titular profession of the true religion, although they be devils incarnate in their lives. Look up and down the kingdom ; you shall see some roaring, drinking, dicing, carding, whoring, in taverns and blind alehouses; others belching out their oaths, their mouths ever casting out, like raging seas, filthy, frothy speeches; others, like Ismaels, scoffing at the best men; yet these are confident they shall be saved. Why, (say they,) they are no Papists; hang them, they will die for their religion, and rather burn than turn again, by the grace of God. Thus the Jews boasted they were Abraham's seed; so our carnal people boast: Am not I a good Protestant? Am not I baptized? Do I not live in the church? and therefore, resting here, hope to be saved. I remember a judge, when one pleaded once with him for his life, that he might not be hanged because he was a gentleman ; he told him that therefore he should have the gallows made higher for him: so when thou pleadest, I am a Christian and a good Protestant, (yet thou wilt drink, and swear, and whore, neglect prayer, and break God's Sabbath,) and therefore thou hopest to be saved; I tell thee thy condemnation shall be greater, and the plagues in hell the heavier.

3. If men have no peace here, then they fly to, and rest in, the goodness of their insides. You will have many a man, whom, if you follow to his chamber, you shall find very devout; and they pray heartily for the mercy of God, and forgiveness of sins; but follow them out of their chambers, watch their discourses, you shall find it frothy and vain, and now and then powdered with faith and troth, and obscene speeches. Watch them when they are crossed, you shall see them as angry as wasps, and swell like turkeys, and so spit out their venom like dragons. Watch them in their journeys, and you shall see them shoot into an alehouse, and there swill and swagger, and be familiar with the scum of the country for profaneness, and half drunk, too, sometimes. Watch them on the Lord's day ; take

them out of the church once, and set aside their best clothes, and they are then the same as at another time ; and, because they must not work nor sport that day, they think they may with a good conscience sleep the longer on the morning. Ask, now, such men how they hope to be saved, seeing their lives are so bad ; they say, though they make not such shows, they know what good prayers they make in private ; their hearts, they say, are good. I tell ye, brethren, he that trusteth to his own heart and his good desires, and so resteth in them, is a fool. I have heard of a man that would haunt the taverns, and theaters, and whore houses at London all day ; but he durst not go forth without private prayer in a morning, and then would say, at his departure, Now, devil, do thy worst ; and so used his prayers (as many do) only as charms and spells against the poor, weak, cowardly devil, that they think dares not hurt them, so long as they have good hearts within them, and good prayers in their chambers ; and hence they will go near to rail against the preacher as a harsh master, if he do not comfort them with this — that God accepts of their good desires.

4. If their good hearts can not quiet them, but conscience tells them they are unsound without, and rotten at core within, then men fall upon reformation ; they will leave their whoring, drinking, cozening, gaming, company-keeping, swearing, and such like roaring sins ; and now all the country saith he is become a new man, and he himself thinks he shall be saved ; (2 Pet. ii. 20 ;) they escape the pollutions of the world, as swine that are escaped and washed from outward filth ; yet the swinish nature remains still ; like mariners that are going to some dangerous place, ignorantly, if they meet with storms, they go not backward, but cast out their goods that endanger their ship, and so go forward still ; so many a man, going toward hell, is forced to cast out his lusts and sins ; but he goeth on in the same way still for all that. The wildest beasts, (as stags,) if they be kept waking from sleep long, will grow tame ; so conscience giving a man no rest for some sins he liveth in, he groweth tame : he that was a wild gentleman before remains the same man still, only he is made tame now ; that is, civil and smooth in his whole course ; and hence they rest in reformation, which reformation is, commonly, but from some troublesome sin, and it is because they think it is better following their trade of sin at another market ; and hence some men will leave their drinking and whoring, and turn covetous, because there is more gain at that market ; sometimes it is because sin hath left them, as an old man.

5. If they can have no rest here, they get into another start-

ing hole: they go to their humiliations, repentings, tears, sorrows, and confessions. They hear a man can not be saved by reforming his life, unless he come to afflict his soul too; he must sorrow and weep here, or else cry out in hell hereafter. Hereupon they betake themselves to their sorrows, tears, confession of sins; and now the wind is down, and the tempest is over, and they make themselves safe. (Matt. xi. 1.) They would have repented; that is, the heathen, as Beza speaks, when any wrath was kindled from Heaven, they would go to their sackcloth and sorrows, and so thought to pacify God's anger again; and here they rested. So it is with many a man; many people have sick fits and qualms of conscience, and then they do as crows, that give themselves a vomit by swallowing down some stone when they are sick, and then they are well again; so when men are troubled for their sins, they will give themselves a vomit of prayer, a vomit of confession and humiliation. (Is. lviii. 5.) Hence many, when they can get no good by this physic, by their sorrows and tears, cast off all again; for, making these things their God and their Christ, they forsake them when they can not save them. (Matt. iii. 14.) More are driven to Christ by the sense of the burden of a hard, dead, blind, filthy heart than by the sense of sorrows, because a man rests in the one, viz., in sorrows, most commonly, but trembles and flies out of himself when he feels the other. Thus men rest in their repentance; and therefore Austin hath a pretty speech which sounds harsh, that repentance damneth more than sin; meaning that thousands did perish by resting in it; and hence we see, among many people, if they have large affections, they think they are in good favor; if they want them, they think they are castaways, when they can not mourn nor be affected as once they were, because they rest in them.

6. If they have no rest here, then they turn moral men; that is, strict in all the duties of the moral law, which is a greater matter than reformation or humiliation; that is, they grow very just and square in their dealings with men, and exceeding strict in the duties of the first table toward God, as fasting, prayer, hearing, reading, observing the Sabbath: and thus the Pharisees lived, and hence they are called "the strict sect of the Pharisees." Take heed you mistake me not; I speak not against strictness, but against resting in it; for except your righteousness exceed theirs, you shall not enter into the kingdom of heaven. You shall find these men fly from base persons and places, like the pest houses, commend the best books, cry down the sins of the time, and cry against civil or moral men, (the

eye sees not itself,) and cry up zeal and forwardness. Talk
with him about many moral duties that are to be done toward
God or man, he will speak well about the excellency and necessity of it, because his trade and skill, whereby he hopes to get
his living and earn eternal life, lieth there; but speak about
Christ, and living by faith in him and from him, and bottoming
the soul upon the promises, (pieces of evangelical righteousness,) he that is very skillful in any point of controversy is as
ignorant almost as a beast, when he is examined here. Hence,
if ministers preach against the sins of the time, they commend it
for a special sermon, (as it haply deserves, too;) but let him
speak of any spiritual, inward, soul-working points, they go away
and say he was in their judgment confused and obscure; for
their part they understood him not. (Beloved,) pictures are
pretty things to look on, and that is all the goodness of them; so
these men are, (as Christ looked on and loved the natural young
man in the gospel,) and that is all their excellency. You know,
in Noah's flood, all that were not in the ark, though they did
climb and get to the top of the tallest mountains, they were
drowned; so labor to climb never so high in morality, and the
duties of both tables, if thou goest not into God's ark, the Lord
Jesus Christ, thou art sure to perish eternally.

7. If they have no rest here in their morality, they grow hot
within, and turn marvelous zealous for good causes and courses;
and there they stay and warm themselves at their own fire : thus
Paul (Phil. iii. 6) was zealous, and there rested. They will
not live, as many do, like snails in their shells, but rather than
they will be damned for want of doing, they are content to give
away their estate, children, any thing almost, to get pardon for
the sin of their soul. (Micah vi. 7.)

8. If they find no help from hence, but are forced to see and
say, when they have done all, they are unprofitable servants, and
they sin in all that which they do, then they rest in that which
is like to evangelical obedience; they think to please God by
mourning for their failings in their good duties, desiring to be
better, and promising for the time to come to be so, and therein
rest. (Deut. v. 29.)

9. If they feel a want of all these, then they dig within themselves for power to leave sin, power to be more holy and humble,
and so think to work out themselves, in time, out of this estate,
and so they dig for pearls in their own dunghills, and will not be
beholding to the Lord Jesus; to live on him in the want of all;
they think to set up themselves out of their own stock, without
Jesus Christ, and so, as the prophet Hosea speaks, (xiv. 3, 4,)

thinĸ to save themselves, by their riding on horses, that is, by their own abilities.

10. If they feel no help here, then they go unto Christ for grace and power to leave sin and do better, whereby they may save themselves; and so they live upon Christ, that they may live of themselves; they go unto Christ, they get not into Christ, (Ps. lxxviii. 34, 35,) like hirelings that go for power to do their work, that they may earn their wages. A child of God contents himself with, and lives upon, the inheritance itself the Lord in his free mercy hath given him. But now we shall see many poor Christians that run in the very road the Papists devoutly go to hell in.

First. The Papist will confess his misery, that he is (and all men are) by nature a child of wrath, and under the power of sin and Satan.

Secondly. They hold Chirst is the only Saviour.

Thirdly. That this salvation is not by any righteousness in a Christ, but righteousness from a Christ, only by giving a man power to do, and then dipping men's doings in his blood, he merits their life. Thus the wisest and devotest of them profess, as I am able to manifest; just so do many Christians live.

First. They feel themselves full of sin, and are sometimes tired and weary of themselves, for their vile hearts, and they find no power to help themselves. Secondly. Hereupon hearing that only Christ can save them, they go unto Christ to remove these sins that tire them, and load them, that he would enable them to do better than formerly. Thirdly. If they get these sins subdued and removed, and if they find power to do better, then they hope they shall be saved : whereas thou mayest be damned, and go to the devil at the last, although thou dost escape all the pollutions of the world, and that not from thyself and strength, but from the knowledge of Jesus Christ. (2 Pet. ii. 20.) I say, woe to you forever if you die in this estate; it is with our Christians in this case as it is with the ivy, which clasps and groweth about the tree, and draws sap from the tree, but it grows not one with the tree, because it is not ingraffed into the tree; so many a soul cometh to Christ, to suck juice from Christ to maintain his own berries, (his own stock of grace :) alas ! he is but ivy, he is no member or branch of this tree, and hence he never grows to be one with Christ. 2. Now, the reasons why men rest in their duties are these : —

First. Because it is natural to a man out of Christ to do so. Adam and all his posterity were to be saved by his doing: " Do this and live; " work, and here is thy wages; win life, and wear it.

Hence all his posterity seeks to this day to be saved by doing; like father, like son. Now, to come out of all duties truly to a Christ, hath not so much as a coat in·innocent, much less corrupted nature; hence men seek to themselves. Now, as it is with a bankrupt, when his stock is spent, and his estate cracked, before he will turn prentice, or live upon another, he will turn peddler of small wares, and so follow his old trade with a less stock : so men naturally follow their old trade of doing, and hope to get their living that way; and hence men, having no experience of trading with Christ by faith, live of themselves. Samson, when all his strength was lost, would go to shake himself as at other times : so when men's strength is lost, and God and grace are lost, yet men will go and try how they can live by shifts and working for themselves still.

Secondly. Because men are ignorant of Jesus Christ and his righteousness; hence men can not go unto him, because they see him not; hence they shift as well as they·can for themselves by their duties. (John iv. 14.) Men seek to save themselves by their own swimming, when they see no cable cast out to help them.

Thirdly. Because this is the easiest way to comfort the heart, and pacify conscience, and to please God, as the soul thinks; because by this means a man goes no farther than himself.

Now, in forsaking all duties, a soul goeth to heaven quite out of himself, and there he must wait many a year, and that for a little, it may be. Now, if a fainting man have *aqua vitæ* at his bed's head, he will not knock up the shopkeeper for it. Men that have a balsam of their own to heal them will not go to the physician.

Fourthly. Because by virtue of these duties a man may hide his sin, and live quietly in his sin, yet be accounted an honest man, as the whore in Prov. vii. 15, 16, having performed her vows, can entice without suspicion of men or check of conscience : so the scribes and Pharisees were horribly covetous, but their long prayers covered their deformities, (Matt. xxiii. 14;) and hence men set their duties at a higher rate than they are worth, thinking they shall save them because they are so useful to them. Good duties, like new apparel on a man pursued with hue and cry of conscience, keep him from being known.

Take heed of resting in duties ; good duties are men's money, without which they think themselves poor and miserable; but take heed that you and your money perish not together. (Gal. v. 3.) The paths to hell are but two. The first is the path of sin, which is a dirty way. Secondly, the path of duties, which (rested in) is but a clearer way. When the Israelites were in distress, (Judg. x. 14,) the Lord bids them go to the gods they served: so when thou shalt lie howling on thy death bed, the Lord will say, Go unto the good prayers and performances you have made, and the tears you have shed. O, they will be miserable comforters at that day.

Objection. But I think thou wilt say, no true Christian man hopes to be saved by his good works and duties, but only by the mercy of God and merits of Christ.

Answer. It is one thing to trust to be saved by duties, another thing to rest in duties. A man trusts unto them when he is of this opinion, that only good duties can save him. A man rests in duties when he is of this opinion, that only Christ can save him, but in his practice he goeth about to save himself. The wisest of the Papists are so at this day, and so are our common Protestants. And this is a great subtlety of the heart, that is, when a man thinks he can not be saved by his good works and duties, but only by Christ: he then hopeth, because he is of this opinion, that when he hath done all he is an unprofitable servant; (which is only an act or work of the judgment informed aright;) that, therefore, because he is of this opinion, he shall be saved.

But because it is hard for to know when a man rests in duties, and few men find themselves guilty of this sin, which ruins so many, I will show two things : —

1. The signs of a man's resting in duties.

2. The insufficiency of all duties to save men ; that so those that be found guilty of this sin may not go on in it.

First. For the signs whereby a man may certainly know, when he rests in his duties, which if he do, (as few professors especially but they do,) he perisheth eternally.

First. Those that yet never saw they rested in them, they that never found it a hard matter to come out of their duties. For it is most natural for a man to stick in them, because nature sets men upon duties; hence it is a hard matter to come out of resting in duties. For two things keep a man from Christ : —

1. Sin. 2. Self. Now, as a man is broken off from sin by seeing and feeling it, and groaning under the power of it, so is a man broken from himself. For men had rather do any thing than come unto Christ, there is such a deal of self in them ; therefore, if thou hast no experience, that at no time thou hast rested too much in thy duties, and then didst groan to be delivered from these entanglements, (I mean not from the doing of them, — this is familism and profaneness, — but from resting in the bare performance of them,) thou dost rely upon thy duties to this day.

These rest in duties, that prize the bare performance of duties

9 *

wonderfully; for those duties that carry thee out of thyself unto Christ make thee to prize Christ. Now, tell me, dost thou glory in thyself? Now I am somebody. I was ignorant, forgetful, hard-hearted; now I understand, and remember better, and can sorrow for my sins: if thou dost rest here, thy duties never carried thee farther than thyself. Dost thou think, after that thou hast prayed with some life, Now I have done very well, and now thou dost verily think (meaning for thy duties) the Lord will save thee, though thou never come to Christ, and sayest, as he in another case, "Now I hope the Lord will do good to me, seeing I have got a priest into my house." (Judg. xvii. 13.) Dost thou enhance the price of duties thus, that thou dost dote on them? Then I do pronounce from God, thou dost rest in them. "These things" (saith Paul) "I counted gain," (that is, before his conversion to Christ, he prized them exceedingly,) but "now I account them loss." And this is the reason why a child of God, commonly, after all his prayers, tears, and confessions, doubts much of God's love toward him; whereas another man, that falleth short of him, never questions his estate; the first sees much rottenness and vileness in his best duties, and so judgeth meanly of himself; the other, ignorant of the vileness of them, prizeth them, and esteemeth highly of them; and setting his corn at so high a price, he may keep them to himself; the Lord never accepteth them, nor buyeth them at so high a rate.

Thirdly. Those that never came to be sensible of their poverty and utter emptiness of all good; for so long as a man hath a penny in his purse, that is, feels any good in himself, he will never come a-begging unto Jesus Christ, and therefore rests in himself. Now, didst thou never feel thyself in this manner poor, viz., I am as ignorant as any beast, as vile as any devil. O Lord, what a nest and litter of sin and rebellion lurk in my heart! I once thought at least my heart and desires were good, but now I feel no spiritual life. O dead heart! I am the poorest, vilest, basest, and blindest creature that ever lived. If thou dost not thus feel thyself poor, thou never camest out of thy duties; for when the Lord bringeth any man to Christ, he brings him empty, that so he may make him beholding to Christ for every farthing token.

Fourthly. Those that gain no evangelical righteousness by duties, rest in duties; I say, evangelical righteousness, that is more prizing of acquaintance with, desire after, loving and delighting in union with the Lord Jesus Christ; for a mortal man may grow in legal righteousness, (as the stony and thorny ground seed sprang up, and increased much, and came near unto maturity,) and yet rest in duties all this while. For as it is with tradesmen, they rest in their buying and selling, though they make no gain of their trading. Now Jesus Christ is a Christian's gain, (Phil. i. 21 ;) and hence a child of God asks himself after sermon, after prayer, after sacrament, What have I gained of Christ ? Have I got more knowledge of Christ, more admiring of the Lord Jesus ? Now, a carnal heart, that rests in his duties, asketh only what he hath done, as the Pharisee : " I thank God I am not as other men ; I fast twice a week, I give alms," and the like ; and thinks verily he shall be saved, because he prays, and because he hears, and because he reforms, and because he sorrows for his sins ; that is, not because of the gaining of Christ in a duty, but because of his naked performance of the duty ; and so they are like that man that I have heard of, that thought verily he should be rich, because he had got a wallet to beg : so men, because they perform duties, think verily they shall be saved. No such matter : let a man have a bucket made of gold ; doth he think to get water because he hath a bucket ? No, no ; he must let it down into the well, and draw up water with it : so must thou let down all thy duties into Christ, and draw light and life from his fullness, else, though thy duties be golden duties, thou shalt perish without Christ. When a man hath bread in his wallet, and got water in his bucket, he may boldly say, So long as these last, I shall not famish ; so mayest thou say, when thou hast found and got Christ, in the performance of any duty, So long as Christ's life lasteth, I shall live ; as long as he hath any wisdom or power, so long shall I be directed and enabled in well doing.

Fifthly. If thy duties make thee sin more boldly, thou dost then rest in duties ; for these duties, which carry a man out of himself unto Christ, ever fetch power against sin ; but duties that a man rests in arm him and fence him in his sin. (Is. i. 14.) A cart that hath no wheels to rest on can hardly be drawn into the dirt ; but one that hath wheels cometh loaded through it : so a child of God that hath no wheels, no duties, to rest upon, can not willingly be drawn into sin ; but another man, though he be loaden with sin, (even sometimes against his conscience,) yet having duties to bear him up, goeth merrily on in a sinful course, and makes no bones of sin. When we see a base man revile a great prince, and strike him, we say, Surely, he durst not do it unless he had somebody to bear him out in it, that he rests and trusts unto : so when we see men sin against the great God, we conceive, certainly, they durst not do it, if they had not some duties to bear them out in it, and to encourage them in their way, that they trust unto.

For, take a profane man : what makes him drink, swear, cozen, game, whore ? Is there no God to punish ? Is there no hell hot enough to torment ? Are there no plagues to confound him ? Yes. Why sinneth he so then ? O, he prayeth to God for forgiveness, and sorroweth, and repents in secret, (as he saith,) and this bears him up in his lewd pranks.

Take a moral man : he knows he hath his failings, and his sins, as the best have, and is overtaken sometimes as the best are : why doth he not remove these sins then ? He confesseth them to God every morning when he riseth. Why is he not more humbled under his sin then ? The reason is, he constantly observeth morning and evening prayer, and then he craves forgiveness for his failings, by which course he hopes he makes his peace with God ; and hence he sinneth without fear, and ariseth out of his falls into sin without sorrow. And thus they see and maintain their sins by their duties, and therefore rest in duties.

Sixthly. Those that see little of their vile hearts by duties, rest in their duties ; for if a man be brought nearer to Christ, and to the light, by duties, he will spy out more motes ; for the more a man participates of Christ, his health, and life, the more he feeleth the vileness and sickness of sin. As Paul when he rested in duties before his conversion, before that the law had humbled him, he was alive ; that is, he thought himself a sound man, because his duties covered his sins, like fig leaves. Therefore ask thine own heart if it be troubled sometimes for sin, and if after thy praying and sorrowing thou dost grow well, and thinkest thyself safe, and feelest not thyself more vile. If it be thus, I tell thee, thy duties be but fig leaves to cover thy nakedness, and the Lord will find thee out, and unmask thee one day ; and woe to thee if thou dost perish here.

Secondly. Therefore behold the insufficiency of all duties to save us ; which will appear in these three things which I speak, that you may learn hereafter never to rest in duties : —

First. Consider, thy best duties are tainted, poisoned, and mingled with some sin, and therefore are most odious in the eyes of a holy God, (nakedly and barely considered in themselves ;) for, if the best actions of God's people be filthy, as they come from them, then, to be sure, all wicked men's actions are much more filthy and polluted with sin ; but the first is true—"All our righteousnesses are as filthy rags ; " for as the fountain is so is the stream ; but the fountain of all good actions (that is, the heart) is mingled partly with sin, partly with grace ; therefore every action participates of some sin, which sins are daggers at God's heart, even when a man is praying and begging for his life ; therefore there is no hope to be saved by duties.

Secondly. Suppose thou couldest perform them without sin; yet thou couldst not hold out in doing so. (Is. xl. 6,) "All flesh and the glory thereof is but grass." So thy best actions would soon wither if they were not perfect; and if thou canst not persevere in performing all duties perfectly, thou art forever undone, though thou shouldest do so for a time, live like an angel, shine like a sun, and, at thy last gasp, have but an idle thought, commit the least sin, that one rock will sink thee down even in the haven, though never so richly laden; one sin, like a penknife at the heart, will stab thee; one sin, like a little firestick in the thatch, will burn thee; one act of treason will hang thee, though thou hast lived never so devoutly before, (Ezek. xviii. 24;) for it is a crooked life when all the parts of the line of thy life be not straight before Almighty God.

Thirdly. Suppose thou shouldest persevere; yet it is clear thou hast sinned grievously already; and dost thou think thine obedience for the time to come can satisfy the Lord for all those rents behind, for all those sins past? as can a man that pays his rent honestly every year satisfy hereby for the old rent not paid in twenty years? All thy obedience is a new debt, which can not satisfy for debts past. Indeed, men may forgive wrong and debts, because they be but finite; but the least sin is an infinite evil, and therefore God must be satisfied for it. Men may remit debts, and yet remain men; but the Lord having said, "The soul that sinneth shall die," and his truth being himself, he can not remain God, if he forgive it without satisfaction. Therefore duties are but rotten crutches for a soul to rest upon.

But to what end should we use any duties? Can not a man be saved by his good prayers, nor sorrows, nor repentings? What should we pray any more then? Let us cast off all duties, if all are to no purpose to save us; as good play for nothing as work for nothing.

Though thy good duties can not save thee, yet thy bad works will damn thee. Thou art, therefore, not to cast off the duties, but the resting in these duties. Thou art not to cast them away, but to cast them down at the feet of Jesus Christ, as they did their crowns, (Rev. iv. 10, 11,) saying, If there be any good or graces in these duties, it is thine, Lord; for it is the prince's favor that exalts a man, not his own gifts: they came from his good pleasure.

But thou wilt say, To what end should I perform duties, if I can not be saved by them?

For these three ends:—

First. To carry thee to the Lord Jesus, the only Saviour. (Heb.

vii. 25.) He only is able to save (not duties) all that come unto God (that is, in the use of means) by him. Hear a sermon to carry thee to Jesus Christ; fast and pray, and get a full tide of affections in them to carry thee to the Lord Jesus Christ; that is, to get more love to him, more acquaintance with him, more union with him; so sorrow for thy sins that thou mayest be more fitted for Christ, that thou mayest prize Christ the more; use thy duties as Noah's dove did her wings, to carry thee to the ark of the Lord Jesus Christ, where only there is rest. If she had never used her wings, she had fallen into the waters; so, if thou shalt use no duties, but cast them all off, thou art sure to perish. Or, as it is with a poor man that is to go over a great water for a treasure on the other side, though he can not fetch the boat, he calls for it; and, though there be no treasure in the boat, yet he useth the boat to carry him over to the treasure. So Christ is in heaven, and thou on earth; he doth not come to thee, and thou canst not go to him; now call for a boat; though there is no grace, no good, no salvation, in a pithless duty, yet use it to carry thee over to the treasure — the Lord Jesus Christ. When thou comest to hear, say, Have over Lord by this sermon; when thou comest to pray, say, Have over Lord by this prayer to a Saviour. But this is the misery of people. Like foolish lovers, when they are to woo for the lady, they fall in love with her handmaid that is only to lead them to her; so men fall in love with, and dote upon, their own duties, and rest contented with the naked performance of them, which are only handmaids to lead the soul unto the Lord Jesus Christ.

Secondly. Use duties as evidences of God's everlasting love to you when you be in Christ; for the graces and duties of God's people, although they be not causes, yet they be tokens and pledges of salvation to one in Christ: they do not save a man, but accompany and follow such a man as shall be saved, (Heb. vi. 9.) Let a man boast of his joys, feelings, gifts, spirit, grace, if he walks in the commission of any one sin, or the omission of any one known duty, or in the slovenly, ill-favored performance of duties, this man, I say, can have no assurance without flattering himself. (2 Pet. i. 8, 9, 10.) Duties, therefore, being evidences and pledges of salvation, use them to that end, and make much of them therefore; as a man that hath a fair evidence for his lordship, because he did not purchase his lordship, will he therefore cast it away? No, no; because it is an evidence to assure him that it is his own; and so, to defend him against all such as seek to take it from him, he will carefully preserve the same; so, because duties do not save thee, wilt thou cast away good duties? No; for they are evidences (if thou art in Christ) that the Lord and mercy are thine own. Women will not cast away their love tokens, although they are such things as did not purchase or merit the love of their husbands; but because they are tokens of his love, therefore they will keep them safe.

That God the Father of our Lord Jesus Christ may be honored by the performance of these duties, therefore use them. Christ shed his blood that he might purchase unto himself a people zealous of good works, (Tit. ii. 14,) not to save our souls by them, but to honor him. O, let not the blood of Christ be shed in vain! Grace and good duties are a Christian's crown; it is sin only makes a man base. Now, shall a king cast away his crown, because he bought not his kingdom by it? No; because it is his ornament and glory to wear it when he is made a king. So I say unto thee, It is better that Christ should be honored than thy soul saved; and, therefore, perform duties, because they honor the Lord Jesus Christ. Thus use thy duties, but rest not in duties; nay, go out of duties, and match thy soul to the Lord Jesus; take him for better and for worse; so live in him and upon him all thy days.

Fourthly. By reason of man's headstrong presumption, or false faith, whereby men seek to save themselves by catching hold on Christ, when they see an insufficiency in all duties to help them, and themselves unworthy of mercy; for this is the last and most dangerous rock that these times are split upon. Men make a bridge of their own to carry them to Christ. I mean, they look not after faith wrought by an omnipotent power, which the eternal Spirit of the Lord Jesus must work in them, but they content themselves with a faith of their own forging and framing; and hence they think verily and believe that Christ is their sweet Saviour, and so doubt not but they are safe, when there is no such matter; but even as dogs they snatch away children's bread, and shall be shut out of doors (out of heaven hereafter forever) for their labor.

All men are of this opinion, that there is no salvation but by the merits of Jesus Christ; and because they hold fast this opinion, therefore they think they hold fast Jesus Christ in the hand of faith, and so perish by catching at their own catch, and hanging on their own fancy and shadow. Some others catch hold of Christ before they come to feel the want of faith and ability to believe, and catching hold on him, (like dust on a man's coat, whom God will shake off, or like burs and briers, cleaving to one's garment, which the Lord will trample under foot,) now say they, they thank God, they have got comfort by this means, and though God killeth them, yet they will trust unto him. (Micah iii. 11.)

It is in this respect a harder matter to convert a man in England than in the India, for there they have no such shifts and forts against our sermons; to say they believe in Christ already, as most amongst us do, we can not rap off men's fingers from catching hold on Christ before they are fit for him ; like a company of thieves in the street, you shall see a hundred hands scrambling for a jewel that is fallen there, that have least, nay, nothing to do with it. Every man saith, almost, I hope Christ is mine ; I put my whole trust and confidence in him, and will not be beaten from this. What! must a man despair? must not a man trust unto Christ? Thus men will hope and trust, though they have no ground, no graces to prove they may lay hold and claim unto Christ. This hope, scared out of his wits, damns thousands ; for I am persuaded, if men did see themselves Christless creatures, as well as sinful creatures, they would cry out, " Lord, what shall I do to be saved ? "

This faith is a precious faith. (2 Pet. i. 2.) Precious things cost much, and we set them at a high rate; if thy faith be so, it hath cost thee many a prayer, many a sob, many a salt tear. But ask most men how they come by their faith in Christ, they say very easily ; when the lion sleeps, a man may lie and sleep by it; but when it awakens, woe to that man that doth so : so while God is silent and patient, thou mayest befool thyself with thinking thou dost trust unto God ; but woe to thee when the Lord appears in his wrath, as one day he will; for by virtue of this false faith, men sinning take Christ for a dishclout to wipe them clean again, and that is all the use they have of this faith. They sin indeed, but they trust unto Christ for his mercy, and so lie still in their sins : God will revenge with blood, and fire, and plagues, this horrible contempt from heaven.

Hence many of you trust to Christ, as the apricot tree, that leans against the wall, but it is fast rooted in the earth : so you lean upon Christ for salvation, but you are rooted in the world, rooted in your pride, rooted in your filthiness still. Woe to you if you perish in this estate ; God will hew you down as fuel for his wrath, whatever mad hope you have to be saved by Christ. This, therefore, I proclaim from the God of heaven : —

1. You that never felt yourselves as unable to believe as a dead man to raise himself, you have as yet no faith at all.

2. You that would get faith, first must feel your inability to believe : and fetch not this slip out of thine own garden ; it must

come down from Heaven to thy soul, if ever thou partakest thereof.

Other things I should have spoken of this large subject, but I am forced here to end abruptly ; the Lord lay not this sin to their charge who have " stopped my mouth, laboring to withhold the truth in unrighteousness." And blessed be the good God, who hath stood by his unworthy servant thus long, enabling him to lead you so far as to show you the rocks and dangers of your passage to another world.

THE

SOUND BELIEVER.

A

TREATISE OF EVANGELICAL CONVERSION.

DISCOVERING THE WORK OF CHRIST'S SPIRIT IN RECONCILING OF A SINNER TO GOD.

Matt. xviii. 11. — "I came to save that which was lost."

Sir: Many strugglings I have had about publishing these notes. I have looked up to God, and at last been persuaded upon these grounds: —

1. The many desires both of friends and strangers, both by private speeches and letters, which I thought might be the voice of Christ.

2. Some good (as I hear) those which are already out have done, and which the rest might do, which I have looked on as a testimony of the Lord's acceptance of them.

3. I know not what the Lord's meaning should be to bring to light by his providence, without my privity, knowledge, or will, the former part, unless it was to awaken and enforce me (being desired) to publish the rest; our works, I thought, should resemble God's works, not to be left imperfect.

4. I considered my weak body, and my short time of sojourning here, and that I shall not speak long to children, friends, or God's precious people, — I am sure not to many in England, — to whom I owe almost my whole self, whom I shall see in this world no more; I have been therefore willing to get the wind, and take the season, that I might leave some part of God's precious truth on record, that it might speak (O that it might be to the heart!) among whom I can not (and when I shall not) be. I account it a part of God's infinite grace to make me an instrument of the least good. If the Lord shall so far accept of me in publishing these things, it is all that I would desire; if not, yet I have

10 *

desired forgiveness in the blood of his Son, for whatever errors or weaknesses may be in it, or are in myself, which may hinder success, and frustrate its end ; only what I have in much weakness believed, I have written, and sent it unto you, leaving it wholly with yourself, whom I much love and honor, that you would add or detract any thing you see meet, (so as it be not cross to what I have writ;) and if you then think it meet for public view, you see upon what grounds I am content with it; but if you shall bury it, and put it to perpetual silence, it shall be most pleasing to him who thinks more meanly of it than others can.

THO. SHEPARD.

THE SOUND BELIEVER.

CHAPTER I.

AS THE GREAT CAUSE OF THE ETERNAL PERDITION OF MEN IS OF THEMSELVES, SO THE ONLY CAUSE OF THE ACTUAL DELIVERANCE AND SALVATION OF MAN IS JESUS CHRIST.

Hosea xiii. 9, "O Israel, thou hast destroyed thyself, but in me is thy help."

Section I.

These words, as they are set down in the Hebrew, are (according to the style of this prophet) very short and sententious, and therefore difficult to translate into English without some periphrasis; but the sense is here truly expressed, "In me is thy help;" which you may see confirmed from verse 4: "There is no Saviour beside me;" and verse 14: "I will ransom them from the power of the grave; O death, I will be thy plague; O grave, I will be thy destruction." Suppose the prophet should speak here of temporal salvation, help and ransom, (which he doth not;) yet the argument is strong; if there be no Saviour from temporal woe and misery but only the Lord Jesus, how much more is there from woes eternal? Only understand me here aright; I am not now speaking of man's deliverance and salvation by price in way of satisfaction to justice, (for that I have already handled,) but of his deliverance and salvation by power; not of man's purchased deliverance, which is by the blood of Christ, but of man's actual deliverance, which is by the efficacy and power of the Spirit of Christ. Some captives among men are redeemed by price only, some by power without price; but such is the lamentable captivity of all men, under the severity of justice and power of sin, that without the price of Christ's blood, (Eph. i. 7,) and the power of Christ's Spirit, (John viii. 36,) there is no deliverance; the Lord Jesus having paid the price for our deliverance. Yet it is with us as with a company of captives in prison: our sins like strong

115

chains hold us ; Satan, our keeper, will not let us go ; the prison doors, through unbelief, are shut upon us, (Rom. xi. 32 ;) and thereby God and Christ are kept out from us. What power now can rescue us, that are held fast under such a power, even after the price is paid ? Truly it can be no other but that in my text, " In me is thy help." When our ransom is paid, the Lord must come himself and fetch us out by strong hand. (Is. liii. 1,) " To whom is the arm of the Lord revealed ? Truly to very few, yet to some it is ; and certainly look as they make Christ no Saviour, indeed, who deny his salvation by price and satisfaction, so those also make him an imperfect Saviour who deny salvation and actual deliverance of man to be only the almighty arm and efficacy of his Spirit and power : excellent therefore is the speech of the apostle, (Acts v. 30, 31,) " God hath exalted Jesus to give repentance and remission of sins to Israel." Look as Jesus was abased to purchase repentance and remission, so he is now exalted actually to give and apply repentance and remission of sins. Whose glory is it to remit sins, but God's in Christ, and by Christ only ? Whose glory is it to give repentance, (which in this place comprehends the work of conversion and faith, as Beza observes,) whereby we apply remission, but the same God only ? The one is as difficult to be conveyed as the other, and we stand in as much need of Christ to do the one as the other ; all the power of Christ exalted is little enough to give us repentance and remission, the condition of the covenant expressed in repentance, and the blessings in the covenant, summed up in the forgiveness of sins ; the Socinians deny redemption and salvation by prize ; the Arminians by Christ's power, leaving suasion only to him, but power of conversion to the power and liberty of the will of man. O adulterous generation, that are thus hacking at and cutting the cords of their own salvation ! I shall here speak only to one question, which is the principal, and most profitable, and that is this : How doth Christ redeem and save us by his power, out of that miserable estate ? and consequently what is the way for us to seek, and so to find and feel deliverance by the hand of Christ's power ?

As there are four principal means and causes, or ways, whereby man ruins himself, — 1. Ignorance of their own misery ; 2. Security and unsensibleness of it ; 3. Carnal confidence in their own duties ; 4. Presumption or resting upon the mercy of God by a faith of their own forging, — so, on the contrary, there is a fourfold act of Christ's power, whereby he rescues and delivers all his out of their miserable estate.

The first act or stroke is conviction of sin.

The second is compunction for sin.

The third is humiliation or self-abasement.

The fourth is faith; all which are distinctly put forth (when he ceaseth extraordinarily to work) in the day of Christ's power; and so ever look for actual salvation and redemption from Christ, let them seek for mercy and deliverance in this way, out of which they shall never find it; let them begin at conviction, and desire the Lord to let them see their sins, that so being affected with them, and humbled under them, they may by faith be enable to receive Jesus Christ, and so be blessed in him. It is true, Christ is applied to us next by faith, but faith is wrought in us in that way of conviction and sorrow for sin; no man can or will come by faith to Christ to take away his sins, unless he first see, be convicted of, and loaded with them. I confess the manner of the Spirit's work, in the conversion of a sinner unto God, is exceeding secret, and in many things very various; and therefore it is too great boldness to mark out all God's footsteps herein; yet so far forth as the Lord himself tells us his work, and the manner of it in all his, we may safely resolve ourselves, and so far, and no farther, shall we proceed in the explication of these things. It is great profaneness not to search into the works of common providence, though secret and hidden. (Ps. xxviii. 5, and xcii. 6.) Much greater is it not to do this unto God's work of special favor and grace upon his chosen.

I shall therefore begin with the first stroke — Christ's power, which is conviction of sin.

SECTION II.

The first Act of Christ's Power, which is Conviction of Sin.

Now, for the more distinct explication of this, I shall open to you these four things : —

1. I shall prove that the Lord Christ by his Spirit begins the actual deliverance of his elect here.

2. What is that sin the Lord convinceth the soul thus first of.

3. How the Lord doth it.

4. What measure and degree of conviction he works thus in all his.

1. For the first, it is said, (John xvi. 8, 9,) that the first thing that the Spirit doth when he comes to make the apostles' ministry effectual, is this : it shall " reprove or convince the world of sin;" it doth not first work faith, but convinceth them that they have no faith, (as in verse 9,) and consequently under the

guilt and dominion of their sin; and after this he " convinceth of righteousness," which faith apprehends. (Ver. 10.) It is true, that the word *conviction*, here, is of a large extent, and includes compunction and humiliation for sin; yet our Saviour wraps them up in this word; because conviction is the first, and therefore the chief in order; here the Lord, not speaking now of ineffectual, but effectual, and thorough conviction expressed in deep sorrow and humiliation. Now, the text saith, the Lord begins thus not with some one or two, but with the world of God's elect, who are to be called home by the ministry of the word, which our Saviour speaks (as any may see who considers the scope) purposely to comfort the hearts of his disciples, that their ministry shall be thus effectual to the world of Jews and Gentiles; and therefore can not speak of such conviction as serves only for to leave men without excuse for greater condemnation, (as some understand the place;) for that is a poor ground of consolation to their sad hearts. Secondly. I shall hereafter prove that there can be no faith without sense of sin and misery; and now there can be no sense of sin without a precedent sight or conviction of sin; no man can feel sin, unless he doth first see it; what the eye sees not, the heart rues not. Let the greatest evil befall a man — suppose the burning of his house, the death of his children; if he doth not first know, see, and hear of it, he will never take it to heart, it will never trouble him: so let a poor sinner lie under the greatest guilt, the sorest wrath of God, it will never trouble him until he sees it and be convinced of it. (Acts ii. 37.) " When they heard this, they were pricked;" but first they heard it, and saw their sin before their hearts were wounded for it. (Gen. iii. 7.) They first saw their nakedness before they were ashamed of it. Thirdly. The main end of the law is to drive us to Christ. (Rom. x. 4.) If Christ be the " end of the law," then the law is the means subservient to that end, and that not to some, but to all that believe: now, the law, though it drives us to Christ by condemnation, yet in order it begins with accusation. It first accuseth, and so convinceth of sin, (Rom. iii. 20,) and then condemneth. It is folly and injustice for a judge to condemn and bring a sinner out to his execution before accusation and conviction; and is it wisdom or justice in the Lord or his law to do otherwise? and therefore the Spirit, in making use of the law for this end, first convinceth as it first accuseth, and lays our sins to our charge. Lastly. Look, as Satan, when he binds up a sinner in his sin, he first keeps him (if possible) from the very sight and knowledge of it; because, so long as they see it not, this ignorance is the cause of **all their woe, why they feel it not, why they desire not to come** out of it; the Lord Jesus, who came to untie the knots of Satan, (1 John iii. 8,) begins here, and first convinceth his, and makes them see their sin, that so they may feel it, and come to him for deliverance out of it. O, consider this, all you that dream out your time in minding only things before your feet, never thinking on the evils of your own hearts; you that heed not, you that will not see your sins, nor so much as ask this question, What have I done? what do I do? how do I live? what will become of me? what will be the end of my foolish courses? I tell you, if ever the Lord save you, he will make you see what now you can not, what now you will not; he will not only make you to confess you are sinners, but he will convince you of sin: this shall be the first thing the Lord will do with thee.

But you will say, What is _that sin which the Lord first convinceth of? which is the second thing to be opened. I answer in these three conclusions: —

The Lord Jesus by his Spirit doth not only convince the soul in general that it is a sinner and sinful, but the Lord brings in a convicting evidence of the particulars: the first is learnt more by tradition, (in these days,) by the report and acknowledgment of every man, rather than by any special act of conviction of the Spirit of Christ; for what man is there almost but lies under this confession that he is a sinner? The best say they are sinners, "and if we say we have no sin, we deceive ourselves," and "I know I am a sinner;" but that which the Spirit principally convinceth of is some sin or sins in particular; the Spirit doth not arrest men for offences in general, but opens the writ and shows the particular cause — the particular sins. (Rom. iii. 9.) We have proved, saith the apostle, that Jews and Gentiles are under sin; but how doth the apostle, (being now the instrument of the Spirit,) in this work of conviction, convince them of this? Mark his method, verses 10–18, wherein you shall see it is done by enumeration of particulars; sins of their natures, there is none righteous; sins of their minds, none understandeth; sins in their wills and affections, none seek after God; sins in their lives, all gone out of the way; sins of omission of good duties, there is none that doth good; their throats, tongues, lips, are sepulchers, deceitful, poisonful; their mouths full of cursing, their feet swift to shed blood, etc. And this is the state of you Jews, (ver. 19,) as well as of the Gentiles; that all flesh may stand convinced as guilty before God. If it be here demanded, What are those but particular sins which the Lord convinceth men of? I answer, In variety of men there is much variety of special sins, as there

is of dispositions, tempers, and temptations; and therefore the
Lord doth not convince one man at first of the same sins of
which he doth another man; yet this we may safely say: usually (though not always) the Lord begins with the remembrance and consideration of some one great, if not a man's
special and most beloved sin; and thereby the Spirit discovers,
gradually, all the rest: that arrow which woundeth the heart of
Christ most, the Lord makes it fall first upon the head of the
sinner that did shoot it against Heaven, and convinceth, and as
it were hits him first with that. How did the Spirit convince
those three thousand, those patterns of God's converting grace?
(Acts ii. 37.) Did not the Lord begin with them for one principal sin, viz., their murder and contempt of Christ by imbruing
their hands in his blood? There is no question but now they remembered other sinful practices; but this was the *imprimis*
which is ever accompanied with many other items which are
then read in God's bill of reckonings where the first is set
down. Israel would have a king. (1 Sam. viii. 19.) Samuel, for a time, could not convince them of their sin: herein
what doth the Lord do? Surely he will convince them of sin before he leaves them; and this he doth by such a terrible thunder
as made all their hearts ache. And how is it now? What sin do
they now see? They first see the greatness of that particular sin;
but this came not to mind alone, but they cried out, (1 Sam. xii.
19,) "We have added unto all our evils this, in asking to ourselves a king." Look upon the woman of Samaria. (John iv.)
The Lord Christ indeed spake first unto her about himself, the
substance of the gospel, about the worth of this water of life:
but what good did she get until the Lord began to convince her
of sin? And how doth he that? He tells her of her secret whoredom she lived in, the man that she now had was not her husband; and upon the discovery of this, she saw many more sins;
and hence (ver. 29) she cries out, "Come see the man that hath
told me all that ever I did in my life." And thus the Lord
deals at this day: the minister preacheth against one sin, it may
be whoredom, ignorance, contempt of the gospel, neglect of secret duties, lying, Sabbath-breaking, &c. This is thy case, saith
the Spirit unto the soul; remember the time, the place, the persons with whom thou livedst in this sinful condition: and now a
man begins to go alone, and to think of all his former courses,
how exceeding evil they have been; it may be the Lord brings
upon a man a sore affliction, and when he is in chains, crying out
of that, the Lord saith to him as to those, (Jer. xxx. 15,) "Why
criest thou for thy affliction? for the multitude of thine iniquities
I have done this:" it may be, the Lord sometimes strikes a man's

companion in sin dead, by some fearful judgment; and then that particular sin comes to mind, and the Lord reveals it armed with multitude of many other sins, the causes of it, the fruits and effects of it; as the father whips a child upon occasion of one special fault, but then tells him of many more which he winked at before this, and saith, Now, sirrah, remember such a time, such a froward fit, such undutiful behavior, such a reviling word you spake, such a time I called, and you ran away and would not hear me; and you thought I liked well enough of the seways; but now know that I will not pass them by, etc. Thus the Lord deals with his; and hence it is, many times, that the elect of God, civilly brought up, do hereupon think well of themselves, and so remain long unconvinced of their woful estates; the Lord suffers them to fall into some foul, secret, or open sin, and by this the Lord takes special occasion of working conviction and sorrow for sin; the Lord hereby makes them hang down the head, and cry, "Unclean, unclean." Paul was civilly educated; he turned at last a hot persecutor, oppressor, blasphemer: the Lord first convinced him of his persecution, and cried out from heaven to him, "Paul, Paul, why persecutest thou me?" This struck him to the heart, and then sin revived. (Rom. vii. 9.) Many secret sins of his heart were discovered, which I take to begin and continue in special in those three days, (Acts iii. 9,) wherein he was blind, and did (through sight of sin and sorrow of heart) neither eat nor drink. As a man that hath the plague, not knowing the disease, he hopes to live; but when he sees the spots and tokens of death upon his wrist, now he cries out, because convinced that the plague of the Lord is upon him; so when men see some one or more special sins break out, now they are convinced of their lamentable condition; yet it is not always, (though usually thus;) for some men the Lord may first convince of sin by showing them the sinfulness of their own hearts and ways; the Lord may let a man see his blindness, his extreme hardness of heart, his weakness, his wilfulness, his heartlessness; he can not pray, or look up to God, and this may first convince him; or that all that he doth is sinful, being out of Christ; the Lord may suddenly let him see the deceits of his own heart, and the secret sinful practices of his life; as if some had told the minister, or as if he spake to none but him; that he is forced to fall down being thus convinced, and to confess, God is in this man. (1 Cor. xiv. 25.) Nicodemus may first see and be convinced of the want of regeneration, and thereby feel his need of Christ; the Lord may set a man upon the consideration of all his life past, how wickedly it hath been spent; and so not one, but a multitude of

iniquities compass him about; a man may see the godly examples
of his parents or other godly Christians, in the family or town
where he dwells, and by this be convinced, that if their state and
way be good, his own (so far unlike it) must needs be stark
naught: the Lord ever convinceth the soul of sins in particular,
but he doth not always convince one man of the same particular
sins at first as he doth another; whether the Lord convinceth all
the elect at first of the sin of their nature, and show them
their original sin in and about this first stroke of conviction, I
doubt not of it. Paul would have been alive, and a proud Pharisee
still, if the Lord had not let him by the law see this sin, (Rom.
vii. 9 ;) and so would all men in the world, if this should not be
revealed first or last, in a lesser or greater measure, under a distinct or more indistinct notion; and hence arise those confessions
of the saints — I never thought I had such a vile heart; if all the
world had told me, I could not have believed them, but that the
Lord hath made me feel it and see it at last; was there ever such
a sinner, (at least in heart, which is continually opposing of him,)
whom the Lord at any time received to mercy, as I am ?

2. The Lord Jesus by his Spirit doth not only convince the
soul of its sin in particular, but also of the evil, even the exceeding great evil, of those particular sins. The Lord Jesus doth not
only convince of the evil of sin, but of the great evil of sin. O
thou wretch, saith the Spirit, (as the Lord to Cain, Gen. iv. 10,)
what hast thou done, whose sins cry to heaven, who hast thus
long lived with God, and done this infinite wrong to an infinite
God, for which thou canst never make him amends! That God
who could have long since cut thee off in the midst of thy sins
and wickedness, and crushed thee like a moth, and sent thee
down to those eternal flames where thou now seest some better
than thyself mourning day and night, but yet hath spared thee
out of his mere pity to thee, that God hast thou resisted and
forsaken all thy lifetime; and, therefore, now see and consider
what an evil and bitter thing it is thus to live as thou hast done.
(Jer. ii. 19.) Look, as it is in the ways of holiness, many a man
void of the Spirit may see and know them in the literal expressions of them, but can not see the glory of them but by the
Spirit; and hence it is he doth not esteem and prize them and the
knowledge of them above gold. So in the ways of unholiness;
many a man void of the spirit of conviction of sin may and doth
see many particular sins, and confess them; but he doth not, can
not see the exceeding evil of them; and thence it is, though he
doth see them, yet he doth not much dislike them, because he
sees no 'great hurt or evil in them, but makes a light matter of

them; and therefore, when the Spirit comes, it lets him see and stand convinced of the exceeding greatness of the evil that is in them. (Job xxxvi. 8, 9.) In the time of affliction, (which is usually the time of conviction of a wild, unruly sinner,) he shows them their transgressions.; but how? that they have exceeded, that they have been exceeding many and exceeding vile. O beloved, before the Lord Jesus comes to convince, we have cause to pray for and pity every poor sinner, as the Lord Jesus did, saying, "Lord, forgive them; they know not what they do." You godly parents, masters, how oft do you instruct your children, servants, and convince them of their sinfulness, until they confess their faults? yet you see no amendment, but they go on still; what should you now do? O, cry out for them, and say, Lord, forgive them, for they know not what they do. Their sins they know, but what the evil of them is, alas! they know not; but when the Spirit comes to convince, he makes them see what they do, and what is the exceeding evil of those sins they made light of before; like madmen that have sworn, and cursed, and struck their friends, and when they come to be sober again, and remember their mischievous ways and words, now they see what they have done, and how abominable their courses then were. O you that walk on in the madness of your minds now, in all manner of sin, if ever the Lord do good to you, you shall account your ways madness and folly, and cry out, O Lord, what have I done in kicking thus long against the pricks?

The Lord Jesus by his Spirit doth not only convince the soul of the evil of sin, but of the evil after sin; I mean, of the just punishment which doth follow sin; and that is this, viz., that it must die, and that eternally, for sin, if it remain in this estate it is now in. (Rom. iv. 15,) "The law worketh wrath," i. e., sight and sense of wrath. (Rom. vii. 9,) "When the law came, sin revived, and I died;" i. e., I saw myself a dead man by it; so the soul sees clearly God hath said, "The soul that sinneth shall die:" I have sinned, and therefore, if the Lord be true, I shall die; to hell I shall, if now the Lord stop my breath, and cut off my life, which he might justly and may easily do. "Death is the wages of sin," even of any one sin, though never so little; what, then, will become of me, who stand guilty of so many, exceeding the number of the hairs on my head, or the stars in heaven? "Whoremongers and adulterers God will judge;" the minister hath said so, the Lord himself hath told me so. (Heb. xiii. 4.) I am the man; my conscience now tears me, and tells me so; what will become of me? "The Lord Jesus will come in flaming fire to render vengeance against all that know not

God, and that obey not the gospel." This I believe, for God hath said it. (2 Thess. ii. 7–9.) And now I see I am he that hath lived long in ignorance, and know not God; I have had the gospel of grace thus long wooing and persuading my heart, and oftentimes it hath affected me, but yet I have resisted God and his gospel, and have set my filthy lusts, my vain sports, my companions' cups and queans at a higher price than Christ, and have loved them more than him; and therefore, though I may be spared for a while, yet there is a time wherein Christ himself will come out against me in flaming fire. To this purpose doth the Spirit work; for, beloved, the great means whereby Satan overthrew man at first in his innocency was this principle — Although thou dost eat, and so sin against God, yet thou shalt not die. (Gen. iii. 4,) "Ye shall not surely die." The serpent doth not say, "Ye shall not die," for that is too gross an outfacing of the word, (Gen. ii. 17;) but he saith, "Ye shall not surely die;" that is, there is not such absolute certainty of it; it may be you shall live; God loves you better than so, and is a more merciful Father than to be at a word and a blow. Now look, as Satan deceived and brought our first parents to ruin by suggesting this principle, so at this day he doth sow this accursed seed, and plant this very principle in the soul of every man's heart by nature; they do not think they can not believe they are dead men, and condemned to die, and that they shall die eternally for the least sin committed by them; men nor angels can not persuade them of it; they can not see the equity of it, that God, so merciful, will be so severe for so small a matter; nor yet the truth of it, for then they think no flesh should be saved; and thus, when the old serpent hath spit this poison before them, they sup it up, and drink it in, and so thousands, nay, millions of men and women are utterly undone. The Lord Christ, therefore, when he comes to save a poor sinner, and raise him up out of his fall, convinceth the soul by his Spirit, and that with full and mighty evidence, that it shall die for the least sin, and tells him, as the Lord told Abimelech in another case, (Gen. xx. 3,) "Thou art but a dead man for this;" and if the Spirit set on this, let who can claw it off. I tell you, beloved, never did poor condemned malefactor more certainly know and hear the sentence of condemnation passed upon him by a mortal man, than the guilty sinner doth his, by an immortal and displeased God; and therefore those three thousand cry out, (Acts ii. 37,) "Men and brethren, what shall we do to be saved?" We are condemned to die; what shall we do now to be saved from death? Now the soul is glad to inquire of the minister, O, tell me, what shall I do? I once thought myself in a safe and good condition as any in the town or country I lived in; but now the Lord hath let me hear of other news; die I must in this estate, and it is a wonder of mercies I am spared alive to this day. There is not only some blind fears and suspicions that it may possibly be so, but full persuasions of heart, die I must, die I shall in this estate; for if the Spirit reveal sin, and convince not of death for sin, the soul under this work of conviction, being as yet rather sensual than spiritual, will make a light matter of it when it sees no sensible danger in it; but when it sees the bottomless pit before it, everlasting fire before it, for the least sin, now it sees the heinous evil of sin; the way of sin, though never so peaceable before, is full of danger now, wherein it sees there are endless woes and everlasting deaths that lie in wait for it. (Rom. vi. 21.) And now, saith the Spirit, you may go on in these sinful courses as others do, if you see meet; but O, consider what will be the end of them; what it is to enjoy the pleasures of sin for a season, and to be tormented forever for them in the conclusion; for be assured that will be the end: and hence the soul, seeing itself thus set apart for death, looks upon itself in a far worse estate than the brute beasts, or vilest worm upon the earth; for it thinks, When they die there is an end of their misery; but O, then is the beginning of mine forever. Hence also arise those fears of death and of being suddenly cut off, that, when it lies down, it trembles to think, I may never rise again, because it is convinced, not only that it deserves to die, but that it is already sentenced for to die: hence also the soul justifies God, if he had cut him off in his sin; and wonders what kept him from it, there being nothing else due from God unto it: hence, lastly, the soul is stopped and stands still, goes not on in sin as before; or if it doth, the Lord gives it no peace. (Jer. viii. 6.) Why doth the horse go on in the battle? Because it sees not death before it; but now the soul sees death, and therefore stops. O, remember this, all you that never could believe that you are dead, condemned men, and therefore are never troubled with any such thoughts in your mind. I tell you that you are far from conviction, and therefore far from salvation: if God should send some from the dead to bear witness against this secure world concerning this truth, yet you will not believe it, for his messengers sent from heaven are not believed herein; woe be to you if you remain unconvinced of this point.

But you will say, How doth the Lord thus convince sin, and wherein is it expressed? which is the third particular.

All knowledge of sin is not conviction of sin; all confession of

11 *

sin is not conviction; there is a conviction merely rational, which is not spiritual; there are three things in spiritual conviction.

There is a clear, certain, and manifest light, so that the soul sees its sin, and death due to it, clearly and certainly; for so the word (John xvi. 9) ελεγχειν signifies to evidence a thing by way of argumentation, nay, demonstration. The Spirit so demonstrates these things, that it hath nothing to object; a man's mouth is stopped; he hath nothing to say but this: Behold, I am vile; I am a dead man; for if a man have any strong arguments given him to confirm a truth, yet if he have but one objection or doubtful scruple not answered, he is not fully as yet convinced, because full conviction by a clear sunlight scatters all dark objections, and hence our Saviour (Jude 15) will one day convince the wicked of all their hard speeches against him, which will chiefly be done by manifesting the evil of such ways, and taking away all those colors and defenses men have made for their language. Before the Spirit of Christ comes, man can not see, will not see his sin for punishment; nay, he hath many things to say for himself as excuses and extenuations of sin. One saith, I was drawn unto it, (the woman that thou gavest me,) and so lays the blame on others: another saith, It is my nature: others say, All are sinners; the godly sin as well as others, and yet are saved at last, and so I hope shall I: others profess they can not part with sin; they would be better, but they can not, and God requires no more than they are able to perform: another saith, I will continue in sin but a little while, and purpose hereafter to leave it: others say, We are sinners, but yet God is merciful, and will forgive it: another saith, Though I have sinned, yet I have some good, and am not so bad as other men: endless are these excuses for sin. In one word, I know no man, though never so bad, though his sin be never so grievous, but he hath something to say for himself, and something in his mind to lessen and extenuate sin; but, beloved, when the Spirit comes to convince, he so convinceth as that he answers all these, pulls down all these fences, tears off all these fig leaves, scatters all these mists, and pulls off all these scales from the eyes, stops a man's mouth, that the soul stands before God, crying, O Lord, guilty, guilty; as the prophet Jeremy told them, (Jer. ii. 23,) "Why dost thou say, I am innocent? look upon thy way," etc. So the Spirit saith, Why dost thou say thy sin is small? it is disobedience, as Samuel said to Saul, (1 Sam. xv. 23,) which is rebellion, and as the sin of witchcraft; and is that a small matter? The Spirit of conviction, by the clear evidence of the truth, binds the understanding that it can not struggle against God any more; and hence let all the world plead to the contrary, nay, let the godly come to comfort them in this estate, and think and speak well of them, yet they can not believe them, because they are certain their estates are woful: hence also we shall observe the soul under conviction — instead of excusing sin, it aggravates sin, and studies to aggravate sin. Did ever any deal thus wickedly, walk thus sinfully, so long against so many checks and chidings, light and love, means and mercies, as I have done? And it is wonderful to observe that those things which made it once account sin light make it therefore to think sin great; *ex. gr.*, my sin is little. The more unkind thou (saith the Spirit) that wilt not do a small matter for the Lord. My sin is common. The more sinful thou that in those things wherein all the world rise up in arms against God, thou joinest with them. God spares me after sin. The greater is thy sin, therefore, that thou hast continued so long in, against a God so pitiful to thee. The dearest sins are now the vilest sins; because, though they were most sweet to him, yet the Spirit convinceth him they were therefore the more grievous unto the soul of God. You poor creatures may now hide, and color, and excuse your sins before men; but, when the Lord comes to convince, you can not lie hid. Then your consciences (when Jesus Christ the Lord comes to convince) shall not be like the steward in the gospel that set down fifty for a hundred pounds. No; the Lord will force it to bring in a true and clear account at that day.

There is a real light in spiritual conviction. Rational conviction makes things appear notionally; but spiritual conviction, really. The Spirit, indeed, useth argumentation in conviction; but it goeth further, and causeth the soul not only to see sin and death discursively, but also intuitively and really. Reason can see and discourse about words and propositions, and behold things by report, and to deduct one thing from another; but the Spirit makes a man see the things themselves, really wrapped up in those words. The Spirit brings spiritual things as well as notions before a man's eye; the light of the Spirit is like the light of the sun — it makes all things appear as they are. (John iii. 20, 21.) It was Jerusalem's misery she heard the words of Christ, and they were not hid from them; but the things of her peace, shut up in those words, were hid from her eyes. Discourse with many a man about his sin and misery, he will grant all that you say, and he is convinced, and his estate is most wretched, and yet still lives in all manner of sin. What is the reason of it? Truly, he sees his sin only by discourse, but he doth not, nay, can not, see the thing sin, death, wrath of God, until the Spirit come, which only convinceth or showeth that really. A man will not be afraid of a lion when it is painted only upon a wall. Why? Because therein he doth not see the living lion : when he sees that he trembles. So men hear of sin, and talk of sin and death, and say they are most miserable in regard of both ; yet their hearts tremble not, are not amazed at these evils, because sin is not seen alive, death is not presented alive before them, which is done by the Spirit of conviction only, revealing these really to the soul ; and hence it is that many men in seeing see not. How can that be? Thus, in seeing things notionally they see them not really. And hence many that know most of sin know least of sin, because, in seeing it notionally, they see it not really. And therefore happy were it for some men, scholars and others, that they had no notional knowledge of sin ; for this light is their darkness, and makes them more uncapable of spiritual conviction. The first act of spiritual conviction is to let a man see clearly that he is sinful and most miserable. The second act is to let the soul see really what this sin and death is. O, consider of this. Many of you know that you are sinful, and that you shall die ; but dost thou know what sin is, and what it is to die ? If thou didst, I dare say thy heart would sink. If thou dost not, thou art a condemned man, because not yet a convinced man. If you here ask how the Lord makes sin real, I answer, by making God real ; the real greatness of sin is seen by beholding really the greatness of God, who is smitten by sin ; sin is not seen because God is not seen. (3 John v. 11,) "He that doth evil hath not seen God." No knowledge of God is the cause why blood toucheth blood. The Spirit casts out all other company of vain and foolish thoughts, and then God comes in and appears immediately to the soul in his greatness and glory, and then the Spirit saith, Lo, this is that God thy sins have provoked. And now sin appears as it is ; and, together with this real sight of sin, the soul doth not see painted fire, but sees the fire of God's wrath really, whither now it is leading, that never can be quenched but by Christ's blood ; and, when the Spirit hath thus convinced, now a man begins to see his madness and folly in times past, saying, I know not what I did ; and hence questions, Can the Lord pardon such a wretch as I, whose sins are so great? Hence also the heart begins to be affected with sin and death, because it sees them now as they are indeed, and not by report only. A man accounts it a matter of nothing to tread upon a worm, wherein here is nothing seen worthy either to be loved or feared; and hence a man's heart is not affected with it. Before the Spirit of conviction comes, God is more vile in man's eye than any worm. As Christ said in another case of himself, (Ps. xxii.,) "I am a worm, and no man," so may the Lord complain, I am viler in such a one's eyes than any worm, and no God; and hence a man makes it a matter of nothing to tread upon the glorious majesty of God, and hence is not affected with it; but when God is seen by the spirit of conviction in his great glory, then, as he is great, sin is seen great; as his glory affects and astonisheth the soul, so sin affects the heart.

There is a constant light; the soul sees sin and death continually before it; God's arrows stick fast in the soul, and cannot be plucked out. "My sin is ever before me," said David, (in his renewing of the work of conversion.) For, in effectual conviction, the mind is not only bound to see the misery lying upon it, but it is held bound; it is such a sunlight as never can be quenched, though it may be clouded. When the Spirit of Christ darts in any light to see sin, the soul would turn away from looking upon it, would not hear on that ear, Felix-like. But the Spirit of conviction, sent to make thorough work on the hearts of all the elect, follows them, meets them at every turn, forceth them to see and remember what they have done. The least sin now is like a mote in the eye; it is ever troubling. Those ghastly, dreadful objects of sin, death, wrath, being presented by the Spirit near unto the soul, fix the eye to fasten here. They that can cast off at their pleasure the remembrance and thoughts of sin and death, never prove sound, until the Lord doth make them stay their thoughts, and muse deeply on what they have done, and whither they are going. And hence the soul, in lying down, rising up, lies down and rises up with perplexed thoughts. What will become of me? The Lord sometimes keeps it waking in the night season, when others are asleep, and then it is haunted with those thoughts, it can not sleep. It looks back upon every day and week, Sabbath, sermon, prayer, speeches, and thinks all this day, this week, etc., the goodness of the Lord and his patience to a wretch hath been continued; but my sins also are continued; I sin in all I do, in all my prayers, in all I think; the same heart remains still not humbled, not yet unchanged.

And hence you shall observe, that word which discovered sin at first to it, it never goes out of the mind. I think, saith the soul, I shall never forget such a man, nor such a truth. Hence also if the soul grow light and careless at some time, and casts off the thoughts of these things, the Spirit returns again, and falls a-reasoning with the soul: Why hast thou done this? What hurt hath the Lord done thee? Will there never be an end? Hast not thou gone on long enough in thy lewd courses against God, but that thou shouldest still add unto the heap? Hast thou not wrath enough upon thee already? How soon may the Lord stop thy breath! and then thou knowest thou hadst better never to have been born. Was there ever any that thus resisted grace? that thus adventured upon the sword point? Hast thou but one Friend, a patient, long-suffering God, that hath left thy conscience without excuse long ago, and therefore could have cut thee off? and dost thou thus forsake him, thus abuse him? Thus the Spirit follows; and hence the soul comes to some measure of confession of sin: O Lord, I have done exceeding wickedly; I have been worse than the horse that rusheth into the battle because it sees not death before it; but I have seen death before me in these ways, and yet go on, and still sin, and can not but sin. Behold me, Lord, for I am very vile. When thus the Spirit hath let into the soul a clear, real, constant light to see sin and death, now there is a thorough conviction.

But you will say, In what measure doth the Spirit communicate this light?

I shall therefore open the fourth particular, viz.: The measure of spiritual conviction in all the elect, viz., so much conviction of sin as may bring in and work compunction for sin; so much sight of sin as may bring in sense of sin: so much is necessary, and no more. Every one hath not the same measure of conviction; yet all the elect have and must have so much; for so much conviction is necessary as may attain the end of conviction. Now, the *finis proximus*, or next end, of conviction in the elect, is compunction or sense of sin; for what good can it do unto them to see sin, and not to be affected with it? What greater mercy doth the Lord show to the elect therein than unto the devils and reprobates who stand convinced, and know they are wicked and condemned, but yet their hearts altogether unaffected with any true remorse for sin? "Mine eye," saith Jeremy, "affecteth my heart." The Lord opens the ears of men and sealeth instruction, that he may hide pride from man. Some think that there is no thorough conviction without some affection. I dare not say so, nor will I now dispute whether there is not something in the nature and essence of that conviction the elect have different from that conviction in reprobates and devils. It is sufficient now, and that which teacheth the end of this question, to know what measure of conviction is necessary. I conceive the clear discerning of it is by the immediate and sensible effect of it, viz., so much as affects the heart truly with sin.

But if you ask, What is that sense of sin, and what measure

of this is necessary? that I shall answer in the doctrine of compunction.

Let not therefore any soul be discouraged, and say, I was
never yet convinced, because I have not felt such a clear, real,
constant light to see sin and death as others have done. Consider thou if the end of conviction be attained, which is a true
sense and feeling of sin, thou hast then that measure which
is most meet for thee, more than which the Lord regards not
in any of his. But you that walk up and down with convinced
consciences, and know your states are miserable and sinful, and
that you perish if you die in that condition, and yet have no sense
nor feeling, no sorrow nor affliction of spirit for those evils, I tell
thee the very devils are in some respects nearer the kingdom of
God than you be, who see, and feel, and tremble. Woe, woe to
thousands that live under convicting ministries, whom the word
often hits, and the Lord by the Spirit often meets; and they
hear and know their sins are many, their estates bad, and that
iniquity will be their ruin if thus they continue; yet all God's
light is without heat, and it is but the shining of it upon rocks
and cold stones; they are frozen in their dregs. Be it known
to you, you have not one drop of that conviction which begins
salvation. Before I pass from this to the second work of compunction, let me make a word of application.

If the Spirit begins thus with conviction of sin, then let all
the ministers of Christ co-work with Christ, and begin with their
people here; be faithful witnesses unto God's truth, and give
warning to this secure world that the sentence of death is passed,
and the curse of God lies upon every man for the least sin. "Lift
up thy voice like a trumpet," was the Lord's word to Isaiah, (Is.
lviii. 2,) "and tell them their sin." Those bees we call drones
that have lost their sting. When the salt of the earth (the ministers of Christ, Matt. v.) have lost their acrimony and sharp-
ness, or saltness, what is it good for but to be cast out? Our
hearers will putrefy and corrupt by hearing such doctrines only
as never search. When the Lord inflicted a grievous curse upon
the people, (Ezek. iii. 26,) the Lord made Ezekiel dumb that
he should not be a reprover to them. What was the lamentation
of Jeremy? "Thy prophets have seen vain and foolish things
for thee, and have not discovered thine iniquity." How would
you have the Lord Jesus by his Spirit to convince men? Must
it not be by his word? Verily you keep the Spirit of Christ
from falling down upon the people if you refuse to endeavor to
convince the people by your word. Other doctrines are sweet
and necessary; but this is in the first place most necessary.

Beware of personating, beware of bitterness and passion ; but
O, convince with a spirit of power and compassion ; and he that
shall be instrumental unto Christ in this or any other work for
Christ's sake, unto him the Lord will be the principal agent, and
by him will attain his own ends, finish his great work, gather
in his scattered sheep who are in great multitudes throughout
the kingdom scattered from him, if once they be thoroughly
convinced that they are utterly lost, and gone out of the way.

May not this also be sad reproof and terror to them that stand
it out against all means of conviction, and will not see their
sin, nor believe the fearful wrath of God due to them for sin ?
Not a man scarce can be found that will come to this conclusion : I am a sinful man, and therefore I am dead ; I am a condemned man ; but, like wild beasts, fly from their pursuers into
their holes, and thickets, and dens — their sinful extenuations,
excuses, and apologies for sin and for themselves ; and if they
be hunted thither, and found out there, then they resist, and arti-
cle against that truth which troubles them. " They flatter themselves in their own eyes until their iniquities be found most
hateful." Many a man dislikes the text, the use, especially the
long-use, wherein his sin is touched, and his conscience tossed —
especially if it be his darling sin, his Herodias, his Rimmon —
especially if withal he thinks that the minister means him, he
will not see it nor confess it — especially if he apprehends he
shall lose his honor, or his silver shrines, and profit by it. He
will not see his sin that he may not be troubled in conscience
for his sin, that so he may not be forced to confess and forsake his sin, and condemn himself for it before God and men.
O Lord, I mourn that I can scarce meet with a man that either
cares to be, or will be, convinced, but hath something always to
say for himself : their sins are not so great, they are not so
bad, but have some good, and therefore have some hope ; and,
if God be merciful, it is no great matter though they be exceeding sinful, or some such thing ; their mouths are not stopped
to say any thing for themselves but guilty. There is less conviction in the world in this age than many are aware of ; for I
believe that all the powers of hell conspire together to blind men's
eyes and darken men's minds in this great work of Christ.
Principiis obsta. It is policy to stop Christ in his entrance in
this first stroke upon the soul ; but O, little do you think what
you do herein, and what woe you work to yourselves hereby.
Dost thou stifle and resist the first breathings of Christ's Spirit
when he comes to save thee ? What hurt will it be to know the
worst of thy condition now, when there is hope hereby of coming

out of it, who must else one day see all thy "sins in order before thee," to thy eternal anguish and terror? (Ps. l. 21.) When the Lord shall say unto thee as to Dives, "Remember in thy life-time thou hadst thy good things," remember such a time, such a place, such a sin; which then you would not see. But now thou shalt see what it is to strike an infinite God. Remember thou wast forewarned of wrath to come, but thou wouldest not believe thyself accursed, that so thou mightest have felt thy need of Him that was made a curse to bless thee; and therefore feel it now: O, you will wish then that you had known this evil in that your day. What dost thou talk of grace? thou thinkest thou hast grace, when as thou hast not the first beginning, nay, not the most remote preparation for it in this work of conviction: what should we do for such as these, but with Jeremy, (Jer. xiii. 17,) "If you will not hear, my soul shall weep in secret for your pride"?

O, be persuaded, therefore, to remember your sins past, and to consider of your ways now. All the profaneness of thy heart and life, all the vanity of thy youth, (Eccl. xi. 9,) all your secret sins, all your sins against light and love, checks and vows; all that time wherein thou didst nothing else but live in sin; thus God's people have done, (Ezek. vi. 9.,) thus all the elect shall do. O, consider the Lord remembers them all, and that with grief of heart against thee, because thou forgettest them. (Hos. ii. 7.) He that numbers thy hairs, and tells the sparrows that fall, numbers much more thy sins that fall from thee; they are written down in his black book. They are no trifles, for he minds not toys; the books must be opened. O, reckon now you have yet time to call them to mind, which it may be shall not continue long; it is the Lord's complaint (Jer. viii. 6) of a wicked generation, "that he could hear no man say, What have I done?" "Winnow your-selves," (as the word is, Zeph. ii. 1,) "O people not worthy to be beloved." I pronounce unto you from the eternal God, that ere long the Lord will search out Jerusalem with candles; he will come with a sword in his hand to search for all secure sinners in city and country, unless you awaken; he will make inquisition for blood, for oaths, for whoremongers, which grow common; for all secret sins we are frozen up in. O, be willing, be but willing that the Lord should search you and convince you, now in this evening time of the day, before the night come, wherein it will be too late to say, I wish I had considered of my ways in time: of all sins, none can so hardly stand with uprightness as a secret unwilling-ness to see and be convinced of sin. (John iii. 20, 21.) The helps and means for attaining hereunto are these:—

Bring thy soul to the light, desire the Lord in prayer, as Job did. "What I see not, O Lord, show me." (Job xxxiv. 32.) Set the glass of God's law before thee; look up in the ministry of the word unto the Lord, and say, O Lord, search me: the sun of this holy word discovers motes: on the Sabbath day attend to all that which is spoken as spoken unto thee; then examine thyself when thou hast leisure. When David saw (Ps. xix.) how pure the law was, he cries out, "Who knows his errors?"

Look upon every conviction of thy conscience for sin as an arrest and warning given from the Lord himself; for sometimes the word hits, and conscience startles, and saith, This is my sin, my condition; yet how usual it is then for a man to put a merry face upon a foul conscience! how oft do men think this is but the word of a man who hath a latitude given him of reproving sin in the pulpit, and we must give way to them therein! or else their hearts rise and swell against the man and word also. And why is it thus? Because he thinks it is man only that speaks; whereas did he see and believe that this was a stroke, a warning, an arrest, a check from the omnipotent God, would he then grapple, think you, with him? Would it pass lightly by him then? When Eli heard Samuel denounced sad things against his house, "It is the Lord," said Eli. (1 Sam. iii. 18.) When Paul saw Jesus speaking, "Why persecutest thou me?" (Acts ix.,) he falls down astonished, and dares not kick against the pricks any longer; an arrest in the king's name comes with authority, and awes the heart of the man in debt.

Do not judge of sin by any other rule but as God judgeth of it, according to the rule of the word by which all men's ways shall be judged at the last day. What made Saul (1 Sam. xv.) extenuate his sin to Samuel? He judged not of it as the Lord in his word did; for had he done so, he would have seen disobedience to a command as bad as witchcraft, as Samuel told him; which also made his proud heart sink, and say, I have sinned: remember for this end these scriptures, (Rom. i. 18; Rom. ii. 9; Rom. vi. 23; Gal. iii. 10,) by which thou mayest see, either I must die, (in the state I am,) or God himself must lie. Remember that an angry look or word is murder in God's account; a wanton eye, an unchaste thought, is adultery before a holy God, before whose tribunal thou must give an account of every vain thought and word. And therefore do not judge of sin by the present pleasure, gain, honor, or ease in it; for this is a false rule: Moses forsook the pleasures of sin for a season," (Heb. xi. 25;) nor yet by not feeling any punishment for it, for God reserves wrath (Nahum i. 2) till the day of reckoning; nor yet by the esteem that others generally have of it, who make no more of wounding the Son of God by sin than they do of crushing vermin under their feet; nor yet by the practice of others: Every man sins, and therefore I hope I shall do as well as others; nor yet seeing thyself better, and thanking God thou art not as other men: it may be so, thou didst never steal, nor whore, nor murder as yet: that is not the question; but hast thou had any one vain thought in prayer? hast thou heard one sermon unprofitably? hast thou sinned? then know God spared not the angels that sinned, and how wilt thou escape, unless the Lord die for thee? — nor yet, lastly, judge of it by thy own opinion of God, in thinking God is like unto thee, that as thou makest light of it, so he maketh less. (Ps. l. 21.) O, take heed of judging the evil of sin by any of these rules: O, remember all men are apt to think of themselves better than they are: "Are we also blind?" say the Pharisees: take heed that by judging of sin by these false rules you deceive not yourselves.

Let this, lastly, be a use of thankfulness to all those whose eyes the Lord hath opened to see, and so convincing you of your sins. When David was going, in the heat of his spirit, to kill Nabal, and Abigail met him and stopped him, what said he? "O, blessed be the Lord for thy counsel;" so when thou wert going on, in the heat and pursuit of thy sin, toward eternal death, that the Lord should now meet thee in thy way, and convince thee of thy folly, and so stop thee, what a world of sin else wouldst thou have committed! how vile wouldest thou have been! O, say, therefore, Blessed be that minister of the Lord, and blessed forever be the name of the Lord that gave me that counsel. It is said, Christ will "send the Comforter to convince of sin:" is it a comfortable thing to see sin? Yes, it shall one day be matter of unspeakable comfort to you that ever you saw sin; that ever he showed thee that mystery of iniquity in thy heart and life, those *arcana imperii*, those secrets of the power and dominion of sin over thee: Thou shalt not hate, but reprove thy brother. If the Lord should secretly keep thy sin glowing in his own bosom against thee, and never reprove thee for it, nor convince thee of it, no greater sign of God's everlasting hatred against thee. O, it is infinite love that he hath called thee aside and dealt plainly and secretly with thee, and will you not be thankful for this? The Lord might have left thee in thy brutish estate, and never made known thy latter end; never have told thee of thy sin or flood before it comes.

It may be you will say, If I felt my sin, and were deeply humbled for it, I could then be thankful that ever I saw it: what is it to see sin?

This is a favor the Lord shows not to all mankind; many have no means to bring them to the knowledge of it, and those that have yet are smitten with a deep sleep under those means, that they know not when death is at their doors, nor what sin means; and this, it may be, is the condition of some of thy poor friends and acquaintance, that think it strange that thou runnest not with them in the same way as they do.

Suppose some reprobates do see sin; yet the Lord puts a secret virtue in that work of conviction upon thee, which makes thee cry to Heaven for a spirit of brokenness for sin, which, without this sight of sin, thou wouldest never so much as have desired; and this they have not.

However, conviction is a work of the Spirit, though it should be but common; and wilt not thou be thankful for common mercy, suppose it be outward? How much more for this that is spiritual, though it should be common! especially considering that it is the first fundamental work of the Spirit, and is seminally all. Sense of sin begins here, and ariseth hence; as ignorance of sin is seminally all sin. Remember that the discovery of Faux in the vault was the preservation of England: we use to remember the day and hour of the beginning of some great and notable deliverance: O, remember this time, wherein the love of Christ first brake out in convincing thee of thy sin, who else hadst certainly perished in it. And thus much of this first work of conviction. Now the second follows — compunction.

SECTION III.

The second Act of Christ's Power, in working Compunction, or Sense of Sin.

COMPUNCTION, pricking at the heart, or sense and feeling of sin, is different from conviction of sin: the latter is the work of the understanding, and seated in that principally; the other is in the affections and will, and seated therein principally: a man may have sight of sin without sorrow and sense of it. (Dan. v. 22, with 20, 21. James i. 24. Rom. ii. 20, 21.) Yet that conviction which the Spirit works in the elect is ever accompanied with compunction, first or last. For the better unfolding this point, let me open these four things to you: —

1. That compunction or sense of sin immediately follows conviction of sin in the day of Christ's power.
2. The necessity of this work to succeed the other.
3. Wherein it consists.
4. The measure of it in all the elect.

That compunction follows conviction is evident from Scripture and reason. (Acts ii. 37.) When they heard this, that is, when they saw and were convinced of their sin in crucifying the Lord of life, which they did not imagine to be a sin before, what follows next? It is said, "They were pricked at the heart." Lo, here is compunction. Ephraim, also, in turning unto God, (Jer. xxxi. 19,) hath these words: "After that I was instructed, I smote upon my thigh," (as men in great calamity befallen them use to do.) "I was ashamed, even confounded, because I did bear the reproach of my youth." The men of Nineveh hearing by the prophet they were all to die within forty days, it is said "they believed God," (in the work of conviction,) and then they fell to sackcloth and ashes, (in the work of compunction,) which did immediately follow. Josiah, (2 Chron. xxxiv. 27,) in his renewed return unto God, after he heard the words of the law, "his heart melted, and he wept before the Lord." For what is the end of conviction? Is it not compunction? for if the Lord should let a man see his sin, and death for sin, and yet suffer the heart to remain hard and unaffected, the Lord did but leave him without excuse; nay, the Lord should but leave him under great misery, and under a more fearful judgment, viz., for a man to see and know his sin, and yet unaffected with it, and hardened under it: hardness of heart is one of the greatest judgments; to see sin, and not to be affected with it, argues greater hardness. For it is no wonder if they that see not and know not sin remain senseless of sin; alas! they know not what they do; but for a man to be enlightened, and see his sin, and yet unaffected, Lord, how great is this hardness, and how unexcusable will such a man be left before God, when the Lord shall reckon with him for his hardness of heart! What is the end of that light the Lord lets into the understanding in other things? Is it not that thereby the heart might be affected throughly with it? Why doth the Lord let in the light of the knowledge of Christ and of his will? Is it that this knowledge should, like froth, float in the understanding, and be imprisoned there? No, verily, but that the heart might be throughly and deeply affected therewith. And do you think the Lord will, in the light of conviction, imprison it up in the mind? Is there not a further end that by this light the heart might be deeply affected with sin? If any say that the end of conviction is to drive the soul to Christ, I grant that is the remote and last end of it; but the next end is compunction. For if the understanding be convinced of misery, and the heart remain hard, the mind may see indeed that righteousness and life only are to be had in Christ; yet the heart

12 *

remaining hard, the will and affections will never stir toward
Christ; it is impossible a hard heart, remaining such, wholly un-
affected with sin or misery, should be truly affected with Jesus
Christ; but of this more hereafter.

What necessity is there of this compunction, to succeed conviction? I speak now of necessity in way of ordinary dispensation,
not of God's usual and extraordinary way of working, where he
useth neither law nor gospel (as ordinarily he doth) to work
by. Many have been nibbling lately at this doctrine, and demanded, What need is there of sorrow and compunction of
heart? A man may be converted only by the gospel, and God
may let in sweetness and joy without any sense of sin or misery,
and in my experience I have found it so; others, godly and
gracious, also feel it so; why, therefore, do any press such a
necessity of coming in by this back door unto Christ? This
point I conceive is very weighty, and much danger in denying
the truth of it; yet, withal, there needs much tenderness in
handling of it, lest any stumble; and therefore, before I lay
down the reasons to show the necessity of it, give me leave to
propound these rules both for the clearing of the point, and
answering sundry objections usually about this point : —

In this work of compunction, do not think that the Lord hath
not wrought any true sense of sin, because you find it not in
such a measure as you imagine you should desire to have, and
that others feel; sense of sin admits degrees. I doubt not but
Joseph's brethren were humbled; yet Joseph must be more; he
must be cast into the ditch, and into the prison, and the iron
must enter not only into his legs, but into his soul. (Ps. cv. 18.)
He must be more afflicted in spirit, because he was to do greater
work for God, and was to be raised up higher than the rest, and
therefore did need the more ballast: some are educated more
civilly than others, and thereby have contracted less guilt and
stoutness of heart against God and his ways; therefore these
have not such cause of trouble ; and being less rugged, have less
need of axes to hew them: some men's sorrow breaks in upon
them more suddenly, like storms and breaches of the sea, and
the Lord is resolved to hasten and finish his work in them more
speedily, and it may be more exemplarily, (for every Christian
is not a fair copy,) as in those, Acts ii. 37. In others their
sorrows soak in by degrees ; *Gutta cavat lapidem ;* the Lord
empties them by continual droppings, and hence feel not that
measure of sorrow that others do : every Christian is not a
Heman, (Ps. lxxxviii.,) who suffers "distracting fears and terrors
from his youth up," (ver. 15,) who is "afflicted with all God's

ways," (ver. 7,) for he was a man of exceeding high parts and gifts, as you may see, 1 Kings iv. 31 ; and therefore the Lord had need of hanging some special plummets on his heart to keep it ever low, lest it should be lifted up above measure. Some sense of sin the Lord will work in all he saves, but not the same measure ; the Lord gives not always unto his that which is good in itself, (it is good, I confess, to be deeply affected and humbled,) but that which is fit, and therefore best for thee.

Do not think there is no compunction or sense of sin wrought in the soul because you can not so clearly discern and feel it, nor the time of the working and first beginning of it. I have known many that have come with complaints — they were never humbled, they never felt it so, nor yet could tell the time when it was so; yet there hath been, and many times they have seen it, by the help of others' spectacles, and blessed God for it. When they in Isaiah lxiii. 17, complained, " Lord, why hast thou hardened our hearts from thy fear ? " do you think there was no softness nor sensibleness indeed? Yes, verily, but they felt nothing but a hard heart; nay, such hardness as if the Lord had plagued them with it by his own immediate hand, and not born and bred with them only, as with other men. Many a soul may think the Lord hath left it, nay, smitten it with a hard heart, and so make his moan of it; yet the Lord hath wrought real softness, under ·self-hardness, as many times in reprobates there is felt softness when within there is real hardness. The stony ground hearers were ploughed and broken on the top, but were stony at the bottom. Some men may be wounded outwardly and mortally; this may easily be discerned. The Lord may wound others, and they may bleed out; their sorrow is more inwardly and secret, and therefore can not point with their finger to the wound as others can.

Do not think the Lord works compunction in all the elect in the same circumstantial work of the Spirit, but only in the same substantial work; the Lord works a true sense of sin for substance and truth of it, yet there are many circumstantial works, like so many enlargements and comments upon one and the same text. Ex. gratia, the same sin that affects Paul, it may be, doth not affect Lydia or Apollos. The same notions for the aggravation of sin in one do not come into the mind of the other; the same complaints, and prayers, and turnings of spirit in the one, may not be in the same circumstances, and with the like effects, as in the other, and yet both of them feel sin, and therefore complain ; they both feel sin, yet by means of various apprehensions and aggravations. This I speak, because you may the better understand the meaning of God's servants in opening the work of humiliation. You may hear them say, The soul doth this, and thinks that, and speaks another thing; it may be every one does not so think in the same individual circumstances, and therefore is to be understood as producing only *exemplum in re simili:* something like this, or for the substance of this, is here wrought.

In this work of compunction we must not bring rules unto men, but men to rules; crook not God's rules to the experience of men, (which is fallible, and many times corrupt,) but bring men unto the rule, and try men's estates herein by that; for many will say some men are not humbled at all, never had any precedent sorrow for sin, God's mercy only hath melted their hearts; and experience proves this, and many find this, who are sincere and gracious Christians.

I answer, We are not in this or any other point to be guided by the experience of men only, but attend the rule; if it be proved that according unto the rule men must be broken and affected with their sin and misery before mercy can be truly apprehended or Christ accepted. What tell you me of such or such men? Let the rule stand, but let men stand or fall according to the rule; many are accounted gracious and godly for a time, much affected with mercy and Christ Jesus; yet afterward fall or wizen into nothing, and prove very unsound.

What is the reason?

Truly the cause was here: their first wound and sorrow for sin was not right, as hereafter shall be made good; many thousands are miserably deceived about their estates by this one thing, of crooking and wresting God's rules to Christians' experience. Let all God's servants tremble and be wary here; rack not the Holy Scriptures, nor force them to speak as thou feelest, but try all things by them. (1 Thess. v. 21.)

Do not make the examples of converted persons in Scripture patterns in all things of persons unconverted; do not make God's work upon the one run parallel with God's work upon the other.

Some say that many in Scripture are converted to Christ without any sorrow for sin, and produce the examples of Lydia, whose heart God sweetly opened to receive Christ; and the eunuch, (Acts viii.,) converted in the same manner.

I answer, These are examples of persons converted to God before, who did believe in the Messiah, but did not know that this Jesus was the Messiah, which they soon did when the Lord sent the means to reveal Christ; and therefore Lydia, a Jewish proselyte, is called a worshiper of God, (Acts xvi. 14,) and so

was the eunuch, (Acts viii. 27;) and in the same condition was
the centurion, (Acts x. 2,) who feared God, and whose prayers
were accepted, (ver. 4,) (which can not be without faith) yet did
not know that this Jesus crucified was the Messiah, until Peter
came unto him. So that, suppose here was no sense or sorrow
for sin, at this time; doth it therefore follow they never had
any when the Lord at first wrought upon them? are these examples in persons converted fit to. show forth God's work in
persons unconverted? In some things, indeed, they are examples,
in others not so; their examples of believing in Christ are not
in that act examples of sorrow for want of Christ. And yet let
me add, to say that God opened Lydia's heart to believe in
Christ, and yet opened not her heart to lament her sin and
misery in her estate without Christ, (suppose she were without
Christ,) is more than can be proved from the text; for it is said
her heart was opened to attend unto the things that were spoken
by Paul; and can any think that Paul, or an apostle, ever
preached Christ without preaching the need men had of him?
and could any preach their need of Christ without preaching
men's undone and sinful estate without Christ? and do you think
that Lydia was not made to attend unto this? do you think that
when Philip came to open the fifty-third chapter of Isaiah to
the eunuch, that "Christ was bruised for our iniquities;" that
he did not let him understand the infinite evil of sin and misery
of all sinners, and of him in special, unless the Lord Jesus was
bruised for him?

In examples recorded in the Scripture of God's converting
grace, do not think they had no sorrow for sin, because it is not
distinctly and expressly set down in all places; for the Scripture
usually sets down matters very briefly; it oftentimes supposeth
many things, and refers us to judge of some by other places; as
(Acts vi. 7) it is said, "many of the priests were obedient to the
faith:" doth it therefore follow that they did immediately believe,
without any sense of sin? Look to a fuller example, (Acts ii.,)
and then we may see, as the one were converted to the faith,
so were the other, having a hand in the same sin. (1 Tim.
i. 13, 14,) Paul, he was a "persecutor, but the Lord received
him to mercy;" and that "God's grace was abundant in faith and
love," doth it hence follow that Paul had no castings down, because not mentioned here? If we look upon Acts ix., we shall
see it otherwise.

Do not judge of general and common workings of the Spirit
upon the souls of any to be the beginnings of effectual and special
conversion; for a man may have some inward and yet common

knowledge of the gospel, and Christ in it, before there be any sorrow for sin ; yet it doth not hence follow that the Lord begins not with compunction and sorrow, because common work is not special and effectual work ; when the Spirit thus comes, he first begins here, as we shall prove.

The terrors, and fears, and sense of sin and death be in themselves afflictions of soul, and of themselves drive from Christ; yet in the hand of Christ, by the power of the Spirit, they are made to lead, or rather drive unto Christ, which is able to turn mourning into joy, as well as after mourning to give joy ; and therefore it is a vain thing to think there is no need of such sorrows which drive from Christ, and that Christ can work well enough therefore without them ; when as by the mighty power and riches of mercy in Christ, the Lord by wounding, nay, killing his of all their carnal security and self-confidence, saves all his alive, and drives them to seek for life in the Son.

These things thus premised, let us now hear of the necessity of this work to succeed conviction.

Else a sinner will never part with his sin ; a bare conviction of sin doth but light the candle to see sin ; compunction burns his fingers, and that only makes him dread the fire. " Cleanse your hands, ye sinners, and purify your hearts, ye double-minded " men, saith the apostle James, (chap. iv. 8.) But how should this be done ? He answers, (ver. 9,) " Be afflicted, and mourn, and weep ; turn your laughter into mourning. " So Joel ii. 12. The prophet calls upon his hearers to turn from their sin unto the Lord ; but how ? " Rend your hearts, and not your garments." Not that they were able to do this, but by what sorrow he requires of all in general ; he thereby effectually works in the hearts of all the elect in particular ; for every man naturally takes pleasure, nay, all his delight and pleasure is in nothing else but sin ; for God he hath none, but that. Now, so long as he takes pleasure in sin, and finds contentment by sin, he can not but cleave inseparably to it. O, it is sweet, and it only is sweet ; for so long as the soul is dead in sin, " pleasure in sin is death in sin." (1 Tim. v. 6.) So long as it is dead in sin, it is impossible it should part with sin ; no more than a dead man can break the bonds of death. And therefore it undeniably follows, that the Lord must first put gall and wormwood to these dugs, before the soul will cease sucking, or be weaned from them ; the Lord must first make sin bitter, before it will part with it ; load it with sin, before it will sit down and desire ease. And look, as the pleasure in sin is exceeding sweet to a sinner, so the sorrow for it must be exceeding bitter, before the soul will part from it.

It is true, I confess, a man sometime may part with sin without sorrow; the unclean spirit may go out for a time, before he is taken, bound, and slain by the power of Christ. But such a kind of parting is but the washing of the cup; it is unsafe and unsound, and the end of such a Christian will be miserable: for a man to hear of his sin, and then to say, I will do no more so, without any sense or sorrow for it, would not have been approved by Paul, if he had seen no more in the careless Corinthians, in tolerating the incestuous person; but their sorrow wrought this repentance. No, the Lord abhors such whorish wiping the lips; and therefore the same apostle, when he reproves them for not separating the sinner, and so the sin from them, he sums it up in one word: "You have not mourned, that such a one might be taken from you;" because then sin is severed truly from the soul, when sorrow or shame, some sense and feeling of the evil of it, begins it. Not only sin is opposite to God, but when the Lord Jesus first comes near his elect in their sinful estate, they are then enemies themselves by sin unto God. And hence it is they will never part with their weapons, until themselves be thoroughly wounded; and therefore the Lord must wound their consciences, minds, and hearts, before they will cast them by. Now, if there be no parting with, no separation from sin, but sin is as strong, and the sinner as vile, as ever before, hath Christ (who now comes to save his elect from sin) the end of his work? What is the man the better for conviction, affection to Christ, name what you can, that remains still in his sins? When the apostle would sum up all the misery of men, he doth it in those words, "Ye are yet in your sin." So I say, thou art convicted, but art yet in thy sin; art affected with Christ, and takest hold of Christ, but art yet in thy sin: "He that confesseth and forsaketh his sin shall find mercy."

You will say, May not the sweetness of Christ in the gospel, and sense of mercy, separate from sin, without any compunction?

I answer, 1. Sense of mercy and Christ's sweetness (I conceive) serve principally to draw the soul unto Christ. (Jer. xxxi. 3,) "With loving kindness have I drawn thee." But compunction or sense of sin principally serves, in the hand of Christ, to turn the soul from sin. Aversion from sin is distinct from, and in order goes before, our conversion unto God.

2. Sense of the sweetness of God's grace in Christ keeps out sin, but it doth not thrust out sin at first.

3. Christ can not be effectually sweet, unless sin be first made bitter; there may be some general notice of Christ's excellency, and some thirty pieces given for him; some esteem of his grace,

and hope of his mercy, which may occasion sorrow ; but I dare not say, that this is any sound or thorough work, till after sorrow. (Is. l. 4.) Christ hath "the tongue of the learned given him to speak a word in season." Unto whom ? It is added, "unto the weary ; " they are the men that will prize mercy, and they only to purpose ; they that have felt the bitterness of sin and wrath find it exceeding hard to prize Christ, and to taste his sweetness ; how shall they do it indeed that find none at all ? Sweetness before sense of sin is like cordials before purging of a foul stomach ; which usually strengthen the humor, but recover not the man.

Because, without this, no man will either care for Christ, or feel a need of Christ ; a man may see a want of Christ by the power of conviction, but he will never feel a need of Christ, but by the spirit of compunction. " The whole need not the physician, but they that are sick." A whole man may see his want of a physician, but a sick man only feels his need of him, will prize him, send for him. By the whole you are not to understand such as have no need indeed of Christ, (for what sinner but hath need of him ?) but such as feel no need of him ; as by sick can not be meant such as are sinful and miserable, for then Christ should come actually to save all men ; but those that did feel themselves so, as a sick man that feels his sickness : these only are the men that feel a need and necessity of Christ ; these only will come to Christ, and be glad of Christ, and be truly thankful for their recovery of Christ. And hence ariseth the great sin of the world in despising the gospel, not at all affected with the glad tidings of it, because they are not affected with their sin and misery ; or if they be affected but in part with the gospel, it is because they are not throughly affected with their misery before.

And hence it is, that when the Lord called his people to him, yet they would not come to him, because they were the Lord's, and well enough without him. Why did not they come to the supper, being invited ? It was because they had farms, and oxen, and wives to attend unto ; they felt no need of coming, as the poor, lame, blind, and halt did. The prodigal cares not for father nor father's house, until he comes to see, Here I die. It is true, the grace of the gospel draws men unto Christ ; but it is very observable, that the gospel reveals no grace but with respect and in reference unto sinners, and men in extreme misery ; the gospel saith not that Christ is come to save, but to save sinners, and to save his people from their sins. It reveals not this, that God justifies men, but he justifies the ungodly ; it reveals not this, that Christ died for us, but that he died for them that were weak, for sinners, for enemies. And if so, can any man imagine that this news will be sweet, unless men see and feel the infinite misery of sin, and the fruits of it? Will not men say or think, What great matter is there in that? Suppose we be sinners and enemies, yet we are well enough; before Christ comes, a man's life lies in his sin. Now, suppose any should proclaim to a company of men the great favor of their prince toward them, that he is such a gracious prince as will take away all their lives; will this be glad tidings? Gospel grace can not be set out, much less felt, but in reference to sin and misery, which must be first felt, before it can be sweet. Because Christ will never come but only unto such as feel their misery; for you will say, A man may come to Christ without it: I say again, If he doth, (as he hath many followers,) yet Christ will not come to him, nor commit himself to him: "I came not to call the righteous, but sinners, to repentance;" in which place note, that as by the righteous is not meant such as are sincerely so, but such as think and feel themselves so; so by sinners is not meant all manner of impenitent and hard-hearted sinners, but such as think and feel themselves such, and lament under it: now, God the Father sent him only unto such; he is sent not to heal the hard-hearted, but the broken-hearted; indeed, he is sent to make men broken hearted who have hard hearts; but he is not sent to heal them until then; the Lord leaves the ninety-nine that need no repentance to wilder forever; the one lost sheep, who feels itself so, and feels a need of a Saviour to come and find it out, who can not come and find out him, the Lord Jesus will come unto, and unto him only, leaving all the ninety-nine.

This may lastly appear by considering the end of man's fall into sin, and the publishing of the law to reveal sin; and of the gospel also in reference unto sin and misery. Why did the Lord suffer the fall of man? What was his great plot in it? It is apparent this, that thereby way might be made for the greater manifestation of God's grace in Christ. The serpent poisons all mankind, that the seed of the woman might have the glory of recovering some: this was God's last end; the perdition of some (of themselves) being but subordinate unto this. (Rom. ix. 22, 23.) Surely Adam might have glorified grace if he had stood, and God had revealed his grace in preserving him (made mutable) from fall. But the Lord saw grace should not be sufficiently advanced to its highest dignity by this, and therefore suffers him actually to fall, and that into an extreme depth of misery. Now, consider man's fall in itself can not be a mean of glorifying grace, but rather obscures all the glory of God. How shall the Lord attain his end then hereby? Truly, if the Lord let men see and feel their fall and misery by it, now grace offered will be accepted and glorified. And therefore the Lord sends the law to reveal sin, and make it exceeding sinful, and death for sin, that this end might be attained. (Gal. iii. 22.) And therefore feeling of sin, and death, and misery, being the means, must precede the other as the end; and therefore, as grace may be seen by conviction of misery, so the sweetness of it only can be felt by feeling misery in this work of compunction.

But you will say, What is this compunction, and wherein doth it consist?

This is the third particular to be opened; in general it is whereby the soul is affected with sin, and made sensible of sin; but more particularly, compunction is nothing else but a pricking of the heart, or the wounding of the soul with such fear and sorrow for sin and misery as severs the soul from sin, and from going on toward its eternal misery; so that it consists in three things: —

1. Fear.   2. Sorrow.   3. Separation from sin.

The Lord Jesus when he comes to rescue his elect, look as Satan held them in their misery: First, by blinding their eyes from seeing of it; secondly, by hardening their hearts from feeling of it: so the Lord Jesus, having cut asunder the first cord of Satan by conviction, breaks asunder the second by compunction, and causing the soul to feel and be affected with its misery; and as the whole soul is unaffected before he comes, so he makes the whole soul sensible when he comes, and therefore he fills the conscience with fear, and the heart with sorrow and mourning, so as now the will of sin is broken, which was hardened before these fears and sorrows seized upon it. Let me open these particularly, that you may taste and try the truth of what now I deliver.

I say the Lord Christ, in this work of compunction, lets into the heart of a secure sinner a marvelous fear and terror of the direful displeasure of God, of death, and hell, the punishment of sin. O beloved, look upon most men at this day; this is the great misery lying upon them — they do not fear the wrath to come, they fear not death nor damning, even then when they hear and know it is their portion; but their hearts are set to sin. (Eccl. viii. 11.)

The Lord Christ therefore lets in this fear, that look as the Lord when he comes to conquer the Canaanites, (Ex. xxiii.

27, 28,) "he sent his hornets before him," which were certain fears, which made their hearts faint in the day of battle, and by this subdued them; so the Lord Christ, when he comes to conquer a poor sinner that hath long resisted him, and would go on to his own perdition, lets in these fears, that the soul shrinks in with the thoughts of its woful estate, and cries out secretly, Lord, what will become of me if I die in this condition? Paul trembles, astonished at his misery and wickedness, and now he begins to cry out; the jailer was very cruel against Paul, but when the Lord Jesus comes to rescue him from this condition, you shall see him trembling. The Lord had let in that fear, that now he is content to do any thing to be saved from the danger he saw he was now in: when a man sees danger, and great danger, near and imminent, now man naturally fears it: before Christ come, the soul may see its misery, but it apprehends it far off, and hoping to escape it, and hence doth not fear it; but when the Lord Jesus comes, he presents a man's danger, death, wrath, and eternity near unto him, and hence hath no hope to escape it, as now he is, and therefore doth fear; and seeing the misery exceeding great, he hath an exceeding great (though ofttimes deep) fear of it; as men near death, and apprehending it so, begin then to be troubled, and cry out when it is too late. The Lord Jesus deals more mercifully with the elect, and brings death and eternity near them before they draw near to it, whilst it is called to-day: the poor jailer began to think of killing himself when fears were upon him; and so many, under this stroke of Christ, have the same thoughts, because they see no hope; but this measure is not in all; this work is in all.

"Put them in fear, O Lord, that they may know they be but men." Before this fear comes, men are above God, and think they can stand it out against him; the Lord therefore lets in this fear to make them know they be but men, and that as proud, and stout, and great as they are, yet that they are not above God, and that it is vain to kick against the pricks, and go on as they have done; for if they do, he will not endure it long. "The spirit of bondage makes men fear." Before the Spirit of adoption comes, these fears therefore are such, as the regenerate, after they have received the Spirit of adoption, never have; and therefore they are such as pursue the soul with some threatening of the word, pronouncing death and perdition to him in that estate. *Ex. gr.*, "He that believes not is condemned already:" thus the word speaks to conscience. (John iii. 17.) Thou believest not, saith a man's own conscience, the Spirit witnessing with it; therefore thou art condemned, saith conscience; now the spirit

of bondage is the testimony of God's Spirit, witnessing to both
the premises and conclusion : now. this Spirit no regenerate man,
indeed, ever hath after this time; but the fears he hath arise
from another principle of corruption of conscience and malice of
Satan through the present desertion of the Spirit leaving him;
not from any positive witness of the Spirit of any such untruth,
which yet is truth, while the soul is under this stroke, and not
regenerate.   Mark therefore diligently that this fear is the work
of the Spirit of the Lord Jesus, and hence it follows, —

1. That these fears are not merely natural, (as those Rom. ii.
15,) arising from natural conscience only, which only accuse of
sin, but never effect ; but they are supernatural ; they are arrows
shot into the conscience by the arm of the Spirit, so dreadful
that no word nor meditation of death and eternity can beget
such fears, but creates them.

2. Hence it follows that they are clear fears; (for the Spirit's
work is ever clear before he leaves it,) (Eph. v. 13 ;) they are not
blind, confused fears, and suspicious and sad conjectures, whereby many a man is afraid, and much afraid, and affrighted like
men in a dream, that think they are in hell, yet can not tell
what that evil is which they fear ; but they are clear fears,
whereby they distinctly know and see that they are miserable,
and what that misery is.

3. Hence it follows that they are strong fears, because the
almighty hand of the Spirit sets them on, and shakes the soul ;
they are not weak fears, which a man can shake off, or cure by
weak hopes, sleep, or business, etc., like some winds that shake
the tree, but never blow it down ; but these fears cast down the
tallest cedar, and appall the heart, and cool the courage and boldness of the most impenitent and audacious sinner; the Spirit
presenting the greatest evil in eternal separation from God :
hence no evil in the world is so dreadful as this.   I had better
never been born than to bear it, (saith the soul,) and hence casts
off all other thoughts, and can not be quiet ; and hence it is
that these fears force a man to fly and seek out for a better condition.   A man like Lot lingers in his sin ; but these fears, like
the angel, drive him violently out, the Lord saying to him, Away,
for thy life, lest thou perish with the world, for thy sins are
come up to heaven ; thou must die before one day be at an end,
and then what will become of thee ?   Ah, thou sinful, wretched
man ! may not the Lord justly do it ? Are not thy sins grown
so great and many that they are an intolerable burden for the
soul of God to bear any longer ? And hence you shall observe,
if the soul, after sad fears, grows bold and careless again, the

Spirit pursues it with more cause of fear; and now the soul cries out, Did the Lord ever elect thee? Christ shed his blood to save his people *from* their sins; thou livest yet *in* thy sins. Did he ever shed his blood for thee? Thou hast sinned against conscience after thou hast been enlightened, and fallen back again. Hast not thou therefore committed the impardonable sin? Thou hast had many a fair season of seeking God, but hast dallied and dreamt away thy time. Is not the day of grace therefore now past? It is true the Lord is yet patient and bountiful, and lets thee live on common mercy; but is not all this to aggravate thy condemnation against that great and terrible day of the Lord which is at hand? Are there not better men in hell than thou art that never committed the like sin? Thus the Spirit pursues with strong fears till proud man falls down to the dust before God. The soul is now under fears, not above them, and therefore can not come out of these chains by the most comfortable doctrine it hears, nor particular application of it by the most merciful minister in the world, until the Lord say, (as Lam. iii. 57,) "Fear not." The Lord only can assuage these strong winds and raging waters, in which there is no other cry heard of this soul tossed thus with tempests but O, I perish! Only the Lord, making way for the Spirit of adoption by these in his elect, drives them out to seek if there be any hope: and so they are not properly desperate fears, yet, as I say, strong fears, not alike extensively, yet alike intensively, strong in all. A small evil, when tidings are brought of it, doth not fear; but if the evil be apprehended great and near too, the very suspicion of it makes the heart tremble. When a house is on fire, or a mighty army entered the land, and near the city, children that know not the greatness of the evil fear them not; but men that know the danger are full of fear. The wrath of the Lord, that fire, those armies of everlasting woes, are great evils. The blind world may not much fear them; but all the elect, whose minds are convinced to see the greatness of them, can not but fear, and that with strong and constant fears. Nor is it cowardice, but duty, to fear these everlasting burnings; and hence the soul in this case wonders at the security of the world, dreads the terrors of the Lord that are near them, and usually seeks to awaken all its poor friends. I once thought myself well, and was quiet as you be; but the Lord hath let me see my woe, which I can not but fear. O, look you to it.

Thus the Lord works this fear in some in a greater, in others in a lesser, measure. O, consider whether the Lord hath thus affected your hearts with fear. O secure times, what will God

13 *

do with us? many of you having heard the voice of the lion roaring, and yet you tremble not. The Lord hath foretold you of death and eternal woe for the least sin. Do you believe it, and yet fear it not? How art thou then forsaken of God? Many of you, that, like old mariners, can laugh at all foul weather, and, like weathercocks, set your faces against all winds ; and if you be damned at last, you can not help it ; you must bear it as well as you can : and do you hope to do it as well as others shall do? O, how far are such from the kingdom of God, the Lord not yet working nor pricking thy heart so much as with fear !

2. Sorrow and mourning for sin is the second thing wherein compunction consists. And look, as fear plucks the soul from security in seeing no evil to come, so sorrow takes off the present pleasure and delight in sin in a greater measure than fear doth. The Lord therefore having smitten the soul, or shot the arrows of fear into the soul, it therefore grows exceeding sad and heavy, thinking within itself, What good do wife or children, house or lands, peace and friends, health and rest, do me, in the mean time condemned to die, and that eternally ; it may be reprobated never to see God's face more ; the guilt and power of sin in heart and life lying still upon me? And hereupon the soul mourns in the day, and in the night desires to go alone and weep, and there confesseth its vileness before God, all the days of vanity and sins of ignorance, thinking, O, what have I done ! and seeks for mercy ; but not one smile, nothing but clouds of anger, appear ; and then thinks, If this anger, the fruit of my sin, be so great, O, what are my sins the cause hereof ! When the angel had set out the sin of the Israelites in making a league with the Canaanites, and told them that they should be thorns in their sides, they sat down, (ver. 4,) and lifted up their voices and wept. So it is with a contrite sinner. Note narrowly that eminent place of Scripture, (Is. lxi. 3,) the Lord Christ is sent to " appoint beauty for ashes, and the oil of joy for the spirit of heaviness to them that mourn." Out of which note these four things for the explication of this sorrow or mourning : —

First. It is such a mourning as is precedent unto spiritual joy. And hence it is not said, I will not give the spirit of gladness to beget mourning, (though the Lord doth so after conversion,) but this goes in order before that. Ephraim-like, who seeing what an unruly beast he had been, unaccustomed to God's yoke, smites upon his thigh, and bemoans himself. It is God's method (after God's people have sinned) to sad their hearts, and then to turn mourning into joy. Much more at first beginning of God's work upon the soul. They shall first mourn, and lament, and smite upon the thigh. If God wounds the soul for sin, it shall smart, and bleed too, before God will heal.

Secondly. It is a great mourning, because it is called a spirit of mourning, as a spirit of slumber is a deep slumber. When the poor Jews shall be converted, their great sin shall then be presented before them of cursing and crucifying the Lord of life, as it was to those, Acts ii. 36. And by reason of this there shall be a great mourning, that they shall desire to go alone in secret, every one apart, and take their fill of mourning, before the Lord open the fountain of grace. It is not a summer cloud, or an April shower, that is soon spent, but a great mourning; for, —

1. Before this spirit of sorrow come, a man's heart takes great delight in his sin. It is his god, his life, and sweeter than Christ and all the joys of heaven, and therefore there must be great sorrow ; sin must be made exceeding bitter. A man that is very hungry and thirsty after his lust must find such meat and drink exceeding bitter, else he will feed on it. Solomon took great content in women ; but what saith he when the Lord humbled him? "I find a woman more bitter than death." Hear this, you harlots, and you that live in your wanton lusts. The Lord will make your sweet morsels more bitter than death to you, if the Lord saves you.

2. Because the greatest evils are the objects of this sorrow, viz., sin and death. It is true a man may mourn for smaller evils sooner ; but when the Spirit sets on the greatest evils, then they sad much more. "Mine iniquities are too heavy to bear." Why so? Many a man can bear them without sinking. True, but in the elect the Spirit sets on, loads the soul herewith. "A wounded spirit who can bear?" Because the greatest evils lie upon the most tender part of a tender soul, pressed down by the omnipotent hand of Christ's Spirit. For now the multitude of sins, more than the hairs on the head, come now to mind, as also the long continuance in them cradles sins. No sooner, saith the soul, did I begin to live but I began to sin. Obstinacy also in them lies very heavy. I have had warnings, checks, resolutions against them, and yet have gone on. The power of sin also sads it, that it is said, (Prov. xxi. 9,) "When the wicked reign, the people mourn." So doth the soul when it feels sin reign. I can not subdue it, nay, the Lord will not, that I fear the Lord hath left me over to it. The increase of sin it feels makes it mourn also. I grow worse and worse, saith the soul. The leak comes in faster than he can cast it out. The greatness of sin makes it mourn. Was there ever

such a sinner as I ? And lastly, the sense of condemnation for sin lies upon him; this is the fruit of your evil ways, saith the Spirit. The soul doth not let sin pass by it now as water down the mill, but being stopped by conviction and fear of the evil of it, it swells very high, and fills the heart full of grief and sorrow, that many times it is overwhelmed therewith.

3. Because Christ will not be very sweet, unless this mourning under misery be very great : the healing of a cut finger is sweet, but of a mortal wound is exceeding sweet ; a little sorrow will make Christ sweet, but great sorrow under sense of deadly wounds is exceeding sweet ; and without this Christ hath not his honor due to him, if he be not only sweet, but also exceeding sweet and precious.

4. Because it is such a sorrow as nothing but that that hath wounded the soul can heal it. Let men have the greatest outward troubles, outward things can cure them, or else they will wear away. As if a man be sick, or in debt, physic and money can cure these ; but this wound neither can or ever shall be healed but by the hand that wounded it. And hence a man can take no comfort in meat, drink, sleep, friends, mirth, nor pastime, while this wound, this sorrow lasts ; for if any thing else can heal it, it is not the right wound, or sorrow, the Lord breeds in his elect. An adulterous heart, indeed, may be quieted with other lovers. Cain can build away his sorrow. Nay, I will say more : this wounded soul can not comfort itself by any promises till the Lord come : David had a promise of pardon from Nathan, yet he cries out to the Lord to make him hear the voice of joy or gladness, that his broken bones might rejoice. Did not the Lord make him hear the voice of joy by Nathan? Yes, outwardly ; but the Lord that had broke his bones must make him hear inwardly. Nay, when the Lord comes himself to comfort, much ado the Lord hath to make him hear it; as the Israelites that "hearkened not to Moses' voice, because of their hard bondage," that unless the Lord did invincibly comfort, it would lie bleeding to death, and never live. It must needs, therefore, be great sorrow, which all the world, men, nor angels can remove.

5. You may be confirmed in this, if, lastly, you consider the many ways the Lord takes to beget great mourning, if the soul will not be sorrowful ; as, sometimes, great afflictions ; Manasseh must be taken in the bushes, and be cast into chains. Sometimes strange temptations, hellish blasphemies : Is there a God ? are the Scriptures his word ? why should the Lord be so cruel as to reprobate any of his creatures, to torment it so long ? etc. Sometimes long eclipsing of the light of God's countenance ; no prayers

answered, but daily bills of indictment. And sometimes it thinks
it hears and feels a secret testimony from God, that he never had
thought of peace toward it, and that his purpose is immutable.
Sometimes it questions, Can God forgive sins so great? Can it
stand with his honor to put up so much wrong? Sometimes it
feels its heart so extreme hard and dedolent, that it thinks the
Lord hath sealed it up under this plague till the judgment of
the great day. And sometimes the Lord makes melancholy a
good servant to him to further this work of sorrow. But thus the
Lord rebukes many a hard-hearted sinner that will not bear the
yoke, nor feel the load; and now the Lord turns the beauty of
the proudest into ashes, and withers the glory of all flesh. Nay,
sometimes you shall observe the Lord, though he comes not out
as a lion to rend, yet as a moth he frets out, by secret pinings and
languishings, the senseless security of man, that he shall mourn
to purpose before he leave him. I do not mean by this, as if all
men had the like measure of sorrow; but a great sorrow it is in
all. Every child is delivered by some throes; those that stick
long in the birth may feel them longer and very many.

Nor yet do I press a necessity of tears, or violent and tumultuous complaints; the deepest sorrows run with least noise. If
a man can have tears for outward losses, and none for sins, it is
very suspicious whether he was ever truly sorrowful for sin;
otherwise, as the greatest joys are not always expressed in laughter, so the greatest sorrows are not always expressed in shedding
of tears; what the measure of this great sorrow is, we shall hear
hereafter.

Thirdly. It is a constant mourning, for so it is here called, a
spirit of heaviness; as that woman that had a spirit of infirmity,
and was bowed down many years: Hannah, constantly troubled,
is called a woman of a sorrowful spirit. (1 Sam. i. 12, 15.) As
"the spirit of pride and whoredom" (Hos. iv. 12) is a constant
frame, where, though the acts be sometimes suspended, yet the
spirit remains, so a spirit of mourning is such sorrow, as, though
the acts of mourning be sometime hindered, yet the spirit and
spring remain. Hypocrites will mourn under sin and misery;
but what is it? It is the hanging down the head like a bulrush in
bad weather for a day. O, how many have pangs and gripes of
sorrow, and can quickly ease themselves again! these mourners
come to nothing in the conclusion. I grant the sorrow and sadness of spirit may be interrupted; but it returns again, and
never leaves the soul until the Lord look down from heaven.
(Lam. iii. 48–50.) The cause continues, — guilt and strength
of sin, — and therefore this effect continues.

Fourthly. It is such a sorrow as makes way for gladness, for so it is here said, " The Lord gives beauty for " these " ashes ; " and hence it is no desperate, hellish sorrow, but usually mixed with sense of some mercy, at least common, and some hope ; not that which apprehends the object of hope particularly, (which is done in invocation,) but that the Lord may find out some way of saving it, (Jonah iii. 9 ; Acts ii. 37,) which hope, with sense of mercy waiting so long, preserving from hell and death so oft, etc., doth not harden the heart, (as in reprobates,) but serve to break the more, and to load it with greater sorrow ; thus the Lord works this sorrow in all his elect. I know it is in a greater measure, and from some other grounds after the soul is in Christ ; but this sorrow there is for substance, mentioned for the reasons given : if Christ hate you, you shall mourn, but never till it be too late ; if he love you, you must mourn now : how great and many are your sins ! how near is your doom ! The Lord only knows how fearful your condemnation will be, you have oft heard ; but yet how few of your hearts are sad and very heavy for these things ! Sin is your pleasure, not your sorrow ; you fly from sorrow as from a temptation of Satan, who comes to trouble you, and to lead you to despair : David's eyes ran down with rivers of waters, because others brake God's law, and Jeremy wished he had a cottage in the wilderness to mourn in ; and yet you do not, you can not pour out one drop, nor yet wish you had hearts to lament your own sins : but O, know it, that when the Lord Christ comes, he will sad thy soul ; when he comes to search thy old sores by the Spirit of conviction, he will make them smart and bleed abundantly, by the spirit of compunction.

3. Separation from sin is the third thing wherein compunction consists : such a fear and sorrow for sin under a sinful estate, as separates the soul from sin, is true compunction ; without which the Lord Christ can not be had : the soul is cut and wounded with sin by fear and sorrow, but it is cut off by this stroke of the Spirit, not from the being, but from the growing power of sin ; from the will to sin, not from all sin in the will which is mortified by a spirit of holiness, after the soul is implanted into Christ ; for compunction, contrition, brokenness of heart for sin, (call it what you will,) is opposite to hardness of heart, which is in every sinner whilst Christ leaves him ; now in hardness (as in a stone) there is, first, insensibleness ; secondly, a close cleaving of all the parts together, whereby it comes to pass that hard things make resistance of what is cast against them : so in compunction there is not only sensibleness of the evil of sin and death, by fear and sorrow, but such as makes a separation of that close union between

sin and the soul; and hence it is that the Lord abhors all fastings, humiliations, prayers, tears, unless they be of this stamp, and are accompanied with this effect. The Lord flings the dung of their fastings and sorrows in their faces, because they did not break the bonds of wickedness; to mourn for sin and misery, and yet to be in thy sin, is the work of justice on the damned in hell, and all the devils at this day, that are pinched with their black chains not loosened from them; and not the work of the grace of Christ in the day of his power. "He that confesseth his sins shall have mercy:" that is true; but remember the meaning of that confession in the next words, "and forsaketh," he shall find mercy. What is the end of the mother in laying wormwood and gall upon her breast, but that the child, by tasting the bitterness of it, might be weaned, and have his stomach and will turned from it? What is the end of fear and sorrow, but by this to turn away the soul from sin? This point is weighty and full of difficulty, of great use, and worthy of deep meditation. For as the first wound and stroke of the Spirit is, so it is in all after works of it, both of faith and holiness in the soul: if this be right, faith is right, holiness is right; if this be imperfect, or nought, all is according to it afterward: the greatest difficulty lies here, to know what measure of separation from sin the Spirit makes here; for after we are in Christ, then sin is mortified: how, then, is there any separation of the heart from it, before it doth fully believe? or what measure is there necessary? Here, therefore, I shall answer to the fourth and last particular, viz.: —

Fourthly. What is that measure of compunction the Lord works in all the elect?

So much compunction or sense of sin is necessary as attains the end of it. Now, what is the end of it? No other but that the soul, being humbled, might go to Christ, (by faith,) to take away his sin; the *finis proximus*, or next end, of compunction is humiliation, that the soul may be so severed from sin as to renounce itself for it; the *finis remotus*, or last end, is, that, being thus humbled, it might go unto Christ to take away sin; for, beloved, the condemnation of the world lies not so much in being sinful under guilt and power of sin, as in being unwilling the Lord Jesus should take it away: this, I say, is the greatest hinderance of salvation. (John iii. 19. John v. 40.) "O Jerusalem, wilt thou not be made clean?" (Jer. xiii. 17.) That was their great evil; they were not only polluted, but they would not be made clean; the Lord Jesus therefore rolls away this stone from the sepulcher, beats down this mountain; and because it must first believe in Christ before it can receive grace from Christ, it must come to Christ to take

away sin, before the Lord will do it; hence so much loosening
from sin as makes the soul thus to come is necessary. So much
fear and sorrow as loosens from sin, and so much loosening from
sin as makes the soul willing, or at least not unwilling, that the
Lord Jesus should take it away, is necessary; for whoever comes
to Christ, or is not willing Christ should come to him to take away
all his sin, hath (whatever he thinks) some antecedent loosening
and separation from sin.

O, saith a poor sinner, when the Lord hath struck his heart,
and he feels guilt, and terror, and mighty strength of corruption,
if the Lord Jesus would take away these evils from me, though
I can not, means can not, that will be exceeding rich mercy. The
Lord doth not wound the heart to this end, that the soul should
first heal itself, before it come to the Physician, but that it might
seek out, or, feeling its need, be willing and desirous of a Physician, the Lord Jesus, to come and heal it. It is the great fault
of many Christians, either their wounds and sorrows are so little,
they desire not to be healed; or, if they do, they labor to heal
themselves first, before they come to the Physician for it; they
will first make themselves holy, and put on their jewels, and then
believe in Christ. And hence are those many complaints, What
have I to do with Christ? Why should he have to do with me,
that have such unholy, vile, hard, blind, and most wicked heart?
If I were more humbled, and more holy, then I should go to him,
and think he would come to me. O, for the Lord's sake, dishonor
not the grace of Christ. It is true, thou canst not come to Christ
till thou art loaden, and humbled, and separated from thy sin.
Thou canst not be ingrafted into this Olive, unless thou beest cut,
and cut off too from thy old root. Yet remember forever, that
no more sorrow for sin, no more separation from sin, is necessary
to thy closing with Christ, than so much as makes thee willing, or
rather not unwilling, that the Lord should take it away. And
know it, if thou seekest for a greater measure of humiliation
antecedent to thy closing with Christ than this, thou showest the
more pride therein, who wilt rather go into thyself to make thyself holy and humble, that thou mightest be worthy of Christ,
than go out of thyself, unto the Lord Jesus, to take thy sin away;
in a word, who thinkest Christ can not love thee, until thou makest
thyself fair, and when thou thinkest thyself so, (which is pride,)
wilt then think otherwise of Christ. The Lord, therefore, when
he teacheth his people how to return unto him after grievous sins,
directs them to this course — not to go about the bush to remove
their iniquities themselves, or to stay and live securely in their
sins, until the Lord did it himself; but bids them come to him, and

say, "Take away (Lord) all inquities." (Hos. xiv. 1–3.) You shall see "Ephraim bemoaning himself." (Jer. xxi. 18.) But how? Doth he say he feels his sins now all removed? No, but he desires the Lord to turn him, and then (saith he) I shall be turned.

As if he should say, Lord, I shall never turn from this stubborn, vile heart, nor so much as turn to thee, to take it away, unless thou dost turn me, and then I shall be turned to purpose. What saith the penitent church? "Come," say they, "let us go unto the Lord." They might object and say, Alas! the Lord is our enemy, and wounds us, and hath broken us to pieces; we are not yet healed, but lie dead as well as wounded; shall such dead spirits live? Mark what follows: True indeed, "He hath wounded us;" let us therefore go to him, that he may heal us, and "after two days he will revive us." The Lord requires no more of us than thus to come to him. Indeed, after a Christian is in Christ, labor for more and more sense of sin, that may drive you nearer and nearer unto Christ. Yet know before you come to him, the Lord requires no more than this; and as he requires no more than this, so it is his own Spirit (not our abilities) that must also work this: and thus much he will work, and doth require of all whom he purposeth to save. If thou wilt not come to Christ to take away thy sins, thou shalt undoubtedly perish in them. If the Lord work that sorrow, so as to be willing the Lord should take them away, thou shalt be undoubtedly saved from them.

If you would know what measure of willingness to have Christ take away sin is required, you shall hear when we come to open the fourth particular in the doctrine of faith.

If you further ask, how the Spirit works this loosening from sin in the work of compunction, —

I answer, The Spirit of Christ works this by a double act. 1. Moral. 2. Physical.

As in the conversion of the soul by faith unto God, the Spirit is not only a moral agent persuading, but also a supernatural agent physically working the heart to believe, by a divine and immediate act; so in the aversion of the soul from sin, the Spirit doth affect the heart with fear and sorrow morally; but this can never take away sin, as we see in Judas and Cain, deeply affected and afflicted in spirit, and yet in their sin. And therefore the Spirit puts forth its own hand physically or immediately, and his own arm brings salvation to us, by a further secret immediate stroke, turning the iron neck, cutting the iron sinews of sin, and so makes this disunion or separation. You think it is easy to be willing that Christ should come and take away all your sins;

I tell you, the omnipotent arm of the Lord, that instructed Jeremy in a smaller matter, can only instruct you here ; both these acts ever go together according-to the measure mentioned; the latter can not be without the first, the first is in vain without the latter.

But what evil in sin doth the Spirit morally affect the heart with, and so physically turn it from sin ?

He affects the soul with it as the greatest evil; by sin I mean not as considered without death, (for at this time the soul is not so spiritual as that sin without consideration of death and wrath due to it should affect it,) but sin and death: sin armed with wrath, sin working death, pricks the heart as the greatest evil, and so lets out that core at the bottom, as may fit the soul for healing. For, —

1. If the Spirit make a man feel sin truly, the soul feels it as it is ; it is not the name and talk of the danger of sin that troubles - it, but the spirit (ever making things real) loads the soul with it indeed, and as it is : now it is the greatest evil, and therefore so it feels sin. Believe it, you never felt sin indeed as it is, if you have not felt it thus.

2. Else no man will prize Christ as the greatest good, without which no man shall have him.

3. Else a man will live and continue in sin. If sin had been a greater evil to Pilate than the loss of Cesar's friendship, he would never have crucified Christ. If sin had been a greater evil to Jehu than the loss of his kingdom, he had never kept up the two calves. If sin were a greater evil than poverty, shame, grief in this world, many a professor would never lose Christ and a good conscience too, for a little gain, profit, or honor. Beloved, the great curse and wrath of the Lord upon all men in the world almost is this, that the greatest evils should be the least of all felt, and the smallest evils most of all complained of. What is death, that only separates thy soul from thy body, to sin, that separates God blessed forever from thy soul ? and therefore the Lord Jesus will remove this curse from whom he saves.

But you will say, What is that evil the soul sees at this time in sin, that thus affects the heart with it, as the greatest evil ? This is the last difficulty here.

There is a threefold evil especially seen in sin : —
1. The evil of torment and anguish.
2. The evil of wrong and injury to God.
3. The evil of separation of the soul from God.

The first may affect reprobates, as Saul and Judas, who were sore distressed when they felt the anguish of conscience for sin.

The second is only in those who are actually justified, called, and sanctified, who lament sin as it is against God, and a God reconciled to them, and as it is against the life of God begun in them; and hence they cry out of it as a body of death.

The third the elect feel at this first stroke and wound which the Spirit gives them; the anguish of sin indeed lies sore upon them, but this much more. Christ is come to seek that which is lost. The sheep is lost, when first it is separated and gone from the owner; secondly, when it knows not how to return again, unless the shepherd find it and carry it home: so that soul is properly and truly lost that feels itself separated and gone from God, knowing not how to return to him again, unless the Lord come and take it upon his shoulders, and carry it in his arms; this lies heavy upon it, viz., that it is gone from God, and wholly separated from all union to him, and communion with him. You may observe, (John xvi. 9,) that the Spirit convinces of sin. How? "Because they believe not in me." 1. Because they shall see and feel themselves quite separated from me; they shall hear of my glory and riches of mercy, and that happiness which all that have me shall and do enjoy; but they shall mourn that they have no part nor portion in these things; they shall mourn that they live without me, and that they have lived so long without me.

I confess many other considerations of the evil of sin come now in, but this is the main channel where all the other rivulets empty themselves. And hence it is that the soul, under this stroke, is in a state of seeking only, yet finds nothing; it seeks God and Christ, and therefore feels a want, a loss of both by sin; for the end of all the fears, terrors, sorrows, etc., upon the elect, is to bring them back again to God, and into fellowship with God, the only blessedness of man. Now, if the soul ordained and made for this end should not feel its present separation from God by sin, and the bitterness of the evil of it, it would never seek to return again to him as to his greatest good, nor desire ever to come into his bosom again; for look as sin wounds the soul, so the soul seeks for healing of it; if only the torment of sin wound, ease of conscience from that anguish will heal it: so if separation from God wound the heart, only union and communion with God will heal it, and comfort it again. The Lord Christ therefore having laid his hand upon the soul to bring it back to himself first, and so to the Father, being designed to gather in all the outcasts of Israel, those he ever makes to feel themselves outcasts, as cast away out of God's blessed sight and presence, that so they may desire at last to come home again : reprobates not made for this end have not this sense of sin, the means of their return. And hence it is that the souls of those God saves are never quiet until they come to God, and have communion with him; but they mourn for their distance from him, and the hiding of his face, until the Lord shine forth again : whereas, every one else, though much troubled, yet sits down contented with any little odd thing, that serves to quiet them for the time, before the Lord return to them, or they enter into their rest, in that ineffable communion with him.

Let me now make application of this, before I proceed to open the next particular of humiliation.

This may show us the great mistake of two sorts.

1. Such as think there is no necessity of any sense of misery before the application of the remedy or their closing with Christ; because, say they, where there is sense there is life, (all sense and feeling arising from life,) and where there is life there is Christ already. And hence it is that they would not have the law first preached in these days, but the gospel: the other is to go round about the bush.

I answer, that for my own part this doctrine (of seeing and feeling our misery before the remedy) is so universally received by all solid divines, both at home and abroad, that I meet with, and the contrary opinion so cross to the Holy Scriptures, and general experience of the saints, and the preaching of the other so abundantly sealed to be God's own way by his rich blessings on the labors of his servants faithful to him herein, that were it not for the sake of some weak and misled, I should not dare to question it; the Lord himself so expressly speaking, that he " came not to call the righteous," but on the contrary, only to heal the sick, who know and feel their sickness chiefly by the law. (Rom. iii. 20.) Dost thou think, therefore, that there is spiritual life wherever there is any sense ? Then I say the devils and damned in hell have much spiritual life, for they feel their misery with a witness.

As for the preaching of the gospel before the law to show our misery, it is true that the gospel is to be looked at as the main end; yet you must use the means, before you can come to the end, by the preaching of the law, or misery in despising the gospel. End and means have been ever good friends, and you may join them well together; you can not sever them without danger. I do observe that the apostles ever used this method : Paul first proves Jews and Gentiles to be under sin, in almost the first three chapters of the Romans, before he opens the doctrine of justification by faith in Christ. I do not observe that ever there was so clear and manifest opening of man's misery as by Christ and his apostles, who brought in the clearest revelations of the remedy. I do not read in Moses, or in all the prophets, such full and plain expressions of our misery as in the New Testament — "The worm that never dies," "The fire that never goes out," "The wrath to come," etc.; and therefore, assuredly they thought this no back door, but faith the door to Christ, and this is the way to faith. To say that a man must first have Christ and life, before he feel any spiritual misery, is to say that a Christian must first be healed, that he may be sick; cured, that he may be wounded; receive the Spirit of adoption, before he receive; and that he may receive the spirit of bondage to fear again.

If ministers shall preach the remedy before they show misery, woe to this age, that shall be deprived of those blessings which the former gloried in, and blessed the Lord for. Mark those men that deny the use of the law to lead unto Christ, if they do not fall in time to oppose some main point of the gospel. For it is a righteous thing, but a heavy plague, for the Lord to suffer such men to obscure the gospel, that in their judgments zealously dislike this use of the law. You must preach the remedy; that is true; but you must also first preach the woe and misery of men, or rather so mix them together, as the hearts of hearers may be deeply affected with both; but first with their misery. It argues a greater consumption of the Spirit of grace when Christians' lives are preserved only by alchymy and choice cordials, notions about Christ, nay, choice ones, too, or else the old and ordinary food of the country will not down. I tell you, the main wound of Christians is want of deep humiliations and castings down; and if you believe it not now, it may be, pestilence, sword, and famine shall teach you this doctrine, when the Lord shall make these things wound you to the very heart, and put you to your-wits' end, that were not, that would not in season be, wounded at the heart with sin.

Are we troubled with too many wounded consciences in these times, that we are so solicitous of coining new principles of peace? What is every man by nature but a kind of an infinite evil? All the sins that fill earth and hell are in every one man's heart, for sin in man is endless; and canst not thou endure to be cast down? Nothing is so vile as Christ to a man not unhumbled; and can you so easily prize him, and taste him, without any casting down?

2. Such as think there is a necessity of sense of misery by

the work of the law, before Christ can be received; but they think there is no such feeling of misery as hath been mentioned, but that it is common to the reprobate as to the elect, and consequently that in sense of sin there is no such special work of the Spirit as separates the soul from sin before it comes unto Christ, but that this is done after the soul is in Christ by faith, viz., in sanctification, being first justified by faith.

This is the judgment of many holy and learned;. and therefore, so long as there is no disagreement in the substance of this doctrine, it should not trouble us; only let it be considered, whether what is said is not the truth of Christ; and if it be, let us not cast it aside. The Jewish rabbins have a speech at this day very frequent in their writings — *Non est in lege unica literula a qua non magni suspensi sunt montes.* It is much more true of every truth, and if I mistake not, much depends upon the right understanding of this point.

That, therefore, 1. There must be some sense of misery before the application of the remedy.

2. That this compunction or sense of misery is wrought by the Spirit of Christ, not the power of man to prepare himself thereby for further grace.

3. That these terrors and sorrows in the elect do virtually differ from those in the reprobate; the one driving the soul to Christ, the other not: these are agreed on all hands. The question only is, Whether there is this further stroke of severing the soul from sin, conjoined with the terrors and sorrows in the elect before their closing with Christ, which is not in the reprobate; or in one word, whether there is not a special work of the Spirit, turning (at least in order of nature) the soul from sin, before the soul returns by faith unto Christ.

For the affirmative I leave several considerations.

That there is *gratia actualis*, or actual grace, as well as *habitualis*, or habitual grace: learned Ferrius makes a vast difference between them; and therefore to think that there can be no power of sin removed but by habitual or sanctifying grace, is unsound; for actual grace may do it; the Spirit may take away sin mediately by habitual grace, and yet it can do it immediately also by an omnipotent act, by that which is called actual, actuating, or moving grace; Christ can and must first bind the strong man, and cast him out by this working or actual grace, before he dwells in the house of man's heart, by habitual and sanctifying grace. The gardener's knife may immediately cut off a scion from a tree, thereby taking away all its power to grow there any more, before it hath a power to bring forth any fruit, which is wrought only by implanting it into another stock. New creation (which is at first conversion,) may well be without habitual graces that are but creatures.

Whether any man since the fall is a subject immediately capable of sanctifying or habitual grace; or whether any unregenerate man is in a next disposition to receive such grace; as the air is immediately of light, out of which the darkness is expelled by light, and so the habits of grace do expel the habits and power of sin, (say some.) I suppose the affirmative is most false, and in near affinity with some gross points of Arminianism. Adam, in his pure naturals, and considered merely as a living soul, was such a subject; like a white paper, fitted immediately to take the impression of God's image; but since, by his fall, sin is fallen like a mighty blot upon the soul, whereby a man not only wants grace, as the dark air doth light, but also resists grace. (John xiv. 17.) Hence this resistance must be first taken away, before the Lord introduce his image again. To say that a man can of himself dispose himself unto grace, was Pelagianism in Aquinas's time: yet some disposition is necessary, saith Ferrius; not unto actual grace, or that which is wrought upon a man, *per modum actus*, (as he saith,) but unto the reception of habitual or sanctifying grace, it being in the soul *per modum formæ*, no form being introduced but into *materiam dispositam*, i. e., matter fitted or prepared, or into such a vessel which is immediately capable of it.

There is in man a double resistance against grace.

1. Of a holy frame of grace, by original corruption, which is opposite to original and renewed holiness, or to this holy frame.

2. Of the God of grace himself when he comes to work it. (Job xxi. 14. Ezek. xxiv. 14.)

The first is taken away in that which we call the spirit of sanctification, after faith; the second is taken away not only in the act of it, as by terrors it may be in reprobates, (Ps. lxvi. 2,) but in some measure in the inward root and disposition of it, (only in the elect,) there being (as hath been said) no more separation from sin, at this time required, than so much as may make the soul come to the Lord to take it away, or at least not unwilling, not resisting the Lord, when he comes to do it himself.

Whether doth not the work of union unto Christ go before our communion with Christ. I suppose it is undeniable, that union must be before communion; and that union to Christ is a work of grace as peculiar to the elect as communion with him.

Now, justification and sanctification are two parts of our communion with him, and follow our union. (Rom. viii. 1.) Our union therefore must be before these, of which there are two parts, or rather two things on our part, necessarily required to it: —

1. Cutting off from the wild olive tree, the old Adam. 2. Implanting into the good olive tree, the second Adam. The first must go before the second ; for where there is perfect resistance, there can be no perfect union. But take a man growing upon this old root of nature, there is nothing but perfect resistance, (Rom. viii. 7;) and therefore that resistance must first be taken away, before the Lord draw the soul to Christ, and by faith implant it into Christ. In a word, I see not how a man can wholly resist God and Christ, and yet be united unto him at the same instant; and therefore the one (in order of nature at least) goes before the other: and therefore let any man living prove his union to Christ, and to his lust also, if he can. You will believe in Christ, many of you, and yet you will have your whores, and cups, and lusts, and pride, and world too, and oppose all the means that would have you from these also. I tell you, you shall find one day how miserably deceived you have been herein. "You can not serve God and Mammon. How can ye believe," saith Christ, (John v. 44,) "that seek honor one of another ? " If you can have Christ, and be ambitious too, take him ; but how can you believe till the Lord hath broken you off from thence ?

Whether vocation (as peculiar to the elect as sanctification) doth not go before justification and glorification. (Rom. viii. 30.) Whether also there are not two things in effectual vocation.

1. Is not Christ that good, the term to which the soul is firstly called ?

2. Is not sin and world that evil, the term from which the soul is called ? I suppose it is evident that the soul is effectually called, and therefore actually and firstly turned from darkness to light, from the power of Satan unto God. First from darkness, then unto light; first from the power of Satan, then unto God ; as is evident by the apostle's own words, (Acts xxvi. 18,) where he methodically lets down the wonderful works of Christ's grace by his ministry : the first is, " to turn them from darkness to light, and from Satan's power unto God," which are the two parts of vocation, " that they may receive forgiveness of sins " in justification, (vocation being a means to this end,) that they may receive an inheritance in glorification among such as, being justified, are sanctified also by faith in his name. The apostle doth not say that he was to return men to light and unto God, and so turn them from darkness and from the power of Satan, (though this is true in some sense,) but he was first to turn from darkness and Satan, and so to return them unto light, and God in Christ. For how is it possible to be turned unto Christ,

and yet then also to be turned to sin and Satan? Doth it not imply a contradiction, to be turned toward sin, (which is ever from Christ,) and yet to be turned toward Christ together? All divines affirm generally that in the working of faith the Lord makes the soul willing to have Christ, (Ps. cx. 2, 3,) but withal they affirm that of unwilling he makes willing; and therefore it follows that the Lord must first remove that unwillingness before it can be willing, it being impossible to be both willing and unwilling together.

Whether the cause of all that counterfeit coin and hypocrisy in this professing age doth not arise from this root, viz., not having this wound at first, but only some trouble for sin without separation from it, sore throes without deliverance from sin. Is not this the death of most, if not all, wicked men living? How many are there that clasp about Christ, and yet prove enemies to the cross of Christ — fall from Christ scandalously or secretly afterward! What is the reason of it? Certainly, if the Lord had cut them off from their sin, they had never fallen to everlasting bondage in sin again; but there the Spirit of God forsook them, the Lord not owning so much love to them. Consider seriously why the stony and thorny ground hearers (Matt. xiii.) came to nothing in their growth of seeming faith and sanctification. Was the fault in the seed? No; verily, but only in the ground. The one was broken, but not deep enough. The other was broken deep, but not through enough. The roots of thorns choked them. The lusts and cares of the world were not destroyed first, and therefore they destroyed that ground.

I conclude therefore with that of Jeremy, "Break up your fallow grounds." Seek to the Lord to break them for you, "and sow not among thorns." Take heed of such brokenness which removes not the thorns of sinful, secret stubbornness, "lest the wrath of the Lord break out against you, and burn that none can quench it." Do not cut off John Baptist's head, you that can be content to hear him gladly, and do many things. But he must not touch your Herodias, and make a divorce there; but suffer him to come in the spirit and power of Elias, nay, of Christ Jesus, to beat down your mountains, fill up your valleys, make your crooked, rough ways smooth, that you see the glory of the Lord Jesus, without which he shall be ever hid from you. Cry, you faithful servants of the Lord, that "all flesh is grass, and all the glory of man," of sin, of world, "is a withered flower," that the Lord Jesus may be revealed ever fresh, and sweet, and precious in the eyes of the saints.

The evidence of this truth in the general put blessed and

learned Pemble upon another way; for when he perceived (as himself confesseth) that it is the general doctrine of all Orthodox divines, viz., that actual faith is never wrought in the soul, till, beside the supernatural illumination of the mind, the will be also first freed in part from its natural perverseness, (God making all men of unwilling, willing,) hereupon he concludes that this is done by the spirit of sanctification, and one supernatural quality of holiness universally infused in all the powers of the soul at once, so that the Spirit instantly first sanctifies us and puts life in us ; then it acts in sorrow for, and detestation of, sin ; and so we come actually to believe. And because he foresaw the blow, viz., that in this way Christians are sanctified before they be justified, he answers, Yes, we are justified declaratively after this.

Others (who follow him) answer more roundly, viz., that we are sanctified before we are really and actually justified, and herein differ from him.

Now, when it is objected against this, viz., that our vocation is that which goes before our justification, sanctification being a part of glorification following after, (Rom. viii. 30,) hereupon some others (treading in his steps) affirm that vocation is the same with sanctification, and not comprehended with glorification.

Others perceiving the evil of this error, viz., to place sanctification before justification, good fruits before a good tree, they do therefore deny any saving work, whether of vocation or sanctification, before justification. And hence, on the other extreme, they do place a Christian's justification before his faith in vocation, or holiness in his sanctification ; so that by this last opinion a Christian is not justified by faith, (which was Paul's phrase,) but rather (as he said wittily and wisely) faithed by his justification. Before I come to clear the truth in these spiritual mysteries, let this only be remembered, viz., that sanctification, which Pemble calls our spiritual life, may be taken two ways : —

1. Largely.　2. Strictly.

1. Largely ; for any awakenings of conscience, or acts of the Spirit of life ; and so it is true we are quickened by these acts, and so in a large sense sanctified first.

2. Strictly ; for those habits of the life of holiness which are opposite to the body of death in us ; and that we are not first sanctified before we are justified in this sense, we shall manifest by and by. Only let me begin to show the error of the last opinion first, viz., 1. That a Christian is not first justified before faith or vocation, may appear thus : —

1. It is professedly cross to the whole current of Scripture, which saith, " We are justified by faith," and therefore not before

faith ; and to say that the meaning of such phrases is, that we are justified declaratively by faith, or to our sense and feeling *in foro conscientiæ*, is a mere device; for our justification is opposed to the state of unrighteousness and condemnation going before, which condemnation is not only declarative, and in the court of conscience, but real, and in the court of Heaven; for so saith the Scripture expressly, (John iii. 18,) " He that believeth not is condemned already; " and, (ver. 36,) " The wrath of God abideth on him ; " and, (Gal. iii. 22,) " The Scripture (which is the sentence in God's court) hath concluded all under sin." Hence a second argument ariseth : —

2. If a man be justified before faith, then an actual unbeliever is subject to no condemnation. But this is expressly cross to the letter of the text, " He that believeth not is condemned already, (John iii. 18,) and the wrath of God doth lie upon him." The subjects of non-condemnation are those that be in Christ by faith, (Rom. viii. 1,) not out of Christ by unbelief. (Rom. xi. 20.) There is indeed a merited justification by Christ's death, and a virtual or exemplary justification in Christ's resurrection, as in our head and surety; and both these were before not only our faith, but our very being ; but to say that we are therefore actually justified before faith, because our justification was merited before we had faith, gives us a just ground of affirming that we are actually sanctified while we are in the state of nature unsanctified, (Eph. ii. 1,) because our sanctification was merited by Christ before we had any being in him.

We must indeed be made good trees by faith in Christ's righteousness before we can bring forth any good fruits of holiness. God makes us not good trees without being in Christ by faith, no more than we are bad trees in contracting Adam's guilt without our being first in him. God gives us first his Son, (offered in the gospel, and received by faith,) and then gives us all other things with him. He doth not justify us without giving us his Son ; but having first given him, gives us this also.

2. That sanctification doth not go before justification may appear thus : —

1. If guilt of Adam's sin go before original pollution, (Rom. v. 12,) then imputation of Christ's righteousness before renewed sanctification.

2. To place sanctification before justification is quite cross to the apostle's practice, (which is our pattern,) who first sought to be found in Christ, (Phil. iii. 9,) (in the work of union,) not having his own righteousness in the work of justification, (which in order follows that,) that he may then know him in the power of

his death and resurrection in sanctification, (here comes in sanctification,) if by any means he might attain to the resurrection of the dead in glorification, (the last of all.)

3. This is quite cross to the apostle's doctrine which makes justification the cause of sanctification, and therefore must needs go before it. (Rom. v.) As sin goes before spiritual and eternal death, so righteousness goes before spiritual life in sanctification and eternal life in glory. The Lord holds forth Christ in the gospel first as our propitiation, (Rom. iii. 24,) and then comes dying to sin, and living to God, in sanctification. (Chap. vi. 1.) Holiness is the end of our actual reconciliation. (Col. i. 21, 22.)

4. If sanctification go before justification by faith, then a Christian's communion with Christ goes before his union to him by faith; but our union is the foundation of communion, and it is impossible there should be communion without some precedent union. (1 Cor. i. 30.) " Christ is made righteousness and sanctification." Unto whom? Read the beginning of the verse, and you shall see it is only to those that be in Christ, which is by faith.

Let none say here (as some do) that we have union to Christ, first by the Spirit, without faith, in order going before faith; for understanding of which, let us a little consider of our union unto Christ. Our union to Christ is not by the essential presence of the Spirit, for that is in every man, as the Godhead is every where, in whom we live and move. This is common to the most wicked man, nay, to the vilest creature in the world. Hence it follows, that our union is by some act of the Spirit peculiar to the elect, (who only shall have communion with Christ,) working some real change in the soul, (for of real, not relative union, I now speak;) this act can not be those first acts of the spirit of bondage, (for they are common unto reprobates;) they are therefore such acts as are essential unto the nature of union. Now, look, as disunion is the disjunction or separation of divers things one from another, so union is the conjunction or joining of them together that were before severed. Hence that act of the Spirit in uniting us to Christ can be nothing else but the bringing back the soul unto Christ, or the conjunction of the soul unto Christ and into Christ, by bringing it back to him, that before this lay like a dry bone in the valley separated from him. Thus, (1 Cor. vi. 17,) " He that is joined, or (as the word signifies) glued to the Lord, is one spirit with him." The Spirit, therefore, brings us to the Lord Christ, and so we are in him. Now, the coming of the soul to Christ, what is it but faith? (John vi. 35.) Our union, therefore, is by faith, not without it;.

for by it only we that were once separated from him by sin, and especially by unbelief, (Heb. iii. 12,) are now come not only unto him, as iron unto the loadstone, (John vi. 37,) but (which is most near) into him, as branches into the vine, and so grow one with him; and hence those phrases in Scripture, to believe in Christ, or into Christ. I speak not this as if we were united to Christ without the Spirit on his part, (for the conjunction of things several must be mutual, if it be firm;) I only show that we are not united before faith by the Spirit unto Christ, but that we are by faith, (wrought by the Spirit,) whereby, on our part, we are first conjoined unto him, and then, on his part, he, by the person of the Spirit, is most wonderfully united unto us. The Spirit puts forth variety of acts in the soul; as it acts us to good works, it is the spirit of obedience; as it infuseth habits of grace, so it is the spirit of sanctification; as it assists us continually, and guides us to our end, and witnesseth favor, it is the spirit of adoption; as it works fears of death and hell, it is the spirit of bondage; but as it drives us from sin to Christ, so it is the spirit of union; and therefore to imagine union before and without faith by the Spirit, is but a spirit indeed, which when you come to feel it, you shall find it nothing, without flesh, or bones, or sinews. As our marriage union to Christ must have consent of faith on our part, wrought by the Spirit, or else the Lord Jesus is a vain suitor to us, so now the Spirit, on Christ's part, must apprehend our faith, and dwell in us, who otherwise shall suddenly go a-whoring from him. (1 Pet. i. 5. Eph. iii. 17.)

3. That vocation is not all one with sanctification may appear thus: —

1. Vocation is before justification. (Rom. viii. 30.) But sanctification is not before justification, as we have proved, and therefore they are not the same.

2. Sanctification is the end of vocation. (1 Thess. iv. 7.) Therefore it is not the same with it.

3. Faith is the principal thing in vocation: the first part of it being God's call, the second part being our answer to that call, or in coming at that call (Jer. iii. 22.) Now, faith is no part of sanctification, strictly taken, because it is the means and instrument of our justification and sanctification. (Acts xxvi. 18.) Our hearts are said to be purified by faith, (Acts xv. 9;) not our lives only in the acts of holiness and purity, but our hearts in the habitual frame of them. "I live by the faith of the Son of God," saith Paul. "We pass from death to life by faith," (John v. 24;) therefore it is no part of our spiritual life. "You will not come to me" (which is faith) "that you may have life;"

(John v. 40; vi. 50, 51;) therefore faith is the instrumental means of life, and therefore no part of our life: as faith comes by hearing, and therefore hearing is no part of faith, so justification comes by faith, and therefore no part of sanctification: all our life both of justification and sanctification is laid up in Christ our head; this life, according to God's great plot, shall never be had but by coming to Christ for it, (Heb. vii. 25,) else grace and Christ should not be so much dishonored. (Rom. iv. 16,) "It is of faith, that it might be of grace." Sanctification therefore is the grace applied by faith, faith the grace applying; by coming to Christ for it, we have it; and therefore have it not when first we come.

I am sorry to be thus large in less practical matters; yet I have thought it not unuseful, but very comfortable, to a poor passenger, not only to know his journey's end and the way in general to it, but also the several stadia or towns he is orderly to pass through; there is much wisdom of God to be seen not only in his work, but in his manner and order of working; for want of which I see many Christians in these days fall very foully into erroneous apprehensions in their judgments, the immediate ground of many errors in practice; the objections made against what hath been delivered are for the principal of them answered; the main end, my beloved, of propounding these things is, that you would look narrowly to your union; O, take heed you miss not there: if you close with Christ, believe in Christ, and yet not cut off from your sin, viz., that spirit of resistance of Christ, you are utterly and eternally undone. This is the condemnation of the world, not that men love darkness wholly, and hate light, but that they love darkness more than light; not that the unclean spirit is not gone out, but that he is not so cast out as never to return again; the wound of all men, yea, the best of men that profess Christ, and yet indeed out of Christ, lies in this: they were never severed from their sin by all their prayers, tears, fears, sorrows; and hence they never truly come to Christ; and hence perish in their sin.

Trouble me no more, therefore, in asking whether a Christian is in a state of happiness or misery in this condition. I answer, He is preparatively happy; he is now passing from death to life, though not as yet wholly passed. Nor yet, whether there is any saving work before union. I answer, No; for what is said is one necessary ingredient to the working up of our union, as cutting off the branch from the old stock is necessary to the ingrafting it into the new: indeed, without faith it is impossible to please God; nor do I say that this work doth please; i. e., it doth not pacify God, (for that is proper to Christ's perfect right-eousness received by faith;) yet as it is a work of his own Spirit upon us, it is pleasing to him, (as the afterwork of sanctification is,) though it neither doth pacify him; nor do I see how this doctrine is any way opposite to the free offer of grace and Christ, because it requires no more separation from sin than that which drives them unto Christ; nay, which is less, that makes them (by the power of the Spirit) not resist, but yield to Christ, that he may come unto them and draw them: you can not repent nor convert yourselves. "Be converted, therefore," (saith Peter, Acts iii. 19,) "that you may receive remission of sins;" and in this offer the Spirit works; and verily he that can truly receive Christ without that sense of misery as separates him from his sin, (as explained to you,) let him believe notwithstanding all that which is said, and the God of heaven speak peace to him; his faith shall not trouble me, if he be sure it shall not one day de-ceive himself.

Of lamentation for the hardness of men's hearts in these times: as it is said the Lord Jesus "mourned" when he saw "the hard-ness of the people's hearts," (Mark iii. 5,) are there not some so far from this, as that they take pleasure in their sins, they are sugar under their tongues, as sweet as sleep, nay, as their lives? and you come to pull away their limbs when you come to pluck away their sins. Though they have broke Sabbaths, neglected prayer, despised the word, hated and mocked at the saints, been stub-born to their parents, cursed and swore, (which made Peter go out and weep bitterly,) though lustful and wanton, (which broke David's bones,) though guilty of more sins than there be motes in the sun or stars in heaven, though their sins be crimson, and fill heaven with their cry, and all the earth with their burden, yet they mourn not; never did it one hour together; nay, they can not do it, because they will not. If you are weary and loaden, where are your unutterable groans? If wounded and bruised, where are your dolorous complaints? If sick, where is your equity for a physician? If sad, where are your tears, in the day, in the night, morning and evening, alone by yourselves, and in company with others? O, how great is the wrath of God, hardening so many thousands at this day! Whence comes it that Christ is not prized, but from this senselessness? Name any reason why the blessed gospel of peace, and all the sweet prom-ises of life are undervalued, but from hence: and what do you hereby, poor creatures, by only aggravate your sins, and make those that are little exceeding great in the eyes of God? Whence it is that you "treasure up wrath against the day of wrath."

(Rom. ii. 2–5.) This hardness is that which blunts the edge of God's ordinances, whence God's poor ministers sit sorrowful in their closets, seeing all God's seed lost upon bare rocks. O, this is the condition of many a man, and which is most fearful, the means which should make the heart sensible make it more proud and unsensible. Tyre, and Sidon, and Sodom are more fit to mourn than Chorazin and Capernaum, that have enjoyed humbling means long. Nay, how many be there that mourn out their mournings, confess out their confessions, and by their own humiliations grow more senseless afterward! Did we ever live in a more impenitent, secure age? We shall seldom meet with one broken with sin; but how few are broken from sin also! And hence it is many a tall cedar that were set down in the table book for converted men, once much humbled, and now comforted; stay but a few years, you shall see more dangerous sins of a second growth; one turns drunkard, another covetous, another proud, another a sectary, another a very dry leaf, a very formalist, another fully of humorous opinions, another laden with scandalous lusts. Woe to you that lament not now; for you shall mourn. Dost thou think that Christ should ever wipe off thy tears, that sheddest none at all? Dost thou think to reap in joy, that sowest not with these showers? Verily God will make his word good, (Prov. xxix. 1,) "He that hardens his own heart shall perish suddenly." Hear this, you secure, sorrowless sinners: if ever God's hand be stretched out suddenly against thee, in blasting thy estate, snatching away thy children, the wife of thy bosom, the husband of thy delight; in staining thy name, vexing thee with debts and crosses, sharp and sore, or lingering sicknesses, know that all this comes upon thee for a hard heart: but O, mourn for it now, you parents, children, servants; the tokens of death are upon you; desire the Lord to break your hearts for you; lie under God's hammer; be not above the word, and suffer the Lord to take away that which grieves him most, even thy stony heart, because it grieves the least: meditate much of thy woful condition; chew the bitter pill; remember death and rotting in the grave; that many are now in hell for their sins; that Christ must die, or thou die for the least sin; remember how patient and long suffering the Lord hath been to thee, and how long he hath groaned under thy burden, that, it may be, though he would, yet he can not bear the load long: let these things be mused on, that thy heart may be at last sorrowful before it be too late. But O, the sad estate of many with us, that can mourn for any evil except it be for the greatest — sin, and death, and wrath that lie upon them!

Of exhortation. Labor for this sense of misery, for this spirit of compunction. How can you believe in Christ, that feel not your misery without him? A broken Christ can not do thee good without a broken heart; be afflicted and mourn, ye sinners; turn your laughter into mourning; tremble to think of that wrath which burns down to the bottom of hell, and under which the eternal Son of God sweat drops of blood. Great sins, which thou knowest thou art guilty of, cause great guilt, and great hardness of heart, and therefore are seldom forgiven or subdued without great affliction of spirit; they have loaded the Lord long, they must load thee. Little sins are usually slighted and extenuated, and therefore the Lord accounts them great; and therefore thy soul must be in bitterness for them before the Lord will pass them by. It is not every trouble that will serve the turn. Look that it be such as separates thy soul from sin, or else it will separate between thy soul and God. I know it is not in your power to break your own hearts, no more than to make the rocks to bleed; yet remember, he that bids thee " cast up and prepare the way of the Lord," he hath promised that " every mountain shall be brought low, and the crooked ways made plain, and the rough smooth, and the valleys filled." He only can do it for thee, and will do it for some, it may be for thee. He that broke the heart of Manasseh and Paul, after their blood and blasphemies, when they never desired any such thing, he can break thine much more when thou art desiring him to do it for thee. Here are many of you that fear you were never humbled nor burdened enough. I say, fear it still. Fear lest there be a stone in the bottom; not so as to discourage and drive thy heart from Christ, but so as to feel a greater need of his grace to soften thy heart, and to take thy senselessness away. The Lord doth purposely command thee " to plow up thy fallow ground," that thou mightest feel thy impotency so to do, and come to him to take it away. Every thing will harden thee more and more until the Lord come and take thy stony heart away by his own hand. All God's kindness will make thee more bold to sin, and all God's judgments more fierce and obstinate in sin, unless the Lord put to his hand. If Pharaoh's heart be softened for a time, it will grow hard again, if the Lord take it not away. The means, therefore, for thee to get this compunction is, 1. To feel the evil of thy hard heart; no surer token of reprobation than hardness, if continued in — especially for thy heart to grow hard under or after softening means, as it was in Pharaoh; 2. To look up to the Lord in all ordinances, that he would take it away.

Have not you great cause of abundant thankfulness, into

15 *

whose hearts the Lord hath let in fears and sorrows concerning your estates? The blind world looks upon all troubles of conscience as temptations of the devil to despair, and the very way to run mad. And consider what the Lord hath done for you that have such. What if the Lord had left you without all feeling, as those in Eph. iv. 19? What if the Lord had smitten you with a spirit of slumber, as those Rom. xi. 8? Would not your estate have been then lamentable? And have you no hearts to acknowledge his unspeakable goodness in a-weakening of you, in shaking thy very foundations? Dost thou think that any ever had such a hard heart as thou hast? Dost not say so in secret before the Lord sometimes? O, then what rich grace is this to give thee any sense and feeling of thy sin and danger by it, though it be never so little in thine eyes! Some think these terrors are a judgment. It is true, if they were merely imaginary, or worldly and desperate; but saith the apostle, (2 Cor. vii. 7,) "I thank God I made you sorry." Suppose thy sorrow should be only in regard of the punishment of sin, yet this is the Lord's goodness to make thy heart so far sensible, that once didst go like a beast to the slaughter, fearing no danger at all. The very means to prize favor from God is to feel wrath, (as well as sin,) and the very reason why the Lord hath let thee feel thy punishment heavy is, that thy soul might feel the evil of sin, by considering that if the fruits be so bitter, what is then the cause. Be not therefore weary of thy burden, so as to think the Lord pours out his vengeance on thee while thy trouble remains. O, consider that this is the hand of the Lord Jesus, and that he is now about to save thee, when he comes to work any compunction in thee — especially such as whereby he doth not only cut thy heart with fears and sorrows, but cut thee off from thy sin, so far only as humbles thee, and drives thee to the Lord Christ to take them away. And so I come to the third particular, of humiliation.

Section IV.

The third Act of Christ's Power, which is Humiliation.

The Lord Jesus, having thus broken the heart by compunction, is not like a foolish builder that leaves off his work before he hath fully finished it; and therefore, having thus wounded a poor sinner, he goes on to humble him also; for though, in a large sense, a wounded, contrite sinner is a humble sinner, yet, strictly taken, there is a great difference between them; and therefore he is said "to dwell with the contrite and humble;" i. e., not only with those that be wounded with sin, but humbled for sin, although it is certain the soul is seldom or never effectually wounded but it is also humbled at the same time. A man may be wounded sore even unto death, and yet the pride of the man is such that he will not fall down before him that smites him. So it is with many a poor sinner. The Lord hath sorely wounded him that he will resist no more; yet he will rather fly to his duties to heal him, or die alone, and sink under his discouragements, than stoop. O beloved, man must down before the Lord Christ will take him up; and therefore, in Is. xl. 5–7, the glory of the Lord is promised to be revealed. But what means must be used for this end? "Cry," saith the Lord. "What shall I cry?" saith he. The Lord answers that all flesh is grass, and that the glory of it fades, and that the people are this grass; i. e., not only that men's sins are vile, but that themselves also are grass; nay, their glory and excellency is withering and fading; and therefore not only mountains must be pulled down, but all flesh and the glory of it wither, before the Lord shall be revealed.

I shall briefly open these four things: —
1. What is this humiliation?
2. What need there is of it.
3. What means the Lord useth to work it.
4. What measure of it is here required.

What is this humiliation?

Look, as pride is that sin whereby a man conceited of some good in himself, and seeking some excellency to himself, exalts himself above God, so humiliation (in this place) is that work of the Spirit whereby the soul, being broken off from self-conceit and self-confidence in any good it hath or doth, submitteth unto, or lieth under, God, to be disposed of as he pleaseth. (1 Pet. v. 6. Lev. xxvi. 41.) That look, as compunction cuts the sinner off from that evil that is in him, so humiliation cuts it off from all high conceits and self-confidence of that good which is in him, or which he seeks might be in him; and so the soul is abased before God.

What need or necessity is there of this? Because, —
1. When the Lord hath wounded the hearts of his elect, this is the immediate work of their hearts, (if the Lord prevent them not by his grace, as many times he doth,) — they look to what good they have; or, if they find little or none, they then seek for some in themselves, that thereby they may heal their wound, because they think thus, that as their sins have provoked

God to anger against them, so if now they can reform and leave those sins, or, if not, repent and be sorry for them, if now they pray, and hear, and do as others do, they have some hope that this will heal their wound, and pacify the Lord toward them. When they see there is no peace in a sinful course, they will therefore try if there be any to be found in a good course; and look, as Adam, when he saw his own shame and nakedness, hid himself from God in the bushes, and covered his nakedness with fig leaves, so the soul, not being able to endure to see its own nakedness and vileness, not knowing Christ Jesus, and he being far to seek, doth therefore labor to cover his wickedness and sinfulness, which now he feels, by some of these fig leaves. And hence (Micah vi. 7) they inquire " wherewith they should come before the Lord; should they bring rivers of oil, or thousands of lambs, or the first born of their body to remove the sin of their soul?" Paul did account these duties gain, and set them at a high rate, because he thought that God did so himself. When the Lord hath wounded the soul, the first voice it speaks is, What shall I do? Do? saith conscience; leave thy sins, do as well as others, do with all thy might and strength, pray, hear, and confer; God accepts of good desires, and requires no more of any man but to do what he can. Hence the soul plies both oars, though against wind and tide, and strives, and wrestles with his sins, and hopes one day to be better; and here he rests. And observe it, look, as sin is his greatest evil, so the casting away of his sins, and seeking to be better, is very sweet to him; and being so sweet, rests in what he hath, and seeks for what he wants, and so hopes all will be well one day, and so stays here; although (God knows) it be without Christ, nor can not rest on him, though he hath heard of him a thousand times. And hence it is, if they can not do any thing to ease themselves, then their hearts sink, or, it may be, quarrel with God, that he makes them not better. But, beloved, it is wonderful to see how many times men rest in a little they have and do.

2. But whiles it is thus with the soul, he is incapable of Christ; for he that trusts to other things to save him, or makes himself his own Saviour, or rests in his duties without a Saviour, he can never have Christ to save him. (Rom. ix. 32.) It is said the Jews lost Christ's righteousness, because they sought it not by faith, but sought salvation by their own righteousness. " He that maketh flesh his arm," (as all duties and endeavors of man be, when trusted to,) the Lord saith, " cursed be that man." (Jer. xvii. 5, 6.) Only the Lord doth not leave his elect here; he that is married unto the law (Rom. vii.) can not be matched

unto Christ, till he be first divorced, not from the duties themselves, but from trusting to them, and resting in them. And
therefore, saith Paul, "I through the law am dead to it, that I
might live unto God." He that trusteth to riches can not enter into
the kingdom of heaven, no more than a camel through a needle's
eye, because it is too big for so narrow a room; so he that trusteth
to his duties and abilities is too big to enter in by Christ. The
Lord must cut off this spirit, and lay it low, and make it stoop as
vile before God, before it can have Christ in this estate; the
Lord must not only cut it off from this self-confidence in duties,
but also so far forth as that the soul may lie under God, to be
disposed of as he pleaseth. And the reason is, because such a
soul is unwilling to stoop, is unhumbled; and he that is so doth
not only on his part resist God, but the Lord also resists him.
(Lam. iv. 7, 8.) And hence you shall observe, many a one hath
lain long under distress of conscience, because they have either
rested in their duties, which could not quiet, or because they
have not so cast off their confidence in them, so as to lie down
quietly before God, that he may do what he will with them;
being so long objects of God's resistance, not of his grace. By
what means doth the Lord work this?

In general, by the Spirit, immediately acting upon the soul;
but after a Christian is in Christ, he hath by the habit of humility, and the virtue of faith, some power to humble himself;
but now the Spirit of Christ doth it immediately by its own omnipotent hand; else the proud heart would never down; for we are
first "created in Christ" (which is by God's omnipotent immediate
act) unto good works, before we do from ourselves, or by the power
of faith, put forth good works. (Eph. ii. 10.) These acts of
self-confidence may not be stirring in all Christians; but in all
men there is this frame of spirit, never to come to Christ if they
can make any thing else serve to heal them or save them; and
therefore the Spirit cuts off this sinful frame in part in all the
elect; he hews the roughness and pride of spirit off, that it may
lie still upon the foundation it is now prepared for. Now, though
the Spirit works this, yet it is not without the word; the word
it works chiefly by is the law. (Gal. iii. 19,) "I through the
law am dead to it," (i. e., from seeking any life or help from it,)
"that I might live unto God."

Now, the law doth this by a fourfold act.

1. By discovering the secret corruption of the soul in every
duty, which it never saw before. It once thought, I shall perish
for my sins, if I continue therein, without confession of them, or
sorrow for them; but it also did think that this confession,

sorrow, and trouble for sin, will serve to save it, and make God accept of it; but the law (while the soul is earnestly striving against his sin) discovering that in all these there is nothing but sin, even secret sins it did never see before, hereupon it begins thus to think: Can these be the means of saving of me, which being so sinful, can not but be the very causes of condemning of me? I know I must perish for the least sin, and now I see that in all I do, I can do nothing else but sin. What made Paul "alive without the law"? You shall find (Rom. vii. 7) it was because he did not know that lust, or the secret concupiscences and first risings of the soul to sin, were sin: he saw not these secret evils in all that which he did; and hence he rested in his duties, as one alive without Christ; but the Lord, by discovering this, let him see what little cause he had to lift up his hand, for any good he did. So it is here, when the soul sees that all its righteousness is a menstruous cloth, polluted with sin; now, those duties, which, like reeds, are trusted to before, run into the hand, nay, heart of a poor sinner; and therefore now it feels little cause of resting on them any longer; now it sees the infinite holiness of God by the exceeding spiritualness of the law, it begins to cry out, How can I stand or appear before him with such continual pollutions?

2. By irritating or stirring up of original corruption, in making more of that to appear than ever before; that if the soul thinks, All I do is defiled with sin, yet my heart is good, and so it rests there; the Lord therefore stirs that dunghill, and lets it see a more hellish nature than ever before, in that the holy and blessed command of God (to its feeling) makes it worse, more rebellious, more averse from God. "When the commandment came, sin revived," saith Paul, and that "which was for life was death to him," sin taking occasion by the law; and hence Paul came "to be slain and die" to all his self-confidence. It was one of Luther's first positions in opposing the pope's indulgences, that *Lex et voluntas sunt duo adversarii sine gratia irreconciliabiles ;* for the law and man's will meeting together, the one holy, the other corrupt, make fierce opposition when the soul is under a lively work of the law; and by this irritation of the law, the Lord hath this end in his elect, to make them feel what wretched hearts they have, because that which is in itself a means of good makes them (through man's corruption) more vile to their feeling than ever before; and hence come those sad complaints on a soul under the humbling hand of Christ: I am now worse than ever I was; I grow every day worse and worse. I have lost what once I had; I once could pray and seek God with delight, and never well but when one duty was done, to be in another; but now I am worse; all that joy

and sweetness in seeking of him, and in holy walking, is gone; I could once mourn for sin, but now a hard heart takes hold of me, that I have not so much as a heart to any thing that is good, nor to shed a tear for the greatest evil. It is true, I confess you may grow (to your feeling) worse and worse, and it is fit you should feel it, that the Lord hereby might pull down your proud heart, and make you lie low; it is the Lord's glorious wisdom to wither all your flowers, which refreshed you without Christ, that you might feel a need of him; and therefore I say the Lord pulls away all those broken planks the soul once floated and rested upon, that the soul may sink in a holy despair of any help from any good it hath; the Lord shakes down all building on a sandy foundation, and then the soul cries out, It is ill resisting here.

3. By loading, tiring, and wearying the soul by its own endeavors, until it can stir no more, — for this is in every man by nature, — when he sees that all he doth is sinful, and all he hath, his heart and nature, to be most sinful; yet he will not yet come out of himself, because he hopes, though he be for the present thus vile, yet he hopes, for future time, his heart may grow better, and himself do better than now; and hence it is that he strives, and seeks, and endeavors to his utmost, to set up himself again, and to gain cure to all his troubles by his duties : now, the law, whose office is to command, but not to give strength, and the Spirit that should give strength withdrawing itself, because it knows the soul would rest therein without Christ; hence it comes to pass that the soul, feeling itself to labor only in the fire and smoke, and to be still as miserable and sinful as ever before, hereupon it is quite tired out, and sits down weary, not only of its sin, but of its work; and now cries out, I see now what a vile and undone wretch I am ; I can do nothing for God or for myself; only I can sin and destroy myself; all that I am is vile, and all that I do is vile; I now see that I am indeed poor, and blind, and miserable, and naked. And the truth is, beloved, here come in the greatest dejections of spirit ; for when the Lord smites the soul for sin, it hopes that, by leaving of sin and doing better, it may do well; but when it sees that there is no hope here of healing the breach between God and itself, now it falls low indeed; and I take this to be the true meaning of Matt. xi. 28, " Ye that labor," i. e., you that are wearied in your own way, in seeking rest to your souls by your own hard labor or works, (as the word κοπιῶντες signifies,) and are tired out therein, and so are now laden indeed with sin and the heavy pressure of that, finding no ease by all that which you do : " Come to me," saith

Christ, "and you shall then find rest unto your souls." The
Jews, seeking to establish their own righteousness, — seeking, I
say, if by any means they might establish it, — lost Christ: the
Lord, therefore, will make his elect know they shall seek here
for ease in vain, and therefore tires them out.

4. By clearing up the equity and justice of God in the law,
if the Lord should never pity nor pardon it, nor show any
respect or favor to it; for this is the frame of every man's heart,
if he can not find rest in his duties and endeavors, as he once
expected he should, but sees sin and weakness, death and condemnation, wrapping him about (like Jonah's weeds) in all he
doth, then his heart sinks, and quarrels, and falls off farther
from Christ by discouragement, and grows secretly impatient
that there should be no mercy left for him; because it thinks
now the Lord's eternal purpose is to exclude him; for if there
were any thoughts of peace toward him, he should have found
peace before now, having so earnestly and frequently sought the
Lord, and having done so much, and forsaken his sinful ways,
according to his own commandment from him. And hence it
is, you shall find it a certain truth that the soul is turned back
as far from God by sinking discouraging sorrows for sin, as ever
it was to a state of security by the pleasures of sin; and hence
sometimes it thinks it is vain to seek any more, and hence leaves
off duties; and if conscience force it to them, yet it sinks again,
because its foot is not stablished upon the rock Christ, but upon
the weakness of the waters of its own abilities and endeavors.
What, therefore, should the soul do in this case to come to God ?
It knows not; it can not fly from him, it dare not, it shall not;
the Spirit, therefore, by revealing how equal and just it is for
the Lord never to regard or look after it more, because it hath
sinned and is still so sinful, makes it hereby to fall down
prostrate in the dust before the Lord, as worthy of nothing
but shame and confusion, and so kisseth the rod, and turns the
other cheek unto the Lord, even smiting of him, acknowledging,
if the Lord show mercy, it will be wonderful; if not, yet the
Lord is righteous, and therefore hath no cause to quarrel against
him for denying special mercy to him, to whom he doth not owe
a bit of bread. And now the soul is indeed humbled, because
it submits to be disposed of as God pleaseth. Thus the church,
in her humiliation, (Lam. iii. 22,) having, in the former part
of the chapter, "drunk the wormwood and the gall," at last lies
down and professeth, "It is the Lord's mercy it is not consumed;" and verse 29, "He puts his mouth to the dust if there
may be any hope ;" and verse 39, "Why should a living man

complain for the punishment of his sin?" You think the Lord doth you wrong, and neglects your good and his own glory too, if he doth not give you peace and pardon, grace and mercy, even to the utmost of your asking, and then think you have hence good cause to fret, and sink, and be discouraged. No, no; the Lord will pull down those mountains, those high thoughts, and make you lie low at his feet, and acknowledge that it is infinite mercy you are alive, and not consumed; and that there is any hope or possibility of mercy; and that you are out of the nethermost pit; and that if he should never pity you, yet he doth you no wrong, but that which is equal and just, and that it is fit your sinful, froward wills should stoop to his holy, righteous, and good will, rather than that it should stoop and be crooked according unto yours. Believe it, brethren, " he that judgeth not himself" thus, " shall be judged of the Lord :" how can you have mercy that will set yourselves up in God's sovereign throne to dispose of it, and will not lie down humbly under it, that it may dispose of you? For are you worthy of it? hath the Lord any need of you? have you not provoked him exceedingly? was there ever any that dealt worse with him than you? O beloved, lie low here, and learn of the church, (Micah vii. 9,) " I will bear the indignation of the Lord, because I have sinned against him." It was a most blessed frame of spirit in Aaron, when he saw God's hand against him in cutting off his children; "and Aaron held his peace;" so, if the Lord should cast thee off, cut thee off, never take pleasure in such a polluted, broken vessel, unfit for any use for him, hold thou thy peace; quarrel not, be silent before him, and say as they did, (2 Chron. xii. 5,) " The Lord is righteous, but I am vile; let him do with me what seemeth good in his own eyes;" and thus the Lord Jesus, by the law, doth dead the soul to the law, until it be made to submit like wax, or like clay to the hand of the potter, to frame it a vessel to what use he pleaseth; and as the apostle most excellently (Rom. vii.) divorceth it from its first husband, (i. e., sin and the law) that it may be married unto Jesus Christ. In a word, when the Lord Christ hath made the soul feel not only its inability to help itself, — and so saith Paul, (Gal. ii. 20,) " It is not I," — but also its own unworthiness, that the Lord should help it, and so cries out with Job, " Behold I am vile;" now, at this instant, it is *vas capax* — a vessel capable (though unworthy) of any grace. (Lam. iv. 6.)

The last question remains, What measure of humiliation is here necessary?

Look, as so much conviction is necessary which begets compunction, and so much compunction as breeds humiliation, so so much humiliation is necessary as introduceth faith, or as drives the soul out of itself unto Christ; for, as the next end of conviction is compunction, and that of compunction is humiliation, so the next end of humiliation is faith, or coming to Christ, which we shall next speak unto.

And hence it is that the Lord calls unto the weary and heavy laden to come unto him. (Matt. ii. 27.) So much as makes you come for rest in Christ, so much is necessary, and no more. If any can come without being thus laden and weary, in some measure, let them come and drink of the water of life freely; but a proud heart that will make itself its own Saviour will not come to the Lord Jesus to be his Saviour; he that will be his own physician so long can not send out for another. Nay, let me fall one degree lower: if the soul can not come to Christ, (as who feel not themselves unable when the Lord comes to draw?) and find not the Lord Jesus coming unto them, to draw them and compel them in, yet if the soul be so far humbled as not to resist the Lord, by quarrelling with him, and at him, as unworthy of the least smile, as worthy of all frowns, verily, the Lord will come to it, and no more is requisite than this; and thus much certainly is, for thus the whole Scripture runs : " He gives grace to the humble." (James iv. 6.)   " I dwell with the contrite and humble." (Is. lvii. 16.)   " The poor afflicted shall not always be forgotten." (Ps. ix. 12, 18.)   " When their uncircumcised hearts are humbled, so as to accept of the punishment of their iniquity, the Lord then remembers his covenant." (Lev.) xxvi. 41, 42.)   Conceive it thus: there can be no union to Christ while there is a power of resistance and opposition against Christ. The Lord Christ must, therefore, in order of nature, (for I now speak not of order of time,) first *removere prohibens*, remove this resistance before he can, and that he may, unite.   I do not mean resistance of the frame of grace, but, as was said, of the Lord of grace, whereby he comes to work it.

Now, there is a double resistance, or two parts of this resistance, like a knife without edges.

1. A resistance of the Lord by a secret unwillingness that the Lord should work grace.   Now, this the Lord removes in compunction, and no more brokenness for sin or from sin is necessary there than that.   2. A resistance of the Lord by sinking discouragements, and a secret quarrelling with him, in case the soul imagines he will not come to work grace or manifest grace.   Now, this the Lord takes away in humiliation; and no more is necessary here than the removal of the power of this,

which makes the soul, in the sense of its own infinite vileness and unworthiness, not to quarrel at the Lord, and, devil-like, grow fierce and impatient, before and against the Lord, in case he should never help it, never pity it, never succor it. "The Lord will not forsake forever, if the soul thus lies down and puts its mouth in the dust." (Lam. iii. 30, 31.)

Which consideration is of unspeakable use and consolation to every poor empty nothing that feels itself unable to believe, and the Lord forsaking it from helping it to believe. And I have seen it constantly that many a chosen vessel never hath been comforted till now, and ever comforted when now ; they never knew what hurt them till they saw this, and they have immediately felt their hurt healed when this hath been removed. In comforting Christians under deep distress, tell them of God's grace and mercy, and the riches of both, you do but torment them the more, that there should be so much, and they have no part nor share in it, and think they never shall, because this is not the immediate way of cure. Tell them, rather, when they are full of these complaints, that they are as they speak, vile and sinful, and therefore worthy never to be accepted of God, and that they have no cause to wonder that they have their lives, and are on this side hell, and so turn all that they say to humiliation and self-loathing ; verily, you shall then see, if the Lord intends good, he will by this do them good, and the weakest Christian that cannot come to Christ, you shall see, first or last, shall see cause to lie down and be silent, and not quarrel, though the Lord should never come to him. And that this is- necessary may appear thus: otherwise, —

1. The Lord should not advance the riches of his grace. The advancement of grace cannot possibly be without the humiliation and abasement of the creature ; the Lord not only saves, but calls, things that are not, that "no flesh might glory." (1 Cor. i. 28, 29.)

2. Otherwise the Lord should not be Lord and Disposer of his own grace, but a sinful creature who quarrels against God, if it be not disposed of, not as the Lord will, but as the creature will. If a stranger comes to our house, and will have what he wants, and if he hath not, he quarrels and contends with the master of the house, what would he say ? "Away, proud beggar ! dost think to be lord of what I have ? dost draw thy knife to stab me if I do not please thee and give thee thy asking ? No, thou shalt know that I will do with my own as I see good ; thou shalt lie down on the dust of my threshhold before I give thee any thing." So it is with the Lord. "It is not in him that willeth, nor in him that runneth, but in God that showeth mercy." It is his princi-

pal name, "I will be merciful to whom I will be merciful;" and therefore if you will not believe me, yet believe the Lord's oath. (Is. xlv. 23,) "Unto me shall every knee bow;" and do you come to lord it over him, and quarrel and fret, and sink and grow sullen, and vex, if the Lord stoop not unto your desires? No, no; you must and shall lie upon his threshhold; nay, he will make thee lay thy neck upon the block, as worthy of nothing but cutting off, and then, when this "valley is filled, all flesh shall see the glory of the Lord." (Is. xl. 5.) Thus humiliation is necessary in this measure mentioned. Not that I deny any subsequent humiliation, after a Christian is in Christ, arising from the sense of God's favor in Christ, than which nothing makes a Christian of an evangelical spirit more ashamed of himself; yet I dare not exclude this, which is antecedent, arising from the spirit of power immediately subduing the soul to Christ that it may be exalted by Christ. (1 Pet. v. 6.) It is true, all things that pertain to life and godliness are received by faith; (2 Pet. i. 3;) yet faith is less a saving work, which is not received by any precedent faith. Faith, therefore, is to be excepted, not only as begotten in us, but as it is in the begetting of it in the conviction and humiliation of every sinner.

Hence, see what is the great hinderance between the mercy of God and the soul of many a man; if it be not some sin and hardness of heart under it, whereby he cares not for Christ to deliver him, then it is some pride of spirit arising from some good he hath, whereby he feels no need of Christ, hoping his own duties shall save him; or else is above Christ, and not under him, willing to be disposed of by him. And hence the Lord makes this the highway of mercy, (Lev. xxvi. 40,) if first they shall confess their sins; secondly, humble themselves, (both which I know the Lord must work,) then he will remember his covenant. Look as it is with a vessel before it can be fit for use: it must first pass through fire, and the earth and dross severed from it; then it must be made holy and empty, which makes it *vas capax*, a vessel capable of receiving that which shall be poured into it. If (O brethren) the Lord hath some vessels of glory, which he prepares beforehand, and makes capable of glory, (Rom. ix. 21, 22;) if the Lord doth not sever you from sin in compunction, and empty you of yourselves in humiliation, you can not receive Christ, nor mercy — you can not hold them; and if ever you miss of Christ by faith, your wound lies here. How many be there at this day, that were once profane and wicked, but now by some terrors and outward restraints upon them they leave their sins, and say they loathe them, and purpose never to run riot as they have done; and hence, because they think themselves very good, or to have some good, they fall short of Christ, and are still in the gall of bitterness, in the midst of all evil. It were the happiness of some men, if they did not think themselves to have some good because this is their Christ. O you that live under precious means, and have many fears you may perish and be deceived at the last! But why do you fear? I know you will answer, "O, some secret and unknown sin may be my ruin." It is true, and you do well to have a godly jealousy thereof. But remember this also, not only some sin, but some good thou thinkest thou hast, and restest in without Christ, and lifting thee up above Christ, may as easily prove thy ruin; because a man's own righteousness rested in doth not only hide men's sins, but strengthens them in some sin by which men perish. Trusting to one's own righteousness, and committing iniquity, are couples. (Ezek. xxxiii. 13.) Nor do I hereby run into the trenches of that wicked generation of the Familists, denying all inherent graces; evidence of favor from any Christian obedience, or sanctification in holy duties; or that a Christian should profanely cast off all duties, because they cannot save themselves by them. No, no; the Lord will search with candles one day for such sons of darkness, and exclude such foolish virgins, that they have neither oil in their vessels nor light in their lamps. I only speak of that good, that righteousness which is rested in without Christ, and lifts up men above Christ, which in deed and in truth is not true righteousness, but only a true shadow of it. And, therefore, as Beza well observes from Rom. ix. 32, "Why did not Israel, that followed after righteousness, attain it? Because they sought it not by faith, but as it were by the works of the law;" they were not fruits of sincere obedience to the law, but as it were the works of the law; now this, saith the apostle, (ver. 33,) is the stumbling stone in Zion. Christ will have all flesh veil, and be stripped naked, and made nothing before him, before they shall ever be built upon him. Now, this men stumble at; they must bring something to him; they will not be vile, emptiness, and nothingness, that he may be all to them. Verily, observe yourselves, and you shall find, if there be little humiliation, there is little of Christ; if much humiliation, much of Christ; if unconstant humiliation, uncertain fruition of Christ; if real humiliation, real possession of Christ; if false humiliation, imaginary fruition of Christ. Know it, you can not perish if you fall not short here — you must perish if you do.

Be exhorted, therefore, to lie down in the dust before the Lord, and under the Lord; nay, entreat the Lord that he would

16 *

put thee upon his wheel, and mold thy heart to his will; why will you rest in any good you have? O, remember thy father was a Syrian, ready to perish, and thyself polluted, an infinite, endless evil. Whatever good thou dost, is it not a polluted stream of a more polluted spring? Nay, suppose the Spirit works any good in thee, yet is it not polluted by thy unclean heart? Nay, suppose any actions should be perfect, yet remember that the Lord spared not the angels that sinned; perfection present can not satisfy justice for pollution past. Cry out, therefore, and say, O Lord, now I see not only that my sin is vile, but that myself and all my righteousness is vile also; and now, though the Lord stands at a distance, speaks no peace, hears no prayers, yet because thou art very vile, lie down under him, that if he will he may tread upon thee, and thereby exalt himself, as well as lift thee up and exalt thee. Be not careless whether the Lord help or no, but be humbled, not to quarrel in case he should not. For, —

1. Suppose thou art not only miserable, but sinful, and the Lord (thou sayest) takes it not away; yet remember, that to quarrel with God for withdrawing his hand is a sin also, (Lam. iii. 39 ;) and wilt thou add sin to sin?

2. Why art thou quiet and still when the Lord denies thee any common mercy? Is it not because the Lord will have it so? Now, look as we say of him that hates sin as sin, that he hates all sin; so he that is meekened with God's good pleasure in any one thing because of his good pleasure in it, upon the same ground will at least desire to stoop in every thing. Suppose, therefore, it be the Lord's good pleasure to deny thee mercy; I grant you must pray for it, yet with submission to the good will of the Lord, saying, The Lord's will is good, but mine is evil; otherwise thou hast no meekness in any thing — thou art not meekly subject to his will in every thing.

3. The greatest pride that is in man appears here; for suppose the Lord should deny thee bread, or water, or clothes, was it your duty to murmur now? nay, was it not pride, if the heart would not lie down, and say, Lord I am worthy to have my bread plucked from my mouth, and my clothes from my back? Now, if it be pride to murmur in case the Lord denies you smaller matters, the offals of this life, dost not thou see that it is far greater pride for thee to sink and quarrel with him if he denies thee greater, and the things of another life? Is he bound to give thee greater, that doth not owe thee the least? Suppose a beggar murmur at thy door if thou dost deny him bread, or a cup of drink, wilt thou not account him a proud, stout beggar? But if thou givest him that, and then he quarrel and murmur at

thee because thou dost not give him a thousand pounds, or thy whole estate when he asks it, will you not say, I never met with the like insolency? The Lord gives you your lives, blessed be his name, but you ask for treasures of grace and mercy, thousands of pounds, Christ himself, and all that he is worth, and the Lord seems to deny you, and now you sink and grow sullen, and discontent, and quarrel, and murmur at God, not directly, but secretly and slyly; may not the Lord now say, Was there ever such pride and insolency? And therefore, as Christ spoke of himself, (John xii. 24, 25,) "A corn of wheat can not live unless it die first," so know it, you shall never live with Christ; unless you die and perish in yourselves, unless you be sown and lie under the clods of your own wretchedness, faith will never spring up in such a soul. As it is in burnings, the fire must be first taken out, before there can be any healing, so this impatient spirit, which torments the soul, must first be removed, before the Lord will heal thee.

4. Consider the approaching times; I do believe the Lord at this day is coming out to shake all nations, all hearts, all consciences, all conditions, and to tear and rend from you your choicest blessings, peace and plenty, both external and internal also; for there is need of it; our age grows full, and proud, and wanton; a man's price is fallen in the market, unless his locks and new fashions commend him to the world. O, consider when God comes to rend all from you, then you may find a need of the exercise of this duty; it may be the time is coming wherein you shall have nothing to support your hearts, you shall find rest in no way but this; I know assurance of God's love may quiet you; but what if the Lord shake all your foundations, and deprive you of that? What will you do then? And therefore, as Zephaniah, (ii. 3,) having foretold of the evil day, cries unto his hearers, "Seek meekness, ye meek of the earth;" seek meekness; so say I to you; for you will find all little enough. Come down from thy throne, and be the footstool and threshhold of Christ Jesus, before the days of darkness come upon you; be content to be a cipher, a stepping stone, the very offal of the world.

But you will say, Wherein should I express this humiliation and subjection?

Be highly thankful for any little the Lord gives. (Lam. iii. 22, 23.) Be humble, and judge thyself worthy of nothing when the Lord denies; and verily you shall find the Lord Jesus ere long speaking peace unto you, and giving thee rest in his bosom, that now art quietly contented to lie still at his feet.

For some helps thereunto, —

1. Remember whose thou art; viz., the Lord's clay, and he thy potter, and therefore may do with thee what he will. (Rom. ix. 20.)

2. Remember what thou art; viz., a polluted vessel, a kind of infinite, endless evil, as I have oft said. See the picture of thy own vileness in the damned in hell, who are full, and shall through all eternity pour out all manner of evil. (Job xl. 3, 4.)

3. Remember what thou hast been, and how long thou hast made war against Christ with all thy might, and heart, and strength; why should the Lord therefore choose thee before others, (Jer. iii. 5,) when as, (ask thy conscience,) was there ever such a wretch since the world began as thou hast been?

4. Remember what thou wilt be: fit for no use to Jesus Christ, good for nothing but to pollute his holy name when thou meddlest with it; and why should the Lord take up such a dry leaf, (Is. lxiv. 6,) and breathe upon such a dry bone?

5. Remember how good the Lord's will is, even when it crosseth thine; he shall have infinite glory by all his denials to thee of what thou wouldest; he shall gain that, though thou losest thy peace and quietness, that good which thy foolish, sinful will desires at his hand, (John xii. 27, 28;) and if so, blessed be his name; let God live, but let man die and perish, that he may be exalted of vile man.

6. Remember the sweet rest thou shalt have by this subjection to the Lord; nothing is man's cross but man's will; a stubborn will, like a stubborn heifer in the yoke, galls and frets the soul. Learn meekness, saith our Saviour, of me, in taking my yoke on you, and then you shall find rest. Hell would not be hell to a heart truly humbled. Sometimes you find enlargements, then you are glad; sometimes none, then you sink; sometimes you have hope of mercy, then you are calm; sometimes you lose your hopes, then the sea works. When the Lord pleaseth you, then you are well; but if a little cross befall you, then your spring is muddy, and a little thing troubles. O, be humble and vile in thine own eyes, and verily such uncertain fits of peace and trouble are done, and the days of all your mourning are now ended.

Of thankfulness, to all those whom the Lord hath truly humbled. Time was, when the Lord first convinced you, that so long as you could make any shift, find rest in any duties, you would never lie down at Christ's feet; now the Lord might have left you to have stumbled at that stumbling stone, and to have stuck in those bushes; but you may see that the Lord will save you even then when you would not be saved by him; and especially take notice of two passages of God's dealings with you, wherein

usually you find matter of discouragement, rather than of acknowledgment of God's goodness to you therein. 1. That the Lord
hath withdrawn all feeling of any good which it may be once you
felt, and that the Lord hath let out more of the evil of your hearts
than ever you imagined was in them; nay, so much evil that you
think there is none like unto you, who hast now no heart nor
power to stir, think, desire, will, or do any thing that is good.
O, bless the Lord for this, for this is God's way to humble, and
empty, and make thee poor; the Lord saw, though it may be you
did not, that you rested in that good you felt, and was or would
be lifted up by these; and therefore the Lord hath broken
those crazy crutches, famished now, brought you down to nothing,
made you like dry deserts; all the hurt the Lord aimeth at in this
being only to humble you, and though these desertions be bitter
for the present, yet that by these he might do you good in your
latter end. O brethren, the apostle stands at a stay, and desires
the Corinthians to consider. "You see your calling," saith he.
(1 Cor. i.) "Not many mighty, not many wise, but things that
are not doth he call, that no flesh might glory." "The Lord,"
saith Moses, (Deut. viii. 2, 3,) "suffered thee to want," (that was
the first,) and then "fed thee, that he might prove thee and
humble thee; remember this," saith he. So say I to you,
remember this mercy, that when the Lord makes you worst of
all, not real, but in your own eyes, that then the Lord is about
this glorious work.

2. That the Lord hath kept you (it may be a long time, too)
from sight and sense of his peculiar love: one would wonder why
the Lord should hide his love so much, so long, from those to
whom he doth intend it; the great reason is, because there is in
many a one a heart desirous of his love; and this would quiet
them, if they were sure of it: but they never came to be quieted
with God's will, in case they think they shall never partake of his
love; but are above that, oppose, and resist, and quarrel with
that, unhumbled under that; the Lord therefore intending to bestow his favor only upon a humbled sinner, he will therefore hide
his face until they lie low, and acknowledge themselves worthy of
nothing but extremity of misery, unworthy of the least mercy.
"The people of God (Lam. i. 16) cry out that "the comforter
which should refresh their soul was far from them." What was
God's end in this? you shall see the end of it; (ver. 18,) "The
Lord is righteous," (here the church is humbled,) "for I have
rebelled;" or, (as Zanchius reads it,) "I have made his mouth
bitter," that the Lord speaks no peace to me, but bitter things.
The cause is in my own self, and therefore if he never comfort

me, nor speak good word unto me, yet he is righteous, but I am vile; and you will find this certain, that as the Lord therefore humbles that he may exalt, so the Lord never refuseth to exalt, (in hiding his face) but it is to humble. And is this the worst the Lord aims at, and will you not be thankful? Why are you, then, discouraged when you find it thus with you? Do not say the Lord never dealt thus with any as with me; suppose that; the reason then is, because the Lord sees, never had any such a high heart as thou hast; but O, be thankful that, notwithstanding this, he will take the pains to take it down.

Thus much for humiliation. I come now to the fourth and last, which is faith.

Section V.

The fourth and last Act of Christ's Power is the Work of Faith.

The Lord having wounded and humbled his elect, and laid them down dead at his feet, they are now as unable to believe as they were to humble their own souls; and therefore now the Lord takes them up into his own arms, that they lean and rest on the bosom of their beloved by faith. After Joseph had spoken roughly to his brethren, and thereby brought the blood of their brother to remembrance, and so had humbled them; and then he can contain no longer, but discovers himself to them, and tells them, " I am Joseph, whom you wickedly sold, yet fear not ; " so doth our Saviour carry it toward his elect, when he laid them low : now is the very season for him to advance the glory of his grace ; he can not now contain himself any longer ; but having torn and taken away that vail of sin and of the law from off their hearts, now they see the Lord with open face, even the end of that which was to be abolished. (2 Cor. iii.) The explication of this great work is of exceeding great difficulty; nothing more stirring than faith in a true Christian, because he lives by it, yet it is very little known ; as children in the womb, that know not that navel string by which they principally live : I shall therefore be wary, and leaving larger explications, acquaint you with the nature of faith, in this brief description of it.

Faith is that gracious work of the Spirit, whereby a humbled sinner receiveth Christ; or whether the whole soul cometh out of itself to Christ, for Christ and all his benefits, upon the call of Christ in his word.

Before I open this particularly, give me leave to premise some general considerations. Faith is the complement of effectual vocation, which begins in God's call, and ends in this answer to that call; the Lord prevents a poor humbled soul with his call, either not knowing how, or not able, or not daring to come; and then the soul comes, and hence men called and believing are all one. (Rom. ix. 24, with 33.) Many a wounded sinner will be scrambling after Christ from some general reports of him, before the day and hour of God's glorious and gracious call. Now, for any to receive Christ, or come to Christ before he is called, is presumption; to refuse Christ when called is rebellion; to come and receive when called is properly and formally faith, and that which the Scripture styles the "obedience of faith." (Rom. i. 5.) And now Christ at this instant is fully and freely given on God's part, when really and freely come unto and taken on our part.

This receiving of Christ, or coming to Christ, is for substance the same, though the words be diverse; the Holy Ghost useth to express one and the same thing in variety of words, that our feebleness might the better understand what he meaneth. And hence in Scripture, *believing, coming, receiving Christ, rolling, trusting, cleaving to the Lord,* etc., set out one and the same thing; and therefore it is no wonder if our divines have different descriptions of faith in variety of words; which, if well considered, do but set out one and the same thing: and I do conceive they do all agree in this description I have now mentioned; I know there are some who tread awry here, whom I shall briefly note out, and so pass on to what we intend.

1. The Papists, with some others of corrupt judgments, at least of weak apprehensions among ourselves, describe faith to be nothing else but a supernatural assent to a divine truth, because of a divine testimony; *ex. gr.*, to assent to this truth, that Christ is come, that he is the Son of God, that he was dead and is risen again, that he is the Saviour of the world, etc.; and to confirm this they produce Matt. xvi. 16; 1 John iv. 3.

It is granted that this assent is in faith, for faith always hath respect to some testimony; for man by his fall hath lost all knowledge of divine and supernatural truths; hence God reveals them in his word; hence faith sees them and assents to them, because God hath spoken them: to see and know things by vision is to see things in themselves intuitively and immediately; but to see things by faith is to see them by and in a testimony given of them. (John xx. 20,) "Blessed is he that hath not seen," (i. e., Christ immediately,) "but believed," i. e., his testimony, and on him in it; this assent, therefore, is in faith, for we must believe Christ before we can believe in him; but this comprehends not the whole nature of faith; I mean of that faith

we are now speaking of, viz., as it unites us to Christ, and possesseth us with Christ. For, —

1. This description placeth faith only in the understanding,
whereas it is also in the will, as the words *trusting, rolling*, etc.,
intimate.

2. This assent is merely general, without particular application, which is ever in true faith. (Gal. ii. 20.)

3. This is such a faith as the devils may have, (James ii. 19,)
and reprobate men may have. (2 Pet. ii. 20, 21. Heb. xx. 26.)
There is a wilful refusing of the known truth.

4. It is the Papist's aim to vilify faith hereby, by describing
it by that which is one ingredient in it, but excluding that which
is principal; those phrases, therefore, of "believing Christ is
come in the flesh," (1 John iv. 3,) and that "he is the Son of
God," (Matt. xvi. 16,) as if this were the only object to faith,
are not to be understood exclusively, excluding other acts of faith,
which the Scripture in other places sets down clearly; but in-
clusively, as supposing them to be contained herein; for as we
in our times, describing faith by relying upon Christ for salvation, do not exclude hereby our believing that he is the Messiah,
but we include it, or suppose it, because that is not now questioned, the truth of the gospel being so abundantly cleared, so
in those times, they described faith by one principal act, to believe
that he was the Son of God, and come into the flesh, because this
was the main and principal thing in question then : and if the
Lord had not set our faith by other acts in Scripture, we should
not vary from our compass in such expressions in the word in
these days; for their faith then is exemplary to us now; because
the word doth more fully set it out in more special acts, hence
we set it out also by them; for it is evident, as the Jews did believe in a Messiah to come, so they did also believe, and look for
all good from him.   (John iv. 25,) "He will teach us all things
when he comes : " and therefore their faith did not confine itself
to that historical act that a Messiah should come, or that this was
the Messiah, but they did expect and look for all good from him :
and hence the apostle expounding this saying, viz., believing that
Christ is dead and risen again, we shall hereby be saved : "If
thou believest" (saith he) "with thine heart" this truth, "thou
shalt be saved." Now, to believe with the heart, as it doth not
exclude assent, so it necessarily includes the acts of the will and
affections in relying upon him, and coming to him. And hence,
when Peter had made that confession, (Acts xvi. 16,) Christ
tells him, "Thou art Peter;" i. e., a stone resting upon the rock,
(as some good interpreters expound it;) and therefore Peter's

faith did not exclude these principal acts of resting on Christ, cleaving to Christ, but did include and suppose them.

2. Some run into another extreme, and make faith nothing else but a persuasion or assurance that Christ died for me in particular, or that he is mine. That which moves some thus to think, is the universal redemption by the death of Christ; they know no ground or bottom for faith but this proposition, Christ died for thee, and hence makes redemption universal: and hence the Arminians boast so much of their *quod unusquisque tenetur credere*, etc. But, 1. This is a false bottom, for Christ hath not died for all, because he hath not prayed for all. (John xvii. 2.)

3. This is a sandy bottom and foundation, which when a Christian rests upon, it shakes under him, when the soul shall think, Though Christ hath died for me, yet no more for me than for Judas, or thousands of reprobates now in hell. Indeed, after faith, a Christian is bound to believe it, as Paul did. (Gal. ii. 20. 1 Cor. xv. 1, 2.)

I conceive, therefore, those holy men of ours who have described faith by assurance, have not so much aimed at a description of what faith is in itself, as it possesseth us with Christ; but of what degree and extent it may be, and should be, in us; they describe it therefore by the most eminent act of it, in full assurance: and therefore consult with the authors of this description, and inquire of them, Is there no doubting mixed with faith? Yes, (say they,) man's doubtings sometimes are even unto a kind of despair, but then (say they) it should not be thus. The Papists commend doubtings, and deny assurance, place faith in a general assent; our champions, that were to wrestle with them, maintained it to be a particular application, (and not only a general assent,) and that with a full assurance of persuasion, which, being the most eminent act of faith, excludes not other inferior acts of it, which as they are before it, so may possess the soul with Christ without it. Although with all, it is certain, that there is no true faith but it hath some assurance, of which afterward.

Let me now come to the explication of the description given, where note these five things : —

1. The efficient cause of faith ; it is a work of the Spirit.

2. The subject, or matter in which it is seated, viz., the soul of a humble sinner.

3. The form of it, viz., the coming of the whole soul to Christ.

4. The end of it, viz., for Christ and all his benefits.

5. The special ground and means of it, viz., the call of Christ in his word.

1. The efficient cause of faith.

Faith is a gracious work of the Spirit of Christ; the Spirit, therefore, is the efficient cause or principal workman of faith; the Spirit doth not believe, but causeth us to believe; it is not *principium quod*, the principle which doth believe, but *principium quo*, the principle by which we do; the souls of all the elect (especially when humbled) are, of all other things, most unable to believe: nay, look, as, before compunction and humiliation, Satan held the soul captive chiefly by its lusts and sins, so now, when the Lord hath burnt those cords, and broken those chains, all the powers of darkness strengthen themselves, and keep the soul under mightily, by unbelief. What do you tell me of mercy? (saith the soul:) it is mercy which I have continually resisted, desperately despised: why do you persuade me to believe? Alas! I can not; it is true, all that which you say is true, if I could believe, but I can not see Christ, I can not come at Christ; I seek him in the means, but he forsakes me there, and I am left of God desolate; and here, beloved, the soul had not formerly so many excuses for its sin, as now it hath clouds of objections against believing; the Spirit therefore takes fast hold of the souls of all the elect, draws them unto Christ; and therefore it is called "the spirit of faith," (2 Cor. iv. 13;) and that by an omnipotent and irresistible power. (Is. liii. 1,) "Who hath believed? and to whom is the arm of the Lord revealed?" that the soul must and shall believe now. "Compel them to come in," saith the lord of the supper. (Luke xiv. 23.) This the Arminians will not believe, for (say they) the question is not, whether we are enabled to believe by grace; but, whether it be after this manner, and by this means, viz., *modo irresistibili*. Consider, therefore, these reasons to clear this point : —

1. Whence doth our call and coming to Christ arise, but from God's immovable and unchangeable purpose? The Lord therefore must either alter his purpose, or prevail with the soul to believe, and overpower the heart thereunto.

2. Is not Christ Jesus bound by office and promise to the Father to bring in all his lost, scattered sheep, that so the Father and he may be glorified in them? (John xx. 16,) "Other sheep I have; those I must bring home, and they shall hear my voice." You that complain you can not believe, nay, that you have no heart to believe, the Lord must fetch you in; and you shall hear the bridegroom's voice with joy.

3. Is not the act of believing wrought by a creating power? (Eph. i. 9; ii. 10. Is. lvii. 18, 19,) "I create the fruit of the lips peace, peace to him that is near and afar off." And is not a creating voice irresistible, though there be nothing for it to

work upon? So, though you have no ability, heart, head, or strength to believe, yet the Lord will create the fruit of the lips of God's messengers peace, peace.

4. Doth not the Lord let in that infinite and surpassing sweetness of grace, when he works the soul to believe, standing in extreme need of that grace, that it can not but come and cleave to it? (Ps. lxiii. 2, 3,) " I long to see thee," saith David, " for thy loving kindness is better than life." It is impossible for a man to cleave to his life; much more to that which is better than life. The light is so clear, it can not but see and wonder at grace; the good is so sweet, it can not but taste and accept what God so freely offers; and therefore the poor Canaanitish woman (Matt. xv.) could not be driven away, though Christ bid her in a manner begone; but she made all the objections against her arguments for her, (as usually faith doth, when under this stroke of the Spirit:) "The violent take the kingdom of heaven by force;" the Spirit puts a necessity upon them, and irresistibly overpowers them, and this is the cause of it.

And is not this matter of great consolation to all those who feel themselves utterly unable to believe? You think the Lord would give peace and pardon, life and mercy, if I could believe. O, consider the Lord hath overtaken in the covenant of grace to work in all his the condition of the covenant, as well as to convey thee good of it. (Jer. xxxi. 31–34.) He hath done this for others by an irresistible power. (Heb. xii. 1, 2.) Look up to Jesus, the Author and Finisher of your faith; he came out of his Father's bosom, not only to give life by his death, but to enable his to eat and close with him by faith, that they might never die. (John vi. 50.) So the Lord may work it in thee; it is true, also, he may not; yet it is unspeakable comfort to consider, that if the Lord had put it over unto thee to believe, it is certain thou shouldest never have believed; but now the work is put into the hand of Christ; that which is impossible to thee is possible, nay, easy, with him; he can comprehend thee when thou canst not apprehend him. This is exceeding sweet when thy body is sick, and soul is deserted, incredible things to be believed are propounded, an impossible work to thy weakness urged, upon pain of God's sorest and most unspeakable wrath; to consider it is not in me, but in the Lord's own hand; and it is his office, his glory to work faith, and, as the apostle speaks, to show mercy unto them that are shut up, not only under sin, but also unbelief. (Rom. xi. 32.) But why hath the Lord made thee feel thy inability to believe? Truly, the end of our wants is not to make us sin and shift for ourselves, but to ask and seek for supply; and the end of the continuance of those wants is, that we should continue to ask and seek. And dost thou think thou shalt seek to the Lord by his own hand to create faith, and fetch thee in, and will not the Lord take his time to work it? He that believes, saith the apostle, (Rom. x. 11,) shall not be ashamed. Why so? Because the Lord, saith he, who is over all, is rich unto all that call upon him. (Ver. 12.) If thou hast not a heart shut up from asking of it, the Lord, who hath power, hath not a heart shut up toward thee from working it.

But withal be thankful exceedingly, all you whose hearts the Lord hath drawn and overcome. He came to his own people the Jews, and would oft have gathered them, but they would not; and therefore he forsook them, and left their habitations desolate. O, how oft would the Lord have gathered you, and you would not! Yet the Lord hath not forsaken you, but called you in, whether you would or no; the Lord hath taken many a man at his first word, and left him at the first repulse, shaken off the dust of his feet against him presently, (Matt. x. 14,) without any more entreaties to accept of mercy. Yet thou hast not only refused, but even crucified the Son of God; yet he hath not been driven from thee, but his bowels have been oft kindled together, when he hath been ready to give thee up; when thou hast been under the hedges, and in the highways that lead to death, and didst never think of him, nor didst desire him, yet he hath compelled thee to come in; he hath made thee feel such an extreme need of him, and made himself so exceeding sweet, that thou hast not been able to resist his love, but to cry out, Lord, thou hast overcome me with mercy, I am not able to resist any more; nay, which is more wonderful, when thou hast been gathered, and gone from him, and lost thyself and him also again, and it may be hast been offended at him, yet he hath gone before thee into Galilee, and gathered thee up when thou hast been as water spilt upon the ground: what should be the cause of this, but only this? the work of faith lies upon him, both to begin and finish; he must gather in all his lost sheep, and therefore he hath put forth an irresistible power of his Spirit upon thy heart, which must carry thee captive after him.

I am afraid my faith hath been rather presumption, a work of my own power, than faith wrought by the Spirit's power: how may I discern that?

If you are wrapped up in God's covenant, if any promise be actually yours, it is no presumption to take possession by faith of what is your own. Dost thou seriously will Christ, and resolve never to give the Lord rest until he give thee rest in him?

Then see Rev. xxii. 17, "Whosoever will, let him take of the water of life." Dost thou thirst after Christ? Then read Is. lv. 1–3. John vii. 37, "If any man thirst, let him come unto me and drink." When Christ "saw their faith," (Matt. ix. 1, 2,) what said he? "Son, be of good cheer; thy sins be forgiven:" the word signifies, be confident. It is no presumption to believe pardon of sins now thou art come unto me, not only for the healing of thy body, but especially for pardon of sin. It is the great sin of many saints, when they do thirst, and believe, and come to Christ, and so are under the promise of grace; yet they think it presumption now to believe and take possession of all those treasures that be in Christ, but look that the Lord should first make them feel, and then they will believe; whereas faith should now receive and drink in abundantly of the fullness of Christ. Shall it be accounted presumption for any man to eat his own bread, and drink his own drink, and put on his own clothes? The promise makes Christ and all his benefits your own; therefore it is no presumption to apply them.

Suppose you can not find yourself within any promise, and you see no reason to believe, only you have the Lord's call and command to believe; do you now, in conscience and obedience to this command, or to God's invitation and entreaty in the gospel, believe, because thou darest not dishonor God by refusing his grace? thou dost therefore accept of it; this is no presumption, unless obedience be presumption. Nay, the most acceptable obedience, which is the "obedience of faith," (John vi. 38;) for what was the ground on which those three thousand believed? (Acts ii. 38, 39, etc.) Peter said, "Repent, that you may receive remission of sins:" now, what follows? "They that gladly received the word were baptized." O, that word "repent" — i. e., as Beza expounds it, "return to God and come in" — was a most sweet word to them, and therefore they received it; this was no presumption, either, for Peter to exhort them to repent, or for them to take the Lord (as that godly man said) at his first word. I know there is a subjection to the gospel, arising only from slavish fear and carnal hopes, (Ps. lxvi. 3, xviii. 44:) this may be in presumptuous reprobates; but there is a subjection arising from the sense of the sweetness and exceeding goodness of God's call and promise. (Ps. cx. 2, 3.) As a woman that is overcome with the words of her loving suitor; the man is precious, and hence his words are very sweet, and overcome her heart to think, Why should such a one as I be looked upon, by one of such a place? It is no presumption now, but duty to give her consent; so it is here, when the Lord

17 *

is precious and his words (O, accept me, O, come to me) are exceeding sweet; and hereupon, out of obedience, gladly yields up
itself to the Lord, takes possession of the Lord, this is no more
presumption than to sanctify a Sabbath, or to pray, or
hear the word, because the Lord's commands are herein very
sweet.

If repentance accompanies faith, it is no presumption to believe.
Many know the sin, and hence believe in Christ, trust to Christ,
and there is an end of their faith; but what confession and sorrow
for sin, what more love to Christ, follows this faith? Truly none.
Nay, their faith is the cause why they have none; for they think,
If I trust to Christ to forgive them, he will do it, and there is an
end of the business. Verily, this hedge faith, this bramble faith,
that catches hold on Christ, and pricks and scratches Christ by
more impenitency, more contempt of him, is mere presumption,
which shall one day be burnt up and destroyed by the fire of
God's jealousy. Fie upon that faith that serves only to keep
a man from being tormented before his time. Your sins would
be your sorrows, but that your faith quiets you. But if faith be
accompanied with repentance, mourning for sin, more esteem of
God's grace in Christ, so that nothing breaks thy heart more
than the thoughts of Christ's unchangeable love to one so vile,
and this love makes thee love much, and love him the more;
as thy sin increaseth, so thou desirest that thy love may increase;
and now the stream of thy thoughts runs, how thou mayest live
to Him that died for thee. This was Mary's faith, who sat at
Christ's feet weeping, washing them with her tears, and "loving
him much, because much was forgiven;" who, though she was
accounted a presumptuous woman by Simon, (and Christ himself suffered in his thoughts for suffering of her to come so near
unto him,) yet the Lord himself clears her therein, and justifies
her before God and men. Many a poor believer thinks, If I
should believe, I should but presume, and spin a spider's web
of faith out of my own bowels; and hence you shall observe,
this not believing stops up the work of repentance, mourning,
and love, and all cheerful obedience in them; and, on the
contrary, if they did believe, it would be with them as themselves think many times, If I knew the Lord was mine, and my
sins pardoned, O, how should I then bless him, and love him,
and wonder at him! how would this break my heart before
him! etc. Now, I say, let all the world judge, if that which thou
thinkest would be presumption be not rebellion, because it makes
thee worse, and stops up the Spirit of grace in thee. Whereas
that faith which lets out those blessed springs of sorrow, love,

thankfulness, humbleness, etc., what can it be else but such a saving faith as is wrought by the Spirit, because it lets in the Spirit more abundantly into a dry and desolate heart?

2. The subject or matter of faith.

This is the second thing in the description of faith ; the soul of a humbled sinner is the subject or matter of faith. I do not mean the matter out of which faith is wrought, (for there is nothing in man out of which the Spirit begets it,) but that wherein faith is seated. I mean also the habit of faith, not the principle of it ; for that is out of man in the Lord Jesus, who is therefore called " our hope," as well as " our strength ; " the soul, therefore, is the subject of faith, called " the heart ; " (Rom. x. 9, compared with Matt. vi. 21 ;) for we can not go or come to Christ in this life with our bodies ; we are " here absent from the Lord," (2 Cor. v. ;) but the soul can go to him, the heart can be with him ; as the eye can see a thousand miles off, and receive the species or image of the things it sees into it, so the soul, enlightened by faith, can see Christ afar off ; it can long for, choose, and rest upon the Lord of life, and receive the lively image of Christ's glory in it. (2 Cor. iii.)

If Christ were present upon earth, the soul (not the body) only could truly receive him. Christ comes to his elect only by his Spirit, and hence our spirits only are fit to receive him and close with him. Thousands hear Christ outwardly, that inwardly are deaf to all God's calls ; their spirits see not, taste not, feel not ; it is, therefore, the soul that is the subject of faith ; and I say it is a humble, empty soul which is the subject, for a full, proud, broken spirit can not, nay, will not, receive Christ, as we have proved ; and therefore (Luke xiv.) the servant is commanded to bid the " poor, halt, and blind, and lame to come in ; " they would not make excuses as others did ; they that were stung to death with fiery serpents were the only men that the brazen serpent was lifted up for them to look upon, and to be healed, (John iii. 14 ;) and therefore the promise doth not run, " If any man have wisdom, let him ask it ; " but, " If any man want wisdom," (Lam. i. 5 ;) so, if any man want light, life, want peace, pardon, want Christ and his Spirit, let them ask, and the Lord will give. Away with your money, if you come to these waters to buy, and take freely. " If any man would be wise, let him be a fool," (saith the blessed apostle,) an empty nothing. A soul, in a perishing, helpless, hopeless condition, is the subject of faith ; such only feel their need of Christ, are glad at the offer of Christ, and therefore such only can and will receive Christ, and come unto Christ by faith ; and truly, if we had

but hearts, the consideration of this might be ground of great comfort and confidence unto all God's people whose souls come unto
Jesus Christ, for that which was in Thomas (John xxi.) is in all
men naturally, — if we could see Christ with our eyes, and feel
him with our hands, and embrace him (as Mary did) with our
arms, if we could hear himself speak, we could then believe ; as
they said, " If he will come from the cross," so we say, If he
will come down from heaven thus unto us, we will then believe ;
if we want this, we fear we may be at last deceived, because we
want sense, and can not come to close with our eyes and hands
the objects of our faith. But O, consider this point : we are
made partakers of Christ's life and salvation by him only, yet
certainly by faith. Now, this faith is not by seeing him with our
eyes, coming near to him with our bodies, but coming to him
with our souls ; the soul is the seat of faith. Now, this you may
do, though you never thus saw him, " whom though you see not,
yet believing you rejoice." This coming of the soul to Christ
doth make a firmer union between thee and Christ than if thou
wert bodily present with him in heaven ; for many touched and
crowded him that never were truly united to him, or received
virtue from him. If our souls were in the third heaven with
Christ, who of us would then doubt of our portion in him ? I tell
you, if our souls go out of sin and self unto Christ Jesus, and
there rest, this makes you nearer to him than if your souls were
under his wing in the highest heavens. The poor seaman, when
he is near dangerous shores, when he can not go down to the
depth of the sea to fasten his ship, yet if he can cast his anchor
twenty or forty fathom deep, and if that holds, this quiets him
in the sorest storms. When we are tossed and can not come to
Christ with our bodily presence, yet if our souls can come, if
our faith, our anchor, can reach him, and knit us to him, this
should exceedingly comfort our hearts.

How and where should my soul come to Christ, who is now
absent from me ?

Christ comes to you in his word and covenant of grace ; there
is his Spirit, his truth, goodness, love, faithfulness ; receive this,
you receive him ; embrace this, you embrace him. As among
ourselves, you see great estates are conveyed and surrendered
by bonds and writings. (Acts ii. 41,) When they received the
word they received Christ. (John xv. 7,) " If my words abide
in you," i. e., if I abide in you by my words, you shall be fruitful.

By the word let thine eye pitch upon the person. Do not
only account the promise true, but, with Sarah, account him
faithful who hath promised : and then let thy heart roll itself

upon that grace and faithfulness revealed in this word, lean upon the breast of this beloved; and thus the soul, by the chariot wheels and wings of the word, is professor of Christ in it, and carried up to Christ's cross, as dying, (Gal. iii. 1,) and from thence to his glory in his kingdom by it. (Heb. x. 19–21.) As a man that gives a great estate, by some writing, to us, we believe it as if he were present; and by this we do not only believe the writing to be true, but the man to be faithful and loving to us; and hereupon our hearts are carried after the man himself, though afar off from us. Thus we ascend to Christ in the cloud of faith; as Jacob, though he could hardly believe, yet as soon as he was persuaded Joseph was yet alive, his spirit presently revived, and it was immediately with him, before his body came to him. So it is with faith: the soul goes unto Christ before our bodies and souls, both together, shall have immediate communion with him.

3. The form of faith.

This is the third thing in the description of faith: the coming of the whole soul out of itself unto Christ is the form of faith, and that wherein the life and essence of it consists, and which doth difference, is from all other graces of the Spirit. The first act of faith, as it unites us to Christ, is not assurance that he is mine, but a coming to him with assurance, and hereby he is become mine. "Come unto the waters," and "so buy wine and milk;" i. e., now make them your own. The "weary and heavy laden" shall not have rest unless they come to Christ for it. Faith doth nothing for life, — for that is the law of works, — it only receives him who hath done all for it, it comes out of all it hath or doth — like Abraham, that left his servants behind him when he went up to God in the mount — unto Christ for life. Conceive it thus. Adam had a principle and stock of life in himself, in his own hand, and therefore was to live by this, to live of himself and from himself, and therefore had no need nor use of faith. He lived by the law of works, which the apostle sets in a direct opposition to the law of faith; but Adam, being now fallen, hath lost his life, and become, not like the man that fell among thieves, betwixt Jerusalem and Jericho, stripped, wounded, and half dead, but wholly dead. (Eph. ii. 1.) So that, let any man seek life from himself, it is impossible he should live; for, if there had been a law that could have given life, our righteousness should have been thereby. (Gal. iii. 21.) Hence it follows, if any man will have life, he must go out of himself to another, viz., the Lord of life, for it. (John v. 40; vi. 27–29.)

Now, observe it, this very coming, this very motion of the soul to Christ — a grace which Adam neither had, nor had power to use — is faith ; the Spirit of Christ moving or drawing the soul, the soul is thence moved, and comes to Christ. (John vi. 64, 65.) The soul, by sin, is averted from God, and turns his back upon God ; the turning or coming of the soul (not unto duties of holiness, for that is obedience properly, but) unto God, in Christ again, is properly and formally faith. All evil is in man's self, and from himself; all man's good is in Christ and from Christ. The souls of all God's elect, seeing these things, forsake and renounce themselves, in whom and from whom is all their evil, and come unto Christ, in whom and from whom is all their good. This motion of the soul between these extremes, throughout that vast and infinite distance that is between a sinful, wretched man and a blessed Saviour, is faith ; for by faith, principally, we " pass from death to life." (John v. 24.) The soul of a poor sinner, wounded and humbled, sometimes knows not Christ, and then cries out, as those, Acts ii. 37, What shall I do ? Whither shall I go ? sometimes dares not, sometimes can not ; it hath no heart to stir or come ; it therefore looks up, and longs, and goes unto the Lord to draw it, like poor Ephraim. (Jer. xxxi. 18.) " O, turn me, Lord, and then I shall be turned," (Lam. v. 21;) and this is the lowest and least degree of faith. But at some other time, the soul mourning for wnnt of the Lord, the Lord comes unto it with great clearness, glory, and sweetness of grace and peace ; and hence the soul can not but come and close with him, and cry, Rabboni, and say, O Lord, it is thy good pleasure to have respect to such a clod of earth, to tender such riches of grace to one so unworthy, and to bid, nay, to beseech me to come and take. Lord, behold, I come. This is faith. Would you have a proof of it ? Consider, therefore, these particulars; 1. Consider these Scriptures: (John vi. 35,) " I am the bread of life; he that cometh to me shall never hunger, and he that believeth in me shall never thirst ; " where you see coming to Christ and believing in Christ all are one. So, (John vii. 37,) " In the last day of the feast, the Lord Christ cries out with much vehemency, If any man thirst, let him come unto me and drink." Now, in the next verse, (38,) our Saviour expounds this coming; for saith he, " He that believeth on me, out of his belly," etc.

So to come to Christ, as upon this to drink in of Christ's fullness, is believing in Christ. So (Heb. xi. 6) the apostle saith, " Without faith it is impossible to please God ; " and then, in rendering the reason of this, explains what he meant by faith, viz., to be our coming unto God upon a double testimony, believing first that he is, secondly, that he is a rewarder of them that seek him diligently, or (which is all one) who do come unto him. So, (John i. 12,) " So many as received him," (which is all one with coming,) " he adopted them as sons, even to them that believe in his name." And hence we shall observe, that the Scripture doth not attribute our righteousness and life to our believing of Christ, but to our believing on Christ, in Christ, (a phrase peculiar to heavenly language, and therefore not found in any human writer,) because it is not the bare believing of a testimony that saveth us, unless we so believe it as to believe in Christ, which can not be but by coming to him, and as it were in him, or into him, our union with Christ being made complete hereby.

2. That upon which the Lord promiseth life, and salvation, and mercy, can not be works, but faith, (Gal. iii. 21 ; Heb. xi. 6 ;) but throughout all the Old and New Testament, the Lord promiseth life and salvation to comers, or to them that return. (Jer. iii. 12. Ex. xxxiii. 10. Joel ii. 12, 13. Heb. vii. 25. John v. 40.)

3. If unbelief be nothing else but a departing from God, faith can be nothing else but a coming unto God ; but that is the nature of unbelief. (Heb. iii. 12 ; x. 38. John vi. 64–69 ; xii. 37–40.) The Lord's great plot is to gather all his elect under the wings of Christ, (Matt. xxiii. 37 ; Eph. i. 9, 10,) and therefore calls them to come under them, by the voice of the gospel. The coming under them, therefore, can be nothing else but faith, the proper obedience to the gospel, as works are under the voice of the law. Thus faith is the coming of the soul to Christ. But you will say, Did not many come to Christ that were never saved by him?

Yes, many came to him with their bodily presence, that were excluded from him. (John vi. 36.)

But you will say, Do not many men's souls come, are not many men's hearts moving, toward Christ, and yet excluded from Christ? Do not many cry, Lord, Lord? are not many enlightened, and taste of this heavenly gift, and yet fall away? I confess it is very true ; and therefore it is set down in this description of faith, that it is the coming of the whole soul unto Christ. Never did any yet come to Christ, and receive him with their whole souls, with all their hearts, but they had fruition of him, and blessedness by him. Faith, therefore, is not the coming of the soul, but the coming of the whole soul unto Jesus Christ, and this you may be established in upon these grounds.

1. The Scripture expressly calls for this : (Prov. iii. 5,) " Trust in the Lord with all thy heart." (Acts viii. 37,) "If thou believest with thy heart, thou shalt be saved." (Joel ii. 13,)

"Turn unto the Lord with all your hearts." (Jer. xxix. 13,) "You shall find the Lord when you seek him with your whole hearts." As when we have a great gift to bestow, and we ask a poor man to whom we intend to give it, whether he will accept of it or no : Yes, saith he, with all my heart: so it is here; the Lord asks those he intends to bestow his Son upon, and saith to them, You have lived thus long without him, and thus long abused him; will you now have him and accept of him? Yes, Lord, with all my heart. This is all the Lord requires. Doth the Lord require no more of me but to come? Lord, this voice is most sweet; I come with all my heart, I come.

2. Because Christ is worthy of the whole heart; all must be sold away to buy this field, this treasure. (Matt. xiii. 44,) "He that loveth father or mother more than me is not worthy of me." A filthy lust, a base harlot hath had thy whole heart, and dost thou think the Lord Christ will have it divided? is not one heart too little for him? are not ten thousand souls too few to embrace him, or cleave to him? 3. Because without this your coming to him is but feigned. (Jer. iii. 10,) "They return to me, not with their whole heart, but feignedly." To cleave to Christ and a lust, to Christ and a proud heart, can not be unfeigned faith; to go to your lusts in time of peace, and fly to Christ in times of extremity, is damnable hypocrisy. When conscience troubles you, you then go to Christ to ease you; and when your unruly wills and lusts trouble you, you go to the world to ease you; and so your hearts are divided, and you come not wholly and only unto Christ for rest. Believe it, it is such a faith by which you may, as Samuel did on Saul's garment, take hold of him, but the Lord will never take hold of you. Set a branch in the stock, if it stays loosely in it, it will wither in time; and this is the great cause of withering Christians, and of so many apostates in these evil times. Those that came to Christ, (John vi.,) and followed him for a time, but afterward fell away, (ver. 66,) what was the reason of their fall? viz., when they were offended at Christ, they knew whether to go from Christ; but what saith Peter? "Lord, whither should we go?" (ver. 68.) If you lay the pipes that are to convey water from a full fountain, but one foot or one inch short of it, there can not be any water derived from thence. O beloved, what is the reason that many a man's faith doth him no good, derives no life, spirit, blood, efficacy, peace, power, from the Lord Jesus? Is it because Christ is a dry Christ, and un-willing to communicate? No, no; the wound is in their faith; that pipe is laid but half way to him, they fall one foot short of him, their souls come, but their whole souls do not come to him,

and hence they never reach Christ; they lie not in Christ, and therefore receive not from Christ; Christ is precious, (here their souls come,) but not exceeding precious ; preciousness itself, as the word is, (1 Pet. ii. 7,) (here the whole soul doth not come;) they cleave to Christ and rest upon Christ, (here their souls come,) but they cleave not to Christ only, (thus their whole souls do not come.) 4. If the whole soul by unbelief departs from God, then the whole soul must return and come again unto God.

5. If the want of this be the great cause why men are rejected of God, then the whole soul must return to him ; but this is the cause why all men under the means are rejected of God. " Israel would none of me," i. e., would not be content alone with me, would not " take quiet contentment in me," (as the Hebrew word signifies;) the Lord was not good enough for them; but their hearts went out from him to other things, and therefore " the Lord gave them up to their own hearts' lust, and they walked in their own counsels." The woman that forsakes the guide of her youth, and sets her heart as much upon other men as her husband, is an adulteress, for which only she shall have a bill of divorce.

6. Because, as the gospel first reveals Christ to the mind, and then offers him to the will, so faith, which runs parallel with the gospel, first sees Christ, (there the mind, one part of the soul, goes out,) then receives Christ gladly, (there the other part, the will, goes out,) and so the whole soul comes to Christ. The gospel comes to all the elect, first in great clearness and evidence of the truth of it, (1 Thess. i. 5,) to which the understanding assents, and is persuaded of; secondly, in great grace and goodness, surpassing beauty and sweetness, (Lam. iii. 24,) with which the will is drawn, and so the whole soul comes unto Christ ; for the gospel is not only true, but glad tidings to all the elect, especially when humbled at God's feet, (1 Tim. i. 15,) " in whom," saith the apostle, (Eph. i. 12, 13,) " you believed after that ye heard the word of truth," (there is the object of the understanding,) " the gospel of your salvation," (there is the goodness of it, the object of the will,) so that the whole soul is drawn to Christ in the work of faith. He that understands how *liberum arbitrium* may be in two faculties, must not wonder if one grace be seated in both faculties of understanding and will ; no grace can be completely seated in divers faculties, but gradually and imperfectly it may : the work of faith is not complete, when the understanding is opened only to see and wonder at the mystery of mercy in the gospel; but when the will adheres and clasps about that infinite and

surpassing good it sees, then it is perfected, and not before. (John vi. 40.) And this is the reason why saving faith (as it is called) doth not look only to a bare testimony and assent unto it, as human faith doth; because, in the gospel, not only divine truth is propounded to the mind to assent unto, but an infinite and eternal good is offered to the heart and will of man to embrace, and thence it is that it is not sufficient for a Christian to believe God or to believe Christ, but he must also believe in him, or else he can not be saved; the object of believing of him being *verum*, or truth; the object of the second, *bonum*, or good: take heed, therefore, a poor, lost sinner, undone in its own eyes forever; not knowing what to do, unless it be to lie down, and lie still at God's feet, as worthy of nothing but hell. What doth the Lord now do? the Lord Christ, by his gospel, first lets in a new light, and it sees the Lord Jesus there bleeding before its eyes, and held forth as a propitiation to all that believe, to all that come to him; the mind sees this mystery, this exceeding rich grace and free mercy, and thinks, Happy are they that share in this mercy? but will the Lord look upon such a nothing as I? can such infinite treasures be my portion? The Lord, therefore, calls, and bids him come away and enter into the possession of it. Thy sins, indeed, are great, saith the Lord; yet remember bloodthirsty Manasseh, persecuting Paul, were pardoned. Nay, remember my grace is free, for whose sake I invite thee. I beseech thee to come in; thy wants indeed are many; yet remember that thou hast, therefore, the more need and more cause to come, and that it is I that have made thee empty and poor on purpose, that thou mightest come: it is true, I have an eternal purpose to exclude many thousands from mercy, yet my purpose is unchangeable, never to cast off any that do come for it; I never did it yet, I will not do it unto thee, if thou dost come; it is true, many may presume, yet it is no presumption, but duty, to obey my great command; and it is the greatest sin that ever thou didst or canst commit, now to reject it, and refuse this grace: come, therefore, poor, weary, lost, undone creature. Hereupon the heart and will come, and rest, and roll themselves upon these bowels, and there rest; thus the whole soul comes, and this, I say again, is faith. Just as it is with the loadstone drawing the iron; who would think that iron should be drawn by it? but there is a secret virtue coming from the stone which draws it, and so it comes and is united to it; so who would think that ever such an iron, heavy, earthy heart should be drawn unto Christ? yet the

Lord lets out a secret virtue of truth and sweetness from himself, which draws the soul to Christ, and so it comes.

May not the consideration of this be of great consolation to those that want assurance, and therefore think they have no faith ? O, remember that if thou comest unto Christ, as that poor woman of Canaan, — she had no assurance she should be helped of Christ; nay, Christ tells her to her teeth, that he would not cast children's bread to such dogs ; yet she came to him, and looked up to free mercy, and clasped about him, and would not away. You will say, Was this faith ? yes, our Saviour himself professeth it before men and angels, " O, great is thy faith." (Matt. xv. 28.)

So I say unto all you poor creatures whom the Lord hath humbled, and made vile in your own eyes, unworthy of children's bread as dogs; yea, you look up unto and rest upon mercy with your whole heart ; this is precious faith in the account of Christ.

But how shall I know when the whole soul comes to Christ?

When the eye of the soul so sees Christ, and the heart so embraceth and resteth upon Christ, as that it resteth in Christ, as in its portion and all-sufficient good : many rest upon Christ that do not rest in him ; that is, that are not abundantly satisfied with him ; and hence their souls go out of Christ to other things to perfect their rest, and so their hearts are divided between Christ and other things. O, "fear" this, saith the apostle, (Heb. iv. 1,) " lest, there being a promise left us of entering into his rest, any of you fall short of it ; " for (saith he) " we that have believed do enter into rest." (ver. 3.) So say I to you : of all delusions, fear this, lest, when you come to Christ, and rest upon Christ for life and salvation, that you rest not in Christ. " I tell you," saith Christ to those that came to him, and were constant followers of him, (John vi. 53,) "except you eat the flesh and drink the blood of the Son of God, you have no life in you." What is this eating and drinking? verily, sipping and tasting is not properly eating and drinking ; tasting your meat will not satisfy you, and therefore will not nourish life in you. To eat and drink Christ is to receive him, as to satiate and satisfy the soul with him, to quench all your desires, your hungering and thirsting in him, until thy soul saith, as he said in another case, " It is enough that Joseph lives ; " so, Lord, I have enough now I have this love, this grace of Christ to be my portion ; now you rest in Christ. For if there be some great good a man enjoys, if there be any good wanting in it, it is not possible that his whole heart should be set upon it ; ex. gr., a man hath food, but if he wants clothes, and his bread will not clothe him, his

whole heart will not be set upon his food, but upon that which
may clothe him also ; so, on the contrary, if there be an eminent
good, wherein he finds all in one, no good out of it that is wanting in it, it is certain that the whole soul is carried after this
good ; so it is here, when the soul so comes to Christ, as that it
comes for all good to him, and so finds all good in him, that he
now only supports the sinking soul, verily the whole soul is now
come, because, as it felt before it came all wants and evils out of
him, so now it finds all fullness in him ; and whither should the
whole soul be carried but after such a good ? when the Lord calls
to the soul to come and take all with nothing, take all or nothing.
And hereupon it comes and drinks, as it is John vii. 37, satisfying itself there, and professing, Lord, I now desire no more ; I
have enough.   O brethren, what faith there is among men at this
day I can not tell, but this I am sure was Abraham's faith, (Gen.
xvii. 1,) and David's faith, (2 Sam. xxiii. 5,) and Peter's faith,
(John vi. 68,) and Paul's faith, (Phil. iii. 8, 9.   Gal. vi. 14.)
When the soul thus rests upon the rock Christ, the gates of hell
may avail, but never prevail against such a one : he that hath
set the whole world at his heels, and sold himself out of all for
this pearl, and this abundantly recompenseth all his losses, such a
one hath Christ his own, and shall never be deprived of him
again ; the Lord never gives his elect any rest out of Christ,
that they may find rest at last in Christ.   When thus the soul
is entered into rest, the whole soul is drawn here, and this is the
great reason why many men famous in their generations and
times in the eyes of others for faith, yet rotten at the heart, and
thence turn apostates, one proves covetous, another ambitious,
another voluptuous, another grows conceited, another grows contentious, another grows formal.   What is the reason of this ?
Verily, they did rest upon Christ, but did never find rest in
Christ, and therefore their whole soul never came to him ; Christ,
after some time of profession, grew a dry and common Christ
unto them, though at first they wondered at him, and he was
very sweet unto them ; and hence they departed from him as
from an empty, dry pit in summer time, where they found nothing to refresh them.   But the Lord Jesus carries it toward all
the faithful as Elkanah did toward Hannah ; though she was in
a fit, much vexed and troubled for want of children, yet because
he loved her exceeding dearly, he quiets her again with this :
"Am not I better unto thee than ten sons ?"   So, though they may
be unquiet for some odd fits for want of many things, yet because
Christ loves them, he brings them back unto their rest, saying,
Am not I better than all friends, all creatures, all abilities, all

spiritual created excellences? and hereby they find rest to their souls in him again.

But is there any believer's heart so knit unto Christ but that there is a heart also after other vanities? Do they find such rest in him as that they find no disquietness? Is there not an unregenerate part and much unbelief remaining? Is any man's faith made perfect that the whole soul must come, or else there is no true faith?

It is true, there is an unregenerate and a regenerate part in a godly man, but not a heart and a heart, (the note of a wicked man in Scripture phrase.) There are disquietings in the hearts of saints, after that they be in Christ; even Solomon himself may sometimes seek out of Christ for rest in his orchards and gardens, knowledge and wisdom; yet there is a great difference between these that are in the saints, arising from the unregenerate part, and those that be in the wicked, arising from a heart and a heart, or a double heart; and this difference is chiefly seen in two things.

A double-minded man, who hath a double heart, makes not a daily war against that heart which carries him away from resting only in Christ; for Christ quiets his conscience, and the world comforts his heart; Christ gives him some rest; and because this is not full, his heart runs out to the creature and to his lusts for more; and so between them both he hath rest, and he is quieted with this, because he feels what he sought for; and therefore he must needs have Christ, else his conscience can not be quiet; and he must needs have his lusts, his ease, and this world too, else his heart is most unquiet; but let him have both, he is now quiet. (Micah iii. 11.) The priests teach for hire, (there the world quiets them,) yet they will lean upon the Lord too, because this also comforts them; what do they do? do they make war against this woful frame? No, no, but bless themselves in it, saying, "No evil shall come to us." But a poor believer, whose heart is upright, it is true there are many runnings out of his heart after other vanities, and much unquietness of spirit, yet the regenerate part makes war against these, as God's enemies and the disturbers of the peace of Christ's kingdom. (Ps. xlii.) David professeth his tears were his meat day and night, (ver. 3,) and his heart was wofully sunk and fallen; yet what doth he? First he chides himself: "Why art thou cast down, O my soul?" And then, secondly, he makes his moan to the Lord of it, (ver. 5, 6,) "Lord, my soul is cast down; O Lord, pity me." You shall see, also, (Ps. lxxiii. 2,) his eyes were dazzled with the glory of the world and the wicked in it,

18*

that he had almost forsaken God ; yet within a little while after he gets into the sanctuary of God, and then loathes himself for such brutish and foolish thoughts, and loseth with God again, saying, " Whom have I in heaven or earth but thee ? " (ver. 25.) All the outrunnings of the hearts of the faithful, and their disquietness of spirit thereby, make them to return to their rest again, and give them the more rest in the conclusion. David was a bird out of his nest for a time, and therefore when he considered how the Lord had saved his eyes from tears, his soul from hell, returns again, and saith, " Return to thy rest, O my soul." Ps. xxv. 13, it is said, " his soul shall dwell at ease," or (as the word signifies) " shall lodge in goodness ; " some hard work, full of trouble, some strong lust, or sad temptation, desertion, affliction, the Lord exerciseth the soul withal for some time ; and so long as the soul is in heaviness and much weariness of spirit, as it is 1 Pet. i. 6, yet when this day's work is done, when the sin is subdued, and the temptation hath humbled him, then a believer's soul shall lodge in goodness ; he shall have an easy bed and soft pillow to rest on at night. When have the faithful sweeter naps in Christ's bosom than after sorest troubles, longest eclipses of God's pleased face ? when do their souls cleave closer to the Lord than when they are ready to forsake the Lord, and the Lord them ? Certainly fire is wholly carried upward, when that which suppresseth it makes it at last break out into greater flame. Peter falls from Christ ; yet he is *Peter*, a stone cleaving most close unto Christ, above all other the apostles, because, his fall being greater, his faith clave the closer to the Lord Christ forever after it. Solomon's heart certainly never clave so unseparably unto the Lord as after his fall, wherein he did more experimentally find and feel the emptiness and vanity of those things wherein he did imagine before something was to be found ; but he that hath a double heart never enters into rest, but the longer he lives, the more common Christ, his truth, and promises grow ; they are but fading flowers, whose beauty and sweetness affect him for a time ; but they wither before the sunset. And, therefore, the longer he lives, the less favor he finds in these things, and therefore takes less contentment therein ; the Lord Jesus and all his ordinances grow more flat and dry things to him ; and therefore, though at first he might rejoice (as John's hearers, John v. 35) in these burning and shining lights, yet it is but for a season ; at last he discovers himself — not by a renewed returning to his rest, but by a wearyish forsaking of it.

The raven never returned to the ark again, because it could

live upon the floating carrion on the waters; whereas the dove, finding no rest there, returns again.

Fourthly, the end of faith.

This is the fourth particular in the description of faith: The whole soul cometh to Christ, for Christ and all his benefits; and this is the end of faith, or of a believer's coming unto Christ. The end of faith is sometimes expressed by a general word, *life*, (John v. 40,) but you must remember that hereby is meant the Lord of life first, and so all the blessings of life. The falseness and hypocrisy of Christ's followers appeared in this, (John vi. 26:) You seek me, saith Christ, for loaves; that was their end; as many a one in these days, if they be in outward misery, seek unto Christ for outward mercy; corn in time of famine, health in time of sickness, peace upon any terms in time of war; and if they be in any inward distress, now they seek to Christ for comfort and quiet; and so, like many sick patients, desire the physician, not to have him married to them, but for some of his physic only, to be healed by him. But what saith our Saviour to these persons? (ver. 27,) "Labor not for the meat that perisheth;" what should be the end of their labor then? he tells them, "but for that bread that endures to everlasting life." What is this bread? (see the 33d, 35th, and 48th verses:) he tells them, "I am the bread of life;" seek for me therefore, come for me; and look, as none can have life from the bread, unless he first feed upon the bread itself, so none can have any life or benefit from Christ that comes not first to Christ for Christ. Conceive of this thus: God in Christ is the complete object of faith under a double notion. First, as sufficient, in being all we want unto us; secondly, as efficient, in communicating all to us, and doing all for us. In the first respect, he is Elshaddai in his promise; in the second respect, he is Jehovah, (Ex. vi. 3,) in making good his all-sufficient promise. Hence faith comes to him for a double end: first, that he would give himself and be all to it; secondly, that he would communicate all his blessings and the benefits also, and so do all for it. For in the covenant of grace, the Lord doth not only promise a new heart, pardon of sin, with the rest of those spiritual benefits, but also himself: "I will be their God, and they shall be my people." Hence faith comes first for that which the Lord principally promiseth, viz., God himself, and then for all the rest of those heavenly and glorious benefits; and hence it is, if any man come for Christ himself, without his benefits, and regard not the conveyance of them, as the Familists at this day do, who abolish all inherent graces, and some of them all ordinances, because Christ is all to them;

or if any come for the benefits of Christ without Christ himself, as many among ourselves do, who never account themselves happy in him, but only by some abilities they receive from him ; neither of these come with a single eye, nor fix a right end in their closing with Christ: you must first come for Christ himself, and so for all his benefits.

For establishing your hearts in which truth, consider these things : —

1. Consider what drives any man to Christ. Is not sense of wants no main thing ? Now, what are a Christian's wants, when the Lord hath humbled him ? Are they not, first, want of Christ; and secondly, of all the benefits of Christ? viz., righteousness, peace, pardon, grace, glory. (John xvi. 9.) If, therefore, the souls of all the elect feel a want of both, doth not faith come to Christ for both ? (John iv. 10,) " If thou knewest the gift of God," (i. e., the worth of him, and thy want of him,) " thou wouldest ask, and he would give thee water of life."

2. What doth the Lord offer in the gospel? Is it not first Christ himself, and then all the benefits of Christ ? (Is. ix. 6, 7,) " To us a Son is born, to us a Son is given ; " in the receiving therefore of Christ by faith, what should the soul aim at, but that it may have the Son himself, and so all his benefits with him ?

3. Can any man have eternal life that not only hath not the benefits flowing from the Son, but that wants the Son himself? I am sure the apostle expressly affirms it ; (1 John v. 12,) " He that hath the Son hath life, he that hath not the Son hath not life : " faith therefore must come for Christ himself: as in marriage the woman consents first to have the man, and so to have all other benefits that will necessarily follow upon this.

4. The happiness of all the saints consists in two things : first, union to Christ; secondly, communion with Christ. Faith, therefore, pitcheth first upon Christ himself, that it may have sure and certain union to him, (for our union is not unto any of the benefits flowing to us from Christ ; we are not united unto forgiveness of sins, nor peace of conscience, nor holinesss, etc., but unto the person of the Son of God himself ;) and then, secondly, cometh for the communication of all the benefits arising only from union ; as Paul (Phil. iii. 9, 10) esteems " things dung and loss," first, " to be found in him, that so he might have his righteousness " in justification, " and feel the power of his death and resurrection " in sanctification, etc. In one word, faith first buys the pearl itself, and then seeks to be enriched by it ; it finds the treasure of grace, glory, peace, mercy, favor, reconciliation, in Christ;

but then buys the field itself, that it may have the treasure also. (Matt. xiii. 44.) The Lord Christ's great desire is, that "all his might be with him to see his glory," (John xxiv. 14;) and faith desires first to have him and be forever with him, and so to partake of that glory: the Lord's great plot is, first to perfect the saints in Christ; (Col. ii. 10,) "ye are complete in him;" then to make them like to Christ by communicating life, grace, peace, glory from him. (Col. iii. 3, 4. 1 John iii. 1, 2.) Faith, therefore, first quiets itself in him, then seeks for life from him; it comes first for Christ, and then for all the benefits of Christ.

O that this truth were well considered! How would it discover abundance of rotten, counterfeit faith in the world; some seeking for peace and comfort, and catching at promises without seeking first to have the person of Christ himself, "in whom only all the promises are yea and amen." Others despising the benefits of Christ, especially grace, holiness, and life from him; because, say they, Christ is all in all to them. Ask them, Have you any grace, change of heart, etc.? Tush! what do you tell them of repentance, and faith, and holiness? They have Christ, and that is sufficient; they have the substance, what should they do now with shadows of ordinances, ministries, or sacraments? They have all graces in Christ; why should they look either for being of, or evidence from, any grace inherent in themselves? They have a living holy head, but Christ's body, they say, is a dry skeleton, a dead carcass, and they are but dry bones; and is it so indeed? Then look that God should shortly bury thee out of his sight; assuredly, you that want and despise the benefits coming from him, shall never have part nor portion in him at the great day of account. Christ is a Saviour to save men from their sins, not to save men and their sins; Christ is king and priest of his church, "holy and separated from sins," (Heb. vii. 26;) and if you have any part or portion in him, he hath made you kings and priests also to God and his Father, and hath not left you in your pollution, but washed you from it in his own blood. (Rev. i. 5, 6.) The law of God is written on the heart of Christ, (Ps. xl. 8, with Heb. x. 5–7;) and if ever he wraps you up in the covenant of grace, he will write his law in your hearts also. (Heb. viii. 10.)

Let all deluded Familists tremble at this, that, in advancing Christ himself, and free grace, abolish and despise those heavenly benefits which flow from him unto all the elect. Let others also mourn over themselves, that have with much affliction been seeking after Christ's benefits, peace of conscience, holiness of heart and life, promises to assure them of eternal glory, but have not sought first to embrace and have the person of the Lord Jesus himself.

O, come, come therefore unto the Lord Jesus for Christ himself, and for all his benefits ; I say for all his benefits. This is that which the apostle prays for with bended knees for the Ephesians, that they might — not take in a little, but — comprehend the height, depth, length, breadth of Christ's love, that so they might be filled with all the fullness of God. This is that which our Saviour expressly with much vehemency calls for; (John vii. 37,) " Let all that thirst come unto me and drink ; " not sip and taste a little, as reprobates and apostates do, (Heb. vi. 4, 5,) but drink, and drink abundantly, as it is. (Cant. v. 1.) And observe it, that upon these very terms the Lord tenders grace and mercy. (Rom. v. 17.) The apostle doth not say, They that receive a little, but abundance of grace, shall reign by righteousness unto eternal life. " Open thy mouth wide, and I will fill it." (Ps. lxxxi. 11, 12.) And most certainly this is one principal difference between the faith of the elect and the reprobates, — and if I mistake not, the principal, — the elect close with Christ for that end, for which the Father offers him, which is, that they might possess his Son, and all his benefits, and therefore come poor and empty for all ; the reprobate come not for all, but for so much and no more than will serve their own turn; in misery they would have Christ to deliver them ; but what care they for spiritual mercies ? In trouble of conscience, or after their soul falls into filthy lusts and sins, they come to Christ to forgive them and comfort them ; but what care they for holiness and a new nature ? Some sins they would have Christ save them from, but they regard not redemption from all. They can not come to Christ, that all the powers of darkness may be perfectly subdued, that their own sins, and selves, conceits, and wills, may be led away captive by this mighty conqueror; that Christ, in all his authority, grace, peace, life, glory, might be forever advanced in them and by them. It was Austin's complaint in his time of many of his hearers, that *Christum assequi*, to have Christ, was pleasing to them; but *sequi Christum,* to follow Christ, this was heavy. To close with Christ's person is sweet to many; but to close with his will, and to come to him that he would give them a heart to lie under it, this benefit they desire not. All Christ is useless and needless ; but something from Christ is precious to them ; for the Lord Jesus' sake, beloved, take heed of this delusion. If any thing hath been bought for us at a dear rate, and cost much ; if the man should offer to hold any part of it back, we will not abate him any thing, we will have it all because it cost dear. I tell you pardon of sin, peace with God, the adoption of sons, the spirit of grace, perseverance to the end, the kingdom of glory, the riches of mercy, have been bought for you by a dear and great price, the precious blood of Christ; and therefore, if the justice of God should hold back any thing, or thy own belief tell thee these are too great and many for so vile a creature as thou art to enjoy, yet abate the Lord nothing; say thou art vile, yet Christ's blood, that bought not some, but all these, is very precious, and therefore take them all to thyself, as thy portion forever, and "bless the Lord," as David doth, (Ps. xvi. 7,) "that gave thee this counsel." Whiles you are in peace, it may be you may neglect so great salvation; but the time of distress and anguish may come, wherein you may feel a need of all, even of those hidden depths of mercy above your reach and reason; and therefore, as bees, gather in your honey in summer time, and, with Joseph, lay up in these times of plenty, wherein the exceeding riches of grace is opened and poured out at your heels for those times of approaching famine, and for those many years of spiritual desertion and distress; wherein you may think, Can it stand with the honor of God to save such a poor sinful creature as I am? What iron heart is not drawn by this love, for the Lord to invite you to possess all or nothing? Dives, in hell, was desirous of a drop to cool his tongue; and behold the very depths and seas of grace are opened for thee to come in and partake of, if the Lord Jesus should be offered unto thee to pardon some sins, but not all; to pardon all sins, but not to heal thy nature also; or to heal some backslidings, but not all; to supply thy spiritual wants, but not outward also, as may be best for thee; or to supply outward, but not inward and spiritual; if he should offer to do thee good in this life, but not in death nor after death, you might refuse to come in; but when all is offered, all that mercy which no eye ever saw to pity thee; all that love wherewith Abraham, David, Paul, etc., were embraced; now to refuse to come up and possess these, how can you escape the sorest vengeance of a jealous God, that neglect so great salvation? O Lord! what extremity of anguish and bitterness wilt thou one day be in, when the contempt of this grace, gowing upon thy conscience, shall press thee down with these thoughts: I am now under all misery, but I might have had all God's grace, all Christ's glory; but, wretch that I am, I would not. Methinks, if your own good hereby should not draw you, yet the exceeding great glory the Lord shall have thereby should force you to accept all this grace; for, if thou didst receive a little grace, believe a little mercy toward thee, this makes thee sometimes exceeding thankful; doth it not? And the very hope of more makes thy heart break forth into a holy boasting and glorying in Christ: "Who is a God like unto thee?" Suppose therefore you drank in all, and received all, that which the Lord freely offers, should not the Lord be exceedingly magnified then? Couldest thou contain thyself then without crying out, "O Lord, now let thy servant depart in peace, for mine eyes have seen" (and my soul has now possession of) "thy salvation"? Wouldest not call to the hills, and seas, and earth, and heavens, and saints, and angels, to break forth into glorious praises, and bless this God?

But what have I to do to come, that am so poor, and empty, and full of woes, and wants, and sins? Never was any so miserable, and blind, and naked, as I.

If faith cometh for all to Christ, and fetcheth all from him, then never be discouraged because thou hast nothing to begin unto him; let all thy wants and miseries be arguments and motives therefore to come unto him. (Rev. iii. 17, 18,) "Because thou art poor and naked," nay, because thou "knowest it not," and art not affected with it, therefore come unto me, and "buy eye salve, and gold, and white raiment." "Lord, pardon my sin," saith David, "because it is great; have mercy upon me, for I am consumed with grief, and am in trouble. Let mercy and truth continually preserve me, for innumerable evils have compassed me round about. Let us return unto the Lord, because he hath wounded us." I am a dog, therefore let me have crumbs, said the woman of Canaan. O, this is cross to sense and reason, and we can not believe, while we are so exceeding poor, empty, vile, that the Lord should look upon us; but, beloved, you little think what wrong you do to yourselves and the Lord Jesus hereby: for by this means Christ is not so much exalted, nor the creature humbled, — both which, concurring in faith, make those acts of faith most precious, — for while you stand upon something, and would have something to bring to Christ, you hereby exalt yourselves; but when you come with sense of nothing else but woes and wants, and see Christ now making of you welcome, O, this is not only mercy, but ravishing mercy. If you should come with sense of somewhat to Christ, and to see his love to you, you might glorify mercy in the height, and length, and breadth of it, but not in the depth of it; unless you see it reaching its hand to you, when you are fallen into so low and poor a condition as nothingness, and emptiness, and misery itself. And therefore do not come to Christ only for the benefits of the covenant, but for the condition of it also.

When you feel a want of faith itself, as Hezekiah did, (Is. xxxviii. 14,) "Lord, I am oppressed, undertake for me," (1 Kings viii. 57, 58,) do not undertake to fulfil any part of the covenant, or any condition in it, or any duty required of thee, of thyself, but go empty to Christ, and say as David, "Lord, I will run the ways of thy salvation, if thou wilt set my heart at liberty." (Ps. cxix. 32, 33.) "Quicken me, and I will call upon thy name." (Ps. lxxx. 18.) Be strong in the Lord, and the power of his might, but not of thine own.

But I come for all, and am never a whit the better, but as poor and miserable still as ever I was.

If the Lord keeps you poor and low, yet the same motive that made thee come, let it make thee stay ; it may be the Lord sees thou wouldest grow full and lifted up if he should give thee a little, and therefore keeps thee low; better be humble than full and proud. "Let us go unto the Lord, because he hath wounded, broken, and slain us." But they might object, We do come, but find no help, no cure. It may be so ; yet it is said, "After two days he will revive us, and the third day we shall live in his sight, and we shall know him, if we shall follow on to know him." (ver. 6.) His goings forth are prepared as the morning ; it may be night for a time, but the Sun of righteousness will arise gradually and gloriously upon thy soul.

Truly, brethren, when I see the curse of God upon many Christians that are now grown full of their parts, gifts, peace, comforts, abilities, duties, I stand adoring the riches of the Lord's mercy to a little handful of poor believers, not only in making them empty, but in keeping of them so all their days ; and therefore come to the Lord, poor, empty, naked, nothing, cursed in the sense of thy want of all things, for all things, and then receive with gladness, yet boldness and holy confidence, not only pardon of some sins, but of all. Believe, answer not to some prayers, but all; embrace in thy bosom not some few promises, but all. It is a great ease of conscience. When may a Christian take a promise without presumption as spoken to him, and given to him in particular? And the rule is very sweet, but certain: when he takes all the Scripture and embraceth it as spoken unto him, he may then take any particular proper promise boldly. My meaning is, when a Christian takes hold and wrestles with God for the accomplishment of all the promises of the New Testament; when he sets all the commands before him, as his rule, and compass, and guide to walk after; when he applies all the threatenings to drive him nearer unto Christ the end of them, — this no hypocrite can do, this the saints should do, and by this may know when the Lord speaks in any particular to them. Go, I say again, therefore unto the Lord for all, and in the sense of all your emptiness be abundantly comforted ; that, though you do not find supply from Christ, yet you come unto the Lord Christ for it. It is a certain rule, you shall not always want that good which you come to Christ to supply, nor always be mastered with that sin which you come to Christ with, to take away ; only then be sure you come for all, otherwise you do not come truly. Come first for Christ himself, and then (as I said) for all his benefits.

To conclude: this is the direct and compendious way of living by faith, so much urged and pressed of God's servants ; for to live by faith properly is to live upon the promise in the want of the thing, or to apprehend the thing in the promise. (Heb. xi. 1.) Now, the promises are not given to the elect immediately, without Christ, but first Christ is given, i. e., offered in the gospel and received by faith, and then with him all things also ; and therefore the Scripture runs thus, (Is. lv. 1–4 :) " Come unto the waters and drink, and then I will make an everlasting covenant," (which contains all the promises,) " even the sure mercies of David." The apostle expressly disputes the case, and saith, " Where there is a testament," (containing evangelical promises,) " there must first be the death of the testator," (Heb. ix. 15, 16,) to whom we must first " come by faith," before we can have right to any promise. (Heb. vii. 22–25, and 10, 16–18, 22.) " Being justified by faith," now " we have peace with God ; " nay, " we have access to God ; " nay, now " we are of sure standing," now " we hope in and glory to come," (Rom. v. 1–4 :) all follow the first.

How shall a Christian, therefore, live by faith ? Truly, first receive Christ and come to him for the end I mention ; and then thou mayest be sure all other things shall be given to thee. As for example: dost want any temporal blessing ? — suppose it be payment of debts, thy daily bread, provision for thy family, a comfortable yoke-fellow, etc., — look now through the Scripture for promises of these things, and let thy faith act thus : If God hath given me Christ, the greatest blessing, then certainly he will give me all these smaller matters as may be good for me ; but the Lord hath given me Christ, and therefore I shall not want. (Ps. xxiii. 1.) " The Lord is my shepherd," saith David ; what follows ? " I shall not want." There is the like reason in all other things, — suppose it be in care of protection from enemies, — if the Lord hath given me Christ to save me from hell, then he will save me from these fleshly enemies much more. You shall see (Is. vii.) a promise given that "Syria should not prevail against Judah;" they doubted of this. How doth the Lord seek to assure them? You shall see, (ver. 14,) it is by promising "a virgin shall conceive and bear a son, and his name shall be Immanuel;" this is a strange reason; yet you may see the reason of it if you consider this point. So, (Is. ix. 5, 6,) "The oppressor's rod shall be broken. For unto us a Son is born, a Son is given. By faith they put to flight the armies of aliens, brake down the walls of Jericho, did wonders in the world." What did they chiefly look to in this their faith? You shall see, (Heb. xi. 39, 40,) it was by respecting the promise to come, and the better thing, Christ Jesus himself, which we now see with open face, and therefore he concludes, (Heb. xii. 1–3,) "Having such a cloud of witnesses," that thus lived and died by faith, "let us look unto Jesus, the Author and Finisher of ours." The prophet Habakkuk (Hab. ii. 5) affirms that the "just shall live by faith." What faith is that? Consult with the place, you shall see it was in the promise of deliverance from the Chaldean tyranny; yet the apostle Paul applies it to faith in Christ's righteousness, and that truly, because if their faith had not respected Christ himself, in the first place, they could never have expected any deliverance by the promise of deliverance from the Chaldeans; but thus they might.

5. The special ground of faith.

The last thing in the description of faith is, that the soul thus comes upon the call of Christ in his word; and this is the special ground of faith, wherefore the soul comes to Christ. Take a sinner humbled and broken for sin, he can not prevent the Lord by coming of himself unto Christ, and therefore the Lord prevents him, by his gracious call and invitation to come in. "Whom God hath predestinated, them hath he called." Our translation from darkness into God's marvelous light is by being called. The soul is lost in humiliation; the Lord Jesus, who is come to save that which is lost, seeketh it out in vocation, or calling. Sanctification is the restoring of us to the image of God we once had in Adam, as corruption is the defacing of that image; vocation is the calling of the soul unto Christ: this voice Adam never heard of; he did not need any call to come to Christ, and therefore was immediately sanctified, as soon as he was made: but we need vocation unto Christ, before we can be sanctified by Christ; we need this call to make us come to Christ, to put us into Christ, and therefore much more before we can receive any holiness from Christ; the ground of our coming by faith is God's call: (2 Thess. ii. 13, 14,) "Chosen to salvation through sanctification," (the remote end of vocation,) "and belief of the truth," (the next end of it,) "whereunto he hath called you:" there is the ground of it.

The explication of this call is a point full of many spiritual difficulties, but of singular use and comfort to them that are faithful and called. I shall omit many things, and explicate only those things which serve our purpose here in these three particulars:—

1. I shall show you what this call is, or the nature of it.

2. The necessity of it.

3. How it is a ground. of coming, and what kind of ground for faith.

1. The nature of this call I shall open for your more distinct understanding in several propositions, or theses. Our vocation or calling is ever by some word or voice, either outward or inward, or both; either ordinary or extraordinary; by the ministry of men, or by immediate visions and inspirations of God. I speak not now of extraordinary call, by dreams and visions, and immediate inspirations, as in Abraham and others, before the Scriptures were penned and published; nor of extraordinary call, by the immediate voice of Christ, as in Paul and in some other of the apostles; for these are ceased now, (Heb. i. 1,) unless it be among people that want ordinary means, and elect infants, etc., whose call must be more than by ordinary means, because they want such means; we speak now of ordinary call by the ministry of men.

2. This voice in ordinary calling home of the elect to Christ is not by the voice of the law, (for the proper end of that is to reveal sin and death, and to cast down a sinner,) but by the voice of the gospel bringing glad tidings; written by the apostles, and preached to the world. "He hath called you by our gospel. These things are written that you might believe. By the foolishness of preaching, the Lord saveth them that believe." I mean preaching at the first or second rebound, by lively voice, or printed sermons at the time of hearing, or in the time of deep meditation, concerning things heard; the Spirit indeed inwardly accompanies the voice of the gospel, but no man's call is by the immediate voice of the Spirit without the gospel, or the immediate testimony of the Spirit breathed out of free grace without the word. (Eph. i. 12, 13.) And therefore that a Christian should be immediately called without the Scripture, and the Scripture only given to confirm God's immediate promise, as a prince gives his letter to confirm his promise made to a man before, (as Valdesso would have it,) is both a false and a dangerous assertion.

3. This voice of the gospel is the voice of God in Christ, or the voice of Jesus Christ, although dispensed by men, who are but weak instruments for this mighty work, sent and set in Christ's stead; but the call, the voice, is Christ's; it is the Lord's call. (Rom. i. 6.) It is certain some of the messengers of Christ called the Romans by the gospel; yet Paul saith, "They were called by Christ Jesus; the dead hear his voice, and arise, and live;" and when the time of calling comes, they listen to it as his call: and hence it is styled, (Heb. iii. 1,) because the Lord Christ from heaven speaks, takes the written word in his own lips, as it were, (Cant. i. 1, 2,) and thereby pierceth through the ears, to the heart, through all the noise of fears, sorrows, objections against believing, and makes it to be heard as his voice; the bowels of Christ now yearn towards a humbled, lost sinner, bleeding at his feet, therefore can contain no longer, but speaks, and calls, and makes the soul understand his voice: so that this call is not a mean business, because the Lord Jesus himself now speaks, whose voice is glorious.

4. The substance of this call, or the thing the Lord calls unto, is to come unto him: for there is a more common calling (or, as some term it, a particular calling) of men, as some to be masters or servants, (1 Cor. vii. 20, 21, 24,) or to office in church or commonwealth, as Aaron, (Heb. v. 4;) and the voice there is to attend unto their work to which they are called. There is also a remote end of vocation, which is to holiness, (1 Thess. iv. 7,) and unto glory also, (2 Thess. ii. 14; Phil. iii. 14;) but we now speak of more special calling, the next end of which is to come unto Christ; the soul hath lived many years without him, the Lord Jesus will now have the lost prodigal to come home, to come to him; the soul is weary and heavy laden, and the Lord Jesus would easily ease it without its coming to him: but this is his will; he must come to him for it: (Matt. xi. 27 ; Jer. iii. 7, 22,) "I said, after she had done these things, Turn unto me, come unto me, ye backsliding children; I will heal your backslidings." (Jer. iv. 1,) "If thou returnest, return unto me." This voice, " Come unto me," is one of the sweetest words that Christ can speak, or man can hear, full of majesty, mercy, grace, and peace; a poor sinner thinks, Will the Lord ever put up such wrongs I have offered him, heal such a nature, take such a viper into his bosom, do any thing for me? If there be but one in the world to be forsaken, is it not I ? The Lord therefore comes and calls, " Come unto me, and I will pardon all thy sins, I will heal all thy backslidings, I will be angry no more." (Jer. iii. 12, 13.) " Though thou hast committed whoredom with many lovers, yet return unto

me, saith the Lord.” (Jer. iii. 1.) Though thou hast resisted my
Spirit, refused my grace, wearied me with thine iniquities, yet
come unto me, and this will make me amends; I require nothing
of thee else but to come: for God’s call is out of free grace,
(Gal. i. 6,) and therefore calls for no more, but only to come up
and possess the Lord’s fullness. (Luke xiv. 17. 1 Cor. i. 9.)

5. This call to come is for substance all one with the offer of
Christ, which consists in three things : —

1. Commandment to receive Christ as present and ready to
be given to it ; as when we offer any thing to one another, it is
by commanding them to take it. (1 John iv. 23.) And this binds
conscience to believe, as you will answer for the contempt of this
rich grace at the great day of account.

2. Persuasion and entreaty to come and receive what we
offer ; for in such an offer, wherein the person is unwilling to
receive, and we are exceedingly desirous to give, we then persuade ; so doth Christ with us.

3. Promise ; to offer a thing without a promise of having it,
if we receive it, is but a mock offer ; and hence you shall find in
Scripture some promise ever annexed unto God’s offer, which is
the ground of faith. (Jer. xxii.)

6. This call or offer hath three special qualifications. First, it
is inward as well as outward ; for the Lord calls thousands outwardly, who yet never come, because they want an inward call to
come; an inward, whispering, still voice of God’s Spirit; and
therefore it is said, “ He that hath heard and learned ” (not of man
only, but) “of the Father cometh unto me.” (John vi. 45.) The
Lord doth not stand at the outward door only, and call to open,
but the Lord Jesus comes in ; he comes near unto the very heart
of a poor sinner, and makes that understand, (Hos. ii. 14 ;) and
the Lord makes his grace glorious, and his mercy sweet unto the
hearts of his elect. Look, (saith the Lord Jesus,) how I have
left thousand thousands in the world, and have had greater cause
so to have left thee ; but behold, I am come unto thee ; O, come
thou unto me.

2. It is a particular call ; for there is a general call and offer of
grace to every one. Now, though this be a means to make it
particular, yet the Spirit of Christ, which is wont to apply generals unto particulars particularly, makes the call particular, that
the soul sees that the Lord in special means me, singles out me
in special to believe ; otherwise the souls of the elect will not be
much moved with the call of God, so long as they think the Lord
offers no more mercy to me than to any reprobate ; and therefore the Spirit of Christ makes the call particular. (Is. xliii. 1.)

" I have called thee by name." (John x. 5,) " He calleth all his
sheep by name ; " not that the Lord calls any by their Christian
name, (as we say,) as the Lord did extraordinarily call Samuel,
Samuel, and Paul, Paul ;. but the meaning is, look, as the Lord
from before all worlds writ down their name in the book of life,
and loves them in special, so in vocation, (the first opening of
election,) the Lord makes his offer and call special, and so special
as if it were by name ; for the soul at this instant feels such a
special stirring of the Spirit upon it, which it feels now, and
never felt before ; as also its particular case so spoken unto, and
its particular objections so answered, and the grievousness of its
sin in refusing grace so particularly applied, as if God, the only
Searcher of hearts, only spake unto it ; and so dares not but think
and believe that the Lord meaneth me.

3. It is effectual as well as inward and particular. (Luke xxiv.
33.) " Compel them to come in." (John x. 16.) Christ's other
sheep shall hear Christ's voice, and those he must bring home ;
for every inward call is not effectual. There came a man in
without his wedding garment, (Matt. xxii. 6–8 ;) whence our
Saviour saith, "Many are called, but few chosen ; " but this I now
speak of, as a calling out of purpose, (Rom. viii. 28 ;) and
therefore never leaves the soul until it hath real possession of
Christ, and rests there. This call falls upon a sinner humbled,
not hard hearted ; and hence the call is effectual. (Matt. ix. 12,
13. 2 Chron. xxx. 10, 11.) It is such a call as was in creation.
(Rom. iv. 17.) And hence the soul can not but come, and when
it is come it can not depart, like Peter, " Lord, whither should we
go ? " And therefore, though it hath never so many objections
in coming to Christ, never so much weakness or heartlessness to
close with Christ, yet the Lord brings it home, and there keeps
it ; and now it infinitely blesseth God that ever the Lord gave it
an eye to see, a heart to come and seek after Jesus Christ.
Thus much of the nature of this call : now follows the necessity
of it, which appears in these three particulars : —

1. No man should come unless first called ; as it is in calling
to an ordinary office, so it is in our calling much more unto
special grace. The apostle saith, (Heb. v. 4,) that " no man
takes this honor but he that is called of God ; " so what hath
any man to do with Christ, to make himself a son of God, and
heir of glory thereby, but he that is called of God ? What have
we to do to take other men's goods, unless called thereto ? What
have we to do to take the riches of grace and peace, if not called
thereto ? It is presumption to take Christ whilst uncalled, but not
when you are called thereunto.

2. Because no man would come without the Lord's call. (Matt. xx. 6, 7,) " Why stand you here all the day idle ? " The answer was, " No man hath hired," or " called us thereto." When there is an outward call only, yet men will not come in. (Matt. xxiii. 37.) And therefore there must be an effectual call to bring men home. (Is. lv. 5.) And therefore you shall see many ; let there be a legal command, suppose to sanctify a Sabbath, or to speak the truth ; they have no objections against obedience unto this. But press them to believe, show them God's call for it, they have more fears and objections rising against this than there be hairs on their head, because the soul would not close with this.

3. Because no man could come, unless called. (John vi. 44.) " No man can come unto me, unless the Father draw him." And how doth the Father draw any man, but by this call ? If the Lord should not come and speak himself, and make his call the most joyful tidings and the sweetest message that ever came to it, it would say, I have no heart, I can not, I am not able, for (Rom. ii. 32) " we are shut up under unbelief ; " and therefore the Lord Jesus (Luke xv. 5) must bring his sheep home upon his shoulders, else it will lie in the wilderness of its own droopings ; whereas, when the Lord effectually speaks, the soul can not but come. Lastly, how this call is a ground of faith, and what ground of faith. For answer hereunto, I do make this call, considered without the promise, the ground on which faith rests, (for that is God's free grace in the promise,) but the ground by which it rests, or wherefore it rests upon the promise. The mind sees, (1.) The freeness of mercy to a poor sinner in misery ; and this breeds some hope the Lord may pity it. (2.) The fullness and plenteous riches of mercy ; and this gives very great encouragement to the soul to think, The Lord (if I come to him) surely will not deny me a drop. (Ps. cxxx. 7, 8.) The prodigal comes home because of bread enough in his father's house, though he was not certain he should have any. (3.) The preciousness and sweetness of mercy make the soul long vehemently for it, (Ps. xxxvi. 6, 7,) and makes it set all other things at a low rate to enjoy it ; but when unto all this the Lord sends a special commandment, and a special message on purpose, and calls it to come in and accept of it, and take mercy as its own, and that for no other reason but because it is commanded and called to accept of it, this puts an end unto all doubts, all fears, all discouragements, and the soul answers as those, (Jer. iii. 22,) " Behold, we come ; thou art the Lord our God." As a man in great want of bread, one comes and freely offers him bread to preserve his

life; the man takes it; if you ask him, Why do you take it? you are a poor fellow unworthy of it, never did yet one hour's work for it, he answers, It is true, I am unworthy; but yet because it is offered to me to preserve life, I gladly take it: the man doth not promise absolutely to me that this bread is mine, and shall feed me; but he tells me, if I do receive it, it shall certainly be mine to feed me. And this is the main ground of his receiving of it. Just so it is in faith. Ask a humbled sinner, Why do you believe? Why do you take Christ as your own? Hath the Lord said absolutely that he is yours? No, saith the soul, but the Lord freely offers himself unto me, who am undone without him, and saith, if I do receive him, he shall be forever mine, to give life to me; and therefore I thankfully accept of him: this is the ground of faith. The Scripture sets out this in a lively similitude of a great supper, to which many were invited. What was the ground of their coming to it? Behold, all things are ready if you come and eat; they are not yours if you do not come; but if you come at my call and invitation, then all things shall be yours. And hence it is that they that came not were excluded; they that came were received with welcome.

I know it is a question of some difficulty among some, viz., whether an absolute testimony of actual favor and justification be not the first ground of faith. They that make faith to be an absolute assurance of God's favor must of necessity maintain this assertion, and then those things will follow.

1. That a Christian must be justified before he believe; for the cause of faith must go before faith.

This proposition, "thou art justified, reconciled," is, according to this assertion, the cause of faith; for no proposition can therefore be true because we are persuaded that it is true, but it must be first true before I am persuaded of it; the wall is not white because my eyes see it so, but it must first be white, and then I see it so. Now, to make actual justification before faith, is cross to the whole current of Scripture. We believe that we might be justified, (Gal. ii. 16;) we are not justified that we might believe. We pass from death to life by faith, (John v. 24;) we are not in a state of life before faith. When the Lord Jesus saw their faith, (Matt. ix. 2,) he then said, "Be of good comfort; thy sins are forgiven thee." The word saith, "He that believeth not is condemned already," (John iii. 18,) and therefore (unless the Spirit's witness be cross to the word) it doth not say to one that believeth not, that he is absolved already. To be justified by faith, and to be justified by Christ's righteousness, is all one in the

Scripture's phrase and meaning. (Gal. ii. 16, 17.) And therefore we may as well say that we are justified before and without
Christ, as before and without faith. And, indeed, this doctrine
of being justified by faith, and by this means to have remission
of sins, the apostle Peter affirms to be the doctrine of all the
prophets. (Acts x. 43.) To him give all the prophets witness,
that whosoever believe in him shall receive remission of sins ; not
that they had remission of sins before they did believe. I know
not any one Protestant writer that maintains our justification
before and without faith, except learned Chamier, who not knowing how to avoid the blow of Bellarmine's horned argument,'that
if faith be an assurance of our actual justification, then we are
first justified before we believe, he affirms we are justified before
faith ; and therefore, that when the Scripture saith we are justified by faith, the reason of that (saith he) is not because our
faith doth *efficere justificationem*, i. e., is a cause (meaning instrumental) of our justification ; but because *efficitur in justificato*,
i. e., is wrought in a justified person ; but if that be the reason of
the phrase, we may affirm our justification to be as well by love,
and sanctification, and holy obedience, as by faith, because these
are wrought in a justified person also.

Then no man's ministry, nor the doctrine delivered by the
faithful ministers of Christ from out of the Scriptures, can be
any ground of faith, for before faith, no minister of Christ can
say to any man in particular, or any men in general, that they
are already justified and reconciled, and therefore believe it ;
but to deny that doctrine which is opened out of the Scriptures
by the ministers of Christ to be the ground of faith, is expressly
cross to the testimony of the Scriptures, and the end of the ministry, and of the messengers of Christ, who have the keys of office
given to them, that what they bind on earth is bound in heaven ;
what they loose on earth is loosed in heaven ; whose sins they remit, they are forgiven ; whose sins they retain, they are retained.
(Matt. xvi. 16. John xx. 23.) Most excellent for this purpose
is the apostle's dispute, (Rom. x.) "You need not go up'to
heaven, nor down to hell, to fetch Christ himself to tell you
whether you shall be justified and saved," (ver. 6, 7,) "for the
word is nigh them," (ver. 8,) that opens Christ's heart unto thy
heart. But what word, might some say, is this ? Is it not the
internal word of the Spirit only? The apostle answers, "It is
that word which we preach;" hereby you shall know whether
you shall live or no. But what is that word Paul preached ?
Is it not an absolute testimony that all your sins are already
pardoned by Christ, and therefore believe it ? No ; but if thou

believest with thine heart that God raised up Christ from the dead, thou shalt be saved. (ver. 9, 11, 12.) What can be more full? Yet consider that one place more, (John xvii. 20,) "I pray for all them that shall believe on me, through their word." What is the ground or means of believing in Christ? It is said here expressly, "their word." Is it not the word of Christ, rather than the word of the apostles and of their successors, in the doctrine they delivered? Is it their word? Truly, that which they delivered was the word of Christ, and that which is opened from their doctrine in the Scriptures is the word of Christ, yet as they open it and apply it, so it is their word; and this word is the ground by which all that Christ prays for do believe in Christ; the bare word I grant can not persuade without the Spirit, yet the Spirit will not give ground of faith without the word, but as by it, so upon it, will build the souls of all the elect, who are built upon the foundation of the apostles and prophets, "Jesus Christ being the chief corner stone." (Eph. ii. 20.) "How can they believe without a preacher?" (Rom. x. 14.)

3. Then when wicked men and reprobates are commanded to believe, (as they are commanded, John iii. 19; Luke xiv. 17. John vi. 38; Heb. iv. 2,) they are commanded to believe a lie, viz., that their sins are pardoned and they actually justified; for if this testimony be the ground of faith, then when they are commanded to believe, they are commanded to be persuaded of this testimony. But the sins of wicked men, especially repro-bates, are not, nor never shall be, forgiven; and therefore this can not be the ground of faith. 4. When the Spirit of adoption, which witnesseth that God is our Father, and that we are his sons reconciled to him, goes before faith; but the apostle express-ly denies this, "Ye are the children of God by faith," (Gal. iii. 26,) "and because ye are sons, he hath sent unto you the spirit of sons, crying Abba, Father." (Gal. iv. 6.)

5. If such a testimony should be the first ground of faith, then no man should believe but he that hath such a testimony antece-dent to his faith; but this is to cross the Scripture. (Is. l. 10,) "He that sits in darkness, and sees no light, let him stay himself upon his God." When Jonah is cast out of God's sight to his own feeling, yet he is bound to look again unto the temple.

6. This absolute testimony is either the testimony of the word, or of the Spirit. Not of the word, as is proved; if of the Spirit, then let it be considered, whether that can be the testimony of the Spirit which is not according to the word; nay, contrary to the word, for the word to say none are justified before faith; for the Spirit to testify some are justified before faith. If it be said,

that the Spirit doth not witness these to any man before and without faith, but yet it is without respect unto, or showing a man his faith, — for those that exclude sanctification from being any evidence, they mean faith as well as any other renewed work of holiness, and so exclude that also, — then I say the testimony of the Spirit (which of itself is exceeding clear) is an obscure and dark testimony ; because it clears up the predicate of this proposition, " Thou believer art justified." It witnesseth to a man, " thou art justified ; " but clears not up the subject of it, viz., " thou believer." It makes a man believe a testimony without understanding the full meaning of it ; for the Spirit, testifying to any man " thou art justified," his meaning is, " thou believer art justified." And I do beseech the God and Father of all lights, that his poor people may be led into the truth in this particular. For want of establishment here, you little think how many delusions you may fall into about your spiritual condition. I remember, that when Satan came to overthrow the faith of Christ, in his second temptation, (Matt. iv. 6,) he brought a promise out of the Scriptures to him, because he saw he held close to them, (ver. 4 ;) and by this promise sought to lead him into temptation. How so ? Observe the text, and see if it was not by hiding part of the meaning of the promise from him ; and in special, that very condition required in the person to whom the promise is made ; for he tells him, that if he " cast himself down headlong, the Lord hath not" only said it, but "writ it, He shall give his angels charge over him, to keep him from dashing his foot against a stone ; " whereas if you consult with the place whence it is cited, viz., Ps. xci. 11, the condition is set down, " in all thy ways," which he purposely hides from our Saviour, as much as in him lay. O, take heed therefore of receiving any testimony from word or Spirit without the meaning of it ; without knowing the person thus and thus qualified, to whom it belongs ; otherwise, Satan will hurry you headlong to a world of delusions ; and you shall find the word of God, appointed to direct you, (through your misapplication of it,) the word of Satan, to deceive and damn you. Do not think that this is building faith upon works ; but to believe that they that believe in Christ are justified, reconciled, and saved, is building faith upon God's promise ; yea, and his free promise too : for saith the apostle, " It is of faith that it might be of grace." (Rom. iv. 16.) It is believing to have the end by the means, not the end without the means of faith. It is true, we may see God's favor and love to us in the cause as well as in the effects of sanctification ; but what is that cause ? The meritorious cause is

Christ's righteousness, and the instrumental cause of applying this is our faith ; so that we are justified by faith. So, seeing this, we may say assuredly, with Paul, " Being justified by faith, we have peace with God." (Rom. v. 1.) It is true, we can not see our justification by faith, nor the work of faith without the shining of the Spirit into our hearts ; but the question is, not whether the Spirit helps us to see our justified estate, but by what means, by what proposition in the word, we come to see it, which we may say is not by any such absolute testimony. Thou art justified already, and therefore believe ; but if thou believe and come to Christ, here is then pardon of sin, peace with God ; yea, all the blessings of Christ ready for thee, which God intends to give and never to take away, if thou thankfully receive what God freely offers, and as it were lays down at thy feet. The call of Christ, therefore, is the ground by which we first believe ; and that you may be confirmed further herein, do but consider the glory and excellency of this ground.

It is a constant ground of faith, for if you come to Christ because you have assurance, or because you feel such and such graces, and heavenly impressions of God's Spirit in you, you may then many a day and year keep at a distance from Christ, and live without Christ ; for the feeling of graces, and assurance of favor, are not constant ; but this call is always sounding in thine ears, " O, come," not only because thou feelest holiness in thee, but come, because poor, hungry, empty, naked, lost, blind, cursed, forsaken, full of sin. There is not one moment of the day of grace but the Lord beseecheth thee to receive his grace, (2 Cor. vi. 1–3 ;) this is an open door to Christ at all times, an open harbor to put in at all storms, a heart-breaking word. O thou tossed with tempests and not comforted, come unto me and thou shalt find rest to thy soul. Many ask, How should I come to Christ, seeing that I have no promise belonging to me ? What have dogs to do with children's bread ? Be it so ; yet God's call, command, beseechings to come in, should be ground unto thee to come ; as a poor beggar, that hath no promise absolutely given him of relief, yet if a rich man sends to him, and bids him come to his door and wait, he thinks he hath good ground and warrant to come.

It is a sure ground against all fears, all doubts of presumption, all sense of unworthiness, and of the greatness of the good promised, etc. For the saints have many fears whereby they dare not come ; they fear they may presume, they see themselves most vile, and unworthy of the least smile ; the benefits are so exceeding great, to which they are called, that they think it is too good for them, etc. But, beloved, when the soul sees evidently, the Lord invites me, persuades me, commands me, waits for me, strives with me, that I would come in, and because his grace is free, therefore requires no more but only to "come and take, come and drink," this forceth the soul to confess, I am sure it is no presumption to obey the call of Christ; and what though I am unworthy, and this good is exceeding great and precious, yet if it be the Lord's grace to call such a poor wretch to receive and accept of it, why should not I rather thankfully receive it, than out of my own head superstitiously refuse it? But this I am sure and certain of, the Lord calls me thus to do. If God should speak from heaven to you to come to his Son, it is not so sure a ground as the call of God from out of the oracle of his word, and the blessed gospel of his dear Son.

It is a strong ground, and of great power and efficacy, to force the soul to come ; for you may object, No man can believe, or should believe, and come out of himself. I say so too; but how would you have the Spirit of Christ enable you to come? Verily, it is by this call; and therefore, (Jer. iii. 22,) when the Lord said, " Return, ye backsliding children," they presently answered, " Lord, we come ; the dead shall hear this voice of the Son of God, and live." (John v. 25.) " Thou saidst, Seek ye my face ; my heart answered, Lord, thy face will I seek." O, iron, stony, adamantine heart, that canst hear so sweet a voice as this word " come," and yet not be overcome !

This call honors grace most, for what more free than for the Lord to say, " Come, and take of the water of life freely "? what more free than for a rich man to inquire of his debtor only to receive so many thousands of him to pay his debts, and set him up again? Verily, brethren, as the Lord honors his grace by commanding us to come, so we honor it when, through the mighty power of the same call, we do come.

Thus much for explication of this call. Now let me put an end to it in a word of application.

Let this persuade all sorts of persons, young and old, one and another, to whom the gospel is sent, to come in to Jesus Christ ; for those that God calls should come : but the Lord calls (at least outwardly) all sorts of persons, nay, every individual person, to come in : (Mark xvi. 15, 16,) Paul told the stout jailer, " If thou believest, thou shalt be saved : " and look, as the law speaks particularly to every man, " Thou shalt have no other gods," etc., so doth the gospel, also, (Rom. x. 9,) that so every man might look upon himself as spoken to in particular. And, indeed, if there were not such a particular call, then men should not sin by refusing the gospel, nor should the Lord be angry for so doing, but their sin and condemnation is great that so do. (John iii. 19.) And the Lord is more wroth for this sin than any other. (Ps. ii. 12. Luke xiv. 18. Heb. iii. 10, 11, 19.) In one word, either the Lord would have thee (who ever thou art) to receive Christ or to reject, and so despise Christ; and if the Lord would have you reject him, he would then have you sin and continue in it, which can not stand either with the honor of God's holiness or of his rich grace. I shall here, therefore, open two things.

1. Set down means to enable you to come. 2. Show you how and in what manner you should come. The means.

1. Consider who it is that doth call you; is it man or ministers? think you; you might never come then; no, it is Jesus Christ himself that calls you by them. Why do many discouraged spirits refuse to come? It is because they think deceitful men or charitable men call them, but the Lord hath no respect unto them ; O, foolish conceit! I tell you their ministry is not an act of their charity, wishing well to the salvation of all; but it is an act of Christ's love and sovereign authority. (Matt. xviii. 18–20.) So that what they do, it is in Christ's stead, (2 Cor. v. 19, 20;) if Christ was present, he would call thee to him with more bowels than any compassionate minister can: and I assure you, to receive them is to receive Christ; to despise them is to despise Christ; (John xiii. 20;) and therefore, (Eph. ii. 14,) although the apostles preached to the Ephesians, yet it is said that Christ came and preached to them. "If any minister preacheth any other doctrine of grace than what Christ hath delivered, let him be accursed ;" but if they publish his mind and his call, look upon them as if the Lord himself called unto you, lest the Lord accurse you, and all their ministry to you; the Lord Jesus did not cast off the Jews for crucifying of him and shedding his blood, until the gospel of grace published by his messengers came to them, and that was rejected; and then Paul waxed bold, and said, "Because you put away the word from you, we leave you." (Acts xiii. 46.)

O beloved, if you did believe Christ called you poor prodigals (that have run riot, and sinned against him as much as you could) home unto him; suppose Christ was present, would it not draw you in? Suppose he was with thee in the chamber, where thou art crying after him, or in the church, where thou art waiting for him, and he should appear visibly before thine eyes, open his bosom, and bowels, and blood before thee, and calling unto thee to this purpose, I do beseech thee, and entreat thee, by all these tears I have shed for thee in the days of my flesh, by all those bitter agonies I have suffered for thee, by all these tender bowels which have been rolled together toward thee, come unto me, embrace me, lay thy wearied head in this blessed bosom of mine, crucify me no longer by thy sins, tread me not under foot by thy unbelief any more ; and I will pardon all thy sins, though as red as crimson, I will heal thy cursed nature, I will carry thee in my own bowels up to glory with me, where all sins, and tears, and sorrows shall be abolished, etc. ; who would not now come in to him? Let me see that man that hath a heart of adamant that would not melt and come in at this. O, my beloved, this very call is done as really by Christ in his ministry now, though not so visibly and immediately as I now describe; and, therefore, take heed how you refuse to hear him that "speaks from heaven." (Heb. xii. 25.)

Consider whom the Lord calls, and that is thee in particular, whoever thou art, to whom the gospel of Christ is sent; for if you think Christ calls some only, that are so and so deeply humbled only to come, and not unto you in particular, you will never come in; but we have proved this, that the Lord calls all in general, and consequently each man in particular: the consideration of this may bring you in. Men fear to commit murder and steal, etc., but you fear not unbelief; but the apostle bids you fear that, "for the gospel is preached' (saith he) " unto you, as well as unto those that fell by unbelief." (Heb. iv. 1, 2.) Do not say he calls me indeed, but it is no more than what he doth to reprobates; true, in the outward call it is so; yet upon this ground you may think the Lord commands not, calls not you to sanctify a Sabbath, or to honor God's name, because this is as common to reprobates as unto you; do not say, I am not able to come, and therefore I am not called; no more are you able to attend the rules of the moral law ; yet you look upon them as appertaining to you, and because you can not do them, you entreat the Lord to enable you, and so because you can not come, you should look up to the Lord to draw you : and verily, many times the great reason why the Lord doth not draw you is, because you do not deeply consider that he doth really and affectionately call you: do not say, I am a dry tree, the Lord can not look upon me, whose condition is worse than ever I heard or read of; yet remember what the Lord speaks to such. (Is. lxv. 3–7.) Look not thou to thy barren and dead heart, but give glory unto God, as Abraham did; (Rom. iv. 19, 20 ;) and receive his grace with more thankfulness than any else, because none ever so miserable as thyself. You young men, hear this ; though you have spent the flower of your years in vanity, madness, and filthy lusts, yet the Lord calls you in to him ; you old men, grown gray headed in wickedness, though it be the last hour of the day in your life, yet behold, the Lord would hire you, and calls you to come in, before the sorest wrath of a long-provoked God break out upon you ; you that have despised God's messengers, crucified the Lord Jesus afresh, imbrued your hands in his blood, scorned and hated the saints, and the word of God's grace, hear what wisdom saith, (Prov. i. 22, 23,) " Return, ye scorners." O, consider, thou that art ignorant of Christ, that never sought after Christ many a year together, that have " continnually provoked him to his face," how the Lord calls you, (Is. lxv. 1–3 ;) you, even you, are all those the Lord calls, and will you not come ? Consider why the Lord calls thee ; is it because he hath any need of you to honor him? I tell you he could have gone to others, that would have given his gospel better welcome than it hath had from you ; he could have gone to many kings and princes, and out of that golden metal have made himself vessels of honor, rather than out of such base mold as thou art made of ; he could have honored himself in thy ruin, as in many millions of other men, and lose nothing by thee neither ; he could have been blessed without you in the bosom of his Father ; or is it because thou hast done any thing for him ? Alas ! thou hast not returned him thy nutshells, thou hast not had so much as a form of religion, thou hast done as much mischief to him as thou couldest. (Jer. iii. 5.) Thou hast wearied him with thine iniquities, and made him serve with thy sins, and hath subdued his heart exceedingly by strong impenitency. (Is. xliii. 24.) The only reason that hath moved him to call upon thee hath been to pity thee, seeing thee running to the fire that never can be quenched, without stop or stay ; (2 Chron. xxxvi. 15, 16 ;) and "because thou art fallen by thine iniquities." (Hosea xiv. 1.) And shall this bring you home ?

Consider for what end the Lord calls thee. Is it not to come and take possession of all the " grace of Christ," (Gal. i. 6,) nay, of all the " glory of Christ," (1 Thess. ii. 12,) nay, to a most near, sweet, and everlasting "fellowship with Christ himself"? (1 Cor. i. 9.) And can I say any more ? Can you desire any more than this ? If the Lord should say unto any of us, Come into the garden, and there watch and pray with me, sorrow and suffer with me, who of us would not account ourselves unworthy of such honor ? But for the Lord to say, Come and enter into your rest ; the land, the kingdom of grace and glory, is before you, go up

20 *

and possess it; O, where are our hearts, if this call will not draw? If the Lord should say at the day of judgment, when the heavens and earth shall be on a light fire, and the Lord Jesus set upon the throne of his glory, admired of all his saints and angels, Come, you blessed, and take the kingdom prepared for you, would you not gladly come at that call? O beloved, the Lord Jesus now on the throne of his glory in heaven, behold he calls you unto a better good than that kingdom; he calls you to come and take himself and all his precious benefits prepared for you, though in thyself accursed; and would he have you take possession of all this? Is it "not the praise of the riches of his grace"? (Eph. i.) If this be his end, then if thou wilt not come for thy own good, yet for his sake, his grace' sake, come.

How long the Lord hath called thee! how oft he would have gathered thee! He hath stood so long, until "his locks are wet with dew of the night." (Cant. v. 1, 2.) It may be you are afraid, it hath been so long that now time is passed; O, no, for whilst the Lord calls by his word and spirit, "now is the acceptable time." (2 Cor. vi. 2.) I confess there is a time wherein the Lord will not be found; but whilst the Lord is near unto thee by his ministry, by his Spirit, convincing, affecting, stirring, knocking at thy heart, the time is not yet passed, the sun is not yet set; so long as those beams appear, (Is. lv. 6,) those thoughts which discourage thee from coming to Christ, whilst the voice of his call is heard, can not be of Christ, but Satan, whose principal work is to lay such stumbling blocks in our way to him.

Consider the greatness of your sin in not coming to him.

1. This is the condemning sin; for no sin should condemn thee, if thou didst "come to him;" (John iii. 17–19;) thou shouldest please him, and as it were make him amends for all the wrongs thou hast done him, by coming to him. (Heb. xi. 5–7.)

2. This aggravates all other sins. "If I had not spoke to them," (saith Christ,) "they had had no sin," i. e., comparatively; "but now they have no cloak for their sin." Can the sin of devils be so great as thine, that never had a Saviour sent unto them? Yet thou hast one sent and come out of heaven to thee, calling to thee from heaven, and yet thou despisest him.

3. This provokes the Lord to most unappeasable and unquenchable wrath. (Heb. iii. 11,) "I swore in my wrath they should not enter into my rest." After sins against the law, the Lord did not swear that man should die; (for that notes an unchangeable purpose;) but let Christ be despised, the Lord now swears in his wrath against such a one: "He that draws back, my soul shall take no pleasure in him." (Heb. x. 38.) After sin

against the law, the Lord took pleasure in glorifying his grace upon man fallen; but if you draw back from the grace of Christ in the gospel, the Lord will take no pleasure in you.

4. It provokes the sorest and most unsupportable wrath. "Take heed you despise not him that speaketh, for if they did not escape who refused him that spake on earth, much less shall we, that despise him that speaks from heaven." (Heb. xii. 25.) Take heed therefore you despise not him that speaketh. The word *despise* signifies in the original to despise or refuse upon some color of reason; every man hath some seeming reason against believing: one thinks time is past; another thinks he is excluded by some antecedent decree of election; another thinks he is not humbled, nor holy enough; another makes excuse, not by pretending his alehouse and whorehouse, but his farm and merchandise, (Matt. xxii;) another thinks he is well enough without Christ, etc. O, take heed, for the wrath of God most intolerable is your portion; the lowest dungeon of darkness is thy place in hell for this sin. "Hear, ye despisers," and wonder, "for I will work" (saith the Lord) "a work in your days, which you shall not believe though it be told you." (Acts xiii. 41.) I pray you what is this work? Certainly a work of wrath and vengeance; but what is it? You will not believe though you be told of it, O you secure sinners; but what is it that they will not believe? Nay, truly, the Lord himself is silent there, and saith nothing, as if it was so great and dreadful, that the glorious Lord himself is not able to express it; and truly no more am I. O, therefore, be not worse than that generation of vipers that came in to John, because some had "forewarned them to escape the wrath to come," (Matt. iii.,) but come unto a Saviour, that you may be ever blessed with him. But you will say, —

How should we come to him?

Come to him mourning, and loathing yourselves for your long continuance in refusing of him. (Jer. xxxi. 9. Ezek. vi. 9.) Come mourning for all thy sins, but especially for this, that thou hast slighted him, and not sought him, shed his blood, rent his bowels; and if thou canst not come, yet come to him and make thy moan to him of thy unbelief and inability to come.

Come with confidence that "they that do come he will never cast away," and that thou being come, he will never cast thee away. (John vi. 37. Heb. x. 22.)

Come gladly and willingly, glorifying his grace, but abasing thyself. "With gladness shall they be brought and enter into the king's presence." (Ps. xlv. 15.) Do not receive God's grace as a common thing, but thankfully, and with all thy heart; for the end why the Lord gives Christ to any man is the glory of his grace; if the Lord attains this end he desires no more, for why should he, when he hath his end?

Do not come and taste, but "come and drink." (John vii. 37.) You may famish to death, and pine away in your iniquities, and prove apostates, even to commit the impardonable sin, if you do but taste of him, as those did, Heb. vi. 4, 5; but "drink abundantly, O ye beloved of the Lord." (Cant. v. 1.) If you can not satisfy your souls by what you feel already received from him, then satiate your souls by what you may find in him. (Is. xlv. 24.) Take possession of all the grace, glory, peace, promises of the Lord Jesus, and leave not a hoof behind thee, and be forever refreshed and comforted therein   So come to him, as that " you keep your confidence," and keep your savor of him and joy in him, (Heb. iii. 14, with vi.) Let the word that called you be ever sweet and precious, as David said, (Ps. cxix. 53,) " I will never forget thy precepts, for by them thou hast quickened me." Let the Lord Jesus be ever fresh, (Heb. iii. 6,) and as " an ointment poured out;" take heed that the blood wherewith you are sanctified do not grow a common thing, and promises withered flowers, and sermons of Christ and his grace (unless there be some new notions about them) as dead drink, for this is the great sin of this age; the old truths about the grace of Christ and the simplicity of the gospel are as water in men's shoes; ministers must preach novelties, and make quintessential extracts out of the Scriptures, and it may be, press blood out of them sometimes rather than milk, or else their doctrines are too many as almanacs out of date, or as news they heard seven years since, and they knew this before. O, the wrath of God upon this God-glutted, Christ-glutted, gospel-glutted age; unless it be among a very few poor believers, whose souls are kept empty, poor, and hungry by some continual temptations or afflictions, and they are indeed glad of any thing, if it be any thing of Christ! Verily I am afraid such a dismal night is toward of spiritual desertions, and of outward, but sore afflictions of famine, war, blood, mortality, deaths of God's precious servants especially, that the Lord will fill the hearts of all churches, families, Christians, that shall be saved in those times, with such rendings, tearings, shakings, anguish of spirit, as scarce never more in the worst days of our forefathers; and that this shall continue, until the remnant that escape shall say, " Blessed is he that cometh in the name of the Lord;" blessed be the face and feet of that minister that shall come unto us in Christ's name, and tell us that there is a Saviour for sinners, and that he calls us for to come.

And thus I have done with this divine truth, viz., that the Lord Jesus, in the day of his power, saves us out of our wretched and sinful estate, by so much conviction as begets compunction, so much compunction as brings in humiliation, so much humiliation as makes us come to Christ by faith.

CHAPTER II.

THAT EVERY SINNER, THUS BELIEVING IN CHRIST, IS AT THAT IN-
STANT TRANSLATED INTO A MOST BLESSED AND HAPPY ESTATE.
— *John v.* 24. *Phil. ii. ult.*

IF the question be, What is that happy condition they are made partakers of?

I answer, this appears in these six privileges, or benefits, principally, —

1. Justification: all their sins are pardoned.
2. Reconciliation: peace with God.
3. Adoption: they are made the sons of God.
4. Sanctification: they are restored to the image of God.
5. Audience of all their prayers to God.
6. Glorification, in the kingdom of heaven, in eternal communion with God.

SECTION I.

Justification.

THIS is the first benefit which immediately follows our union unto Christ by faith, that, look, as we are no sooner children of Adam, and branches of that root by natural generation, but we immediately contract the guilt of his sin, and so original pollution, so we are no sooner made branches of the second Adam by vocation, and so united unto Christ by faith, but immediately we have the imputation of his righteousness to our justification; after which we receive in order of nature (not time) our sanctification. There is no truth more necessary to be known than this, it being the principal thing contained in the gospel, (Rom. i. 17,) the law showing how a man may be just and live; but it hath not the least word how a sinful man may be just and not die; this is proper to the revelation of the gospel; let me, therefore, give you a taste of the nature of it.

Our justification is wrought by a double act: 1. On God the Father's part; he, by a gracious sentence, absolves and acquits a sinner, and accepts of him as righteous. 2. On God the Son's part, procuring the passing of this sentence by his satisfaction imputed and applied. The Father, being the person principally wronged, hath chief power to forgive; yet in justice he can not acquit, nor in truth account a man unrighteous as righteous, unless the Son step in and satisfy, for whose sake he forgives, as the apostle expressly saith, (Eph. iv. ult.;) so that our justification is wholly out of ourselves, and we are merely passive in it. Justification is not to make us inwardly just, as the Papists dream, but it is a law term, and is opposed against condemnation. (Rom. viii. 33.) Now, look, as condemnation is the sentence of the judge condemning a man to die for his offences or sin, so justification is the sentence of God the Father, absolving a man from the guilt and punishment of sin, for the sake of the righteousness of Christ. That you may more particularly understand me, take this description of it: —

Justification is the gracious sentence of God the Father, whereby, for the satisfaction of Christ, apprehended by faith, and imputed to the faithful, he absolves them from the guilt and condemnation of all sin, and accepts them as perfectly righteous to eternal life.

Let us open the particulars herein briefly, in several queries, what it is, in general, to justify.

It is to pass sentence of absolution, to pronounce a sinner righteous; it is God's pardon, remission of sins. This appears from the opposition mentioned it stands in unto condemnation, as a judge pardons a man when he saith he shall live; or as a man manifestly forgives another when he gives him a promise or a bill of discharge; so that — note this by the way, that — our justification is not God's eternal purpose to forgive, but it is God's sentence published; a sinner is justified intentionally in election, but not actually, till this sentence be past and published. The difficulty only here is, where this sentence is pronounced; for answer whereof, note that there is but a double court where this is passed: 1. Publicly, in the court of heaven, or in the court rolls of the word; for there is no other court of heaven where God speaks but this. 2. Privately, in the court of conscience. By the first we are justified indeed from personal guilt; by the second we feel ourselves justified by the removal of conscience guilt. The first is expressly mentioned, (Acts x. 43, and Rom. i. 17;) the second is expressly set down also. (Ps. xxxii. 4.) The first is the cause and foundation of the second; the second ariseth from the first; otherwise, peace of conscience is a mere delusion. The first is sometimes long before the second, (Ps. lxxxviii. 15,) as the sentence of condemnation in the word is sometimes long before a man feels that sentence in his own conscience ; the second comes in a long time after in some Christians. The first is constant and unchangeable ; the second very changeable : he that hath peace in his conscience to-day, may lose it by to-morrow. So that you are not (in seeking the testimony of your justification) to look for a sentence from heaven immediately pronounced of God, but look for it in the court of his word, (the court of heaven,) which, though we hear not sometimes, yet it rings and fills heaven and earth with the sound of it, viz., " There is no condemnation to them that believe :" for hereby the Lord mercifully provideth for the peace of his people more abundantly. As when a poor creditor is acquitted, or a malefactor pardoned, I beseech you, (saith he,) let me have an acquittance, a discharge, a pardon under your own hand, and this quiets him against all accusers. So it is here ; the Lord gives us an acquittance in his word, under his own hand and seal, and so gives us peace. (Heb. vi. 18.)

Who is this that justifieth ?

It is " God the Father." (Rom. viii. 34.) " Father, forgive them," saith Christ. And hence, Christ " is an advocate with the Father." (1 John ii. 2.) All the three persons were wronged by sin ; yet the wrong was chiefly against the Father, because his manner of working appeared chiefly in creation, from the righteousness of which man fell by sin. The Father forgives primarily by sovereign authority ; the Son of man, Christ Jesus, forgives by immediate dispensation and commission from the Father, (John v. 22 ; Matt. ix. 6 ;) the apostles and their successors forgive ministerially. (John xxi. 23.) The Father forgives by granting pardon, the Son by procuring, the ministers (where the Spirit also is) by publishing or applying pardon ; so that this is great consolation, that God the Father, the party chiefly incensed, it is he that justifieth, it is he that passeth this gracious sentence ; and then who can condemn ?

Why doth the Father thus justify ?

It is merely his grace, and out of his grace. And hence I call it his " gracious sentence," (Rom. iii. 24 ;) " justified freely by his grace." What is his " grace " ? The prophet Isaiah expounds it to be, not our grace, or works of grace, (although wrought by grace,) but " his own name's sake." In some respect indeed it is just for God to forgive, viz., in regard of Christ's satisfaction. (1 John i. 7. Rom. iii. 20.) The mercy seat and the tables of the law in the ark may well stand together, but that Christ was sent to satisfy justice, and that thy sins were satisfied for, and not another's : thus it is wholly of grace. If therefore you think the Lord pardons your sins because you have been less sinners than others, or if you think the Lord will not pardon your sins because you are greater sinners than any else, you sin exceedingly against the riches of God's grace in this point.

What are the means by which the Father doth thus justify ?

It is for the satisfaction or by the price of the redemption of Christ, (Rom. iii. 24 ; v. 10 ; Eph. i. 7 ;) for mercy would, but justice could not forgive, without satisfaction for the wrong done. Hence Christ satisfies, that grace and mercy might have their full scope of forgiving. So that neither works before conversion, which are but glistering sins, (Rom. i. 18,) nor works of grace in us after conversion, can be causes of our justification ; for Abraham, when he was justified and sanctified, yet " had not whereof to boast," but " believed in him that justified the ungodly." (Rom. iv. 5.) And the apostle Paul saith expressly, " We " that believe " have believed that we might be justified." (Gal. ii. 16.) It is therefore the price of Christ's redemption which doth procure our justification. But understand this aright, for this price is not applied to each particular man as the " common price," redeeming all, (for then every believer should be accounted a saviour and redeemer of all,) but as the price of those souls in particular, to whom it is specially intended and particularly applied. Christ's righteousness is sufficient to justify all to whom it is imputed ; but it is no further imputed than to the attaining the end of imputation, viz., to justify and save me in particular, not to make me a head of the church or a common saviour. It argues a man weakly principled that denies the necessity of Christ's satisfaction to our justification, because, forsooth, every believer should then be a redeemer. By " satisfaction," I understand the whole obedience of Christ unto the very death, — which is both active and passive, — by which we are justified. (Heb. x. 10. Phil. ii. 8.) That righteousness of Christ (wrought in his satisfaction) is imputed, which satisfies the law and divine justice, (Gal. iv. 1–4,) which is both active and passive. The very reason why the law requires perfect obedience of us — which we can not possibly bring before God — is, that we might seek for it in Christ, that fulfilled all righteousness : and therefore he is called " the end of the law for righteousness." (Rom. x. 3, 4.) And it is strange that any should deny justification by Christ's active obedience, upon this ground, viz., because that " by the works of the law " (which satisfy the law) " shall no sinner be justified ; " and yet withal say that we are justified by that which satisfies the law.

This righteousness of Christ is not that of the Godhead, (for then what need was there for Christ to do or suffer?) but that which was wrought in the manhood.

And hence it is infinite in itself, though infinite in value, in that it was the righteousness of such a person. This righteousness of God may be considered two ways ; first, absolutely in itself; secondly, respectively, as done for us.

1. Christ's absolute righteousness is not imputed to us, viz., as he is Mediator, head of the church, having the Spirit without measure, (which is next to infinite,) etc. ; for though these things are applied for our good, yet they are not imputed as our righteousness ; and therefore the objection vanisheth, which saith we can not be justified by Christ's righteousness, because it is of such infinite perfection.

2. The respective or dispensative righteousness, which some call *justitia fide jussoria*, is that whereby Christ is just "for us" in fulfilling the law, in bearing God's image, we once had, and have now lost by sin ; and thus we are truly said to be as righteous as Christ, by imputation, because he kept the law for us. And here observe, that the question is not whether all that Christ did and had is imputed to us as our righteousness, but whether all that he did, *pro nobis*, for us as a surety in fulfilling the law, be not "for substance," our righteousness ; and therefore to think that we are not justified by Christ's righteousness, because then we are justified by his working of miracles, preaching of sermons, — which women are not regularly capable of, — is but to cast blocks before the blind ; so that, though Christ doth not bestow his personal wisdom and justice upon another, yet what hinders but that that which Christ doth by his wisdom and righteousness for another, the same should stand good for him for whom it is done ? For thus it is in sundry cases among men. Christ's essential righteousness, infinite wisdom, fullness of spirit without measure, etc., is not imputed to us ; yet these have conspired together to do that for us, and suffer that for us, by which we come to be accounted righteous before God : he shall be called "the Lord our righteousness." (Jer. xxiii. 6.) This righteousness therefore imputed to us, justifies us. (Rom. v. 18.) We are said to be made "the righteousness of God in him ; " not the righteousness of God whereby "he is just," but whereby "we are just ; " opposed to the righteousness of man, which is called "our own righteousness." (Rom. x. 3 ; i. 17.) Not righteousness *from* him, (as the Papists dream,) but righteousness *in* him ;

nor remission by Christ only, by righteousness in Christ; this imputed justifies; as sin imputed condemns.

Who are the persons the Lord doth justify?

They are believers; we are justified " by faith," (Rom. v.,) or " for Christ's righteousness apprehended by faith," (Phil. iii. 9 :) it is by faith not as a work of grace, but as by an instrument appointed of God for this end. Christ did not die that our sins should be actually and immediately pardoned, but mediately " by faith," (John iii. 16, 17, 20 ;) and the Lord in wisdom hath appointed this as the only means of applying righteousness, because this, above all other graces, casts down all the righteousness of man in point of justification, and so all cause of boasting, and advanceth grace and mercy only, (Rom. iii. 27 ; iv. 5; 16 ; ix. 30–32 :) the faithful account themselves ungodly in the business of justification, and thence it is said that " Abraham " (though a godly man in himself, yet) " believed in him that justifies the ungodly:" he only is righteous whom God pronounceth and saith is righteous. Now, faith, above all other graces, believes the word; and a believer saith, I believe I am righteous before God, not because I feel it so in myself, but because God saith I am so in his Son, so that you are not justified before you believe; nor then only, when you have performed many holy duties, but at the first instant of your closing with Christ, you are then to see it, and by faith to admire God's rich grace for it.

What is the extent of this sentence?

The description saith, that Christ's satisfaction thus applied, the Father doth two things.

1. He absolves them from all guilt and condemnation of sin, so that, in this sense, " he sees no iniquity in Jacob;" chastisements they may now have after justification, but no punishments, crosses, nor curses,, such as destroy their sins, no punishments to destroy their souls : hence those phrases in Scripture, " scattering sins as a mist, blotting them out, remembering them no more, setting them as far as east is from the west." For Christ being made sin for his people, and this being imputed, he " abolishing all sin, by one offering," (Heb. x.,) hence all are forgiven; and hence it is that there can be no suit in law against a sinner, the law being satisfied and the sinner absolved ; nay, hence sin is condemned, and the sinner spared, (Rom. viii. 3 :) as Christ died for us, so he was acquitted for us, and we in him ; we in him in redemption, we by him in actual faith and application. Whether all sins, past, present, and to come, are actually forgiven at the first instant of believing, I will not, dare

not determine; this is safe to say: 1. That the sentence of pardon of all thy sins is at an instant, (Rom. viii. 1,) but not the sense nor execution of pardon: actual sentence of pardon, not actual application of pardon till they be actually committed. (Col. ii. 13. Heb. ix. 12; x. 1, 2. Rom. iii. 25.) There is a pardon, of course, (some say,) for sins of infirmities; I say there is also a pardon, of course, for sins of wilfulness, — all manner of sins; but not sense of pardon always. He accepts and accounts us perfectly righteous. (Rom. iv. 3.) Faith " is accounted for righteousness;" not the act of faith, as the Arminians would, but the object of it apprehended by faith. (Rom. v. 17.) The Lord accounts us as righteous through Christ's righteousness, as if we had kept all the law, suffered all the punishments for the breach of it. " Who can lay any thing to the charge of God's elect, whom God hath justified?" saith the apostle. (Rom. viii.) Satan may answer, Yes, I can, for the law saith, " The soul that sins must die:" Christ answers, But I have died for him, and satisfied the utmost farthing to justice in that point. True, may Satan say, here is satisfaction for the offence, but the law must be kept also. The Lord Christ answers, I am the end of the law for righteousness, I am perfectly holy and righteous, not for myself, (for I am a common person,) but for this poor sinner, who, in himself, is exceedingly and wholly polluted; and hence the Lord covers sins as well as pardons sins; clothes us with Christ, as well as remits sin for Christ's sake; and as we are accounted sinners by imputation of Adam's legal unrighteousness, so are we accounted righteous by the second Adam's legal righteousness, and that unto eternal life. (Rom. v. 17, 18.) Thus you see the nature, now the Lord opens your eyes to see the glory of this privilege; you that never felt the heavy load of sin, the terrors of a distressed conscience arising from the sense of an angry God, can not prize this privilege; but if you have, you can not but say as he did, " O, blessed are they whose iniquities are forgiven, and whose sin is covered;" and again, " Blessed is the man to whom the Lord imputes no sin." (Ps. xxxii. 12.) The Lord pity us; how many be there in these times, that know there is no justification but by Christ's righteousness, and yet esteem it not? let me, therefore, give you one glimpse of the glory of it in these particulars: 1. This is the righteousness by which a sinner is righteous: the law shows you how a man may be righteous, but there is not the least tittle of the law, which shows you how a sinner may become righteous; this could never have entered into the thoughts of angels how this could be; it is cross to sense and reason for a man accursed and sinful in himself to be at that very time blessed and righteous in another; to say, "Lord, depart from me, for I am a sinful man," (Luke v. 8,) is the voice of natural conscience awakened, not only concerning God out of Christ, but even when God appears in Christ as he did then to Peter; but that the Lord should become our righteousness, when we think no sinners like ourselves: no cases, no afflictions, no desertions like ours, who can believe this? yet thus it is; the very scope of the fourth chapter to the Romans is not to show how a just man may be made righteous, but how a sinner may; our own duties, works, and reformation may make us at the best but less sinful, but this righteousness makes a sinner sinless. 2. By this a sinner is righteous before the judgment seat of God: what man that hath awakenings of conscience but trembles exceedingly when he considers the judgment seat of God, and of his strict account there? but by this we can look upon the face of the Judge himself with boldness. "It is God that justifies; who shall condemn?" (Rom. viii. 32.) Can Christ condemn? He is our Advocate. Can sin condemn? Why did Christ die and was made sin then? Can Satan condemn, if God himself justify us? If the Judge acquits us, what can the jailer do? Can the law condemn? No, the Lord Christ hath fulfilled it for us, to the utmost. O, the stings that many have, saying, What shall I do when I die and go down to the dust? May not the Lord have something against me at the day of reckoning that I never saw, nor got cancelled? O, poor creature! Is Christ now before God without spot? Hath he cleared all reckonings? Verily, as he is before him, so are you, through that righteousness which is in him for you.

By this you have perfect righteousness, as perfectly righteous as Christ the righteous. (1 John ii. 1, 2, and iii. 7.) All your own righteousness, though it be the fruit of the Spirit of grace, is a blotted, stained righteousness, very imperfect and little; but by this, the faith of David, Peter, Paul, was not more precious than thine is, because thou hast the same righteousness as they had. (2 Pet. i. 2.) What sincere soul but esteems of perfect holiness more than of heaven itself? O, consider thou hast it (in this sense I now speak of) in the Lord Jesus.

By this you have continual righteousness. What dost thou complain of daily? Is it not because thou feelest new sins, or the same sins confessed and lamented, and in part subdued? nay, some to thy feeling wholly subdued; but they return upon thee again, and the springs in the bottom fill thy soul again, that thou art weary of thyself and life. O, but remember, this is not a cistern, "but a fountain opened," (Zech. xiii. 1,) for thee to wash in; as "sin abounds, so grace in this gift of righteousness abounds much more; the Lord hath changes of garments for thee," (Zech. iii. 1–7,) by means of which there shall never enter into the Lord's heart one hard thought toward thee of casting thee off, or of taking revenge upon any new occasion or fall unto sin.

By this you have eternal righteousness, that never can be lost; if the Lord should make thee as perfectly righteous as once Adam was, or angels in heaven are, and put on thy royal apparel again, thou wast in danger of losing this, and of being stripped naked again; but now the Lord hath put your righteousness into a safer hand, which never shall be lost. (Heb. vi. 12. Dan. ix. 24.)

By this you please God, and are more amiable before him than if you had it in yourself. Do not say this is a poor righteousness, which is thus out of thyself in another. Why do you think righteousness in yourself would be best? Is it not because hereby you think you shall please God? Suppose thou hadst it, yet thy righteousness should be at the best but man's righteousness; but this is called " the righteousness of God," which can not but be more pleasing to him than that in thyself. (2 Cor. v. 20.) What is angelical righteousness to the righteousness of God? It is but a glowworm before the sun: the smell of Esau's garments, the robes of this righteousness of the Son of God, are of a sweeter odor than thine can be or ever shall be. (Eph. v. 1, 2.) It is said, " By faith Abel, Enoch, etc., pleased God:" their persons were sinful, their own duties were weak, yet by faith in this they pleased God. Thou thinkest when thou goest to prayer, If I had no sin, but perfect holiness in me, surely God would hear me. I tell you, when you bring this offering of Christ's righteousness, the Lord had rather have that than all you can do; you bring that which pleaseth him more than if you brought your own. For ask thy own conscience if it be possible for the righteousness that is done by thyself to be more pleasing to God than the righteousness of the Son of God, the Lord of glory himself, done and perfected for thee.

7. By this you glorify God exceedingly, as "Abraham believed, (Rom. iv.,) and gave glory unto God." " In the Lord shall all the seed of Israel be justified, and shall glory." (Is. xlv. 25.) For, —

1. By this you glorify him perfectly in an instant; for you continue to do all that the law requires that instant you believe. The apostle propounds the question, (Rom. iii. 21,) whether a Christian " by faith doth make void the law." No, saith the apostle, " but we establish the law." How is that? Paræus

21 *

shows three ways : one is this : because that perfect righteousness which the law requires of us, we perform it in Christ by faith. So that in one instant thou continuest to do all that the law requires, and hence ariseth the impossibility of a true believer's apostasy, as from one principal cause — they that deny satisfaction by Christ's doing of the law, because by our own works and doings we can not be justified before God, may as well deny satisfaction by Christ's sufferings, because by our own sufferings we can not be justified; our obedience to the law in way of suffering is as truly the works of the law as our obedience in way of doing.

2. By this you glorify God's justice ; whatever justice requires to be done or suffered, you give it unto God, by faith in Christ.

3. By this you glorify grace and mercy, (Eph. i. 7,) for by this means mercy may over-abound toward you, and you may triumph in it as sure and certain to you. What a blessed mystery is this ! Doth it not grieve you that you can not glorify God in your times and places ? Behold the way ; if thou canst not do it by obedience, thou mayest by faith ; and thereby make restitution of all God's glory lost and stolen from him by thy disobedience to him.

By this you have peace in your consciences : by this Christ's blood is sprinkled upon them, and that cools the burning torments of them. (Rom. v. 1.) The comers unto the Levitical sacrifices and washings (types of this offering of Christ) could not thereby be perfected and be without the guilty conscience of sin ; none of your duties can pacify conscience but as they carry you hither to this righteousness, but the comers to this have no more terrors of conscience for sin ; I mean they have no just cause to have any. This rainbow appearing over your heads is a certain sign of fair weather, and that there shall be no more deluge of wrath to overwhelm thee.

By this all miseries are removed: when thy sins are pardoned, there is something like death, and shame, and sickness, but they are not. It is said, (Is. xxxiii. ult.,) "There shall be none sick among them." Why so ? " Because they shall be forgiven their iniquities." It is no sickness in a manner, no sorrow, no affliction, if the venom, sting, and curse be taken away by pardon of sin ; thy sickness, sorrow, losses, death itself, is better now than health, joy, abundance, life ; you may here see death, hell, grave, swallowed up in victory, and now tread upon the necks of them. (1 Cor. xv.) You may see life in death, heaven in the deepest hell, glory in shame, when thou seest all thy sins done away in the blood of Christ Jesus. This is the blessedness of all you poor believers and comers to the Lord Jesus : what should you do but believe it, and rejoice in it? If the wicked, that apply this righteousness presumptuously, say, Let us sin that grace may abound, and make no other use of forgiveness but to run in debt and sin with a license, why should not you say, on the other side, Let me believe and own my portion in this righteousness, that as my sins have abounded, so my love may abound ; as my sins have been exceeding great, so the Lord may be exceeding sweet; as my sins continue and increase, so my thankfulness, glory in God, triumph over death, grave, sins, through Christ, may also increase; as you see righteousness in Christ forever yours, so you may from thence expect from him such a righteousness as may make you righteous also, as he is righteous. Tremble, thou hard-hearted, impenitent wretch, that didst never yet come to Christ, nor feel thy need of him, or prize his blood; this is none of thy portion ; all thy sins are yet upon thee, and shall one day meet thee in the day of the Lord's fierce wrath, when he shall appear as an everlasting burning before thine eyes, and thou stand guilty before him as chaff and stubble.

Section II.

Reconciliation.

This is the second benefit which in order of nature follows our justification, although sometimes in a large sense it is taken for the whole work of justification; strictly taken, it follows it. (Rom. v. 1,) " Being justified by faith, we have peace with God; " i. e., not only peace from God in our consciences, but peace with God in our reconcilement to him, and his favor toward us : " Being justified, we shall be saved from wrath; " i. e., not only the outward fruits of. wrath, but wrath from whence those come; Christ is first King of Righteousness, then King of Peace, (Heb. vij. 2 ;) for is not sin the cause of God's anger? Must not sin, therefore, be first removed in our justification, before we can have God's anger allayed in our reconciliation? So that as in our justification the Lord accounts us just, so in our reconciliation (himself being at peace with us) he accounts us friends; indeed, our meritorious reconciliation is by Christ's death ; as the king's son who procures his father's favor toward a malefactor, who yet lies in cold irons and knows it not. And this is before our justification or being, (Rom. v. 9 ;) but actually and efficacious reconciliation, whereby we come to the fruition and possession of it, is after our justification. (Rom. iii. 24, 25.) Christ is a propitiation by faith; and here the malefactor hath tidings of favor, if he will accept of it, (Eph. ii. 15, 17,) and of this I now speak: God and man were once friends, but by sin a great breach is made; the Lord, only bearing the wrong, is justly provoked, (Is. lxv. 2, 3;) man, that only doth the wrong, is notwithstanding at enmity with him, and will not be entreated to accept of favor, much less to repent of this wrong. (Jer. viii. 4–8.) The Lord Jesus, therefore, heals this breach by being Mediator between both; he takes up the quarrel, and first reconciles God to man, and man to God, in himself, in redemption, and after this reconciles God and man, by himself, in (or immediately upon) our justification.

This reconciliation consists in two things chiefly:—

1. In our peace with God, whereby the Lord lays by all acts of hostility against us. (Rom. v. 1.)

2. In love and favor of God. I do not mean God's love of good will, for this is in election; but his love of complacency and delight, for till we are justified, the Lord behaves himself as an enemy and stranger to us who are polluted before him, but then he begins thus to love us. (1 John iv. 10, 16. Col. i. 21, 22.) A gardener may intend to turn a crab-tree stock into an apple tree; his intention doth not alter the nature of it, until it actually be ingrafted upon: so we are "by nature the children of wrath." (Eph. i. 3.) The intention of God the Father, or his love of good will, doth not make us children of favor and sons of peace, until the Lord actually call us to and ingraft us into Christ, and then, as Christ is the delight of God, so we in him are loved with the same love of delight. Peace with God and love of God are of different degrees of our reconciliation. A prince is at peace or ceaseth war against a rebel, yet he may not bring the rebel before him, into his bosom of special favor, delight, and love; but the Lord doth both toward us enemies, strangers, rebels, devils, in our reconciliation with him.

O, consider what a blessed estate this is to be at peace with God. It was the title of honor the Lord put upon Abraham to be the friend of God. (Is. xli. 8.) I am not able to express what a privilege this is; it is better felt than spoken of; as Moses said, (Ps. lx,) " Who knows the greatness of his wrath ? " So I may say, Who knows the greatness of this favor and love ?

1. That God should be reconciled with thee after anger, this is exceeding glorious. (Is. xii. 1, 2.) What is man that the Lord should visit him, or look upon him, though he never had sinned ? But to look upon thee, nay, to love thee, after provocation of sin,

after such wrath, which like fire hath consumed thousand thousands, and burnt down the bottom of hell, and is now and ever shall be burning upon them; O, blessed are they that find this favor!

2. That the Lord should be pacified wholly and thoroughly, that there should be no anger left for you to feel. The poor, afflicted church might object against those sweet promises made here, (Is. xxvii. 1–3,) that she left no love. " You are mistaken," saith the Lord, " fury is not in me." (ver. 4.) Indeed, against briers and thorns, and obstinate sinners, that prick and cut me to the very heart by their impenitency, I have, but none against you. Out of Christ, God is a consuming fire, but in Christ he is nothing else but love, (1 John iv. 16;) and though there may be fatherly frowns, chastisements, reproofs, and rods; though he may for a time hide his face, shut out thy prayers, defer to fulfill promises, etc., yet all these are out of pure love to thee, and thou shalt see it, and feel it so in thy latter end. (Heb. xii. 8, 9.) Never did David love Jonathan (whose love exceeded) as the Lord loves thee from his very heart, now thou art in Christ by faith.

3. That the Lord shall be pacified eternally, never to cast thee off again for any sins or miseries thou fallest into, this is wonderful. Those whom men love they forsake, if their love be abused; or if their friends be in affliction, they then bid them good night; but the Lord's love and favor is everlasting. (Is. ix. 7.) " The mountains may depart out of their places, and the hills cast down to the valleys, but the Lord's kindness never shall, never can; he hath hid his face a little moment," whilst thou didst live in thy sin and unbelief; but now, " with everlasting mercy he will embrace thee." Nay, which is more, " the abounding of thy sin " is now the occasion " of the abounding of his grace." (Rom. v. 20.) Thy very wants and miseries are the very causes of his bowels and tender mercies. (Heb. iv. 15, 16.) O, what a privilege is this! Did the Lord ever show mercy and favor to the angels that sinned? Did not one sin cast them out of favor utterly? O, infinite grace, that so many thousand thousands every day gushing out of thy heart against kindness and love, nay, the greatest, dearest love of God, should not incense his sorest displeasure against thee! The Lord that poured out all his anger upon his own Son for thee, and for all thy sins, can not now pour out, nay he hath not one drop left (though he would) to pour out upon thee for any one sin.

4. That the Lord should be thus pacified with enemies. A man may be easily pacified with one that offends him a little;

but with an enemy that strikes at his life, (as by every sin you do,) this is wonderful; yet this is the case here. (Rom. v. 7, 8.)

5. That the Lord should be pacified, even with enemies, by such a wonderful way as the blood of Jesus Christ, (Rom. v. 7, 8,) this is such love, as one would think the infinite wisdom of a blessed God could have devised no greater; by this (ver. 6) he commended and set out his love, which though now it grow a stale and common thing in our days, yet this is that which is enough to burst the heart with astonishment and amazement, to think that the party offended (who therefore had no cause to seek peace with us again) should find out such a way of peace as this is. Woe to the world that despise this peace!

6. That, being thus pacified, you may come into God's presence with boldness at any time, and ask what you will. I wonder what he can deny you if he loves you, (Rom. v. 2,) and which is yet more, that now all creatures are "at peace with you," (John v. 23,) as when the captain of the army is pacified, none of his soldiers must hurt or strike that man; nay, that hereby all your enemies should be forced to do good to you; "O death, where is now thy sting?"

I have oft wondered, if Christ hath borne all our miseries, and suffered death for us, why then should we feel any miseries, or see death any more; and I could never satisfy my own heart by any answers given better than by this, viz., that if the Lord should abolish the very being of our miseries, they should, indeed, then do us no hurt, but neither could they then do us any good; for, if they were not at all, how could they do us good? Now, the Lord Jesus hath made such a peace for us as that our enemies shall not only not hurt us, but they shall be forced (himself ordering of them) to do much good unto us; all your wants shall but make you pray the more, all your sorrows shall but humble you the more, all your temptations shall but exercise your graces the more, all your spiritual desertions shall but make you long for heaven, and to be with Christ, the more; it is now part of your portion not only to have "Paul, and Apollos, and world," but "death" itself to do you good. O Lord, what a blessed estate is this, which, though thousands living under the gospel of peace hear of, yet they regard not; they can strain their consciences in a restless pursuit of the favor of men, and in seeking worldly peace, yet to this day (though born enemies to God) never spent one day, it may be not one hour, in mourning after the Lord for favor from him, nor care not for it, unless it be upon their own terms, viz., that God would be at peace with them, but they may still remain quietly in their sins, and war against God; and thence it is that the Lord will shortly take away peace from the whole earth, and plague the world with war and bloodshed, as it is in Zach. xi. 6: " Deliver every man into the hand of his neighbor, and into the hand of his king, and they shall smite the land;" even for this very cause, for despising the peace and reconciliation with God, you might and should have accepted in the gospel of peace.

SECTION III.

Adoption.

THIS is the third benefit which, in order of nature, follows our rēconciliation, whereby the Lord accounts us sons, and gives us the spirit and privilege of sons; for, in order, we must be first beloved before we can be loved so as to be accounted sons. (1 John iii. 1, 2.) For the Lord of unjust to account us just in our justification is much; but for the Lord to account us hereby as friends, this is more; but to account us sons also, this is a higher degree and a further privilege; and hence, our adoption follows our faith, (John i. 12; Gal. iii. 26;) and if adoption, then the Spirit of adoption much less doth not precede faith. By Christ's active obedience (our divines say) we have right unto life; by adoption we have a further right; the one destroys not the other; for a man may have right unto the same thing upon sundry grounds. We know there are two sorts of sons: 1. Some by nature, born of our own bodies; and thus we are not sons of God, but children of wrath. 2. Some by adoption, which are taken out of another family, and accounted freely of us as our sons; and thus Moses was, for a time, the son of Pharaoh's daughter. And of this sonship by adoption I now speak, the Lord taking us out of the family of hell to be his adopted sons. Christ is God's Son by eternal generation, Adam by creation; all believers are sons of adoption. Now, adoption is twofold.

1. External, whereby the Lord takes a people by outward covenant and dispensation to be his sons, and thus all the Jews were God's " first born," (Ex. iv. 22,) and unto them did " belong the adoption," (Rom. ix. 4, 5 ;) and hence their children were accounted " sons " as well as saints, and " holy," (1 Cor. vii. 14; Ezek. xvi. 20, 21 ;) but many fall from this adoption, as the Jews did.

2. Internal, whereby the Lord, out of everlasting love to particular persons in special, he takes them out of the family of

Satan, and, by internal love and special account, reckons them
in the number of sons, makes them indeed sons, as well as calls
them so. Isaac, by special promise, was "accounted for the
seed," (Rom. ix. 8;) and of this we now speak. Now, this is
double.

1. Adoption begun, (1 John iii. 1, 2,) now we are the sons of
God. To which of us, (though sons indeed,) yet the Lord behaves himself toward them for some time, and for special
reasons, as unto "servants," exercising them with many fears.
(Gal. iv. 1, 2.) Some spirits will not be the better for the love
of their Father, but worse, and therefore the Lord keeps a hard
hand over them; to others the Lord behaves himself with more
special respect, in making them cry with more boldness, "Abba,
Father," (Rom. viii. 15, 16,) who will be more easily overcome,
and bent to his will, by love.

2. Adoption perfected, when we shall receive all the privileges
of sons, not one excepted, (Rom. viii. 23,) where we are said
" to wait for our adoption, the redemption of our bodies." By
the first we are sons, but not seen nor known as such. (1 John
iii. 1, 2.) By the second, we shall be known before all the world
to be such. We now speak principally of adoption begun, whereby we are sons in God's account, and by real reception of the
spirit of sons. The manner of this adoption is thus : —

1. God loves Jesus Christ with an unspeakable love, as his
only Son, and as our elder brother.

2. Hence, when we are in Christ his Son, he loves us with the
same love as he doth his own Son.

3. Hence, the Lord accounts us sons. (Ephes. i. 5, 6.) God's
love is not now toward us as to Adam, his son by creation, viz.,
immediately diffused upon us ; but in loving his own Son immediately, hence he loves us, and hence adopts us, and accounts us
children.

O that the Lord would open our eyes to see this privilege.
" Behold it," saith John, (1 John iii. 1,) stand amazed at it, that
children of wrath should become the sons of the most high God ;
for a beggar on the dunghill, a vagabond, runagate from God,
a prodigal, a stranger to God, whom the Lord had no cause to
think on, to be made a son of God Almighty.

If sons, then the Lord doth prize and esteem you as sons. If
a man hath twenty sons, he esteems the poorest, least, sick child
he hath, more than all his goods and servants, unless he be an
unnatural father ; I tell you that the least of you, the poorest and
most feeble believer, is accounted of God, and more esteemed
than all his household stuff, than heaven, earth, and all the glory

in it, and all the kings and great men in the world, (Is. xliii. 4–6 ;) not because thou hast done any thing worthy of this, but only because he accounts thee freely as his son.

If sons, then the Lord surely will take care for you as for sons ; a godly father hath a double care of his children. First, of their temporal ; secondly, and chiefly, of their eternal estate ; we are ready to question, in times of want, what we shall eat, drink, how we shall live. O, consider, art thou a son of God, and will not He that " feeds the ravens, and clothes the lilies," provide for thee ? Yes, verily, he will take care for thy temporal good. It is true, you may be brought into outward straits, wants, miseries ; yet then the Lord is thereby plotting for thy eternal good ; for hence come all God's corrections, (Deut. viii. 5 ; Heb. xii. 8 ;) the Lord took all they had from them by their enemies in war, and carried them away captive into a strange land ; yet (Jer. xxiv. 5) this was for their good : we think the Lord many times takes no care for us, and so make him of a worse nature than the savage beasts, or bloody men, toward their young ; but this is certain — he never denies any thing to us in outward things, but it is to further our eternal bliss with him, to do us good in our latter end : what say godly parents ? it is no matter what becomes of my children, when I am dead, if the Lord would but give them himself to be their portion ; if at last they may see the Lord in glory : do not wonder, then, if the Lord keeps you short sometimes.

If sons, then he loves you as sons, as a father doth his sons ; you think the Lord loves you not, because you do not always feel his love, nor know his love. Is thy son not thy child, because while it is young it knows not the father that begot it, or because thou art sometimes departed from it, and hast it not always in thine own arms ? " Israel saith, My God hath forsaken me and forgotten me," (Is. xlix. 14 ;) and yet no mother tenders her child as the Lord did them ; you think, because you have so many sins and afflictions one upon another, that the Lord loves you not : judge righteously ; hath thy child no father because it is sick long together, and therefore kept under unto a spare diet ? no, he knows our mold, and that we are but dust, and freely chooses us to be his sons, and hence, loves, notwithstanding all our sins. (Ps. lxxxix. 32, 33.) If he sees Ephraim bemoaning his stubbornness, as well as his sickness and weakness, (Jer. xxxi. 20,) doth not the Lord profess, " Is he not my only son ? "

If sons, then we are " heirs and co-heirs with Christ," saith the apostle, (Rom. viii. 17 ;) sons by nature are not always heirs, but all sons by adoption are : we are heirs with Christ, the Lord

Christ as our elder brother, managing all our estate for us, because unable to do it ourselves; we are heirs, 1. Of the kingdom of glory. (1 Pet. i. 4, 5.) 2. Heirs of all this visible world, (1 Cor. iii. 22;) not that we have the whole world in our own hand, (it would be too cumbersome to us to manage,) but the Lord gives us the rent of it, the blessing and good of it, though it be possessed by others. 3. We are heirs of "the promise," (Heb. xi. 9; vi. 17;) whereby Jehovah himself comes to be our inheritance and portion forever; and look, as Christ was in the world an heir of all, though trod under foot by all, so are we; what can we desire more?

If sons, then we have, and shall ever have, the spirit of sons, (Rom. viii. 15, 16;) and what are we the better for this spirit? Truly, hereby, First, we cry unto him; we are enabled to pray who could not pray before, because guilt stopped our mouths. Secondly, we cry, Abba, Father; and this Spirit witnesseth that we are sons of this Father: it is not said that it witnesseth *to* our spirits, but συ ηνχτυρει̃, it witnesseth *with* our spirits, i. e., our renewed conscience, thus: All believers called and justified of God are sons; but I am such a believer; therefore I am a son: now, the Spirit bears witness with us in every part, both premises and conclusion, only it being the clearest and strongest witness, it testifies the same thing our consciences do, but yet more clearly, more certainly, more comfortably and sweetly, ravishing the soul with most unspeakable peace and joy, especially in the conclusion. I know there is a Noetic testimony, but it is lastly resolved into this: I will not now dispute it, only this is certain; that this testimony all the sons of God have by means of their adoption. They may not indeed sometimes hear it; if they do, they may object against it through the unbelief in part remaining in them; or if it be sometimes suspended, what you want in the witness and comfort of it, you have it in the holiness of it; and, therefore, the Spirit sealing is called "the Holy Spirit," (Eph. iv. 30; 1 Pet. i. 6–8;) and is not this a great privilege? Thirdly, hereby you are led and guided, and that continually, toward your last end. For as, if Adam had stood, he should have had the Spirit of God; this very Spirit to have kept him and all his posterity from falling at any time from God, so Christ, having stood for us, justified us before God, sends the immutable constant assistance of the Spirit in adoption, which, though it doth not always quicken us, nor comfort us, nor assure us, etc., yet it is every moment guiding and leading of us unto our utmost end. From hence it is, that the same sins which harden others, at last humble us, the same temptations by which others fall and perish, serve at last to purify us ; hence our decay in grace leads us to growth at last, hence our fears and doubts serve to establish at last, hence our wilderings from God for a time make us esteem more of the presence and ways of God at last, because this Spirit of adoption is that by which we are led, and constantly assisted and carried toward our latter end. O, mourn, thou that art as yet no son, but a slave to Satan and unto thy filthy lusts; a servant at best, working for wages only, and fear of the whip, who shalt not only abide in God's house as sons shall do ; nay, it may be, hast hated and reviled the sons of God ; time shall come that you shall wonder at their glory, who are not known now.

Section IV.

Sanctification.

This is the fourth benefit which follows in order of nature — our justification, reconciliation, and adoption ; for, upon our being sons in adoption, we receive the image of our heavenly Father in sanctification, because we are under grace. Hence it comes to pass that we are freed from the " reigning power of sin," (Rom. vi. 14,) so that our sanctification follows our justification, and adoption goes not before it. In justification, we have the love and righteousness of the Son ; in reconciliation, the love of the Father ; in adoption, the love of a Father and presence of the Spirit assisting, witnessing; in sanctification, the image of our Father by the same Spirit : and this I conceive, with submission, is "the seal of the Spirit" mentioned Eph. i. 13 ; the " seal sealing" is the Spirit itself; the " seal sealed" consists. first, in the expression of it in adoption ; secondly, in the impression of it in sanctification, and that he only shall pass as current coin that hath both these. I know the most full and clear expression and testimony of the Spirit is after all God's work is finished in glorification ; but the beginning of it is here in adoption, a fuller measure of it in sanctification ; God's seal is ever set to some promise, (as men's seals to some bond, not to blanks ;) the Lord's promise of actual justification and reconciliation pertains only to men sanctified or called : in adoption, therefore, we receive the Spirit, which looks both ways, testifying either thou sanctified, art justified, or thou called, art justified and reconciled. I speak not now of external sanctification by outward show and profession, and common illumination and operation of the Spirit upon men, from which many fall away, (Heb. x. 29,) but of internal and special, the nature of which you may best conceive in these three degrees : —

1. It is the renewing of a man. So that by it a man is morally made a new man — another man. "All things are become new ; " he hath new thoughts, new opinions of things, new desires, new prayers and praises, new dispositions, regeneration not differing from it.

2. It is a renewing of the whole man, (1 Thess. v. 23 ;) for as every part and faculty of man is corrupt by the first Adam, so they are renewed by the second Adam ; not that we are perfectly renewed in this life by Christ, as we are corrupt by Adam, but in part in every faculty, (Rom. vi. 19 ;) and from hence ariseth our spiritual combat and warfare with sin, yea, with all sin ; it is not because of our sanctification simply, (for if it were perfect, we should war and wrestle no more,) but from the imperfection of it. And this renewal in part is in every part, even in the whole man ; and as the first Adam propagates sin chiefly and radically in the soul, especially into the heart of man, and from thence it diffuseth itself like leaven into the whole lump of our lives, so the Lord Jesus chiefly communicates this renewal into our hearts, and thence it sweetens our lives, and hence it is called " the inner man." (Rom. vii. 22. Eph. iii. 16.) You see a little holiness in a Christian ; I tell you, if he be of the right make, there is a kind of infinite endless holiness within him from whence it springs, as there is a kind of infinite endless wickedness in a wicked man, from whence his sins spring : if a man be outwardly holy, but not within, he is not sanctified, no more than the painted sepulchres of the proud Pharisees ; if any man say his heart is good, though he makes no show in his life, he speaks not the truth, if the apostle may be believed, (1 John i. 6 ;) for sanctification is a renewal of the whole man, within and without ; it is not for a man to have his teeth white, and his tongue tipped, and his nails pared ; no, no, the Lord makes all new where he comes.

3. It is a renewal unto the image of God, or of God in Christ ; an unsanctified man may be after a sort renewed in the whole man, his outward conversation may be fair, his mind may be enlightened, his heart may taste of the heavenly gift, etc., (Heb. vi. 4, 5,) he may have a form of godliness, (2 Tim. iii. 5,) he may have strong resolutions within him unto godliness, (Deut. v. 29,) and hence with the five foolish virgins may be received into the fellowship of the wise, and not discerned of them neither, till the gate is shut ; but they are never renewed in their whole

man "after the image of God:" i. e., they do not know things and judge of them, as God doth; they do not love and will holiness and the means thereto, as God doth; they hate not sin, as God doth; they do not delight in the whole law of God; it is not writ in their hearts, and hence they love it not as God doth; and this is the cut of the thread between a sanctified and unsanctified spirit; by sanctification a man is renewed unto God's image, once lost, but here again restored. (Eph. iv. 24. John i. 16.) We receive from Christ grace for grace, as the seal on the wax hath tittle for tittle to that in the seal itself; we are changed into the same image of Christ by beholding him in the glass of the gospel by faith. (2 Cor. iii. 18.) " I delight in the law of God in my inward man," (Rom. vii. 23;) and hence a Christian, by the life of sanctification, lives like unto God; at least hath a holy disposition and inclination (the habits of holiness) so to do. (Gal. ii. 19.) " I live unto God; he calleth us from darkness into his marvelous light, that we might show forth his virtues ; " and that this is true sanctification may thus appear; because our sanctification is opposed to our original corruption, as our justification to our original and contracted guilt of sin: now, as original corruption is the defacing of God's image by contrary dispositions to sinfulness, so our sanctification can be nothing else but the removal of this pollution, by the contrary habits and dispositions to be like unto God again; our sanctification is to be holy, (Lev. xx. 7;) our holiness hath no other primary pattern but God's holiness, so that our sanctification is not the righteousness and holiness as it is inherent in Christ, for that is the matter of our justification, and therefore sanctification must be that holiness which is derived unto us from Christ, whereby we are made like unto him; and thus Christ is made " sanctification unto us." (1 Cor. i. 30.) There should be no difference between Christ our righteousness and sanctification, if that holiness which is in Christ should be both unto us. Hence, also, sanctification is not the immediate operation of the Spirit upon us, without created habits of grace abiding in us, as the spirit that came upon Balaam, and mightily affected him for a time, but left him as destitute of any grace or change of his nature as the ass he rode on. No, no ; it renews you unto the image of God himself, if you be truly sanctified. And therefore let all those dreams of the Familists, (denying all inherent graces, but only those which are in Christ, to be in the saints,) let them vanish and perish from under the sun, and the good Lord reduce all such who in simplicity are misled from this blessed truth of God. I will not now enter

22 *

into that depth concerning the means of our sanctification, in mortification by Christ's death, and vivification by the resurrection of Christ : this may suffice for explication of the nature of it. Only see and forever prize this privilege, all you blessed souls, whom the Lord hath justified ; thou hast many sad complaints : What is it to me, if I be justified in Christ, and be saved at last by Christ, and my heart remain all this while unholy and unsubdued unto the will of Christ; that he should comfort me, and my holy heart be always grieving of him? what though the Lord save me from misery, but saves me not from my sin? O, consider this benefit. It is true thou findest a woful, sinful nature within thee, cross and contrary unto holiness, and leading thee daily in captivity ; yet remember, the Lord hath given thee another nature, a new nature ; there is something else within thee, which makes thee wrestle against sin, and shall in time prevail over all sin, (Matt. xii. 20 ;) this is the Lord's grace sanctifying of thee. O, be thankful that the Lord hath not left thee wholly corrupt, but hath begun to glorify himself in thee, and to bless thee in turning thee from thine iniquities.

1. By this thou hast a most sweet and comfortable evidence of thy justification and favor with God: he that denies this must (whatever distinction he hath) abolish many places of Scripture, especially the Epistles of James and John, who had to do with some spirits that pretended faith and union to Christ, and communion with him; and so long as it was thus, this was evidence sufficient to them of their justified estates. What saith James? Thou sayest thou hast faith; show it me then ; prove it for my part, saith he. I will prove by the blessed fruits and works which flow from it, as Abraham manifested his. (James ii. 18, 22.) What saith John ? You talk (saith he) of fellowship and communion with Christ, and yet what holiness is there in your hearts or lives? If you say you have fellowship with him, and walk in darkness, we lie and do not the truth ; but if you walk in the light, then, although your holiness, and confession, and daily repentance for sin doth not wash away sin, vet the blood of Christ doth wash us. (1 John i. 6, 7.) Again : you say you know Christ, and the love and good will of Christ toward you, and that he is the propitiation for your sins : how do you know this ? Saith he He that saith, I know him, and keepeth not his commandments, is a liar." (1 John ii. 4.) True, might some reply, he that keeps not the commandments of Christ hath thereby a sure evidence that he knows him not, and that he is not united unto him ; but is this any evidence that we do know him, and that we are united to him, if we do keep his

commandments? Yes, verily, saith the apostle, "Hereby know we that we know him, if we keep his commandments," (ver. 3;) and again, (ver. 5:) "Hereby know we that we are in him." What can be more plain? What a vanity is this, to say that this is running upon a covenant of works! Is not sanctification, the writing of the law in our hearts, a special benefit of the covenant of grace, as well as justification? (Heb. viii. 10, 12;) and can the evidencing, then, of one benefit of such a covenant, by another, be a running upon the covenant of works? is it a truth contained in the covenant of grace, viz., that he that is justified is also sanctified, and he that is sanctified is also justified? and is it an error against grace to see this truth, that he that is sanctified is certainly justified, and that therefore he that knows himself sanctified may also know thereby that he is justified? Tell me, how will you know that you are justified? You will say, By the testimony of the Spirit; and can not the same Spirit shine upon your graces, and witness that you are sanctified as well? (1 John iv. 13, 24. 1 Cor. ii. 12.) Can the Spirit make the one clear to you, and not the other?

O beloved, it is a sad thing to hear such questions, and such cold answers also, that sanctification possibly may be an evidence: may be? is not certain? Assuredly, to deny it is as bad as to affirm that God's own promises of favor are true evidences thereof, and, consequently, that they are lies and untruths; for search the Scripture, and consider sadly how many evangelical promises are made unto several graces, that is, unto such persons as are invested with them; you may only take a taste from Matt. v. 3, 4, etc., where our Saviour (who was no legal preacher) pronounceth, and consequently evidenceth, blessedness by eight or nine promises, expressly made to such persons as had inherent graces of "poverty, mourning, meekness," etc., there mentioned; the Lord Jesus leaving those precious legacies of his promises unto his children that are called by those names of "mourners," "poor in spirit," "pure in heart," etc., that so every one may take and be assured of his position manifested particularly therein; that I many times wonder how it comes to pass that this, so plain and ancient principle of catechism, (for so it was among the Waldenses many hundred years since,) grounded on so many pregnant scriptures, should come to be so much as questioned in our days: sometimes I think it ariseth from some wretched lusts men have a mind to live quietly in; desirous to keep their peace, and yet unwilling to forsake their lusts; and hence they exclude this witness of water, the witness of sanctification, to testify in the court of conscience whether they are beloved of God and sincere hearted, or no, because this is a full witness against them, and tells them to their faces that "there is no peace to the wicked," (Is. lvii. ult.; Deut. xxix. 19, 20,) and that they " have nothing to do to take God's name in their lips," that seriously " hate to be reformed." (Ps. l. 16.)　In others, I think it doth not arise from want of grace, but because the spirit of grace and sanctification runs very low in them; it is so little that they can scarce see it by the help of spectacles; or, if they do, they doubt continually of the truth of it; and hence, because it can speak little, and that little very darkly and obscurely for them, they have no great mind that it should be brought in as any witness for them.　Others, I think, may have much grace and holiness, yet, for a time, cast it by as an evidence unto them, because they have experienced how difficult and troublesome it is to find this evidence; and, when it is found, how troublesome to read it, and keep it fair, and thereby have constant peace and quietness; and hence arise those speeches, Why do you look to your sanctification, a blotted evidence? you may have it to-day, and lose it to-morrow, and then where is your peace? and I do believe the Lord deprives many of his precious saints from the comfort of this evidence, either because they look only to this, and not unto Christ, and their justification by faith, (Rom. v. 1,) or else because there is some secret lust or guile of spirit, (Ps. xxxii. 1, 2,) which the Lord, by sore and long shakings about their call and sanctification, would first winnow out, or because there is a perverse frowardness of spirit, whereby, because they feel not that measure of sanctification which they would, do therefore vilify, and so come to deny what indeed they have; because they " feel a law of sin in their members, leading them away captive;" will not, with Paul, take notice of the law of their minds, whereby that "inner man delights in the law of God," and mourns bitterly " under the body of death," by which they might see, with Paul, that there is "no condemnation" to such. (Rom. viii. 1.)

To conclude: whatever is the cause of this crookedness of judgment, I do believe that the general cause is, want of attendance and standing unto the judgment of the Scriptures in this controversy; for if this was stood unto, men would not produce their own experience, viz., that they would never find any evidence from sanctification, but they have met with it in another way, by the immediate witness of the Spirit only; nor would men cry it down, because grace being mixed with so much corruption, it can hardly be discerned, and so will be always left in doubts, and that the heart is deceitful, and many that have evidenced their estates hereby have been deceived.　I confess thus the Popish doctors argue against assurance of faith from the Scriptures without special and extraordinary revelation; but what is all this to the purpose, if the Scriptures make it an evidence? Away, then, with thy corrupt experience; shall this be the judge, or the Scriptures rather? What though many, judging of themselves by marks and signs, have been deceived; yet, if the Scripture make it an evidence, (as we have proved,) then, though men, through their own weakness or wickedness, have been deceived in misapplying promises, yet the Scriptures can not deceive you. What though it be difficult to discern Christ's grace in us; yet if the Scriptures will have us try our estates by that rule, which in itself is easy, but, to our blindness and weakness, difficult many times to see, who shall, who dares condemn the holy Scriptures? which, as they shall judge us at the last day, should judge us now. Suppose that divers books and many ministers sometimes give false signs of grace and God's favor; yet doth the Scriptures give any? I shall propose one thing to conscience, as the conclusion of this discourse. Suppose thou wert now lying upon thy death bed, comforting thyself in thy elected and justified estate; suppose the Spirit of God should now grapple with thy conscience, and tell thee, if thou art " justified " then thou art " called and sanctified." (2 Thess. ii. 13, 14.) Is it thus with thee? What wilt thou answer? If thou sayest thou art not sanctified, the word and Spirit will bear witness then against thee, and say, Then thou art not elected nor justified; if thou sayest thou knowest not, thou lookest not to sanctification, or fruits of the Spirit, they will then reply, How then canst thou say that thou art elected or justified? for it is a truth as clear as the sun, and as immovable as heaven and earth, none are elected and justified, but they are also sanctified, and they that are not sanctified are not justified. (Rom. viii. 1, 13.) And now tell me, how can you have peace, unless you make your faces like flint before the face of God's eternal truth, or heal your conscience by such a plaster as will not stick? If, therefore, the Lord ever made sin bitter to thee, let holiness be sweet; if continuance in sin hath been an evidence unto thee of thy condemnation, O, let the riches of the grace of Christ, in redeeming thee from the lamentable bondage and power of sin, be an evidence to thee of thy salvation. O, bless God for any little measure of sanctification; do not scorn or secretly despise this spirit of grace, as many in this degenerate age begin to do, saying, You look to graces, and fruits, and marks, and signs, and a holy frame of heart, and sanctification; what is your sanctification? O, let it be the more precious to thee, mourning that thou hast so little, and blessing the God and Father of all grace for what little thou hast, wearing it as a bracelet of gold about thy neck, knowing hereby thou art born of God, and that "the whole world lieth in wickedness," and shall perish without this. (1 John v. 18, 19.)

2. This is your glory and beauty, this is glorification begun ; what greater glory than to be like unto God? To be like unto God is to be next to God ; and therefore this is called glory ; (2 Cor. iii. 18,) " We are changed into the same image from glory to glory." Every degree of grace is glory, and the perfection of glory in heaven consists chiefly in the perfection of grace; what is the work of some men at this day but to cast reproach upon sanctification, our glory ?

3. This will give you abundance of sweet peace, and therefore (Heb. xii. 11) it is called the quiet fruit of righteousness ; for from whence come the sore troubles and continual doubts of God's favor in many men's consciences? Is it not some decay or guile here ? (Ps. xxxii. 1, 2.) Is it not some boldness to sin, that they "walk not in fear," and therefore not in the "consolation of the Holy Ghost"? Is it not their secret dalliance with some known sin, continued in with secret impenitency? Is it not because they labor with some strong unmortified corruption, pride, or passions, that they are in daily pangs and throes of conscience for? (Ps. xxxii. 1–4.) What was the rejoicing of Paul? Was it not that "in all sincerity and simplicity he had his conversation among men"? (2 Cor. i. 12.) What was Hezekiah's peace when dying, as he thought? was it not this — "Lord, remember I have walked before thee uprightly"? (Is. xxxviii. 2, 3 ;) not that this was the ground of their peace, for that only is free grace in Christ, but this is the means of your peace ; (John xiv. 22, 23 ;) it is a cursed peace which is kept by looking to Christ, yet loving thy lust.

4. This is that which will make you fit for God's use. (2 Tim. ii. 20, 21.) A filthy, unclean vessel is good for nothing till cleansed. God will not delight to glorify himself much by an unsanctified person. What are thy wife, children, friends, family, the better for thee, if thy heart remain unsanctified ?

5. A little holiness is eminently all, springing up to eternal life ; this little spring shall never cease running, but it shall fill heaven itself, and thy soul in it, with abundance of glory. (John iv. 14, and vii. 38.) You despise it because it is but little ; I tell you this little is eminently all, and contains as much as shall be poured out by thee so long as God is God. It is true, thou sayest it is weak and oft soiled, and gives thee not complete power and victory over all sin; yet know that this shall, like the house of David, "grow stronger and stronger," and it shall at last

prevail, and the Lord will not break thee though thou art bruised by sin daily, until judgment come to victory, and the prince of this world be judged, and thy soul perfected in the day of the Lord Jesus.

Section V.

Audience of all Prayers.

This is the first benefit, which, though it be a fruit of other benefits, yet I name it in special, because I desire first that it might be specially observed; and I place it after our sanctification, because of David's speech, "If I regard iniquity in my heart, the Lord will not hear my prayer," (Ps. lxvi. 18;) and that of the apostle, (1 John iii. 22,) "We believe whatever we ask we receive, because we keep his commandments, and do those things which are pleasing in his sight." As the Lord hath respect to the prayers of his people, not only in regard of their justification, but in some sense in regard of their sanctification also, a justified person, polluted with some personal or common sins of the times, may want that audience and acceptance of his prayers I am now speaking of. That God will hear all the petitions of his people, can there be a greater privilege than this? Yet this our Saviour affirms twice together, because it is so great a promise that we can hardly believe it. (John xiv. 13, 14,) "Whatsoever you ask the Father in my name, that will I do." Mark the scope of the words. Our Saviour had promised that "he that believes in me shall do greater works than I have done." Now, because this might seem strange and impossible, the Lord in those verses tells them how; for saith he, "Whatsoever you ask in my name I will do for you." I will do indeed all that is to be done, but yet it shall be by means of your prayers. Christ did great works when he was upon the earth; but for him to do whatever a poor sinful creature shall desire him to do, what greater work of wonder can there be than this? "This is our confidence," saith the apostle, "that whatever we ask according to his will, he heareth us." (1 John v. 15.) The greatest question here will be, What are those prayers the Lord Jesus will hear? I confess many things are excellently spoken this way; yet I conceive the meaning of this great charter is fully expressed in those words, "in my name." If they be prayers in Christ's name, they shall be heard, and it contains these three things: —

1. To pray in Christ's name is to pray with reliance upon the grace, favor, and worthiness of the merits of Christ; thus this phrase is used, "to walk in the name of their God," is in confi-

dence of the authority, and excellency, and favor of their God, that they will bear them out in it. So to pray in Christ's name is to pray for Christ's sake; thus (Eph. ii. 18) through him (i. e., through his death and sanctification rested upon) we have access with confidence to the Father, (Eph. iii. 12,) in whom we have boldness, and access with confidence, by the faith of him. There are three evils that commonly attend our prayers when we see God indeed: 1. Shame and flight from God. The apostle saith, therefore, that "by faith in Christ we have access." 2. If we do accede and draw near to him, there is a secret fear and straitness of spirit to open all our minds; therefore saith he, we have boldness; the word signifies liberty of speech to open all our minds without fear or discouragement. 3. After we have thus drawn near and opened all our desires and means before God, we have many doubts; viz., Will the Lord hear such a sinner, and such weak, and imperfect, and sinful prayers? And therefore he also affirms, that we have confidence and assurance of being heard; but all this is by faith in him; for look, as Christ hath purchased all blessing for us by his death, and hence makes his intercession for those things daily, according to our need, so we are much more to rest upon and make that satisfaction the ground of our intercession, because Christ's blood purchased this; therefore, O Lord, grant this.

2. To pray in his name is to pray from his command, and according to his will; as when we send another in our name, we wish him to say thus: Tell him that I desire such a thing of him, and that I sent you; so it is here, and thus the phrase signifies, (John v. 43,) "I am come in my Father's name," i. e., by his authority and command.

To pray in Christ's name, therefore, is to pray according to the will of Christ, and from the will of Christ, when we "take those words" the Lord puts into our mouths, (Hos. xiv. 1–3,) and desire those things only that the Lord commands to seek, whether absolutely or conditionally, "according to his will" revealed, and "with submission to his will" concealed. (1 John v. 14.) "Whatever we ask according to his will, he hears us." (Ps. xxvii. 8. Rom. viii. 26.) If you ask any thing not according to God's will, you come in your own name; he sent you not with any such message to the Father.

3. To pray in his name is to pray for his ends; for the sake and use of Christ, and glory of Christ. Thus the phrase is used, (Matt. x. 41, 42,) "to receive a prophet in the name of a prophet," i. e., for this end and reason, because he is a prophet. A servant comes in his master's name to ask something of

another, when he comes as from his command, so also for his master's use. So, when we pray for Christ's sake, i. e., for his ends, not our own, these ever prevail. (Lam. iv. 3.) "You ask and have not, because you ask amiss, to spend it on your lusts." (John xii. 27, 28. Ps. cxlv. 18.) This is to "ask in truth," to act for a spiritual end ; to make it our utmost end, ariseth from a special, peculiar, supernatural presence of the Spirit of life, and consequently a spirit of prayer which is ever heard. And hence you shall observe, the least groan for Christ's ends is ever heard, because it is the groaning of the Spirit, because it is an act of spiritual life, the formality of which consists in this, that it is "for God." (Gal. ii. 19.) The Lord can not deny what we pray for Christ's ends, because then he should crush Christ's glory. And therefore let a Christian observe, when he would have any thing of God that concerns himself, not to be solicitous so much for the thing, as to gain favor and nearness to God, and a heart subject unto God in a humble contentedness, to be denied as well as to be heard, and he shall undoubtedly find the thing itself. A lust is properly such a desire (though for lawful things) wherein a man must have the thing because it pleaseth him ; as when Rachel asked for children, she must have them, else she must needs die. "Give us water that we may drink," was their brutish cry, (Ex. xvii. 1, 2 ;) not that we may live to Him that gives it. Holy prayers or desires (opposed unto lusts) are such desires of the soul, left with God, with submission to his will, as may best please him. Now, the Lord will hear the desires indeed of all that fear him, but not fulfill their lusts. These three are the essential properties of such prayer as is heard, or, if you will, of that which is properly or spiritually prayer : fervency and assurance, etc., are excellent ingredients ; but yet the Lord may hear prayer without them. It is true, the Lord may sometimes not hear us presently, for our praying time is our sowing time ; we must not look presently for the harvest. "The Lord hears the prayer of the destitute," (Ps. cii. 17 :) the original word is, of the "shrub," or "naked place of the desert," which the prophet saith (Jer. xvii. 6) "sees no good when good comes;" yet such as feel themselves such, the Lord doth regard them, and will have a time to answer them ; and though the Lord may not give us the thing we pray for, nor so good a thing of the same kind, yet he ever gives us the end of our prayers : he that is at sea, and wants stiff winds to carry him to his port, yet hath no cause to complain if the Lord secretly carries him in by a strong current of the sea itself ; and it is certain, at the end of all God's dealing with you, you shall then see how the Lord hath not failed to answer you in any one particular. (Josh. xxiii. 14.) O, therefore, see and be persuaded of this your privilege. That God will now hear every prayer, many make a question, How may we know when the Lord grants us any blessing as an answer to prayer? Many things are said to this purpose; but the simplicity and plainness of the answer lie in this, viz., if it be a prayer, God hears it; if it be put up in Christ's name, it is then a prayer: and that you may believe this, and glory in this, consider these reasons, to confirm this truth.

From the promise of Christ as in this place, (John xiv. 13, 14.) which was a promise in special, to be accomplished when he came to his kingdom; and therefore, though it is true God's grace is free, and therefore you think the Lord may as well refuse to hear you as hear, yet consider that by his promise he hath bound himself to hear.

From the fatherly disposition that is in God, (John xvi. 26, 27;) and hence "he loves us," and hence can not but hear us.

Because all prayers put up in Christ's name, Christ "makes intercession" that they may be heard. (Heb. vii. 25.) He hath laid down his blood that all our prayers might be heard, (as we have proved;) and indeed, hence ariseth the infinite efficacy of prayer, because it is built upon that which is infinitely and eternally worthy.

Because all prayers of the faithful arise from the Spirit of prayer, (Rom. viii. 26;) because, as that which is for the flesh, is of the flesh, so that which is for the Spirit, or for the sake of Christ, for spiritual ends, is ever of the Spirit. (John vii. 18.)

Because of the glory of Christ, that the Father may be glorified in the Son. Can not Christ be glorified unless he hear all prayers? Yes, he could; but yet his will is to reveal his glory by this means; so that though thou and thy prayers be vile, and therefore deservest no acceptance or answer, yet remember that his glory is dear. It is the glory of kings to hear some requests and petitions, but they can not hear nor answer all; it is the glory of Christ to hear all, because he is able, without the least dishonor to himself, thus to do. O, be persuaded of this; how should your joy then be full! how should you then delight to be oft with him! how would you then encourage all to come unto him! how would you then be constrained to do any thing for him, who is ready to do all for you! But O, woe unto our unbelief, for that which the apostle saith (1 John v. 14) was ground of his confidence, viz., that "whatever we ask according to his will, he hears us," is no ground to us ; and we may say, and mourn to think, (this is our diffidence,) that, Whatever I ask according to Christ's will, he hears me not. But O, recover from such a distrustful frame, and from all dead-heartedness in this duty withal, lest the Lord send taskmasters and double our bricks, and then we groan, and sigh, and cry, and learn to pray that way, that will not pray nor believe now. If the Lord will but give us hearts, assuredly you might not only rule yourselves and families, but, by the power of prayer, pull down and raise up kingdoms, dispose of the greatest affairs of the church, nay, of the world ; you might hereby work wonders, by means of Him, who, ruling all things, yet is overcome by prayer. (Hos. xii. 4, 5.)

Section VI.

Glorification.

THIS is the sixth and last privilege and benefit, and you all know is the last thing in the execution of God's eternal purpose toward all his beloved and chosen ones ; whom he hath "predestinated, called, justified," them he hath also "glorified," (Rom. viii. 30 ;) hereby we are made perfect in holiness; no more sin shall stir in us ; perfect also in happiness; no more tears, nor sorrows, nor temptations, nor fears, shall ever molest us, (Heb. xii. 13 ; Rev. xiv. 13 ;) and all this shall be in our immediate communion with God in Christ. (Col. i. 18. John xvii. 23, 24.) "We shall be then," saith Paul, "forever with the Lord." If the Lord would but open our eyes, and give us one glimpse of this, what manner of persons should we be ! How should we then live ! How willingly then should we embrace fagots and flames, prisons and penury ! The light afflictions here, would not they work for us glory ? Nay, the apostle useth such a phrase which I believe may pose the most curious orator in the world to express to the life of it — "an exceeding weight of glory." (2 Cor. iv. 17.) What is our life now but a continual dying, carrying daily about us that which is more bitter than a thousand deaths ? What saith the apostle ? "You are dead, yet when Christ shall appear, you shall appear with him in glory." The general security of these times foretold by Christ, (especially when churches become virgins, and people are seeking after purity of ordinances,) it shall not be in want of watchfulness against the present corruptions of the times, as in a careless want of expectation of the coming of Christ in glory, not having "our loins girt and lamps burning," nor readiness to meet the Lord in glory. (Matt. xxv. 1–5, etc.) O that I were able therefore to give you a blush and a dark view of this glory, that might raise up our hearts to this work!

Consider the glory of the place: the Jews did and do dream still of an earthly kingdom, at the coming of their Messiah; the Lord dasheth those dreams, and tells them "his kingdom is not of this world," and that he "went away to prepare a place for them, that where he is they might be," (John xiv. 2, 3,) and "be with him to see his glory." (John xvii. 23, 24.) The place shall be the third heaven, called our Father's house, built by his own hand with most exquisite wisdom, fit for so great a God to appear in his glory (John xiv. 2, 3) to all his dear children; called also a "kingdom." (Matt. xxv. 31,) "Come, ye blessed, inherit the kingdom prepared for you," which is the top of all the worldly excellency, called also "an inheritance," (1 Pet. i. 3,) which the holy apostle infinitely blesseth God for, as being our own, and freely given to us, being our Father's inheritance divided among his sons, which is a greater privilege than to be born an heir to all the richest inheritance on this earth, or to be Lord of all this visible world; for this inheritance, he tells us, is, 1. "Incorruptible," whereas, "all this world waxeth old as a garment." 2. It is undefiled, never yet polluted with any sin, no, not by the angels that fell, for they fell in paradise, when guardians to man; whereas "this whole creation groaneth under burden and bondage of corruption." (Rom. viii.)

3. This never fadeth away; it is not like flowers, whose glory and beauty soon wither, but this shall be most pleasant, sweet, and ever delightsome, after we have been ten thousand years in it, as it was the first day we entered into it, (for this is the meaning of the word, and so it differs from *incorruptible ;*) whereas in this world (suppose a man should ever enjoy it, yet) there grows a secret satiety and fullness upon our hearts, and it grows common, and blessings of greatest price are not so sweet as the first time we enjoy them; they clog the stomach and glut the soul: but here our eyes, ears, minds, hearts, shall be ever ravished with that admirable glory which shines brighter than ten thousand suns, the very fabric of it being God's needlework, (if I may so say,) quilted with variety of all flowers, in divers colors, by the exactest art of God himself, as the apostle intimates. (Heb. xi. 10.)

Secondly. Consider of the glory of the bodies of the saints in this place: the Lord shall change our vile bodies, which are but as dirt upon our wings, and clogs at our feet, as the apostle expresseth it. (Phil. iii. ult.) Paul was in the third heaven, and saw the glory, doubtless, of some there: see what he saith of them. (1 Cor. xv. 42–44.)

1. It shall be an incorruptible body: it shall never die, nor rot again; no, not in the least degree tending that way; it shall never grow weary, (as now it is by hard labor, and sometimes by holy duties,) nor faint, nor grow wrinkled and withered. Adam's body in innocency *potuit non mori*, we say truly; but this *non potest mori*, it can not die: and hence it is, that there shall be no more sickness, pains, griefs, faintings, fits, etc., when it comes there.

2. It shall be a glorious body: it shall "rise in honor," saith Paul; and what glory shall it have! Verily, it shall be like "unto Christ's glorious body," (Phil. iii. ult.,) which, when Paul saw, (Acts ix.,) did "shine brighter than the sun;" and therefore here shall be no imperfection of limbs, scars, or maims, natural or accidental deformities; but as the third heaven itself is most lightsome, (Gen. i. 1, 2,) so their bodies that inhabit that shall exceed the light and glory thereof, these being more compacted, and thence shining out in greater luster, that the eyes of all beholders shall be infinitely ravished to see such clods of earth as now we are advanced to such incomparable beauty and amiableness of heavenly glory.

3. It shall be a "powerful, strong body: it is sown in weakness," saith Paul, "it shall rise in power;" it shall be able to help forward the divine operations of the soul, which are now clogged by a feeble body; it shall be able to bear the weight of glory, the joy unspeakable and full of glory, which our weak bodies can not long endure here, but we begin to burst and break in pieces (like vessels full of strong spirits) with the weight and working of them; and therefore the Lord in mercy keeps us short now of what else we should feel; it shall be able to sing hallelujahs, and give honor, glory, power, to the Lamb that sits upon the throne, forevermore, without the least weariness.

4. It shall be a spiritual body: our body now is acted by animal spirits, and being earthly and natural, grows, feeds, eats, drinks, sleeps, and hath natural affections and desires after these things, and is troubled if it wants them; but then these same bodies shall live by the indwelling of the Spirit of God poured out abundantly in us and upon us, and so acting our bodies, and swallowing up all such natural affections and motions as those be here; as Moses, being with God in the mount forty days and nights, did not need any meat or drink, the Lord and his glory being all unto him: how much more shall it be thus then! I do not say we shall be spirits like the angels, but our bodies shall be

23 *

spiritual, having no natural desires after any earthly blessing, food, raiment, etc., nor troubled with the want of them : and hence also the body shall be able as well to ascend up as now it is to descend down; as Austin shows by a similitude of lead, which some artists can beat so small as to make it swim : we are now earthly, and made to live on this earth, and hence fall down to the center; but we are made then to be above forever with the Lord, the Lord proceeding from imperfection to perfection, as the apostle here shows; not first spiritual, and then natural; but first that which is natural, (in this life,) and then that which is spiritual.

5. Consider the glory of the soul: now we know but in part, and see but in part; now we have joy at sometimes, and then eclipses befall us on a sudden; but then "the Lord shall be our everlasting light," (Is. lx. 19;) then we shall "see God face to face." (1 John iii. 1, 2.) We shall then know and see those things that have been hid, not only from the wicked, but from the deepest thoughts of the saints themselves in this world. (2 Cor. xii. 4.)

Paul saw some things "not fit to be uttered," or that he "could not utter:" we shall be swallowed up in those depths of grace, glory, immediate vision; God shall be all in all. The souls shall now enjoy, 1. The accomplishment of all promises which we see not here made good unto us. (1 Cor. xv. 24.) Then you shall have restitution of all these at times of refreshing, wherein your sins shall be publicly blotted out from the presence of the Lord. (Acts iii. 19.) If Joshua said, (Josh. xxiii. 14,) when the people's warfare was ended, "See if the Lord hath been wanting in one word to you," much more will the Lord Jesus say unto you then.

2. Then you shall receive a full answer to all your prayers: all that grace, holiness, power over sin, Satan, fellowship with God, life of Christ, blessing of God, which you sought for, and wept for, and suffered for here, you shall then see all answered.

3. Then you shall find the comfort of all that you have done for God. (Rev. xiv. 13.) Your work in this sense shall follow you ; you shall then infinitely rejoice that ever you did any thing for God ; that ever you thought of him, spoke to him, and spoke for him; that ever you gave any one blow to your pride, passions, lust, natural concupiscence, etc.; you shall then enjoy the reward of all your sufferings, cares, sorrows for God's Christ, fastings, and days of mourning, whether publicly or secretly, for God's people. (2 Cor. iv. 17.) The same glory God hath given Christ, the Lord shall at that time give unto you. (John xvii. 22.)

It shall not be with us there as it was with the wicked Israelites, who when they came into the good land of rest, they then forgot the Lord and all his works past: no, no, all that which God hath done for you in this world, you shall then look back and see, and wonder, and love, and bless, and suck the sweet of, forevermore. It is a fond, weak question, to think whether we shall know one another in heaven. Verily, you shall remember the good the Lord did you here; by what means the Lord humbled you; by what ministry the Lord called you; by what friends the Lord comforted and refreshed you: and there you shall see them with you. Do you think you shall forget the Lord and his works in heaven, which (it may be) you took little notice of, and the Lord had little glory for here?

Fourthly. Consider the glory of the company and fellowship you shall have here. 1. Angels. (Heb. xii. 23, 24.) They will love you, and comfort you, and rejoice with you, and speak of the great things the Lord hath done for you, as they did on earth to the shepherds. (Luke ii. 10.) "Be not afraid," saith the angel, (Matt. xxviii. 5;) "I know you seek Jesus." So will they say then, Be ever comforted, you blessed servants of the Lord, for we know you are loved of the Lord Jesus. 2. Saints. You shall sit down with Abraham, Isaac, and Jacob in the kingdom of God; be taken into the bosom of Abraham, and there we shall speak with them of the Lord's wonders, of his Christ and kingdom, (Ps. cxlv. 11,) and every sentence and word shall be milk and honey, sweeter than thy life now can be unto thee. We shall know, and love, and honor one another exceedingly. 3. The man Christ Jesus: when Mary clasped about him, (John xx. 17,) "Let me alone," said he; "touch me not; I am not yet ascended to my Father." As if he had said, (saith Austin,) Then shall be the place and time wherein we shall embrace one another forevermore. Never were husband and loving wife so familiar one with another as the Lord Jesus will be, (not carnally and in an earthly manner, but) in a most heavenly, glorious, yet gracious manner, with all his saints. "Come, ye blessed," will he then say to them: we shall then ever be, not only in the Lord, but with the Lord, saith Paul. (1 Thess. iv. ult.; v. 10.) Just as Moses and Elias in his transfiguration, that talked with him, (which was a glimpse of our future glory,) so shall we then, (Luke xii. 37,) and you shall then see that love of his, that blessed bosom of love opened fully, which the apostle saith "passeth knowledge." (Eph. iii. 19.) I need not tell you of your fellowship with the Father, also when the Son shall give up the kingdom to him that he may be all in all.

Fifthly. Consider the glory of your work there; which is only to glorify this God.

1. You shall then live like Christ in glory. We shall think and speak all with glory. (1 John iii. 1, 2.) Our strings shall be then raised up to the highest strain of sweet melody and glory.

2. You shall then bless him, (Eph. i. 6; iv. 30,) and that with ravishment; you shall come then to the full acknowledgment of the Son of God; you shall see and say all this is the work and grace of Christ, and then shall cry out, O, let all angels, saints, ever bless him for this. What should I speak any more? You will say, Is this certain? Can this be so? Yes, assuredly, for Christ is gone to prepare this place and glory for you. (John xiv. 2, 3.) We have also the first fruits of this glory, which we feel sometimes, whereby we see, and taste, and drink, and long for more of that joy unspeakable, and peace that passeth understanding, that triumph over the rage and working power of remaining corruption, that dark vision of God, and holy glorying and boasting in him as our everlasting portion, etc., which can not be delusions and dreams, which never feed, but ever leave the deceived soul hungry, but are realities and things indeed, which satiate the weary soul, and fill it up with the very fullness of God himself, (Eph. iii. 19;) and therefore it is certain that we shall have the harvest that thus taste of the fruits, and the whole sum paid us faithfully that have already the earnest penny. The Lord also fits us for this, as the apostle disputes. (2 Cor. v. 4, 5.) What means the Lord to deny our requests in many things as long as we live? What is his meaning not to let us see the accomplishment of many of his promises? Is it because he is unfaithful? or because he would let us know there is a day of refreshing he hath reserved for us, and would have us look for, wherein we shall see it hath not been a vain thing for us to pray, or him to promise? Why doth he afflict us, and keep us more miserable, both by outward sorrows and inward miseries, than any other people in the world? Doth he not hereby humble us, empty us, wean us from hence, and make us as it were vessels big enough to hold glory, which we hope for in another world?

But you will say, Can this glory be thus great? We see it is certain it shall be so; but shall it be so exceeding great and endless? Yes, verily, because, —

1. The price is great which is paid for it. (Eph. i. 14.) It is a purchased possession, (by the blood of Christ we enter into the holy of holies;) a price of infinite value must bring a kind of infinite glory.

2. We are, by Christ, nearer to God than angels are, whose glory we see is very great.

3. Shall not our glory be to set out the glory of Christ? (2 Thess. i. 10 ;) and if so, then if this glory be exceeding great, ours must bear a due proportion, and be very great also.

4. Doth not God pick out the poor and vile things of the world to be vessels of glory? (1 Cor. i. 27 ;) and is not that an argument that he intends exceedingly to glorify himself on such? to raise up a most glorious building, where he lays so low a foundation?

5. Are we not loved with the same love as he hath loved Christ? (John xvii. ult. ;) and shall not our glory abound then exceedingly?

6. Are not the torment and shame of the reprobates to be exceeding great and grievous? doth not God raise them up to make his power known? (Rom. ix. 23.) What then shall we think, on the contrary, of the glory of the saints, wherein the Lord shall set forth his power in glorifying them, as he doth the glory of his power in punishing others? and therefore (2 Thess. i. 9) the punishment of the wicked is expressed by separation of them "from the glory of the Lord's power ;" because that in the glory of the saints the Lord will (as I may so say) make them as glorious as by his power, ruled by wisdom, he is able to make them. This is, therefore, the great glory of all those whom God hath called to the fellowship of his dear Son ; and which is yet more, blessed be God, the time is not long but that we shall feel what now we do but hear of, and see but a little of, as we use to do of things afar off. We are here but strangers, and have no " abiding city ;" we look for this " that hath foundations ;" and, therefore, let sin press us down, and weary us out with wrestling with it ; let Satan tempt, and cast his darts at us ; let our drink be our tears day and night, and our meat gall and wormwood ; let us be shut up in choking prisons, and cast out for dead in the streets, nay, upon dunghills, and none to bury us ; let us live alone as pelicans in the wilderness, and be driven among wild beasts into deserts ; let us be scourged, and disgraced, stoned, sawn asunder, and burnt ; let us live in sheep skins and goat skins, destitute, afflicted, tormented, (as who looks not for such days shortly ?) yet, O brethren, the time is not long, but when we are at the worst, and death ready to swallow us up, we shall cry out, O glory, glory, O welcome, glory. If our miseries here be long, they shall be light ; if very bitter, they shall be short ; however, long or short, they can not be to us long, who look for an eternal

weight of glory. Who would not (that considers of these things) despise this world, and set it at his heels, who hath all these privileges and benefits, with Christ in his eye? who would not abhor a filthy lust to enjoy such a Christ? who would ever look back unto his flesh pots, or father's house, that hath such welcome made him the first moment he comes to the Lord Jesus, in having present fruition of some of these benefits, but present right unto all; fruition of some by feeling, of all by faith? But O, the wrath of God upon these times, that either see not this glory, or, if they do, despise so great salvation! Christ, and pardon, and peace, adoption, grace, and glory, are brought home to our doors, but their price is fallen in our market, and we think it better to be without Christ with our lusts, than to be in Christ with his benefits. The reproach of Christ was dearer to Moses (as great a courtier, and as strong a headpiece, as our times can afford) than all the riches and honors of Egypt; but the grace, and peace, and life, and glory of Jesus Christ is viler to us than the very onions, and leeks, and flesh pots of Egypt; if you had but naked Christ (our life) for a prey in these evil times, you had no cause to complain, but infinitely to rejoice in your portion; but when with Christ you shall find all these benefits and privileges coming in as to your portion, and yet to despise him! Assuredly the Lord will not bear with this contempt always. Away to the mountains, and hasten from the towns and cities of your habitation, where the grace of Christ is published, but universally despised, you blessed, called ones of the Lord Jesus; for the days are coming wherein for this sin the heavens and earth shall shake, the sun shall be turned into darkness, and the moon into blood, and men's hearts failing for fear of the horrible plagues which are coming upon the face of the earth. Dream not of fair weather, expect not better days, till you hear men say, " Blessed is he that cometh in the name of the Lord," who thus " blesseth his with all spiritual blessings in Christ." (Eph. i. 3.)   I now proceed to the last

CHAPTER III.

ALL THOSE THAT ARE TRANSLATED INTO THIS BLESSED ESTATE ARE BOUND TO LIVE THE LIFE OF LOVE, IN FRUITFUL AND THANKFUL OBEDIENCE UNTO HIM THAT HATH CALLED THEM, ACCORDING TO THE RULE OF THE MORAL LAW. — *Ps. xl.* 7, 8.

THE Lord doth no sooner call his people to himself, but as soon as ever he hath thus crowned them with these glorious privileges, and given them any sense and feeling of them, but they immediately cry out, O Lord, what shall I now do for thee? how shall I now live to thee? They know now they are no more their own, but his, and therefore should now live to him. If you ask Moses, after all the love and kindness the Lord had shown Israel, what Israel should do for him, you shall see his answer full, (Deut. x. 12, 13,) "And now, O Israel, what doth the Lord require of thee, but to fear the Lord thy God, and to love him, and serve him with all thy heart, and to keep his commandments, which I command thee this day for thy good?" If you ask Paul (as evangelical a Christian as ever lived) what now we are to do when we are in Christ, he answers punctually, (2 Cor. v. 14, 15,) "The love of Christ constraineth us, because we thus judge, that Christ dying for those that were dead, they that live should not live unto themselves, but unto him that died for them and rose again." If we ask Peter the question, to what end the Lord hath "called us out of darkness into his marvelous light," he expressly tells you it is "to show forth the virtues of him that hath so called us." (1 Pet. ii. 9.) If we be doubtful whether this be the Lord's mind, the Lord himself resolves it by Zechariah, (Luke i. 74,) and tells us that it is his oath, "that, we being delivered out of the hands of our enemies, we should serve him without fear in holiness" (in all the rules of the first table) "and righteousness" (in all duties of the second table) "all the days of our life," and that all this should not be out of a spirit of bondage and slavish fear, but "without fear," that is, fear of our enemies, sin, death, wrath, and so, consequently, out of love to him that hath delivered us; that one would wonder it should ever enter the heart of any Christian man that hath tasted the love of Christ, as to think that there is no use of the law to one in Christ; and that because they are to live the life of love to Christ, that therefore they are not to look to the law as the rule of their love, expressly cross to the letter of the text, (John xiv. 15,) "If ye love me, keep my commandments;" which commandments are not only faith and love to the saints, but love to enemies, and spiritual obedience unto the moral law, in a far different manner and measure than as the Pharisees instructed the people in those days, as you may see. (Matt. v. 17.) It is true, indeed, obedience to the law is not required of us now, as it was of Adam; it was required of him as a condition antecedent to life; but of those that be in Christ it is required only as a duty consequent to life, or as a rule of life, that seeing he hath purchased our lives in redemption, and actually given us life in vocation and sanctification, we should now live unto him, in all thankful and fruitful obedience, according to his will revealed in the moral law. It is a vain thing to imagine that our obedience is to have no other rule but the Spirit, without any attendance to the law. The Spirit, indeed, is the efficient cause of our obedience, and hence we are said to be led by the Spirit, (Rom. viii. 14;) but it is not properly the rule of our obedience, but the will of God revealed in his word, especially in the law, is the rule. The Spirit is the wind that drives us in our obedience; the law is our compass, according to which it steers our course for us. The Spirit and the law, the wind and the compass, can stand well together. (Ps. cxliii. 10.)

"Teach me to do thy will, O God;" (there is David's rule, viz., God's will revealed;) "thy Spirit is good;" (there is David's wind, that enabled him to steer his course according to it;) "the Spirit of life doth free us from the law of sin and death," but not from the holy, and pure, and good, and righteous law of God. (Rom. viii. 1–3.) "The blood of Christ by the Spirit cleanseth us from dead works, to serve the living God, (Heb. ix. 14,) not to serve our own selves, or lusts, or wills, to do what we please. The law indeed is not a rule of that by which we are to obey, viz., of our faith; yet it is the only rule of what we are to obey; we are not to perform acts of obedience now as Adam was to do, viz., by the sole power of inherent grace; but we are to live by faith, and act by faith, (for "without me you can do nothing," John xv. 5;) we are not united to Christ, our life, by obedience, as Adam was to God by it, but by faith; and therefore, as all action, in living things, comes from union, so all our acts of obedience are to come by faith from the Spirit on Christ's part, and from faith on our part, which makes our union. Noah built by faith, Enoch walked with God by faith, Joshua and his soldiers fought by faith, Abraham traveled, dwelt in his tents, lived and died, by faith; they acted according to the rule, but all by the power of faith. It is a weak reasoning to imagine a man is not bound to pay his debts because he is to go unto another for the money. Obedience is our debt we owe to Christ, (Luke xvii. 10,) though we are to go to Christ poor, and weak, and feeble, to enable us to pay. It is true, Christ hath kept the law for us ; and are we therefore free from it as our rule ? No, verily ; Christ kept the law for satisfaction to justice, and so we are not bound to keep the law. He kept the law also for imitation, to give us a copy and an example of all holiness, and glorifying God in our obedience ; and thus Christ's obedience is so far from exempting us from the law, as that it engageth us the more, having both rule and exercise before us. (1 John ii. 6.) " He that saith he abideth in him ought to walk as he walked." (1 Pet. i. 14–16.) It is true, the law is writ in a believer's heart, and if he hath a law within, what need he, say some, look to the law without? when as our Saviour and David argued quite contrary, (Ps. xl. 7, 8,) "I come; I delight to do thy will, it being written of me that I should do it," because "thy law is within my heart." This argues that you are not to attend the law unwillingly, as bondmen and slaves, but willingly and gladly, because the law, even the law of love in your hearts. (1 John v. 3.) The place alleged by some for this liberty from the law, viz., " the law is not made for a righteous man," (1 Tim. i. 9,) if well considered, fully dasheth this dream in pieces ; for there were divers Jewish preachers of Moses' law, and they had a world of scruples and questions about it, (ver. 4 ;) and Paul and others were accounted of as men less zealous, because they did not sound upon that string so much. Away, saith Paul, with those contentious questions ; " for the end of the commandment " is not scruples and questions, but charity and love, (i. e., both to God and man) " out of a pure heart and faith unfeigned." (ver. 4.) And saith he, " The law is very good " when " used lawfully," that is, for this end, and out of these principles ; (ver. 8 ;) it is not talking, but doing, and that out of love, which is the end and scope of the law ; so that, note by the way, you may as well abolish love as abolish the law, love being the end and scope of the law. But to proceed : " The law is not made " (saith he) " for the righteous," i. e. for the condemnation of the righteous, i. e., of such as, out of a pure heart and faith unfeigned, love God in the first table, love to show all duties of respect to man in the second table ; and therefore they, of all other men, have no cause to abolish the law, as if it was a bugbear, or a thing that could hurt them ; but it is made for the condemnation of the lawless Anomians, — as the original word is, — or, if you will, Antinomians, (transgressors of the first command,) and disobedient, (transgressors of the second command,) for ungodly and sinners, (transgressors of the third command,) for unholy and pro-

fane, (transgressors of the fourth command,) for murderers of
fathers and mothers, (of the fifth command,) for man slayers, (of
the sixth,) for whoremongers and defilers of mankind, (of the
seventh,) for man stealers, (of the eighth,) for liars, (of the ninth,)
and for those that in any thing walk contrary to sound doctrine,
the purity of the law and will of God, (of the tenth ;) so that
this place is far from favoring any of those that run in this channel of abolishing the law as our rule.   No, beloved, the love of
Christ will constrain you to embrace it as a most precious treasure.
It is the observation of some, that in the preface to the moral
law, (Ex. xx. 1, 2,) the Lord reveals himself to be "the Lord
their God that brought them out of the land of Egypt;" the very
scope of which words is to persuade to a reverend receiving and
keeping of that good law. This law all nations are bound to observe, because he is Jehovah the Lord ; but to be thy God in special covenant, and that "redeemed thee from Egypt," and from
that which was typified by it, this belongs to none but unto
them especially that are the people of God, and therefore, of all
other people in the world, they are bound to receive it as their
rule ; for obedience doth not make us God's people, or God our
God; but he is first our God, — which is only by the covenant of
grace, — and thence it is, that being ours, and we his, we, of all
others, are most bound to obey.

To conclude : They that stick in these briers, therefore, cry
down the law as a Christian's rule, because by this means a
Christian shall find no peace ; because he is continually sinning
against this law ; the law, therefore, say they, will be always
troubling of him.

I answer, first, a corrupt heart and putrid conscience can
have no peace by the law ; (Is. lvii. 21,) "There is no peace
to the wicked," and it is good it should be so.

2. A watchful Christian may. (Ps. cxix. 15,) "Great peace
have they that keep thy law." Hezekiah had it when he desired
"the Lord to remember how he had walked before him with a
perfect heart." (Is. lviii. 1–3.) Paul found it "the testimony of
his conscience " bearing him witness, was "his rejoicing herein."
(2 Cor. i. 12.)

3. If a Christian ignorant of maintaining his peace with God
by faith in his justification, notwithstanding all the errors in
his obedience and sanctification ; if, I say, he wants his peace,
shall we, therefore, break the law in pieces ? If a secure Christian
that walks loosely wants peace, by the accusations of the law, it
is God's mercy to him to give him no peace in himself, while he
is at truce with his lust.

4. That peace will end in dismal sorrow which is got by kicking against the law ; it is but daubing for a man to keep his peace by shutting his eyes against the way of peace. A servant may have peace in his idleness by thinking that his master requires no work from him, and by hiding his talent; yet what will his lord say to him when his day is ended, and he comes to reckon with him at sunset ? Bring the law into thy conscience in point of justification ; it will trouble conscience; for there only Christ's righteousness, God's grace, and the promise, are to be looked on, and our own obedience and holiness laid up in the dust ; but bring it before thee as a rule of thy sanctification, and as thy copy to write after and to imitate, and aspire after that perfection it requires, it will then trouble thee no more than it doth a child, who, having a fair copy set him to write after, and knowing that he is a son, is not therefore troubled, because he can not write as fair as his copy ; he knows, if he imitates it, his scribbling shall be accepted : howsoever, though his father may chastise him with rods, if he be careless to imitate, yet he will never cast him therefore off from being his son. The truth is this : it argues a most graceless, carnal, wretched heart, for a man to cast by God's rules, because attendance to them is his trouble and torment, which, unto a gracious heart, are life, and peace, and sweetness : " All the ways of wisdom, to him, are ways of pleasantness, and her paths peace." And it is God's common curse upon them that love not the truth in these days, that because sin is not their sorrow, nor breach of rules their trouble, that, therefore, the observance of the law and attendance unto rules shall be their burden and trouble ; they feel not the plague in their own hearts, and therefore reproofs plague them, and commands are a plague and a torment unto them : crooked feet and crooked wills make them tread awry in such corrupt opinions.

All the called ones of God are therefore to live this life of obedience, and that out of love, which I call the life of love, (Gal. v. 6 ;) for else circumcision avails nothing, nor uncircumcision, no, nor faith itself, unless it be of this nature, as that it works by love. There is much obedience and external conformity to the law in many men, but the principal difference between these formalities and the obedience of the saints is love ; the obedience of the one ariseth from self-love, because it pleaseth themselves and suits with their own ends; the other from the love of Christ, because it pleaseth him, and suits with his ends. (1 Cor. xiii. 4, etc. 1 John v. 3.)

Wherein doth and should this life of love appear ?

In these five particulars : In thinking and musing much on Christ and upon his love, and on what you shall do for him ; he that saith he loves another, and yet seldom thinks on him, or will seldom give him a good look when he meets him, certainly deceives himself; the least degree of love appears in thinking on what we love, because the "loving kindness of God" was "better than life" unto David ; hence he did "remember him upon his bed, and meditate on him in the very night." (Ps. lxiii. 3, 6.) They that "fear the Lord"—i. e., with a son-like fear, where love is chiefly predominant—are such as "think upon his name." (Mal. iii. 16.) "We have thought on thy loving kindness, O Lord, in thy temple." (Ps. xlviii. 9.) Thou that canst spend days, nights, weeks, months, years, and hast thy head all this time swarming with vain thoughts, and scarce one living thought of Christ and his love, that didst never beat thy head, nor trouble thyself in musing, O, what shall I do for him ? nor in condemning thyself because thou dost so little, verily thou hast not the least degree of this life of love.

In speaking and commending of him. Is it possible that any man should love another and not commend him, not speak of him ? If thou hadst but a hawk or a hound that thou lovest, thou wilt commend it ; and can it stand with love to Christ, yet seldom or never to speak of him nor of his love ; never to commend him unto others, that they may fall in love with him also ? You shall see the spouse, (Cant. v. 9, 16,) when she was asked "what her beloved was above others," she sets him out in every part of him, and concludes with this : "He is altogether lovely." "Because thy loving kindness" (saith David) "is better than life, my lips shall praise thee, and I will bless thee whilst I live." (Ps. lxiii. 3, 4.) Can it stand with this life of love to be always speaking about worldly affairs, or news at the best, both week day and Sabbath day, in bed and at board, in good company and in bad, at home and abroad ? I tell you it will be one main reason why you desire to live, that you may make the Lord Jesus known to your children, friends, acquaintance, that so, in the ages to come, his name might ring, and his memorial might be of sweet odor, from generation to generation. (Ps. lxxi. 18.) If, before thy conversion especially, thou hast poisoned others, by thy vain and corrupt speeches, after thy conversion thou wilt seek to season the hearts of others by a gracious, sweet, and wise communication of savory and blessed speeches ; what the Lord hath taught thee thou wilt talk of it unto others, for the sake of him whom thou lovest.

In being oft in his company, and growing up thereby into a

familiar acquaintance with him. Can we be long absent from those we love entirely, if we may come to them? Can we love Christ, and yet be seldom with him, in word, in prayer, in sacraments, in Christian communion, in meditation and daily examination of our own hearts; in his providences of mercies, crosses, and trials? (for Christ is with us here, but those two ways, in his ordinances or providences, " by his Holy Spirit.") " Lord," saith David, " I have loved the habitation of thy house, and the place where thine honor dwelleth," (Ps. xxvi. 8 ;) the ground of which is set down, (ver. 3 :) " Thy loving kindness is before mine eyes ; my soul longeth for thee as in a land where no water is, that I might see thee, as I have seen thee in the sanctuary ; " the reason of it was, " because thy loving kindness is better than life." (Ps. lxiii. 1, 2.)

In doing much for him, and that willingly. Did not Jacob love Rachel? How did he express it? His seven years' service, in frost and snow, in heat and cold, by day and night, were nothing to him, for her sake whom he loved. " Shall I serve the Lord " (saith David) " of what cost me nothing ? " And when he had prepared many millions for the building of the temple, yet he accounted it a small thing for his sake whom he loved, (1 Chron. xxix. 3 ;) he gave it out of his poverty, as he speaks : " This is love, to keep his commandments, and those are not grievous." (1 John v. 3.)

In suffering and enduring any evil for his sake. I confess it is not every degree of love that will carry a man hither ; yet where there is great and singular love, "for a good man, one may be willing to die." (Rom. v. 7.) Assuredly if there be any love to Christ, it will in time increase to this measure. It will think ten thousand lives too little to lay down for Christ's sake, that laid down his precious life for him. " What tell you me," saith Paul, " of bonds and imprisonments? I am ready, not only to be bound, but to die, for the sake of Christ " at Jerusalem ; " my life is not dear to me," no more than a rush at my foot, " that I may finish my course with joy. For thy sake we are killed all the day long." (Rom. viii. 36.) I tell you the love of Christ will make you fall down upon your knees, and bless the Lord, and he will accept of such a poor sacrifice as thy body is, though it be burnt to ashes ; and thou wilt bless him again and again, that whereas he might have left thee in thy sins to have trodden him and his glory and grace under foot, as he hath done thousands in the world, yet that he should call thee to share in this honor, not only to do but to suffer for his sake.

24 *

Now, the good Lord persuade all our hearts unto this fruitful obedience and life of love. O, you young men, you have a fair time before you to do much for Christ in. How pleasing will it be to him to see such young trees hang full of fruit! You aged men have now one foot in your grave, and you have forgotten the Lord Jesus most of your time, and your time which now remains is very little, and then your lamp is out, your sun is almost set, and all your work is yet to be done for Christ; O, therefore awaken now at last before you awake when it is too late. You rich men have abilities and wherewithal to set forward Christ's kingdom in the towns and villages where you live; you poor men may do much by ardent and instant prayers, day and night, for the advancement of the Lord Jesus.

You husbands, wives, masters, servants, remember, if you are not good in your places, you are not good at all, whatever your profession be; a good woman, but a froward wife; a good man, but a hare-brained, curst husband; a good servant, but a very sore tongue; these can not well stand together. If you have any love to Christ, the life of love will make you move best in your proper place. O, therefore love much, and so think much and speak much of, and converse much with, and do much, and suffer much for the Lord Jesus Christ. Content not yourselves with doing small things for him that hath done and suffered much for you; if you can do but little, yet set God on work by being fervent and frequent in prayer, not only that Christ may be honored in yourselves, but also in your families, and in all churches and kingdoms of the world. If you can not do much, yet maintain alive a will to do much, which is accepted as if you did. (2 Cor. viii. 12.) If thou art a poor man, and hast nothing to give, yet keep a heart as liberal as a prince; if you can do but little yourselves, yet encourage others that they may; thou art not a preacher called to convert souls, yet do thou encourage the messengers of Christ in their work, by thy prayers, counsel, help, and at the last day the conversion of souls shall be attributed unto thee, as well as unto them. If thou canst not do any good, yet prevent what evil thou canst in thy place; to keep off judgments, at least to delay them; mourn thou for other men's sins, as if they were thine own, that so the Lord may pity and pardon them, and it may be convert them, who shall do no more good, it may be, than ever thou canst do; let the Lord Jesus be in thy thoughts the first in the morning, and the last at night; do what thou canst, nay, go continually to him to enable thee to do more than thou of thyself canst, and mourn bitterly and lament daily what thou hast not done, either through want of ability or will; remembering his love to thee, that he came out of his Father's bosom for thee, wept for thee, bled for thee, poured out his life, nay, his soul to death for thee, is now risen for thee, gone to heaven for thee, sits at God's right hand, and rules all the world for thee, makes intercession continually for thee, and at the end of the world will come again for thee; who hast loved him here, that thou mightest live forever with him then.

But is this our life, in these evil and lukewarm times? How many be there that believe in Christ, that they may live as they list? If to drink, and whore, and scoff, and blaspheme; if to shake a lock, and follow every fond fashion; if to cross and cringe before a piece of wood; if to be weary of the word, and outwardly zealous for long prayers; if to seek purity of ordinances in churches, and to maintain impurity in hearts, in shops, in families; if to set our hearts upon farms and merchandises, and so to be covetous; if to set up our own selves, and parts, and gifts, with a secret disdain of God's ministers; if to cry down learning, and set up ignorance; if to set up Christ, and destroy sanctification and obedience; if to be a sect master of some odd opinions; if to crack the nut of some superlunary and monkish notions and high-flown speculations; if to hear much and do little; if to have a name to live, and yet dead at the heart, — if this be to live the life of love, we have many that live this life; the Lord Jesus wants no love, if this be to love. But O, woe unto you, if you thus requite the Lord, foolish people and unwise.

The Lord knows we may complain as Paul did, "Every man minds his own things, and not the things of Jesus Christ;" none in comparison of that huge number that think they are religious enough, if they be baptized, and say that they believe in Jesus Christ. Verily the time draws near wherein the Lord will come for fruits of his vineyard; and if he finds it not, assuredly he will not be beholding to us for obedience; he can raise his glory out of other people, and there carry his gospel to them who shall bring forth the fruits of it; the Lord will shortly lay his ax unto the root of our tree, and if we will not serve the Lord in this good land in the abundance of peace and mercy, we shall serve our enemies in hunger, cold, and nakedness; if we will not serve him in love, we must serve our enemies in fear. Do not think that the Lord will be put off with venerable names and titles, shadows and pictures: what is most men's profession at this day but a mere paint, which may serve to color them while they live, but will never comfort them (unless conscience be asleep) when they come to die? O, take heed of such formality. I can never think enough of David's expression, (Ps. cxix. 167,) "I have kept thy commandments, and I love them exceedingly:" should he not have said first, "I have loved thy commandments, and so have kept them?" Doubtless he did so, but he ran here in a holy and most heavenly circle: I have kept them, and loved them; and loved them, and kept them. If we love Christ, we shall live such a life of love in our measure, and his commandments will be most dear, when himself is most precious.

THE

SAINT'S JEWEL;

SHOWING

HOW TO APPLY THE PROMISE.

ACTS ii. 39. — "For the promise is unto you, and to your children, and to all that are afar off, even as many as the Lord our God shall call."

REV. iii. 20. — "Behold, I stand at the door, and knock : if any man hear my voice, and open the door, I will come in to him, and will sup with him, and he with me."

TO THE READER.

Reader, the body may as well subsist without the soul, as the soul can without a promise; and as the body is not wearied with bread, (being the staff of life,) though it hath it every day for nourishment, so, likewise, the fainting, hungry soul can never be cloyed with feeding upon the promises. For which cause I have also adventured this little Sermon, not doubting but it may reap its due fruit from those whose hearts are rightly affected; which God granting, I shall account my labor abundantly requited. Farewell.

Thomas Shepard.

April 2, 1655.
Imprimatur.
Edmund Calamy.

THE SAINT'S JEWEL,

SHOWING HOW TO APPLY THE PROMISE.

---

2 Cor. vii. 1, " Having these promises, dearly beloved, let us cleanse ourselves from all filthiness of the flesh and spirit, perfecting holiness in the fear of God."

THE apostle Paul in the former chapter exhorteth the Corinthians to beware of unequal yoking themselves with unbelievers ; and he gives a double argument for it, one from the unequalness of it, the other from the promises, as in my text, " Having these promises."

In these words are three parts : —

1. A loving appellation, in these words, " Having these promises, dearly beloved."

2. A gracious exhortation, " Let us cleanse ourselves from all filthiness of flesh and spirit, perfecting holiness in the fear of God."

3. An argument for instigation or motive, that he useth to press his exhortation, which is from the nature of the promise.

That which is in the last part of the division is first in order of the words, and therefore we will look upon the words as they lie in order ; and so from the last part and first words I shall handle this doctrine.

That God made many promises unto his people.

I am come to you this day not to set out unto you the excellency of wit or learning, or the creature ; but the excellency of a naked promise, according to that, (2 Pet. i. 4,) " Whereby are given unto us exceeding great and precious promises."

Now, all the promises of God unto his people are such as concern the body, or the body and the soul. Those that concern the body are with this limitation, that is, so far as concerns God's glory and the good of our souls ; but for the body and soul, consider that place, " For the Lord is a sun and shield ;

287

the Lord will give grace and glory, and no good will he withhold from them that live uprightly." (Ps. lxxxiv. 11.)

I come to the reasons why God hath thus made many promises unto his people; and they are three.

The first reason is this: that his people might have a fit object for their faith to lay hold upon; for if you look upon all the creatures in the world, you shall not find in all of them jointly, or any of them apart, a fit object for faith to work upon, or be satisfied in. It is with faith as with a poor woman that hath a child, and hath nothing in the world to give it; she takes the child at her back and goeth from door to door, and what she getteth she giveth to the child; so faith takes the soul, and carrieth it to promise after promise, and whatever she finds there she gives it to the soul.

The second reason why God hath made many promises unto his people is, that they may have a ground of comfort; for as it is the object of their faith, so it is the ground of their comfort; for all other things of this world can not profit or comfort the believing soul. As suppose we should go to friends for comfort; it may be they want comfort for themselves, and so are unfit to comfort us; or it may be they will not comfort us; or it may be they are a great way off, and so can not do it; or perhaps, though able and sometimes willing, yet they are mutable in their comforts, so as though at one time they are willing, and do comfort us, yet another time they fail us. But Christ, to whom the soul is led by the promise, not only hath comfort, and is able to comfort us, but he is willing also to give comfort to us, who knoweth our wants, " and is near to all that call upon him in truth," (Ps. cxlv. 18;) and also he is immutable in his comforts. And were the creature a sufficient ground of comfort to God's people, then to want the creature were a sufficient ground of misery to them. But a man may want health, wealth, liberty, and the like, and yet through and in Christ his soul may have satisfying comfort; but if he want Christ, though he hath a fullness of the creature, he is most miserable and without all satisfying comfort. The promise only is able to afford comfort to the soul in health, in sickness, in life, and in death.

The third reason why God hath made many promises unto his people is, that they may become mutual comforters one of another, by having somewhat by experience from a promise, wherewith they may be enabled to comfort others, so that you may see the promise is not given to comfort ourselves with only, but also one another.

Now for use. Is it so, that God hath made many promises

unto his people ? Let us try ourselves, whether we have any right to the promises or no. I will name but one note that you may the better remember it, and it is a true one, for you shall find it in Scripture. " But the Scripture hath concluded all under sin, that the promise by faith in Jesus Christ might be given to them that believe." (Gal. iii. 22.) So that you may see it is to them, and to them only, that believe. He that can exercise faith in the promise, hath right to the promise, " for ye walk by faith, and not by sight." (2 Cor. v. 7.)

If Christians be in affliction, and see that it doth them good, then it is easy to believe that promise which God hath made. " All things shall work together for the good of them that love God." .(Rom. viii. 28.) But to believe this promise, when we can not see any good come of affliction, that is to believe by faith, and not by sight : but when we can see no good come by affliction, but find ourselves more dead and dull, and also God to frown upon us, and yet we trust in God, and believe the promise, and stay our souls upon God's word ; this is to live by faith, as we are commanded. " Who is among you that feareth the Lord, that obeyeth the voice of his servant, that walketh in darkness and hath no light ? Let him trust in the name of the Lord, and stay upon his God." (Is. l. 10.) Faith maketh things absent to be present, and maketh the promise good to us, though things seem to thwart the promise never so much. " Now, faith is the substance of things hoped for, and the evidence of things not seen " (Heb. xi. 1) with the eye of sense. As Abraham believed against hope, (Rom. iv. 18,) that he should have a child, according as God had promised, so must we trust God upon a naked promise, that if health should be gone, or wealth, liberty, strength, friends, yea, life itself almost gone, and God seems to be gone, and hell to be threatened, yet still to trust in God, and believe — this is to live by faith, and comfort is in the promise for all such ; but I speak now to God's people.

The second use of this doctrine is, that seeing God hath made many promises unto his people, it is a ground of comfort unto them all, that though they go up and down sad, as if they were the worst people in the world, yet have they the only cause to rejoice, and they only in all the world. For here is comfort against all their sins, God hath promised to do them away. " I am he that blotteth out thy sins, for mine own name's sake." (Is. xliii. 25.) Comfort thyself, Christ is thine. "I am my beloved's, and my beloved is mine ; " if, therefore, there be enough in Christ's merits, hold up thy head and take comfort to thyself.

O, but, saith the poor soul, I find sin prevail, and how can I then be comforted?

I answer, Look into that place of Scripture, "I will subdue your iniquities, and cast your sins in the midst of the sea," (Micah vii. 18–20;) and in the twentieth verse you may see the oath of God, for the truth and mercy of the promise was gone forth before.

But saith the soul, The devil will be busy with me wherever I go, and how can I be cheerful?

I answer, God hath said it, "I will tread down Satan under your feet shortly." (Rom. xvi. 20.) Comfort thyself in this, though Satan may trouble thee for a time, yet thou shalt have him under thy feet shortly.

O, but again saith the soul, I shall meet with abundance of opposition in the world, and I am not able to make my party good, and how can I then rejoice?

I answer, Flee thou to the promise against that also, as where it is said, "Though hand join in hand," etc. (Prov. xi. 21.) Though men join themselves together, and strike hands even with the devil against God's children, yet shall they not overcome them.

But alas! saith a poor soul, I am in present want of outward comfort, and how should I be comfortable in such a condition?

I answer, It may be God dealeth with thee in this as a mother with her children, who takes away the victuals from the children for a while, and puts it into the cupboard, but afterward she giveth it them again. So sometimes God taketh away these outward things, and locketh them up for a while in the cupboard, which is in the promise, and when he seeth it best for us, he giveth it us again: and thus he did with Job; he took away all his outward comforts, and left him so poor, as it is a proverb at this day, "as poor as Job," (Job i. 15, etc.;) but after a while, God did not only restore unto him his former comforts, but gave him double. And this was written for thy comfort, and the strength of thy patience: comfort thyself, therefore; happiness is above the creature.

But I shall meet with many mocks and reproaches in the world.

Answer. Let us comfort ourselves against this with God's promises: let us do as the covetous man in the poet, who, being mocked as he went in the streets, went home and looked into his closet, and there seeing his bags of gold, rejoiced in his wealth, and scorned all their reproaches: so when we are mocked and scorned of men of the world, let us look into the Bible, and we shall find bags of promises, true treasure; and therein let us rejoice.

But it may be the poor soul will say, Alas, I can not go to God by prayer to fetch comfort, or if I do pray, it is with so much coldness and deadness, as I can not believe I shall obtain any thing.

I answer, Though it be so, yet believe and thou shalt have thy desire, though it may be thou canst but chatter, and though others, hearing thee, regard it not, yet God will say, Let me hear thee ; and as a father loves to hear his child prattle, though others regard it not, so God loveth to hear his children pray.

But O, I am afraid of death, and that taketh away all my joy and comfort.

I answer, Thou mayest comfort thyself against that, yea, and make death itself a ground of comfort and joy to thyself. If a child be at board from his father's house, though he be at play with his fellows, yet if he see horse and man come to fetch him, he is glad, and leaves his play and companions to go home to his father willingly : so here we are at board in the world, and we are at play, as it were, among the creatures ; but when death comes, which is as horse and man, we should be willing to go to our Father's house, which is best of all.

But I am afraid, if suffering times come, I should never be able to stand out.

If God call thee to sufferings, he will give thee grace suitable to thy condition. "He will not suffer us to be tempted above that we are able ; but will with the temptation also make a way to escape, that we may be able to bear it." (1 Cor. xiii. 10.)

But alas ! I am afraid I shall fall away from God, and that continual fear thereof doth take away all my comfort.

Answer. None can pluck thee out of Christ's hands, neither sin nor devil; she were a cruel mother that would cast her child into the fire; Christ must do so if thou shouldest go to hell ; yea, more, if that should be so, he should rend a member from himself, for he is thy head, and thou art one of his members : therefore, for thy comfort, know this can not be ; the Lord saith, "I will make an everlasting covenant with them, that I will not turn away from them to do them good." But you may say, perhaps, I shall turn from him ; see therefore what followeth in the same verse — "I will put my fear into their hearts, and they shall not depart from me."

This is good news, it may be the poor creature will say, if I had right to the promise ; but alas ! I can not believe, and take a naked promise.

Answer. Dost thou desire to believe and to have Christ, and canst thou say thus ? If it were possible heaven and Christ could be separated, I would rather have Christ without heaven than heaven without Christ; then comfort thyself, for God hath promised, "I will give to him that thirsteth of the water of life freely."

But this is a hard matter, and I can not say I truly desire Christ on such terms as I should.

But is it a grief to thy heart that thou canst not deny thyself, and desirest, rather than be separated from Christ, to close with Christ, even upon any terms? Is it thy burden, because thou canst not desire to believe as thou shouldest? Then comfort thyself; God will accept the will for the deed in this case. (1 Cor. viii. 12.)

But the soul objecteth and saith, Alas! I am so far from being grieved as I ought, that I rather find a heart that will not grieve and mourn for sin; I can not find breakings of heart for it.

For thy comfort, I will come one step lower to thee: hast thou any will to it? Mark this place; if any place in the whole Scripture be for thee, here it is in the last words of this verse. "And whosoever will, let him take of the water of life freely." (Rev. xxii. 17.)

But it may be the wicked will say, I will have Christ: but stay; not every one that saith so shall have Christ; but art thou willing to part with thy sins, and it may be to part with health, wealth, liberty, friends, yea, and your own life also? What say you? Are you willing upon these terms?

But the poor soul saith again, I fear I shall never do this. But art thou willing that Christ should make thee willing, and pitch thee upon a promise, and should hold thee there? If thou canst find these things, then comfort thyself, for thou hast right unto God's promises.

The third use is, seeing God hath made many promises unto his people, this is terror to the wicked. Here are many in this congregation to whom I have not spoken one word in the last use of comfort; now God sends other news to you, therefore put it not off from you. If I prove not what I say by Scripture, believe me not. What I have said for the comfort of God's people, I must say the contrary unto you.

First. As God's children have their names written in God's book, so you have your names written also; but it is in the black book of God's wrath.

Secondly. As God's children have a mark set on their foreheads, so there is a mark set on you; but it is a woful one; for, though I judge you not, yet I am persuaded the devil hath set his black mark with a brand from hell on some of you: yea, a man may gather from your very faces, almost, what some of you are ; but the day of judgment will fully discover you all. But in the mean time, know this : whosoever you are that are under your natural condition, you are under God's curse, as it is, " If any shall hear the words of this curse, and bless himself in his heart, saying, I shall have peace though I walk in the imagination of my heart," etc., then the Lord will not spare him, but the anger of the Lord and his jealousy shall smoke against that man, and all the curses of this book shall be upon him, and the Lord shall blot out his name from under heaven," etc. (Deut. xxix. 19, 20.) Also, " I will heap up mischief upon you, and I will send mine arrows upon you." (Deut. xxxii. 23.) O, what a heavy thing is this, I pray you consider sadly ; not to have right to God's promises is the condition of a man that is cursed, and miserable in his life, at his death, and after his death.

You rich gentlemen and gentlewomen, give me leave to speak to you. I pray you consider thus much : if you have not right to God's promises, the curse of God is stamped upon every cross and penny, and upon every thing you have. See but this place : " I have cursed your blessings, saith the Lord ; " (Mal. ii. 2, 3 ;) as if he should have said, Though I have given plenty of corn, and money, and other things, yet they are to you but as curses ; and is not this a very sad thing ? Give me leave to deal painly ; it is as if a man had but twopence in all the world, and he should go and buy a halter with it, to hang himself ; yea, further, all that thou hast, in this condition, is but as if thou shouldest twist a cord together to hang thy soul in hell. And to you of the poorer sort, that have not a right to the promise, you are in a miserable condition, for you are both miserable here and hereafter also. " Israel hath not returned to him that smote them, neither do they seek unto the Lord ; therefore the Lord will cut off from them both head and tail, branch and rush, in one day." (Is. ix. 13.) Again : whatsoever you do in your calling is accursed unto you ; yea, your praying, reading, hearing, fasting, and mourning, all is sin ; for, " The sacrifice of the wicked is an abomination unto the Lord." (Prov. xv. 8.)

But if it be so, may these wicked men say, that our best duties are sin, why should we perform any duties, either praying, hearing, or the like ?

In answer to this, know for certain whilst thou art in this condition, thou art in a bad condition, for every thing you do is sin. " Unto the pure all things are pure ; but unto them that are defiled, and unbelieving, nothing is pure, but even their minds and consciences are defiled." (Tit. i. 15.) So that to you, to

25 *

perform duty it is sin, or not to perform duty is sin : but yet omit not duty, for though in performing duty thou sinnest, yet not to perform duty is a double sin.

To perform duty, whilst thou art in thy natural condition, is sin for the manner, because, though thou mayest do the duty for substance, as pray, hear, confer, or the like, yet because thou dost want a principle of grace, nothing is done aright, and so wanteth acceptance : but to neglect duty is a sin, in regard of matter and manner also ; for as it is sinfulness itself not to do the duty, so it is sin to have the heart not rightly disposed for the manner of performance. It is with you as it was with the lepers ; they said among themselves thus : " Why sit we here till we die ? If we say we will enter into the city, then the famine is in the city, and we shall die there ; and if we sit still here, we die also. Now therefore let us come and fall unto the host of the Syrians ; if they save us alive, we shall live, and if they kill us, we shall but die." (2 Kings vii. 3, 4.) So say thou with thyself, If I do duty, I sin ; and if I do not perform duty, I commit a double sin ; but I will go to duty : if God will save me, I shall live ; if not, I can but perish : and for thy comfort, consider, it may be God will cast an eye of pity upon thee ; thou art in the way ; that is the means God hath appointed to bring you home to Christ : but yet, until thy condition be changed, all thou dost is sin ; for, " The very thoughts of the wicked are an abomination unto the Lord." (Prov. xv. 26.)

But, O, strange ! though firebrands out of hell be spitted in your faces, yet you are not affected. But it may be some of you think to do it when you are sick, or upon your death bed ; but it may be too late then, when God openeth and awakeneth your conscience, and if you be not awakened here, you shall be sure to be awakened in hell. I remember I heard of a young prodigal, when he was dying, looked on the fire and said, As that fire burneth there, so shall my soul burn in hell. Another said on his death bed, O that I might live, though it were but the life of a toad. God is very careful to send his angels for the godly ; but for the wicked the devils stand ready at his bedside to fetch him into hell as soon as his breath goeth out of his body ; and then they will cry out, O the time of mercy that I have had ! but now it is past ; the gate of mercy is shut, never more to be opened.

But it may be yet some will say, Thanks be to God, I am not in hell yet, and as long as there is life there is hope.

O, fearful ! what ! hope still ? Read that place, and tremble in reading of it : " The Lord of that servant shall come in a day when he looketh not for him, and in an hour that he is not aware of, and shall cut him asunder, and appoint him his portion with the hypocrites; there shall be weeping and gnashing of teeth." (Matt. xxiv. 50, 51.)

O, consider this against the day of judgment; it is a sad day for all such, when mercy, and patience, and Christ shall plead against them; yea, "The dust of ministers' feet shall rise up against them." (Luke x. 11.) O, but if so, then what will their condition be, when drops of blood and sweat shall rise up against them? yea, more, the husband shall rejoice to see the damnation of the wife. "The righteous shall rejoice when he seeth vengeance on the wicked," (Luke xxii. 44; Ps. lviii. 10,) because God hath gotten the glory of his enemies.

The fourth use is, An exhortation to the godly first, and, secondly, to the wicked.

In the first place, to the godly, that complain they can not lay hold on the promise. Go to God to enable you; and that you may so do, —

Consider, in the first place, that not to believe and lay hold on the promise is a sin of unbelief; "and he that believeth not is damned." (John iii. 13.) See the evil of this sin of unbelief in these particulars: —

First. "Hereby we grieve the Holy Spirit of God, whereby we are sealed to the day of redemption." (Eph. iv. 30.) What a grievous thing is it for thee, who desirest to be assured that the promise is thine, that thou, by unbelief, shouldest grieve that Holy Spirit, which sealeth up the promise to thy soul! See that place, "Hear ye now, O house of David: Is it a small thing for you to weary men, but you must weary my God also?" (Is. iii. 17.) If a man promise to do another man a courtesy, and, after some delay, that man comes to him and saith, Will you do as you promised me? He saith, Yes. But saith he, Will you indeed? and thus he pleadeth with him a whole day, and doth not believe him: will not that exceedingly grieve his friend, who promised him so to do, and fully intended no less? Even so is it with all those that are God's people, and will not believe what God hath said unto them, but stand and plead with God two or three years or more. As those that believe glorify God, so those that will not come in rob God of his honor and glory, and grieve him.

It argueth a great deal of pride of heart in them, that they will not believe because they have not what they would; but something they must have of themselves, like women that will not go to a feast, because they have nothing to carry.

Here is a great deal of unthankfulness for all that God hath done for them, yea, even for Christ himself. Where we love, we are very thankful; and where we desire to be thankful, we will be willing to take a kindness.

It argueth a great deal of impatience, when we will not wait in a way of believing upon the promises of grace, and cheerfully attend God's leisure.

He that will not believe gives God the lie; for, " He that believeth," etc. (1 John v. 10.) He that believeth not in every ordinance he comes to, he maketh God a liar, because every ordinance beareth record of Christ. Not to believe is a denying of God's power, for they will not trust God, especially in a great strait; and by this we may see what a many sins even God's people may commit in this case.

Consider again, in the second place, what a safe thing it is to believe ; I speak to God's people. As surgeons, when they let a man blood, bid him look another way, so when the devil letteth you blood, that is, holds you poring on your corruptions, look another way, — I mean on God, — and then you shall be safe from the devil, and the world, and your own corruptions. And that you may lay hold on the promises of God, take heed of those lets and impediments that might hinder you.

Sin is a let; for it will wrest the promise out of our hands. " But your iniquities," etc. (Is. lix. 2.)

The second impediment is, our doubting and wandering in our our prayers ; for " we must pray, lifting up holy hands," etc. (James i. 6.)

The third impediment to believing is slavish fear, when we fear man more than God, contrary to that counsel, " Fear not their fear, nor be afraid," etc. (Is. viii. 12.)

The fourth let is, when we lay down one thing that might afford us help, and draw ourselves to God, and, in the mean time, take up another which can no way help us; as, when we lay down the promise, and take up the threatening.

Fifthly, when we set our mind too much on the creature, or honors, and seek our own baseness, or worldly pleasures.

In the next place, take these helps to lay hold on the promise.

Labor to live by faith in all straits and conditions, and by faith fetch a supply for all your wants, by the promise from Christ.

Secondly, mark the promise well, which is the ground of all comfort, and read them over often.

Do not flutter up and down, from one promise to another, but lie a great while on some one, and wring and squeeze it by meditation upon it.

Thirdly, apply the promise aright; do not think it belongeth not to you, because you have not that presently which is proposed in it : you must know that God setteth not down the time when it shall be fulfilled.

Fourthly, we are to wait patiently and humbly under our present condition; until God grant our desire, God's time is the best time.

Bless God for all his promises, but especially when they are made good to us.

In the next place, to those that yet stand out, and are not closed with the promise, I entreat you, come in to God, take his gracious offer, lay hold on the promise ; which that you may do, take heed of those things that will be lets, and hinder you. (Ps. ciii.)

Take heed of all sin ; for the Lord saith, " Your sins have kept back good things from you."

Take heed of setting your mind too much upon the creatures, for they will shut out God the Creator. Old men, do you come home to God ; young men, do you remember your Creator in the days of your youth. God this day calleth you ; it may be he will never call more. How many hath the Lord struck with death and sickness ! and how soon it may be any of our turns, I know not. Sickness is an unfit time to get Christ, and to make our peace with God. If you stand still, you die ; if you go on in sin, you die : therefore turn from all your sin, and come in and lay hold by faith on the promise, that so ye may live, and this that I have spoken unto you may not be in vain.

CERTAIN SELECT CASES

RESOLVED;

SPECIALLY TENDING TO THE

RIGHT ORDERING OF THE HEART,

THAT WE MAY COMFORTABLY

WALK WITH GOD IN OUR GENERAL AND PARTICULAR CALLINGS.

IN A LETTER TO A PIOUS FRIEND IN ENGLAND.

CHRISTIAN READER.

————

THIS holy letter of that ready scribe of Christ's kingdom is so full of grace and truth, that it needs no other epistle commendatory than itself.

Yet seeing the lot is unexpectedly fallen upon my pen to give it a superscription, that it may pass current from hand to hand, I do heartily, in the first place, dedicate it to thee, thou bleeding, troubled spirit, as a choice, cordial friend; an interpreter — one of a thousand — that doth not only speak thy heart, but by the Comforter (whom Christ hath promised to send) to thy heart.

It may be this paper present is sent on embassy from heaven, on purpose to set thy house in order, to untie thy bosom knots, to bind the strong man, and cast him out of thy doors, that thy heart may be once again set at liberty, to serve the Lord thy God in thy general and particular calling, whose service is thy freedom. What is here sent by this embassador of Christ (who is now the voice of one crying in the wilderness) to a weary and heavy-laden soul in this island, I had rather it should appear to thy judgment in the serious reading, and to thy conscience in the home application thereof, than from my opinion of it. Therefore I shall only add (as the contents of this letter) certain select cases, proposed and resolved in the several paragraphs thereof, as they lie in order in the pages following, viz.:—

301

All which select cases (and many more that collaterally issue
from their sides) are judiciously resolved with much perspicuity
and brevity in these few sheets, by the only Judge of all controversies, the two-edged sword of the Spirit, the word of God.

Thus humbly beseeching thee to read over this epistle of
Christ to thee, with the same spirit of love and of a sound mind
which indited every line in it, I do desire to leave thee at the
throne of grace, in the arms of Christ, with the Father of all
comfort, that thou mayest receive the peace of God, which passeth all understanding, and be crowned with joy unspeakable and
full of glory.   I subscribe myself, friend,

Thine in any spiritual

furtherance of thy faith,

WILLIAM ADDERLEY.

CHARTER HOUSE, LONDON.
  Feb. 1, 1647.

CERTAIN SELECT CASES RESOLVED.

DEAR SIR: I dare not multiply many words in acknowledging and professing my own unfitness and insufficiency to yield your loving and most welcome letter that satisfaction which both yourself desire and it deserves. Neither yet will I be so unfaithful to you, (seeing your expectation puts me to reply,) neither ought I, I think, be so unserviceable to Jesus Christ, who in you, and by you, beckons to me to take this call to write to you, and not to neglect so fair a season; seeing especially it may be possible my dying letter to you, before I depart from hence and return to him, as not knowing but our last disasters and sea straits (of which I wrote to you) may be but preparations for the execution of this next approaching voyage. Yet our eyes are to the hills, and our desires are your prayers; and at this time my endeavor shall be in respect of yourself, to break open that light to you, and to prepare it to you, with that brevity I may, and with what plainness I am able; beseeching the God and Father of our Lord Jesus Christ, who must be, when all fails, the Wonderful Counselor, to give you the Spirit of revelation, and that after you have suffered a while by these outward temptations, doubts, fears, desertions, distractions, which the letter mentions, he would make you perfect, stablish, strengthen, and settle you. And this I verily think will be the unexpected, yet happy, joyful, and most glorious end of them; for since I have observed and seen the lamentable ruins of the soul, and seeming graces of many men, by being rocked asleep in a quiet, still, calm, easy performance of duties, without such awakening temptations and tumults within which itself complains of; I say, since I have observed what a deal of mud is in the bottom of such standing pools, and what a deal of filth is in such moats, which are inwardly at ease, and not emptied from vessel to vessel, next unto the donation of the Lord Jesus to a man, I have accounted tumultuous heart storms and uproars, together with the fruitful strange effects of them, the second mercy. For I never saw that man kept from secret putrefaction and corruption that was not usually salted with such temptations (especially in a Christian's first apprenticeship) which usually preserve him entire till death. And therefore, dear sir, faint not, for Jesus Christ will raise a world of blessings out of your present chaos and confusions. But I make haste to answer. Before your reply to my first letter, your complaints are many.

Your first trouble is, concerning your disturbances in civil affairs, by the secret injection of religious thoughts, so that you know not how to follow the one without hazard of grieving the Spirit, and breaking your peace in not maintaining and nourishing, the same time, the other; and hence being drawn to go two ways at the same time, (which you can not well do,) your heart is disquieted, and your peace much interrupted.

This of yours puts me in mind of the complaint of an honest, yet plain man, to an able minister once, who in bewailing his condition to him, among other miseries, that was not the least, viz., that he was exceedingly troubled with good thoughts, so that he could not follow his place, unless very oft he did stand still and pray, for fear of grieving the Spirit, (as he thought,) and losing his season of being heard in heaven; for said conscience oft unto him, How dost thou know but this may be thy accepted time, and if thou dost not take it, it may be thou shalt never have it again? I have forgot the minister's answer, but I am sure in these complaints you go not alone; I have lately known one very able, wise, and godly, put upon the rack in these kind of thoughts by him that, envying God's people's peace, knows how to change himself into an angel of light. For it being his usual course, in the time of his health, to make a diary of his hourly life, and finding much benefit by it, he was in conscience pressed, by the power and delusion of Satan, to make and take the same daily survey of his life in the time of his sickness, by means of which he spent his enfeebled spirits, cast on fuel to fire his sickness, and had not a friend of his convinced him of his erroneous conscience misleading him at that time, he had murdered his body, out of conscience to save his soul and to preserve his grace; and do you think these were the motions of God's Spirit, which, like those locusts, (Rev. ix. 9, 10,) had faces like men, but had tails like scorpions, and stings in their tails?

Your thoughts, I know, are not likely to produce the same effects, although you have the same efficient; and because you say your peace is hereby disturbed by ignorance, as not knowing what to do in the midst of these civil actions and these religious thoughts, I conceive that two things are to be sadly considered of for the cure of them.

First. How to know when such religious, pious thoughts come from God's Spirit, and when from the devil transforming himself into an angel of light, or from a well-mettled stirring conscience, yet blind. For when you know they come from God's Spirit, you are bound to nourish them; but when not, you are bound not to embrace nor comply with them.

Secondly. Learn how your soul is to behave and carry itself in civil employments. For when you see how you do, and may honor God in following them, your spirit will not be so unquiet, if at any time you embrace not the suggestions of the other.

1. For the first briefly, all good motions and thoughts are not the Spirit's motions, as may thus appear : —

There be three things chiefly by which we may discern the motions, suggestions, and thoughts which come from God's Spirit; all which concurring together in a good action, or thought, or word, (not one alone,) will make discovery whether they are from God's Spirit or not.

1. If it be suggested for God's ends, it is from God's Spirit; to act so high as for a supernatural end must rise from a supernatural principle, which only is God's Spirit. Pharisaical actions were for a double, selfish end, and hence not from God's Spirit, but nature, and their own spirit.

1. To be seen of men.

2. If they did any of them abhor this, yet it was to purchase and gender in their own minds an opinion of holiness before God; and hence Christ gives them this item, in giving alms, that they should not let the right hand know what their left hand doth; for many men will do good acts, lest they should, by the neglect of them, think them hypocrites, and so be troubled for them. Christ would have us not to take notice of what we do for such an end.

If they be animated and quickened from God's command; for the higher measure of holiness for glorious ends, without a warrant from the word, is the more sordid superstition : Christ healed the leper; when he charged him with anger to tell no man, he (no question for a good end) published the miracle the more; this was a good motion, but it was sinful in him, being cross to Christ's command. When Christ would have washed Peter's feet, he had many thoughts that came into his head concerning his own vileness and Christ's glory, and had a good end and meaning in his answers; yet his humility crossing Christ's

26 *

command, the Lord professeth against it, and him for it, that he had no part in him, if he should go on in it.

God's Spirit sets a man on work in due season; for let the duty be commanded and rightly directed, yet if it be not done in season, it is not from God's Spirit: hence, (Ps. i.,) " The righteous bring forth fruit in its season; " and hence Solomon speaks of " words spoken in season are as apples of gold; " and hence we read in Ecclesiastes of " a time and season for every thing under the sun; " and therefore, when there is a season of God's appointing for civil things or business, it is not season now to be molested or perplexed in it, by the injection and evocation of those thoughts which we think to proceed from the Spirit of God. I know, indeed, that the Spirit of God doth enable a man to do whatever good he doth; but as grace makes nature sometimes to serve, so sinful nature brings grace into captivity, which Paul complains of, (Rom. vii.,) and makes grace to serve it. To exhort and reprove another for sin, is from God's Spirit that it is done; but to reprove at an unseasonable time, it is from sinful corruption, abusing God's grace, and making Samson to grind. It is from the excellence of a knife to cut well, but to cut my finger with it when I should be cutting of my meat with it, ariseth not from the end of the knife, nor from the intention of him that made it; so to think of good things, it is from the Spirit, I grant, but to think of them in such a season that God sets you a work to mind and follow other occasions, it is from the enemy of God's Spirit and your own peace; for as it is a sin to nourish worldly thoughts when God sets you a work in spiritual, heavenly employments, so it is, in some respects, as great a sin to suffer yourself to be distracted by spiritual thoughts, when God sets you on work in civil (yet lawful) employments. Such thoughts, I conceive, are but the leaven of monkish holiness, if they divert you from your lawful affairs when the Lord calls you to follow them. For the Lord never calls you to two divers employments at the same time, unless you make the one to be a means to further the good of the other; which such pious thoughts in some civil employments do; it being no piece of Christian wisdom or honesty to turn round in worldly employments so long till by giddiness we fall down, but by secret steps ever and anon to look up to heaven, and to behold the face of God, to whom only therein we are to approve ourselves. But yet it seems your thoughts are so far from being subservient the one to the other, that you are distracted and molested, and your peace interrupted, and your Christian course made troublesome, and a heavy burden, which surely can not be by the yoke of Jesus

Christ; therefore you must first bring your troubles in this particular to this issue — either you may follow your civil affairs, and nourish these thoughts as helps to maintain your peace, and make you heavenly-minded in them, (and if they serve sufficiently to such an end, why are you troubled with them?) or else you can not follow God comfortably in civil actions, unless you banish from you thoughts which do so miserably distract you; and then why do you fear you shall grieve God's Spirit, if at the same time you do not give entertainment to them? the unseasonableness of which speaks plainly they came not from the Spirit's suggestions, besides their hinderance of comfortably walking with God, which the employments themselves can never hinder.

But you will say, When is the season of nourishing such thoughts?

I answer, Entertain those thoughts as (it may be) you have done friends who came to you at that time you have business with strangers, (whom you love not so well as your friends;) you have desired them to stay a while, until you have done with the other, and then you have returned to your friends; and when the other hath been shut out of the doors, the other hath had the welcome, and hath lodged with you all night, and thus you have grieved neither, but pleased both. It is so in this case; worldly employments are our strangers, yet they must be spoke with. Religious thoughts and practices are our friends; these come unto us while God calls us to parley with the other; you can not speak with both at one time, in one place, without much perplexity: take, therefore, this course; make much of the good thoughts, but parley not with them till your business is done with strangers; and toward evening, which is your season, set some time apart every day for meditation, and then make them welcome; then consider and ponder well what was suggested to you in the daytime, and sift every good thought to the bran, for then is your season, and after that let them sup and lodge with you all night, and keep the house with you every day. And surely, when the Lord Jesus shall see what a friend you shall make of his Spirit, and how wisely you walk therein, you shall not need to fear any grieving of it, or unseasonable times: nay, (I say,) you will most fearfully grieve his Spirit if you parley with the conceived suggestions of it at unseasonable times. "What thou dost, do it with all thine heart," saith Solomon. (Eccl. ix.)

Therefore, when you are to pray, confer, or meditate, do it with all your mind, and all your thoughts, and all your strength.

So, when God calls you to worldly employments, do them with all your mind and might; and when the season of meditation comes, take it, which glorious ordinance of God, although many Christians use it occasionally, and against some good time, or when they have leisure meeting with them, yet to set some time apart for it in a solemn manner every day, and that in conscience, as we do for prayer generally, where is the man to be found that does thus? Those men that thus neglect their season of musing and entering into parley with God's Spirit daily, may be well said to grieve the Spirit, through the neglect of which ordinance, God's Spirit is as much grieved by profess-ors in England as by any course I know. The Lord awaken us. But I have run too far already in this first part of my answer.

For the second means, viz., how the soul is to carry itself in civil employments, that so you may not think you do for better, when you listen to good thoughts as you mention.

I say two things: 1. Learn to follow them out of an awful respect to the eye, presence, and command of Jesus Christ, and to do what you do in civil businesses as the work of Christ; when you are riding, or making up breaches between man and man, then think, I am now about the work of Jesus Christ.

Secondly. Seeing yourself thus working in worldly employ-ments for him, you may easily apprehend that for that time God calls you to them, and you attend upon the work of Jesus Christ in them, that you honor God as much, nay, more, by the meanest servile worldly act, than if you should have spent all that time in meditation, prayer, or any other spiritual employment, to which you had no call at that time. It is noted, therefore, by some, of Peter's wife's mother, that when Christ had healed her of her fever, she sat not down at table with Christ in communion with him, which (no question) was sweet, but ministered at the table, and ran to and fro, and so served him, and acted for him, wherein she showed more love, and gave him more honor, viz., in that mean service, and in acting for him, than in having com-munion with him : now, if the Lord would, out of his abundant goodness, set the soul in such an acting frame for him, and if it could do its worldly employments, as the work of Christ, and see how greatly it honors Christ in attending on him, O, what peace should a Christian enjoy, notwithstanding all his distractions every day! And how easily would such devout thoughts you speak of be repelled, like darkness before the light! for the nobleness of those good thoughts you speak of, presenting themselves against the mean and base outsides of civil affairs, makes you ready to honor the one, when you are called to serve the other; but now, by seeing, you do the work of Christ Jesus in them, you shall hereby see a glory in the meanest service you perform in civil affairs, and this will make you cleave unto them. But I have said too much about repelling of good thoughts, in these times, wherein men have so few, though (it may be) little enough to satisfy you.

Your second trouble is this, viz., that your heart is kept from being humbled for sinful distractions, that hinder and interrupt the spiritual performance of holy duties, and that for two reasons : First. Because they be involuntary and accidental. Secondly. Because they can not break the covenant between God and your soul, being but infirmities.

For the latter clause concerning breach of covenant, together with the other, 1. I say, not only infirmities do not, but the greatest sins can not, make a breach of covenant between God and the soul that is once really (not rationally) wrapped up in the covenant of grace. Indeed, gross scandalous sins, nay, infirmities, when they are given way to, and not resisted, may keep the soul from the fruition, for a time, of God's covenant, but never from the eternal *jus* and right unto it; for as the habit of faith or grace gives a man a constant right to the promise and covenant, (which seed ever remains, which habit ever lasts, Jer. iii. 9,) so the act of faith or grace gives a man fruition of the covenant and the benefit of the promise, and hence by the acting and venting of some sins wherein there is included the neglect of the exercise of grace. He that is really in covenant with God may be deprived of the fruition of it; yet seeing the seed of God and the habit of grace ever remain, he can not by any sin break his covenant, for the covenant of grace is absolute, wherein the Lord doth not only promise the good, but to begin, and perfect, and fulfill the condition absolutely, without respect of sin, *ex parte creaturæ.* Indeed, if God's covenant of grace did (as that of works) depend upon man to fulfill the condition, having sufficient grace to fulfill it, then gross sin might well break the covenant; but seeing God hath undertaken to fulfill the covenant absolutely, notwithstanding all the evils and sins of the soul, no sin can possibly break that knot and covenant which so firm and resolute love hath once knit. And therefore, if this be a good argument, infirmities can not break covenant. What cause have I to be humbled for them? so as to say, It is thy mercy, Lord, that I am not consumed for them, (as you write;) you may upon the same ground say so, if the Lord should desert you, or you forsake the Lord, and so fall into the foulest sin, which I suppose corrupt conscience dares not be so bold as to think or allow of.

Secondly. I say least sins or infirmities do break the first covenant of works: and hence you do not only deserve, but are under the sentence of death and curse of God, immediately after the least hair's breadth swerving from the law by the smallest sin, and most involuntary accidental infirmity. According to the tenor of the law, the soul that sinneth shall die; and "cursed is he that continueth not in all things of the law," (Gal. iii. 10;) the least sin being (*ex parte objecti*) in respect of God, against whom it is committed, as horrible and as great as the greatest. For it being an infinite wrong, being the dishonor of an infinite majesty, there can be no greater wrong than an infinite one, unless you can imagine a greater thing than that which is infinite; and therefore in this respect there is as much venom and mischief done against God in the least as in the greatest sin; and therefore it, and whosoever commits it, deserves death for it, as if they had committed the foulest sin in the world; and therefore, after the least and smallest infirmities, you may from hence see what cause you have freely to be humbled, and to confess for them how worthy you are to be destroyed; yea, even to look upon yourself as lying under the sentence of the law and death, immediately after the commission of them, and so to mourn bitterly for them.

But you will say, A Christian that is under the covenant of grace is not within the covenant of works; that bond is cancelled; the last will must stand; and therefore he being out of that covenant, no sins of his can be said to break the covenant; for no man can be said to break that law under which he is not, and which he is not bound to keep.

In answer: Every believer hath a double being or standing, and so there may be put upon him a double respect.

First. He may be considered as united to and having a spiritual being on Christ; and so it is true, he is under grace, and the covenant of grace, and not under the law, nor the covenant of works; and hence not being under the law, nor bound to keep it as a covenant of life, (though it be a rule of life,) no sin can condemn him, there being no condemnation to them that are in Christ Jesus. (Rom. viii. 1.) As Christ is above condemnation, and law, and death, and curse, so is he. And this, truly understood, is the foundation of a Christian's joy, and peace, and glory every day; yet so, as though sin doth not condemn him, yet he hath good reason to say, it is mercy, and mere mercy, Lord, that I am not consumed, that I am not condemned. For sin is the same, nay, grace and God's love aggravate sin; for to sin against the law deserves death without recovery, but to sin when grace hath received me, and loved me; when the blood of Christ hath been shed abundantly to deliver me from sin; O, this makes the most secret silent sin a crying one! So that if you do consider this well, you may see what little cause there is to have your heart rising against the deepest humiliation for the least sin, though you be in Christ, and under grace. For, as Daniel, when he was put into the lions' den, had not he cause to wonder that he was not torn in pieces by them? And why? Because it was not from any defect on their part to tear him in pieces, but from the omnipotent power, and mercy, and grace of his God, that muzzled their mouths: so though no lion can tear, though no sins can hurt or condemn a Christian, as he is considered in Christ, yet hath not he cause to confess and wonder, and say, Lord, it is thy mere grace and mercy that it is not so? (which is the act of humiliation your letter saith you can hardly come unto.) And why? Not because God's grace puts any less evil in sin, but because it is merely grace that keeps it from spitting that venom which otherwise it would.

Secondly. A Christian may be considered in respect of his natural being in himself, and thus he is ever under the law, and as oft as he sinneth, under the sentence of death; and (as the apostle speaks) by nature even we (justified, quickened) are the children of wrath as well as others. And thus, after the least involuntary accidental sin, you may easily see what cause you have to lie down deeply humbled, mourning under the sentence of death, and God's eternal curse, as a condemned man going to the execution; to feel that fire that shall never go out; looking upon yourself as you are in yourself, a forlorn castaway, every moment: and this, truly understood, is the foundation of a Christian's sorrow, shame, and confusion of face, self-loathing, self-forgetting, self-forsaking, and condemning every day. And, believe it, sir, it is no small piece of a Christian's skill and work to put a difference between himself and himself, himself as he is in Christ, and so to joy and triumph, and himself as he is growing on his first root, and so to sorrow, and loathe and condemn himself; so that, (to wind up all that I have said,) look upon yourself as in Christ, you may say, these involuntary infirmities do not, shall not, condemn me.

But, Lord, it is grace, grace that it is not so, and this is evangelical humiliation. Look again upon yourself, as you stand on your own bottom, and live in your own nature, and so you may say, after the least infirmity, I have now broken a most holy and righteous law, and therefore I am already condemned: O, woe is me! I have already undone myself by mine iniquity; and this is legal humiliation, which serves for mortification, as the first for vivification. I know it is very difficult to bring the heart to acknowledge freely it deserves death after so small an involuntary offense ; but when the Lord reveals two things, first, himself in his glory, secondly, how the least sin strikes him, I persuade myself the vilest heart can not but be forced to confess how just God should be in his severest proceedings against him. And withal consider, the more involuntary any sin is, the more strong and natural it is, and the more natural the more horrible, as to be a natural thief is far worse than to be a deliberate thief, who sometimes steals ; and therefore, good sir, take heed of looking no deeper, nor seeing no further, than the bare act, and unvoluntariness, and accidentalness, and suddeness of your infirmities; for if you do, you look through the wrong end of the glass, and they will appear so small that you will find it a very rough work to bring your heart consentively to say, (if I may say and use your own phrase,) It is a mercy, Lord, that I am not consumed for them ; but look upon them as indeed they are, in respect of that infinite glory you strike, doing the greatest mischiefs to God by them, and (which makes them the viler) as they are so strong you can not remove them, and so horrible as that it is natural to you to commit them, etc. And surely you will not (through grace) find such thoughts haunt you long ; not but that they will be, haply, rising and tempting, but never always vexing and prevailing. Satan's ground reaching as far as the minds of God's people, and therefore so far he may come, and there he may walk, (for he came into the mind of innocent Adam, nay, Jesus Christ, by his suggesting temptations;) but the heart is Christ's peculiar possession and purchase ; and if he shall still there offer to come in and vex you, and prevail against you, and to lodge his suggestions this or any other way with you, you have law and Christ on your side, by this little light now given you, to cast him out.

The third thing that troubles you is the disranking of the persons in the Trinity ; for though you think the Holy Ghost is God, yet you have not so high a repute of him as of the Father and the Son, because the Son addresseth himself to God the Father in all his prayers and acknowledgments, in a more immediate manner than unto the Holy Ghost, and therefore you would know if the word *Father*, as in the Lord's Prayer, includes not the Unity in Trinity.

To this briefly consider three things : —

1. Without all question, the same God which lies under that relative property of Father, is the same God with the Godhead

of the Son and the Godhead of the Holy Ghost, there being not three Gods; and therefore the Godhead of the Son and Spirit are not excluded, but included in the Godhead of the Father, when we look upon the Father as God, in the Lord's Prayer, or any where else.

2. But, secondly, the Father, as Father, is never taken for the same Holy Ghost in Scripture, nor the Son, as Son, is taken for the Father, nor the Holy Ghost, as Holy Ghost, is at any time taken for the Son; for it is a rule in theology, though the *res substrata*, the thing that lies under the relative property (viz., the Godhead) of every person, be common and communicated, yet the same Godhead, considered as clothed with his relative property, (as Father, Son, and Spirit,) it is not common, but peculiar. For the Godhead of the Father, as Father, is not the Godhead of the Son, as Son, etc.

3. Hence it follows, that when Christ addresseth himself to the Father, as Father, in Scripture, it is not because he is either a diverse or greater God than the Holy Ghost, but it is for two other reasons: —

1. Because the Father, as Father, received primarily the wrong that sin did against his work of creation. For the Father being the first person in order, and creation the first transient act, (as election and reprobation were the first immanent,) hence this work is attributed chiefly to God the Father, in respect of our orderly apprehension; and hence man sinning then when he was only made, this is chiefly attributed to be against the Father, because his work appeared to be chiefly there, and not against the Son, for his work chiefly appears in redemption, he being the second person, and this the second main and wonderful work; neither against the Holy Ghost, for his work chiefly appears to us in application, being the third person, and this the third main act that ever God will do or show forth to the world in this life: hence God the Father receiving to our apprehension the wrong in creation by sin, he is the person that is to be satisfied, and not the Holy Ghost. And hence Jesus Christ in all his prayers had a most special eye to him, and not to the Holy Ghost, as Holy Ghost, because he came into the world by his death, and inter-cession, and strong cries, to satisfy God the Father, and not God the Holy Ghost as a third person. And hence it is said, (1 John ii. 1, 2,) " If any man sin, we have an advocate with God the Father," (not God the Holy Ghost,) because he was (to our apprehension) the person wronged; and hence we are after sins committed chiefly to address the Father in our prayers, and to go to him for pardon with our advocate with us, because to whom

offense is chiefly offered, from him chiefly pardon and reconciliation is to be expected.

2. Therefore Christ addresseth himself chiefly in his prayers to God the Father, because he is the original and first cause of all good; because he is the first person in order of subsisting, and therefore first too in the manner of conveying. I know the Godhead is the original of all good; but consider the persons one with another, and so the Father is ever the first in operation, as the Holy Ghost is the last in consummation, for all good comes from the Father, (James i. 17,) through the Son, by the Holy Ghost. And hence, in all our prayers we are to look for all good from the Father, for his Son's sake to be conveyed us by the Holy Ghost; and hence it is said, (John vi. 10,) "No man comes to me but whom the Father draws." Why? It is the immediate office and work of the Holy Ghost to draw and apply the soul unto Christ. Why, then, is it said, "unless the Father draw"? The reason is, because that which was perfected and consummated by the Holy Ghost was intentionally and by way of purpose and decree begun originally by the Father; and this is that which Christ's words have chiefly reference unto, viz., the Father, through the Son, by the Holy Ghost, draws.

But I have waded too far in this divinity, the clear knowledge of which is reserved for us in heaven : but thus much to satisfy you. Yet the word *Father*, in the Lord's Prayer, I conceive, under correction, as it doth not exclude any person of the Godhead, so it is chiefly set down there, not so much to denote the person of the Father, as the affection of God, as a Father, to us his sons by Christ, which we are to believe, in our first approaching to your prayers, to be as, nay, to transcend, the affection of any father to his son; when we come to call upon him for those six things which the petitions set down, for those three ends, kingdom, power, and glory, which the prayer concludes withal.

Your fourth trouble is, your aptness to go to God immediately, especially when his graces are most striving in his ordinances, contrary to that of Christ, "Ye believe in God, believe also in me."

So indeed it is usual for religious nature often to outrun and get the start of grace; as it appears in many other, so in this case you put. Look as it is with every man when God awakens him effectually; he first seeks to his kitchen physic to save himself, by his duties, praying, mourning, reforming, endeavoring, repenting, working, before he will seek out to the physician and to Christ to save him. Because it was natural to Adam to seek to live by his working, it is natural to every son and branch of that root to seek to save himself by doing as well as he can, or as God gives him the strength and grace. So it is here. It was natural to Adam to depend upon, and go to God immediately, as a creature to a creator, as a son to go nakedly to God as a father. Christ was not then known, nor seen: so it is natural to every man, when rectified nature is stirred up, to go immediately to God. It is grace in the second covenant that reveals and draws to Jesus Christ, and to God by Christ. (Heb. vii. 25.)

For cure of this distemper, ponder but these three things : —

1. Clearly convince the soul, that the immortal, invisible, and most holy God, that dwelleth in an unapproachable light, hath set out himself to be seen, or made himself only visible in Jesus Christ, so that he would have no man look upon him any other ways than as he hath revealed himself in his Son; in whom, (though in all other creatures his *vestigia* and footsteps are to be seen,) as he is God, the face of God is to be seen, which no creature is able to behold, but there, being the brightness of his glory, and the express image of his person, (Heb. i. 3 ;) and as he is man, the very heart of God, both in respect of affection and will to be seen; so that in and through Jesus Christ, especially his human nature, the glory of the great God breaks out like the sun through the clouds most brightly, in respect of us, and therefore in and through his human nature we are only to behold God, in whom all that a Christian desires to know is to be seen, which is the face and heart of so dear a friend. (1 Cor. iv. 6. John xiv. 9, 10.) For we know, by too lamentable experience, how the whole world, vanishing in their smoky thoughts of the glory of God, as he is considered in himself, and not able to conceive or retain the knowledge of him, did hence invent and set up images as fit objects for their drunken, staggering understanding to fasten upon, and to be limited with, and hence adored God before these, (as our Popish hypocrites do before the altar,) and in these, and at these, as Papists do in respect of their images. Hence the Lord, to cure this inveterate natural malady, hath, in the second person, united himself to man Christ Jesus, through whom we are both able, to our everlasting wonderment, to see him, and also here bound only to behold him, who, as he is a fit handle for our faith, so he is a fit object for our weak minds to behold the glory of the most high God in. Wherefore, then, do you offer to go unto God without Christ, when as you are not so much as to look upon God, but as he appears in Christ? Is not the human nature of the Lord Jesus more easy to be seen and conceived of than the invisible, unlimited, eternal Godhead?

2. Secondly: See evidently that there is not any dram or drop of God you have, especially in God's ordinances, but it issues from the blood, and is purchased by the intercession, and delivered unto you by the hand, of Jesus Christ. (Eph. i. 7. Heb. vii. 25. John v. 22.) You should never have heard the sound of the gospel, nor never have had day of patience, nor never have heard of God's ordinances to find him in, nor never have been comforted, quickened, enlarged, affected by God's ordinances, were it not for Jesus Christ, the efficacy of whose blood, and power of whose glorious intercession, doth, at the very instant you feel any good in God's ordinances, prevail with God the Father for what you feel; for the Father loveth the Son, and "hath put all things into his hands," (John iv. 35,) that all men might honor the Son; all the three persons plotting chiefly for the honor of the second; so that you may see, nay, you are bound to believe, at the time you feel your heart savingly affected in any ordinance now, the Lord Jesus, who is at the right hand of God in heaven, who is now in his glory; now he remembering me, a poor worm on earth; now I feel the fruit of his death. O, what a miserable, forlorn wretch had I been, were it not for Jesus Christ! Mercy could never have helped, enlightened, comforted, quickened, assured, enlarged me, and justice could never have relieved my dead, bloody, perishing, lost soul, had it not been for Jesus Christ, whose Spirit, power, grace, comfort, presence, sweetness, I taste, drink, and am satisfied abundantly with, and now do enjoy.

O, sir, methinks the sad meditation of this should make you, in all God's ordinances, where you are apt to say you go immediately to God, to hasten suddenly in your thoughts, affections, praises, to Jesus Christ. Nay, methinks you should speedily have your heart elevated and lifted up to Jesus Christ, and say, I receive this, and taste this from Jesus Christ. O, but this is but a taste of the honeycomb with the end of my rod, and if this presence of Christ's Spirit I feel now be so sweet, what is himself then?

3. Thirdly: Labor for increase of love and familiarity with Jesus Christ, by taking notice of him, by coming often to him, by musing daily on his love, as on a fresh thing, by banishing slavish false fears of his forgetfulness of you, and want of everlasting love toward you; and then you know love will carry you speedily to him; *amor meus pondus meum;* nay, grant that you have been a stranger to Christ, yet restore the love of Christ to life again in your soul, and when you come to his ordinances, where he dwells, your soul will make its first inquiry for him, neither will

it be satisfied till it hath seen him, as we do them we love, toward whom we have been greatest strangers.

Your fifth trouble is, you know not how to apply absolute promises to yourself, as in Heb. viii., because they are made indefinitely, without condition. Conditional promises you say you can, if you can find the qualification that gives you right to the good of the promise within you.

This useful, fruitful question, how to apply absolute promises to one's particular, deserves a larger time and answer than now, in the midst of perplexities, I am able, yet willing, to give. For when the Lord saith absolutely, without condition, that he will take away the stony heart, and he will put his fear into his people's hearts, etc., and these kinds of promises are made to some, not to all, to those only whom the Lord will, and in general to his people, hereupon the souls of many Christians, especially such as question God's love toward them, are most in suspense. And, therefore, when they complain of the vileness of their hearts, and strength of their lusts, let any man tell them that the Lord hath undertaken, in the second covenant, to heal their backslidings, and to subdue their iniquities, they will hereupon reply, It is true he hath promised indeed to do thus for some absolutely, though they have no good in them ; but I that feel so vile a heart, so rebellious a nature, will he do this for me, or no ? And thus the soul floats above water, yet fears it shall sink at last, notwithstanding all that God hath said. I will answer therefore, briefly, these two things in general.

1. I shall show you to what end, and for what use and purpose, God hath made absolute promises; not only to them that be for the present his people, but to them that in respect of their estates and condition are not.

2. I shall show you how every Christian is to make use of them, and how and when he ought to apply them. For the first of these : —

1. First, I conceive that, as in respect of God himself, there are many ends which I shall not mention, as being needless, so in respect of man, there are principally these two ends, for which the Lord hath made absolute promises : —

1. To raise up the soul of a helpless, sinful, cursed, lost sinner in his own eyes, to some hope (at least) of mercy and help from the Lord. For thus usually every man's soul is wrought, to whom the Lord doth intend grace and mercy. He first turns his eyes inward, and makes him to see he is stark naught, and that he hath not one dram of grace in him, who thought himself rich and wanting nothing before, and, consequently, that he is

27 *

under the curse and wrath of God for the present, and that if the Lord should but stop his breath, and cover his face, and take him away, which he may easily do, and it is to be feared he will, that he is undone forever. Hereupon the soul is awakened, and falls to his kitchen physic, as I spake before ; prays, and hears, and amends, and strives to grow better, and to stop up every hole, and to amend itself of every sin ; but finding itself to grow worse and worse, and perceiving thereby that he doth but stir, and not cleanse, the puddle, and that it is not amending of nature that he must attain to, but he must believe, and make a long arm to heaven, and apprehend the Lord Jesus, (which so few know, or ever shall enjoy,) and hereby quench the wrath of God. I say, finding he can not do thus, no, nor no means of themselves can help him to this, hereupon he is forsaken of all his self-wisdom, and of all his vain hopes, and now sits down like a desolate widow, comfortless, and sorrowful, and thinks there is no way but death and hell, and the wrath of a displeased God to be expected. And if any come and tell this soul of God's mercy and pity to sinners, saith he, It is true, he is even infinitely merciful unto them who are rent for their sins, and that can believe ; but that I can not do, and am sure shall never be able for to do, and therefore what cause have I but to lie down in my sorrow, and to expect my fatal stroke every moment ? Reply again upon this soul, and tell him, that though he can not believe, or loosen his heart from sin, yet that the Lord hath promised to do it — that he will subdue all his iniquities, and he will pardon all his sin, and that he will cause men to walk in his ways, etc. True, saith the soul again, he will do thus for his own people, and for them he hath chosen ; but I never had a dram of grace in my heart, and there is no evidence that the Lord is mine own, or that I am his. Here again the soul lies down, until the Lord discovers to the soul that he will do these things for some that have no grace, or never had grace, for these promises were made to such.

Hereupon the soul thinks thus : These promises are made for some that are filthy ; for why should God pour clean water upon them ? for some that be hard hearted ; for why should he promise to take away the stony heart from them ? etc. And if unto some such, and I being such a one, why may not the Lord possibly intend and include me, seeing he hath not by his promise excluded nor shut me out ? Indeed, I dare not say he will ; but yet how do I, or men, or angels know, but yet I may be one ? Hereupon hope is raised to life again ; seeing God hath undertaken the work for the vilest, it is possible he may do it for me, now when I am vile, and can do nothing for myself. And thus you may see the first end and use of absolute promises to be, as it were, twigs to uphold the sinking spirits of hopeless, helpless, distressed souls. ·

2. The second end and use of·them is this : to create and draw out faith in Jesus Christ in the promises. For as the law begets terror, so the promises beget faith. Now, no conditional promise firstly begets faith, because he that is under any condition of the gospel, in that man there is a presupposed faith. It is God's absolute promise that firstly begets faith, for faith is not assurance, but the coming of the whole soul to Christ in a promise. (John vi. 35.) And then the soul believes in Christ, when it comes to Christ; now this God works in the gospel. First, the soul is raised up by hope. And being raised, it secondly comes to Christ, which is faith, by vehement, unutterable desire. And being come to him, it thirdly embraceth Christ by love ; and thus the march is made, and the everlasting knot is tied.

Now, as you have heard, the absolute promise works hope of relief from Christ; and if it works hope, it also works a desire, or coming to Christ by desire. O that thou, Lord, wouldest honor thy grace, thy power, thy love, thy promise, in helping me, a poor castaway. And thus faith is created (as it were) by this absolute promise ; for it can not but move the heart of any one, that ever felt his want, to cry mightily to the Lord for help, if he hath any hope, seeing the Lord hath promised to do it for some. O, saith the soul, that thou wouldest do it for me. And surely, were it not for this absolute promise of God, no soul would desire, because he would have no hope to be saved, or to seek for any thing as from the hands of God. And thus you see to what end God makes, and to what use a Christian may put, these absolute promises.

2. For the second thing, viz., how and when a Christian may apply these promises, —

I answer : Every Christian is either,

1. Within covenant with God, and knows it ; or,

2. Within covenant with God, and knows it not ; or,

3. Out of covenant indeed, for his present estate and condition ; yet he is *in fieri*, or making toward it.

1. If he be in covenant, and knows it, then you may easily perceive how and when he ought to apply promises unto himself; for he may boldly conclude, if God be his God, then all the promises of God shall be made good unto him ; if he be a son of God, he may boldly challenge at all times, at the hands of God, (nay, in some respects, at the hands of justice itself,) the fulfilling of God the Father's will, delivered in the several lega-

cies of the promise bought by the blood, and sealed by the same blood of Jesus Christ, that they may and shall be made good unto him, that is clear.

2. Secondly, if he be in covenant, and knows it not, and questions hence whether God is his or not, and consequently whether the promises belong unto him, then the rule is to be observed: let him so sue and seek for the good of the absolute promise, until, by reflecting upon his own acts, herein he perceive himself adorned and dignified with the qualification of some conditional promise; and then if he can find the condition or qualification within himself, then, as you judge and write, he may conclude that the conditional promise belongs to him; and if one promise, then all God's promises; and therefore that absolute promises are his own, because at least one conditional promise is. For no unregenerate man is within the compass of any one conditional promise of grace, unless you will say he is under the everlasting love of God, the promises of grace being but the midway between the eternal purpose and decree of love, and the glorious, certain execution of that love in time — the promise being the breakday of God's most glorious love, which must shine out in time.

But here you will say is the difficulty, viz., how I should so seek for the good of absolute promises, as therein to find myself within the compass of some conditional one.

I answer, it is done chiefly by three acts.

1. By being humbly contented, that seeing the Lord hath absolutely promised to work and do all for the soul he intends for to save, even when it can do nothing for itself, and that he hath taken the work into his own hands; so that it is his promise, offer, office, and honor to do all; that therefore you lie down, not sluggishly, but humbly, at the feet of God, and contented to have him to be your God, and forever to be disposed of in any thing by God, if he will fulfill his covenant in you; contented to part with any sin, if he will rend it from you, — contented to know any truth, if he will reveal it to you, — contented to do any duty, if he will enable you, — contented to shine bright with all his glorious graces, if he will create and maintain them in you, — contented to bear any evil, if he may lay his hand under your head, and thereunto strengthen you. And so, seeing the Lord promised to undertake the work for some, put out the work, and put over your soul to him, that he would fulfill the good that his covenant promiseth in yourself. Now, when you do thus, which (no question) you and many a soul doth, many times reflect upon this act, and see if you can not or may not find yourself by it under the condition of some conditional promise; and if you do,

then are you bound to believe all God's promises are and will be yea and amen unto you. Now that you do so by this act, itself speaks plainly, for how many conditional promises are made to the meek, — " Blessed are the meek," (Matt. v.,) — and to the humble, whom God will raise up! For this is not saving meekness, to be quietly contented to be, or to do, or to bear any thing that the Lord will have me from mine own strength and feeling, but to be, to do, or to bear any thing that the Lord will have me, if the Lord enable me. Many a stout heart would gladly have Christ, but if he can not have him in his own terms, viz., Christ and his lusts, Christ and the world too, or by his own strength and power, he will have none of him, but desperately casts him away, and saith, What, shall I look after him any more? I can not pray, I can not believe, I can not break this vile and unruly will, this stony, adamant heart. Thus the pride of a man's heart works. Now, he that is truly meekened and humbled, he is contented gladly to have God his God, and Christ his Redeemer, and that upon Jesus Christ's own terms. First, on his own covenant. Now, what is that? Why, it is this : I will give you the good, and work in you the condition too; I will give you myself, and therefore will not stick to give you an eye to see, and a heart to receive too. This is the covenant. Now, hereupon a humbled soul accepts of Christ according to his covenant, on his own terms, thus, viz., upon that condition, Lord, that thou wilt humble me, teach me, persuade me, cause me to believe, and in every thing to honor thee; Lord, I am contented gladly and joyfully to save thee; do therefore what thou wilt with me. Just as a sick man tells his physician, who comes not to him on these terms, If you will make yourself half-whole, then I will cure you, and do the rest for you; but being utterly unable to cure, or to know how to cure himself, he tells his physician, I am content you should begin and perfect the cure, and so honor your skill and love in me, to be contented to take any thing if you will give it me, and if I offer to resist that, you should bind me, and so do any thing with me.

The second act is, earnestly to long and come to Christ, to cleave unto Jesus Christ by fervent and ardent desire that he would make good those absolute promises to you, seeing that they are made to some, and that they do not exclude you; for when you ponder well, and see what wonderful great things the Lord promiseth to some, whose heart can not but be stirred up to say, as that woman in another case, " Lord, give me of that water to drink ; " and as they in the fifth of John, " Lord, evermore give us that bread." Now, doing this, reflect upon the second act, and see if unto it no conditional promise belongs, and you shall find an affirmative answer from the word. For what is this longing after the good, not of some, (which many hypocrites do,) but of all the promises, but that which the Scripture calls thirsting? who are commanded to "come and drink of the waters of life freely," (Is. lv. 1, 2;) and hungering? to which all good things are promised, (Matt. v. 6,) and which, coming to Christ, (as I spake even now,) who hath given this as the first fruit of eternal election, and which kind of people he will never cast away. (John vi. 37.) Now, when you see these promises belonging unto you, why dare you not conclude but that all these absolute ones are yours also?

3. The third act is this: Seeing God hath promised absolutely such good things in the second covenant, but hath not set down the time when, or how much grace he will give, and seeing only he can help, therefore look up, and wait upon the Lord in the use of all known means, until he makes good what he hath promised to do, and perform, and work for you. Say, as beggars, that have but one door to go to for bread, if none hear, or, hearing, help not; lay themselves down at the door, and say, I will wait here, I am sure I perish if I go away, or quarrel with them in the house, because they help me not so soon as I would, and therefore I will wait, for it may be their compassions may move them as they pass by to help me. So do you. Many a soul comes and longs for the good of the promises; but if the Lord do not speedily help him, he goes with discouragements, fears, and discontents, or despair, or sin, away, and saith one of these two things; either, I shall never have help, or, I come not truly, and hence I feel no help. O, remember that bread is only to be had at the door, to be distributed when the Lord seeth need, not when we would, or think we have need; and therefore wait here and say, If I perish, here I will, at the feet of God, and at the feet of the promises and covenant of God, etc.

Now, reflect upon this act, and see if you may not find some conditional promise annexed unto it, which surely you may, and I will name you but two — Is. xlix. 29–31, and Is. lxiv. 4; and if the conditional promise belongs to such a soul, you may easily conclude the absolute promises are your own, and the chiefest use you are to make of them when you know them that they are your own, is to press God to make them good daily to you, and to believe as verily and really as if you had the performance of them, that they shall. It may be you will ask me, How shall I know whether I have these conditions truly in me? I answer, Sincerity is a very witnessing grace; the frequent meditation of the

Scripture will give you much light to judge of the sincerity of them, and that which St. Paul speaks, (1 Cor. xii.,) I say unto you, " We have not received the spirit of the world, but of God, whereby we know (or may know) the things that are freely given to us of God."

3. Thirdly. If he be out of the covenant, but yet God begins to work with some common work of his grace upon him : all that I would say unto him, and all the use he can make of such absolute promises, consists in these things : —

1. Let him consider the freeness of God's promise, whereby he may be stirred up to conceive some hope it may be made good to him in time. For the promise is very free and large, excluding none, (except those that sin unpardonably,) be their sins and natures never so vile before God, and yet not including any by name, for that is in the conditional promise ; and hence such a one is to make this use of it, Who knows but the Lord may have pity upon me in time ? and so hang thy hope upon him.

2. Let him consider the worth and price of God's promise bought by blood, and for which some men would give a thousand worlds for the benefit and comfort of, and hereby raise up his heart, as by the freeness of it to hope, so by the price of it to esteem of the thing promised, above pearls, and all the honor and pomp of the world.

3. Let him consider the fullness of the promise, which is a plaster as big as his sore, just answerable to all his wants, nay, infinitely more large than his wants. And surely these three things will draw his heart to long for the promise, and then you know what is conditionally promised and bequeathed to them that thirst ; for similitude is the ground of love. Now, when the fullness of the promise is seen, there will appear such a suitableness and fitness of the promise to his soul, that he can not but long for it. Thus much for the fifth trouble.

Your sixth trouble set down in two heads, put into one for brevity, viz., secret unwillingness to seek God in the strictest solemn services, before you enter into them, weariness of them while they last, and glad when they are gone. The reasons which you mention are partly fear of not using them aright, together with melancholy, and lastly, the strictness of them.

It is very true, there is abundance of wildness in our hearts, which naturally seek to have their liberty abroad, and can not endure to be pent in the narrow room of holy performances, extraordinary duties, etc., no more than children can be pent up from their play. And hence it is weary of them, and glad to think of their departures and ends. And truly it is one of the most grievous miseries that a holy heart can feel; and I beseech the Lord of heaven and earth to keep you and me, and all his forever, while we are here in our valley, under the sense of such distempers, as our greatest misery. And therefore me-thought it was a solemn sweet speech of an honest man to his friend, who seeing him oppressed with such distempers as you mention, and perceiving him to droop under them, he came cheer-fully to him, and suddenly said unto him, I can tell you good news, the best that ever you heard, viz. : As soon as ever you are in heaven, you shall serve Christ without weariness ; which words, well thought on, revived the man. That which I would speak with as much tenderness of compassion as I am able to you, I refer to these things.

1. That a child of God is never usually weary of the duty, but rather of his vile heart, to think of, and to look upon, that in the duty Christ's yoke is easy, and his burden light, to him that takes it on his neck, and puts his soul under it. The duty, nakedly considered in itself, is glorious in his eyes and sweet to his soul, and hence sometimes never well, but when he considers his dead, blind, barren, and senseless heart that he is to carry to the duty, and that he fears, and hath felt, will abide with him in the duty. O, this grieves ; here the soul pincheth. A hypocrite is weary of the duty ; a child of God rejoiceth in it, but he is weary of his sin, and unsavoriness and weariness in the duty. I persuade myself, sir, that you may soon mistake your spirit herein : you think you are unwilling to come to the duty, and are weary of it, when indeed it is your glory, joy, and love ; but it is because you fear you can do it no better that troubles you, that you have such a vile heart in it. And if your trouble be from hence, the good Lord increase it in you daily ; and withal, bless the Lord, and say, Lord, though I am weary of my vile heart, in these days of humiliation, in these Sabbaths, yet I bless thee, the days and duties themselves thou knowest are dear unto me ; it is not, Lord, because I am weary of thy word, but because I can do it no better ; I am weary of myself, and this vile heart ; here is much love in such a spirit to the Lord. And believe it, sir, your love wants not its recompenses ; and remember, that the Lord respects you not according to your duties done, but according to your love in them and to them. And therefore those duties you are ashamed to own, the Lord will not be ashamed to crown.

2. Consider, you must and shall be baited with these distem-pers of heart, sometimes more, and sometimes less, as long as you live. It is part of Paul's body of death, which he must carry with him till he come to bury himself.

3. Those means which may help you to be freed from them (a little at least) are these, among many : —

1. Be but truly and really, not by fits and darkly, sensible of them ; men in deep miseries are not unwilling to be helped out.

2. Judge ye not rigorously of God, as though he were a bloody, austere God, as he did of his master whose talent he had, and hence never improved it. But look upon God as having a father's heart and affection toward you, in the meanest and greatest performances ; which is double, either to give you strength to do what you can not, (I can do all things through Christ,) or having come to him for it, to accept of what you would do for him, as if it were done ; and this will make you joy in the poorest performance, that though it be never so full of vileness, yet the Lord, out of his fatherly love, accepts of it as glorious.

3. Renew, morning and evening, by sad and solemn meditation, the sense of God's love to you in Christ, and in every duty that he sets you about ; and love will love and like the yoke, and make the commandments that they shall not be grievous to you.

Thus, I have briefly done with your new troubles, which you mention, you say, because you may not have the like opportunity of writing again. It may be so, and therefore I have desired to satisfy you, which I beseech the Lord himself to do.

Next you come to reply to my first letter, of which I have kept no copy, as I never did of any, and hence may and do forget what I writ then unto you. So much light as your letter lends me to bring things to mind I will gladly take, and be more brief in answer.

You find the strength of grace to be got in you rather by argumentation than inward communication and influence arising from the union to Christ. And this troubles you.

To which I answer these three things : —

1. That, as the old sinful nature is communicated from Adam the first to us, without any argumentation, so the new nature, which is the seed, foundation, and plot of all grace, is diffused into us by the second Adam when we are united to him, without argumentation. It is only by divine operation. The Lord leave not me, nor any friend I have, to a naked Armenian illumination and persuasion.

2. That to the increase of those labors, and drawing out the acts of the new creature, the Lord is pleased to use moral and rational persuasions, as in the instance you gave : Christ died for us, then hence the love of Christ constrains. But remember, withal, it is not the bare meditation, or strength of reason or

persuasion, that elicits such divine and noble acts in the heart and affection ; but it is the blood of Christ, sprinkling these serious meditations, that makes them work such graces in the soul — which I might show at large ; which blood is the salve, though argumentation is the cloth or leather to which it sticks, and by which it is applied ; but from such leather comes no virtue ; all of it is from the blood of Christ, which by argumentation heals the soul. For if it were nakedly in the argumentation to stir your heart, and to work strength of grace, what should be the reason that sometimes you are no more moved by all your argumentations than a mountain of brass is by the winds ? Why should the same truth affect you at one time and not at another, when you are as fitly disposed to be affected as at the first ? Therefore, consider, it is not your reason and argumentation, but Christ's blood, that doth all, by as admirable and yet secret operation.

3. Your union to Christ on your part is begun and partly wrought by the understanding, and hence the good that you get by it at any time, it is from your union, or part of it at least.

Again you ask me, whether Calvin doth not express fully my thoughts about our spiritual union, in his *lib.* 4, *cap.* xvii.

I answer, I have forgot what he hath wrote and myself have read long since out of him, and for the present I have no books about me where I am, and therefore can not satisfy you in this, neither know I when I shall seek to find out the book and place ; if I have leisure, I will write to you, or tell some of your friends before I am gone, what he hath said or writ that way, etc.

Again, thirdly, you desire me to tell you how myself came to the cure of atheistical thoughts, and whether they did wear out, or whether they were rationally overthrown.

I answer, at first they did wear out, meeting with fruitless and dead-hearted company, which was at the university.

2. The Lord awakened me again, and bid me beware lest an old sore broke out again. And this I found, that strength of reason would commonly convince my understanding that there was a God, but I felt it utterly insufficient to persuade my will of it unless it was by fits, when, as I thought, God's Spirit moved upon the chaos of those horrible thoughts ; and this, I think, will be found a truth.

3. I did groan under the bondage of those unbelieving thoughts, looking up, and sighing to the Lord, that if he were as his works and word declared him to be, he would be pleased to reveal himself by his own beams, and persuade my heart by his own Spirit of his essence and being, which if he would do, I should account

it the greatest mercy that ever he showed me. And after grievous and heavy perplexities, when I was by them almost forced to make an end of myself and sinful life, and to be mine own executioner, the Lord came between the bridge and the water, and set me out of anguish of spirit, (as she prayed for a child,) to pray unto him for light in the midst of so great darkness. In which time he revealed himself, manifested his love, stilled all those raging thoughts, gave return in great measure of them; so that, though I could not read the Scripture without blasphemous thoughts before, now I saw a glory, a majesty, a mystery, a depth in it, which fully persuaded, and which light (I desire to speak it to the glory of his free grace, seeing you call me to it) is not wholly put out, but remains, while I desire to walk closely with him, unto this day. And thus the Lord opened mine eyes, and cured me of this misery; and if any such base thoughts come (like beggars to my door) to my mind, and put these scruples to me, I used to send them away with this answer: Why shall I question that truth which I have both known and seen?

But you say this remedy is good, viz., of prayer, but that you can not use it, especially because you question the truth of God.

Yet (dear sir) give not over this trade; you will doubtless find it gainful, when it may be God hath laden you more with these thoughts, and made you loathe yourself for them. But the thing seems strange to me, if I mistake you not, viz., that your heart will not be persuaded, but that you must resolve your doubts concerning the perfection of Scripture, not by seeking to harmonize those passages that seem to cross one another, but by ascribing some humanity or error (if I may interpret you) to the penmen, seeing St. Paul saith, "We prophesy but in part," and seeing one of the evangelists leaves out the doxology in the Lord's Prayer.

Sir, if you take these thoughts, arising from these and the like grounds, as your burden, I do not blame you, but pity you in that respect; but if your judgment indeed think so, I am sorry you should harbor such thoughts one hour within doors; for you know that holy men writ the Scriptures (but so far they might err, but it is added) as they were inspired, or (as the original hath it) as they were moved or carried in the arms of the Holy Ghost, and so how could they err? how could God lie? It is true, Paul did prophesy but in part; and is this an argument, because he did not prophesy fully, therefore in some things he did not prophesy truly? I am persuaded you will say there are many things my poor thoughts have suggested to you, as true; and yet I am persuaded I do in them prophesy (if I may so say) but in part.

The Spirit of God directed the four evangelists to write; yet so as they did not all write what another writ, but in great wisdom left some things doubtful, and short in one, which are more clear and full in another. And hence the doxology is fully set down in one, and not in another; and many reasons I could set you down why, but that it is needless. I grant you ought not to put up all with a charitable opinion of Scripture; but if you can, by reason, reading, and comparing, help your heart to a full persuasion, this is Scripture. But many things you cannot get satisfaction for, by that way and means, but still your spirit will be left dark and doubtful. What course will you here take for resolution, which is Scripture? The Papists say it is so, because the church hath christened it for Scripture; you say you will see reason for it that it is so, or else you cannot be satisfied; then I fear you will never be satisfied. I think, in this case, therefore, these two things you are to do: —

1. To go to God by prayer, to give you a resolution of all your doubts, and by some means or other some light, to see whether this is his word or not. Secondly, if this be his word, that he would persuade your heart of it that it is so. For the least resolution which is Scripture, and which is not, is made by the same persuasion, and sole persuasion, of the same Spirit that writ the Scripture. Concerning the angels that appeared to Mary, see Gerard, and he briefly (I think) will satisfy you. In your answer to the particular scruples about the Scripture sense, and the dissonancy of them, only this I will add to the last clause about these things, that if the Scripture be inspired by the Holy Ghost, and that not in the sum and substance of it, but to every word and sentence of it, which I think you will not doubt of, when you have considered it, then I think it will undeniably follow, that the same Spirit of truth is also a Spirit of order; and hence the method of various penning of it is from the Spirit too, which you say you stick at.

Again, to your third thing, concerning your spirit being burdened with involuntary infirmities, as burdens, but not as sins. I say nothing now, because I perceive, by one part of your reply, that the Lord hath done you some good by the first answer, only it is your grief you can not fear them, nor condemn yourself for them, as damning sins. For satisfaction of which, I hope this reply to your second trouble will give you some satisfaction.

Again, to your fourth question, to know whether these changes you have sometimes, and these movings of the Spirit, are not of natural temper, or God's Spirit. It seems I did a little mistake the meaning, because you meant not the main work of grace, but occasional stirrings and movings of the heart, as by reading some pathetical letter, your spirit is moved with joy or sorrow, which it may be will not be stirred at some other time, as by drinking a cup of wine the spirit is made more cheerful and lively, etc.

I answer these three things : —

1. First. That it is very useful for natural affections to be raised by a natural temper, as by drinking, eating, noveltiness of the gospel, John's candle flies were ravished with the gospel: people are naturally moved sometimes by a thundering minister, yet never a whit the more grace, etc.; and it is a good speech of Dr. Ames, Arminian universal grace (as they describe it) may be the effect of a good dinner sometimes.

2. That though the being of grace depends not upon the temper of the body, yet the exercise of grace, and many gifts of grace, together with the feeling of it, doth. And hence a good dinner, and sometimes wine to a sad, melancholy (if gracious) heart, may remove *rem prohibentem*, that may keep grace, as joy and thankfulness, from working, and so take the grace and draw it out, not create and diffuse the grace. The prophet called (you know) for a minstrel, which some think (and that upon good grounds) was to raise up his heavy heart, and make him cheerful and fit to speak. The body is the instrument, which if it be broken, the best grace will hardly sound, but if whole, then they will.

3. If you would know when these things only draw out grace, or make a thing like unto grace in the soul, I answer, by these two things chiefly : —

1. If it be true grace, it ever makes you more humble and vile in your own eyes, and say, Lord, why dost thou give me any desire to thee, any cheerfulness in serving thee?

2. It makes you more thankful, and to bless the Lord that he thus remembers you; for this is a standing rule, whatever comes from nature and a man's self, it ever builds up itself, and returns to self again; whatever grace comes from Christ, it drives a man out of himself, by making him humble, and draws him unto Christ that sent him, by making him thankful. I think all grace, and stirrings, and movings, that have not this double effect in some measure, are to be suspected, and if they have, it is dangerous to doubt whether they are true or no.

5. Again: your fifth thing about providence. You say you can not see a positive providence, although you do see a negative providence in all your occasions, and comforts, and crosses you meet withal, as, namely, you can thank God for not taking away your life, etc., but you can not see God giving it.

I answer: 1. Consider what I writ to you at first about this question in general.

2. Ponder sadly whether any creature, or appurtenance to it, hath its being from itself, or from the will and word of God, viz., I will have such a man to be, and such a memory to be, etc. I think you will say, Nothing can make itself, therefore here is a positive providence in having life, liberty, etc.

3. Consider whether the same will and word that gives it a being, together with all the appurtenances to it, doth not also give it act and motion. That it is so, I thus demonstrate it. 1. Every creature is made for an end, for no wise efficient, but works for some wise end. 2. That no creature can lead itself to its end, if sinful or irrational. 3. God must and doth lead it by its several acts and movings to that end. Hence, 4. Every act is determined by God.

And 'although I grant some creatures move freely, some necessarily, yet it is from a positive will and providence that they move, act, and see. Therefore you see what cause there is to see a positive providence in every thing.

Concerning the rest of your letter, O that I had time and heart to write more! Yet I hope I have writ enough for this time, and the Lord knows whether ever more or no. However, I thank you heartily for improving me this way of writing, who have my mouth stopped from speaking. I wish I had more such friends to deal thus with me, and myself more time, and a more fruitful head and heart to improve myself, this, or any other like way for them; for who knows what breathings of God's Spirit are lost for want of writing, especially when there is no season of speaking? Truly, sir, I meet with few that are much troubled in that manner as yourself, but they go on in an easy, quiet, and very dangerous way; which troubles (I persuade myself) keep you awaking when other virgins are slumbering, and after which (I am persuaded) the Lord intends to use you for more than common service, if you wade well through them; however, as I said before, be not discouraged, or too much perplexed in sorrow for them. For surely, as far as I can guess, the Lord is preparing you for himself by them. I shall not forget you, though I never saw you; and I beseech you, if you have any spark of affection toward me, kindled by these few lines, remember when you are best able to pray for yourself, to remember to look after me and mine, and all that go with me on the mighty waters, and then to look up and sigh to Heaven for me, that the Lord would out of his free grace but bring me to that good land, and those glorious ordinances, and that there I may but behold the face of the Lord in his temple, though he never delight to use me there, though I and mine should possibly beg there, and that if the Lord should call me to my solemn work and service for the good of his church and people and company that go with me, or are gone before me, that then the Lord Jesus would reveal his secrets to me, and enable me, the little time I have to live, to be fruitful to him, and to have a larger heart than ever for him. As for yourself, I shall desire the Lord to keep you blameless and unspotted in an evil world, and that as he hath begun, so he would perfect and crown his divine graces and work in you, and that you may be preserved from national sins, which shortly bring national and most heavy plagues.

And the presence of the Lord may abide with you, and in you, until the Lord call for you. Remember my kind love to your father, whose name I have forgot, and by whom I could not send these lines, being then hindered by business. Now, the peace of Jesus Christ be with you, and keep you upright and blameless till death. And if I never see you more till the last and great day, then farewell, farewell.

Yours in Jesus Christ,

T. S.

THE

FIRST PRINCIPLES

OF

THE ORACLES OF GOD.

HEB. v. 12. — "For when for the time ye ought to be teachers, ye have need that one teach you again which be the first principles of the oracles of God; and are become such as have need of milk, and not of strong meat."

TO THE

CHRISTIAN READER.

It is no disparagement at all for this wise master-builder to labor sometimes, by the hammer of the word, to fasten these nails of truth in a sure place, — even in the heads and hearts of infant Christians.

Neither is it below the highest scholar in Christ's school to hold fast the form of wholesome words.

The great apostle himself, (who was rapt up into the third heaven,) although he had received a commission of Christ, his Master, to make disciples, yet he was a disciple still; for he not only catechized others, but learned — and that again and again — the first principles of the oracles of God, which are called the mysteries of the kingdom of heaven, and the depths of God; that is, in plain English, those doctrinal truths which are truly fundamental, and absolutely necessary unto salvation; that we may be able, by sound doctrine, both to exhort and convince the gainsayers; and be ready always to give an answer to every man that asketh us a reason of the hope that is in us.

Thus heartily beseeching thee, in the name of Christ, to search the Scriptures, and to give thyself continually to prayer, and the ministry of the word, that you may grow in grace, and in the knowledge of our Lord and Saviour Jesus Christ, I now commend you to God, and to the word of his grace, which is able to build you up, and to give you an inheritance among all them which are sanctified. So be it.

Friend, I am thine, if thou dost love the truth, and our Lord Jesus Christ, in sincerity.

WILLIAM ADDERLEY.

CHARTER HOUSE, LONDON,
February 1, 1647.

(335)

TO THE

CHRISTIAN READER.

BEING desired to peruse and give our opinion of the resolutions in this letter now presented to thy view, we must confess they appeared to us very precious ; for we have seldom seen acuteness, profoundness, and godliness so eminently, equally, and happily matched. There are in Christ's school divers forms, elementaries, and men of exercised wits. The scholar proposing these cases was no puny, and he was happy in meeting with a teacher so able for resolution. Therefore whoever reads and heeds will not repent of his labor. But the more knowing the reader is, and the more experienced in the ways of Christ, the more delight may he take in, and the more profit may he reap by, these pious and profound resolutions. So we are

> Thine, in Christ Jesus,
>
> JOHN GEREE,
> WM. GREENHILL.

March 27, 1648.

SUM OF CHRISTIAN RELIGION,

IN WAY OF QUESTION AND ANSWER.

Question. WHAT is the best and last end of man?

Answer. To live to God. (Rom. vi. 10, 11. Gal. iii. 9. 2 Cor. v. 3, 15.)

Q. How is man to live unto God?

A. Two ways. First, by faith in God. (Ps. xxxvii. 3.) Secondly, by observance of God. (Eccl. xii. 13.)

Q. What is faith in God?

A. It is the first act of our spiritual life, whereby the soul believing God believeth in God, and there resteth, as in the only author and principle of life. (Heb. iv. 3; x. 38; xi. 13. John iii. 33, 36. Rom. iv. 3. Deut. xxx. 20.)

Q. What is God?

A. God only knoweth himself; no man can so know him and live. Yet he hath manifested himself unto us in his back parts, according to our manner or measure of knowing things; and we need know no more than these, that we may live. (1 Tim. vi. 16. Ex. xxxiii. 19, 23.)

Q. What are God's back parts?

A. They are two. First, his sufficiency. (Ps. xxxvi. 9.) Secondly, his efficiency. (Rom. iv. 21.)

Q. What is God's sufficiency?

A. It is his perfect fullness of all good, whereby he is all-sufficient for us in himself. (Ps. xvi. 13. Gen. xvii. 1.)

Q. Wherein stands and appears God's sufficiency?

A. First, in his essence. (Ps. lxviii. 19.) Secondly, in his subsistence or persons. (2 Sam. vii. 20, 25.)

Q. What is God's essence?

A. Whereby he is that absolute first being. (Rev. i. 8. Is. xliv. 6. Ex. iii. 14.)

Q. Can you sufficiently conceive of the glory of this one most pure essence by one act of faith ?

A. No; and therefore the Lord hath manifested it unto us by divers attributes. (Deut. xxix. 29. Ex. xxxiv. 6, 7.)

Q. What are God's attributes ?

A. That one most pure essence diversly apprehended of us, as it is diversly made known unto us. (1 John iv. 16. Is. xliii. 25.)

Q. How many kinds of attributes are there ?

A. There are two sorts of them. First, some showing what God is. Secondly, some showing who God is.

Q. By what attributes know you what God is ?

A. By these : God is a Spirit living of himself. (John iv. 24; v. 26.)

Q. By what attributes do you understand who God is ?

A. By his essential properties, which show to us, First, how great a God he is. (Ps. lxxvii. 13.) Secondly, what a manner of God he is. (Matt. vi. 17.)

Q. What attributes show how great a God he is ?

A. First, his infiniteness, whereby he is without all limits of essence. (2. Chron. ii. 5, 6.) Secondly, his eternity, whereby he is without all limits of beginning, succession, or end of time. (Ps. cii. 25–27. 1 Tim. i. 17.)

Q. What are those attributes which show what a manner of God he is ?

A. His qualities, whereby he acteth with, are of two sorts. First, his faculties, whereby he is able to act. (Is. lx. 16; lxiii. 1.) Secondly, his virtues of those faculties, whereby he is prompt and ready to act. (Ps. lxxxvi. 5.)

Q. What are his faculties ?

A. First, his understanding, whereby he understandeth together and at once all truth. (Heb. iv. 13. Acts xv. 8.) Secondly, his will, whereby he purely willeth all good. (Ps. cxix. 68.)

Q. What are the virtues of those faculties ?

A. First, they are intellectual; the virtues of his understanding, as wisdom, knowledge, and the rest. Secondly, moral; the virtue of his will, as love, holiness, mercy. In the acting of both which consists God's happiness.

Thus much have you seen of God's sufficiency, in regard of his essence. Now follows his subsistence.

Q. What are his subsistences or persons ?

A. That one most pure essence, with its relative properties.

Q. What are those relative properties?

A. They are three. First, to beget. Secondly, to be begotten. Thirdly, to proceed from both.

Q. How many pèrsons learn you from hence to be in God?

A. Three. First, the first is the Father, the first person in order, begétting the Son. (Ps. ii. 7.) Secondly, the Son, the second person, begotten of the Father. (John iii. 6. Heb. i. 3.) Thirdly, the Spirit, the third person, proceeding from them both. (John xv. 26.)

Q. Are these three persons three distinct Gods?

A. No. For they are that one pure essence, and therefore but one God. (John i. 1. Rom. ix. 5. 1 Cor. vi. 16; ii. 10.)

Q. If every person be God, how can they be distinct persons and not distinct Gods?

A. Yes; because one and the same thing may have many relative properties and respects of being, which in the Godhead makes distinct persons. As one and the same man may be a father in one respect, a master in another respect, and a scholar in another respect.

Q. If these three persons be but one God, what follows from hence?

A. That all the three persons are coequal, coeternal, subsisting in, not separating from each other, and therefore delighting in each other, glorifying each other. (Prov. viii. 30.)

Thus much concerning God.

Now concerning the Works of God.

Q. Thus much concerning God's sufficiency. What is his efficiency?

A. Whereby he worketh all things, and all in all things. (Rom. xi. 36. Is. xlv. 7.)

Q. What of God shines forth, and are you to behold, in his efficiency?

A. Two things. First, God's omnipotency, in respect of his essence. Secondly, the coöperation and distinct manner of working of the three persons. (Rom. i. 20. John v. 17.)

Q. What is God's omnipotency?

A. It is his almighty power, whereby he is able to bring to pass all that he doth will, or whatever he can will, or decree. (2 Chron. xx. 6. Phil. iii. 21. Matt. iii. 9. Ps. cxv. 7.)

Q. What is God's decree?

A. It is his eternal and determinate purpose concerning the effecting of all things by his mighty power, according to his counsel. (Eph. i. 11.)

Q. What attributes or glory of God appear in his decree?

A. First, his constancy, whereby his decree remains unchangeable. (Num. iii. 19.) Secondly, his truth, whereby he delivereth nothing but what he hath decreed. (Jer. x. 10.) Thirdly, his faithfulness, whereby he effecteth whatever he decreeth according thereunto. (Is. xlvi, 10.)

Q. What is God's counsel?

A. His deliberation, as it were, for the best effecting of every thing according to his wisdom. (Acts iv. 24. Ps. xl. 24.

Q. What is God's wisdom?

A. It is the idea or perfect platform of all things in the mind of God, which either can be known, or shall be done, according to the good pleasure of his will. (Heb. xi. 3. Prov. viii. 12, 13.)

Q. What is the good pleasure of God's will?

A. It is the most free act of his will, whereby he willeth himself directly, as the greatest good, and all other things for himself, according to his good pleasure. (Matt. xi. 25. Prov. xvi. 4.

Q. What learn you from hence?

A. That God's good pleasure is the first and best cause of all things. (Ps. cxv. 3; xxxiii. 8–11.)

Q. What is the coöperation of the three persons in God's efficiency?

A. Whereby they work the same thing together unseparably. (John v. 17, 19, and xvi. 13, 14.)

Q. If they work the same thing together, how is it that some works are attributed to God the Father, as creation; some to the Son, as redemption; some to the Holy Spirit, as application?

A. This is not because the same work is not common to all the three persons, but because that work is principally attributed in Scripture to that person whose distinct manner of working appears chiefly in the work.

Q. What is God the Father's distinct manner of working?

A. His working is from himself by the Son, and to the Holy Ghost. (Ps. xxxiii. 6. John i. 3.) And hence the beginning, and so the creation of all things is attributed to him.

Q. What is God the Son's manner of working?

A. His working is from the Father, by the Holy Ghost, (John xiv. 16;) and hence the dispensation of all things, and so redemption, is attributed to him.

Q. What is the Holy Ghost's manner of working?

A. His working is from the Father and the Son, (John xiv. 26,) and hence the consummation of all things; and so application is attributed unto him.

Q. Wherein doth God's efficiency or working appear?

A. In two things. First, in his creation of the world. Secondly, in his providence over the world. (Is. xxxvii. 16.)

Q. What is his creation?

A. It is God's efficiency, whereby he made the whole world of nothing, originally exceeding good. (Ps. xxxiii. 9. Gen. i. 31.)

Q. Did the Lord make the world in an instant?

A. No, but by parts, in the space of six days, described at large by Moses. (Gen. i.)

Q. When did the Lord make the third heaven, with the angels their inhabitants?

A. In the first day, in the first beginning of it. (Gen. i. 1. Job xxxviii. 6, 7.)

Q. What is the creation of the third heaven?

A. Whereby he made it to be the heaven of heavens, a most glorious place, replenished with all pleasure which belongs to eternal happiness, wherein his majesty is seen face to face, and therefore called the habitation of God. (2 Chron. ii. 5, 6. Ps. xvi. 11; lxiii. 15.)

Q. What is the creation of the angels?

A. Whereby he created an innumerable number of them, in holiness, to be ministering spirits, with most acuteness of understanding, liberty of will, great strength, and speedy in motion, to celebrate his praises and execute his commands, specially to the heirs of salvation. (Heb. xi. 22. John viii. 44. Heb. i. 14. 2 Sam. xiv. 20. Jude 6. 2 Pet. ii. 11. Is. vi. 2. Ps. cxxx. 20.)

Q. When did God create man?

A. The sixth day. (Gen. i. 27.)

Q. How did God create man?

A. He made him a reasonable creature, consisting of body and an immortal soul, in the image of God. (Gen. ii. 7; i. 28.)

Q. What is the image of God, wherein he was made?

A. That hability of man to resemble God, and wherein he was like unto God, in wisdom, holiness, righteousness, both in his nature, and in his government of himself and all creatures. (Col. iii. 10. Eph. iv. 24. Gen. i. 26.)

Q. What became of man, being thus made

A. He was placed in the garden of Eden, as in his princely court, to live unto God, together with the woman which God gave him. (Gen. ii. 15.)

Thus much of God's creation.

Q. What is his providence?

A. Whereby he provideth for his creatures, being made, even to the least circumstance. (Ps. cxlv. 16. Prov. xvi. 33.)

Q. How is God's providence distinguished?

A. It is either, First, ordinary and mediate, whereby he pro-videth for his creatures by ordinary and usual means. (Hos. ii. 22.) Secondly, extraordinary and immediate, whereby he provides for his creatures by miracles, or immediately by himself. (Ps. xxxvi. 4. Dan. iii. 17.)

Q. Wherein is his providence seen?

A. First, in conversation, whereby he upholdeth things in their being and power of working. (Acts xvii. 28. Ps. civ. 29, 30. Neh. ix. 6.) Secondly, in gubernation, whereby he guides, directs, and brings all creatures to their ends. (Ps. xx. 10; xxxiii. 11.)

Q. Doth God govern all creatures alike?

A. No; but some he governs by a common providence, and others by a special providence, to wit, angels and men, to an eternal estate of happiness in pleasing him, or of misery in dis-pleasing him. (Deut. xxx. 15, 16.)

Q. What of God's providence appears in his special govern-ment of man?

A. Two things. 1. Man's apostasy, or fall. 2. His recovery, or rising again.

Q. Concerning man's fall, what are you to observe therein?

A. Two things. 1. His transgression, in eating the forbidden fruit. (Gen. ii. 17.) 2. The propagation of this unto all Adam's posterity.

Q. Was this so great a sin, to eat of the forbidden fruit?

A. Yes, exceedingly great, this tree being a sacrament of the covenant; also he had a special charge not to eat of it; and in it the whole man did strike against the whole law, even when God had so highly advanced him.

Q. What are the causes of this transgression?

A. The blameless cause was the law of God. (Rom. v. 13.) And hence, as the law did it, so God did it, holily, justly, and blamelessly. (Rom. vii. 10–12.)

Q. What are the blamable causes?

A. Two, principally. 1. The devil abusing the serpent to de-ceive the woman. (Gen. iii. 1.) 2. Man himself, in abusing his own free will, in receiving the temptations which he might have resisted. (Eph. vii. 29.)

Q. What is the devil?

A. That great number of apostate and rebellious angels, which, through pride and blasphemy against God, and malice against man, became liars and murderers of man, by bringing him into that sin. (Luke xi. 18. 1 Tim. iii. 6. 1 John iii. 12; viii. 44.)

Q. What are the effects and fruits of this transgression?

A. They are two. 1. Guilt, whereby they are tied to undergo due punishment for the fault. (Rom. iii. 19.)   2. Punishment, which is the just anger of God upon them for the filth of sin. (Rom. i. 18.)

Q. What are the particular punishments inflicted on the causes of this sin?

A. Besides the fearful punishment of the devils, mentioned Jude vi., and that of the serpent and the woman, (Gen. iii. 14, 16,) the punishment of man was, First, sin original and actual. Secondly, death. (Gen. v. 5.)

Q. What is sin?

A. The transgression of God's law. (John iii. 4.)

Q. What is original and actual sin?

A. First, original sin is the contrariety of the whole nature of man to the law of God, whereby it, being averse from all good, is inclined to all evil. (Eccl. viii. 11.   Gen. vi. 5.   Rom. vi. 20.) Secondly, actual sin is the continual jarring of the actions of man from the law of God, by reason of original sin, and so man hath no free will to any spiritual good. (Is. lxv. 2, 3. James i. 14, 15. Is. i. 11.)

Q. What death is that God inflicts on man for sin?

A. A double death.   1. The first death of the body, together with the beginnings of it in this world, as grief, shame, losses, sicknesses. (Deut. xxviii. 21, 22, 25.)   2. The second death of the soul, which is the eternal separation and ejection of the soul after death, and soul and body after judgment, from God, into everlasting torments in hell.

Q. Is there no beginning of this death, as there is of the other in this life?

A. Yes, at first security and hardness of heart, which can not feel sin its greatest evil.   2. Terrors of conscience. (Hèb. ii. 15.) 3. Bondage of Satan. (Eph. ii. 2.)   4. The curse of God in all blessings, whereby they are fitted for destruction. (Rom. ix. 22.)

Q. What of God's attributes shine forth here?

A. His holiness, whereby he, being pure from all sin, can not away with the least sin in the best of his creatures. (Heb. i. 13.) 2. His justice, whereby he, being most just in himself, can not but punish man for sin, as well as reward him for well doing. (2 Thess. i. 6.)   3. His patience, whereby he useth pity, patience, and bounty to his creatures offending. (Rom. ii. 3.)

Q. Is this sin, and the punishment of it, derived to all men's posterity?

A. Yes. (John iii. 3.   Eph. ii. 3.)

Q. How is it propagated?

A. By the imputation of Adam's sin unto us, and so the punishment must needs follow upon it. (Rom. v. 13.)

Q. Why should Adam's sin be imputed to all his posterity?

A. Because we were in him as the members in the head, as children in his loins, as debtors in their surety, as branches in their roots, it being just, that as if he standing, all had stood, by imputation of his righteousness, so he falling, all should fall, by the imputation of his sin.

Q. Thus have you seen man's apostasy from God. What is his recovery?

A. It is the return of man to the favor of God again, merely out of favor, and the exceeding riches of his free grace. (Eph. ii. 12, 13. Rom. v. 8.)

Q. How are we brought into favor, and what are the parts of this recovery?

A. Two ways. First, by redemption. (2 Cor. v. 19, 20.) Secondly, by application hereof. (Tit. iii. 6.)

Q. What is redemption?

A. The satisfaction made, or the price paid, to the justice of God for the life and deliverance of man out of the captivity of sin, Satan, and death, by a Redeemer, according to the covenant made between him and the Father. (1 Cor. vi. 20. Luke i. 74. Is. lv. 10, 11.)

Q. Who is this Redeemer?

A. Jesus Christ, God and Man. (Matt. i. 23. John i. 14. Col. ii. 19.)

Q. Why is he God-Man?

A. That so he might be a fit Mediator, to transact all businesses between God and man, in the execution of his three offices, whereunto he was anointed of the Father. (1 Tim. ii. 5. Is. xlii. 12.)

Q. What are those three offices of Christ?

A. 1. His prophetical office, whereby he doth reveal the will of the Father. (Acts iii. 22. Col. ii. 3.) 2. His priestly office, whereby he makes full atonement with the Father for us. (Col. i. 20.) 3. His kingly office, whereby he governs his people whom he had taught and reconciled, subduing their enemies, and procuring their eternal peace. (Ps. ii. 6. Is. ix. 6.)

Q. How hath Christ Jesus made satisfaction?

A. By his humiliation, whereby he was made subject, throughout his whole life and death, to the strict justice of God, to perform whatever the same might require for the redemption of man. (Gal. iv. 4, 5.)

Q. What did God's justice require of man?

A. 1. Death, for the breach of the law, and that Christ tasted, in his bitter sufferings, both of body and soul, by being made sin, and so abolishing sin; and this is called his passive obedience. (Heb. ii. 9. Eph. i. 7. 2 Cor. v. 21. Gal. iii. 13.) 2. Perfect obedience, in fulfilling the law perfectly, both in his nature and actions, for the procuring and meriting of life; and this is called his active obedience. (Heb. vii. 26.)

Q. What follows Christ's humiliation?

A. His exaltation, which is his glorious victory and open triumph over all his and our enemies, sin, Satan, and death, in the several degrees of it. (Luke xxiv. 26. Phil. ii. 8, 9. 1 Cor. xv. 5, 7.)

Q. What is the first degree of Christ's exaltation?

A. His resurrection the third day, whereby his soul and body, by the power of the Godhead, were brought together again, and so rose again from death, appearing to his disciples for the space of forty days. (1 Cor. xv. 4. John ii. 19. Acts i. 3.)

Q. What is the second degree of Christ's exaltation?

A. His ascension into heaven, which was the going up of the manhood into the third heaven, by the power of the Godhead, from Mount Olivet, in the sight of his disciples. (Acts i. 11, 12.)

Q. What is the third degree of his exaltation?

A. His sitting at the right hand of God, whereby he, being advanced to the fullness of all glory, in both natures, governeth and ruleth all things, together with the Father, as Lord over all, for the good of his people. (Mark xvi. 9. Ps. cx. 1. 1 Cor. xv. 25. Eph. i. 20–22. 1 Pet. iii. 22.)

Q. What is the fourth and last degree of his exaltation?

A. His return to judgment, which is his second coming into this world with great glory and majesty, to judge the quick and the dead, to the confusion of all them that would not have him rule over them, and to the unspeakable good of his people. (Matt. xix. 28. 2 Tim. iv. 1. Acts xvii. 31. 2 Thess. i. 1, 7–9.)

Q. Thus much of redemption, the first part of his recovery. What is application?

A. Whereby the Spirit, by the word and ministry thereof, makes all that which Christ, as Mediator, hath done for the church, efficacious to the church as her own. (John xvi. 14. Tit. iii. 5–7. John x. 16. Rom. x. 14, 17. Eph. v. 25, 26.)

Q. What is the church?

A. The number of God's elect. (Heb. xii. 23. John xvii. 9–11; x. 16. Eph. i. 22, 23.)

Q. How doth the Spirit make application to the church?

A. 1. By union of the soul to Christ. (Phil. iii. 9, 10.) 2. By communion of the benefits of Christ to the soul.

Q. What is this union?

A. Whereby the Lord, joining the soul to Christ, makes it one spirit with Christ, and so gives it possession of Christ, and right unto all the benefits and blessings of Christ. (1 Cor. vi. 17. John xvii. 21.   Rom. viii. 32.   1 John v. 12.)

Q. How doth the Spirit make this union?

A. Two ways. 1. By cutting off the soul from the old Adam, or the wild olive tree, in the work of preparation. (Rom. xi. 23, 24.)   2. By putting or ingrafting the soul into the second Adam, Christ Jesus, by the work of vocation. (Acts xxvi. 18.)

Q. What are the parts of the preparation of the soul to Christ?

A. They are two. 1. Contrition, whereby the Spirit immediately cuts off the soul from its security in sin, by making it to mourn for it, and separating the soul from it, as the greatest evil. (Is. lxi. 1, 3.   Jer. iv. 3, 4.   Matt. xi. 20, 28.)   2. Humiliation, whereby the Spirit cuts the soul off from self-confidence in any good it hath or doth; especially by making it to feel its want and unworthiness of Christ, and hence submitteth to be disposed of as God pleaseth. (Phil. iii. 7, 8.   Luke xvi. 9; xv. 17–19.)

Q. What are the parts of vocation of the soul to Christ?

A. 1. The Lord's call and invitation of the soul to come to Christ, in the revelation and offer of Christ and his rich grace. (2 Cor. v. 10.)   2. The receiving of Christ, or the coming of the whole soul out of itself unto Christ, for Christ, by virtue of the irresistible power of the Spirit in the call; and this is faith. (Jer. iii. 32.   John vi. 44, 45; x. 16.   Is. lv. 5.)

Q. Thus much of our union. What is the communion of Christ's benefits unto the soul?

A. Whereby the soul possessed with Christ, and right unto him, hath by the same Spirit fruition of him, and all his benefits. (John iv. 10, 14.)

Q. What is the first of those benefits we do enjoy from Christ?

A. Justification, which is the gracious sentence of God the Father, whereby for the satisfaction of Christ apprehended by faith, and imputed to the faithful, he absolves them from the guilt and condemnation of all sins, and accepts them as perfectly righteous to eternal life. (Rom. iii. 24, 25; iv. 6–8; viii. 33, 34.)

Q. What difference is there between justification and sanctification?

A. Justification is by Christ's righteousness, inherent in Christ only; sanctification is by a righteousness from Christ inherent in ourselves. (2 Cor. v. 21.   Phil. iii. 9.)   2. Justification is perfected at once, and admits of no degrees, because it is by Christ his perfect righteousness. Sanctification is imperfect, being begun in this life. (Rev. xii. 1. Phil. iii. 11.)

Q. What is the second benefit next in order to justification, which the faithful receive from Christ?

A. Reconciliation, whereby a Christian justified is actually reconciled, and at peace with God. (Rom. v. 1. John ii. 12.) And hence follows his peace with all creatures.

Q. What is the third benefit next unto reconciliation?

A. Adoption, whereby the Lord accounts the faithful his sons, crowns them with privileges of sons, and gives them the Spirit of adoption — the same Spirit which is in his only-begotten Son. (1 John iii. 2. Rom. viii. 11, 14–17.)

Q. What is the fourth benefit next to adoption?

A. Sanctification, whereby the sons of God are renewed in the whole man, unto the image of their heavenly Father in Christ Jesus, by mortification, or their daily dying to sin by virtue of Christ's death; and by vivification, their daily rising to newness of life, by Christ's resurrection. (1 Thess. v. 23. Eph. iv. 24. Jer. xxxi. 22. Rom. vi. 8.)

Q. What follows from this mortification and vivification?

A. A continual war and combat between the renewed part, assisted by Father, Son, and Holy Ghost, and the unrenewed part, assisted by Satan and this evil world. (Rom. vii. 21–23.)

Q. What is the fifth and last benefit next unto sanctification?

A. Glorification, which hath two degrees — the one in this life, and the other in the world to come.

Q. What is the first degree of glorification in this life?

A. A lively expectation of glory, from the assurance and shedding abroad God's love in our hearts, working joy unspeakable. (Rom. v. 2, 5. Tit. ii. 13.)

Q. What is the second degree in the world to come?

A. Full fruition of glory, whereby being made complete and perfect in holiness and happiness, we enjoy all that good eye hath not seen, nor ear hath heard, in our immediate and eternal communion with God in Christ. (Heb. xii. 23. 1 Cor. xv. 28.)

Thus much of the first part, of living to God by faith in God.

Q. What is the second part, viz., our observance?

A. It is the duty that is to be performed to God of us, through the power of his Holy Spirit, working in us by faith, according to the will of God. (Eph. vi. 6, 7. Ps. cxxxix. 24. Rom. vi. 1. Luke i. 74.)

Q. Wherein consists our observance of God?

A. It is either moral or ceremonial.

Q. Wherein consists our moral observance of God?

A. In two things. 1. In suffering his will, whereby a believer, for the sake of Christ, chooseth rather to suffer any misery than to commit the least sin. (Heb. xi. 26. Acts xxi. 13.) 2. In doing his will, whereby a believer, in sense of Christ's love, performeth universal obedience to the law of God. (Rom. vii. 22. 1 John v. 3. Luke i. 6. Phil. iii. 12.)

Q. Is there any use of the law to a Christian?

A. Although it be abolished to a Christian in Christ, as a covenant of life, (for so Adam and his posterity are still under it,) yet it remains as a rule of life, when he is in Christ, and to prepare the heart for Christ. (Rom. vi. 14, 15. Matt. v. 17–20. Ezek. x. 11. Rom. ix.)

Q. Why is not a Christian so under the law as a covenant of life, so as if he breaks it by the least sin, he shall die for it?

A. Because Jesus Christ hath kept it perfectly for him. (Rom. viii. 3, 4; v. 20, 21.)

Q. Can any man keep the law perfectly in this life?

A. No, for the unregenerate, wanting the Spirit of life, can not perfect an act of life in obedience to it. The regenerate, having the Spirit but in part, perform it only imperfectly. (Rom. viii. 7; vii. 21.)

Q. What befalls the unregenerate upon their disobedience unto it?

A. The eternal curse of God for the least sin, and the increase of God's fierce and fearful secret wrath as they increase in sin. (Gal. iii. 10. Rom. ii. 5.)

Q. What befalls the regenerate after their breach of the law, and imperfect obedience unto it?

A. The Lord may threaten and correct them, but his loving kindness (in covering their sins in their best duties by Christ, and accepting their meanest services so far as they are quickened by his Spirit) is never taken from them. (Ps. lxxxix. 31–33. Zech. iii. 1–8. Is. lvi. 7. Rom. vii. 20.)

Q. What is that imperfect obedience of believers which is accepted?

A. When they observe the will of Christ, as that therein, — 1. They confess and lament their sins. (1 John i. 9. Rom. vii. 24.) 2. They desire mercy in the blood of Christ, and more of his Spirit. (Phil. iii. 9–11.) 3. They return him the praise of the least ability to do his will. (Ps. l. 23. 1 Cor. xv. 10.)

Q. How is the law or ten commandments divided?

A. Into two tables. The first showing our duty to God immediately, in the four first commandments. The second, our duty to man, in the six last commandments.

Q. What rules are you to observe to understand the moral law ?

A. These: 1. That in whatsoever commandment any duty is enjoined, there the contrary sin is forbidden; and where any sin is forbidden, there the contrary duty is commanded. 2. That the law is spiritual, and hence requires not only outward, but inward and spiritual obedience. 3. Where any gross sin is forbidden, there all the signs, degrees, means, and provocations to that sin are forbidden also, and are in God's account that sin. And so, where any duty is commanded, there all the signs, means, and provocations to that duty are commanded also. 4. That the law is perfect, and therefore there is no sin in all the Scripture but is forbidden in it; nor no duty required (if moral) but it is commanded in it.

Thus much of our moral observance of God.

Q. What is our ceremonial observance ?

A. The celebration of the two sacraments, baptism and the Lord's supper.

Q. What is a sacrament ?

A. It is a holy ceremony, wherein external sensible things, by the appointment of Christ, are separate from common use ; to signify, exhibit, and seal to us that assurance of eternal life by Christ Jesus, according to the covenant of his grace. (Gen. xvii. 9, 10.)

Q. Which are the sacraments ?

A. They are two, baptism and the Lord's supper.

Q. What is the external sensible part of baptism ?

A. Water. (John iii. 23.)

Q. What is the inward and spiritual part of baptism, signified, exhibited, and sealed thereby ?

A. Christ's righteousness and his Spirit. 1. Washing away our sin, and so delivering us from death. 2. Presenting us clear before the Father, and so restoring us again to life. (Rom. iv. 1 Cor. ii. 11. Matt. iii. 11.)

Q. What follows from hence ?

A. 1. That it is a sacrament of our new birth, and ingrafting into Christ. (John iii. 5.) 2. That as we are perfectly justified at once, and being new born once, shall never die again. Hence this seal is to be administered but once.

Q. What is the external and sensible part of the Lord's supper ?

A. Bread and wine, with the sacramental actions about the the same.

Q. What is the inward and spiritual part of it, signified, sealed, and exhibited thereby ?

A. The body and blood of Christ crucified, offered and given to nourish and strengthen believers, renewing their faith unto eternal life. (1 Cor. xi. 24. John vi. 54, 55.)

Q. What follows from hence?

A. 1. That it is the sacrament of our growth in Christ, being new born, because it is food given to nourish us, having received life. 2. That therefore it is to be administered and received often, that we may grow. 3. That children and fools, and wicked, ought not to partake of the sacrament, because they can not examine themselves, and so renew their faith. (1 Cor. xi. 28.)

Q. Ought not the sacrament to be administered to carnal people, if they have been baptized?

A. No, because such as are not within the covenant have no right to the seal of the covenant.

Q. Where are believers, who have right unto this sacrament, to seek fruition from it?

A. Because it ought not to be administered privately, (as the Papists would;) hence God's people are to seek to enjoy their right to it in some particular visible church, in joining with them, as fellow-members of the same body. (1 Cor. xi. 20, 22. 1 Chron. x. 17. Acts ii. 42.)

Q. What members ought every particular visible church to consist of?

A. Christ being head of every particular church, and it his body, hence none are to be members of the church but such as are members of Christ by faith. (1 Cor. i. 2. 1 Thess. i.)

Q. But do not hypocrites, and no true members of Christ, creep in?

A. Yes; but if they could have been known to be such, they ought to be kept out; and when they are known, they are orderly to be cast out. (Matt. xxv. 1. 2 Tim. iii. 5. Rev. ii. 20. Tit. iii. 20.)

Q. Are these members bound only to cleave to Christ, their head, by faith?

A. Yes; and to one another also by brotherly love, which they are bound to strengthen and confirm (as well as their faith) by a solemn covenant. (Eph. iv. 15, 16. Col. i. 4. Jer. l. 4. Is. lvi. 45. Zech. xi. 14. Zeph. iii. 9. Ps. cxix. 106.)

Q. What benefits are there by joining thus to a particular church?

A. 1. Hereby they come to be under the special government of Christ in his church, and the officers thereof. (Is. xxx. 20.) 2. Hereby they have the promise of special blessing, and on their children also. (Ps. cxxxiii. 3. Exod. xx. 6.) 3. Herein they have the promise of God's special presence: 1. Revealing unto them his will. (Ps. xxvii. 4; lxiii. 2, 3.) 2. Protecting them. (Is. xliv. 6.) 3. Hearing all their prayers. (Deut. iv. 7. Matt. xviii. 19.)

Q. Are there not some who never find these benefits?

A. Yes. Because many knowing not how to make use of God's ordinances, not feeling a need of God's presence only in them, their sin also blinding, and partly hardening their hearts, and polluting God's house, they then become worse when they have best means. (Matt. xi. 23. Jer. xvii. 5, 6. Heb. vi. 8. 1 Sam. v. 8, 9. Ezek. xiv. 4. 1 Kings viii. 21.)

Q. What are the miseries of those who carelessly and willfully despise, and so refuse to join to God's church?

A. Besides the loss of God's presence in the fellowship of his people, it is a fearful sign (continuing so) God never intends to save their souls. (Acts ii. 47. Is. lx. 12. Rev. ii. 23, 24.)

Q. What therefore ought people chiefly to labor for, and to hold forth unto the church, that so they may be joined to it?

A. A threefold work. 1. Of humiliation, under their misery, death, and sin, as their greatest evil. (Acts ii. 37. Matt. iii. 6.) 2. Of vocation, or their drawing to Christ, out of this misery, as to their greatest and only good. (Acts i. 38, 41.) 3. Of new obedience; how they have walked in Christ since called. (Acts ix. 26, 27. Matt. iii. 8.)

END OF VOLUME I